JEWELRY
GEM BY GEM
MASTERS AND MATERIALS

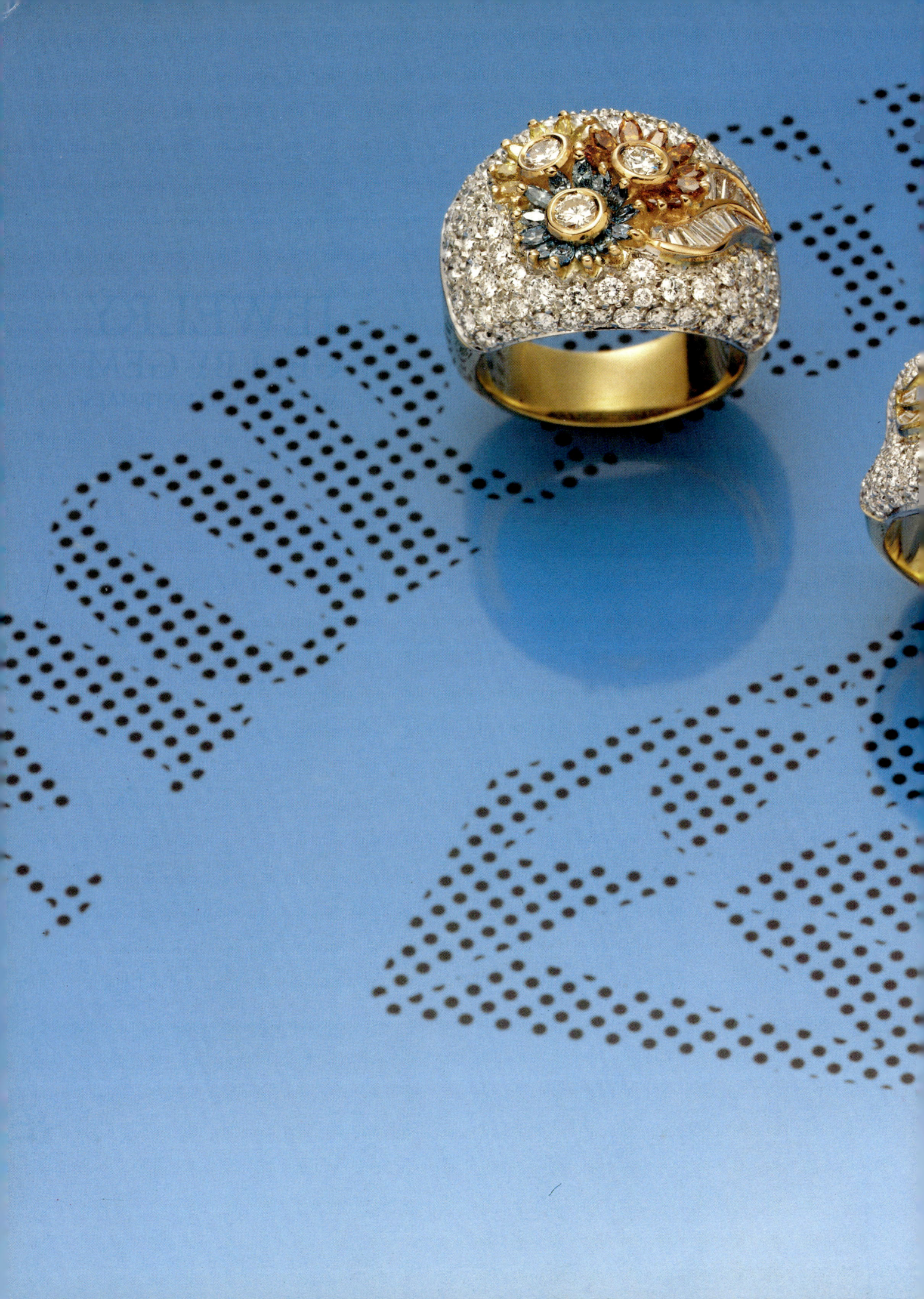

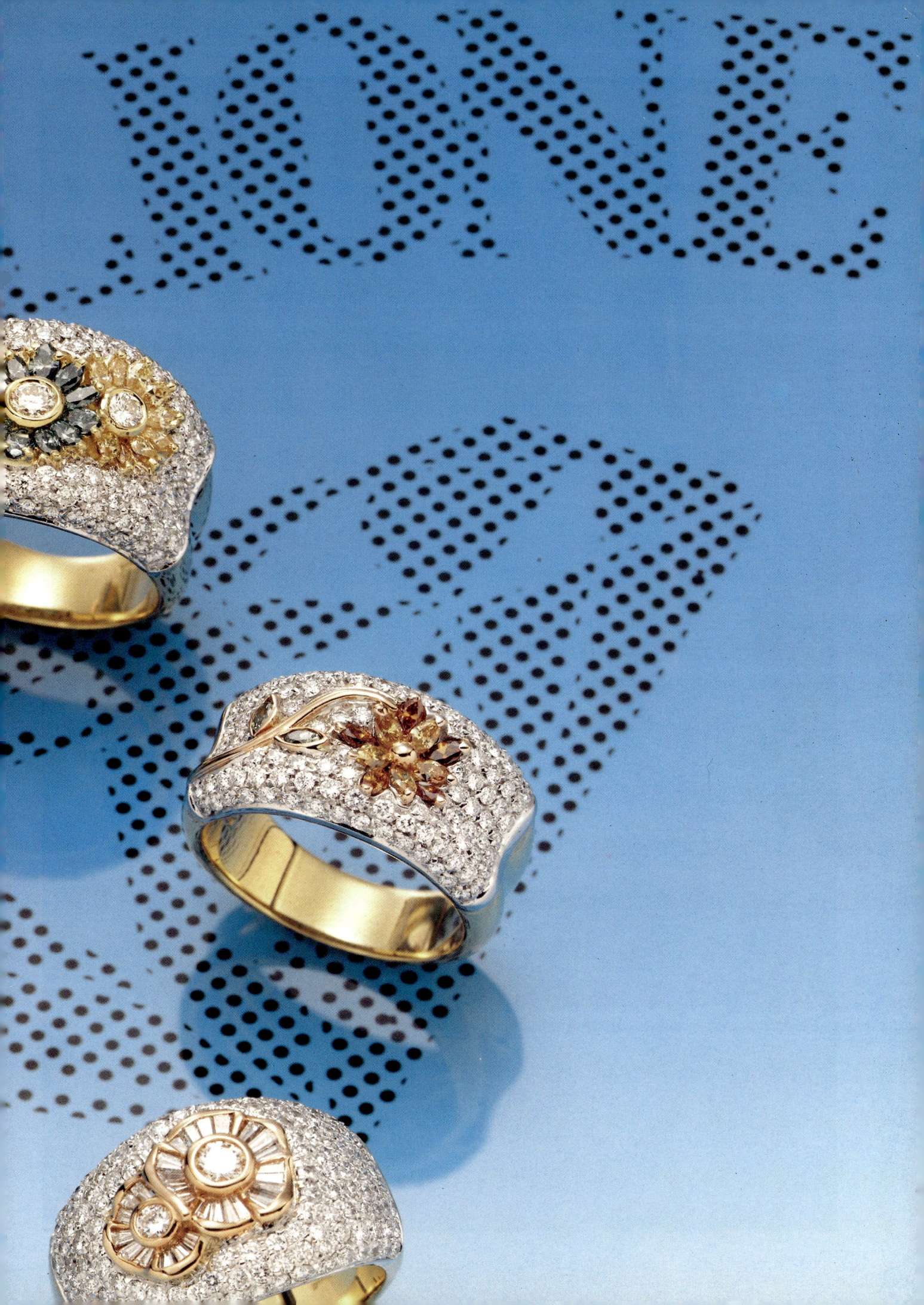

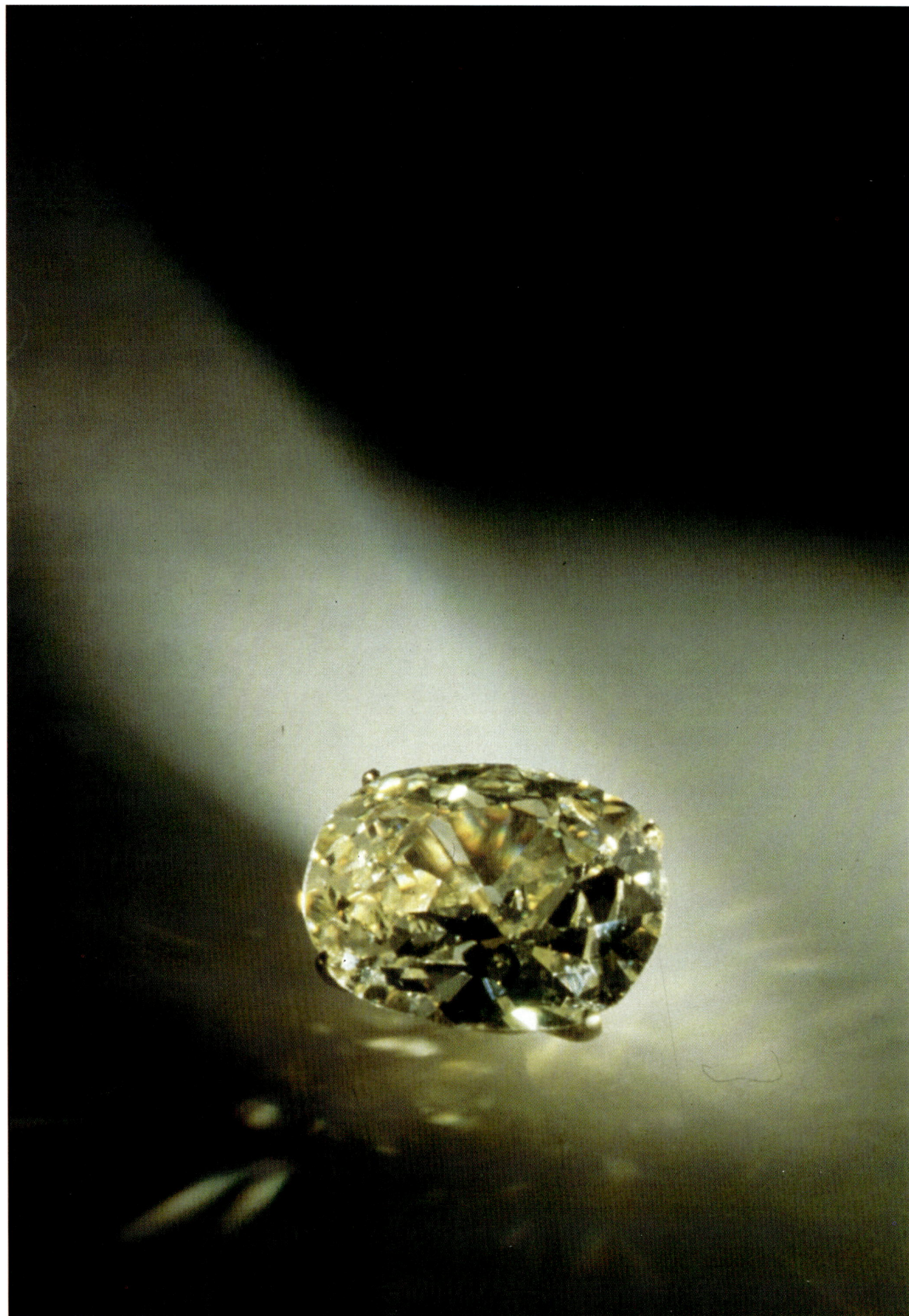

Acknowledgements

Carlo CUMO and Claude MAZLOUM would like to thank the following for their help: ASSOCIAZIONE ORAFA VALENZANA (A.O.V.) and Vincente ALVES, Lena ANTABI, Chantal BIZOT, Marisa BRIATA, Ricardo BRONFEN, Martin COEROLI, Chris COLEMONT, Wagner COLOMBAROLI, Rosanna COMI, Gianni COMMARE, Monica CUMO, Christine DIETZ, Gillian DOWLAND, Emile DUFOUR, David FARDON, Guido GIOVANNINI-TORELLI, Silvia GRASSI, Cheryl KREMKOW, Haidrun KUHLMANN-REIDASCH, Miriam MAMBER, Serena MIAZZO, Beatrice NORMAND, Lino PASINI, Heather QUAYLE, François RENAC, Karen RENDERS, Francesco ROBERTO, Maria Lucia ROCHA CAMPOS, Jules SAUER, Teresa SICUPIRA, Federico STOCCO, Christine STOCK, Paolo VALENTINI, Daniel VERGES-RENAU, Cristiana VILLA, Gabriele WEINMANN.

As well as very special thanks to Dieter BROTZMANN, Director of INTERGEM and ICA GEMBUREAU EUROPE, in Idar-Oberstein, Germany. As for all our previous volumes, Dieter BROTZMANN has once again contributed to our research with up-dated information and exceptional photos principally from the archives of the IDAR-OBERSTEIN TRADE FAIR ASSOCIATION and the ICA INTERNATIONAL COLORED STONE ASSOCIATION. Whenever the "author specialized in gems and jewels" encountered any difficulties, Dieter BROTZMANN and the institutions he represents could always be counted on to help find the best possible solutions.
He generously made available to us all the experience and assistance possible and imaginable, motivated certainly by our shared passion, admiration, and enthusiasm for jewelry and precious stones.

Carlo Cumo   Claude Mazloum

JEWELRY
GEM BY GEM
MASTERS AND MATERIALS

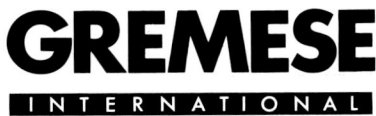

Cover: Exceptional Australian pearls from Rosario Autore (photo Garry Sarre/Rosario Autore Pty Ltd) and rare necklace of Tahiti pearls with gold and diamonds.

End paper: Ring in gold and diamonds by Moraglione (photo Photochrom).

Back cover: Unique creation in gold, diamonds, pearls, and opals by Simonne Muylaert-Hofman (photo Van Cauwelaert).

Translated from the Italian by: Patricia Fogarty
(Introductory material and sections on: Vietnam, Sri Lanka, Angola, Tahiti translated by Sandra E. Tokunaga)

Layout: Fortunato Romani

Jacket design by: Antonio Dojmi

Phototypeset and Photolithography: Graphic Art 6 s.r.l. – Rome

Printed and Bound by: Conti Tipocolor – Calenzano (Florence)

© 1996 Gremese International s.r.l.
P.O. Box 14335 – 00149 Rome, Italy

All right reserved. No part of this publication may be reproduced, stored in a retrieval system or transmitted in any form or by any means, without the prior written permission of the Publisher

ISBN 88-7301-070-9

CONTENTS

Preface *by Paolo Valentini* 11
Introduction *by Carlo Cumo* 13
Introduction *by Claude Mazloum* 15
A Homage to Stone *by Patrizia Macera and Paolo Spalla* 17

Chapter I: RUBY 27
Vietnam: Watch Out for Rubies *by Claude Mazloum* 35

Chapter II: SAPPHIRE 39
Sri Lanka: Precious Stones in All Colors *by Chris Colemont* . . . 47

Chapter III: EMERALD 57
Paris-Muzo: Departure for an Infernal Paradise
 by Claude Mazloum 69

Chapter IV: DIAMOND 73
Angola: Diamond Hunt *by Claude Mazloum* 121

Chapter V: PEARL 127
The Pearls of Tahiti *by Martin Coeroli* 139

Chapter VI: 26 FINE STONES 155

Chapter VII: OTHER STONES 265

Glossary 277

The World's Finest Creators 281
Photographic Credits 283
Index of Stones 285

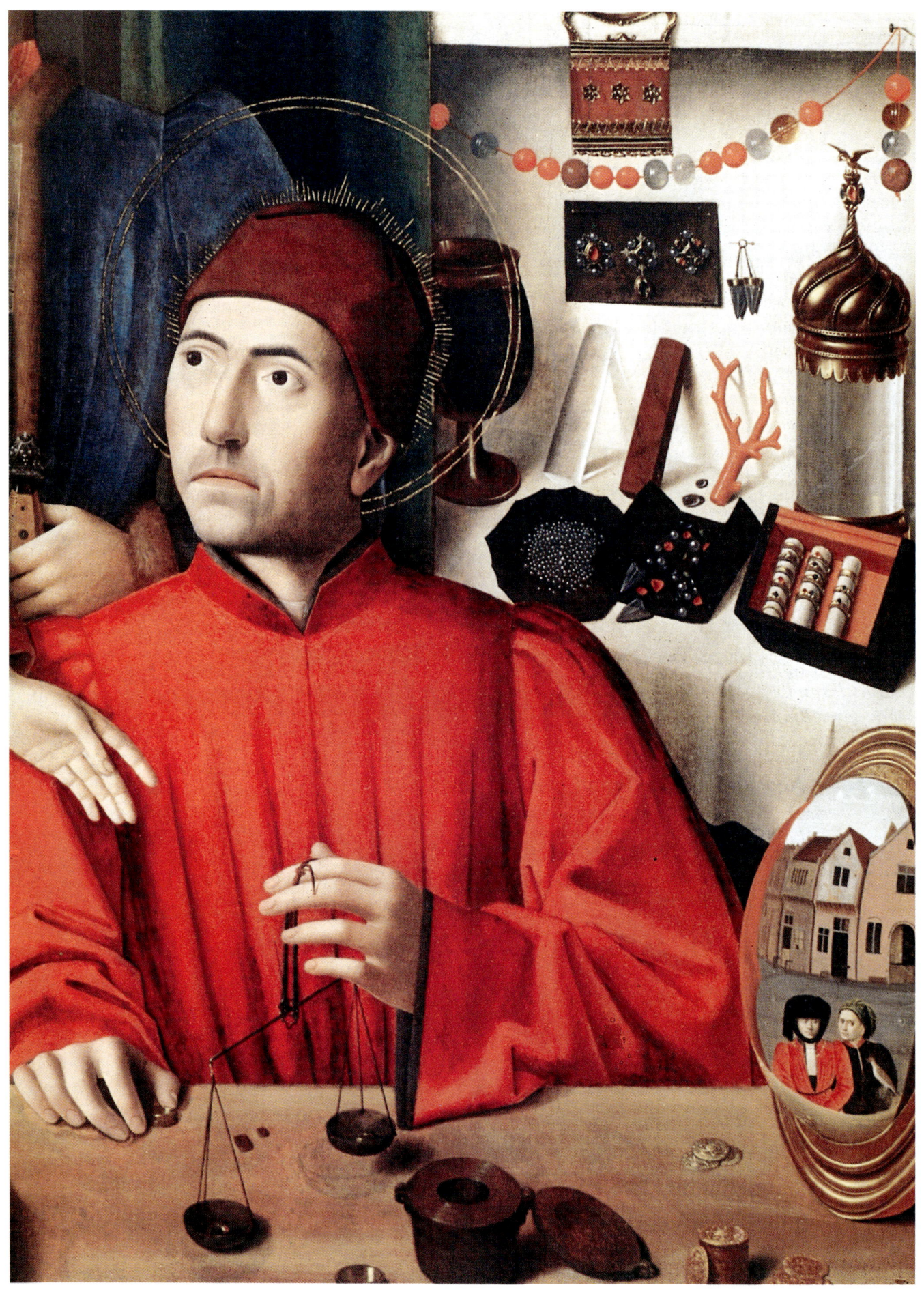

Saint Eligius, patron saint of jewelers and goldsmiths.

Preface

Taking up this book I asked myself, as perhaps many readers, hadn't most everything been said and written about jewelry and gems? And I must admit it was with some skepticism that I began leafing through these pages. But then, turning page after page, I began to be drawn deeper and deeper into its world without even realizing it.

Its style, layout, choice of illustrations, simple and clear approach and easy reference make Jewelry Gem by Gem *the ideal companion not only for those just becoming acquainted with the world of precious stones, but also for professionals active in the field.*

This book shares the pace and personality of all works that reconcile both simplicity and class, attaining a timelessness that make them "jewels" regardless of the materials of which they are made.

But that wasn't all. There was something else, something intriguing that reached out and touched me deeply. I was already reacting to a quiet yet insistent appeal, strongly present throughout all of this work: something to do with the most ancient beliefs Man has always nurtured and still intimately does today, despite progress, success, or technological advances. That mixture of superstition and searching for alternative truths, the response to an ancestral need, as ancient as mankind, to distinguish oneself by the wearing of jewelry. Not only as a manifestation of power but also and above all as an affirmation of one's personality.

This volume is a wonderful experience which induces the reader, by its clear style and informative details, to read on and on, in search of the little "why's" that not only offer responses to scientific curiosity but also to human questions.

We are most grateful and indebted to Carlo Cumo and Claude Mazloum for this fine presentation of the complex world of gems. They have known how to render their wealth of experience in gemmology as well as education accessible to all. For, instead of overwhelming readers with facts and figures that suffocate the imagination, their work is a persuasive and stimulating invitation to expand our knowledge of the world around us.

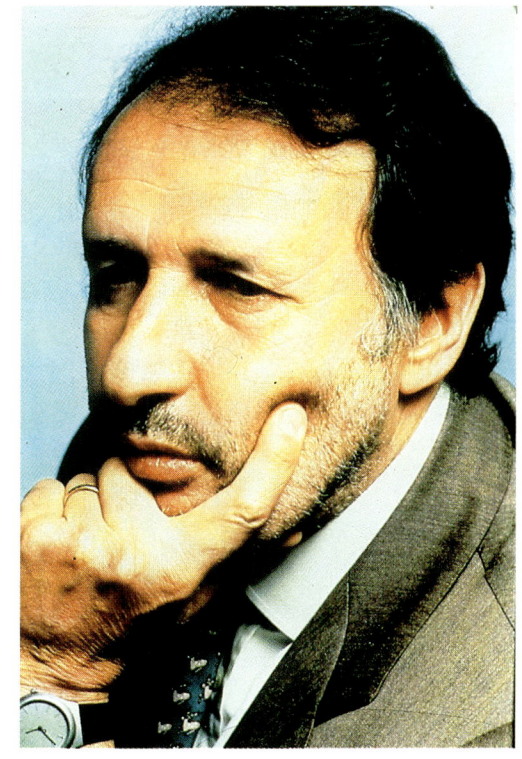

Paolo Valentini
*President ICA
(International Colored Gemstone Association)*

*President Federpietre Italia
(National Federation of Diamond, Pearl, Precious Stone Dealers and Lapidaries)*

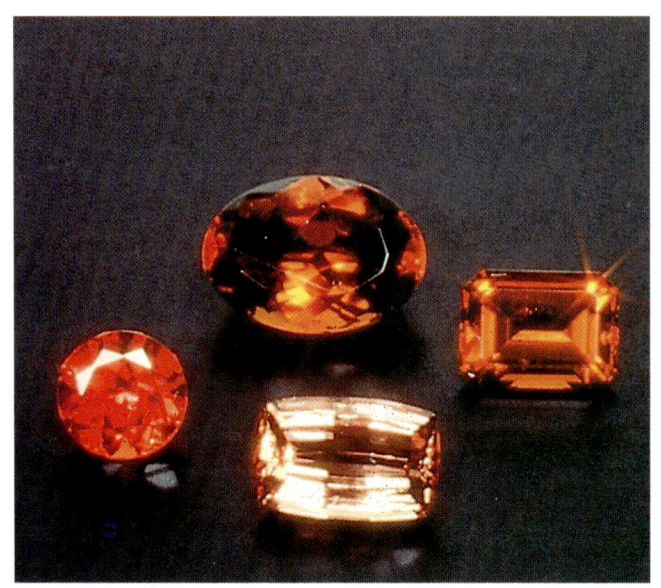

Citrine Quartz
Sapphire   *Garnet*
Topaz

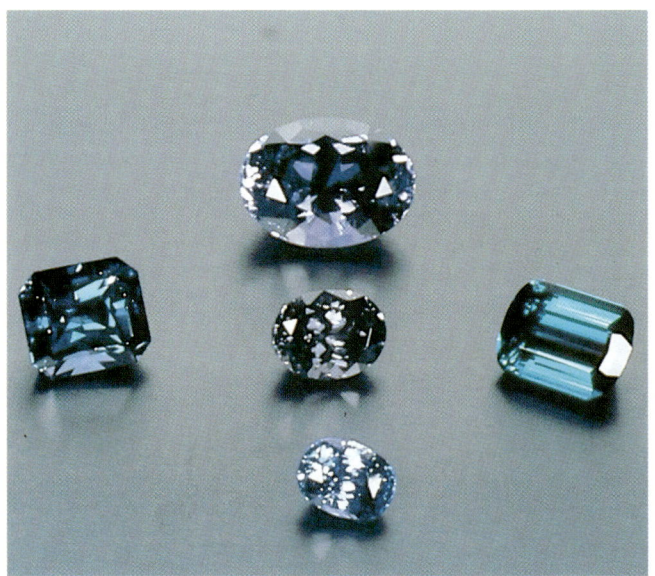

Iolite
Tanzanite   *Spinel*   *Tourmaline*
Sapphire

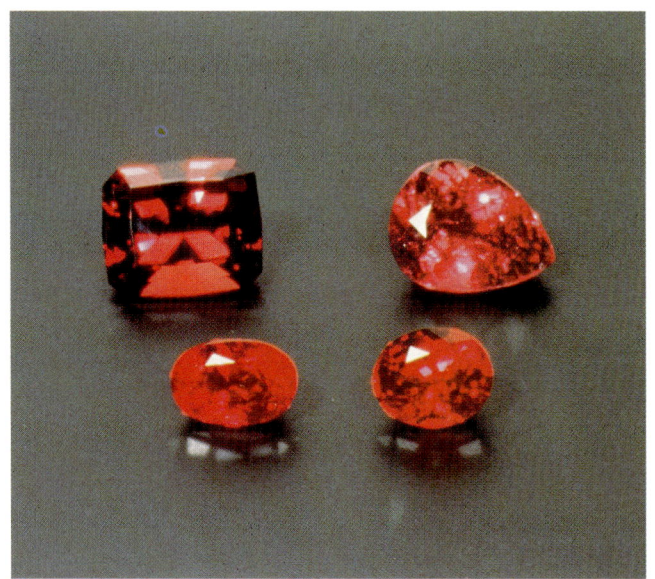

Garnet   *Tourmaline*
Ruby   *Spinel*

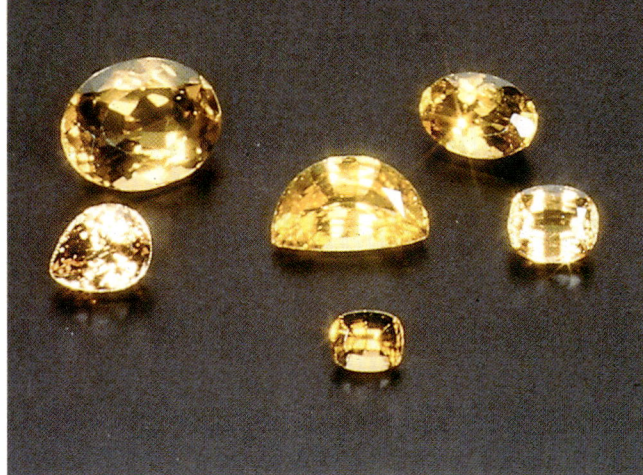

Citrine Quartz   *Beryl*
Topaz   *Sapphire*   *Garnet*
Tourmaline

CARLO CUMO.
Gemmology, the science which studies stones.

Introduction

by Carlo Cumo

When I was asked to participate in drawing up this text and take charge of the gemmology section, I certainly didn't hesitate to accept: partly because analyzing gems is what I do every day of my life; partly because I was sparked by the idea of promulgating this still young science; and then, of course, the world of "stones" has never ceased to fascinate me.

But then the work in hand had to be given a format, a volume that was intended – and here my friend Claude Mazloum and I are in perfect agreement – for anyone and everyone working in the field of jewelry, but also to the jewelry public at large, the purchasers.

And so a book was born. It furnishes all the basic and indispensable information on gems, presented in a language all laymen will find understandable, yet with real scientific rigor. Let me emphasize: Jewelry Gem by Gem *is not written as a textbook for students in gemmology courses; it is designed for all those who wish to learn more about the wide world of gems through a clear and carefully documented presentation.*

The tables of essential data preceding the discussion of each gem in the first section are a good indication of the book's aim.

Provenance of each mineral is provided as a hint to the reader that you are not likely to make an advantageous purchase of a gem outside its country of origin. If this is not possible, you are probably better off buying in your own country unless, of course, you are interested in the gem solely as a souvenir of a pleasurable trip.

The interesting sidelights cited are intriguing anecdotes, and are chiefly calculated as an introduction to a hitherto unknown world which may offer some tantalizing surprises.

And I believe that the chapters describing the stones as seen under a magnifying lens will be of absorbing interest to all those readers who have a keen curiosity about genuine research.

A glossary at the conclusion of this volume gives basic definitions for key terminology used by experts in gemmology, though it will also be useful even if you only want to increase your general understanding of the field.

To all our readers: an emphatic invitation to carefully consider the many photographs that fill these pages for they beautifully demonstrate what fine and exciting jewelry can be created through the knowledgeable use of gems.

And, finally, special thanks to my daughter Monica for her painstaking and dedicated contribution.

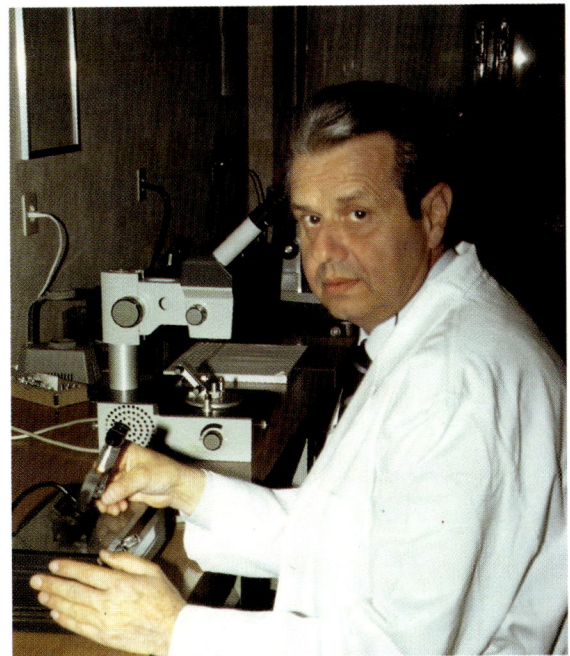

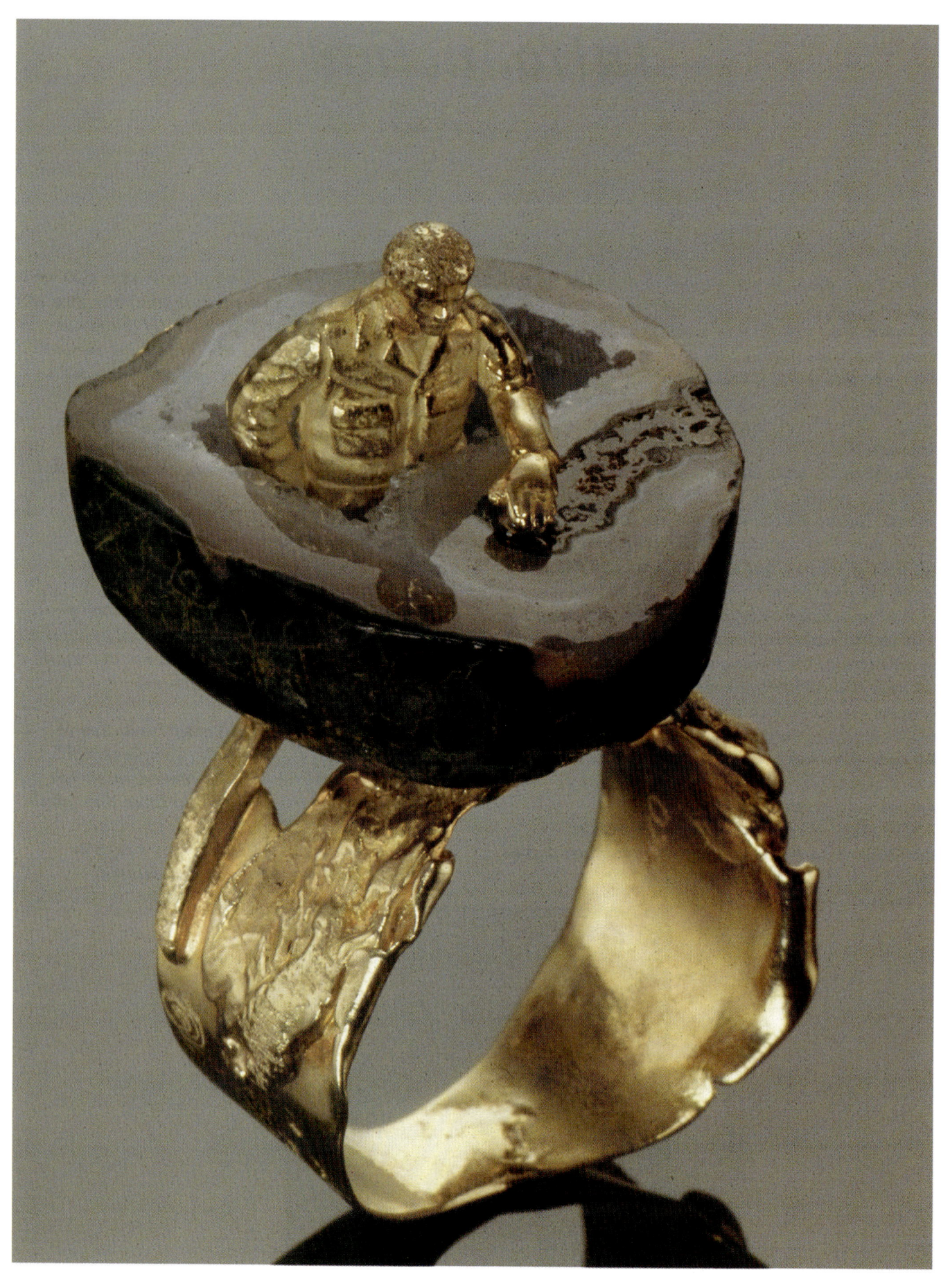

CLAUDE MAZLOUM: "MAN AND STONE"
Gold ring and small agate geode. This piece is on display at Idar-Oberstein's Heimatmuseum and symbolizes the close bond that links man to stone.

Introduction

by Claude Mazloum

Gems... jewels... words that set us dreaming our most fantastic dreams, bursting with light and beauty, luxury, class. When people approach me about gold and precious stones I feel flattered and wonderfully self-indulgent. Yet, hidden behind its glowing façade is a highly complex science, hungry monopolies, and the fate of millions of people.

Since the dawn of time these precious materials have had the power to impassion entire peoples, deeply moving the men who have discovered them, bringing infinite joy to those who have worn them.

As a symbol not only of love but of the power of kings, they have incited men to acts of outrage and been the cause of wars. Though precious and rare, they are familiar everywhere from the far reaches of good to evil. It is said entire lands have been destroyed only for the booty they represented. To own them brings us honor, to be dispossessed of them is humiliation.

The gem's turbulent journey, from the core of the earth to the sensuous cleavage of a woman's plunging neckline, is also part of this history. My professor and friend, Carlo Cumo, joins me in relating this story down to the last detail, in a way we hope will be as clear as it is entertaining. For the reader intent on discovering what truly lies behind the brilliance and colors of the showcase, here is the entire voyage, from the harshness of the mines to the hushed comfort of the velvet-lined jeweler's tray, all via, of course, the gemmologist's microscope.

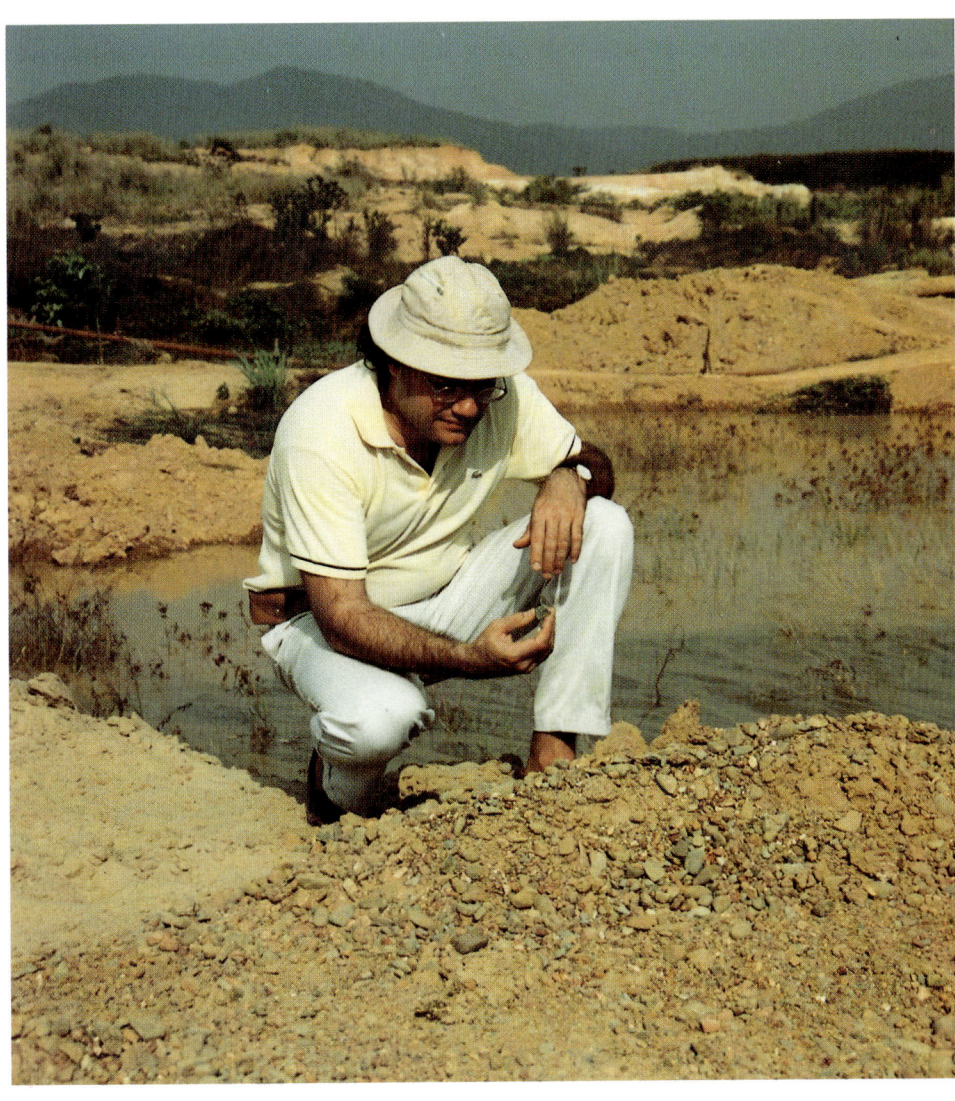

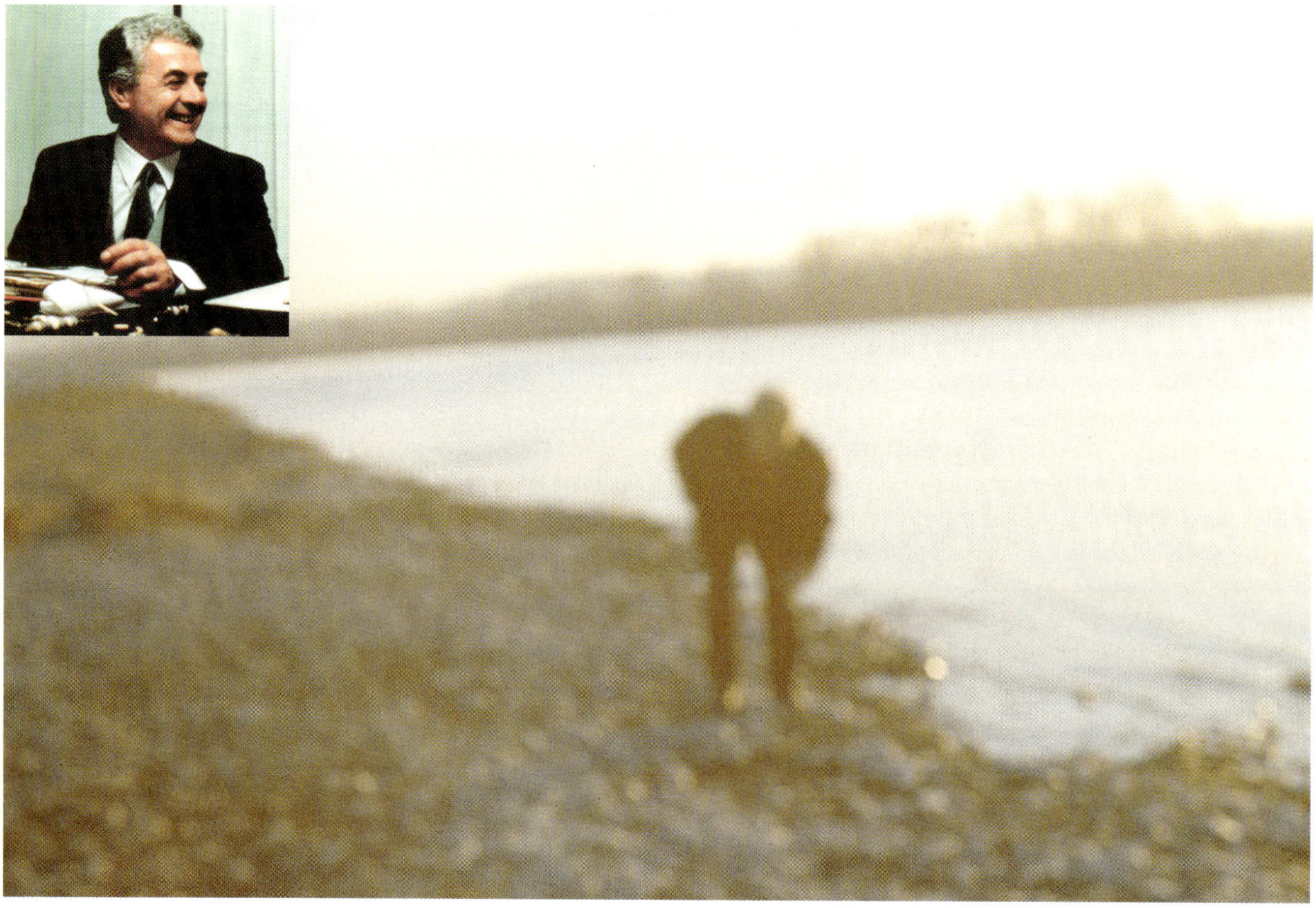

Paolo Spalla along the misty Po.

Patrizia Macera test drilling a rock.

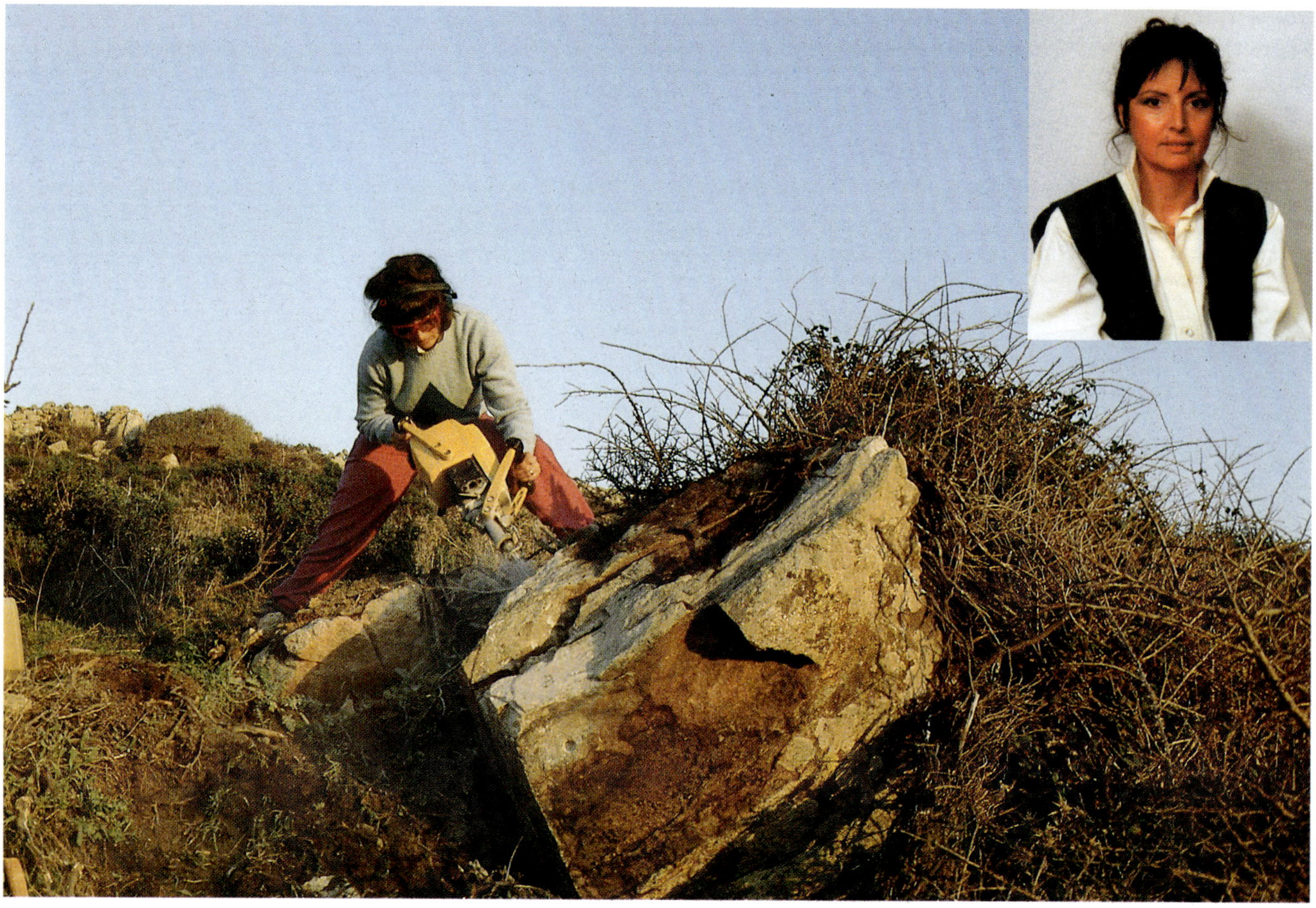

16

A Homage to Stone

Stone is not only rare and therefore precious. For, even if it is ordinary, it is as venerable for its thousand-year history as it is beautiful for its mutations over time. Patrizia Macera of the Department of Earth Sciences at the University of Pisa offers us a poetic and scientific presentation of ordinary stones, and Paolo Spalla, sculptor and jeweler from Valenza Po, illustrates his very special way of transforming stones into rare and precious jewels.

How many times, walking along a riverbank or crossing a stream, have we been struck by the variety of stones and their many colors and sizes, and especially by the rounded forms of most of them, as if they had been sculpted by a great master. If we linger a while longer to look more closely at these natural wonders it also occurs to us that though many of them resemble each other, others are completely different in color and pattern. At this point we might begin to wonder about the origin and history of these stones, indeed a fascinating story.

In science these stones are referred to as "pebbles" and are the result of the decomposition of rocks that at one time existed or still exist in the surrounding areas. Geologists tell us that any type of rock that appears on the surface of the earth is exposed to altering and eroding phenomena caused by atmospheric agents (wind, rain, ice, thawing, watercourses, snow) that effect a slow, gradual, and automatic decomposition of the rock itself.

When the alteration agent is a river, it will have the force to strip the main rock of fragments as large as the current is strong, and in seasons when the river is high it will have a greater capacity of erosion, even carrying away extremely large blocks of rock. The continuous rolling motion of these blocks along the riverbed smooths their angles little by little giving them a rounder shape. The rocks colliding against each other also contribute to this process.

But why are these pebbles sometimes so different from one another? Of course this depends upon the types of rock found along the river's course. And also the fact that in the process of erosion, a river may gouge deep into rock formations and carry away new lithotypes and different layers of rock that are deposited along its course as the river diminishes and flows more slowly. This explains why we might find limestone and sandstone pebbles (from sedimentary rock) mixed in with gabbro, serpentine, jasper, and others (from ophiolitic deposits).

But the history of pebbles does not end here. As the waters of the river rise, the pebbles are eventually deposited at the mouth of the river and, due to the accumulation of more and more of these new deposits, conditions are created that encourage their cementing and formation into a new rock called a "conglomerate." The conglomerate rock, thoroughly formed with the passing of geological time, will again reappear at the surface (due to movements of subsidence) and

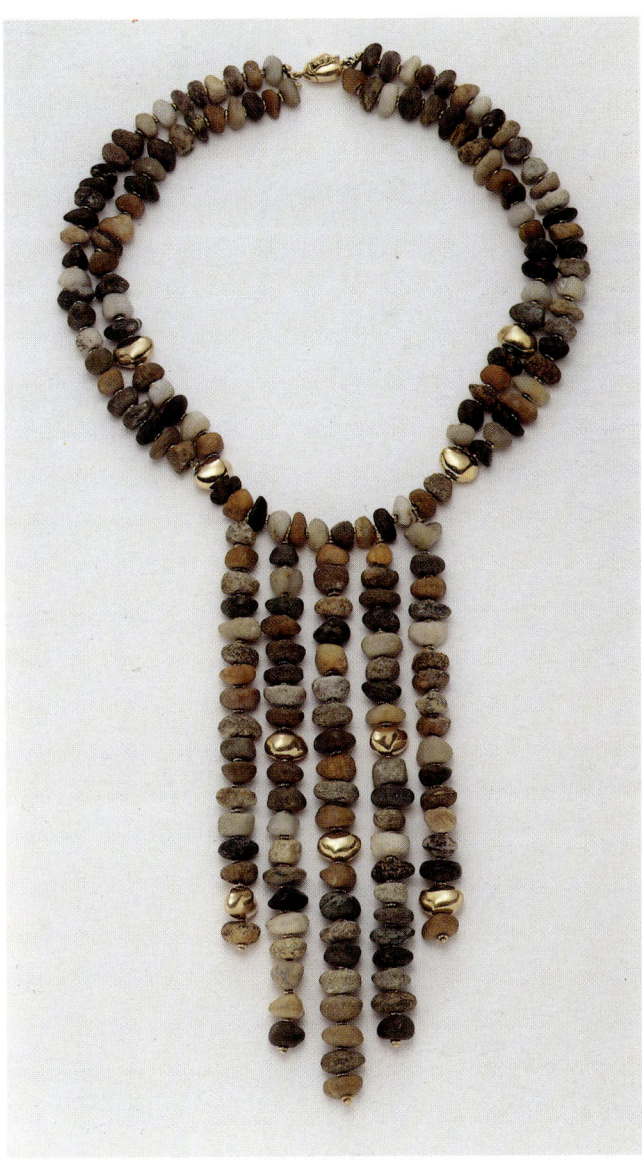

PAOLO SPALLA: *"THE RIVER'S PEBBLY SHORE"*
Collection of gold jewels and stones from the Po with diamonds.
A complete set realized with plain and noble materials in honor of stone.

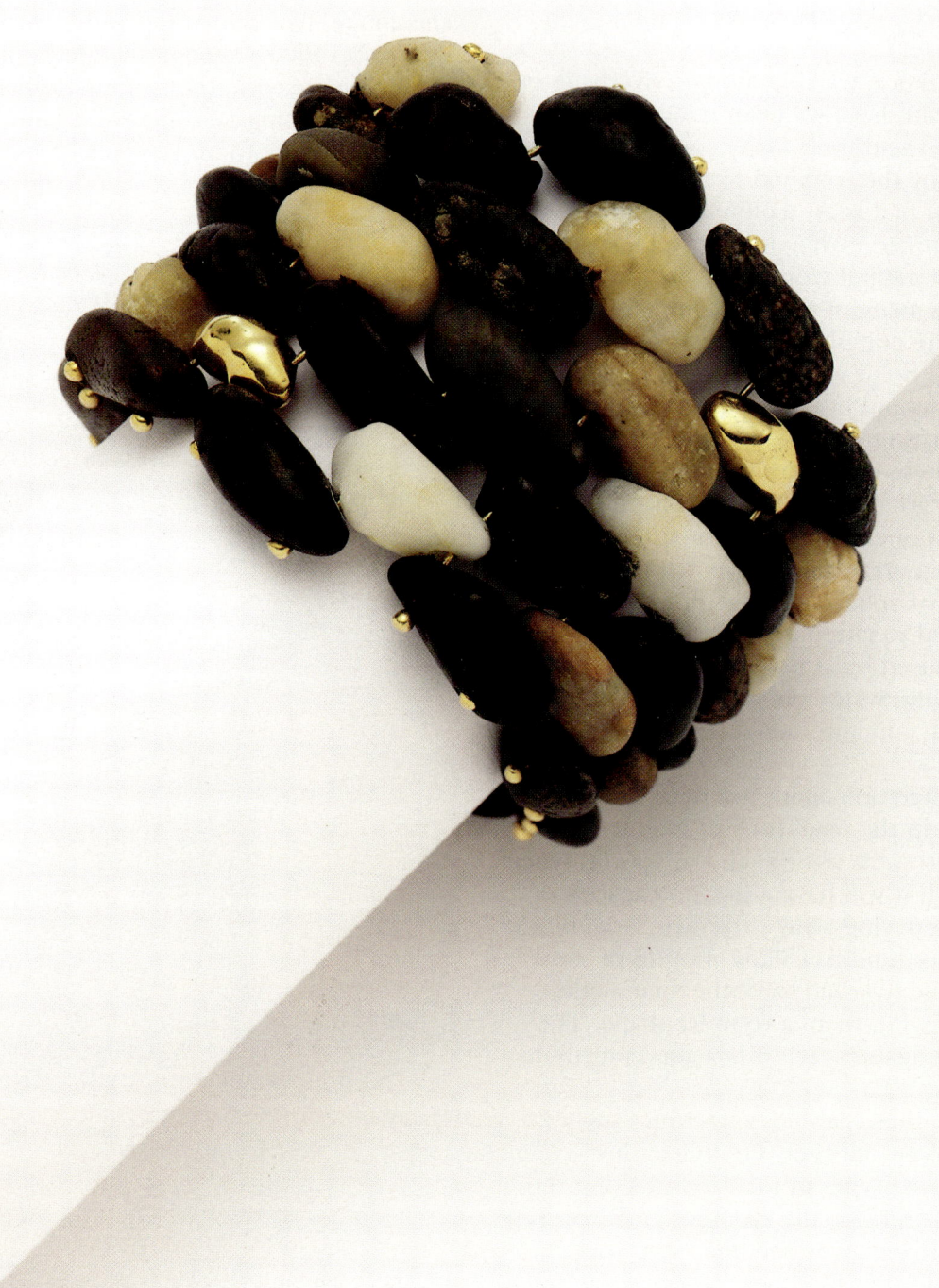

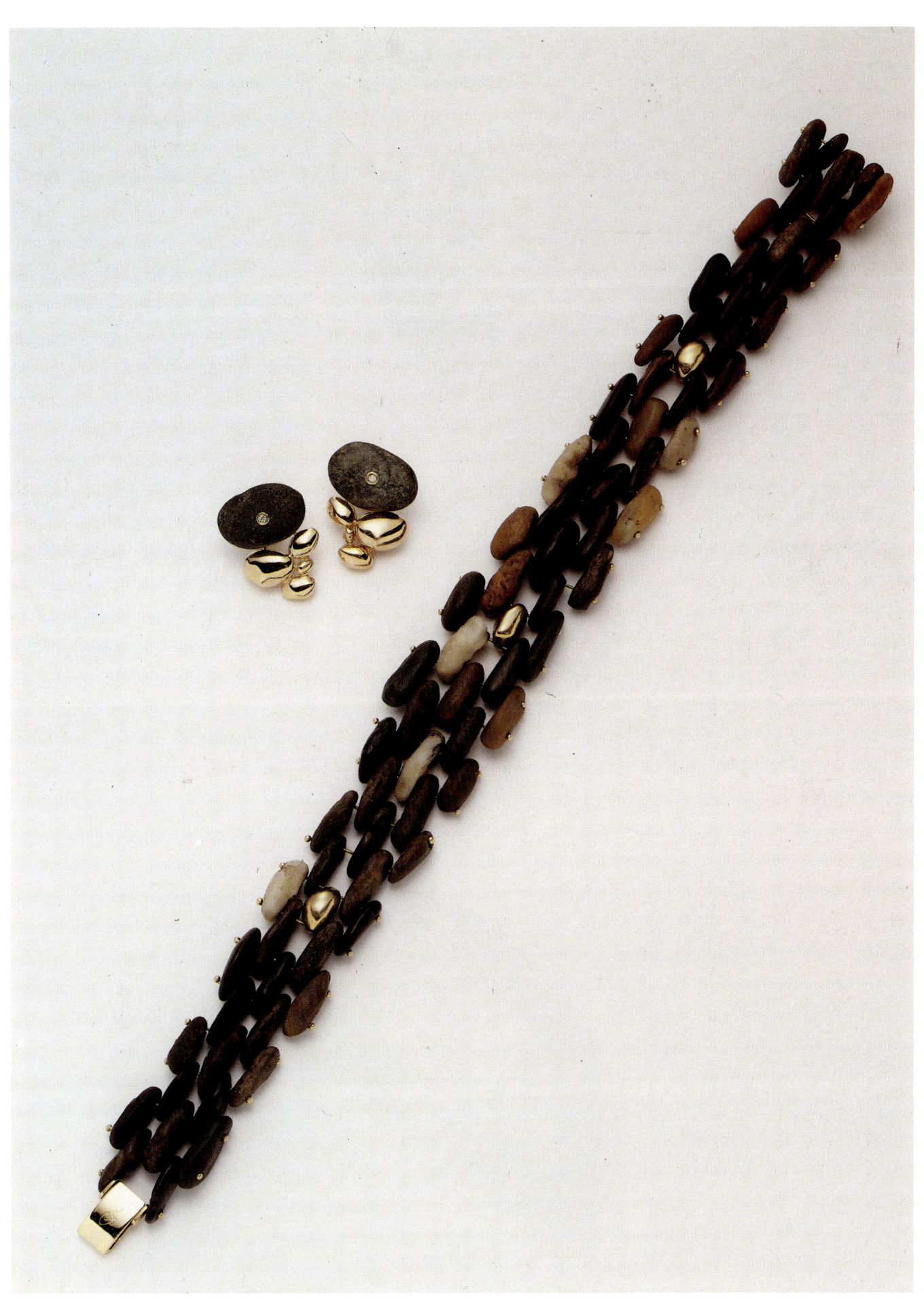

PAOLO SPALLA: "THE RIVER'S PEBBLY SHORE"

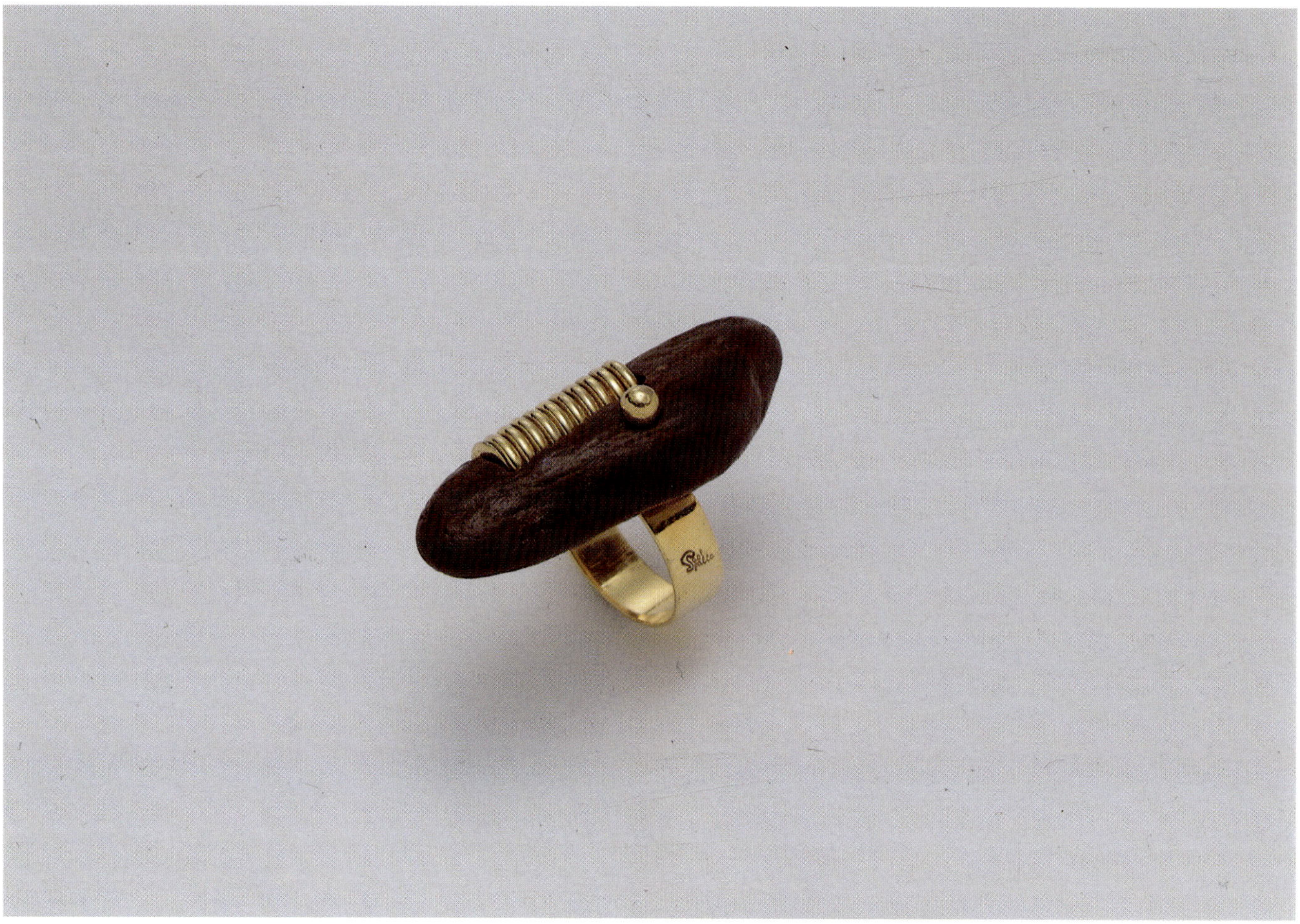

PAOLO SPALLA: "THE RIVER'S PEBBLY SHORE"

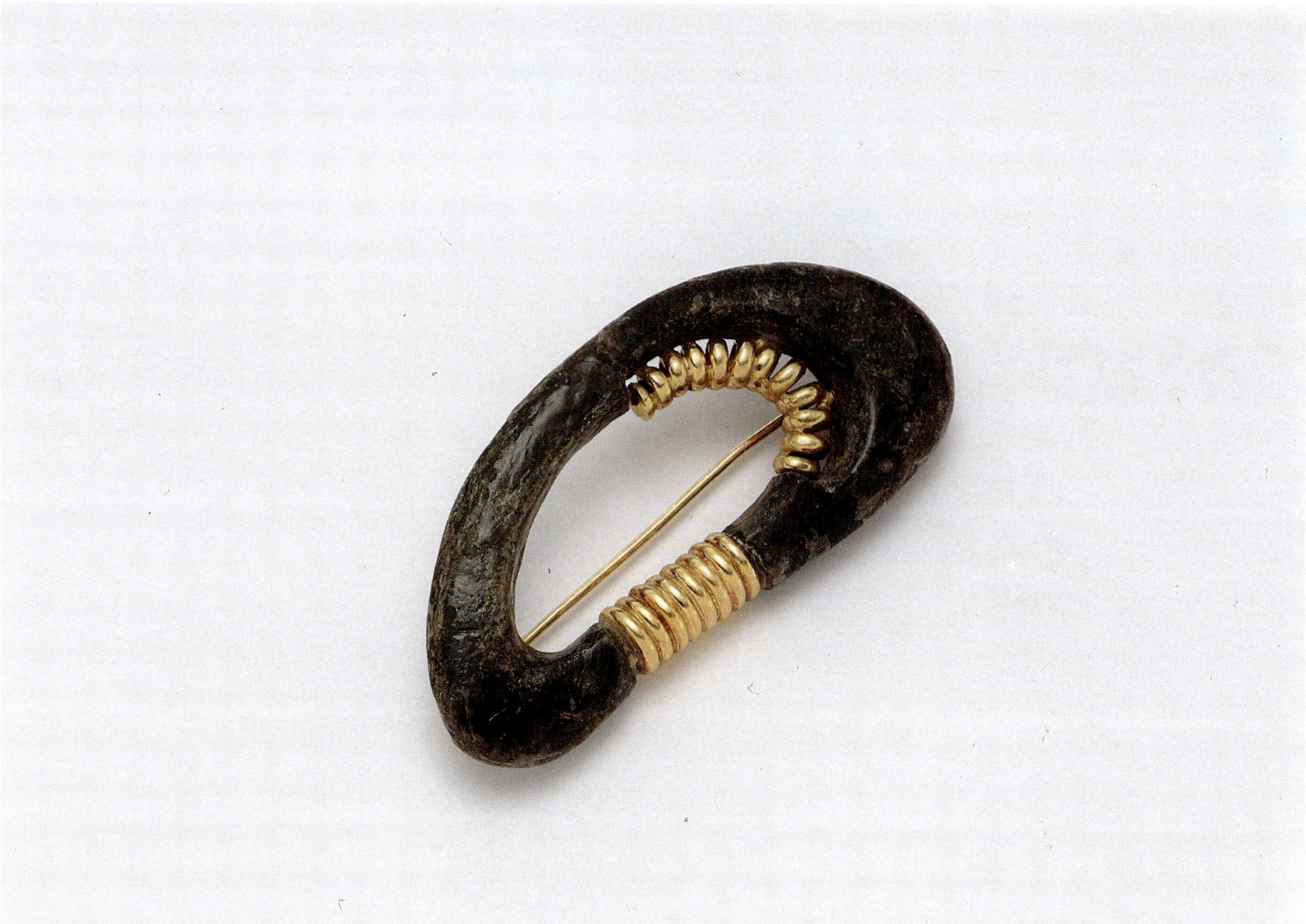

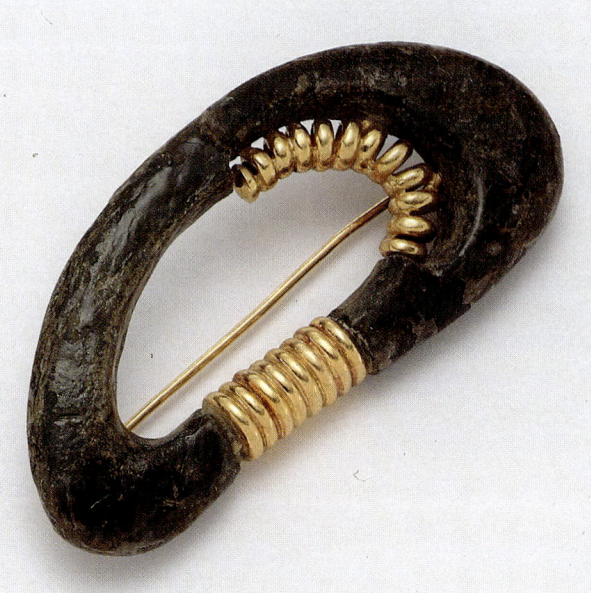

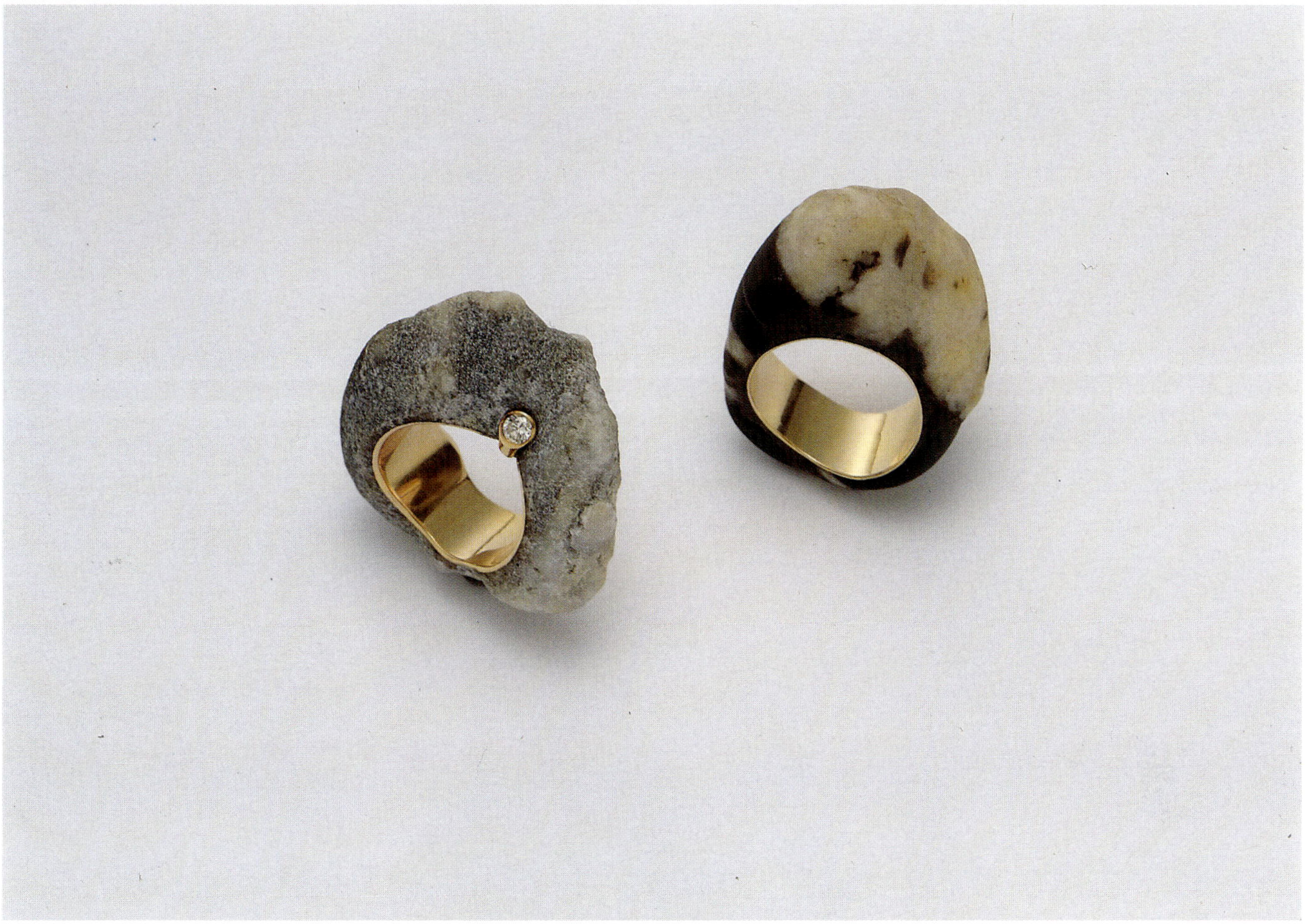

PAOLO SPALLA: "THE RIVER'S PEBBLY SHORE"

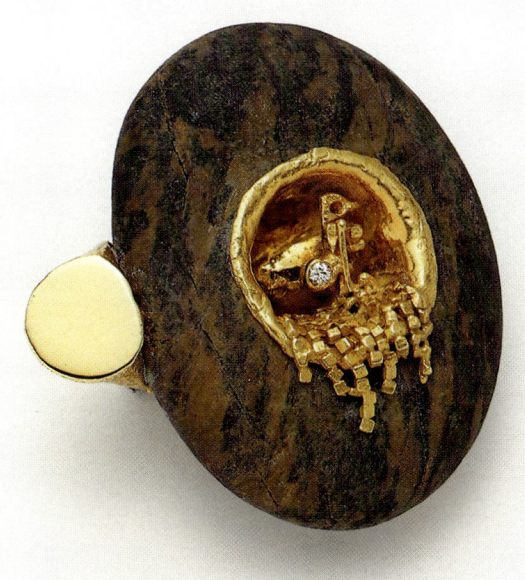

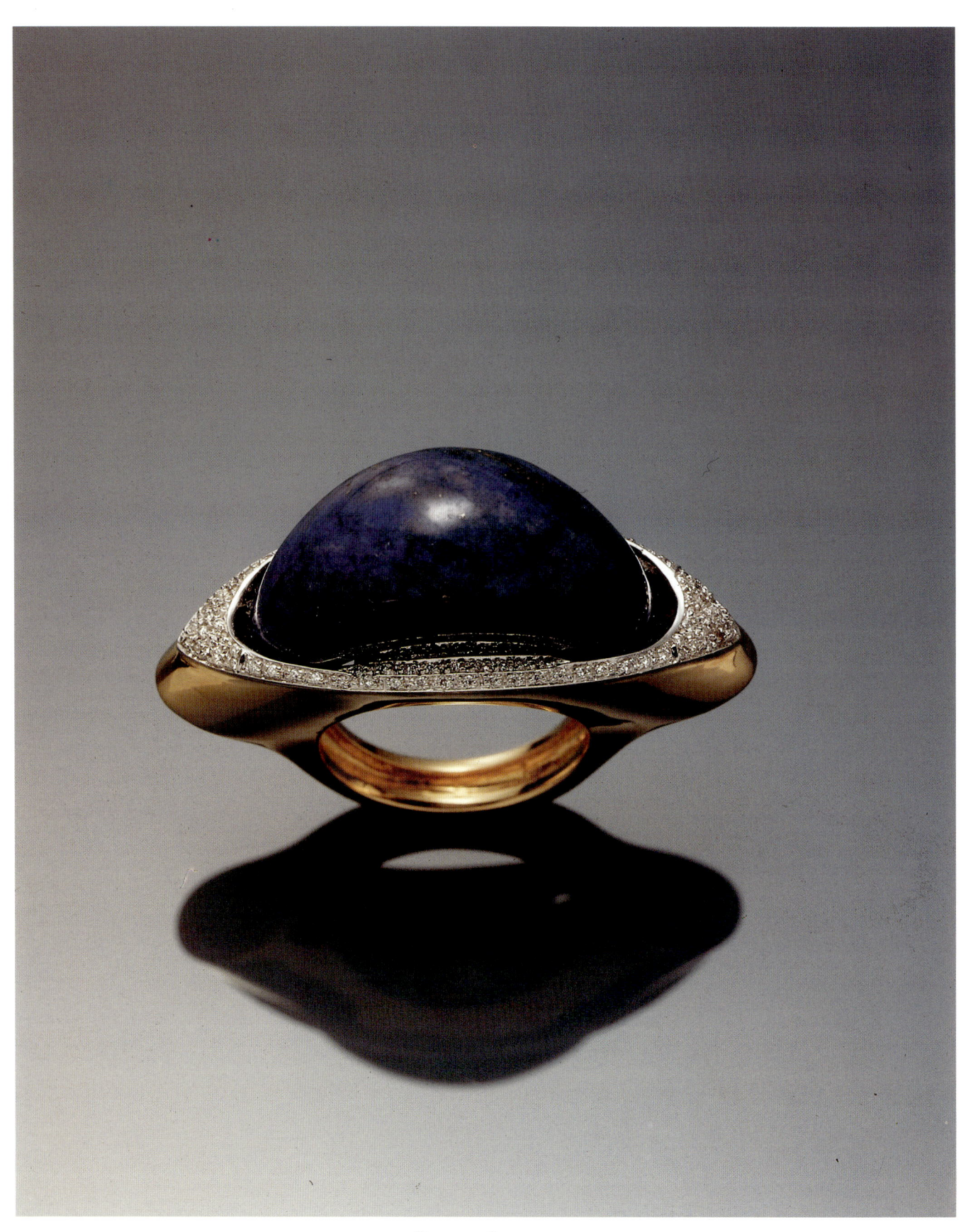

Paolo Spalla.
Gold ring, diamonds and lapis lazuli.

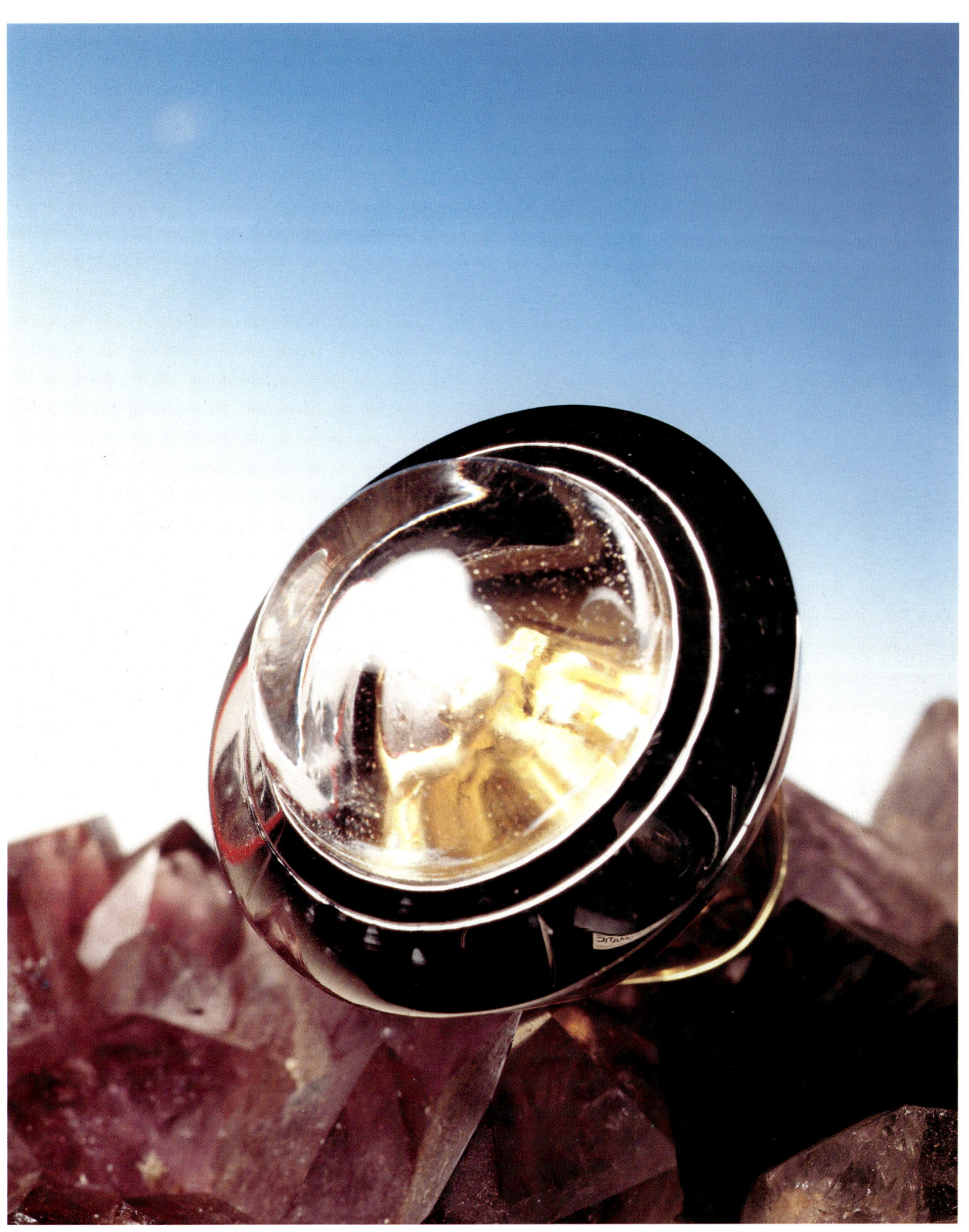

PAOLO SPALLA.
Gold ring, rock crystal and diamond bead.

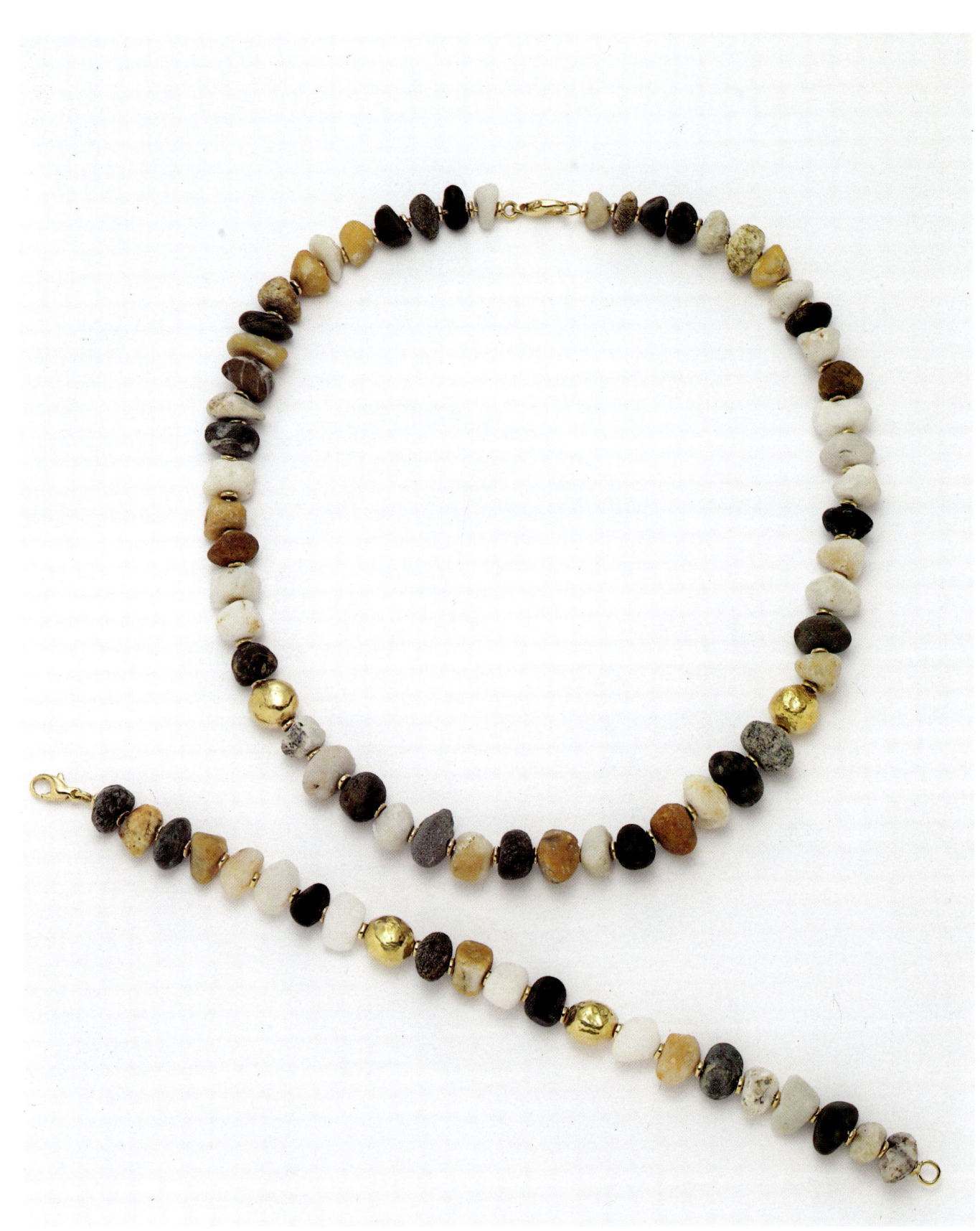

PAOLO SPALLA: "THE RIVER'S PEBBLY SHORE"

begin its cycle of alteration, erosion, and conveyance all over again.

Thus we can see that every pebble on the gravel bank of a river or stream, in fact, has its own story to tell. For each one is part of the immense cycle of the Earth's evolution, one in which all things are in a state of constant and gradual mutation.

Patrizia Macera

How long it has been since as a child I ran to the banks of the river to play. Indeed I never imagined how this would alter the course of my life. Playing by the river Po was a simple game that cost nothing, maybe the only game there was in those days, so far removed from our modern excesses.

My encounter with this world, the pebbly shore singing under my feet, was a necessary condition that came about all by chance…but, no, I don't really believe in chance. I think, instead, that we are called; something seeks us out and, though we cannot name it, we feel this special something deep inside of us. For otherwise how else can you explain that though we were many children to play on the banks of the river, only I was to have this special feeling that apparently left the others indifferent?

This attraction is difficult to describe, like a small yet powerful bond with the divine, the discovery in a stone of the message and power of God. As an adult, driven by this same feeling, I later returned to the river for a few peaceful moments to myself and took a handful of stones home with me. I hadn't chosen *them*, but they had found *me*; stones have a way of revealing themselves!

For me, each stone had a story: where I had found it, what had impressed me about it, what it reminded me of, what it made me feel. I turned each one over and over in my hands, with precise movements, attentively studying their shapes, feeling the energy in them. I began to build jewels around these stones to express myself through them and communicate these feelings to others.

This "ritual" has been going on now for thirty years. The collection that has been born out of it is my "book," my autobiography, the testimony of how profound and loving a bond can be with a place and a material, so simple yet so powerfully real.

In a world constantly on the run, turning at top speed, men never take the time to stop a moment. They assume that this is all there is to our world, they see only the surface of things without wondering what might be contained within… I have learned to stop, to look beyond. I think of great majestic mountains where stones are born and how guiding rivers carry them along, becoming like fathers to them, at times gently, at times impetuously, rounding their sharp angles and strengthening their characters.

Stones allow themselves to be molded by rivers and streams but no one can ever destroy them. If they are broken, they begin a new life, they never disappear but are transformed; rocked by gentle waters, stones hum a peaceful melody but when violent currents rush down fast and hard, they are aggressive, overturning everything in their path. Stones can float if you know how to skim them over the water, but if you don't, they sink heavily to the depths out of sight.

Stones are like men, they resemble each other though not one is identical to another, each one is distinguished by a unique personality. This is the concept I apply to my work. Every object is different from the others and each one of us is attracted to one object in particular. And here again, the idea of the "call." A unique relationship is created between ourselves and an object, almost mystical, when we choose it because it is the one that resembles us the most and truly represents us.

Paolo Spalla

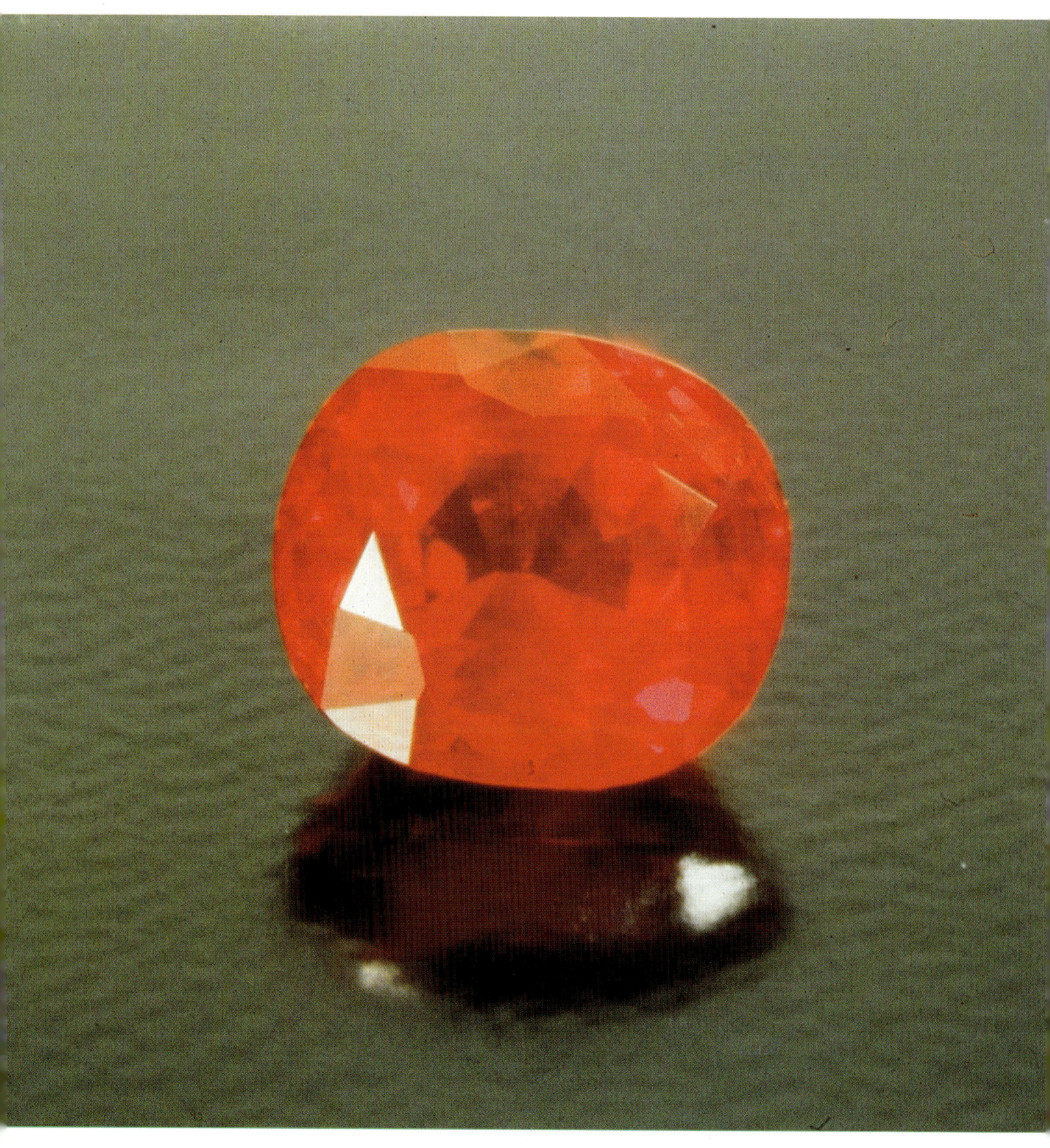

CHAPTER I

Ruby

GENERAL INFORMATION

How it got its name A term that comes down to us from Latin, *rubeus* (red). At one time, rubies, like red spinels and red garnet, were listed generically as carbuncles and it was not until 1800 that they were considered as a separate species.

Varieties To be quite clear: rubies are actually a corundum variety; but they are such extremely precious stones that they are always discussed separately.

Some interesting sidelights That lovely deep red is due to the presence of trivalent chromium atoms. If large stones in prized tints display a brilliant luster and weigh over ten carats, they may be sold for astounding sums; for they are among the rarest of gems, and in no way inferior to the diamond. You may chance upon some specimens made brownish red by the presence of iron, but none of these known shadings have much eye appeal.

In the ruby market we come across fine-sounding names such as "Burmese rubies," "Siamese rubies," "Ceylon rubies" and, lately, even "Vietnamese rubies," though these terms don't exist in the official gemmological dictionary. Rather, they are a fashionable usage invented by dealers on all levels who need a concrete parameter to refer to when describing a particular red shade; such terms do not necessarily identify the country of provenance! And when checking for the mine name, remember that no source of extraction provides uniform material, all with the same qualities in the same degree.

This said, let us add that generally those rubies from ex-Burma (Myanmar) that fulfill all the criteria for a fine stone are truly sumptuous gems, highly prized among all rubies for their great beauty. "Pigeon's blood" is an oft-used term for these specimens; and though this name also has no gemmological referent, it has so caught the public imagination that it is often assumed to represent an official maximum value description.

Princes in India customarily wore extremely valuable rubies and even had them set in their weapons or into the adornment of their thrones.

Rubies in Sanskrit were called *ratnaraj*, which means "King of the precious gems."

Hindus held that the glowing red color was fuelled by what they believed to be eternal flames burning within all rubies.

It was claimed that the owner of a ruby was guaranteed a peaceful and harmonious life, and, on the practical side, would never lose his worldly goods.

A lucky charm in financial matters, rubies are also legendary symbols of passionate, everlasting love. Ayurveda, an ancient Indian folk medicine, proclaimed that rubies stimulated all vital organs, and then improved your mental faculties.

Since rubies are presumed to affect blood circulation, they are also assumed to stop hemorrhaging and cure any inflammation. Further properties: helps

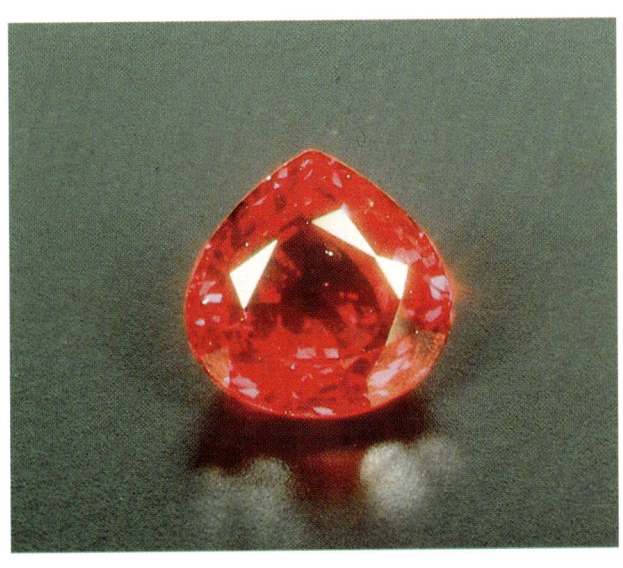

Chemical Formula: *Al_2O_3 – aluminium oxide*
Hardness: *9 (Mohs scale)*
Specific Gravity: *3.90 – 4.10*
Refraction: *biaxial birefringent*
Color: *quite a range of red tones*

eliminate any woman's menstrual pain; or if placed on the navel, it should work wonders for your digestion.

Celebrated rubies The largest stone in history was of Burmese provenance: from its 400-carat rough stone weight three separate gems were obtained.

The most famous rubies known to be in existence today are:

Edward's Ruby (167 carats), housed in the London Museum of Natural History;

Peace Ruby (43 carats), which owes its name to the fact that it was discovered in 1919 at the end of the First World War.

Then, of course, there is the approximately 40-carat Chatrapati Manick Ruby, and the 250-carat stone set in the crown of Charles IV (1346) and now in Prague; again in this city, at the Narodni Museum, there is a Burmese provenance ruby weighing 27.11 carats.

Among the splendid rubies Tavernier described as part of the wonders of his travels, the king of Bijapur possessed one legendary 17.5-carat example cut en cabochon. Of those stones traditionally considered the five most beautiful rubies in the world, one belongs to the Maharani of Baroda.

An exquisite sculpture was created by Harry Derian from a ruby crystal of almost 3,000 carats, provenance Mozambique, and this work of art is now in the United States. For news about stones called "the Timur Ruby" and the "Black Prince's Ruby," however, you will have to turn to "Spinel" under the section "Some interesting sidelights."

Deposits No question about it: the loveliest specimens come from Mogok in Myanmar (ex-Burma), though it seems that only 1% of the material extracted is of gemstone quality. Long famous, indeed, these mines were cited by Marco Polo in the narrative of his travels in Cathay.

Thailand (ex-Siam) is a rich producer, providing about 70% of world production. A substantial part comes from the Chantaburi region, about 300 kilometers from Bangkok. In the southwestern zone of Sri Lanka (ex-Ceylon) a large number of corundums are extracted, including rubies. Vietnam is another good source, with mines in the Yen Bai and Nghe An Provinces.

Additional deposits are in: Kenya (Mangari),

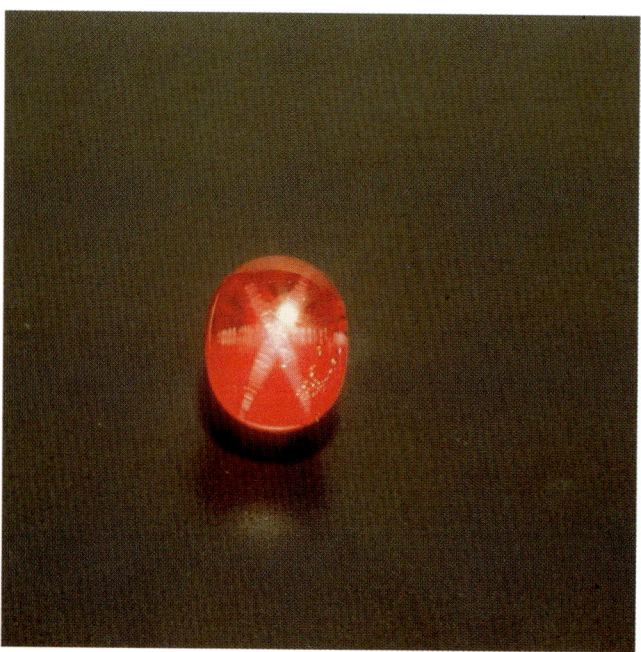

Star ruby from Burma with a cabochon cut.

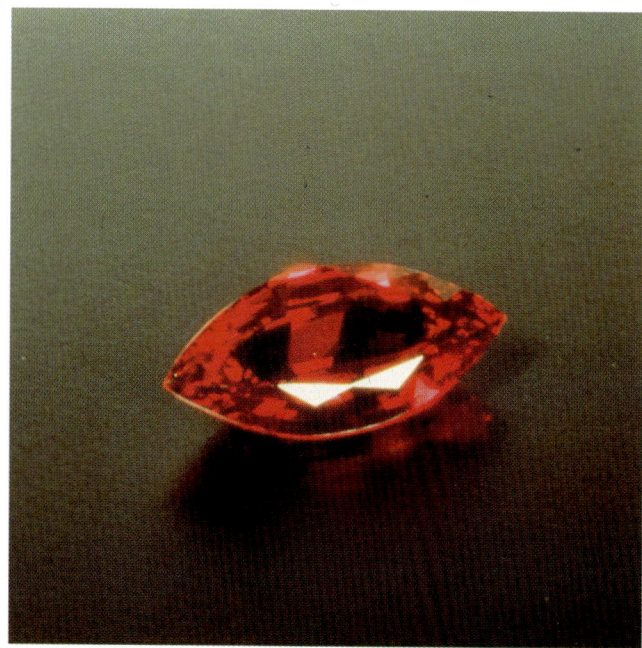

Ruby from Thailand with a marquise cut.

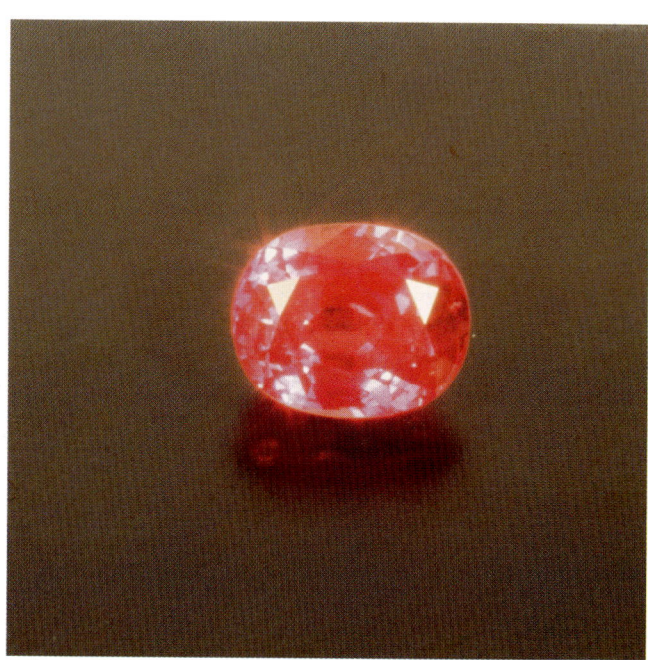

Ruby from Vietnam with a cushion cut.

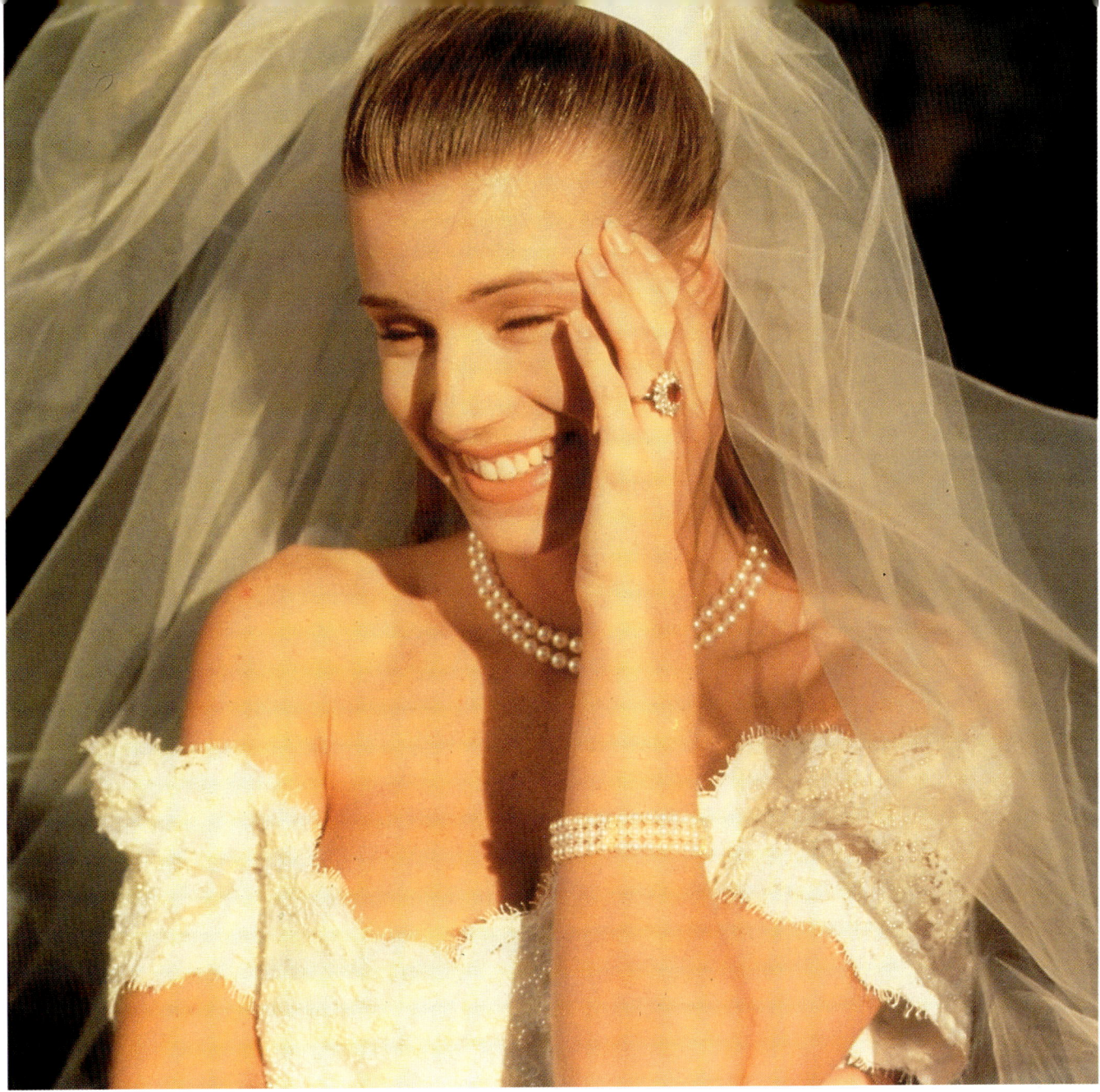

Engagement ring with rubies and diamonds.

Malawi (Chimwadzulu), Tanzania (Morogoro), Afghanistan (Sorobi), and Brazil (Barra Ingedinho).

Cut Rubies are usually best suited for a mixed cut, diamond cut in the upper half and bern cut in the lower.
Outstanding specimens are given the bern or "emerald" cut.

Less transparent specimens are cut en cabochon, or used to produce necklace beads. En cabochon, of course, is used for all specimens displaying the starlike bands of asterism.

Under the lens The radiant glow of asterism (see "Corundum") or a chatoyant effect may be present in some ruby specimens and can always be identified without a lens. For all other ruby specimens, the view through a magnifying lens opens onto a fascinating world.

The chart on the following page is intended to organize and simplify this topic; considering rubies according to provenance, key qualities are listed for important extraction sources.

Let us point out that we may define a stone as natural without having necessarily found all the listed inclusions for each deposit specimen.

Regarding rubies of other provenance, the expert must look for the inclusions listed in the following chart, with the expectation that they will be arranged differently in the sample.

Treatments Very often natural corundums are placed in heat furnaces to improve color and transparency.

Not even ruby is excluded from this operation, which not all experts are inclined to consider a true "treatment." Thailand rubies, in particular, it is believed, may be heated; currently, in fact,

PROVENANCE	INCLUSIONS
Myanmar (ex-Burma) – bright red coloring.	– colorless crystals (at times clearly visible) or even very dark crystals, occasionally evincing halo-effect; – short needles intersecting at 60° and 120° angles with unusual reflection, called "silk"; – colored zonings in hexagonal and straight band shapes; – quite rarely, there are liquid inclusions, conventionally referred to as "finger print" or "fly's wing."
Thailand (ex-Siam) – dark red, occasionally evincing a slightly brownish tinge.	– isolated needles, with tiny pointed branchings; – crystals, generally rounded, often immersed in the numerous liquid inclusions arranged in open weave.
Sri Lanka (ex-Ceylon) – not very deep red, tending toward purple, but fairly bright.	– needles that can produce "silks," as in Burmese rubies, though these are longer specimens; – colorless but also dark crystals; – rather fine liquid inclusions.
Vietnam – purplish red color, occasionally with a milky cast.	– generally, all observed inclusions recall those noted in Burmese rubies; – possible presence of colored zoning and bluish zones.

applying heat treatment to slightly milky material is considered part of routine procedure.

Heating – which is very difficult to detect – will also eliminate unattractive "silks."

Adulteration, effected by inserting glass pieces to fill up small gaps left after the cut, is a process that is severely disapproved of. It is employed, of course, to reduce loss of rough stone and produce a perfect stone without blemishes or breaks.

Fortunately, it is easy to identify this falsification, for glass has a less brilliant sheen, and often the point where ruby and glass join has an irregular, slightly cracked appearance.

At times small air bubbles remain entrapped in these zones and may be observed with a 10x lens.

Under UV rays the glass zone remains inert.

One of the newer ruby treatments involves thermodiffusion applied to only slightly colored, cut natural corundums, a process that creates a red tint.

With careful technique it is even possible to insert chromium atoms – a ruby's chromophore element – until a red coloring is produced. So far, however, none of these treatments have obtained genuinely satisfying reds.

Gemmological analysis laboratories indicate such treatments in their reports with the definition "thermodiffused" rubies; or else they label the stones as "natural corundums whose red coloring has been obtained by thermodiffusion." Under the lens, we see that such color is more marked at angles and that liquid inclusions near the surface have a slightly blackish appearance.

Note that material so treated acquires coloring only on the outer surface while the entire inner stone remains precisely as it was before treatment.

Synthetic rubies Given the importance of this topic, we are considering it separately in order to give a clear overview of the situation.

Initial studies for obtaining synthetic corundums were carried out around 1850. But it was not until 1891 that the first satisfactory results were achieved when E. Fremy and his then assistant, A.V.L. Verneuil, succeeded in obtaining tiny synthetic rubies.

In 1894 Verneuil became Professor of Applied Chemistry at the Museum of Natural History in Paris and continued the research, which he completed at the end of the century when he realized the "Verneuil" process. Today we still employ this method.

Nonetheless, other studies have come along since then, producing various types of synthetic rubies, all bearing the name of their inventor or manufacturing company.

Let's look at a brief summary of the history of synthetic rubies following Verneuil's initial success.

• *Czochralski* (1919). An extraction technique rather similar to Verneuil's; the feeding mass is melted in a crucible in which a technical expert immerses a seed made of a natural ruby crystal. In 1960 there was an attempt to reutilize this method, and today it is ably put to use by the Kyocera Company of Japan, which even manages to produce a synthetic star ruby sold on the market as "Inamori."

- *Chatam* (1960). At first it was believed that these were hydrothermic products; but later Thomas Chatam (son of Carrol Chatam, inventor of the synthesis process) revealed that the technique actually involves a melting and fusing method. However, we can always distinguish these first generation synthetics from the second generation that the San Francisco based Chatam Created Gems began marketing around 1981.

- *Kashan* (1968). Melting and fusion technique. Made by the Ardon Associates Inc., Dallas, Texas.

- *Ramaura* (1981). Fusion and melting method. Produced by the company J.O. Crystal in Redondo Beach, California.

- *Chatam* (1981). Melting and fusion method, probably developed out of the technique invented by them in 1960.

- *Knischka* (1982). To all appearances, this is a melting and fusion method effected with highly specialized techniques. Rubies of this type are produced in Steyr, Austria by the method's inventor, P.O. Knischka.

- *Leichleitner* (1983). Melting and fusion method, adopted to layer-over seeds of natural rubies or even synthetic ones. Manufactured in Austria by the method's inventor, J. Lechleitner.

- *Douros* (1990). Melting and fusion method; produced in Greece.

The chart below is intended to provide an outline of the different sorts of inclusions to be found in varying types of synthetic rubies. Though it may be hard to make out one synthetic from

Synthesis	Viewed under a 10x Lens
Verneuil	– tiny air bubbles, generally isolated but occasionally grouped together; – thin curvilinear striae, resembling grooves in a record.
Czochralski	– inclusions similar to those observed in Verneuil synthetic rubies, though inclusions in the latter are easier to distinguish.
Kashan	– thickly cloudy inclusions that resemble the liquid inclusions observed in natural rubies; – residuum of melting, often in rows; – coloring resembles that found in the finest Burmese rubies.
Ramaura	– fairly widespread cloudy inclusions; – irregularly shaped bright orange fusing residue; – a deep red shade similar to that noted in a number of Thailand rubies.
Chatam	– whitish clouds, sometimes clearly visible, formed of residuum of melting used in the process; – colorless or rose-tinted crystals may be noted; – colored in zones; – color recalls that of finest Burmese rubies.
Knischka	– two-phase (inclusions with simultaneous presence of an air bubble entrapped in a strip of liquid, flattened and arranged like a thin jagged sheeting); – clouds resembling open weave liquid inclusions in Thailand rubies; – color close to that of Chatam's synthetic rubies.
Lechleitner	– in the seed (be it natural or synthetic) there are clear traces of those inclusions found in the natural or synthetic ruby utilized; – clouds and melt residue.
Douros	– residuum of melting similar to that found in Ramaura synthetic rubies; – internal fractures, occasionally quite emphatic; – clouds, which may be whitish with a raylike structure.

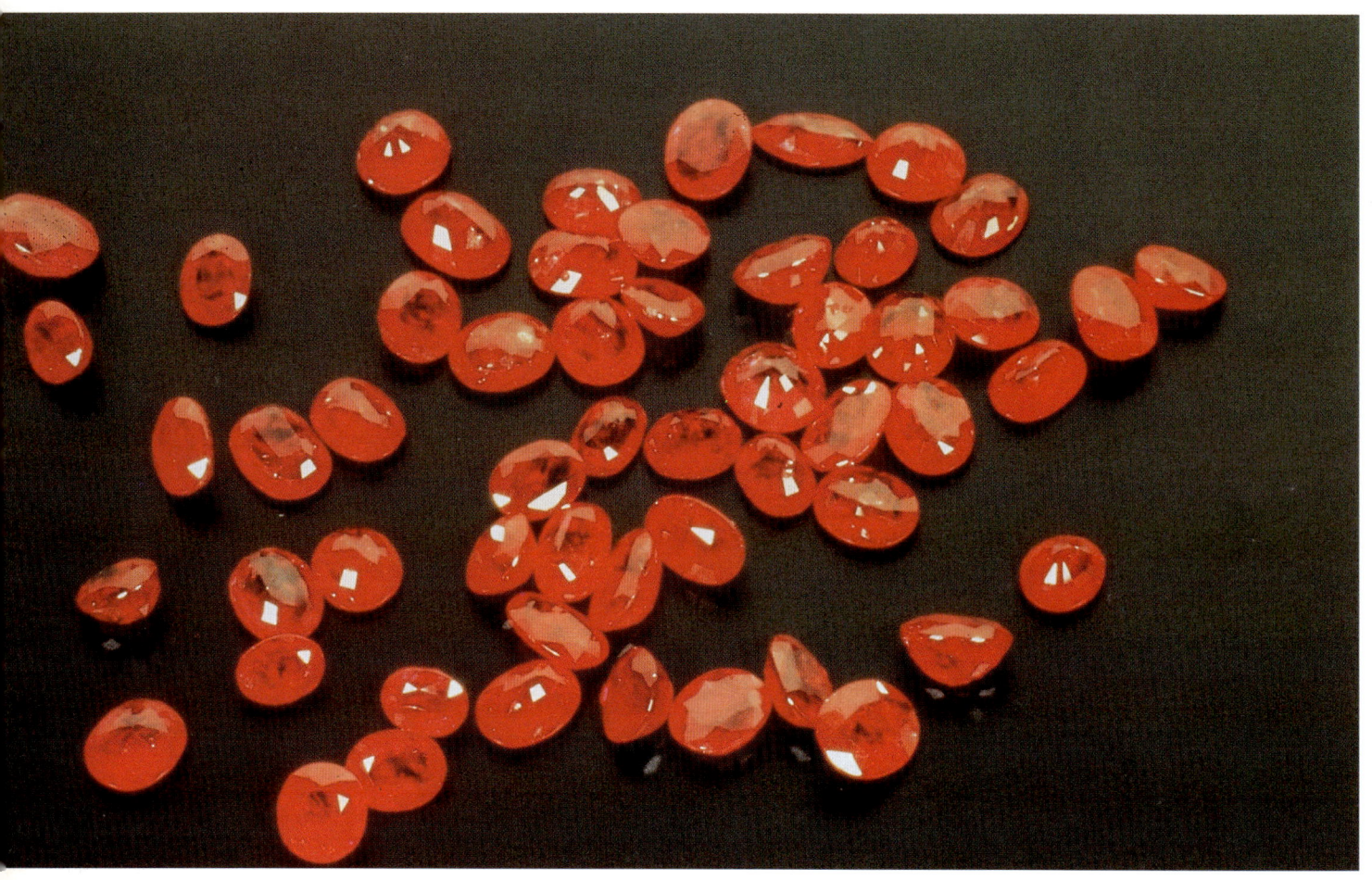

another, in fact it is only really necessary to differentiate between natural and synthetic.

Imitations and similar stones All red-hued stones, even those of little value, may be mistaken for rubies.

There are, however, several mineralogical species that must be distinguished with care such as: garnet (almandine or pyrope), red spinel, red tourmaline (rubellite), topaz, and zircon.

Nor can we overlook simple glass or doppiette imitations. These latter may be put together in such a way that the upper part is formed of a thin sheet of garnet or natural ruby, while the lower part is mere red glass or synthetic ruby.

Among doppiette counterfeits, the most deceptive has a very thin top layer of natural sapphire from Australia (which therefore contains the inclusions found in natural material), and a bottom section of synthetic ruby.

Since this doppiette is almost all lower section, the entire composite seems to be red; moreover, in a superficial examination, the inclusions in the real layer can be misleading. For, sapphirelike ruby is a corundum; so aside from slight differences, the inclusions are almost identical.

An expert will look for signs that reveal where the two parts were attached, with careful attention to the girdle, and examine for possible air bubbles entrapped in the adhesive layer. Our 10x lens is perfectly suited for the job.

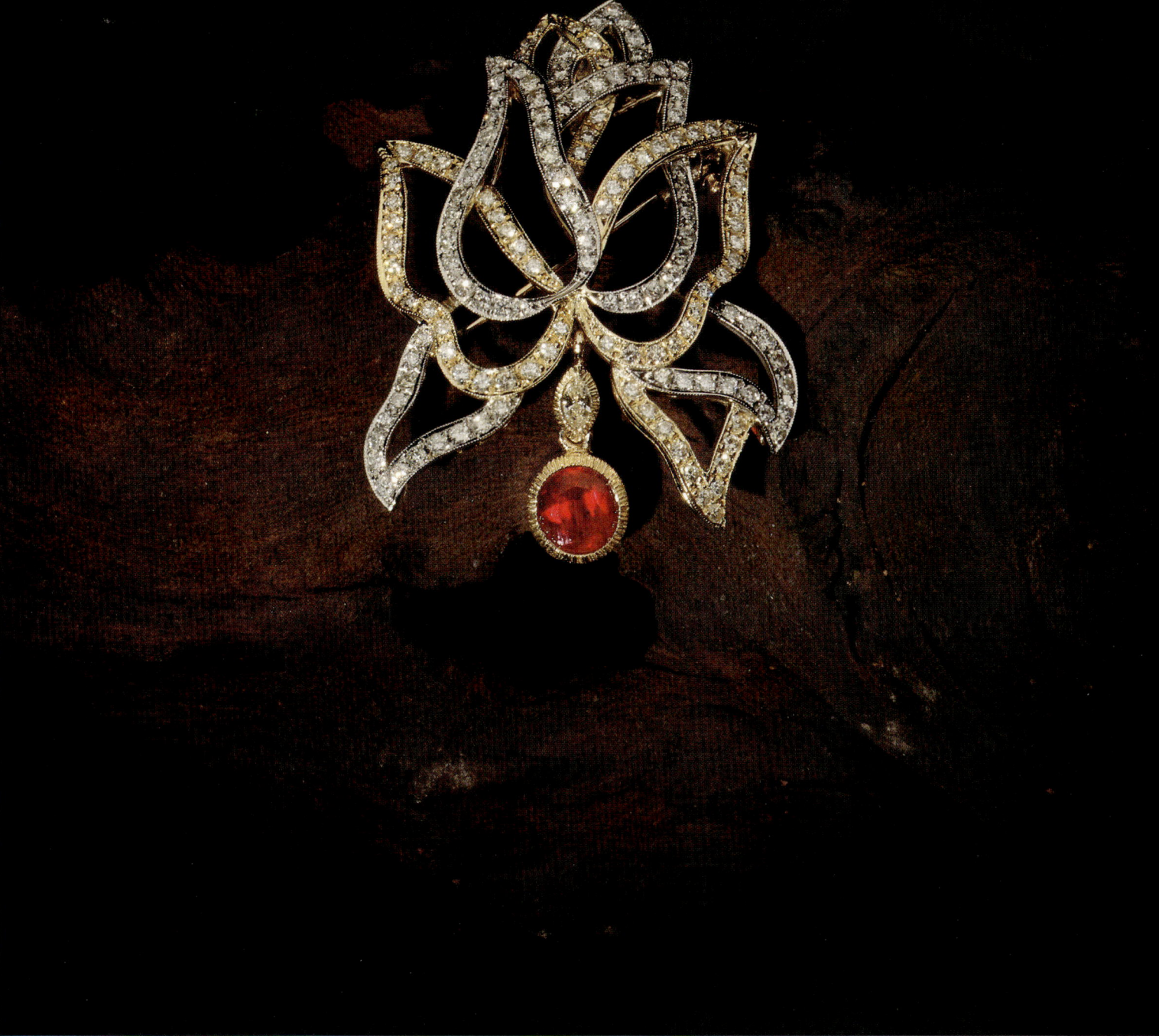

WOO HYUN CHOI: "BUTTERFLY"
Yellow and white gold brooch with a cushion-cut ruby.

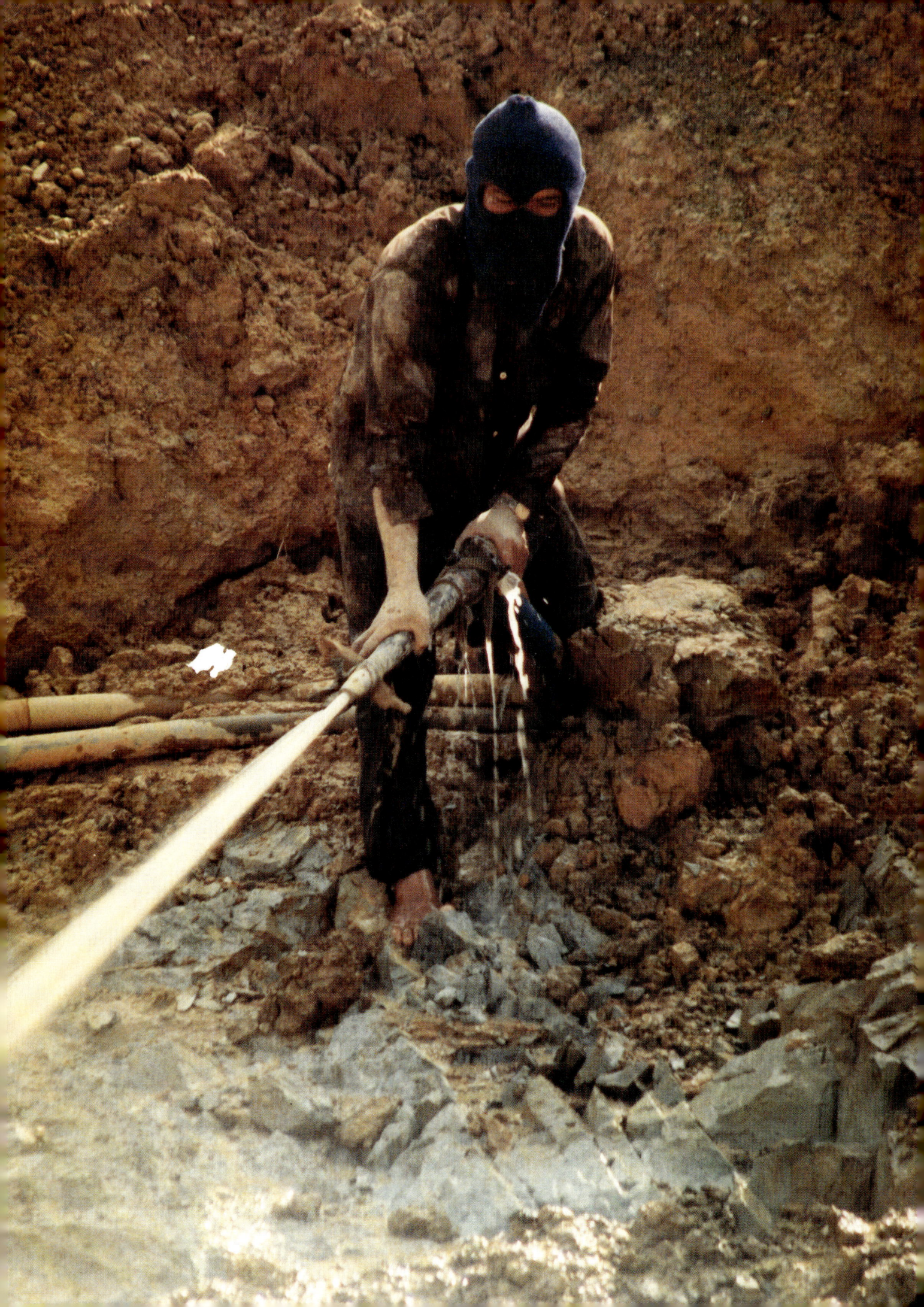

Vietnam:
Watch Out for Rubies

by Claude Mazloum

The Vietnamese embassy in Brussels absolutely refuses to grant me a visa to enter the country, "The purpose of your visit is tourism, for the moment we have no tourism," a good start, I think. At any rate, this minor obstacle is certainly not going to force me to give up my expedition to the new ruby mines in that country, which, according to hearsay, yield specimens as splendid as the Burmese of the Mogok valley.

I leave for Bangkok, the capital of Thailand, where I know I can count on the power and influence of a few of my friends.

As I leave the red and yellow-starred embassy building, not only am I the holder of a visa stamped "Guest of Honor," but I have also been granted a special pass into strictly off-limits zones. The largest deposits being located in the north of the country, I skip Saigon and head directly for Hanoi.

A Surprise Welcome

As I get off the plane, a black limousine is waiting for me, the driver, with a funny Bugs Bunny smile advises, "General Nam O is expecting you for dinner. I am here to drive you to your hotel and then to the General's residence." True, the General and I did have a mutual friend in Bangkok, but I really hadn't expected this kind of welcome.

The General is a fine gentleman, his hair, grown completely white with wisdom and experience, is a rare feature for an Indochinese. He receives me in a luxurious bungalow-type villa with a warm family atmosphere. Wonderful hospitality. Nam O speaks perfect French, particularly thanks to his days collaborating with the Paris troops. We make pleasant small talk, speak of our mutual friend, then come to the heart of the matter, "General, I'm here to visit the new corundum mines."

As a seasoned militaryman, however, caution immediately alters his expression. Though oriental faces are often difficult for Westerners to read, it is all too clear that the General definitely does not approve of my plans. "This would create a lot of problems, political, economic, and most of all a problem of security. The Thais control the situation and are capable of resorting to anything to get what they want. They're supported by the Chinese mafia and some of the army, they would find your presence disturbing. I know clandestine dealing is going on all over the area, even extremely fraudulent transactions in collusion with certain Europeans. An expert like you could denounce them all. No, you would not be welcome there. Listen to me, give it up, I can have full documentation on the world's precious deposits sent to you, photos, everything you need for your report. Please, I beg you, give up the idea."

But I won't be put off, I remind the General that I've been in far more dangerous situations in countries where human life is known to be very cheap... the Vietnamese and Thais are much gentler peoples than, for example, the Colombians. And at least, here, I can make myself understood, "Don't worry, I'll be okay."

The General admires my courage and tenacity, and finally gives in, "Alright then, but let me give you some tips and some names just in case you have any problems."

The Vinh Mines

The Vietnamese deposits are located on two sides of Hanoi, to the north, towards the Chinese frontier, and to the south, towards the Gulf of Tonkin. Heeding the General's advice, I start with those in the South, admittedly less interesting, but also far less dangerous.

At six in the morning I catch a bus, an old Saviem pieced together with Japanese spare parts, that runs between Hanoi and Thanh Hao. The first police check earns me the place of honor next to the driver, it seems I am the only foreign passenger aboard.

From the city to villages, from villages to hamlets, a few army road blocks where documents and luggage are screened and searched, and at noon we arrive in Thanh Hoa, a small, quiet, poor town immersed in wild vegetation. Someone recommends the boarding house across the street from the bus terminal. No point in trying to set out on the overland expedition now, it is already much too late. I make preparations for it though, and inquire about the sites, about people who might be of help.

The guide who has been recommended to me confirms that there will be a good four-hour walk to reach the mines tomorrow, a nice way to start the day. "You should get some sleep, we'll be leaving at three in the morning."

And so it is. Two hours by jeep to cover fifty kilometers of dirt track before reaching the edge of a thick jungle. It is still dark when we start unloading the car, we will both be carrying a backpack of twenty kilos each! As soon as the first rays of the sun appear we enter the jungle.

Ho Chi Minh's men, who exploit the deposits to finance the purchase of arms, have made sure that the mines are virtually impossible to reach. Here and there patches of asphalt, twisted and torn by powerful roots, remind us that at one time good roads existed. The discovery of rubies in the region put an end to life here, condemning the entire area to isolation. Overgrown abandoned villages, first gutted by men's iron bars and then by fire and finally giant trees, testify to the barbarity and violence of the process.

We walk for three hours along paths freshly cleared

by invisible machettes, there is absolutely no one in sight. True, it is only 8:00 in the morning, but I can feel my guide's nervousness. He keeps looking at his compass and notepad until finally he admits, "We should have come to a river, walked along it until we came to a bridge, I don't understand why we're still in this jungle."

I fly into a terrible rage, as violent as it is unusual for me, until he confesses on his knees that he has never set foot in this region and that a friend had simply given him directions in order to pocket the two hundred dollars I had offered for a guide.

So here we are lost. What can we do, I have brought no maps, none exist officially. We stop in a clearing, my guide at least manages breakfast with coffee.

I begin to feel like some character in one of those classic adventure films where the hero suddenly finds himself hopelessly lost in a jungle full of wild beasts. Fortunately, at least, the wild animals seem to be missing here, but the only other difference is that this happens to be reality…

Luckily we had enough foresight to leave some markings to guide us back to the car, and we rest before heading back. I hear cracking sounds suddenly, then rushing noises as half a dozen soldiers appear from out of the bush. The guide's face lights up, finally someone to help us. No doubt they saw our fire. They check my papers, our bags, then kindly offer to help us get our bearings. Indeed, we aren't far at all from our destination. At about eleven we reach the bridge and at noon the mines.

It is like one big sprawling campsite. Makeshift houses, parasols, and tents shelter hundreds of people from the beating sun, the forest having been completely razed. The land has been thoroughly overturned everywhere. Men, women, children, waist-deep in muddy holes of clay and water, are patiently digging, searching. Each one has a small pouch hanging from his neck. When a miner finds a stone, he puts it on his tongue, sucks it clean, spits out the mud then drops the shining stone delicately into his pouch.

Often the stones are rubies, though small ones. The area is quite rich. There is no bickering, no violence among the workers, when someone finds a large stone he shows it proudly to his companions who congratulate him. At day's end, the Thais come and buy up the daily spoils, paying next to nothing for them, then smuggle the gems to Bangkok for cutting.

By early afternoon everyone is visibly exhausted. As the site seems safe enough, I decide to spend the night among the miners. We had foreseen this possibility and have a tent with us and everything we need to set up camp. In any case, it would be almost impossible to get back to our base before nightfall.

That evening I make friends with the miners, who have understood that I am a gemmologist, and they show me their finds. One man, from out of his pouch, produces a tremendous crystal. Another displays a rough stone of beautiful breathtaking colors, someone else, a fragment so pure it seems impossible in a natural specimen. No one tries to sell me anything, the guide has already warned them that I have no money on me, for safety's sake.

The next day, after a very long hike, we get back to our jeep and return to Thanh Hao, and then Hanoi.

The Yen Bai Mines

As soon as I reach the capital, I call the General who has some very good news for me. He has arranged to have me accompanied by one of his lieutenants to the mines in the North.

At nine in the morning our party leaves by jeep for Hanoi. Two men in the front, two in the back, since the lieutenant Nguyen Quoc Phien and I are also accompanied by two soldiers for protection.

The northern route is much richer than the one to the south. I marvel at the lush landscapes that unfold before our eyes at every turn, though I notice my escorts appear much less impressed. From the Red River to the Claire River the ride is absolutely extraordinary.

At noon on the dot we are in Yen Bai province, only a few kilometers from the frontier town of Lao Cai, on the Chinese border. We immediately enter the valley where the gem deposits are located and where the Da River originates.

I am astounded! Here we are at the Cao Yen mine, no mishaps, no adventures, I have never reached a destination so easily in my life. The General should have done this from the beginning.

These deposits are not at all like the ones in the South, even though the corundums mined here are almost identical. Here everything is extremely well organized, there is even electricity to run motors and vibrators. It looks more like Thailand. I see trucks, bulldozers, houses, and even a restaurant with a bar.

I invite the soldiers for lunch. A European is having a drink inside. He is quite drunk, a bright crimson, and, holding up his glass introduces himself in English, "I am Lechner, Max Lechner, professional buyer for the S.S.A. and Co. of Vienna, welcome."

In spite of his state, I invite him to join me at my table and try to find out more. He turns out to be a nostalgic ex-mercenary from the Indochinese War, now turned dealer in rough stones. Alcohol and drugs have taken their toll. A few more drinks and his thick speech begins to flow, he specializes in buying the rough stones that no other merchants are interested in, remnants and leftovers after rough-hewing. At the lowest of prices, of course.

"What do you do with these stones?"

"Oh, in Austria, they can turn a small corundum fragment into a superb ruby, several carats, if you heat them long enough."

A few minutes later a Thai comes over with a pouch of stones and affably offers to sell them to me. Max smiles, "You see, here's where our production goes, everything I buy comes back here, ha!" The Thai sends him an angry look, Lechner bursts out laughing again and nodding in my direction, "He's a gemmologist, he'll never fall for it, he's even written books. Please go home, go home…"

Then, turning to me, "Even professionals, though, have been fooled especially when it comes to those made by our Japanese and American competitors."

I have certainly learned a lot in only a few minutes. New synthetics, extremely difficult to detect, are circulating in the mines. These synthetics are often mixed in with the truck loads of gemmiferous earth taken to the vibrators. The loads of earth are sold at auction to miners who own sorting facilities but have already exhausted the precious substance on their own lands. They buy the earth in order to keep their facilities going and amortize the machinery.

As each day passes and frauds are discovered one after another, uncontrolled powers seem to surpass themselves in inventing more and more Machiavellian ways of recycling these synthetics.

It All Ends Up in Bangkok

In Bangkok I go to one of the many jewelry shops on Silom Road, pretending to be a tourist looking for a large ruby to take back with me to Europe, "A three or four-carat ruby, a very good one, Burmese if possible."

"We have just what you're looking for, a 3.85 cushion cut, Burmese from Mogok. Ten thousand dollars a carat."

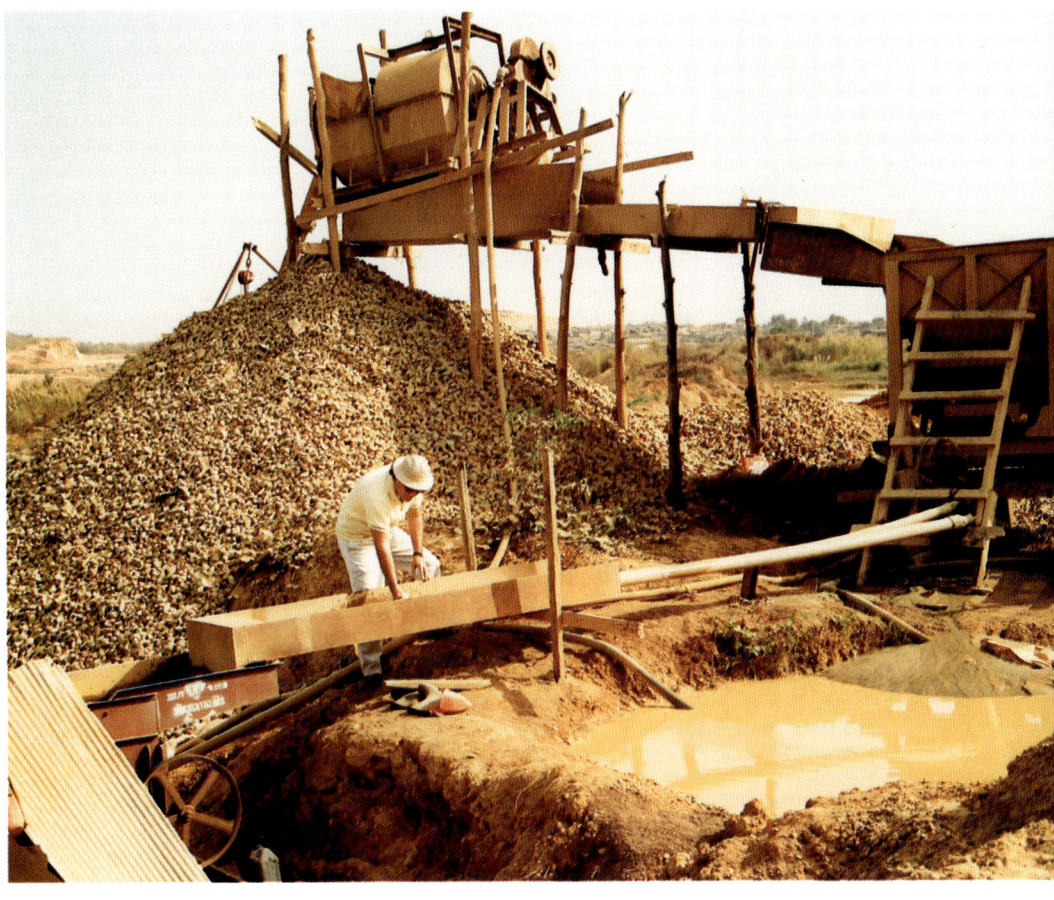

An excellent stone, reasonable price, even quite a good bargain, I must admit, for the quality and weight.

I decide to try my luck: "I can offer you five thousand dollars for the stone, that's all I have."

A general exclamation of surprise and then amusement sweep the shop. Have I done something wrong? At about eight o'clock that evening the front desk tells me someone is at the hotel to see me. To my surprise, it's the jeweler from Silom Road, "I accept your offer of five thousand dollars cash, I've brought you the stone with its certificate of authenticity."

I can't believe it, a 3.85 certified Burmese ruby at five thousand dollars, impossible! I ask him to come up to my room. Of course the ruby isn't sealed. I reveal my true identity to him, he apologizes and leaves.

These so-called jewelers first have a number of real rubies certified, then have perfect imitations made in artificial materials. They don't stop there: to justify the fact that the stones are not sealed, they set them in jewels.

When I told my story to a trustworthy dealer and friend of mine, he also confirmed the practice. A supplier had offered him some small, light, rather dull rubies which he had refused to buy. Once out on the landing, the supplier was seen on video taking another pouch of rubies out of his pocket and adding a fistful of these to his original lot before going to see my friend's neighbor to try to sell them there. Tipped off by my friend, his neighbor carefully examined the lot and found that, true enough, it was a mixture of real and false stones.

From everything seen and heard, I truly wonder if the lots that come to Europe, even if officially declared as genuine rubies, are in fact all authentic. I am also beginning to ask myself if the manufacturers who innocently use these stones realize what they might be mounting on their jewels. Will it perhaps be necessary from now on to check these stones, one by one, thus further adding to production cost?

Finally, in the case a private party has a jewel they have just bought expertised and discover that synthetic stones have been used, who will be held responsible?

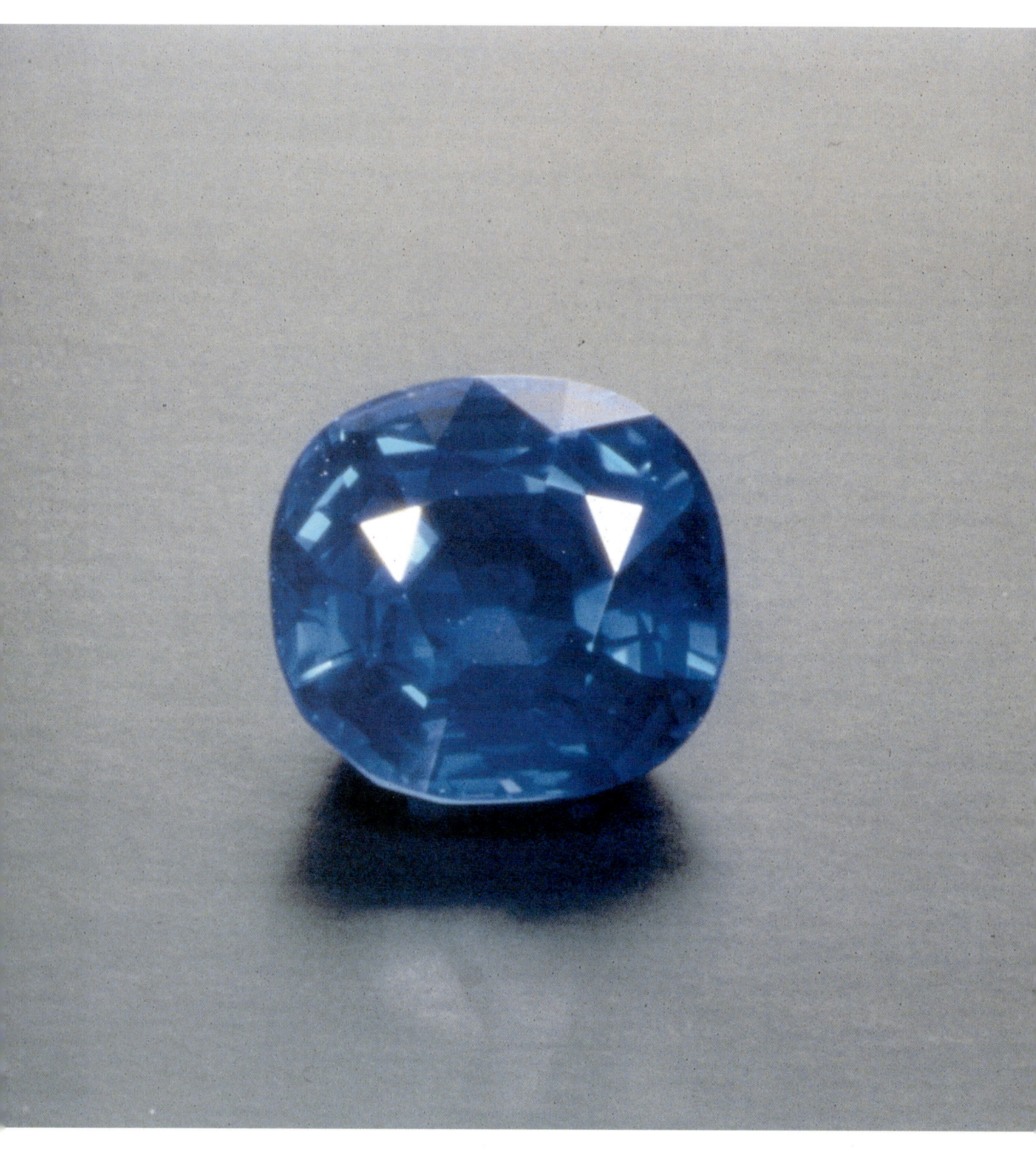

CHAPTER II

Sapphire

GENERAL INFORMATION

How it got its name Either in debt to the Greek color term *sappheiros* for its rich azure shade, or tracing to the Hebrew word for "most beautiful thing" (*sappir*). Until the 1800s almost all blue stones were generically referred to as "sapphire."

Varieties It bears repeating: sapphire is a variety of corundum (see "Corundum"); but, given its immense value as a precious stone, it is always discussed separately.

Some interesting sidelights This intense blue tint is due to the presence of minimum quantities of iron and titanium atoms in the crystal lattice of aluminium oxide.

Reputedly, world sapphire production is twenty times that of ruby, and it is not unusual to find good quality stones weighing over 10 carats.

As with ruby (see "Ruby"), there is much talk of "Burmese sapphires" or "Siamese sapphires" or "Kashmir sapphires"; and we must emphasize that these, again, are not official gemmological referents.

According to Christian belief sapphires are a highly spiritual stone since their color is a perfect match for the hue traditionally assigned to the Virgin's cape in allegorical paintings. Moreover, Pope Innocence III chose sapphire for the bishop's ring.

Buddhists, on the other hand, contend that the gem is an invitation to prayer and is therefore, in itself, spiritually elevating. The stone is also held to be an amulet against bad luck of all kinds. In fact, it has always been a talismanic stone, and such qualities were attributed to the gold pendant, belonging to Charles the Great; enclosing a fragment of Christ's Cross, it is set with two en cabochon-cut sapphires and is now on display in Rheims Cathedral in France.

In India people also believe in the sapphire's positive magic, and point to the Navaratna, a jewel composed of nine gems of which one is a midnight blue sapphire said to unite humanity with the heavenly spheres. Moreover, sapphires are said to change color if the wearer is not a wholly sincere person.

Its medicinal powers are proposed for curing rheumatism and sciatica.

It is also thought to heighten one's powers of observation, increasing your chance of making the right decision; as bonus, it should make you good-natured as well.

Celebrated sapphires The Mineral Museum of Paris displays a historically fabled 133-carat stone which belonged to the French Royal Family. A gorgeous bright blue sapphire weighing 258.8 carats is housed in the Kremlin Museum in Moscow.

For historic echoes, two other famous gems are called the "St. Edward" and the "Stuart" stones, though the latter is also called "Charles II." And we can hardly forget to mention the 2,302-carat gem adopted by Norman Maness to carve the likeness of Abraham Lincoln.

A fairly recent Christie's auction offered a 377.66-carat specimen which was extracted in Sri Lanka and mounted in 1910 by Cartier & Arpels

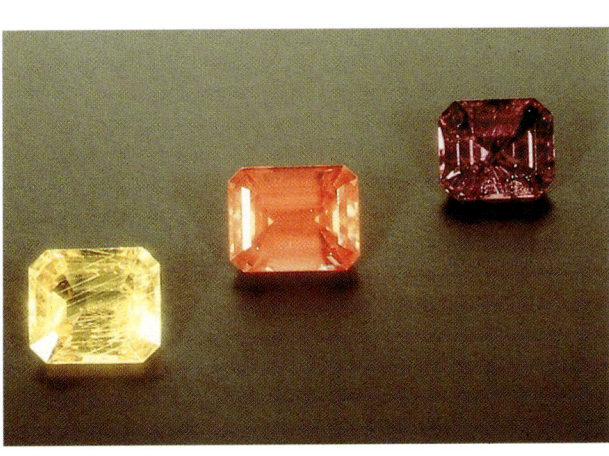

Chemical Formula: Al_2O_3 – aluminium oxide
Hardness: 9 (Mohs scale)
Specific Gravity: 3.95 - 4.05
Refraction: biaxial birefringent
Color: varying tonalities of blue; azure

in a jewel also enhanced with 20 diamonds weighing a total of about 24 carats.

It was not until the end of the Second World War that this stone had its public presentation. Another coincidence: the Cartier gem is identical in weight with the legendary stone owned by Catherine the Great.

Deposits Most important mining areas are: Myanmar (ex-Burma), in the Mogok area; Thailand (ex-Siam), mainly in the area of Battambang and in the Kanchanaburi Province; Cambodia, in Pailin; and Sri Lanka (ex-Ceylon), in the southwestern area.

A cornflower blue variety first found in 1881 in the Zanskar district of Kashmir is quite highly prized though recent extractions have had seesaw results.

Australian mines in Queensland have produced vast quantities of dark, almost inky-blue material but this output is currently very limited. The quality found in Montana, in the United States, has a metallic sheen but comes in quite small pieces.

At the moment there are additional sources of limited importance in: Tanzania (along the Umba River), China (near the city of Mingxi, and on Penglaim, an island of Hainan).

Cut Like ruby, sapphire is best suited to a mixed cut, though for truly beautiful specimens the emerald cut is advised.

Less transparent material is worked en cabochon or may be used for inlays, and any stones evincing asterism are always cut en cabochon.

Under the lens Asterism is a fairly common phenomenon in sapphire and is clearly visible with the naked eye (see "Corundum").

To simplify the mass of information available, the following table clarifies deposits and their characteristics.

The presence of specific inclusions determine an analysis of precise variety, and the presence of even one inclusion guarantees the specimen is natural. Therefore, aside from the provenances cited above, sapphires of whatever origin will be labelled natural if they contain at least one of the inclusions described in some part of the table.

For example, a deep, almost blackish blue Australian sapphire contains both liquid inclusions and color banding, sometimes arranged almost like the sides of an irregular hexagon; its combination of qualities is rather singular, but natural.

Treatments Not all experts are willing to define heating as a treatment as such; for, by now, it has become a routine methodology when treating stones that are a bit milky or have an overly dark cast, as the technique increases transparency and brilliance.

Heating, which resists easy laboratory identification, can almost eliminate unpleasant silks.

When thermodiffusion techniques are employed

PROVENANCE	INCLUSIONS
Myanmar (ex-Burma) – fairly deep velvety blue with very faint purplish overtones.	– rare crystal inclusions; – fairly numerous liquid inclusions (fingerprint); – intersecting short "shoelace" strings; – may have "silks"; – occasional color bands and slightly brownish zonings.
Thailand (ex-Siam) – truly intense blue, at times with a slightly milky cast.	– particle clouds that can create "silks"; – rectilinear bands of coloring; – highly visible liquid inclusions; – crystals often surrounded by liquid inclusions.
Cambodia (Pailin) – electric blue.	– inclusions very like those found in Thailand sapphires.
Sri Lanka (ex-Ceylon) – quite variable shades: from azure to deep blue with occasional gaps in coloring.	– widespread presence of large liquid inclusions; – crystals (including red ones); – overall presence of easily detected rutilated needles; – a number of crystals may have a halo effect; – bands of color, at times broken off in pieces.
Kashmir – slightly milky, cornflower blue	– very small liquid inclusions; – typical zonings of wide milky bands.

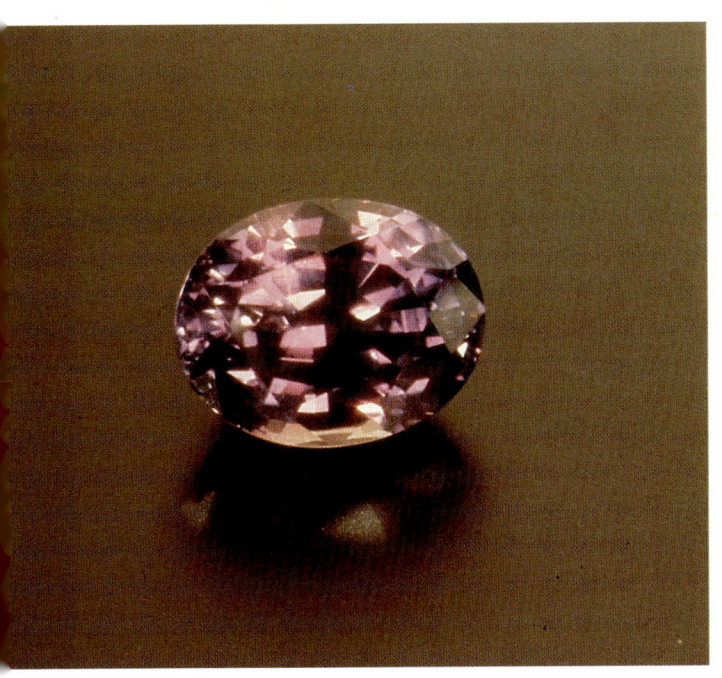
Sapphire which changes color according to the light.

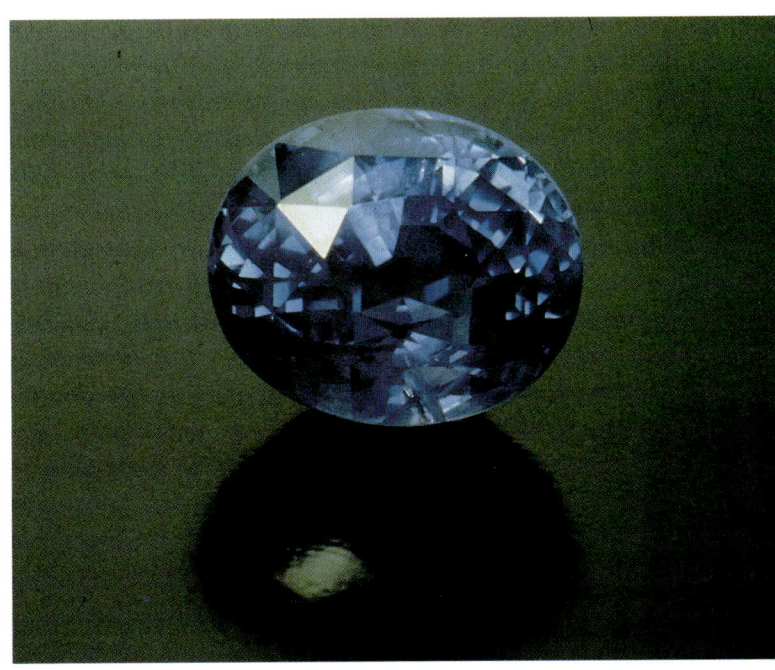
Sapphire from the Sri Lankan mines weighing 30.73 carats.

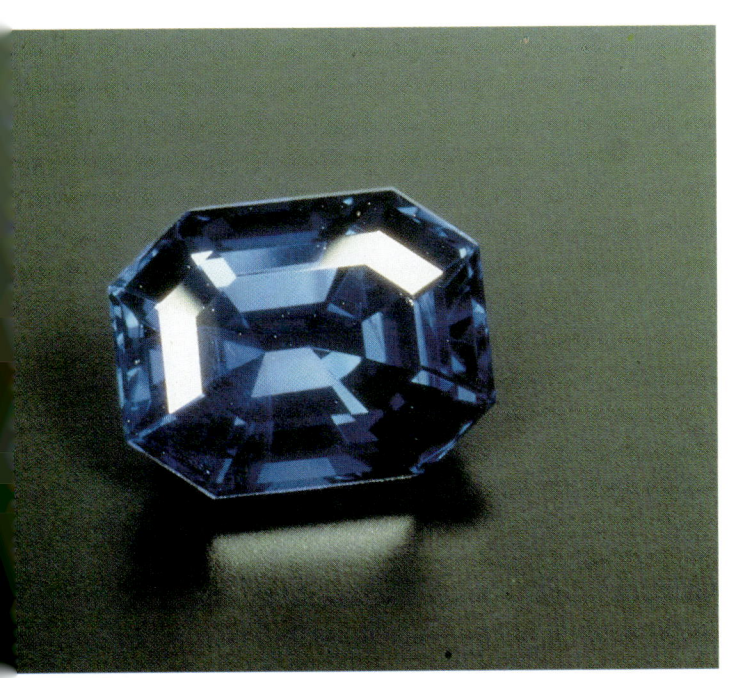
Sapphire from Burma with an emerald cut.

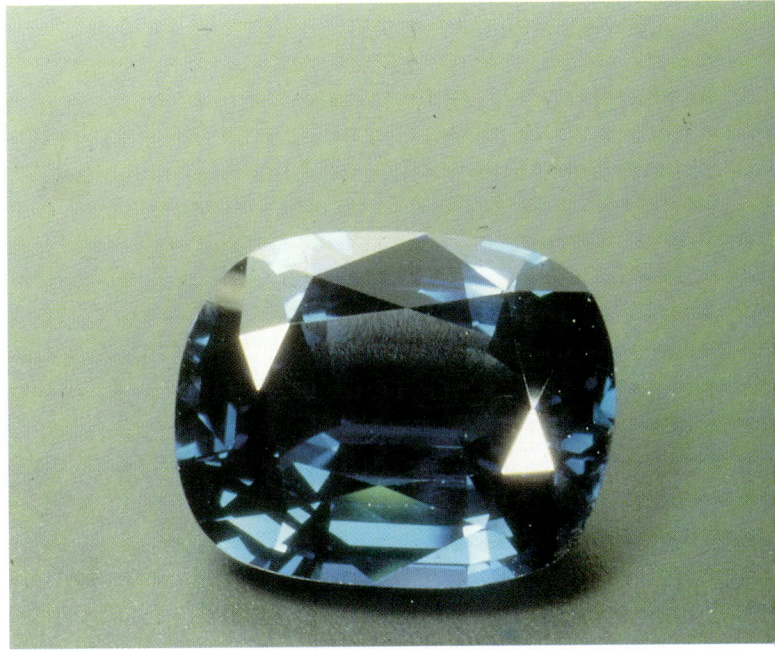
Sapphire from Thailand with a cushion cut.

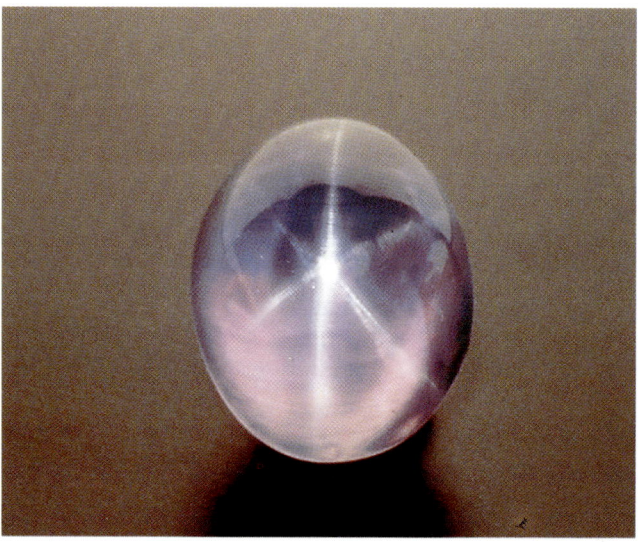

Star sapphire from Sri Lanka with a cabochon cut.

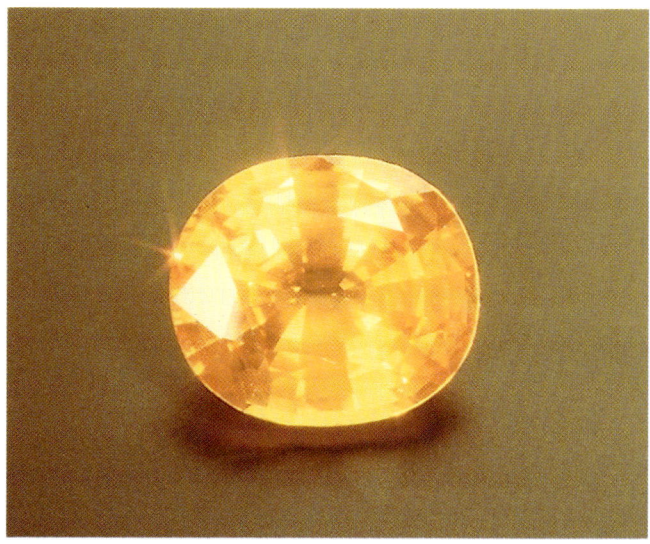

Yellow sapphire with a cushion cut.

they must surely be declared. For, the method creates founts of color that have been created artificially and are actually very, very thin layers. From natural pale corundums that have little value, it is possible to produce a stunning blue material that would certainly be highly prized, were it natural.

It is generally agreed that such a stone must always be correctly labelled as a natural corundum whose color has been produced by thermodiffusion. And it should be noted that the tint is easily removed by energetic polishing on a stone cutter's grinding wheel.

With a 10x lens we can see that such color is more pronounced on the angles and that liquid inclusions near the surface look slightly blackish.

This treatment was first invented in the Italian town of Valenza in a laboratory for gemmological analysis co-owned by one of the authors of this book.

Synthetics and similar stones In theory, all methods employed to obtain synthetic rubies (see "Ruby") can also be used to produce synthetic sapphires; however the only process actually put to use is the flame-fusion method invented by Verneuil.

To best explain such limited use of the numerous synthetic techniques available, perhaps we should take a look at the substantial quantity of material extracted, with its great gamut of colors, all of which affects the cost of natural sapphires and means that there is a market supply that easily satisfies any and all buyer requests.

This does not mean, certainly, that there are no synthetic sapphires on the market; but it does explain the lack of interest in that multitude of sophisticated techniques employed to create synthetics of the far scarcer ruby.

To identify a synthetic sapphire you have only to use the 10x lens and with it hunt for air bubbles – frequently grouped – and for curvilinear striae that look like the grooves in a vinyl record.

Natural sapphire may be confused with other gems such as: benitoite, cordierite, sapphirine, blue spinel, tanzanite, topaz, and tourmaline. It may be counterfeited by doppiettes whose lower section is made of synthetic sapphire (or even just blue-dyed glass substances), while the upper section is formed of natural material, either dark natural sapphire or natural green corundum or even natural garnet; however a simple blue artificial glass is also much employed as imitation sapphire.

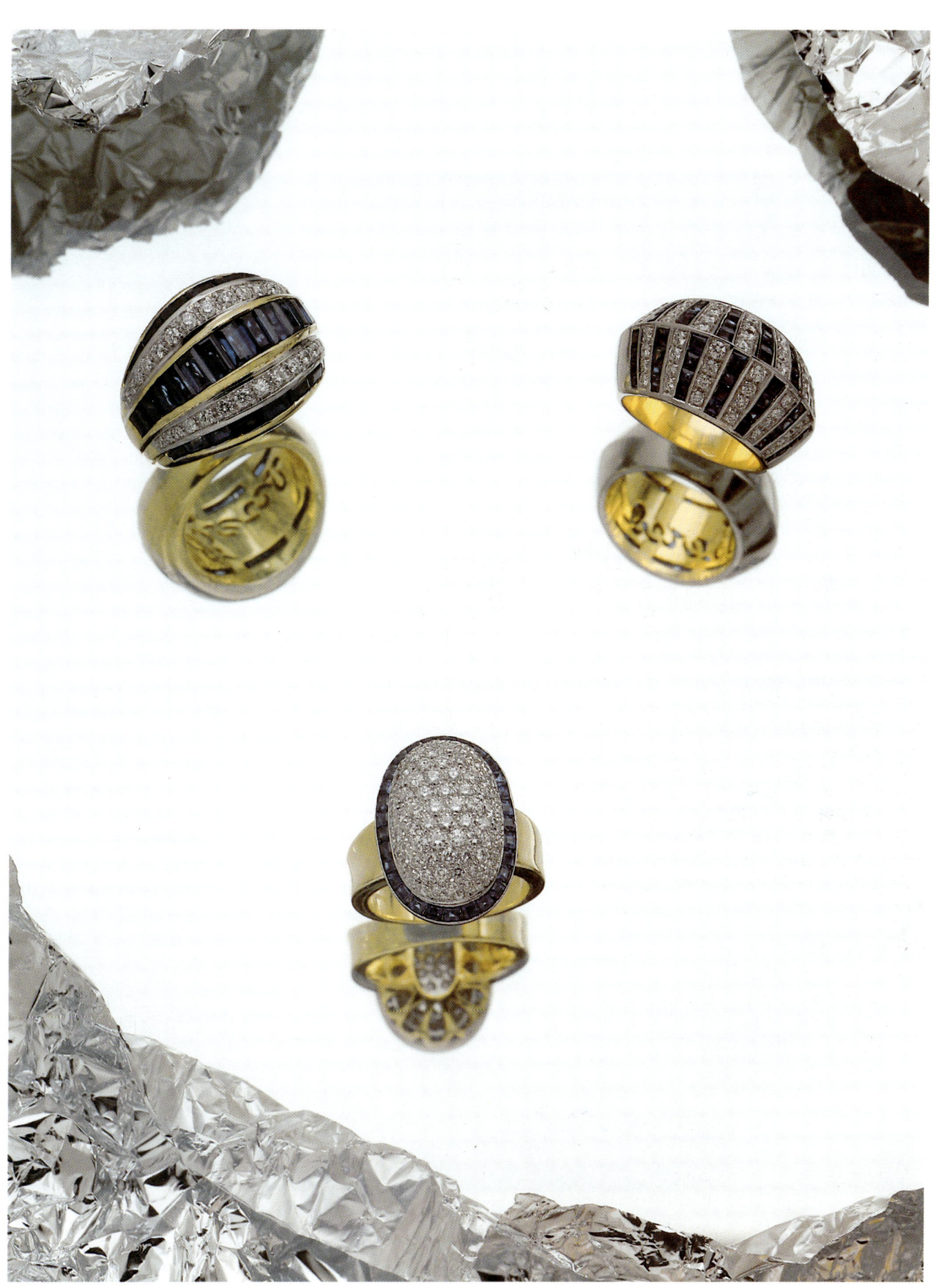

BERCA.
Gold rings with diamonds and sapphires.

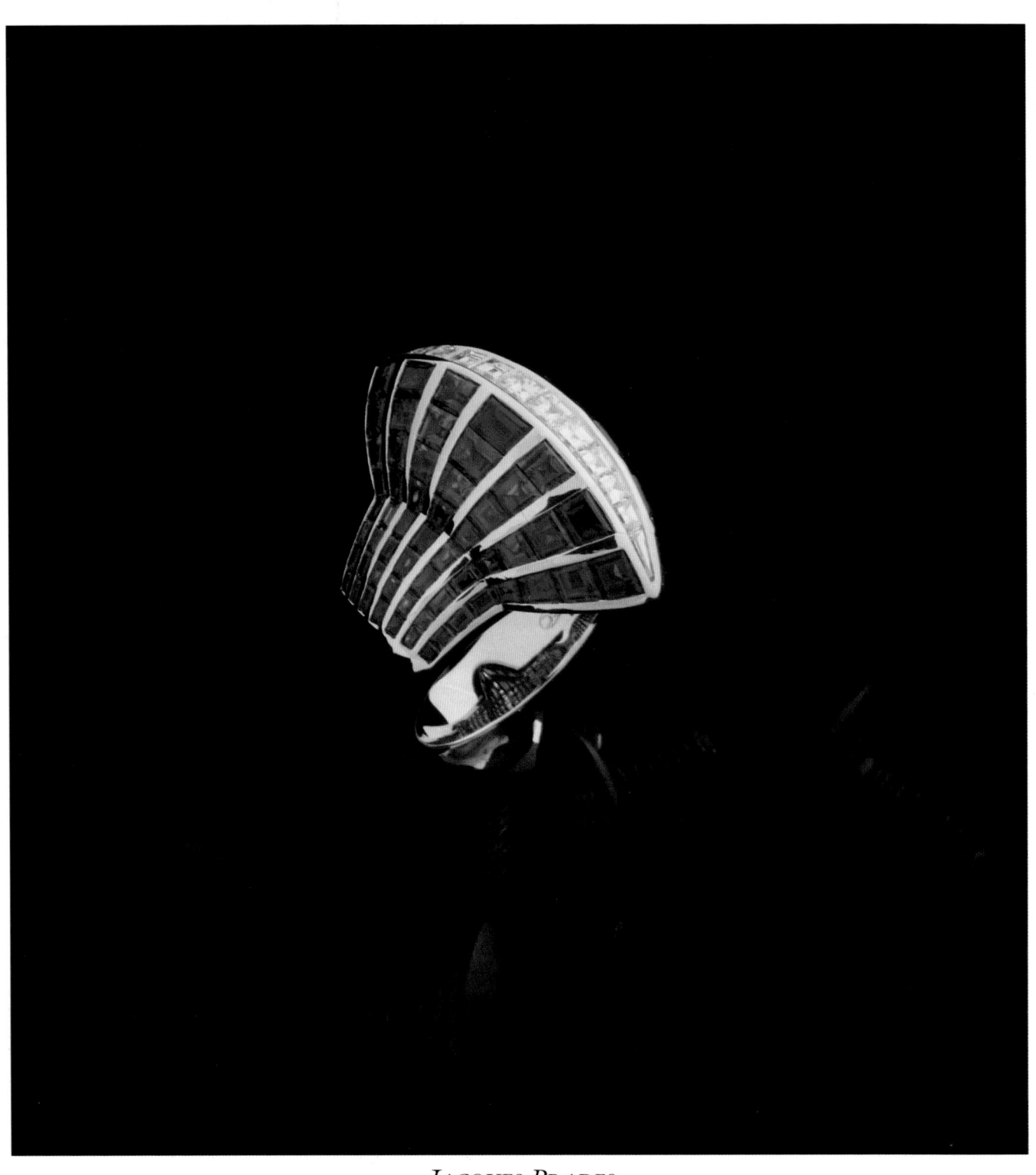

Jacques Prades.
Ring in platinum with diamonds and sapphires.

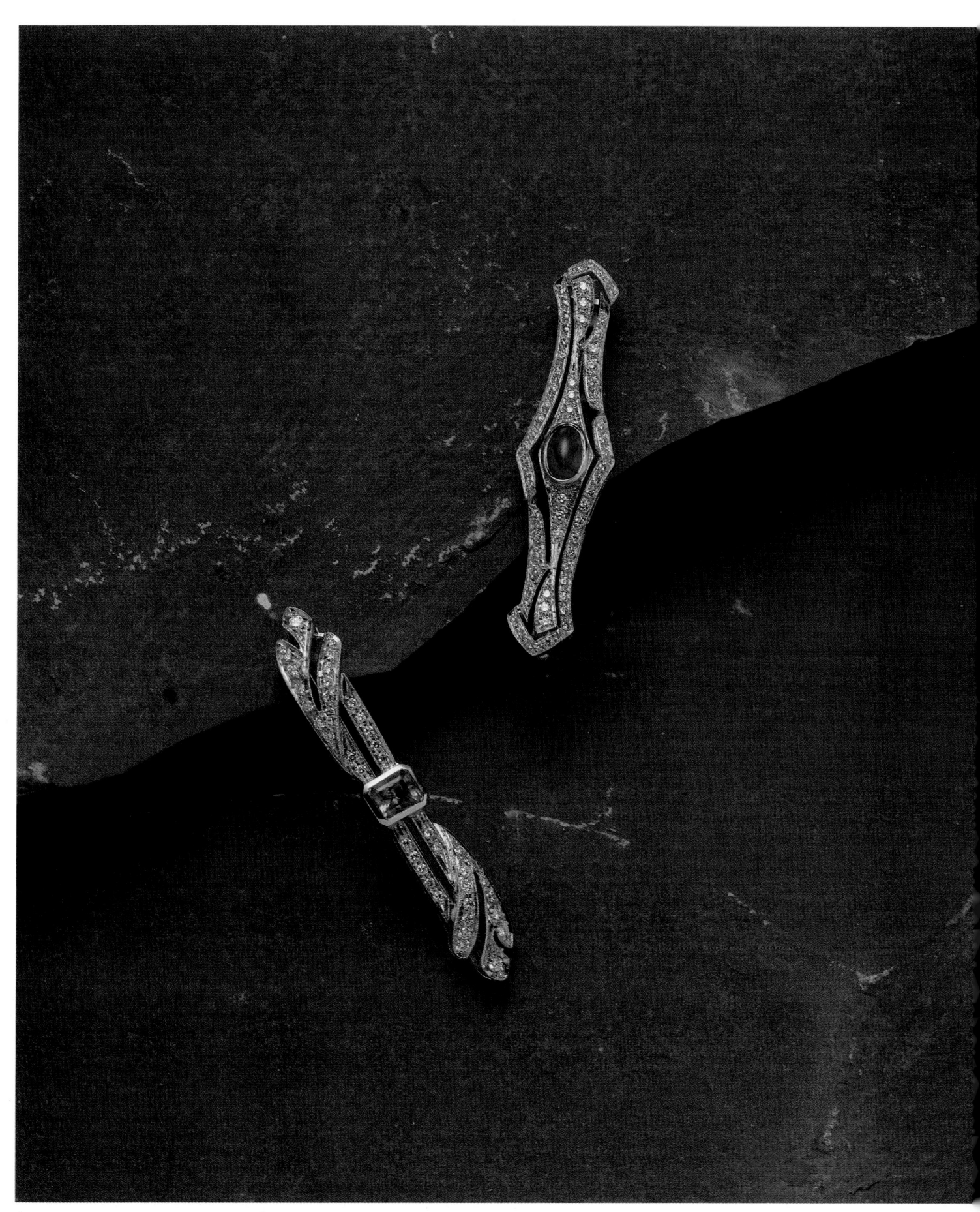

P. Carlo Lenti.
Two 1930s-style brooches with a Burmese en cabochon sapphire,
a Zambian emerald, and diamonds.

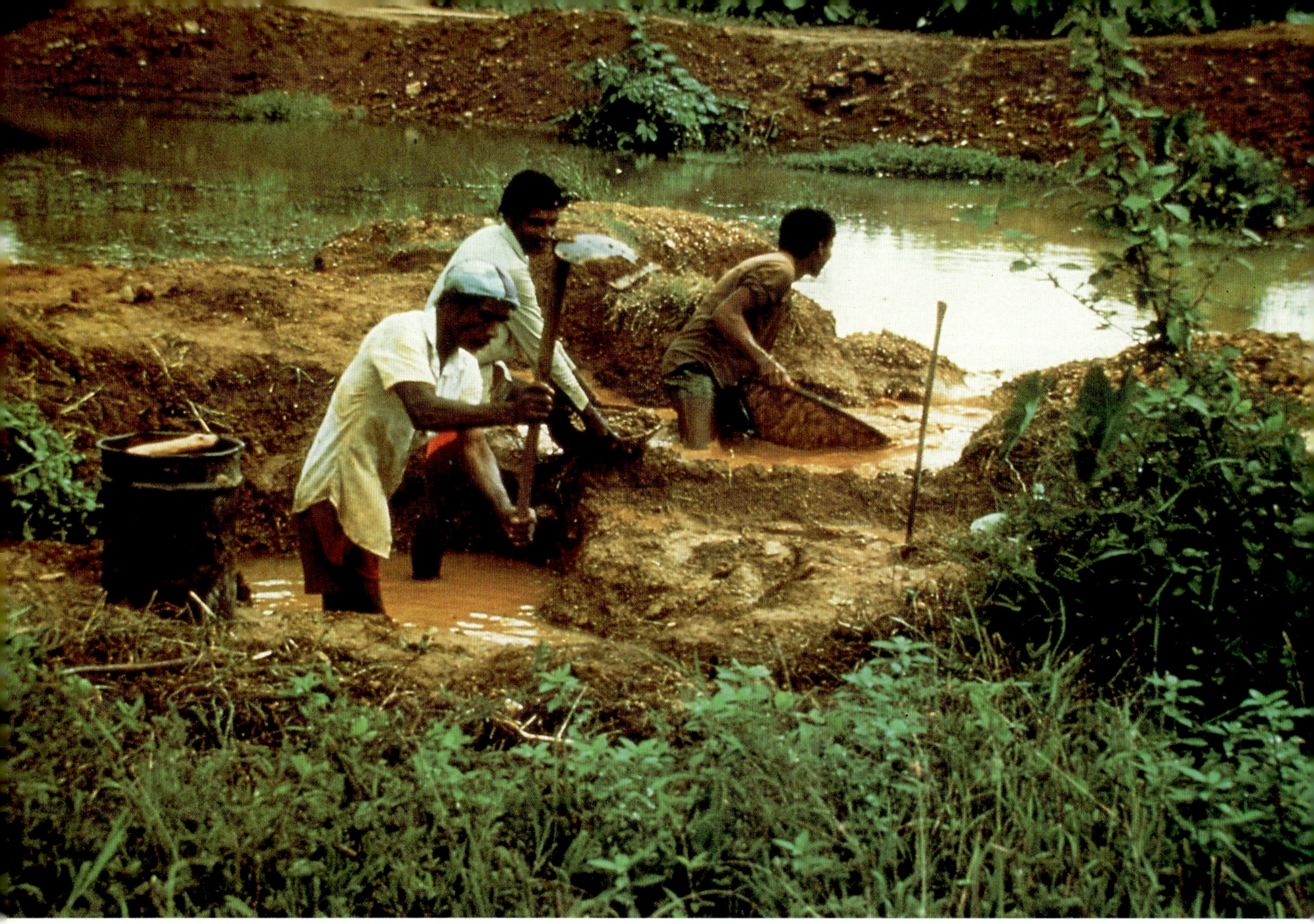

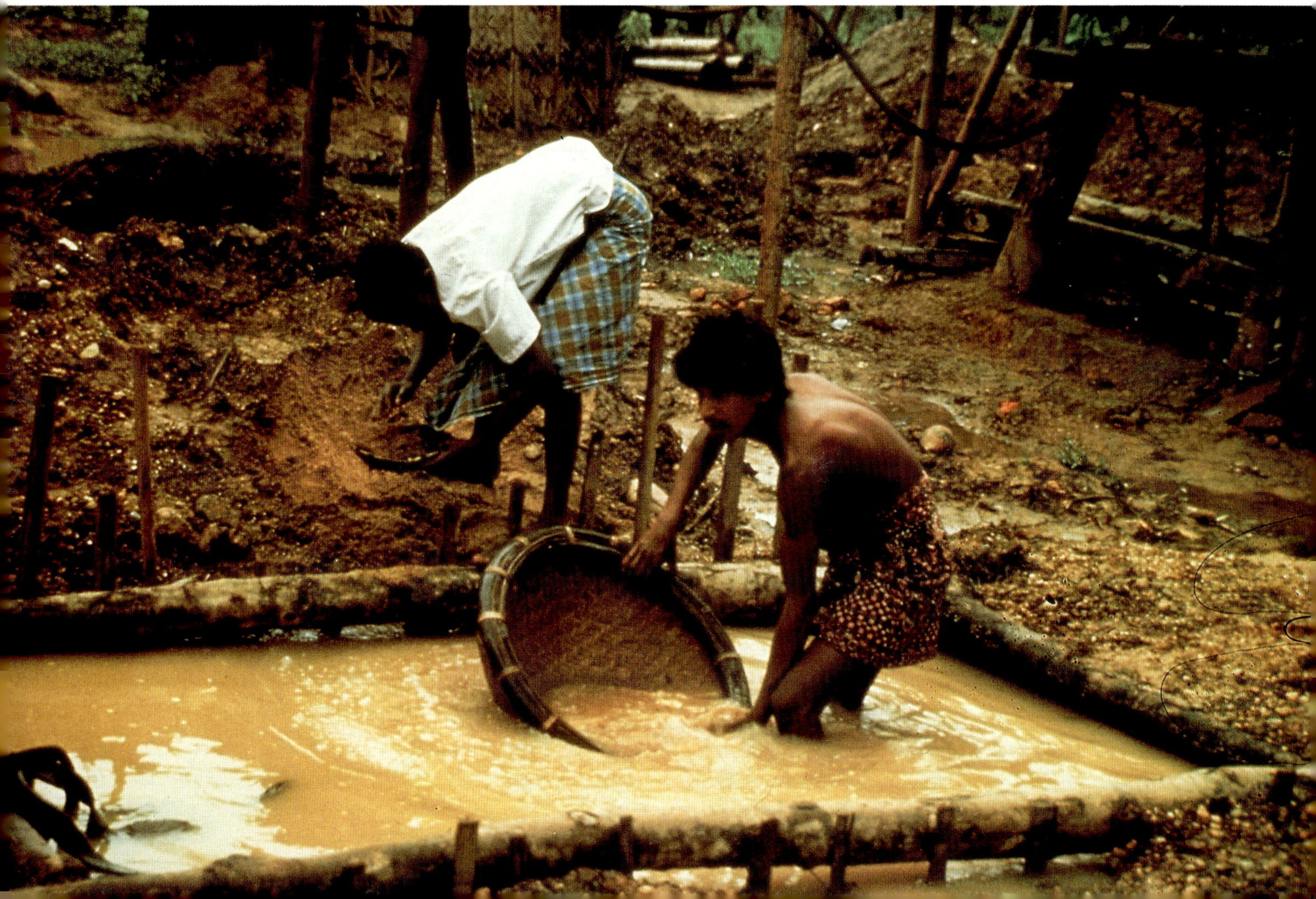

Sri Lanka:
Precious Stones in All Colors
by Chris Colemont

"A *yellow* sapphire?"

My friend is astonished. "but I thought sapphires were blue...and rubies red?"

"Yes, they are blue. That is, sapphires most familiar to us are blue, but they can be many other colors too, though they are considered less valuable, such as transparent sapphires called "white" sapphires, or other types such as green, mauve, violet, or gray sapphires. When not red enough to be considered rubies, another stone of the corundum family, they are called "pink" sapphires. Black sapphires are considered of lesser quality though in countries where they are mined, people often wear rings set with black sapphires since these stones are believed to protect the wearer against the harmful effects of the planets. Yellow sapphires are more sought-after since they are much rarer. In some countries pale yellow is preferred, and in others, a deeper yellow. And then, there's also a sapphire that has a mysterious, some claim "undefinable" color, somewhere between pink and orange and is known by the pretty name *padmaraga*. This name, often used erroneously, comes from the Sinhalese *padma*, which means lotus, and *raga*, which means color, desire, pollen or musical rhythm. Padmaragas are rare and are one of the most expensive kinds of sapphires."

"And blue sapphires? I've seen both pale blue and dark blue ones. Is one worth more than the other, or is it just a matter of personal taste?"

"In nature all different shades of blue can be found. The most highly prized is 'cornflower blue,' also known as 'Kashmir blue.' When a sapphire is a brilliant blue shade, pure, without inclusions, well cut and untreated, it can be worth a fortune! But you have to be careful, since most blue sapphires are heated to deepen their color and many pale yellow ones are irradiated..."

"Sapphires are heated and irradiated?" my friend exclaims to me again.

My head is brimming with technical and scientific data, my heart full of warmth, and the memory too, of smiling faces of the men, women, and children I have met or crossed on my trip. My story of sapphires and Sri Lanka unfolds under the spell of the island's magnificent wild beauty: its national parks set deep in tropical jungle, its mountains as great and imposing as their descent is dizzying, the leaning coconut trees along golden beaches and the crystal sea...

With its thriving tea plantations, rice paddies, rubber trees, herbs and spice cultivation, Sri Lanka, in addition to being the land of gemstones, is also a veritable botanist's paradise. As for gems, ruby and sapphire are mined there, as well as aquamarine, chrysoberyl, spinel, topaz, garnet, zircon, tourmaline, amethyst, quartz, moonstone, and many other stones as well. Those such as andalusites, apatites, cordierites, cornerupines, or sinhalites, are somewhat rarer.

I have just returned from Sri Lanka, its sun still on my face, its warmth in my skin. Where do I begin? How will I find the words? I have learned so much, seen and discovered, appreciated and loved, tasted and felt. But let's see, how did it all happen? A wish, it all began with a little passing thought... and then, it seemed, I was already on my way! A desire to see for myself, right on the spot, in the field, where men dig, dig, dig for gems, precious stones... and have been doing so for the past two thousand years; to truly discover the world that lies behind the brilliant jewels we eventually admire.

In the Beginning, a Passion for Gems

The idea of a study trip came to me when I was taking a gemmology course in Antwerp, a program devoted to cut stones, both natural and synthetic. How were they identified? How could treatments be detected? Simple questions. The answers, however, were complex and required careful study, tests and research. Chemical compositions, crystal systems, physical properties such as hardness, cleaving and fracture, specific weight and gravity; optical properties such as indexes of refraction, birefringence, dispersion, spectrums of absorption, pleochroism and so forth, were taught to us. When we came to the treatment of stones, the course took a decidedly academic and encyclopaedic turn. Gemmology is indisputably a science in constant evolution, and revolution, since the advent of computers. New types of gems are still being discovered even today. The innovation and development of more effective instruments have brought increasing precision to gemmologists' research and have greatly contributed to this revolution. Their application is particularly important in the study of inclusions, and this was of special interest to me during my course, since with the help of these tools the interior life of stones is revealed to us ever more fully. Inclusions, or particles, are carriers of precious information that can help us identify the true nature of stones, to trace their origin and determine their provenance.

In my strong-room laboratory (a matter of security) and surrounded by instruments, I suddenly felt the great need to rediscover the human side of this field, a desire to see these stones in their natural habitat, as they are brought out of the earth, to stand by as they are sorted, washed, cut and polished, long before finally being placed between my fingers to be examined under a microscope. They came up out of the earth as little pebbles and man transformed them into precious stones. This "alliance" between nature and man intrigued me.

And this was how one day I found myself on a flight from London to Colombo, the capital of the Democratic Socialist Republic of Sri Lanka. A young Sinhalese student, obviously overjoyed at the prospect of returning to her native island after several months study and training in the United States, sitting next to me.

Suddenly here is a more modern side of Sri Lanka. For, though it is true that miners still work according to ancestral methods in that country, there is also a younger generation that leaves the island for further studies and returns home, importing the most recent developments in computer science and marketing.

The student asks me what group I'm traveling with and what itinerary I plan to take. When I tell her that I'm not part of any group and that I intend to visit Ratnapura, she smiles and corrects me, "Rrratnapurra." I don't have the right pronunciation. The "r's" are rolled and the stress is on a different syllable. I repeat after her, and she nods.

"There are very beautiful stones mined there I know, but I have never visited the area. Is this your first trip? Are you going there specially for the gems?"

The plane is already beginning its descent and suddenly the island appears, like a dazzling pendant attached to the tip of India, a magnificent jewel in the Indian Ocean.

It is past five when I leave Katunayake International Airport and night is already falling fast, the sky will stay ablaze for just a few minutes more with the breathtaking pinks (tourmaline), reds (ruby), oranges (fire opal), that can only be admired in the tropics. Warmth envelops me, a light breeze suddenly lifts the fatigue from my trip. How wonderful it is to be here. *Ayubovan*. Hello, welcome.

First Stop: Colombo

I ignore the taxi drivers who rush to take my suitcases. There's no hurry...though I guess I really should check in at the hotel. I ask a hostess wearing a saree if she can call me an official taxi.

"Do you want one with air conditioning? It's more expensive."

"No thanks."

The air is fine and light. I get into the taxi, for a few rupees more my baggage is taken care of. We're off to Colombo. I must have been in a daze, I remember absolutely no security at the airport.

I had asked my travel agency in Brussels to reserve a room in an old-fashioned type hotel, just to get a taste of the past too. The local agent apparently decided otherwise, though. I find myself in a full-service palace. An executive suite with a balcony overlooking the sea must compensate for the old-fashioned charm missing. Taking a walk around the grounds, I meet an American tourist who is only too happy to show me where some bullet holes have been left after the terrorist attack here, not even two months ago! Right here in this very garden, near the swimming pool. The tourist relates how a woman armed with explosives entered the garden from "over here," and threw the grenades "over there," and how all the hotel guests dove into the swimming pool or hid under their lounge chairs. Total panic. The hotel guards had fired back immediately and in the confusion a bullet had killed a hotel waiter who was running by, trying to escape. Only two months ago... Before my departure, my family had asked me, "It won't be dangerous, will it?"

"No, I don't think so." The embassy in Brussels hadn't mentioned anything in particular, and it was very difficult to even get a reservation, since all the flights were booked solid for Colombo these days. The region I wanted to visit was not in the north of the island, if there really was any danger...

Life Goes On Under Surveillance

The next morning a soldier in a khaki uniform is standing guard near my room. As I take the elevator, another soldier wearing the same kind of uniform accompanies me. In the lobby, confusion reigns. The hotel guests are asked to pass through a special control, installed for the occasion. I must accept to be searched – by a woman in uniform. Not exactly the normal procedure on your way to breakfast. I go looking for an explanation.

"Please, there's nothing to worry about Madam, it's just security. We have several wedding receptions today at the hotel and our President, Mrs Bandaranaike Kumaratunga, is invited to one of them. We're expecting her any moment now." So that was what all the commotion was about!

My first Sinhalese breakfast is delicious: hoppers, thin delicious pancakes made of rice flour, and tea, Ceylon, of course.

Her Excellency Madam the President has not yet made her appearance when I decide to leave for the Sri Lanka National Gem and Jewellery Authority in a *bajaj*, a rather picturesque motorized tricycle. This seemed much more fun than taking a taxi. However, there is one great disadvantage to this means of transportation, and it doesn't take me long to discover it. In my open seat behind the driver I am at perfect exhaust-pipe level of any bus, car, truck, in short, of any passing vehicle in the streets of the capital.

We drive by the residence of Her Excellency the President. Soldiers stand guard while their comrades lie in waiting behind barriers of sandbags, fingers on the trigger. In the evening this avenue is closed to traffic for security reasons which means a long detour which will cost you several hundred rupees more, though bargaining is always possible, I find out.

The National Gem and Jewellery Authority: A Service For Professionals and Tourists

At 310 Galle Road, Colombo 3, the façade of the Sri Lanka Gem and Jewellery Exchange appears unimpressive. I push the door open and on my left see a young woman in uniform (*again?*), with a neat bun, sitting behind a small desk. Information?

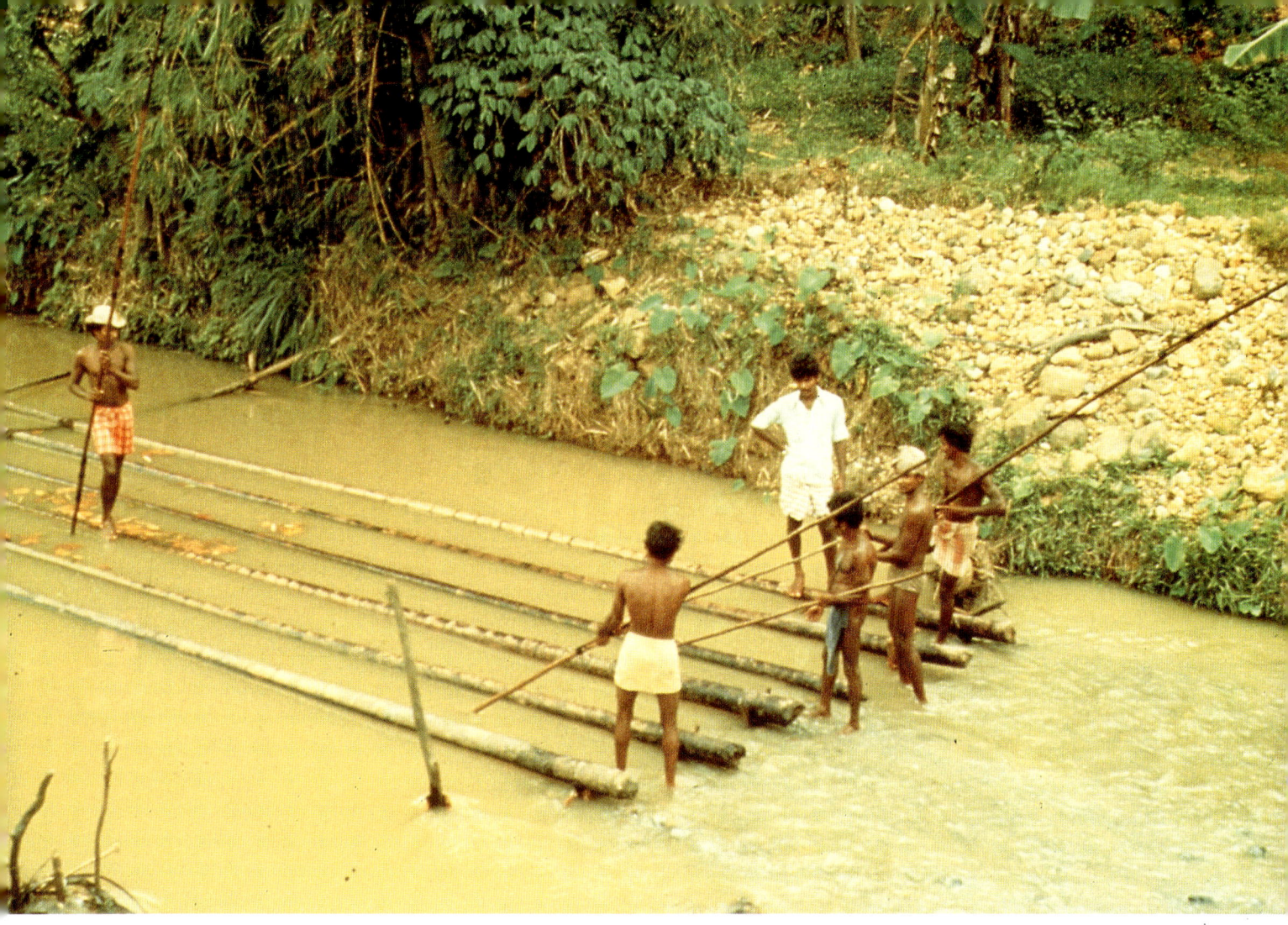

Reception? Security? I see several boutiques on the ground floor, their windows displaying jewels and gemstones. A group of shopkeepers, standing together chatting, come up to me flourishing their business cards and inviting me to follow them to their shops. "*Where you from*?" A question I'll be asked again and again during my trip. "*You want sapphire… ruby ? Come, see, I show the way.*" But it's impossible to even move, I'm completely encircled.

"Please, let me pass! I'm going to the first floor." My words have an instant effect, the crowd parts and I hurry towards the stairs.

The National Authority is a governmental institution whose purpose is to control, assist, and promote the country's gem and jewel industry. It houses several different departments in the building as well as a gemmology laboratory located on the first floor...I'm lucky, the head gemmologist is in and receives me in his office. When I tell him the purpose of my visit, he makes a call, the conversation is brief and to the point.

"It's arranged. You can go to see the regional director of the local office in Ratnapura. He'll help you."

How nice, and what service, what efficiency! A woman, also a gemmologist, joins us. She tells me she studied in Germany and this creates a common bond between us. I compliment her on her light green saree, her earrings are obviously meant to match. She smiles, "Peridot." The head gemmologist chuckles, feminine complicity... I admire the elegance of sarees and the ease with which the women here wear them. The movement of yards and yards of fabric, pleated and draped so gracefully! The women all look like regal princesses. And me, in my shirt and slacks, must certainly not appear very elegant to them!

I am delighted when the head gemmologist shows me the impressive book he has just written on precious stones in Sri Lanka. Much to my disappointment it isn't for sale yet, this is just a first copy. I learn that Ratnapura in the southwest is not the only region rich in gems, though more than three-fourths come from there. There are other gemmiferous areas hidden deep in the jungle, their access extremely difficult. If only I could visit them too!

Other regions that yield precious stones are Avissawella, Eheliyagada, Elahera, Horana, Kandy, Kataragama, Matale, Nivithigala, Nuwara Eliya, Okkampitiya and Polonnaruwa. There is also Meetiyagoda, a small village in the south of the island, known for its moonstones.

The type of terrain and soil vary from one region to another. Terraces, valleys, paddy fields, swamps and alluvial areas, all turned up in the feverish search for gems. In the regions of Pelmadulla and Balangoda some types of stones are mined in streams. I have more than my choice of mines to visit.

The Gem Testing Laboratory, where the head

gemmologist works, is across the hall. This is where any foreign customer or tourist can go and have a gem he has chosen analysed free of charge. For 300 rupees he may obtain a certificate of authenticity, the National Authority thus becoming the official guarantor of all purchases. I recognize the instruments : microscope, spectometer, polariscope, scale, refractometer… A container holds methyloidine, the smell is familiar. We do some tests. Spinel or garnet? We need to do several tests. One of the last ones is conclusive: spinel. Carefully I ask, "And synthetic stones?"

The gemmologists are rather amused, relaxed about my question. "It's a challenge for us. Their presence on the market encourages us to perfect our techniques and keeps us on our guard. There are a lot of synthetics circulating. Even here, how many times have we unfortunately had to announce to a customer that he is the owner of a very nice – synthetic – stone! Be careful!"

I agree. Better safe than... I end up spending the entire day in the building. The export and shipping departments are on the upper floors. The shopkeepers are still chatting on the ground floor, "*What you want?*" I warn them, "I don't want to buy anything, I'm just here to learn about gems." "Okay, come, come in." And then drawers slide open, expert fingers unfold tissue paper holding veritable treasures, each one rarer than the other. Delicately, the seller chooses a small stone and rubs it against his perspiring nose, a curious ritual. The small stone, brighter after this, "reveals" itself even more intensely, "Look, a starred ruby." Cat's eye, alexandrite and others are presented to me. "The Japanese like phenomenal stones." We talk shop and time seems to fly by.

Ratnapura: Gem City

Ratnapura, *ratna* meaning gem, and *pura*, city, is a small town set at the foot of a superb towering rockface. We are in Sabaragamuwa province about two hundred miles, or a three-hour drive, southeast of Colombo. This is in the opposite direction from Jaffna, in the north of the island, which is closed to tourism because of the political unrest there.

So there should be nothing to fear, except perhaps the mosquitoes or other insects that seem to take me for an exotic delight… No tropical habitat exists anywhere without its little creatures to plague you, and I have my share here, including a "surprise party" of monkeys that dance the whole night long on the roof of my room. Needless to say its difficult to get any sleep when monkeys party like that! The hotel staff, sententious, only tell me, "You must be aware, Madam, that there's a jungle here. The monkeys come from the jungle. They damage the roof, eat the telephone cables..."

When I arrive in Ratnapura it's *Poyday*, Full Moon Day. This is also Sri Lanka, the festival of the full moon, a bank holiday. A holiday for the moon, once a

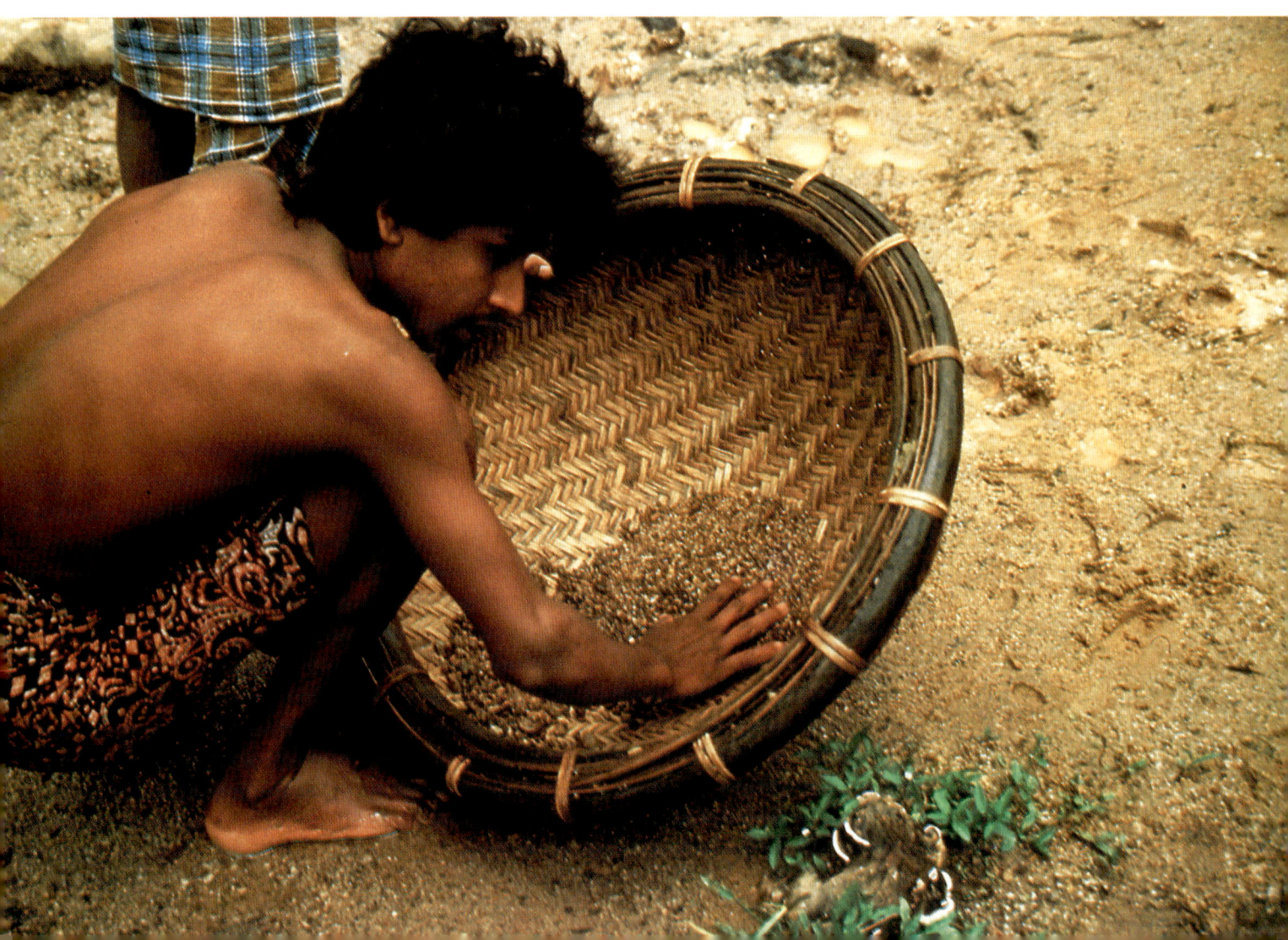

month when it is full? The idea appeals to me. This means the governmental offices are closed. I won't be able to see the regional director of the local bureau, or anyone else today. Tomorrow is Saturday, and then Sunday, three days without any appointments. My evening is devoted to looking for accommodation, this is also part of traveling, and sometimes holds its suprises.

While I'm having breakfast, the hotel manager comes to announce that a gentleman is waiting for me on the veranda. He sells gems. *Already?* Without interrupting my breakfast, which though simpler than the one at the palace in Colombo is just as delicious, I tell the manager that I cannot receive anyone without an appointment. He should leave and, anyway, I'm not interested in buying any gems. If I accept to see him, it will mean a stream of sellers and other merchants for all the days ahead. An hour later, the man is still there and tells me, "Your driver is a good friend of mine. I can show you some gems from my personal collection."

"Oh, he *is* a good friend? That's very interesting, he didn't go by the rate yesterday evening. I had problems!"

"Sorry, Madam! Not such a good friend. He only told me you were here. The hotel manager is my good friend and..."

That's enough. I don't like this at all and ask him even more firmly to leave. Later, when I see the manager in the lobby I tell him, more than ask him, "He said he was a good friend of yours..."

He bursts out laughing, "No, no, not at all. He's a shopkeeper who often comes here when there are tourists. Sometimes it works."

Although the government offices aren't open, I see the shopkeepers never close. I decide to explore the city and begin by visiting the museums. The owner of the hotel also owns a precious stone museum. He's a well-known personage in Ratnapura. Famous gemmologist and one of the biggest gem dealers in the region, he is also a great art lover, collector of rare Sinhalese pieces, philosopher, and musician, botanist and herb specialist. And it is true that his hotel, located a little outside the city, exudes the serenity of his philosophy and is beautifully decorated with the finest of antique art objects.

The evening of my arrival, the hotel manager had stopped the ventilation for a moment, though it was only blowing very gently, "Listen, absolute silence here." And he was right, not one sound from the city came to disturb the extraordinary peace of the place. I had fallen asleep that night rocked by the sounds of tropical nature. Quite honestly, I couldn't recognize all the sounds, such as the nocturnal singing of the frogs right outside my window. The silence of nature is in fact full of the strangest sounds. In the early morning I awoke to the strident singing of tropical birds. Later during the day, sipping a cool glass of lime juice in the shade of the veranda, I would actually see them. The most breathtaking birds imaginable, bursting with color and long white tails, fluttering from branch to branch. Then there was the majestic beauty of the coconut trees, and a multitude of other kinds of trees and shrubs, heavy with fragrant flowers. A part of the grounds was also a lush botanical garden where you could easily imagine Adam and Eve strolling somewhere nearby.

It's not easy to leave this tranquil and ravishing spot and go out into the fields under the merciless sun, but this is what I've come for. Maybe tomorrow?

The hotel owner's museum is located in Getangama, two miles from the city, I take another *bajaj*. The Gem Bureau Museum and Laboratory is well worth the trip, not only for its large range of rough and polished stones but also for its exceptional collection of art objects. The Gemmological Museum in Batugedara, slightly more than a mile away on the road to Badulla, has the added advantage of being next to the Chamber Restaurant where tourists can order a dish of curry and rice to their own taste, that is, not too spicy!

Exhibited at the entrance is a letter from Professor Gubelin, "father" of the study of precious stone inclusions, written when the museum was inaugurated. The process of gemstone mining is clearly illustrated, with photos and models (without the normal dust, mosquitoes, and other insects present in real life). I am pleasantly surprised to find that these museums, as well others belonging to gem dealers, usually not only possess a collection of rough and cut stones from Sri Lanka, but also a very large, even complete selection of minerals, crystals and gems from the world over. If you take the time, you can make your visit a lesson in the study of rare specimens from the four corners of the earth. Even synthetic gems are represented!

I go to see the regional director of the National Gem and Jewellery Authority to organize transportation to some mines. At nine in the morning, there is a pleasant atmosphere in the local bureau. Men in sarongs or in trousers, some women in sarees, have come to negotiate or just to chat. This bureau is where permission to exploit land believed to have gem deposits is granted, usually for a duration of two years.

The director is in Colombo for a meeting and I am asked to leave a message and come back the next morning. The hotel owner is also in Colombo for several days, so I won't have the honor and pleasure of meeting him personally. It is still early, as I talk with more and more people I even meet a young gem dealer and his brother who help me organize an excursion to the mines.

"Why do you want to go out into the fields? It's so hot, and they're mining gems right before your eyes, here, nearby."

True, there are a few pits right near the center of town. I remember seeing a minibus stop there and a dozen Japanese tourists hurrying over to the pits for a souvenir photo. Even though the pump was broken and the pit full of water, it didn't seem important. This was a typical scene at Ratnapura, and I insist upon leaving the city to explore the surrounding areas.

Digging by Hand

The gems are taken from three types of mines. "Shallow pits," "deep pits" which can be more than fifty meters in depth, and "alluvial mines," which are found in rivers. The young man and his brother, of course, cannot leave their shop. They arrange for a driver and a guide who speaks some English and, nice surprise, a magnificent air-conditioned limousine complete with local music.

After a lovely ride, we turn off onto a small path. Things are getting more interesting. For as far as I can see, an expanse of paddy fields. Where are the mines? I never thought rice paddies could be so green! My guides are already striding along the bamboo beams that serve as a walkway across the rice fields. I stop a minute to admire the beauty of the landscape, the border of tropical trees. Far in the distance I can make out a straw roof, it looks like a hut floating in a sea of green. The driver and his friend are making their way towards it. I follow them with little steps, trying not to trip into the water. Finally reaching the hut, everyone is talking, no one is working, the pump is broken. What, again? Just a coincidence? Probably.

The pit under the straw roof is a rectangular hole, filled with dirty water. Impurities of every kind float on the surface. It takes me a while to realize that this is where the men go down into the mines. I can't believe it! "And are the gems down there?" It's hard for me to comprehend. What a sight. So here's my first mine, in the beating heat, in the middle of acres of rice fields. Here I am on the edge of a hole filled with muddy water, next to a broken down pump, in the company of four half-naked miners – later I'll understand why – and a limousine driver. My improvised guide isn't able to offer much of an explanation.

Is there really anything to explain? Traditional mining is remarkably simple. The primitive methods that men have used for centuries are still in use today. When a mining project is undertaken, a few people form a cooperative, called a *karuha vula,* whose principal partners are the investor and the miner. Other members include the landowner, the owner of the waterpump, and the supplier of the wood used for the props. The members of the *karuha vula* share the expenses, the work, as well as the profits made from the sale of the rough stones they mine. A percentage of the profits also goes to the person who runs and knows how to repair the pump! The right to exploit land presumed to have gemstone deposits is granted by a government permit.

Old rubber tires tied to a basket serve as handles. It's strong. The man below, like an ant, has disappeared. Where is he? In a passage leading very far underground. In certain pits, as this one, underground horizontal galleries are dug completely by hand. The miners work in an atmosphere of stifling humidity by candlelight. When one of the flames goes out it's a warning that oxygen is getting low.

We wait an eternity before the man finally comes up again. Not surprising either, since these galleries, called *donava,* are sometimes as far as six to nine yards from the vertical shaft. In the galleries, several men carefully scrape the earth. Fascinated, I'm glued to the pit's edge, watching this backbreaking labor carried out so cheerfully and calmly, without the slightest irritation, though the men are caked in clay from head to toe and literally drowning in sweat.

"Earn your bread by the sweat of your brow," I'm beginning to understand the full meaning of these words. Convinced that riches and happiness are just around the corner, these people accept to work like slaves for next to nothing, a few rupees a day, in these almost unbearable conditions. The price of gems crosses my mind for a moment. How can anyone possibly imagine, admiring these stones in the comfort of a jewelry shop, with what difficulty they are actually mined! From the bowels of the earth, an incredible journey!

My guides wait patiently for me. They still feel there is nothing to see. Yet I can barely tear myself away, if only to go on to another mine. Before leaving on this trip, I could just see myself descending into one of these pits to take my best photos. I must admit, in the field it is quite a different story. I keep my feet firmly on dry ground. As for the photos, the blazing sun doesn't help. The straw roofs and coconut trees give a little shade, and I finally take a few shots. It suddenly occurs to me that though I have seen quite a few pits and several cubic yards of mud, I have still not seen one gem! Pointing to a pile of clay, a miner assures me, "they're there!"

The next day the regional director of the National Gem and Jewellery Authority, who has been given my message, kindly receives me. He suggests I go to see the gem cutting class being held on the third floor. The person responsible for the program, who is also acting as my guide, is told not to let me leave without a few specimens of the different cuts the students are learning. Round, oval, pear, marquise, square, baguette... all work intently.

Luckily there are still a few more days left before my departure, for I learn it will only be "tomorrow" that I can visit the gemmology department, located in another part of the city, where a gemmologist will talk to me about the treatment of stones. We decide to meet in the afternoon since in the morning I want to visit the mines. I change hotels, not that I'm not happy with my garden of Eden, but I want to explore a different region, and change base. My new hotel, three miles from the city and surrounded by dense forest, has everything to satisfy a demanding tourist clientele including a superb swimming pool surrounded by magical gardens. The manager, an important gem dealer's son, has studied hotel management in Switzerland and speaks perfect German. Though it is high tourist season, the hotel, well run and used to accommodating a great number of guests, is practically empty. The political situation has definitely made itself felt, and I begin to understand how much this country is suffering from the fall in tourist trade.

Washing Day

When I inquire about renting a vehicle for another excursion, the clerk smiles, "You can walk there, you'll see, it isn't far!" To the mines on foot? Why not? A beautiful walk across tea and rubber plantations. Along the way I see pits this time without grass huts, without technical facilities. Huge holes simply dug into the ground. For a moment I think to myself that this is all too easy, it can't be true! I learn that this is the shallow pit area. Unlike deep pits which are rectangular, these pits are about two to three yards deep, very wide and round. It seems I've come at the right time since today is "washing day." Here again the scene is fascinating. Miners knee-deep in water handle large baskets filled with dry, gray mud. These recipients are slowly turned in the pit's water, in circular movements. That way the clay is washed away and a first sorting of the stones is made automatically: by their sheer weight, the stones sink down into a cone-shaped basket. Pebbles remain on the surface and are thrown out. After several washings, there is still enough gravel to do another sorting. Well washed, this gravel is called *nambuva*. The miners come out of the water and squat in front of the large basket turned towards the sun. This is the most critical stage of the sorting process. Only the most experienced men are allowed to participate.

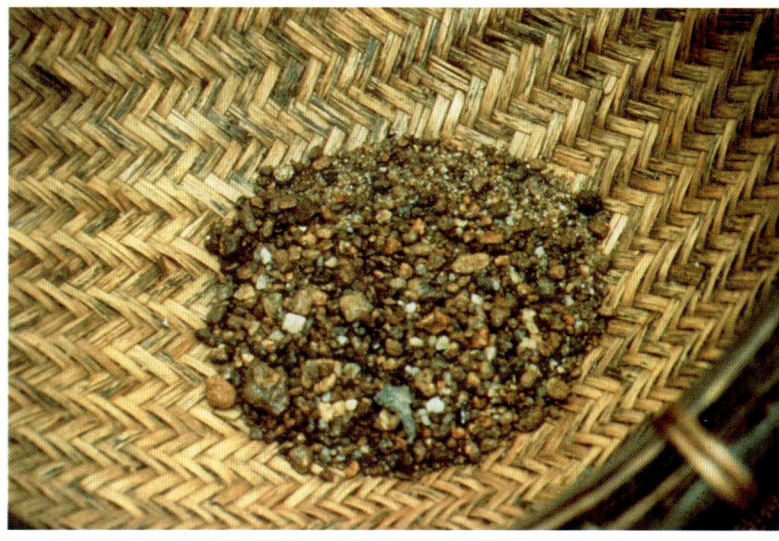

With the help of the sun, they examine the *nambuva*, their fingers brush lightly over the contents like a fan. The movement is quick and delicate. Someone chooses a small stone, rolls it between his fingers then, between thumb and index, examines it against the sun. It's a good one, a dark orange-red hessonite. This stone, which is believed to possess certain powers, is also known as "cinnamon stone," and is very popular on the island. Again, after the same series of movements, a small green zircon appears. Fingers feel and detect, eyes sensitive to the slightest sparkle or transparency. A quartz. Very pretty, it is passed around for all to admire. I'm very curious to see if we'll find a ruby too, rarer in this region. Most rubies range from light red to raspberry red. Too pale, it's a pink sapphire. After an hour or two a small ruby appears. Tiny, tiny, tiny! The men's hands can hardly hold it. In my palm it looks more like a tiny red stain. I am beginning to truly realize what "precious" means! One by one the stones disappear into the mine owner's pocket. The miners are watched closely by their boss as they are sorting. Before they leave, he will choose one stone to give to each miner. This will be their share of the spoils.

The strange water ballet begins again. The miners are stripped to the waist, in short sarongs. If ever they wear shorts, their pockets are sewn up! It isn't by chance that a gem gets lost in a fold of clothing...

The miners use a shovel to fill the basket then "waltz" it around in the muddy water. The worthless pebbles are thrown out. Each time the men emerge from the water and the sorting begins, a religious silence falls over the group, the tension increases. Most of the rough stones are quite small with imperfections. Suddenly, excitement. A beautiful clear blue crystal, it's a sapphire! Not very large, but no inclusions and it is a good even color. Everyone admires it. Our hearts quicken. It's an event!

I am surprised that after sorting each basket, only a few small "semi-precious" stones have been found. The distinction between precious and semi-precious seems unimportant. So few? It's normal, they say.

Sometimes there is nothing at all. That's the way it is. They have understood and accepted this fact for a long time now. But sometimes there will be many, many! And it's enough to make up for all the long grueling hours of labor, the days of unfailing patience. I spend the morning at the washing and learn to recognize the stones: zircons, garnets, quartz, tourmalines, all mixed together as they come out of the same pile of mud from the same pit. Every time a basket is lifted out of the water, we hold our breath. What stones does it hold? Has all this work been for nothing? In a few minutes will everyone be wealthy? No one can say.

When the miners stop for a tea break a little boy comes to play near the gravel. Squatting down as he has seen his father do time and time again, he imitates the miner's movements perfectly. The youngster searches for some pebbles, rubs them with his fingers too, and examines them against the sun. From his pocket he takes out a piece of newspaper where other "treasures" are wrapped and adds this one to his collection. This is definitely the best school, his apprenticeship has begun early.

Instead of drinking tea with the others, I am offered a huge "king coconut" picked from the heights of a tree growing right next to us in this earthly paradise. No need for a cup, one swift chop of the machette is enough. The simplicity of the movement and the kindness with which this delicious coconut is handed to me is in perfect harmony with the peaceful, generous spirit I have found everywhere on this part of the island.

That evening after my meeting with the gemmologists at the National Authority laboratory, I see the owner of the pit again – what a change has come over him. He is absolutely radiant! What has happened? Good news! "Later we found a very large sapphire, a perfect color." His joy is genuine. "I'm convinced there are more sapphires there. We're continuing tomorrow!"

Though I share his happiness, I am of course disappointed not to have been there too when it was found. At least I've seen the mine where it has come from. "May I see it?"

"Of course." Now it is my turn to hold the stone between my fingers. A wonder, even in its natural state. The owner can already imagine it as a cut stone. As they say, "You have to see it to believe it!"

The Art of the Lapidary

The exportation of rough stones from Sri Lanka being forbidden by law, gems are cut before leaving the country. Workshops can be found all over the island where traditional methods are often still employed. The stones must then be recut in Europe. Modern technology, however, has been introduced in the field and has considerably improved the quality of the lapidaries' work. Many young people enroll in a professional training program organized by the National Authority. Women often work at home, others are employed by workshops or in companies with modern facilities, as in Ratnapura.

I am curious standing in front of the skyblue building of the Central Lapidary (Pvt) Ltd. It reminds me of a flying saucer that has just landed out of the blue in this chaotic neighborhood full of small shops and stalls. Then, for a minute, I think I'm dreaming. Three eyes are quietly watching me. No, I'm not talking about a statue of one of the Hindu gods… the dark eyes of a charming hostess and the cold eye of a "see-all" camera have just recorded the image of one amazed tourist holding a camera. And my surprise isn't over yet, for can you believe it, the saucer swallows me up for a visit on board.

Once the heavy door has closed behind me like a vault, I'm in another universe. Black and white monitors reveal the building to me from all angles. I discover that the noises I heard as I walked in are coming from fifty worktables on the first floor where boys and girls all in skyblue shirts and navy blue trousers or skirts, sit in neat rows busily cutting and polishing. Everything is spotless, functional, happy and fresh. The young people work cheerfully though no one speaks: everyone is busy concentrating on their tasks. What a contrast with the bustling market outside, the heat and dust.

I learn that the Central Lapidary opened its doors only ten days ago. Three years of perseverance were needed to realize the ambitious project of creating this modern workshop. The director describes their efforts and philosophy, the adventure of the enterprise.

I watch a young employee's hands at work. The speed and precision of her movements are astonishing. I admire her serene concentration. When the stone is finished, it is registered by a controller and handed over to a colleague for the next phase. Everything is carefully followed and recorded.

I see before my very eyes how a small, rough, imperfect stone becomes a bright shining miracle. After having removed the visible impurities, the stone is mounted on a small stick with the help of a hot lacquer glue and is pre-shaped. The lapidary plays an important role at this stage, when the stone is roughly cut, since this is when he decides on the stone's final shape, the one for which the gem is best suited. Then the facets are cut, one by one, unless the en cabochon cut has been chosen. My eyes can barely follow the quickness of the successive movements necessary to execute the operation. Glued to the holder, the stone is then pressed against a horizontally turning cylinder. The grindstone and abrasive chosen depend upon the stone to be cut. The other end of the stick is held by a device that alters the position of the stone with extreme precision depending upon the angles of the faceting. Each facet is checked with an eyeglass. At this stage the stone is still dull. It is polished on a cylinder, also rotating horizontally, to reveal the stone's transparency and true color.

It's time for tea and everyone stops working. The young employees wave me over and I follow them to the cafeteria, but then, a burst of laughter! For me, tea is served in the director's air conditioned office.

As he speaks to me about his career and the history of the company, R. Perera continues answering the telephone, controlling bills with his accountant, organizing his next business trip, signing documents. He also proudly shows me some of the best examples of stones cut in his shop by people he has trained. He knows their work well, which cutter should be entrusted with a difficult stone, an exceptional gem. He checks each and every stone and never hesitates, if necessary, to cut a fragile gem himself. The director is obviously a man of action. From his early days as a gem cutter, after completing a course offered by the State Gem Corporation, to his successful position today, he has forgotten nothing of the basics of his trade.

Down by the River...

To complete my in-the-field study I'm interested to see how stones are mined in streams, a method still practiced today in Sri Lanka. Since it isn't monsoon season, this will apparently be possible to arrange. The sites are located a few hours by car and I can go there in the morning, the day of my departure, on my way back to Colombo.

I would never know how the misunderstanding came about. I set off with a driver who spoke almost no English towards Haptuale and after about an hour, stopping by the side of the road, he points out a series of mines. By now this type of landscape has become familiar. Rice paddy fields and grass huts. Once out of the city, this is the familiar scenery on both sides of the road.

With a sweeping gesture the driver tells me that the mines are "over there." I get out of the car and set out across the fields. Miners' children run up to me, taking gems out of their pockets, out of their sleeves, from everywhere. What a hubbub! They won't let me go.

"For you, three thousand rupees."

I take a quick look at all the stones and hand them back. More envelopes and white boxes are produced. There is just about everything you could consider "unacceptable," including synthetic cat's eyes, obvious even to the naked eye.

I happen upon a new mine. The work has only begun this morning. Muscular men are at the bottom of the pit, at a depth of about thirty feet. They heave a heavy chunk of earth to other miners precariously balanced above them, who in turn do the same. Little by little the large block is hoisted to the surface by

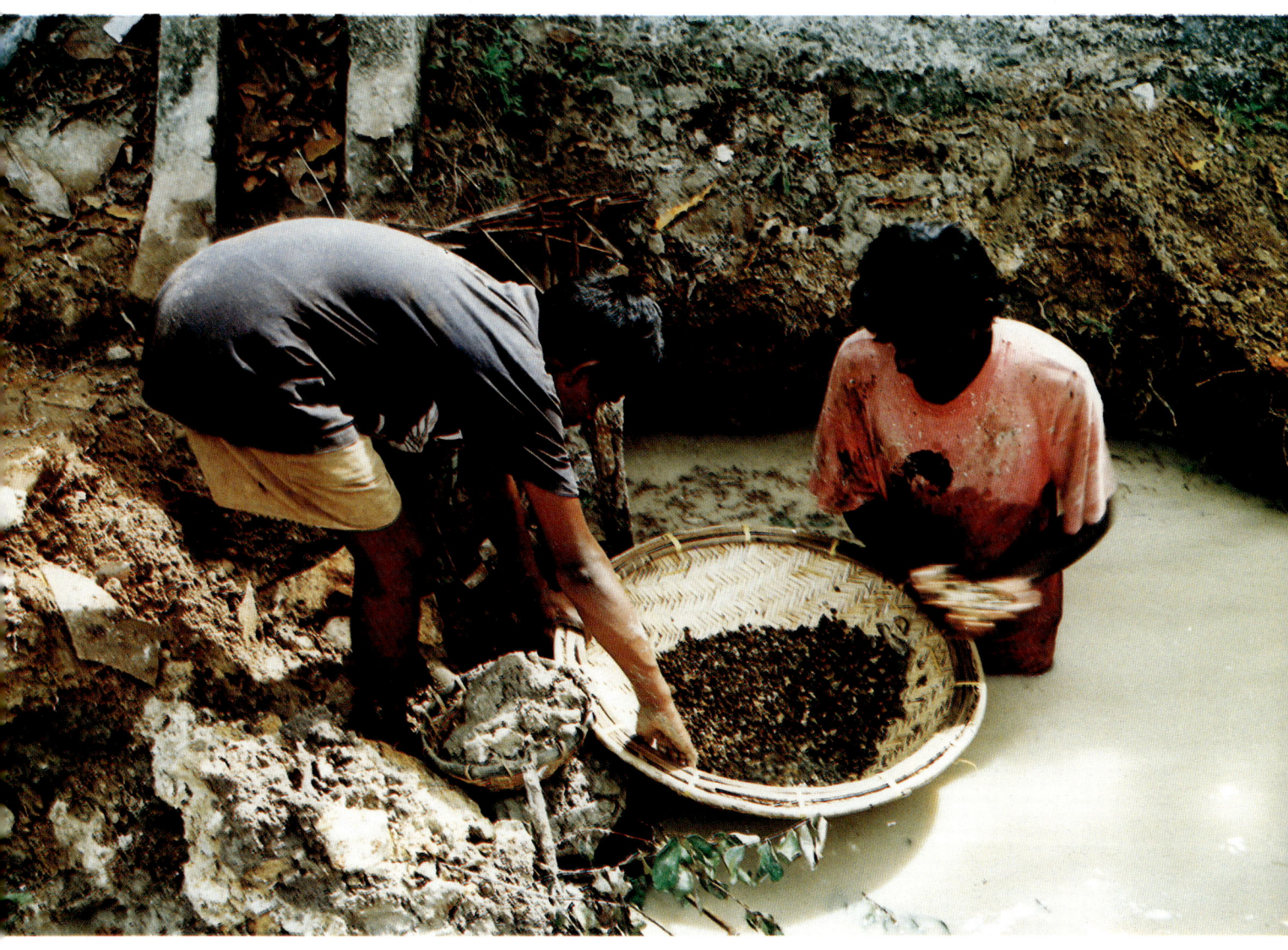

the human chain. Further away I discover wells even deeper than thirty meters. Amazing. Where's the river? Someone offers to take me there.

There it is, flowing along one side of the field in a deep ravine, completely inaccessible. I see no men, no mining activity, nothing. Only water flowing. I've been taken to the "riverside mines." Not exactly what I had in mind! Time is running out, the sun is already intense, I've got a long journey ahead of me… it will have to be for another time. I have a good reason to come back.

Along the road that leads me away from Ratnapura, I watch the landscape go by absent-mindedly. Like a succession of memories, I see men and women, digging, sorting, cutting, polishing and realize that these are the people who are indeed responsible for giving "life" to stones, whose work and care make them become truly "precious."

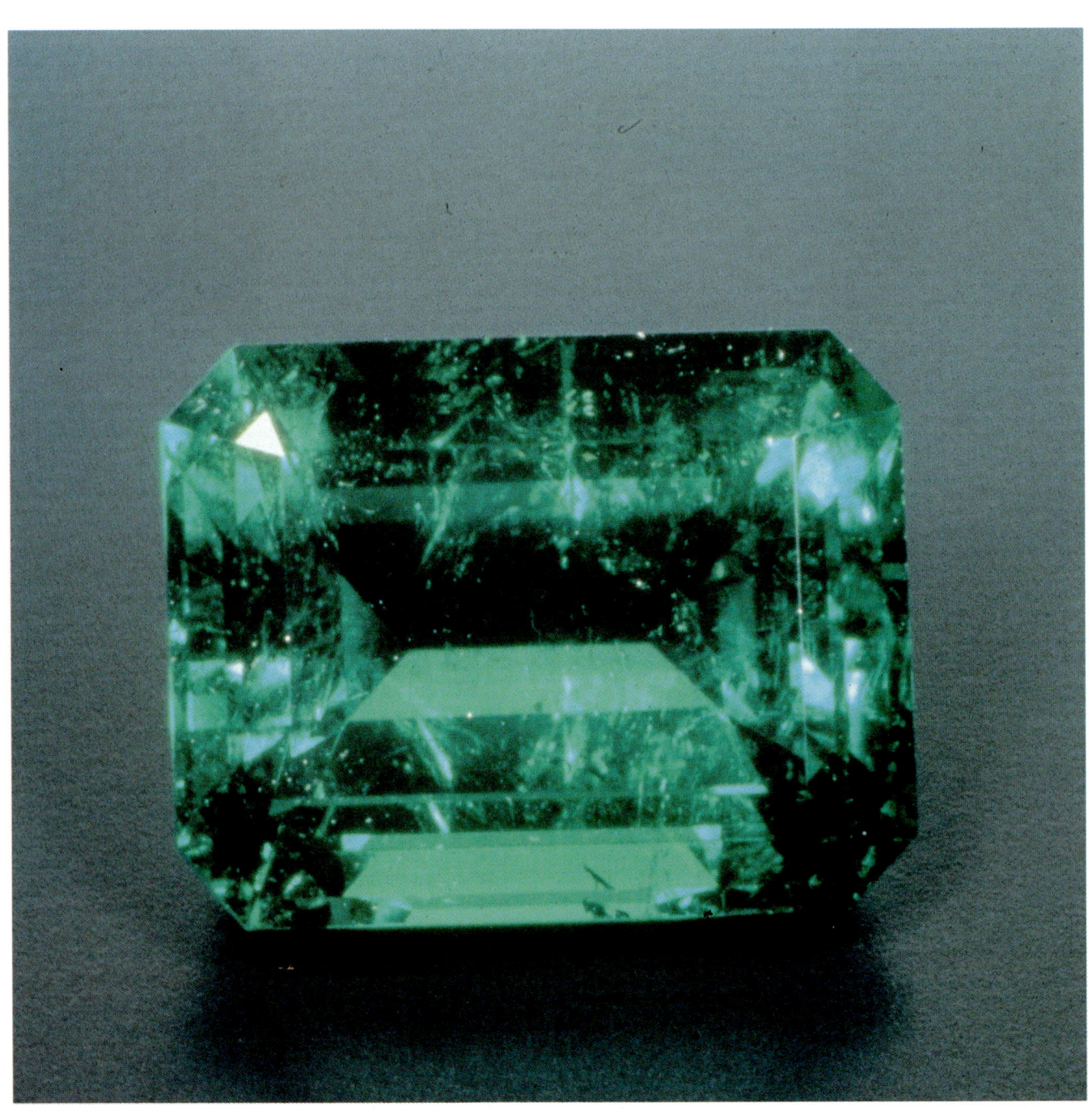

CHAPTER III

Emerald

GENERAL INFORMATION

How it got its name A simple denomination: from the Greek *smaragdos*, meaning "green stone." In turn, the Greek word may go back to ancient Indian or Persian words with the same significance.

Today we are accustomed to hearing people speak of "emerald green," the best, if not the only referent that seems to adequately describe a certain green hue.

Varieties To start, let's underline the fact that emerald is a beryl variety (see "Beryl") which is so precious among gems that it requires a discussion in its own right.

Some interesting sidelights The superb green coloring depends on the presence of chromium atoms – trivalent – and sometimes vanadium atoms in the crystal's lattice.

When an emerald is transparent, has outstanding brilliance, a fine green color and an adequate weight in carats then we are dealing with one of the world's most highly treasured gems. From ample data regarding emerald trade in Babylon, we can deduce that the gem was valuable merchandise as early as 4000 B.C.

The first known mines were situated near the Red Sea and were historically referred to as "Cleopatra's mines." Emeralds found in an ancient Egyptian royal sarcophagus undoubtedly came from these locations.

After the discovery of America, Cortez brought back some stunning examples – including specimens carved by the Aztecs – presenting them to the court of Charles V.

Far and away the most famous deposits today are in Colombia; in fact the current market refers to "Colombian emerald" to specify a truly special green color. It must be added that while these mines regularly produce a considerable amount of prized material, other qualities are extracted as well. So provenance of a gem is not, by itself, guarantee; other data are also required to confirm its true beauty. It has always been held that emeralds improve your eyesight; and so the Emperor Nero watched Colosseum games through a concave green lens that sources cite as emerald.

In India this green beryl is believed to improve your relationships with other people, and even with nature, to the extent that you can thereby learn to understand the entire cosmos.

Should you wish to improve memory and eloquence, wear a ring set with an emerald on your middle finger.

And in Ayurveda canons – that ancient oriental wisdom dedicated to self-healing – emerald disintoxicates kidneys and gall bladder.

For ancient peoples, an emerald was considered highly talismanic for childbirth.

In the Peruvian Mantu Valley there was once a fine emerald stone honored as the Emerald Goddess; men were wont to bring very small stones of the same quality and leave them at her altar; in return she kept their wives faithful.

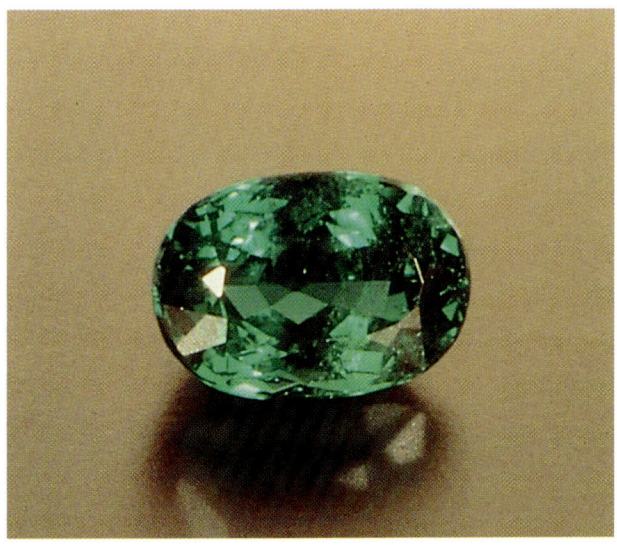

Chemical Formula: *$Be_3 Al_2 Si_6 O_{18}$ – aluminium and beryllium silicate*
Hardness: *7½ – 8 (Mohs scale)*
Specific Gravity: *2.67 – 2.78*
Refraction: *uniaxial birefringent*
Color: *varying shades of green*

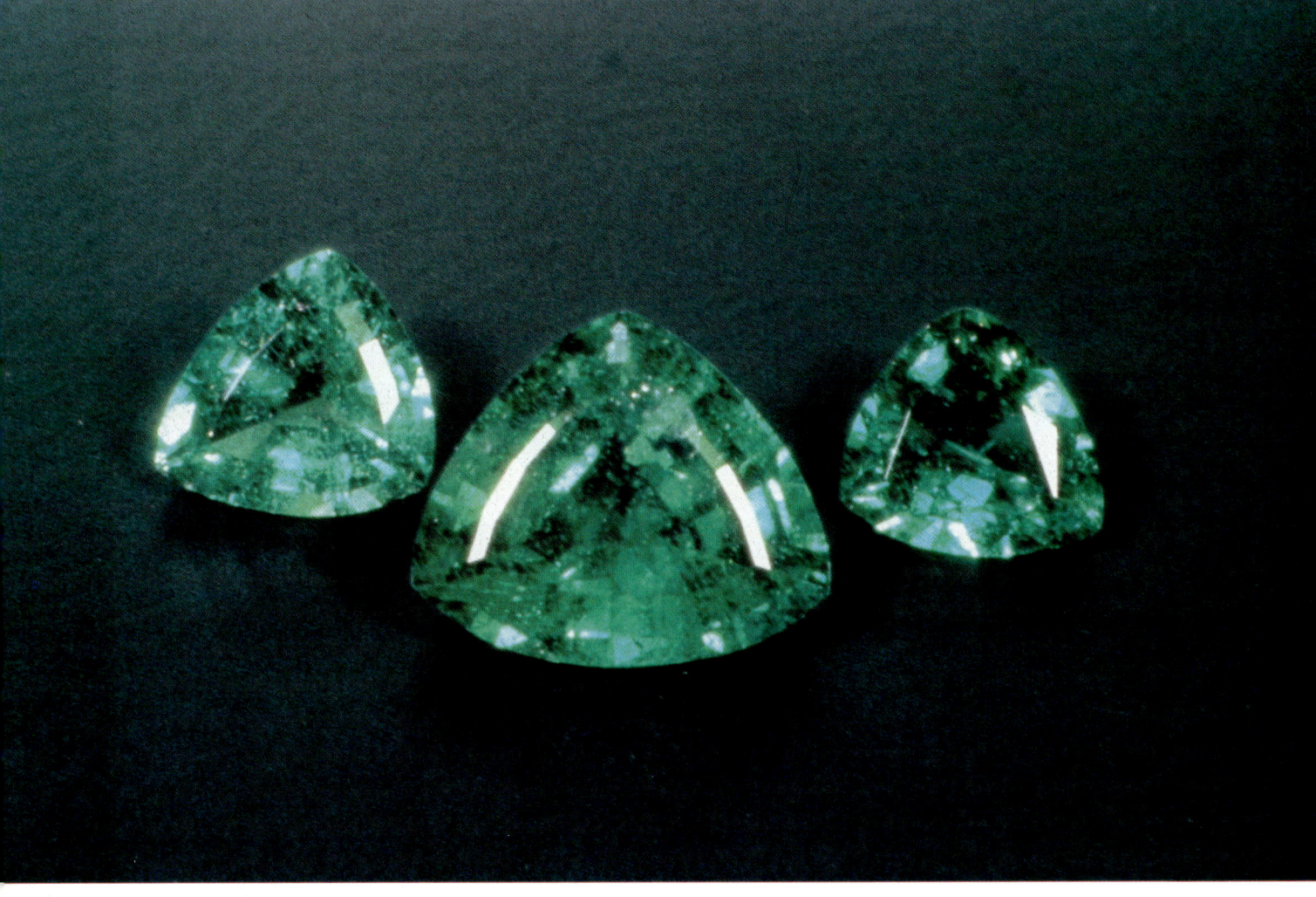

Emeralds from Zambia with a shield cut.

Through the centuries, this gem has symbolized immortality and faith.

Celebrated emeralds The Ataualpa emerald, a 45-carat deep green marvel, has its own very special and unforgettable story. It seems this gem from the Colombian Muzo mines was originally set in the renowned Crown of the Andes in 1593, and was kept until 1650 in the cathedral in Popayan, until one day it was carried off by Captain Morgan's band of pirates. History lost sight of the gem until 1818 when Simón Bolivar found it among the booty left behind by the Spaniards he had driven out. Once again, the gem stone disappears from view; but at last in 1969 the New York league of diamond merchants announces it has this fabled stone in safekeeping.

The following is a list of some of the world's most famous emeralds:

– Kakovin (2,226 grams): owes its name to the stone cutter who attempted to steal it; it now is on view in the Russian Diamond Museum.

– Devonshire (1,384 carats): Colombian crystal from Muzo, in gift from Pedro I Emperor of Brazil to the Dukes of Devonshire, the current owners.

– Patricia (632 carats): Colombian crystal (Chivor), on display at the Museum of Natural History in New York.

– Mogul (217.8 carats): a gemstone slab with floral motif engraved on one side and, on the other, a prayer in Arabic with the inscribed date 1107. Part of the Allan Caplan collection (New York).

– Napoleon (24.38 carats): Napoleon's gift to Josephine in 1800; later owned by the Paris jeweler Mauboussin.

Aside from the list above, we can't forget those genuinely outstanding specimens which, though never "named," have their own historic resonance:

– the emeralds belonging to the collection of the Banco de la República in Bogotá; five marvelous crystals weighing from 220 to 1,796 carats;

– priceless gems conserved in the Topkapi Museum in Istanbul; or, in the same city, in the Seraglio Museum, we can admire a 1,400-carat stone (approximately) designed to adorn the Grand Sultan's tunic;

– a rich gathering of emeralds of highly prized colors in the Iranian Crown Jewel Collection: weights range from 10 to 300 carats; among which, three en cabochon stones weighing 225, 175, and 65 carats each; the last mentioned has been set as turban jewelry;

– a square emerald weighing 136.5 carats, set on a pin; on display in the Kremlin Armor Palace;

– a 2,680-carat emerald vase by Dionisio Misseroni (1642) is owned by the Vienna Museum of Natural History where we may also admire a block of limestone containing ten valuable emerald crystals;

– an emerald cup that belonged to Emperor Jehangir, on show at the American Museum of Natural History in New York.

Deposits Indeed material mined in Colombia cannot be rivaled for beauty. Chief sources here are: the Muzo and Cosquéz mines (in the West), and the Chivor and Ghachaia mines (in the East).

Some experts claim the Muzo emeralds are the most beautiful available; others prefer specimens extracted from the Cosquéz mines. In reality, emeralds found in this latter area bear closer resemblance to those from Chivor as their color is not as strong and definite as the coloring of Muzo emeralds.

The first reports of South American emerald mines concerned Chivor and came down to us from the Spaniard Gonzalez Jiménez de Quesada, who, in 1537, located a mine dubbed "Somondoco," for "god of the green stones," which had long been heavily mined by the natives in the area.

Other emerald producing countries are: Brazil, Zambia and Zimbabwe.

In Brazil, the emerald hunt first began in 1550;

PROVENANCE	INCLUSIONS
COLOMBIA: *Muzo:* – green coloring with slight yellowish shadings; *Cosquéz:* – green coloring with slight bluish shadings; *Chivor:* – green, at times a bit light-toned, with faint bluish shadings and outstanding brilliance; *Ghachaia (Buenavista):* – green with slightly paler center zone.	In general: – three-phase inclusions are characteristic of all Colombian emeralds; in this type a liquid phase (solution) a solid phase (usually a rock salt crystal) and a gaseous phase (bubble) are simultaneously present; – the coexistence of two-phase (liquid and gas) levels and three-phase levels, along with other chaotically arranged inclusions, make for a definite grouping which looks like a "garden of the emerald," and is so named appropriately; – possible crystals. In particular: *Muzo* = brownish crystals (parisite) in bipyramidal shape with hexagonal base; lack of pyrite crystals (resembling small dice with metallic sheen); *Cosquéz* = presence of crystals unusual; marked absence of pyrite; *Chivor* = two and three-phase oblong inclusions, usually arranged parallel to the stone's largest side; *Ghachaia (Buenavista)* = hexagonal structure growth lines which define an almost colorless zone, within the surrounding green zone; usually visible in observation from the pavilion's smallest side.
BRAZIL: – ample range of colors: from pale green to dark green (with heavy bluish green shadings); material extracted at Nova Era is usually a fine yellowish green.	– blackish chromite crystals (defined by some experts as "chrome diopside"), translucent calcite crystals, and pyrite crystals; – widespread talc masses that may even at times obfuscate the material; – brownish bands (biotite); – presence of crystalline aggregates with slightly marblelike aspect;
ZAMBIA: – green colored with slight bluish shadings.	– typical negative crystals (tiny prisms containing a liquid and a bubble) going in a single direction; – oblong crystals in dark green (tourmaline); – brownish bands (biotite); – short needles.
ZIMBABWE (Sandawana): – deep green, sometimes revealing slight yellowish shading.	– typical slightly curved needles (tremolite); – oxidation with dendritic aspect; – crystals, occasionally surrounded by halo effect.

but the first commercially important source was not unearthed until as recently as 1963. But then, with the discovery of rich mines in Salininha, in the State of Bahia, and – soon after – in Itabira (Minas Gerais), in Santa Terezinha (Goiás), and at Nova Era (Minas Gerais), Brazil soon became one of the world's most important emerald sources.

In 1956 the Zimbabwe mines were discovered in the Sandawana Valley; and, in 1970, deposits in Miku and Kafubu, in Zambia, came to light.

Further sources are in: Afghanistan (Panjshir), India (discoveries at Rajasthan in 1943 and at Kaliguman in 1945), Pakistan (the Swat Valley), Russia (near the Takovaya River), South Africa (Gravelotte), and Tanzania (at Maij Moto, on the banks of Lake Manyara); deposits of lesser importance are situated in Australia, Austria (Habachtal), Nigeria, Norway, the United States (Connecticut, Maine, and North Carolina).

Cut Emerald is a stone best suited to a particular rectangular faceted cut, with bevelled corners and flat facets – appropriately called "the emerald cut."

Since emerald is a pleochroic material, the stone's table may look yellowish green or bluish green depending on the relationship of the cut to the direction of the original crystal.

So though the emerald cut is the most popular, all other possibilities may be adopted.

En cabochon is employed for stones containing clearly visible fractures or crystal frost; or the material may be cut into beads, a form often put to use for Indian jewellery. Lastly, emeralds that lack transparency but have a good coloring may be used for engraving.

Under the lens When observed under a 10x magnifying lens, emerald – like ruby and sapphire – will reveal a fabulous inner world that fascinates as it enchants.

To explain the subject in as simple a manner as possible, you may refer to the table indicating typical inclusions and locations of main deposits. A brief list of other locations with respective inclusion is as follows:

– Afghanistan: material bears a resemblance to emeralds from the Muzo mines in Colombia, both for stone color and type of inclusions present.
– India: contains negative crystals.
– Pakistan: dark green coloring, with mica bands (also referred to as "strips") and small crystals.
– Russia: actinolite banding with transverse fractures that look like bamboo canes.
– South Africa: green fuchsite bands.
– Tanzania: mica bands and liquid-filled cavities.
– Austria: actinolite bands.

Oiling Emerald often presents internal fractures that may take on a whitish cast from internal reflections. It is now common practice to remove this blemish effect by injecting a vegetable oil in fractures with surface terminations. However oil may also accidentally enter and penetrate such fracture openings during the cutting phase as the substance is used to reduce attrition and avoid overheating of the stone; of course, such penetration is minimal.

When oil is deliberately and more substantially introduced, in the final dressing phase during ultrasonic cleaning the stone may become more or less opalescent since the oil is partially removed.

If you are wearing a ring set with an oiled emerald be sure to take it off before putting your hands into water containing any proportion of a detergent solution; or else, over a period of time, the stone may be damaged.

Adopting a 10x lens we can note in "oiled' stones:
– a slightly metallic look, resembling a fringed band which appears on the fracture where oil has been placed (this effect depends on the different refractive capacity of the emerald with respect to the oil introduced);
– occasional presence of flat bubbles in the fracture.

Unfortunately, there have been cases in which a green-colored oil has been adopted, to decidedly fraudulent ends.

Opticon treatment In the past few years an infiltration technique for filling fractures using a synthetic, epoxy resin, called "opticon" has been perfected.

Emeralds thus treated reveal a "flash" – similar to the effect created in infiltrated diamonds – with alternating yellow and greenish blue highlights on the fractures so treated. Simply by rotating the gem, you may observe this effect through a 10x magnifier.

Sometimes, on close examination, we can note air bubbles that have remained entrapped in the opticon. Obviously, any use of this treatment must be forthrightly declared.

Synthetic emeralds Efforts to obtain a synthetic emerald began almost a century and a half ago. In fact, it was in 1848 that J.J. Ebelman created the first emerald crystals produced in a laboratory, and these were exceedingly small specimens.

Today the production of synthetic emeralds relies on either one of two totally different and distinct procedures:
– melting and fusion;
– hydrothermal.

> These two methods have met with notable success in the synthesis of emerald.
>
> The following is a list of the syntheses realized after the initial success of J.J. Ebelman, defined either by their creator's name or by their commercial denomination:
>
> *Nachen* (1928). After a long fallow period, he resumed research in this sector.
>
> *Igmerald* (1934). Considered the forefather of today's synthetic emerald obtained by melting and fusion.
>
> *Chatham* (1953). The first synthetic emeralds to achieve a substantial commercial success.
>
> *Lechleitner I* (1959). At first labeled "Emerita," it was later called "Symerald."
>
> *Zerfass* (1963). Cloudy species with characteristic structure termed "beehive."
>
> *Gilson* (1963). Began research in 1950; well known on the market.
>
> *Lechleitner II* (1964). Technique employing a seed on which the synthetic crystal develops; this earlier form has developed into the current product "Lechleitner III."
>
> *Linde* (1965). Today we know this product as "Regency."
>
> In the past twenty years or so, one after the other, a number of synthetics have come onto the market: *Lennix*, *Crescent Vert* (Kyocera), *Biron*, *Bijoreve* (Seiko) and the *synthetic Russian emerald* obtained by hydrothermal treatment and melting and fusing technique (now known as "the Vasar emerald").
>
> And remember: a thorough study of the inclusions found in synthetic emeralds is of fundamental importance in recognizing and distinguishing them.

Melting and fusion

Emeralds obtained with this method reveal residuum of the melting employed entrapped in the resoldered fratures; they contain thick clouding inclusions that are strongly evident. Among the synthetic emeralds obtained by this method we should note: Nachen (Germany), Igmerald (Germany), Chatham (the United States), Zerfass (Germany), Gilson (France), Crescent Vert-Inamori, Kyocera (Japan), Lennix (France), Russian (Russia), Bijoreve (Japan); the last named contains zoned coloring and colorless crystals.

Hydrothermal

Greater attention must be devoted to synthetic emeralds produced with this method as they are certainly more difficult to recognize than the products of melting and fusion.

- *Linde.* Since 1970, this product has been called "Regency." In order to produce the growth of the synthetic gem, a colorless seed was first used, and later a green one was adopted. When samples of the very first production are viewed laterally under a 10x lens we can note a structure that research studies have termed "wafer"; inclusions resembling tiny black nails may also be perceived.

In the latest output we note colorless crystals (phenacite) and two-phase levels.

- *Lechleitner I*. First termed "Emerita" and later "Symerald," this material results from the deposition of a synthetic emerald layer on an already faceted almost colorless natural beryl. Under the lens, the surface of the stone looks as if it were furrowed with miniscule, intersecting surface cracks; of course a view within the stone discloses those inclusions found in natural beryl.

- *Lechleitner II*. A procedure which adopts a colorless seed as nucleus around which a synthetic crystal is grown. Under the lens we may perceive its "wafer" structure, crystals (phenacite) resembling tiny nails arranged in the same direction as the seed, cloudy inclusions and two-phase levels.

- *Lechleitner III*. A further development of the preceding method; it is no longer possible to observe the seed with the magnifying lens, though we may still see nail and cloud inclusions.

- *Biron*. Made in Perth, Australia by Biron International Ltd. At the moment it appears that this particular synthetic has gained wide popularity. Though it first appeared on the market in 1983, first production attempts date back to 1977.

Coloring depends heavily on the presence of vanadium, which makes it inert under UV rays.

Basic characteristics visible under a lens are: two-phase inclusions, color fluidification, gold sightings, phenacite crystals and growth zonings.

The two phases may be subdivided in:
– fingerprints, clouds; in the earliest production these are very easy to identify and may also be arranged in spirals (as in some natural emeralds);
– pinheads; these two phases are arranged in conical cavities with fairly elongated, oblong profile in which bubbles are easily identified. The base of the cone is generally sealed with gold sheeting or phenacite crystals.

Color fluidification, most clearly visible on the surface of the stone, looks very like the slight ruffling of a calm sea.

Gold is found in a vast range of shapes.

It may be surprising to learn that this noble metal is adopted in synthetic productions; actually only the very thinnest sheets are used, to line the container in which the process is effected and to avoid possible secondary reactions which would soon block the formation of the emerald.

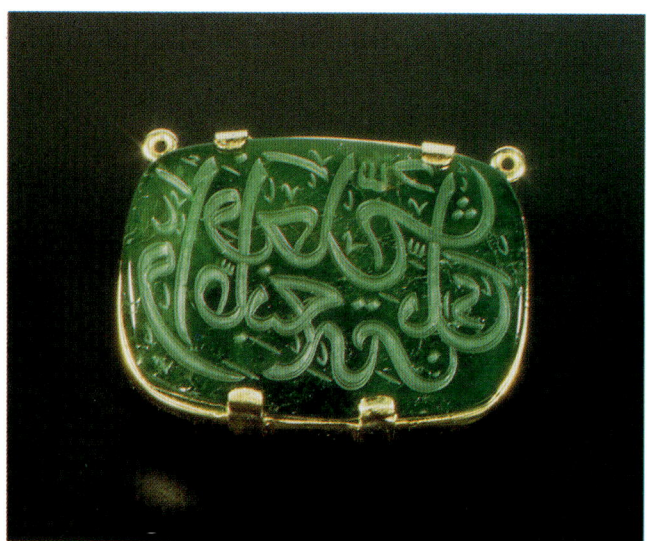

A quotation from a Sura *of the Koran engraved on emerald.*

By slowly rotating this stone under a 10x magnifier we can see the bright gleams given off by these fine golden strips.

Phenacite crystals (Be_2SiO_4) are colorless, rhombohedral-shaped and often found in groupings. They are not to be confused with calcite and dolomite crystals, found in natural emeralds, as these latter crystals are usually isolated and give off a more brilliant glow.

Growth zones are extremely thin stratifications, aptly described as "Venetian blinds," and are always present in hydrothermal synthetic material.

In the latest Biron manufacture, previously numerous inclusions have greatly decreased in number.

An important detail: when the two phases are not clearly visible in this product they quite resemble the two-phase inclusions found in natural emeralds; so even an expert cannot always be sure of classifying these synthetics as such.

• *Russian hydrothermal.* In 1987 a trade magazine first brought news of the arrival of this synthetic on the market. Two-phase oblong inclusions with superimposed phenacite crystal and color fluidification are the most frequently noted inclusions for this material.

We have been fairly detailed in describing a number of inclusions, for though such information is not necessarily decisive in setting one synthetic type apart from another, it will always distinguish a synthetic from a natural stone.

Imitations and similar stones All green stones may be erroneously taken for emerald.

There is, however, a list of materials most likely to be confused with the more valuable gem: green corundum, demantoid, green diopside, dioptase, hiddenite, olivine, green tourmaline, tsavorite, and uvarovite.

Closer examination reveals that demantoid, tsavorite, and uvarovite are garnet varieties and, being monorefringent, are not pleochroic, unlike the emerald which is, even if only to a lesser extent.

As mentioned, in the vast array of imitations, there are even simple green glass counterfeits.

In fact, the most frequently encountered imitation is the doppiette.

The most common are formed of colorless quartz in both upper and lower halves, held together with a green glue; seen from the table, the entire stone seems green. Another doppiette trick is made of colorless natural beryl in both halves, again joined by green glue. In this fraud, too, the stone looks totally green when viewed from the table, and the inclusions found in natural beryl add to the deceptive similarity with the real emerald.

Generally a doppiette is easily discovered: examining the girdle with a 10x lens we can almost always make out the dividing line between the two parts. Then, viewing from the table, we can often note air bubbles entrapped in the adhesive layer.

The reader may refer to the section on rock crystal, in the subdivision "Synthetics and similar stones" for a clear summary of the methods for tinting colorless quartz and thus producing visually appealing synthetics.

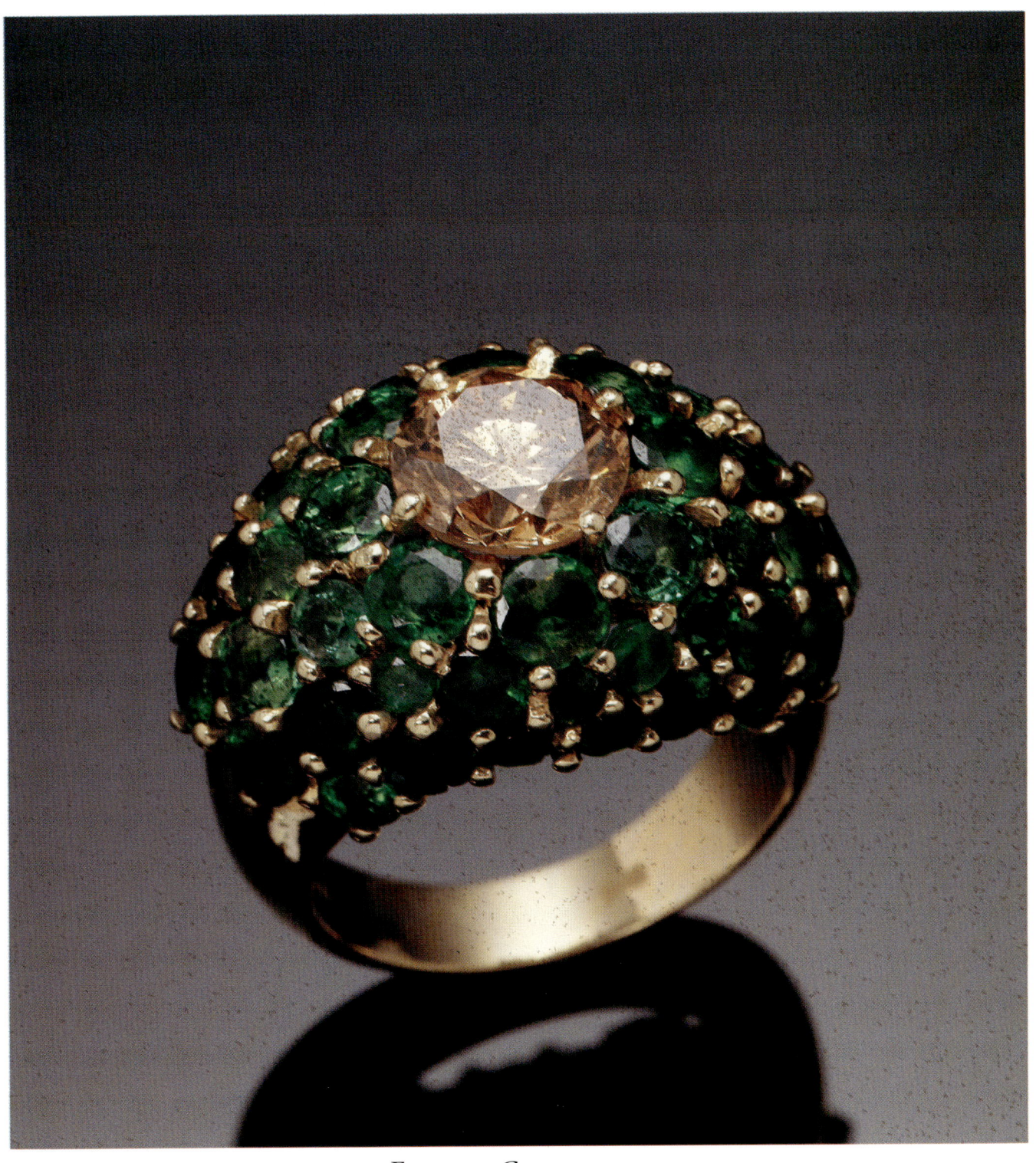

Fabrizio Cantamessa.
Ring in yellow gold with emeralds and a natural-colored diamond.

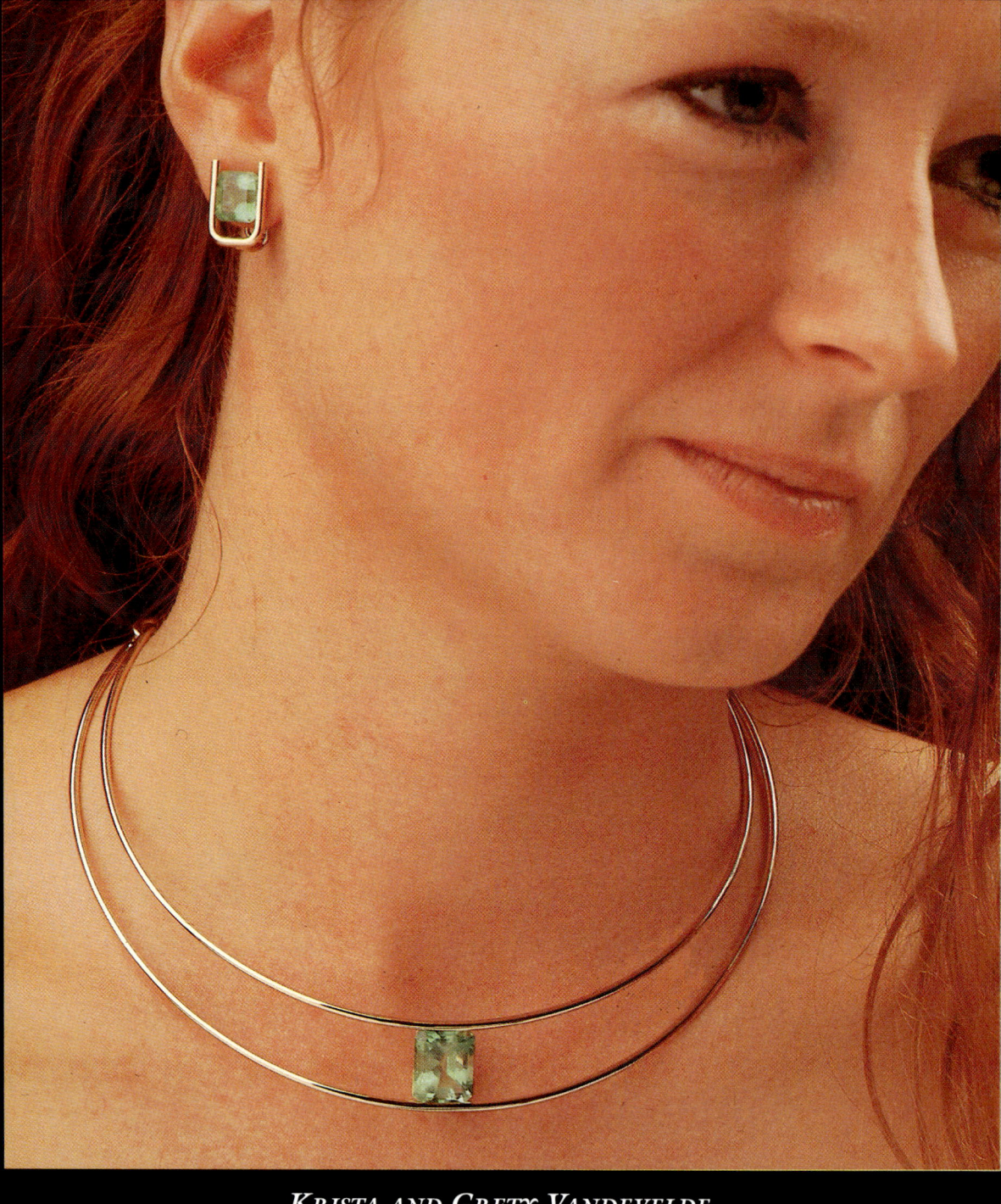
KRISTA AND GRETY VANDEVELDE.
Gold and emerald earrings and necklace.

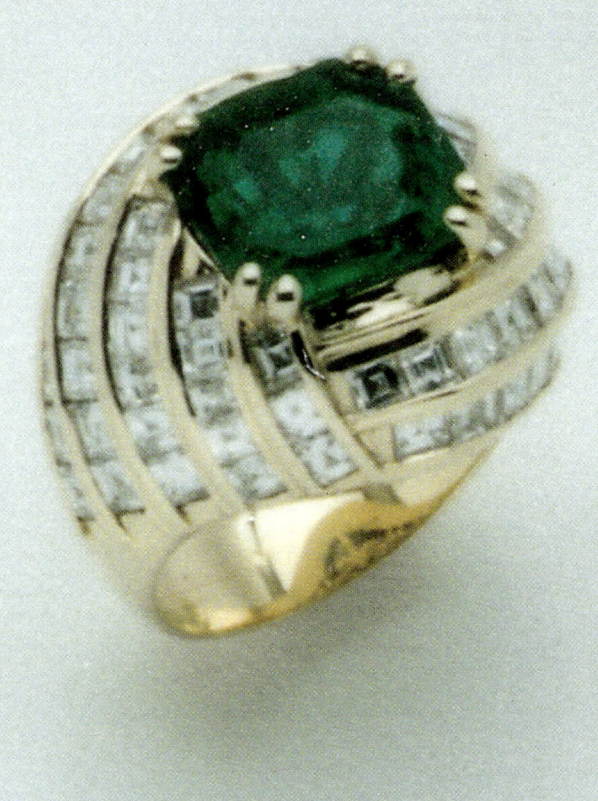

CEVA GIOIELLI: "TURBAN"
Yellow gold ring, 60 square diamonds, and Colombian emerald exceeding 4 carats.

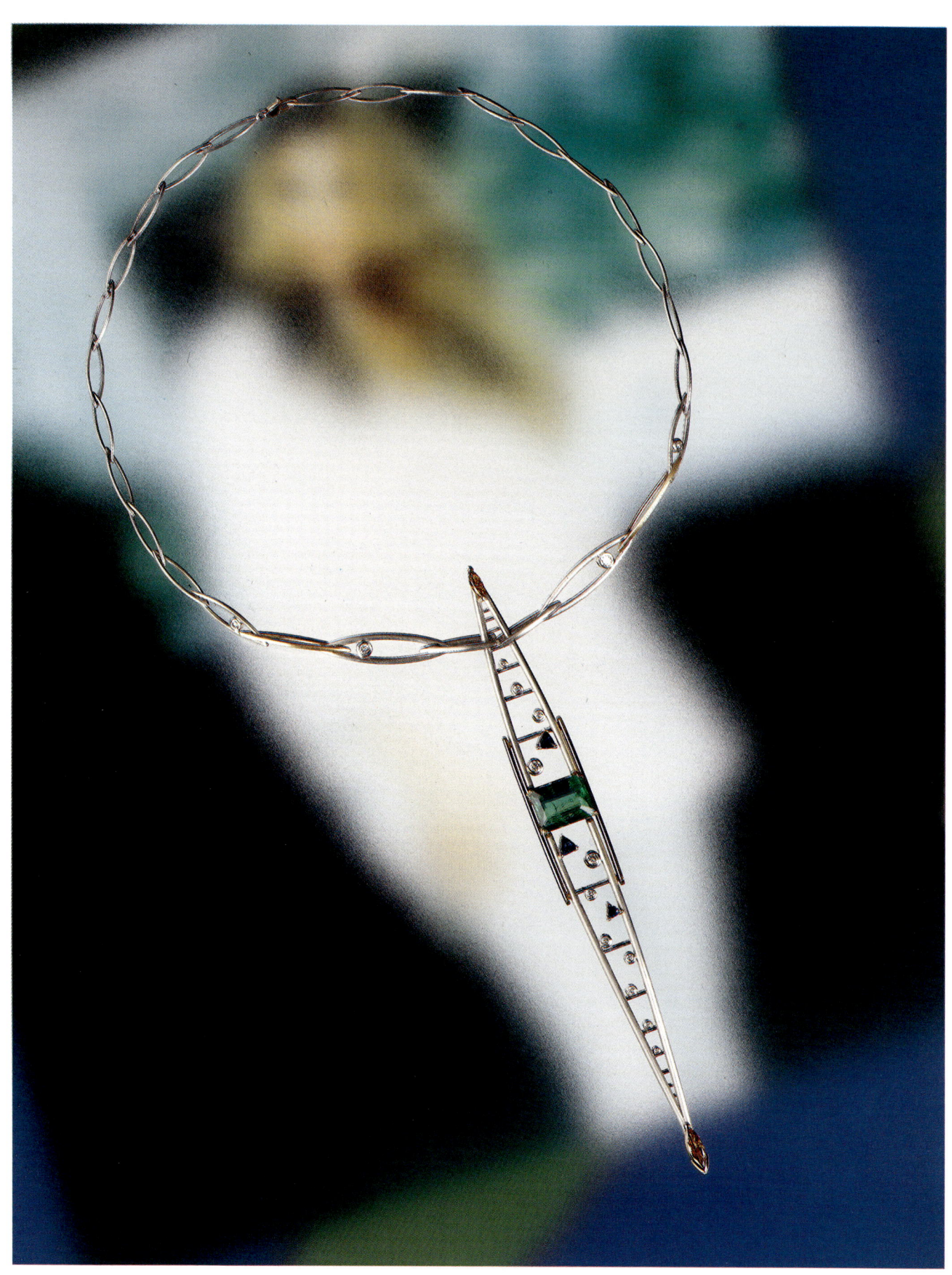

HANS SCHINDLER.
Choker of gold and precious stones including an emerald with an emerald cut.

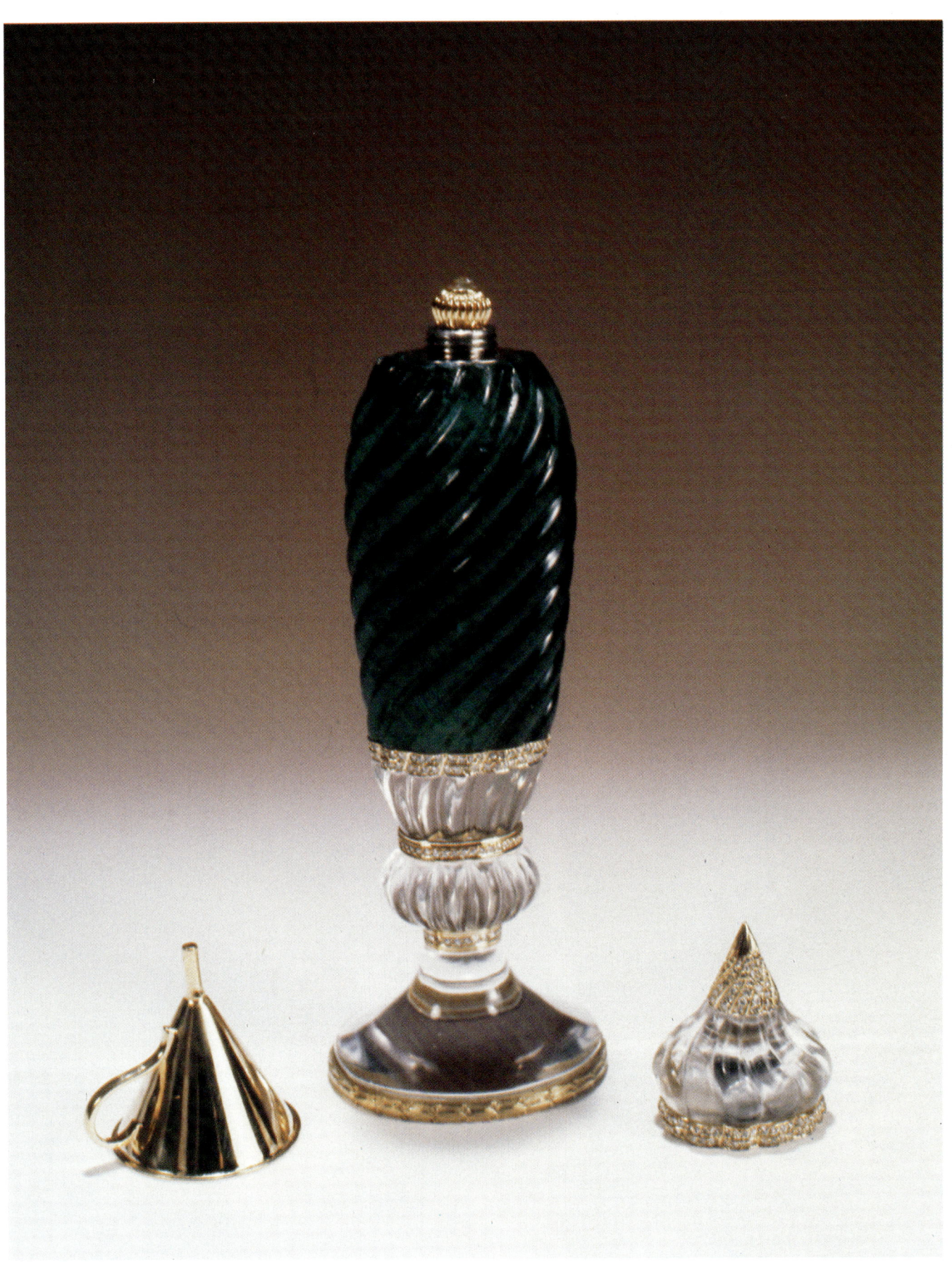

Perfume carrier in emerald.

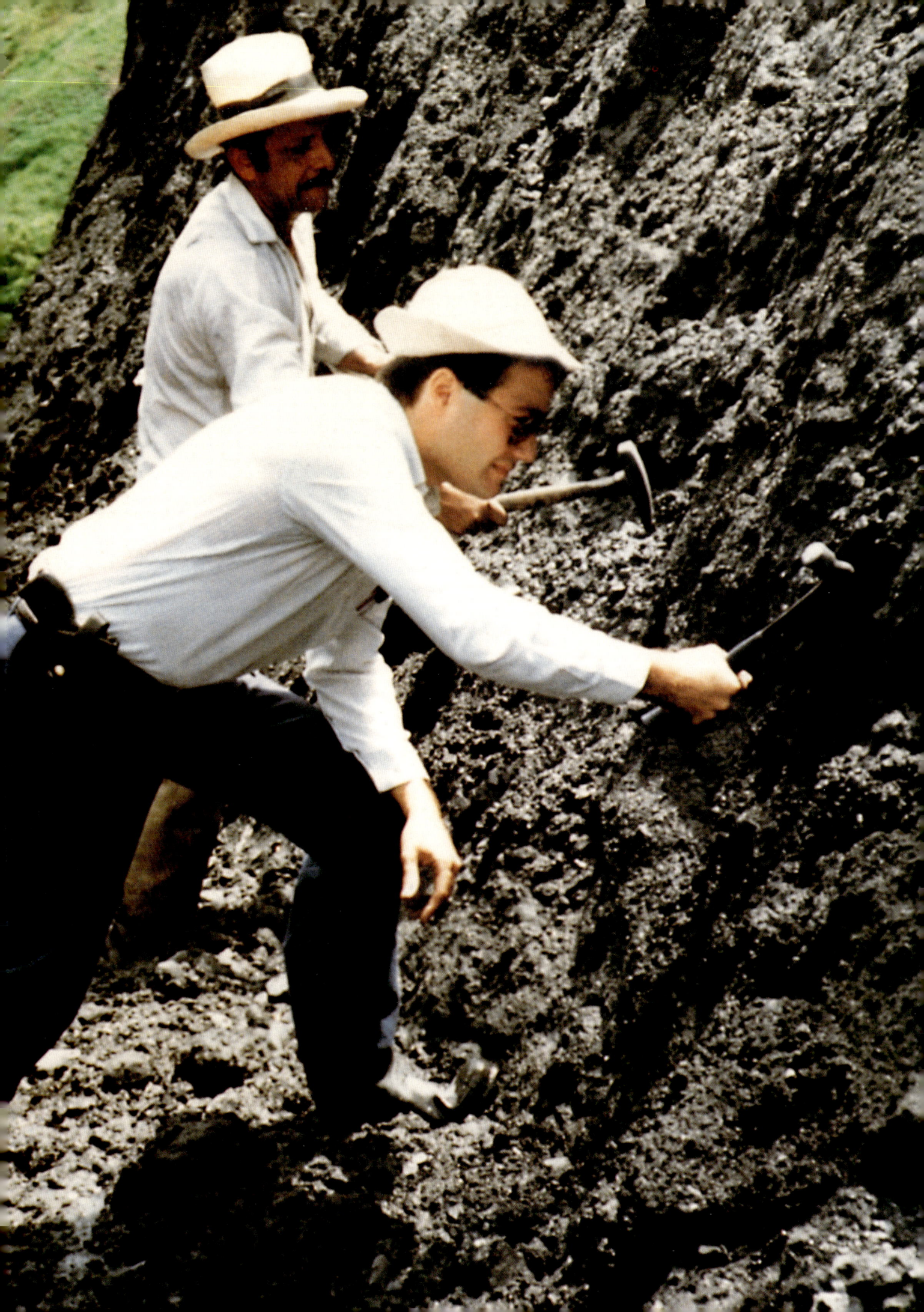

Paris - Muzo:
Departure for an Infernal Paradise
by Claude Mazloum

It all began in the summer of 1986 on the beach at Monte Carlo, where I whiled away the hours totally absorbed by a fascinating book by Marie Thérèse Guinchard entitled *La route des émeraudes (The Emerald Route)*. A journalist for French television, Miss Guinchard had journeyed halfway across the world and back to visit the Colombian emerald mines and on her return had written an account of her amazing adventure.

Coming as I do from a family of jewelers and being myself an expert gemmologist, I was deeply impressed by the fact that a European woman had actually succeeded in reaching Muzo, the most important emerald mine in the world and a place so dangerous that it is generally referred to as a living hell. A place where death by violence is so commonplace that it arouses neither interest nor emotion.

With each page I read I became more and more determined to relive the writer's experience, though I was fully aware of the perils involved in what was nothing more than a highly risky gamble. Indeed, of the few who have been foolhardy enough to venture there, those who have returned can be counted on the fingers of one hand. But I was not to be deterred.

After a twenty-hour flight from Paris, my plane landed at Bogotà at dawn. My only contact in Colombia was in Cali, the country's second largest city; so I stopped in the capital only for as long as it takes to step off one plane onto another. As soon as I arrived, I phoned a long-standing family friend of mine, Paul Ziablof. Ziablof listened politely as I expounded my ambitious project. He did not once interrupt me and wore an expression throughout that I can only describe as inscrutable. His answer was an ominous silence that seemed to go on forever. Up until my arrival, there had been no such word as "impossible" for Paul Ziablof, but I am certain that for those few tense moments even he doubted that my plan could be accomplished. It was sheer madness to go to Muzo, a sinister location where blood is shed as freely as the rain falls. But luckily for me, Ziablof was not a man to balk at the thought of danger. His mind works like a computer and at much the same speed. Striking the desk with his fist, he sententiously pronounced his verdict: "Claude, you shall go to Muzo, I promise you." I cannot describe my feelings as he said this. A mixture of joy, fear, pleasure, anxiety and uncertainty, I think, for I realized that those words, coming from a man like Ziablof, were the culmination of a well-conceived, well-deliberated plan that he already had in mind.

Paul instructed me to leave the very next day for Bogotà, where I was to contact a man named Juan Beetar who, together with Victor Carranza and Gilberto Molina, is indisputably one of the three emerald kings. Thanks to a vast network of contacts, in less than twenty-four hours Paul had moved heaven and earth for me, and I strongly suspect that, had it been necessary, he could have summoned the help of the President of the Republic himself. Paul had accepted the wager and won. He had succeeded in persuading the concessionaires to sanction my visit. That left just a few technical details to be cleared up.

On my arrival at Bogotà, I called don Juan. He was already acquainted with the situation so no explanations were needed. The following day Simon Beetar, don Juan's son, came to fetch me at the hotel and accompanied me to the Guayamarel private airport, where everyone had been informed of my expedition. Journalists and *paparazzi* are viewed with suspicion by the emerald prospectors who have, on many occasions and often unjustifiably, been the victims of defamatory publicity. Consequently, I was thoroughly searched from head to toe before we were allowed to depart.

The sky was clear as we took off, but as we drew near to the district of Boyaca visibility began to diminish as the mists thickened around us. We were but a few kilometers from Muzo when the control tower peremptorily ordered us back to base. I could have screamed with rage and frustration, so near and yet so far, and all because of the weather! It was maddening.

That evening, depressed and disheartened, I was back in my hotel room. Suddenly, the telephone rang. A voice informed me that I would be picked up the following morning for a second attempt. In the meantime, I learned from the hotel porter that during my absence the police had been making inquiries about my business in Colombia. Just before midnight I received a second telephone call telling me that take-off was scheduled for 8:00 a.m. and that I was to make my own way to the airport. I awoke at dawn to find that a note had been pushed under my door during the night. It simply said that the whole thing had been called off and that I was to make my way to an address in town. Nothing more.

Shortly after, my taxi drew up in front of don Juan's sumptuous, and heavily guarded villa. I was greeted by Simon, who placed at my immediate disposal a Range Rover and chauffeur instructed to drive me to Guaymaral.

The weather had actually deteriorated over the last twenty-four hours, but the new captain was a true *cascador* chosen especially for the occasion, and the helicopter was twice as big as the first. We soon found ourselves in the middle of a gale and torrential rain. Chopper champion Angel Salqado Bustos had to literally climb out of the clouds to avoid collision with a mountain, plunging down again through the mist almost to the ground as soon as he was over the top. I had never been so terrified in all my life!

The control tower, with which we had temporarily lost contact, suddenly ordered us to land anywhere we could, but the jungle was so thick that we could find no

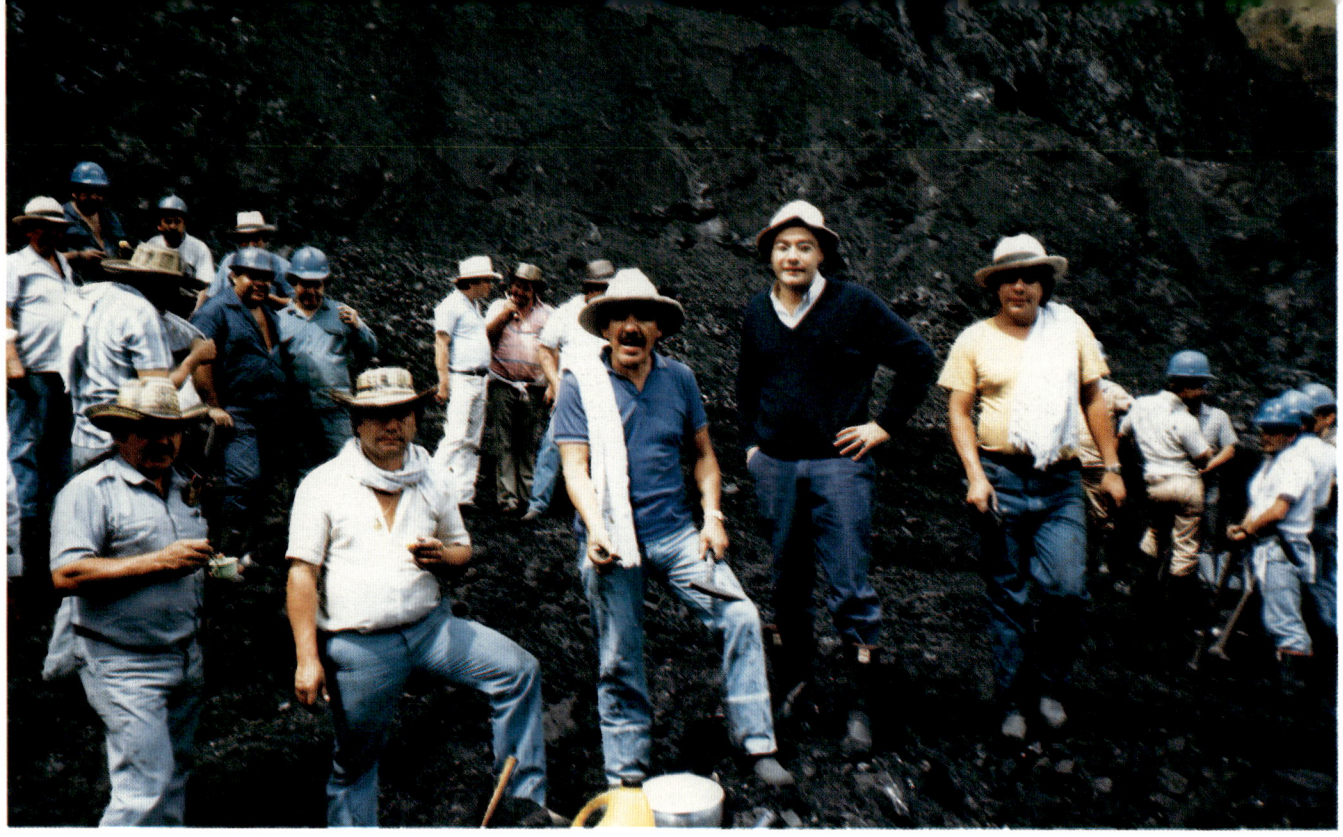

suitable clearing. We were next advised to turn back, but our captain, who was either reckless to the point of insanity or too courageous for his, and our, own good, merely winked at me and informed the control tower that he was in the middle of mist and clouds and had no choice but to go on.

A few kilometers further, beyond the next mountain, and paradise opened up before my eyes. Under a clear blue sky stretched a fairytale land as far as I could see. Bustos gave me the victory sign and pointed to a black spot in the middle of the verdant undergrowth: Muzo.

I could hardly believe what I saw. After a two-hour flight, which should have taken thirty minutes, here at last was our destination. And what a destination! Paradise on earth…

Armed men guarded the landing strip situated on top of a hill overlooking the mine. From the moment I set foot on the ground until I had opened my traveling bag I had a machine gun aimed straight at me. I was not carrying much; nonetheless, security measures had to be followed rigorously, for even the slightest oversight could have caused a bloodbath. Not only was I searched, I was also subjected to a painstaking interrogation, after which my hosts seemed at last convinced that I was really quite harmless. I was handed a pair of rubber boots and Captain Bustos conducted me to the mine where I was introduced to don Victor Carranza and his work team. Millionaire and miner, don Carranza is an amazing man, one of the only three men authorized to operate the Colombian emerald mines. I was proud and thrilled to shake his hand – a hand blackened by years of handling oxides and one that alone had extracted a third of the Colombian emeralds now distributed the world over.

Don Victor spoke only Spanish, but we managed to understand each other by using sign language. Mind you, nobody speaks at Muzo. People communicate with their eyes or with the movement of a single hand, the other being permanently attached to the essential tool of the trade, a pickaxe. Don Victor gestured to the driver of the bulldozer to open up a passage in the rock so that I could see how mining operations were carried out. The scene that appeared before me took my breath away; white veins adorned with green crystals, the famous «drops of oil» which don Victor proceeded to gather up as though he were harvesting apples. He packed them into a large leather bag closed with a padlock which was allowed into the hands of only his most trusted aides.

It was very hot, and the blackness of the surrounding terrain contrasted vividly with the clear blue of the sky. The nearby hill had been sculpted into shape first by the *dynamiteros* then by the bulldozers, and all the ravines in the immediate vicinity had been filled with the earth that had already been removed and verified. At each new phase of the operation don Victor stopped work so that I could take photographs. At a certain point he bent to pick up a crystal from the matrix and handed it to me pronouncing his only word of the day: "Souvenir." I was dumbfounded. Where then was the violence so vehemently described by the few visitors to this hell, which I must admit seemed more and more like paradise with each moment that passed?

"Violence? Just over there, at the foot of the hill," explained Captain Bustos, pointing to some little colored specks that could be distinguished against the black backdrop: *guaqueros*. According to Marie Thérèse Guinchard, who was allowed to approach the *guaqueros* these were men who would not think twice about killing their own mothers for the sake of an emerald, and not of course for its beauty but for its worth. On average, there were five killings a day in the the region. Miss Guinchard actually witnessed the execution of a worker who had stolen a gem, and she was again present when a young girl named Yanara was murdered.

The *guaqueros* (literally "grave-robbers") are allowed the "privilege" of panning the black mud removed from the "official" mine. There are some 20,000 of these men keeping their vigil around the mine, while no more than

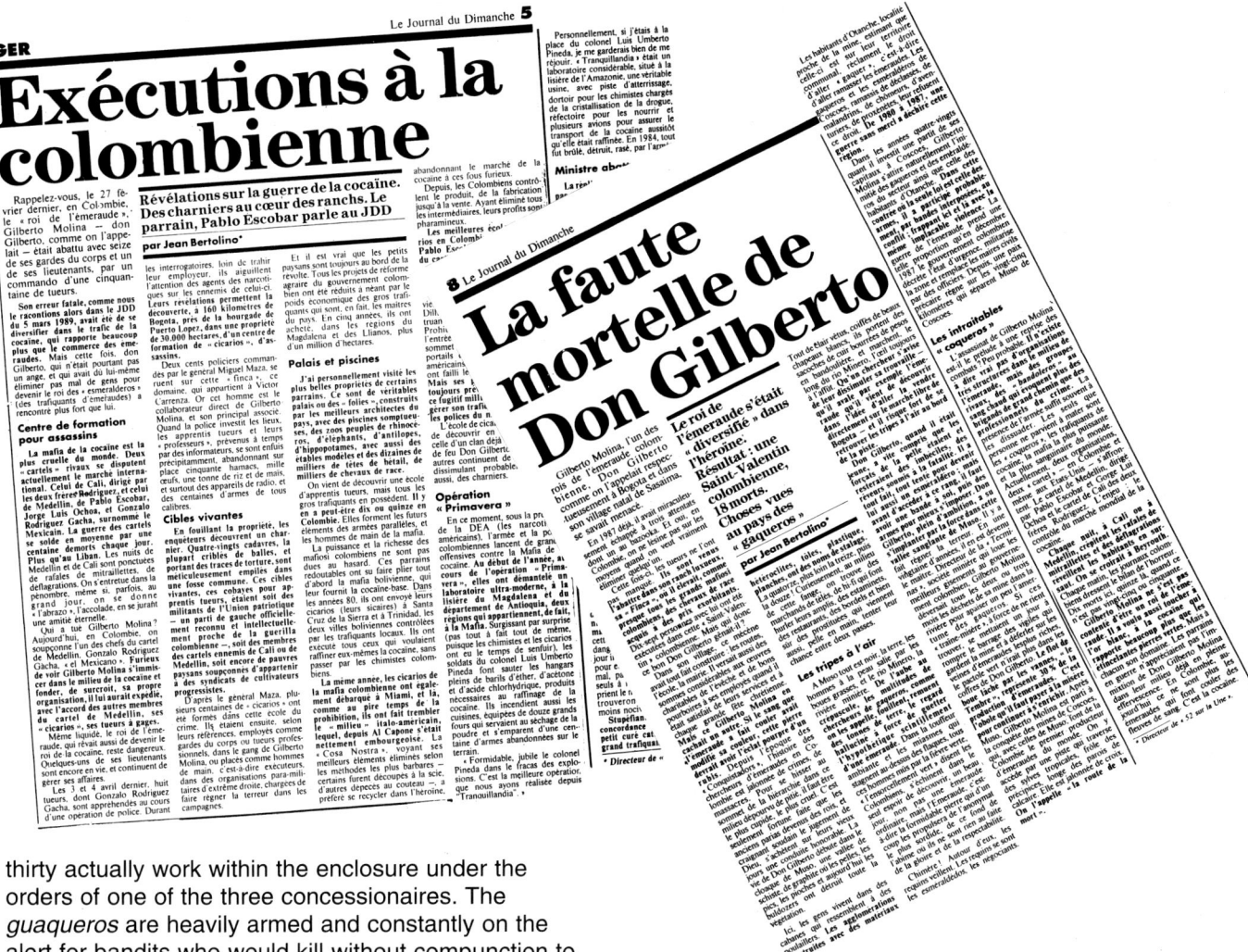

thirty actually work within the enclosure under the orders of one of the three concessionaires. The *guaqueros* are heavily armed and constantly on the alert for bandits who would kill without compunction to lay hold of the day's spoils. Sometimes these amount to as much as 10,000 carats, worth hundreds of thousands of dollars.

On the dot of mid-day, don Carranza invited me to lunch in a make-shift dining room close by the mine: four iron stakes driven into the ground supporting a few sheets of metal to protect us from the sun, a box of dynamite for a table, one glass shared by everybody and two forks, one for don Victor and the other for me. The food was simple and, under the circumstances, quite good. No one spoke or smoked, and there was no coffee, which struck me as most odd, considering where we were.

Our thirty-minute break over, the powerful bulldozer once again began to dig, inch after inch, for the rest of the afternoon. I was beginning at last to relax after my adventurous morning, when one of don Carranza's aides approached me and took from his mouth a magnificent green crystal. "Que piensas?" (What do you think of it?) was his straightforward question. I can honestly say that in my entire career I had never seen such an exquisitely green, exquisitely pure emerald. Only one gem in some 20,000 reaches such perfection. The man held out his pickaxe and launched a challenge: "Muzo te da lo que buscas" (Muzo will give you whatever you find), which in simple terms meant that I could keep any gems I was lucky enough to unearth. Bustos nodded his agreement. He himself was black with digging. Unwittingly I had just caught a disease that only exists in Muzo. A sort of hallucination similar to a mirage in the desert. Your eyes are inexorably drawn to the ground in search of little green stones. In fact, you see nothing but green. It is like being in a state of hypnosis. Black stones became emeralds, and I was convinced I was walking all over them. I was a victim of "green fever," which leads to senseless killing, violence and death at Muzo.

Epilogue

On 27 February 1989 television networks worldwide announced the assassination of one of the "emerald kings." Don Gilberto Molina had been brutally murdered together with seventeen of his aides and bodyguards. Less than two months later, on 10 April 1989, the Colombian Army discovered, at don Victor Carranza's ranch, a mass grave containing eighty bodies heaped one on top of the other. Most of them were riddled with bullets and showed clear evidence of torture. (From a report by Jean Bertolino published in the *Journal du Dimanche* 16 April 1989).

August 1996: the author would like to render special homage to Paul Ziablof, brutally murdered in Cali (Colombia). He was C. Mazloum's last friend in this country.

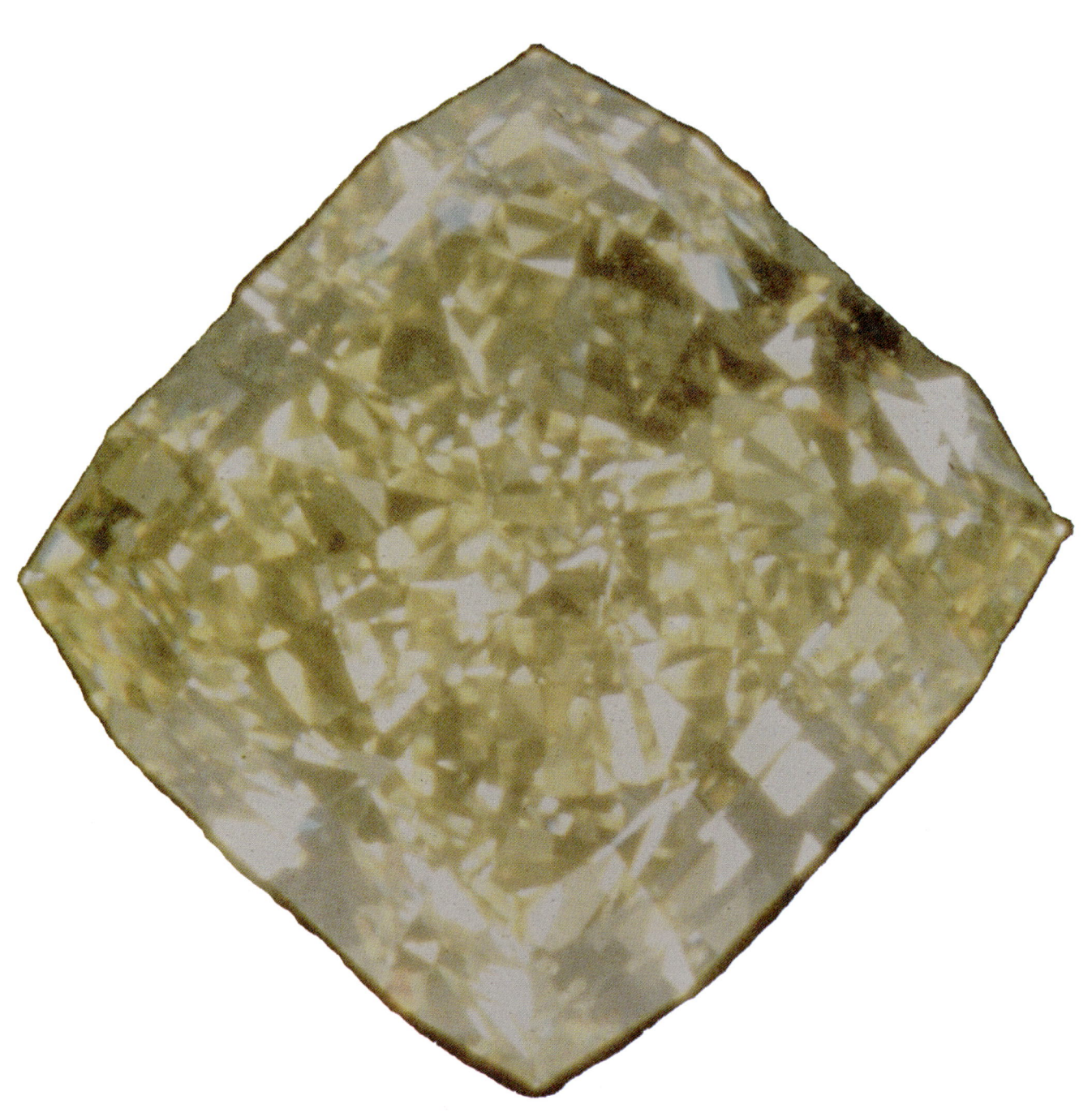

CHAPTER IV

Diamond

GENERAL INFORMATION

How it got its name Harder than any other known mineral, the name "diamond" derives from the Greek *adamas* (unconquerable).

Varieties There are no varieties, unless we decide to take into consideration lonsdaleite, which is only found in meteorites and belongs to the hexagonal rather than cubic order of crystals. Additional reference must be made to two types with exclusively industrial use: the Brazilian "carbonado," an aggregate of microcrystalline diamond; and the Australian "bort," with a structure of small radiating spheres.

Some interesting sidelights To get an idea of just how hard a diamond is we can compare its 10 rating on the traditional hardness index to the 9 rating assigned to a corundum, translating these figures, as it were, into a metric decimal system such as Rosiwal's and we shall see that the diamond is actually 140 times harder than the corundum. So here is a reminder: never put diamonds in the same container as other gems, for the latter will surely be scratched on contact.

One of the first citings for this gem comes in the Bible where it is called by the Hebrew appellation *yahalom*, whilst there was an entire chapter about these stones in Pliny the Elder's *Natural History*.

Diamonds have come down through the centuries as a pledge of everlasting love: the first famous ladies to receive them as such were Agnès Sorel and Marie de Bourgogne.

In Europe the rage for diamonds spread when the noted voyager J.B. Tavernier arrived at the court of the Sun King, reporting his wondrous travels and the magnificence of a brilliant gem encountered in the Indies. Louis XIV actually acquired 44 diamonds of outstanding size, and an amazing 1,122 smaller stones, though his great coup was a 112.5-carat rough blue diamond. Through the years people began to say this stone brought bad luck; later, when cut, it produced the famous Hope Diamond, a rectangular stone in mixed cut with rounded border.

Benvenuto Cellini is supposed to have met his end by eating food mixed with diamond grit. But generally the diamond stands for very positive factors: great strength, equilibrium and loyalty, qualities which greatly increase if the stone is received as a gift.

Ayurvedic folk medicine promises the wearer a cardiac stimulant, a cure for the nervous system, and a total physical purification.

In India it is held that diamonds favor meditation, inspiring spiritual development.

Celebrated diamonds

In the history of this gem there have been a certain number of unusually large specimens, occasionally in fancy colors; rare and

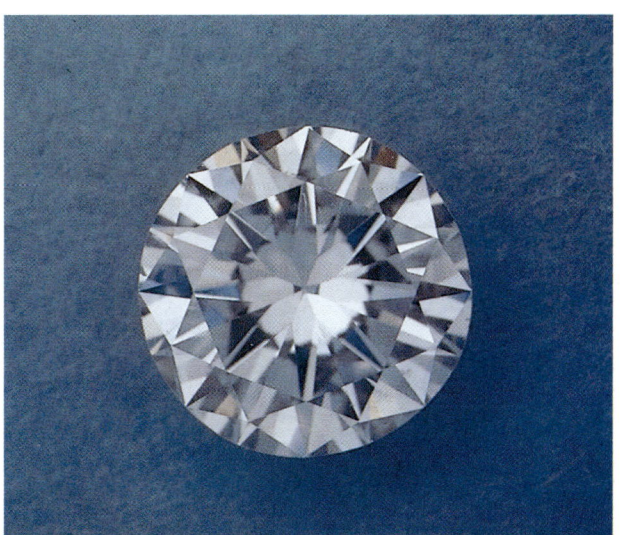

Chemical Formula: C – carbon
Hardness: 10 (Mohs scale)
Specific Gravity: 3.52
Refraction: monorefringent
Color: colorless (or "white") predominantly; more rarely, transparent colored specimens in pale yellow, a brownish tint, grey, black, or fancy color

FAMOUS DIAMONDS

Weight in Carats	Name	Color	Cut	Provenance	Last Report
530.2	Cullinan I	White	Drop	South Africa	Tower of London
317.4	Cullinan I	White	Coussin	South Africa	Tower of London
280	Grand Mogul	White	½ Egg in rose cut	India	–
273.85	Centenary	White	Fantasia, unique	South Africa	De Beers
245.35	Jubilee	White	Coussin	South Africa	Paul-Louis Weiller
234.5	De Beers	Straw-colored	Coussin	South Africa	Sold at auction in Geneva, 1982
205.7	Red Cross	Yellow	Square brilliant	South Africa	Sold at auction in Geneva, 1973
202	Black Star of Africa	Black	–	–	Shown in Tokyo, 1971
189.6	Orlov	Slight shadings of greenish blue	½ Egg with small rose cut on top	India	Kremlin, Moscow
175-195 (Estimated)	Darya-i-Nur	Pale pink	Rectangular in bern cut	India	Teheran, Iranian Crown Jewels
184.5	Jacob, Victoria, Imperial	White	Oval	South Africa	Collection of the Prince of Hyderabad (died in 1977)
140.5	Regent (or Pitt)	White with light blue highlights	Coussin	India	Louvre Museum, Paris
137.27	Florentine	Light yellow	Irregular, double rose cut	India	Until 1920, in possession of the Austrian Imperial Family
133.03	Algeiba Star	Yellow	Square, modified to brilliant cut	South Africa	Private collection
132.42	Golden Hue	Yellow	Coussin	South Africa	Private collection
130	Grand Brasileiro	White	Rectangular	Brazil(?)	Seen in 1956
128.8	Estrèla do Sul	White	Oval	Brazil	Rustomjee Jamsetjee, Bombay
128.51	Tiffany	Yellow	Coussin	South Africa	Tiffany & Co., New York
128.25	Niarchos	White	Drop	South Africa	Niarchos Family
127.02	Portuguez	White	Emerald	Brazil	Smithsonian Institution, Washington
125.65	Jonker	White	Emerald	South Africa	Sold in Hong Kong in 1977
118.05	Meister	Yellow	Coussin	South Africa	Walter Meistyer, Zurich
116.6	Vainer Briolette	Yellow	Briolette	South Africa	Sultan of Brunei
115.06	Taj-i-mah	White	Mogul Cut	India	Teheran, Iranian Crown Jewels
109.26	Cross of Asia	Champagne	–	–	Shown in San Antonio, Texas in 1947
107.07	Cartier	White	Drop	South Africa	Sold to unknown buyer in 1984
105.6	Koh-i-Noor	White	Oval	India	Tower of London
105.54	Soleil d'Or	Yellow	Emerald	–	Private collection
104.95	Golden Door	Yellow	Shield	–	Private collection
102.48	Ashberg	Amber	Coussin	South Africa	Sold at auction in Geneva, 1981
101.25	No name	Yellow	Briolette	–	M. Vainer Ltd., London
90.38	Briolette	White	Drop	–	Sold by Harry Winston in 1971
78.53	English Dresden	White	Drop	Brazil	Probably in India
69.42	Taylor-Burton	White	Drop	South Africa	Said to be in Saudi Arabia
60	Nur Ul-Ain	Pink	Drop	India	National Bank of Teheran
55.23	Sancy	White	Irregular drop	–	Louvre, Paris
44.52	Hope	Blue	Mixed cut	India	Smithsonian Institution, Washington
43.38	Nassak	White	Emerald	India	–
40.7	Dresden Green	Green	Pendeloque	India or Brazil	Dresden Jewel Collection
35.5	Wittelsbach	Dark blue	Fancy in fifty facets	India	Since 1964 in a private collection
30.82	Unzue Heart	Blue	Heart	–	Smithsonian Institution, Washington
20.53	Hortensia	Pale pink	Pentagonal	India	Louvre, Paris
10.73	Eureka	–	Oval coussin	South Africa	Kimberley, South Africa

beautiful, they bear famous names recognized worldwide and closely linked to their stories. Take care to keep the following table of essential data as referent:

In addition to the diamonds enumerated in the table, we often also hear about the "Braganza" stone (weighing 1,860 old carats) and the "Matan" (367 old carats). These, however, are not true diamonds; the former is a colorless topaz, and the latter a rock-quartz crystal.

Historical notes Sanskrit documents reveal that this gem was already known in 400 B.C.; but so far no one has proven the date of its discovery.

Until the first Europeans arrived in India, Orientals had complete control of diamond commerce, save for a brief interval around the time of the fall of the Roman Empire. Yet for all this enormous span of time, there are precious few documents, and those few contain fantastic exaggerations.

From his travels, Marco Polo was able to provide the first account of Hormuz, a Persian City that acted as market for diamonds mined in India. It was from this city that all stones arrived in Armenia, Turkey, and Aleppo, that market area in Arab territory which later became nerve center of the Venetian import monopoly for Europe, a dominion continuing till 1498 when Vasco de Gama opened the new sea route to India, which shifted the European hub to Lisbon.

Meanwhile, a prosperous trade had developed between Venice and Bruges, so aptly dubbed the "Venice of the North," where diamond processing had become a fine art that called for strict exams to accredit its cutters.

As it took over the Venetian hegemony, Lisbon established its own link with Antwerp, which soon became the world diamond cutting center.

Following the Thirty Years War (1618-1648), Antwerp's fame dimmed as the city of Amsterdam offered refuge both to Protestant diamond cutters fleeing Antwerp itself and Hebrew cutters from Portugal, craftsmen who brought the Dutch city to international eminence in the field of diamond cutting. In the end, Amsterdam even became Antwerp's source for rough stones, that parcel remaining after the Dutch first choice.

In 1725 the Minas Gerais deposits were discovered along the Jequitinhonha River in Brazil; and the area was soon named "Diamantina," reflecting a rich output that wreaked havoc with the diamond market as prices fell calamitously. Then yet another mining zone was uncovered in Brazil at Estrèla do Sul. Prices plummeted again in 1866 when Erasmus Jacobs, a Boer, found in South Africa the Eureka diamond, a 21.25-carat specimen that produced a 10.73-carat faceted gem, and signalled another new flow of stones. Ultimately, the real diamond rush was on when a 83.50 rough stone was unearthed and subsequently cut to produce the stunning Star of South Africa.

Since then, the diamond market has looked to the African continent for chief supply, and the history of diamonds has been dramatically effected by the De Beers Consolidated Mines and the De Beers CSO.

A large quantity of very small stones arrived on the European market with the discovery of the mine, Premier, in South Africa and later, a number of alluvial deposits. Antwerp was in prime position to take advantage of the situation having a nearby area ready for small-industry development, with a low-cost labor force.

Yet another epoch battle – the First World War this time – stimulated the emigration of diamond cutters and merchants toward Holland, which had remained firmly neutral. At war's end, however, they returned to Antwerp, thus stimulating many Dutch cutters to make the same move.

Amsterdam was more heavily hit than Antwerp by the worldwide crisis in the thirties, and the latter city survived as diamond center even after the Second World War when many of its Jewish cutters emigrated to Tel Aviv or the United States.

Antwerp's postwar recovery was as dramatic as it was swift: at the beginning of April in 1945 there were 3,480 workers in the diamond sector in Antwerp whereas just eight months later in December there were 11,000.

Even today Antwerp and its Diamond Center are a mecca for cut diamonds, while Amsterdam has only a few hundred workers involved in the industry.

Other cities boasting an important diamond market are Tel Aviv, followed closely by Bombay, Surat, and New York.

In the meantime, it's worth keeping your eye on a number of countries emerging on the market: China, Malaysia, Mauritius, Russia, Sri Lanka, and Thailand.

Deposits Before discussing the principal mine areas, we had best emphasize the difference between *primary* and *secondary* deposits.

Primary deposits are those that rock formations have thrust almost to the surface of the earth's crust. In homage to early diamond

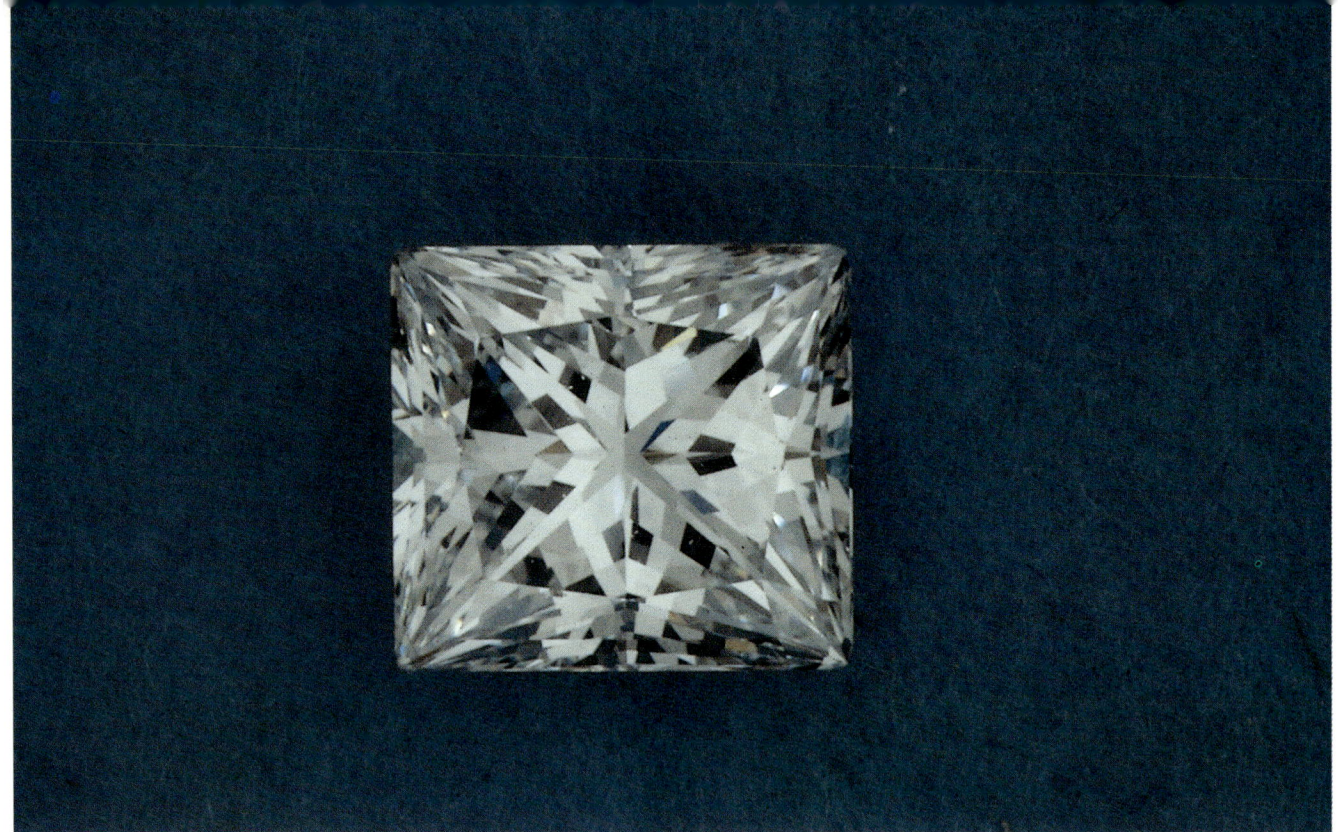

Square diamond.

discoveries in such locations as Kimberley, these rocks are labelled "kimberlite," as well as "blue ground" and "lamproite" (only noted as primary deposits in Australia in 1979). Whatever their name tag, these rocks originally form at a depth of about 150-200 kilometers; however, varying theories are offered to explain the phase of diamond formation and the gradual rise of these rocks towards earth level. We know diamonds are created when two extreme conditions conjoin: a 1700°C temperature and about a 55/60-kilobar pressure. Obviously, diamonds did not form either in kimberlite or lamproite, which only acted as carriers to the diamond furnace in which ancient eruptive phenomena had produced tubular funnels known as "pipes."

Secondary deposits are those alluvial deposits produced by the action of water or wind on primary deposits. Aside from eruptive volcanic situations, all deposits are alluvial.

Generally these secondary sources are rich in good-to-fine quality material that is ideal for cutting: in alluvial deposits in South Africa and Namibia 95% of extracted specimens will have some market value. Nevertheless, to be noted is the apparently contradictory information reported from Zaire where only 5% of the secondary deposit material is said to be idoneous for faceting.

World diamond production Amassed in 1990, the data in the table below gives a fair overview of the world's major diamond producers.

Raw Material Extracted (in millions of carats)

	1980	1990
Australia	0.50	36.00
Zaire	14.00	24.00
Botswana	5.10	17.30
Russia (ex-USSR)	12.00	15.00
South Africa	8.70	8.50
Namibia	1.56	0.80
South America	1.25	1.70

Remember that 48% of our material comes from Africa, 34% from Australia, 15% from Russia, and only 3% from other areas.

Comparing the data expressed in millions of carats of raw diamonds extracted in 1980 and 1990, we observe some significant shifts. Only the major producing countries are shown.

The De Beers Group If you are interested in diamonds, you have undoubtedly already heard of the De Beers Group.

Though it has a single-organization structure it is composed of many juridically distinct but economically dependent units, and is controlled by a single operative unit. The Group was founded on 12 March 1888 with the fusion of the De Beers and Kimberley mines. Today almost 35% of the world diamond production is connected with the De Beers Group.

Chief areas where diamonds are extracted Here is an alphabetical listing which also includes

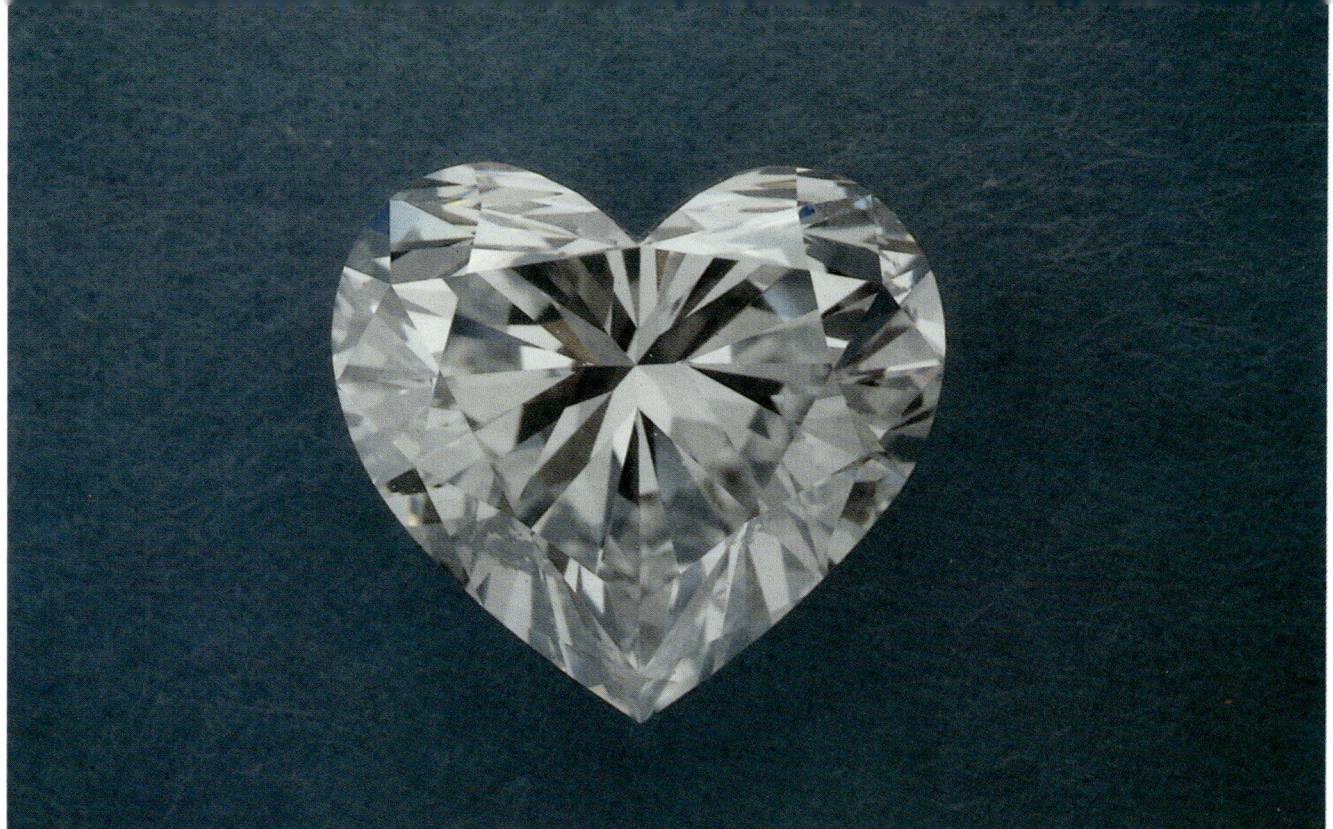

Heart-shaped diamond.

countries already mentioned as major producers of raw material: Angola, Australia, Borneo, Botswana, Brazil, China, the Federation of Russian States, Ghana, Guayana, Guinea, India, Indonesia, the Ivory Coast, Lesotho, Liberia, Namibia, the Republic of Central Africa, Sierra Leone, South Africa, Swaziland, Tanzania, Venezuela, Zaire.

The African continent's predominance is clear: 14 countries out of the 23 names cited.

Diamond types Evaluating the stone's behavior in ultraviolet light, its absorbtion phenomenon under infra-red, the presence of foreign atoms in the crystal lattice, to name some of the more important properties to be analyzed, we may divide the diamond into three types:

Type I. Generally evincing a blue fluorescence and containing azote atoms, this type again divides into two subgroups:

I(a) – subdivides into another two groups:

1) carbon/azote relationship about 1,000,000/1; usually yellow or greenish;

2) carbon/azote relationship about 1,000/1 with groupings of azote atoms; generally colorless (white).

95% of all natural diamonds fall into the I(a) subtype.

I(b) – diamonds with marked presence of azote atoms; only about 0.1% of all natural diamonds fall into this subtype; however all known synthetic yellow diamonds are members.

Type II. Contains only very slight traces of azote atoms and they are rarely fluorescent; very large diamonds frequently belong to this type, which in turn subdivides into:

II(a) – these diamonds are often brown, though occasionally also pink, blue-green and colorless;

II(b) – a blue diamond group, colored by traces of boron atoms.

Type III. Refers solely to lonsdaleite diamonds.

A classification that is interesting for diamond cutters and useful in distinguishing natural from synthetic diamonds.

Key characteristics *The 4 Cs.* When it comes to evaluating stones, today's diamond market is governed by highly restrictive criteria. And it is just these new normative classifications that have renewed consumer faith in diamonds as truly rare and precious gems; moreover, these norms are in public domain and we may all consult them.

A publicity campaign launched by the De Beers Diamond Information Center is spreading the word that correct classification must always refer to the famous *4 Cs*: *carat, clarity, color,* and *cut*.

Carat weight is easily obtained by instrument; in judging the other three *Cs*, we must depend on technicians with highly specialized training.

Carat weight A precision scale is sufficient for loose stones; it will provide weight in carats,

Ø mm		Carats
9.0	○	2.50
8.6	○	2.25
8.2	○	2.00
7.8	○	1.75
7.4	○	1.50
7.0	○	1.25
6.5	○	1.00
6.2	○	0.85
5.9	○	0.75
5.6	○	0.65
5.2	○	0.50
4.8	○	0.40
4.4	○	0.33
4.1	○	0.25
3.8	○	0.20
3.4	○	0.15
3.0	○	0.10
2.7	○	0.07
2.5	○	0.05
2.0	○	0.03
1.5	□	0.02
1.8	□	0.03
2.0	□	0.05
2.5	□	0.08
2.8	□	0.13
3.0	□	0.16
3.5	□	0.23

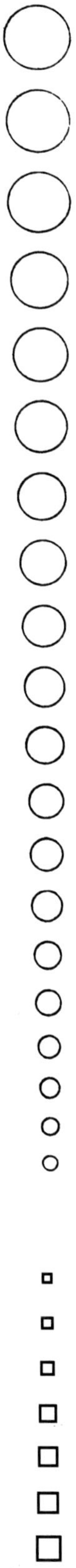

The table on the left allows the weight of a diamond in carats to be calculated from its diameter, provided that the stone is well proportioned. The relative circumference indicated in the diagram corresponds exactly to that of a diamond having the weight and dimensions indicated at the sides.
In the same column, but lower down, an identical measurement can be effected for square-shaped diamonds. The right-hand column can be used for calculating the weight of diamonds with the following types of cut: marquise, emerald, baguette, trapezoidal-baguette. Once again, this is providing that the cut is well proportioned.

Shape	Carats
marquise	3.00
marquise	2.00
marquise	1.50
marquise	1.00
marquise	0.75
marquise	0.50
emerald	3.00
emerald	2.00
emerald	1.50
emerald	1.00
emerald	0.75
emerald	0.50
baguette / trapezoid / marquise	0.30
baguette / trapezoid / marquise	0.20
baguette / trapezoid / marquise	0.15
baguette / trapezoid / marquise	0.10
baguette / trapezoid / marquise	0.07
trapezoid / marquise	0.05

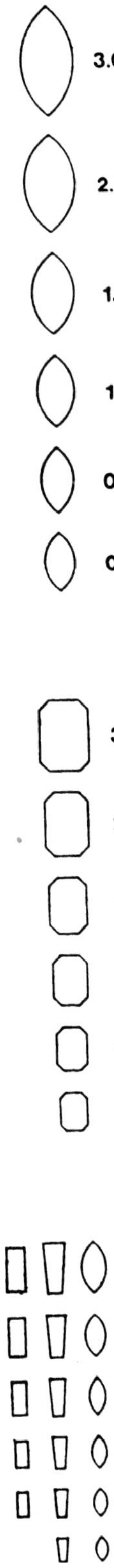

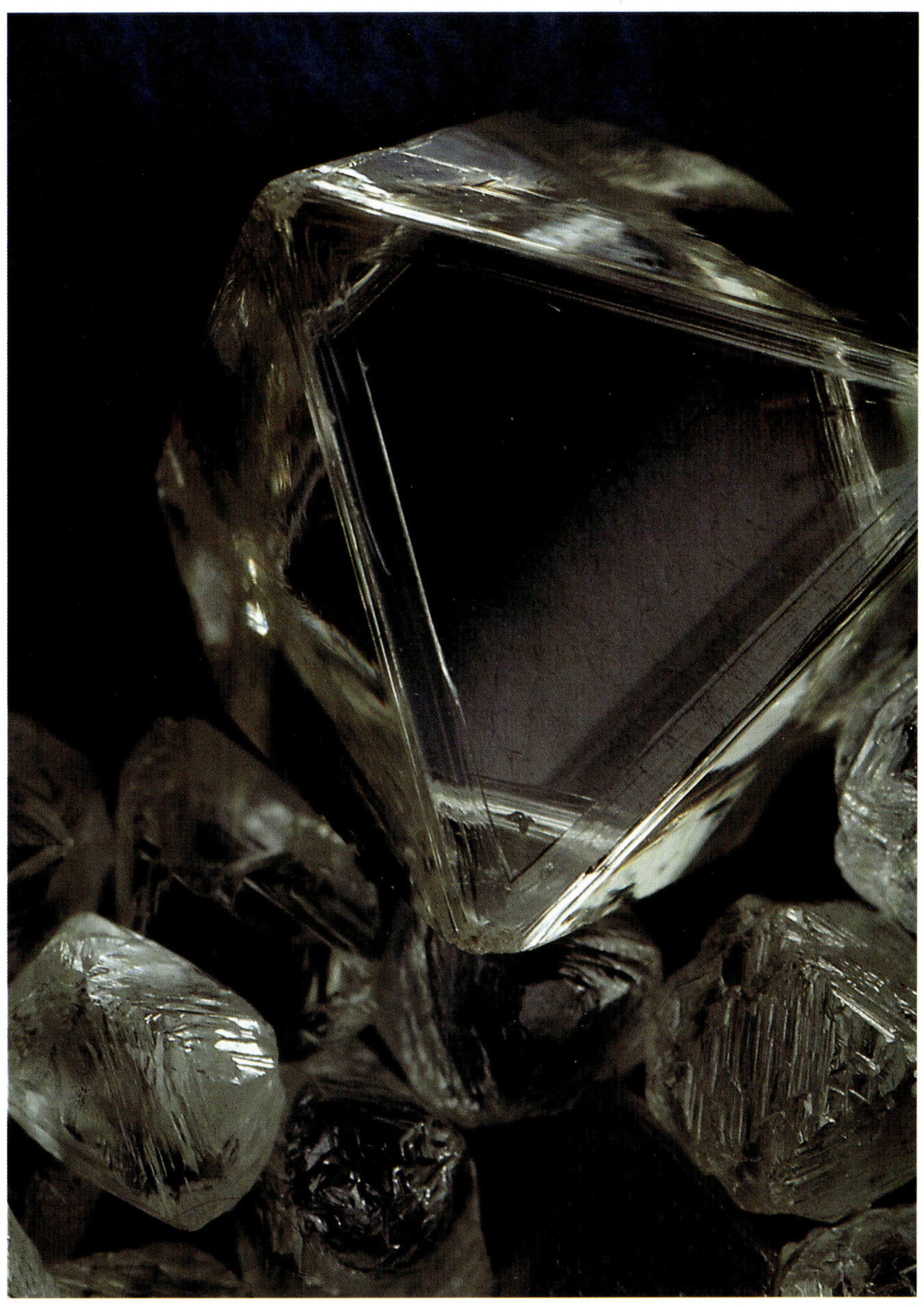
Rough diamonds.

expressed with at least two numbers after the decimal point.

Set stones must be measured with a caliber and the results processed by specific formulas, producing a satisfactory approximation of the stone's weight.

This procedure is possible because diamond has a highly constant density; however if the examiner does not have an instrument with digital data reading, caliber readings should be conducted with great precision.

In tribute to their inventor, these formulas are called "Leveridge."

For all the most important cuts (see also the section "Cut" in this chapter) we apply the formulas listed below, where sizes are expressed in millimeters.

Leveridge formula for round brilliant cut: weight in carats = radius × radius × height × 0.0245 (radius is obtained by taking the sum of the stone's length and width and dividing by two);

Leveridge formula for oval brilliant cut: weight in carats = the same as for round brilliant cut above;

Leveridge formula for drop cut: weight in carats = length × width × height × 0.0062;

Leveridge formula for marquise cut: weight in carats = (length − ⅓ width) × width × height × 0.0077;

Leveridge formula for emerald cut: weight in carats = (length − ⅓ width) × width × height × 0.013.

Clarity The diamond's crystal lattice often reveals interruptions that may be caused by crystal inclusions, cavities, gemination layers, linear structures, cleavages and internal tensions.

Certainly it is far from easy to find a diamond totally free of all the defects we have enumerated. And so, at the start of this century, just after the discovery of large South African deposits, it was decided in a Paris meeting that any diamond examined under the lens and found defect-free would be defined as "pure," having perfect clarity, in contrast to stones that fail to satisfy this criteria and which would, therefore, be classified as "piqué." Internationally, "purity" is a frequent referent for clarity.

Around 1920 the United States proposed a more detailed scale as follows:

Definition	Label
Flawless	FL
Very very slightly imperfect	VVS
Very slightly imperfect	VS
Slightly imperfect	SI
Imperfect	I

Such a scale of decreasing value (from FL to I), brought a serial order to clarity classification, even if several countries were reluctant to accept the term *imperfect*, protesting that you cannot possibly apply this description to the most prized and valuable of all gems.

In 1971 a European supplement to the latter scale was chosen and published in Germany as RAL 560A5E, proposing the added precision of *Einschlusse* (inclusion). Save for the United States, countries the world round soon adopted this certifying definition.

In the following table concerning clarity, we offer scales used both in Europe and the United States (GIA) so that you may compare classifications and remove any doubts about the kind

Europe		United States (GIA)	
Clarity at 10x	Definition	Clarity at 10x	Definition
IF	Internally Flawless	FL IF	Flawless Internally Flawless
VVS1 VVS2	Very very Small Inclusions	VVS1 VVS2	Very Very Slightly Imperfect
VS1 VS2	Very Small Inclusions	VS1 VS2	Very Slightly Imperfect
SI1 SI2	Small Inclusions	SI1 SI2	Slightly Imperfect
P1 P2 P3	Piqué	I1 I2 I3	Imperfect

Clarity scale in use.

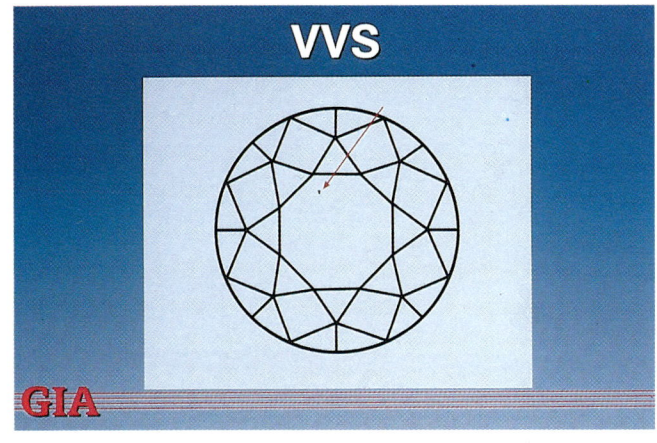 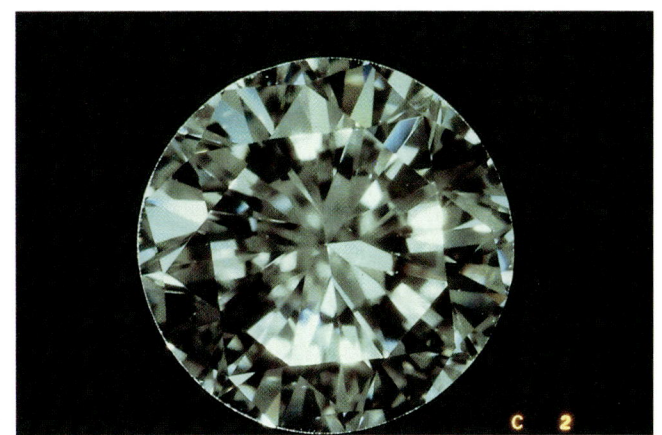

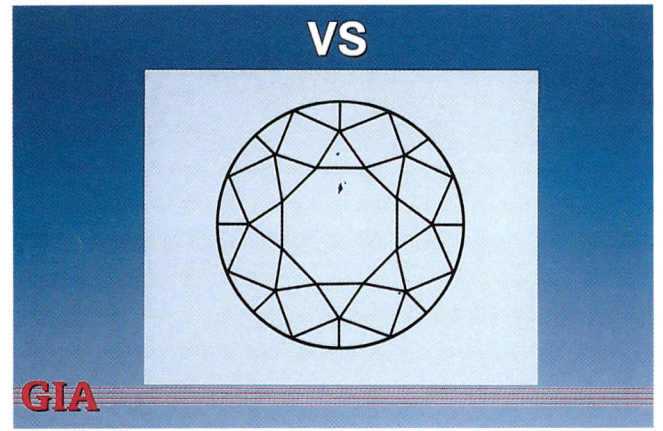 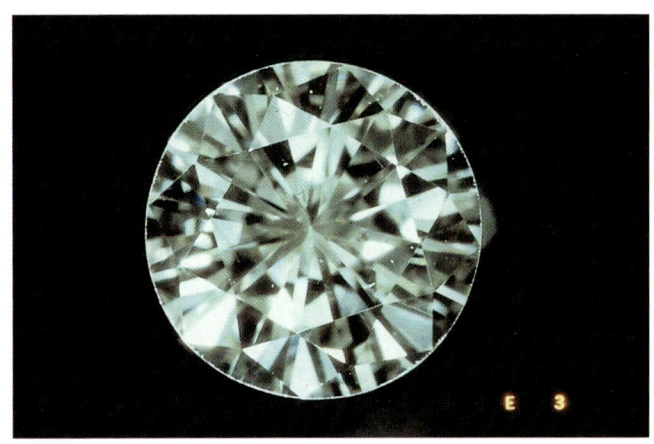

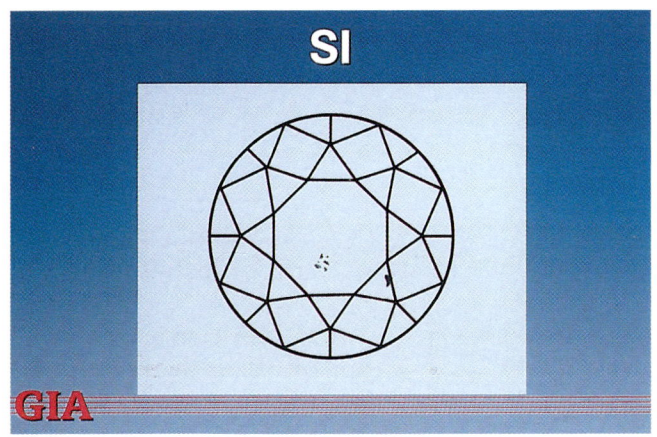 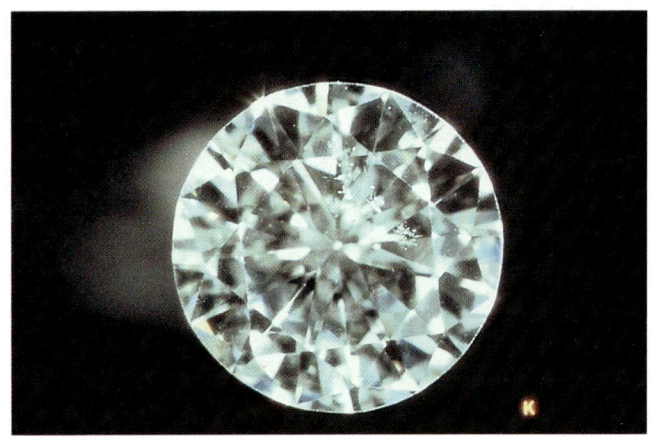

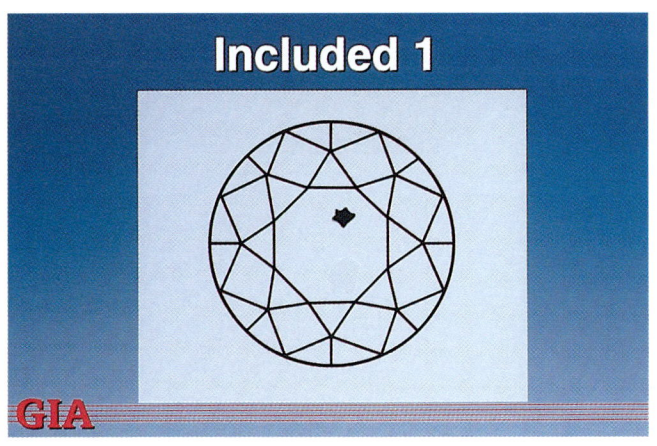 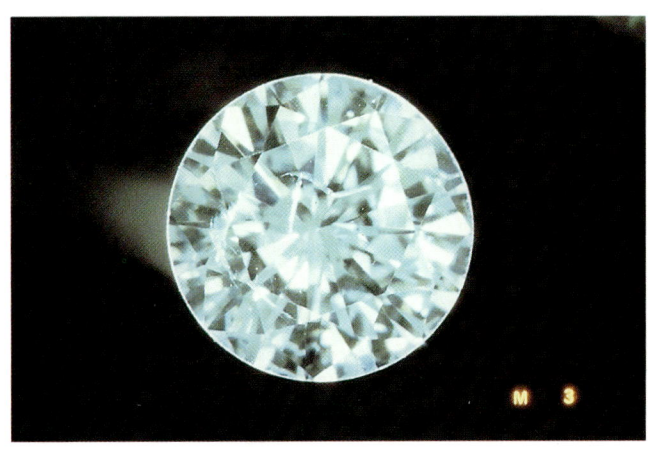

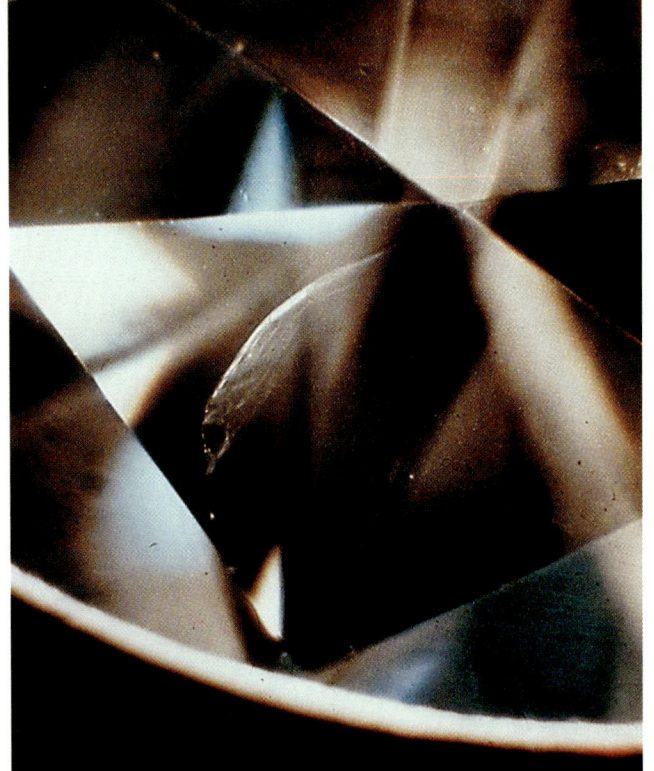

Feather.

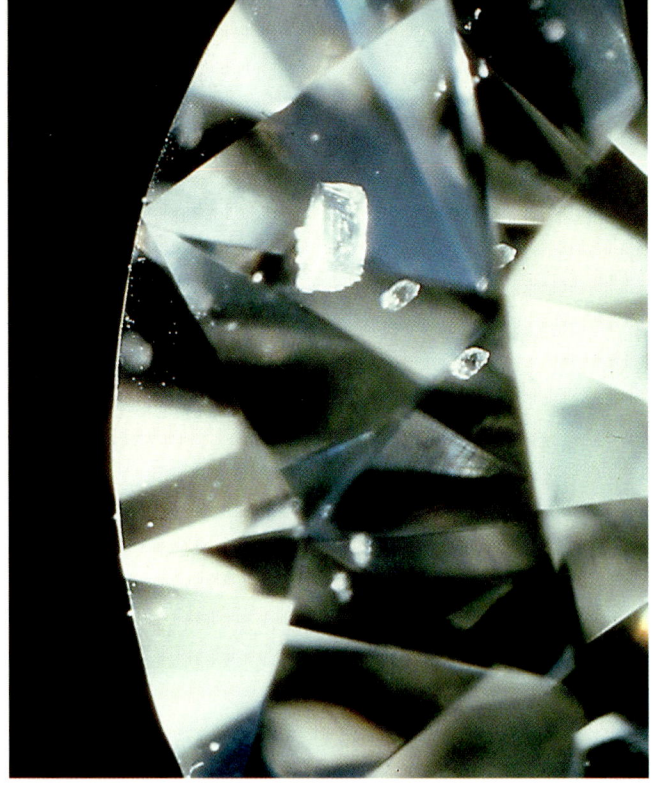

Crystal inclusion.

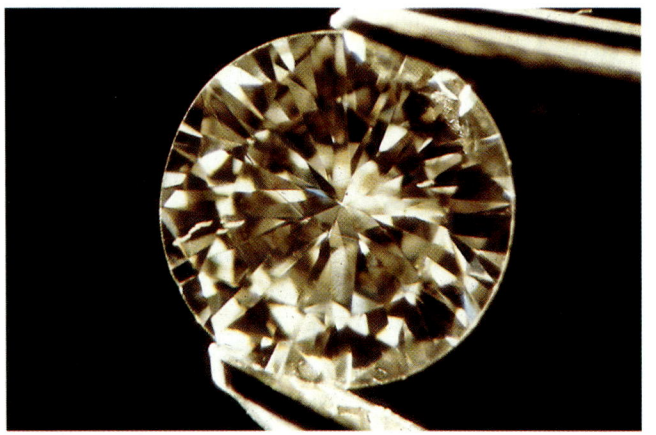

Cloud.

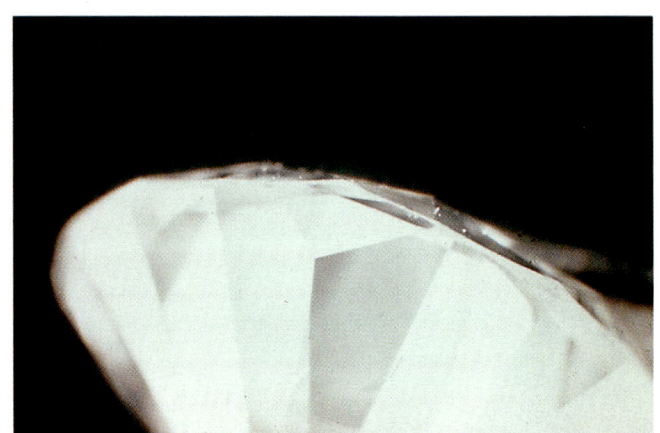

Extra facet.

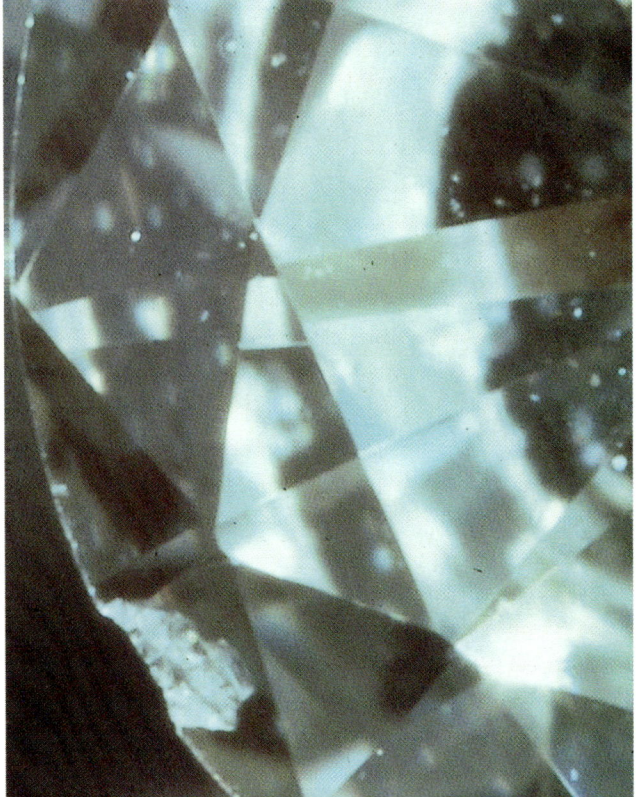

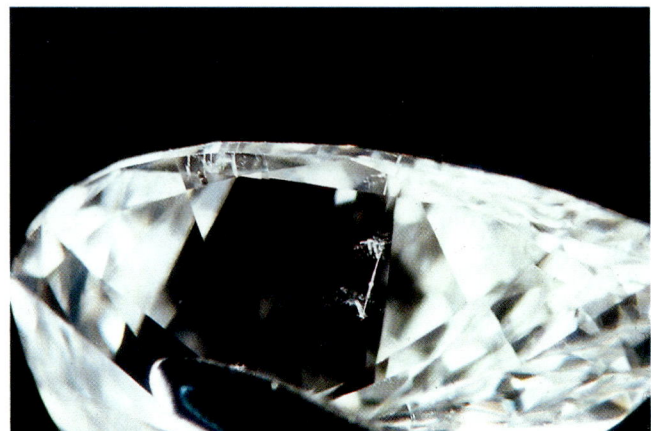

Laser hole.

Cavity.

of authenticity offered by your diamond certificate, whatever its source. It must be emphasized that while the European scale is topped with IF, assuming that minimal external details are not significant, the United States has inserted the IF label in its scale but maintained FL at peak position, possibly for purely historical reasons, though such a deviation creates confusion in any global interpretation of clarity gradations.

Other certificates, such as the HRD issued in Antwerp, substitute the IF label with LC (meaning *loupe clean*, or pure in lens examination); implicitly, a scale of this sort refers to a definition of clarity gradations of diamonds based solely on defects visible under a 10x magnifying lens.

In the two scales mentioned, the VVS, VS, and SI levels are each divided into two subgrades whereas the European P or the I (United States) is subdivided into three subgrades. Recently, it has been suggested that the SI level should be subdivided into three subgrades though the proposal has not yet been accepted.

UNI terminology does not contain the word "inclusion," which has been substituted by "internal characteristic."

Since it is of the utmost importance to achieve maximum homogeneity in classifying degrees of clarity, a set of drawings has been established, representing the varying grades of inclusion (see appropriate tables).

Obviously any correct identification of degree of clarity depends on the ability and experience of the analyst, who will choose the most suitable instruments and rely on a scientifically valid, constant methodology.

GIA AND IDC-CIBJO COLOR SCALE	
GIA	IDC-CIBJO
D	Exceptional white +
E	Exceptional white
F	Rare white +
G	Rare white
H	White
I	Slightly tinted white
J	
K	Tinted white
L	
M	Tinted color
N	
O	
P	
Q	
R	
S	
T	
U	
V	
W	
X	
Y	
Z	

Instruments Anyone employed in defining clarity grade must obviously have: a diamond, a 10x lens, tweezers to hold the stone, and a light source, but – above all – enormous patience and thoroughness since he or she must check out and inspect the table of the stone and then each and every facet, one by one.

Color When a ray of white light passes through any mineral formation, reflection and refraction phenomena may take on certain colorings. Diamond, of course, is no exception to this rule; for, as it is an allochromatic material, under certain conditions it may absorb some wavelengths (i.e. colors) and reflect others.

In the case of diamonds we can make a clearcut distinction between the so-called "Cape series" (all stones ranging from purest white to yellowish stones) and fancy color specimens.

Diamonds in the Cape series Before getting down to detail, a short summary of the evolution of diamond classifications will be useful.

The very first color terms were named after historic deposits such as: Golconda, Bagagem, Canavieiras, Diamantina, and Bahia. A French scale was then adopted at the beginning of the 1900s, but soon after an international table was constructed with English terminology, now defined as the "old terms," although they are still well known: *river, top wesselton, top crystal, crystal, top cape, cape, light yellow, yellow.*

Today we use the color classification established by the GIA (Gemmological Institute of America), which is very precise and easy to handle, based as it is on the letters of the English alphabet running from D to Z, and also the classification established by the IDC-CIBJO (International Diamond Council – Confédération Internationale de la Bijouterie, Joaillerie, Orfèverie, des Diamantes, Perles et Pierres), in which the term *white* (an inexact definition often applied to colorless material) is specified by a series of adjectives (see GIA and IDC-CIBJO).

Despite our precision guides, pinpointing diamond color is really a very delicate matter; because picking out the exact color shade within a vast gamut of tones can present a problem even for an expert, who doesn't have enough practical experience.

Instruments A trained eye can do an adequate job if there is a graduated diamond series ("master diamonds") set as referent.

The examination must take place under standardized artificial light from a special lamp, and the diamond in question should be viewed within an opaque white paper card folded into a V, then compared one by one with the master diamonds until the precise color correspondence is determined. To carry out this operation, the examiner should focus his attention on the pavilion and the crown, giving only slight importance to the table.

With the use of a 10x lens to better view the angles, and after having acquired a little experience, identification will become quite easy. And if you effect brief, but frequent observations, you will little by little eliminate any great doubts – always possible – and, also, avoid excessive eye strain.

Diamonds used for comparison purposes must meet certain requirements of clarity (never less than VS2), weight (not less than 0.50 carats), cut (brilliant with good proportions), fluorescence (none or very weak), and must belong to the Cape series.

A buyer should be aware that, though their color is equal, a diamond visibly larger than another may seem to have a greater saturation grade; this effect is more evident starting with "color I" stones and continuing through the less valuable colorings.

You may come across a master diamonds scale in the market that is not made up of real diamonds, but composed of imitations such as synthetic zirconium oxide (cubic zirconium).

Gemmological analysis laboratories employ only real diamonds for their color scales, for these are the rules and regulations, but should you simply want to practice your skill, a scale of cubic zirconium samples will give satisfying results.

As additional assistance, there are instruments called "colormeters" for diamond classification, though they yield uncertain results when applied to the testing of diamonds evincing fluorescence.

Fluorescence In diamonds, fluorescence, as determined with UV lamps, is usually displayed within a range of blue shades, but can also be yellow, pink or green.

Here we have a physical phenomenon that can create real difficulties in determining a precise color gradation, even when we use direct comparison with a color scale; so before trying to establish classification, it is best to first submit a diamond to fluorescent check in order to establish the possible definition problems that may be involved. When, however, there is no fluorescence, the classification is "null"; its presence, on the other hand, must be graded as weak, medium or strong.

At times fluorescence is so strong that the stone takes on a slightly milky or oily look; not very popular stones, they are called "petrol blue" or "over-blue," and even "Premier," the name of the diamond pipe from which they are extracted.

Fancy color diamonds As an allochromatic mineral, diamond's color may depend on foreign atoms contained in its crystal structure, but the cause, which has been proven, may also be found in defects or dislocations in that structure.

Fancy color diamonds have a truly unusual coloring, and a range so wide that in theory any and all colors are possible. Much sought after by collectors, they can bring extraordinary sums.

Artificially colored diamonds Given the astonishing prices of fancy color specimens, there has naturally been an attempt to produce them artificially, working with natural Cape series material. At the beginning of this century, W. Crookes achieved a green coloring in a few specimens by exposing them to radiations; though with the dangerous side effect that the stones themselves became radiactive.

With the creation of particle accelerators (1932), new treatments were developed for obtaining a fancy color diamond that was not dangerous to the wearer.

At this point a new problem arose: how to identify fancy color diamonds with artificially created coloring. The price difference between the counterfeit and the real one make this identification a critical *sine qua non* of any purchase. Fortunately, by evaluating fluorescence and working with a spectroscope or one of today's more sophisticated instruments, an expert can resolve the problem for us.

Cut Though diamond as a mineral has been known to men since time immemorable, the custom of cutting this stone must be considered relatively recent.

To explain this fact we should remember that the first known diamonds were found in India where, for religious reasons, it was forbidden

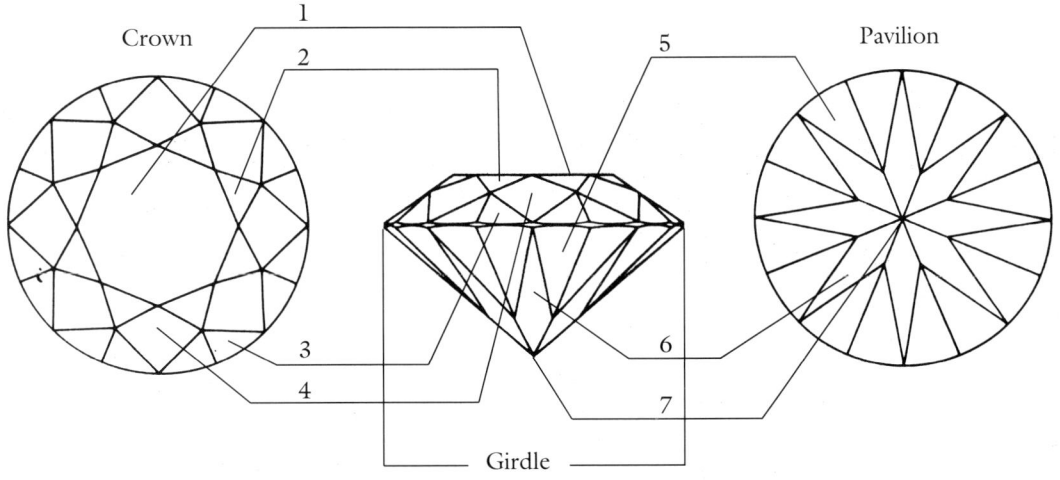

1 = Table
2 = Star facet
3 = Upper cross facet
4 = Upper basic facet

5 = Lower cross facet
6 = Lower basic facet
7 = Culet of the pavilion

Close-up of the various parts of a round brilliant cut.

even to polish them. The first diamond cutting as such took place about halfway through the seventeenth century and was effected in "simple cut," chronologically followed by "double cut" or Mazarin cut (referring to the famous French cardinal), the "triple cut" (created by the Venetian, Vincenzo Peruzzi), and our contemporary "modern cut."

These developments are not simply the result of a technical evolution; careful research and study have been brought to bear upon important laws of optical physics. In fact, the modern cut does not differ from Peruzzi's in number of facets, but rather in the proportions that must be respected to obtain maximum brilliance, that superb diamond fire.

We have all of 142 shapes to choose from, 10 of which are round cuts. Created by Gabriel S. Tolkowsky, the newest cuts in the trade are listed as "Marigold," "Sunflower," "Dahlia," "Fire Rose," and "Zinnia."

For basic guidelines that will aid in unraveling this vast topic, the reader should see our tables, (see pages 89-93), which describe the better known cuts. Note the particular emphasis paid to the number of facets, with their corresponding denomination particularly for the round brilliant cut:

table = one
crown = 8 star facets
8 basic facets on the upper section
16 facets on the side of the crown
pavilion = 8 basic facets on the lower section
16 facets on the side of the pavilion
1 (possible use of a tiny table cut at the base)

Our total for this type of cut is therefore 57 facets in all – plus one, if the optional base cut is adopted; and it is essential to remember that the term "brilliant cut" can only be used for a gem diamond with this faceting and not for other cuts.

Work phases for a diamond are:

– for important rough stones, a prolonged study and careful marking;
– either saw cut or cleavage;
– rough machining for shaping;
– faceting;
– polishing.

Instruments We are not interested here in

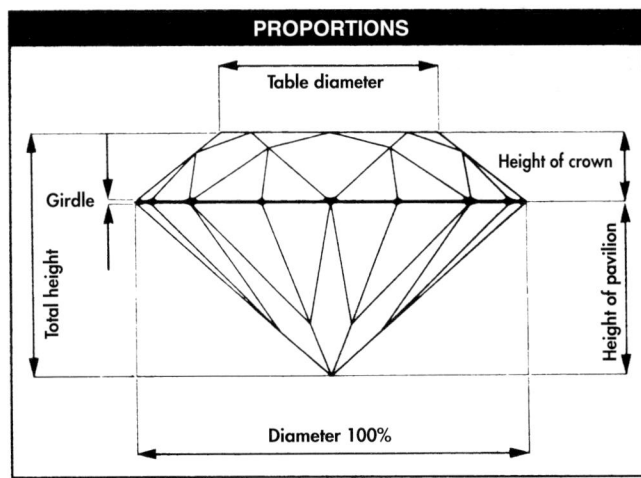

Diagram of the sections for which values have been given based on a diameter of 100%.

Diamonds cut by GABY TOLKOWSKY:

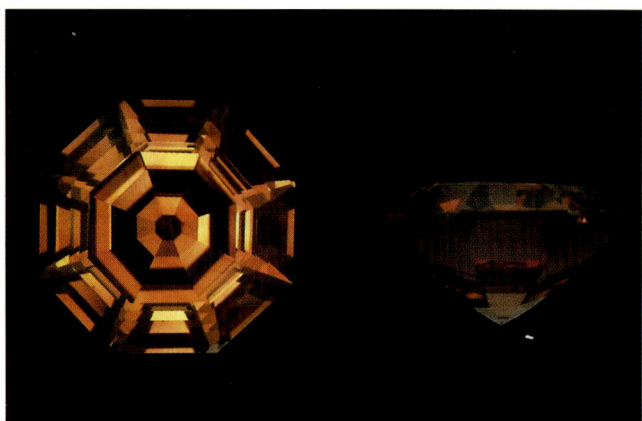

Marigold cut.

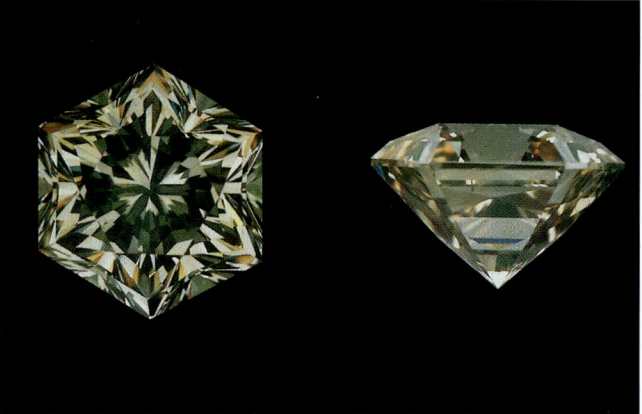

Fire Rose cut.

cutting tools, but in the range of instruments employed to classify cuts.

Given the importance of the cut – one of the famous *4 Cs* – a highly specialized instrument has been produced which allows us to read proportions expressed in percentages. Assigning a theoretical value of 100 to the stone's diameter, all other values are related to it in percentages, and the reading is effected directly on the instrument, a proportionoscope.

For the round brilliant cut the standardized values are expressed as:

– 64% for the table;

– 12% for the height of the crown;

– 43% for the height of the pavilion.

In practice, these values are treated with a bit of flexibility.

Aided by a 10x lens a careful technician will observe the arrangement of the table angles in relation to the star facets and observe the point of the pavilion through the table; and he will be able to decide with a high degree of reliability if a stone – especially a brilliant – has been well cut, or not.

Or a caliber may be put to use: an appropriate tool for determining if a round brilliant cut has been suitably effected.

Glancing back at the table (see page 78) listing the real dimensions of brilliants, with diameter and weight data, we can see that a round diamond, weighing one carat and idoneously cut, has a 6.5 mm diameter. But if we measure the stone and find that though it weighs a carat, it only has a 6.3 mm diameter, then we know that the stone in question does not have a well-proportioned cut.

A diamond cutter must constantly strive to reach the best compromise between maintaining weight and achieving a cut that will bring out maximum fire; unfortunately, this is not always possible.

Treatments In our section on fancy color diamonds, we have already mentioned a number of treatments applied to Cape series minerals in order to produce artificial fancy color stones. Aside from this sort of treatment, it is also possible to improve a diamond's clarity grade, generally operating upon stones with SI and Piqué (or Imperfect, in the United States) impurities.

Such procedures are of fairly recent development and rely on the use of lasers or on the practice of filling fractures with a substance with a high index of refraction.

The laser produces a miniscule opening and attacks the observed impurity – which may even be unpleasantly blackish – until it becomes almost white. Unfortunately the ray's original path is permanently outlined as if it were a very fine needle. At the close of this operation the surface hole is filled with resin.

According to the filling method, a technician may literally fill up those visible fractures that run from the stone's inner section to its surface. They are often referred to in the trade as "filled diamonds."

Yehuda, an Israeli, was the first researcher to achieve this result, and the treatment is named after him, although it has actually had many sequels.

In effect, adopting the Yehuda process, or one of the similar adaptations, we can make a significant difference in the clarity grade, though color occasionally loses on the value scale.

When diamonds treated with these two methods first appeared on the world market, the IDMA (International Diamond Manufacture Association) met in London and immediately took a strong position, announcing that:

Diamonds cut by GABY TOLKOWSKY:

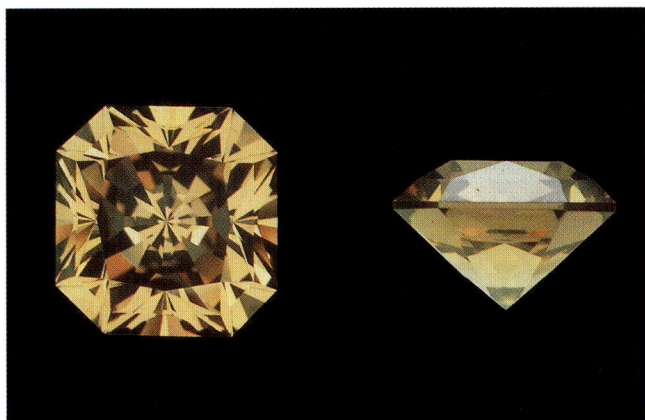

Sunflower cut.

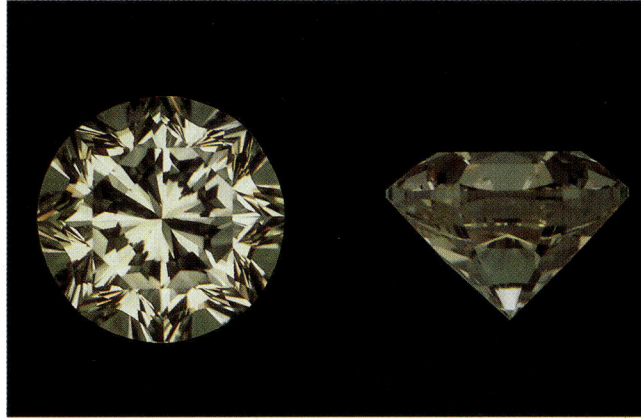

Zinnia cut.

1 – to sell diamonds whose clarity (purity) has been altered by any treatment whatsoever without a declaration to that effect, is to be considered explicitly as fraud;

2 – improving the purity grade of rough stones is fraud;

3 – real or presumed ignorance of the treatment will not exempt a seller from liability;

4 – all receipts on diamonds exported for sale must be accompanied by clear labelling indicating treatments applied, if any.

The GIA refuses to certify diamonds treated with these two methods and simply indicates the type of treatment identified.

In June of 1994 the twenty-one Diamond Exchanges the world over voted to accept this decision. In France the National Board for Diamonds, Precious and Semi-Precious Stones simply, but significantly, made reference to the 1983 law regarding consumer protection, which obliges the seller to check merchandise and verify that it has the qualifications required by law.

Under the lens   Once again, the 10x lens is the proper tool, quite adequate for identifying these two treatments.

"Filled diamonds" present flash effects. Slowly rotating the gem, an expert observes the pavilion attentively; suddenly – and here is our source for "flash" – our expert sights zones of clearly visible colorings.

The very first "filled diamonds" offered alternating blue and orange zonings; today we can glimpse quite a play of colors such as: purple/greenish yellow, purple/bluish green, violet/from bluish green to greenish yellow.

For the owner or buyer, microscope examination and expert techniques offer the fastest and most satisfying results.

Now and then we may discover air bubbles –

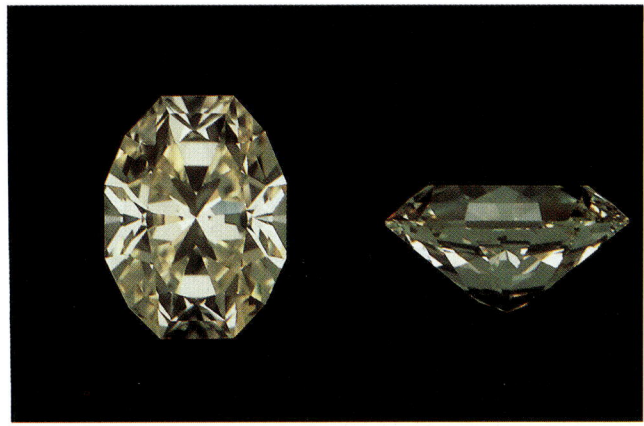

Dahlia cut.

not to be confused with crystal inclusions – which were entrapped in the material when the filling was introduced.

Laser-treated diamonds are easily recognized since, as we have already pointed out, the laser leaves a slight trace behind it, the ray's path as it made its way to, and dissolved, a given impurity.

In the future we can look forward to a new treatment, using the C.V.D. process (see the section "Synthetic diamonds"), which deposits a very thin layer of colored synthetic diamond on a faceted natural diamond which has a poorly esteemed color. Assumedly, the final product will closely resemble a fancy color diamond.

Certification   Above all, your certificate must clearly declare mineral type as natural diamond, and then list related *4 Cs* data: carat, clarity, color and cut.

Each accompanying certificate must further clearly identify the issuer; it must be easy to read, with all abbreviations adhering to the referent code, usually stamped on the certificate cover folder.

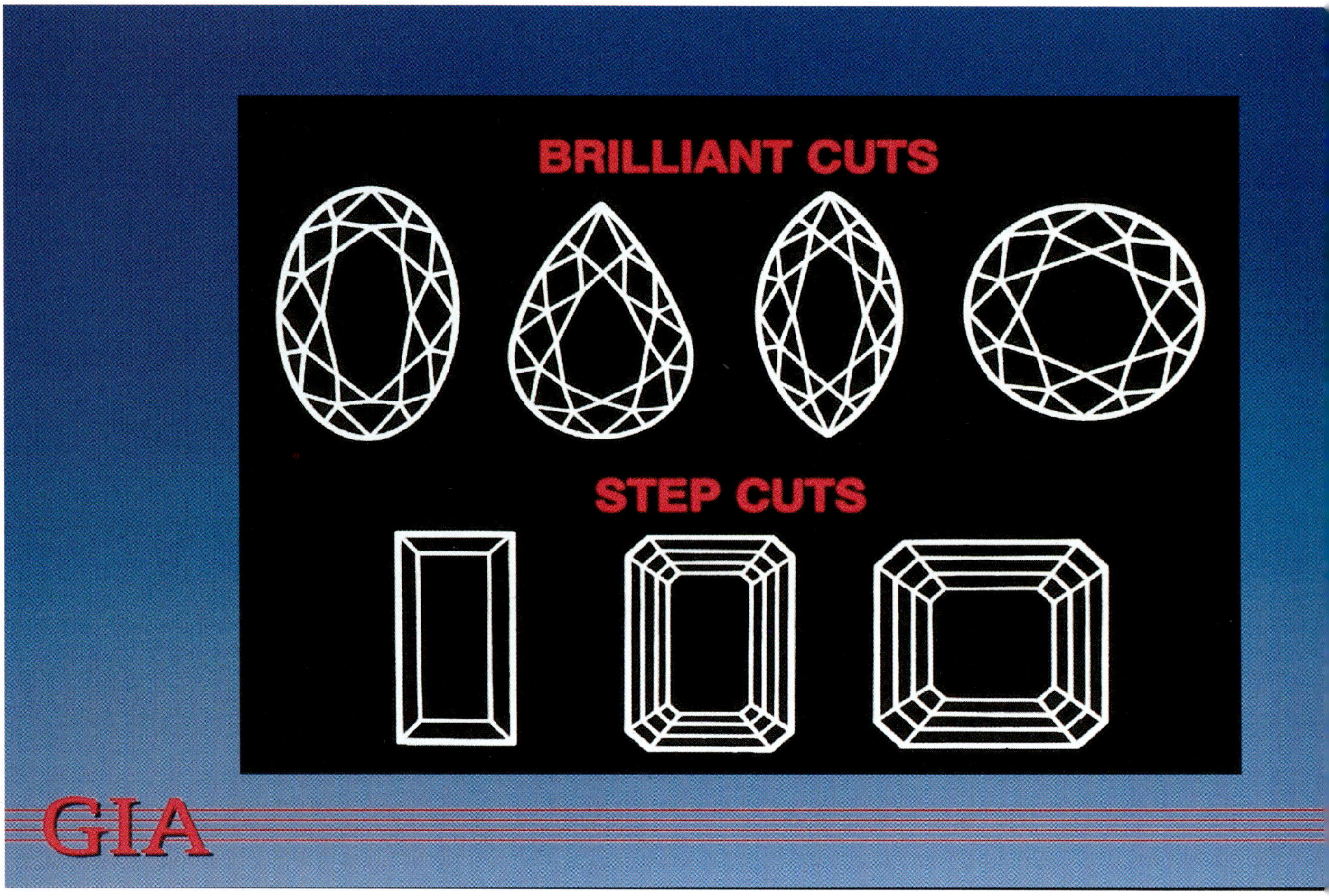

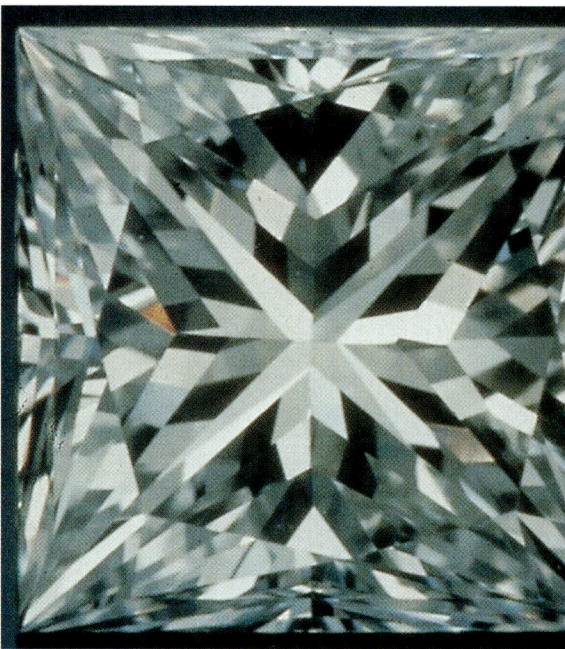

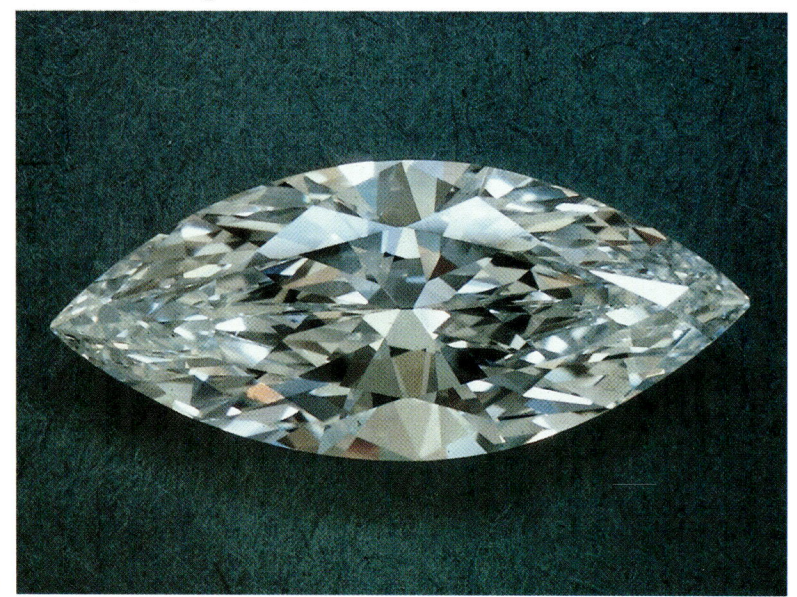

Diamond, marquise cut.

Diamond, princess cut.

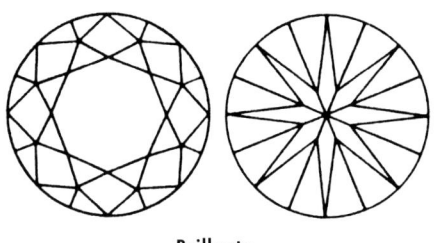
Brillante

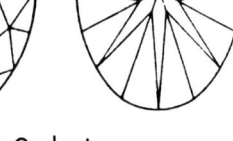
Oval cut

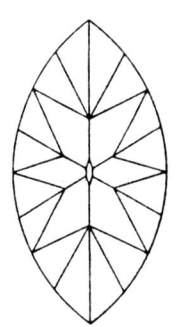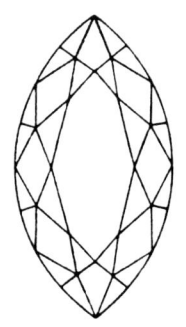
Marquise cut

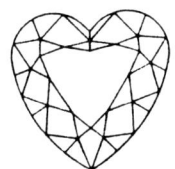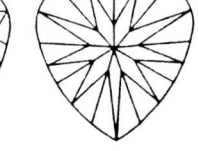
Heart-shaped brilliant cut

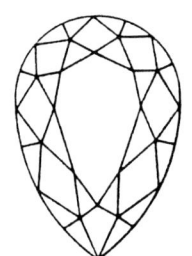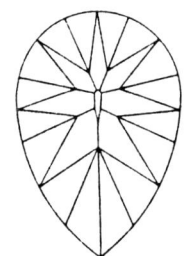
Pear-shaped cut

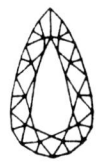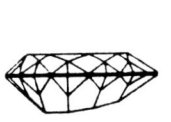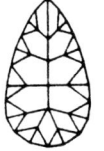
Pendeloque cut

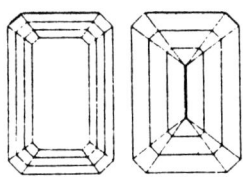
Emerald cut

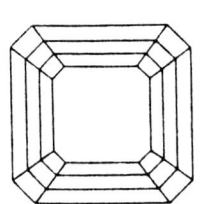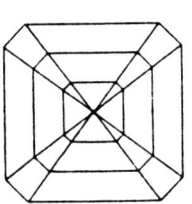
Square emerald cut

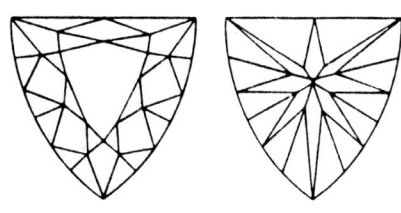
Seminavette

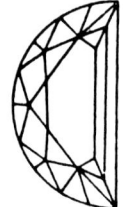 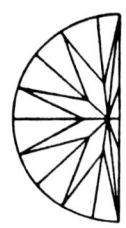
Half-moon cut

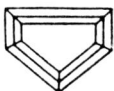 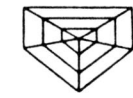
Epaulet (or epaulette) cut

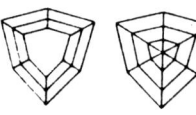
Shield cut

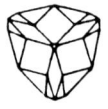 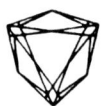
Trilliant cut

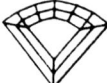 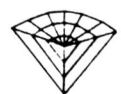
Fan-shaped cut

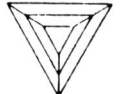 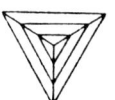
Triangle cut

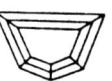 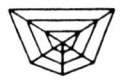
Tapered pentacut

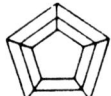 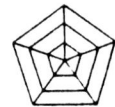
Pentagon cut

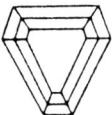 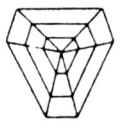
Calf's head

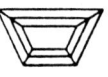 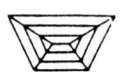
Trapeze cut

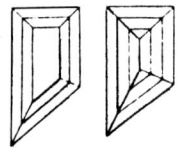
Whistle cut

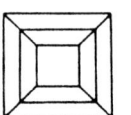 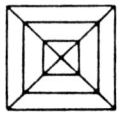
Square cut

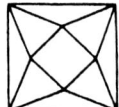 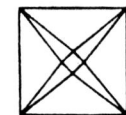
French cut

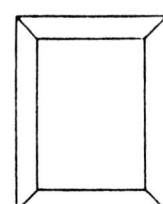 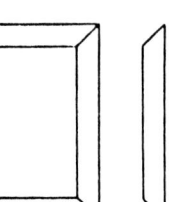
Bevel cut

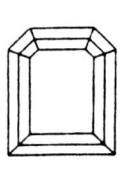 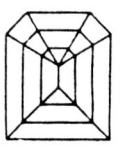
Window cut

90

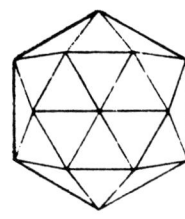
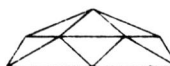
Half-Dutch (or half-Holland) rose cut

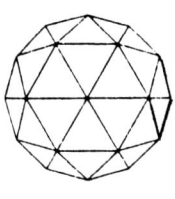
Full-Dutch (or full-Holland) rose cut

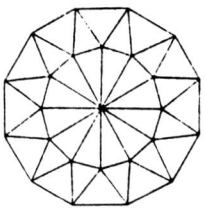
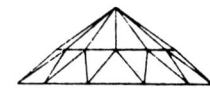
Double-Dutch rose cut

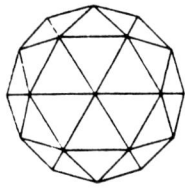
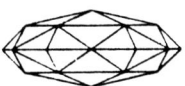
Double rose cut

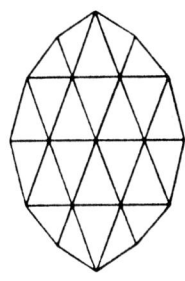
Boat-shaped rose cut

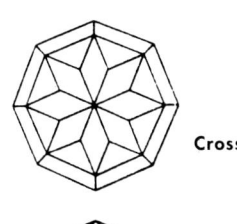
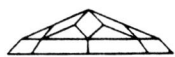
Cross-rose cut

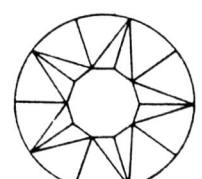
Split-brilliant cut

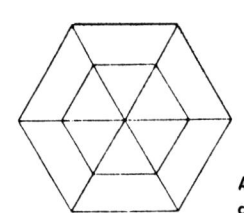
Antwerp (or Brabant) rose cut

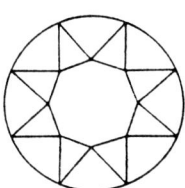
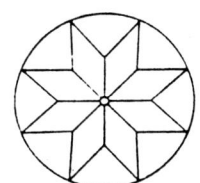
Swiss cut

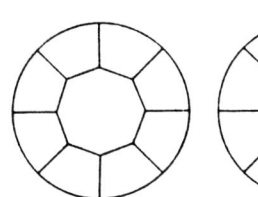
Single cut

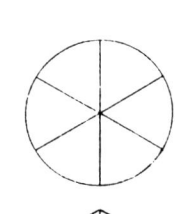
Six-facet rose cut

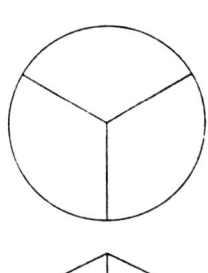
Three-facet rose cut

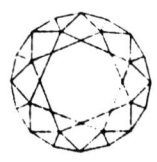
Half-brilliant cut

Princess (Profile) cut
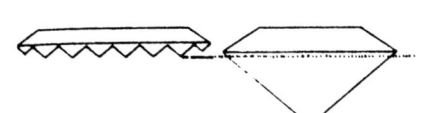
Comparison of Princess (Profile) cut with a brilliant cut

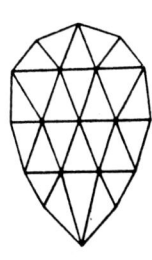
Pear-shaped rose cut

91

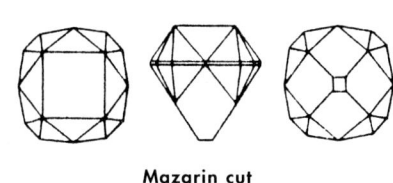
Mazarin cut

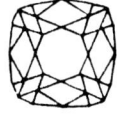 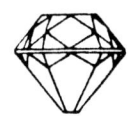 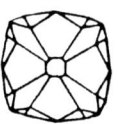
Old-Mine cut

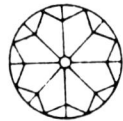 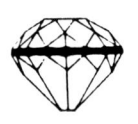 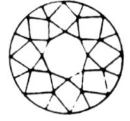
Old-European cut

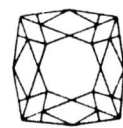 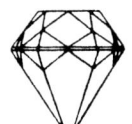 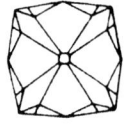
Peruzzi cut

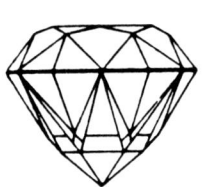 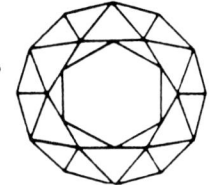
Cairo star cut

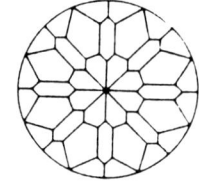 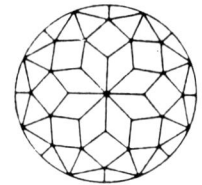
Jubilee cut

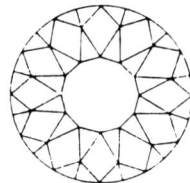 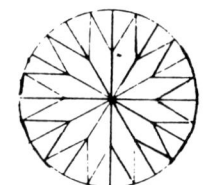
King cut

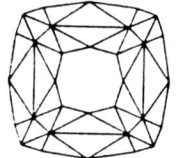 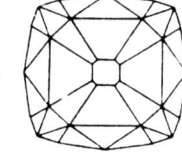
Lisbon cut

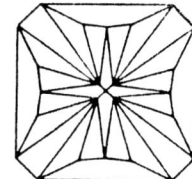 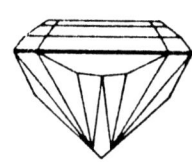
Barion cut

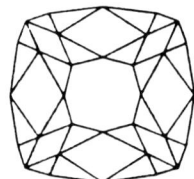 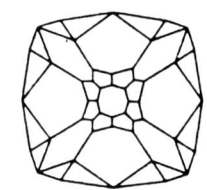
Brazilian cut

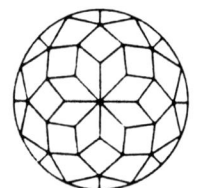 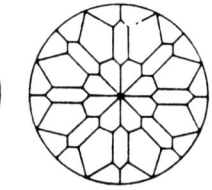
Twentieth-Century cut

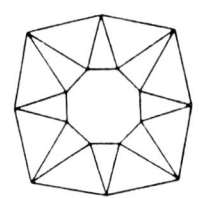 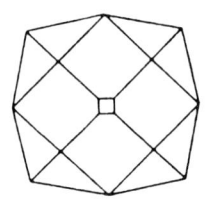
English square-cut brilliant

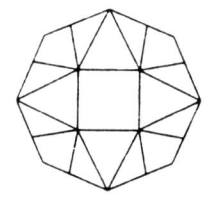 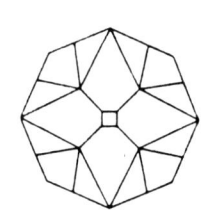
Double-cut brilliant

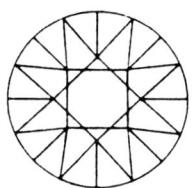 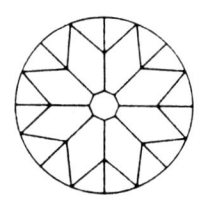
English round-cut brilliant

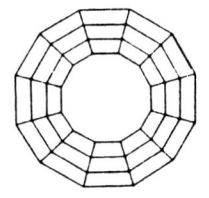 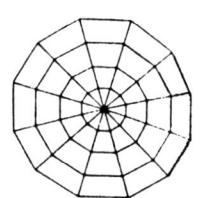
Trap brilliant cut

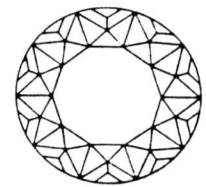 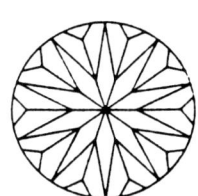
Magna cut

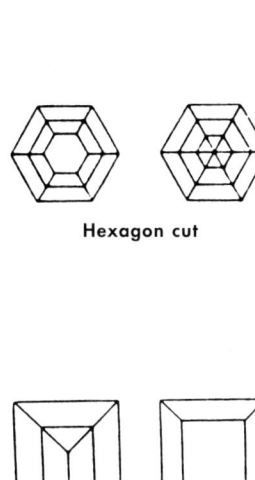
Hexagon cut

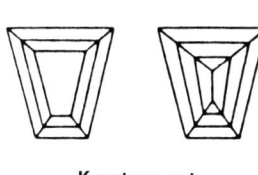
Keystone cut

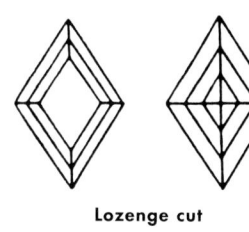
Lozenge cut

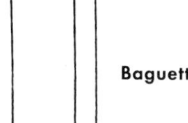
Baguette

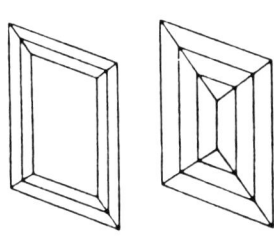
Rhomboid cut

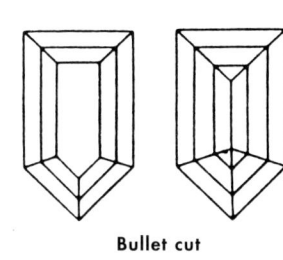
Bullet cut

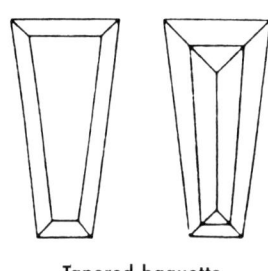
Tapered baguette

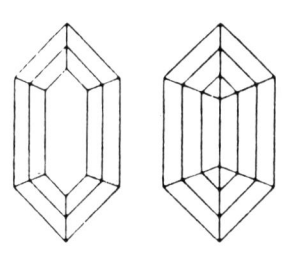
Long hexagon cut

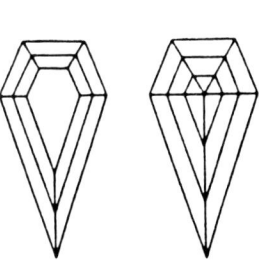
Cut-corner triangle cut

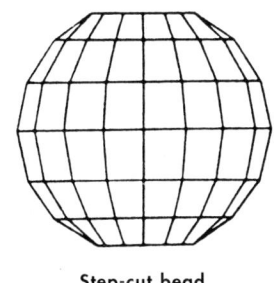
Step-cut bead

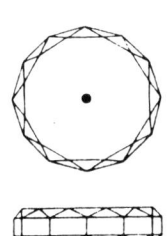
Rondelle

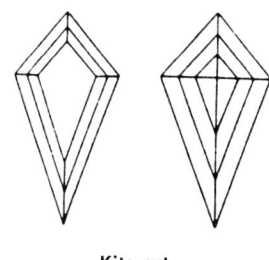
Kite cut

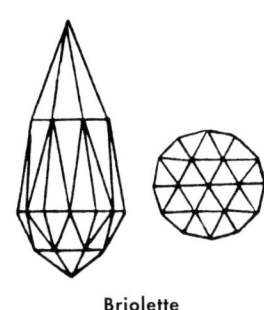
Briolette

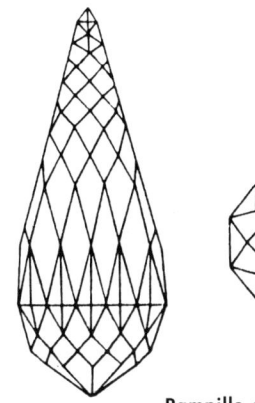
Pampille cut

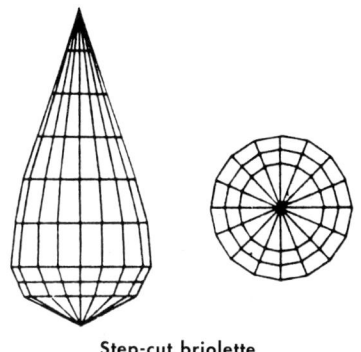
Step-cut briolette

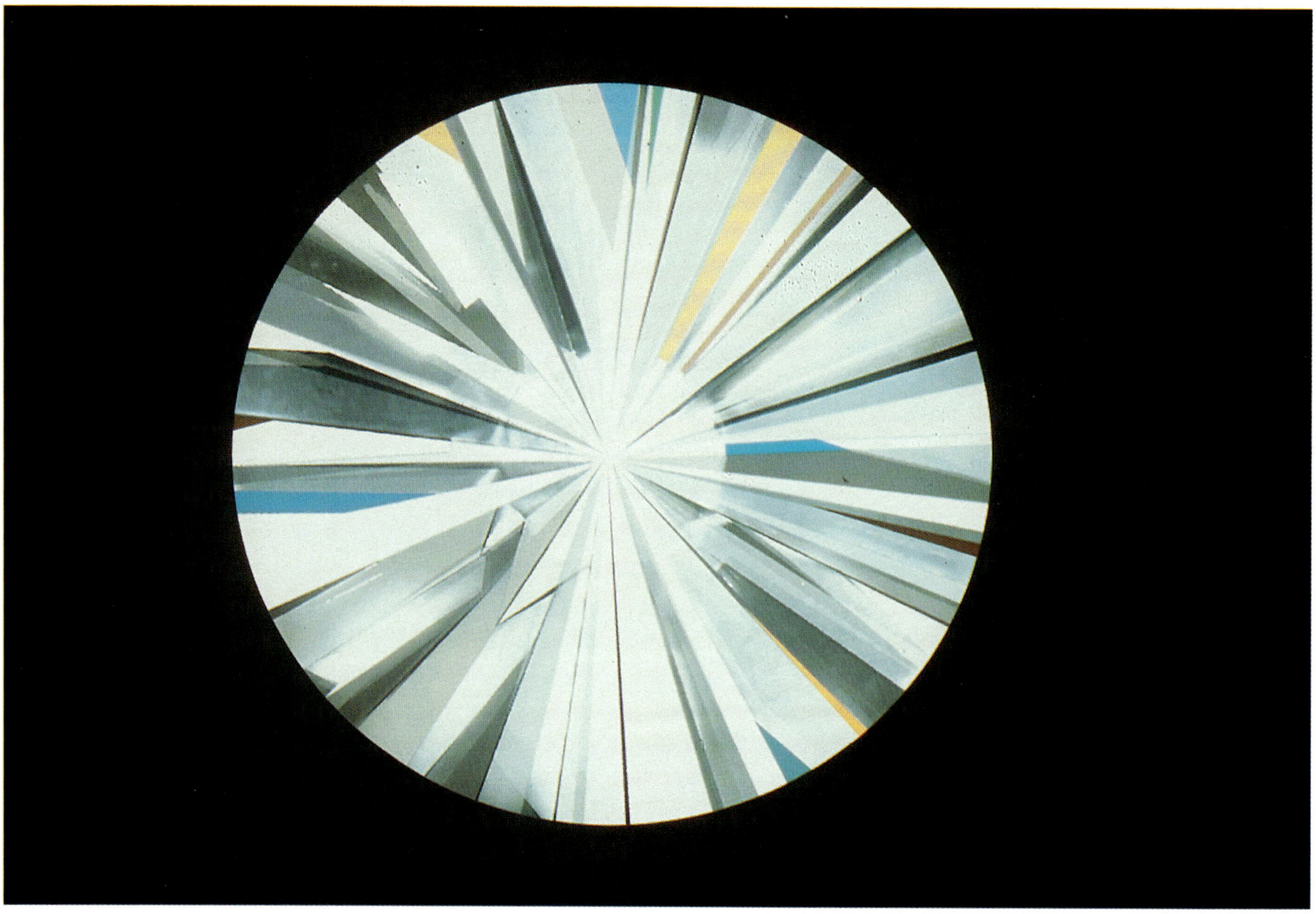

DR. ULRICH FREIESLEBEN: "SPIRIT SUN" *Cut diamond.*

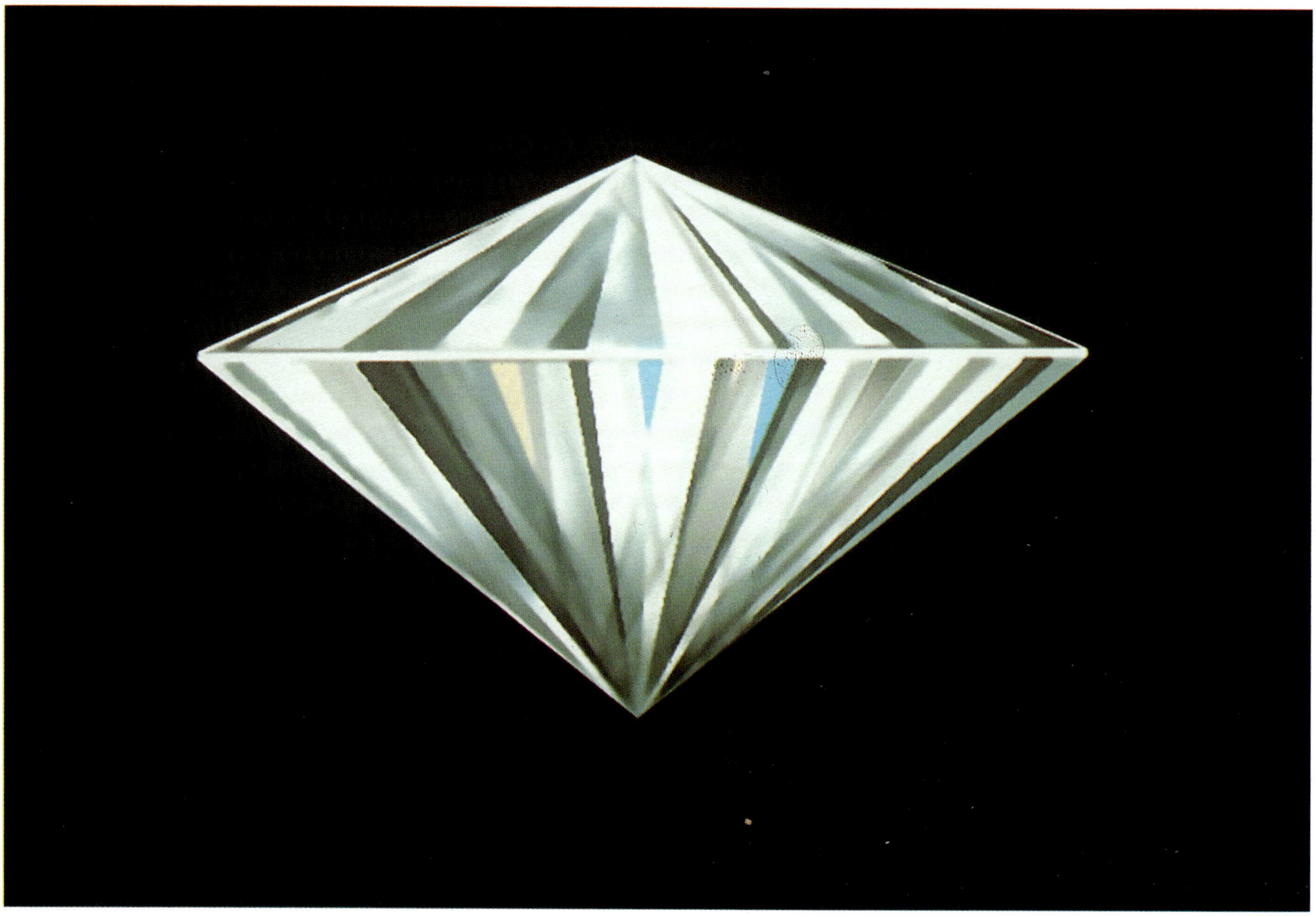

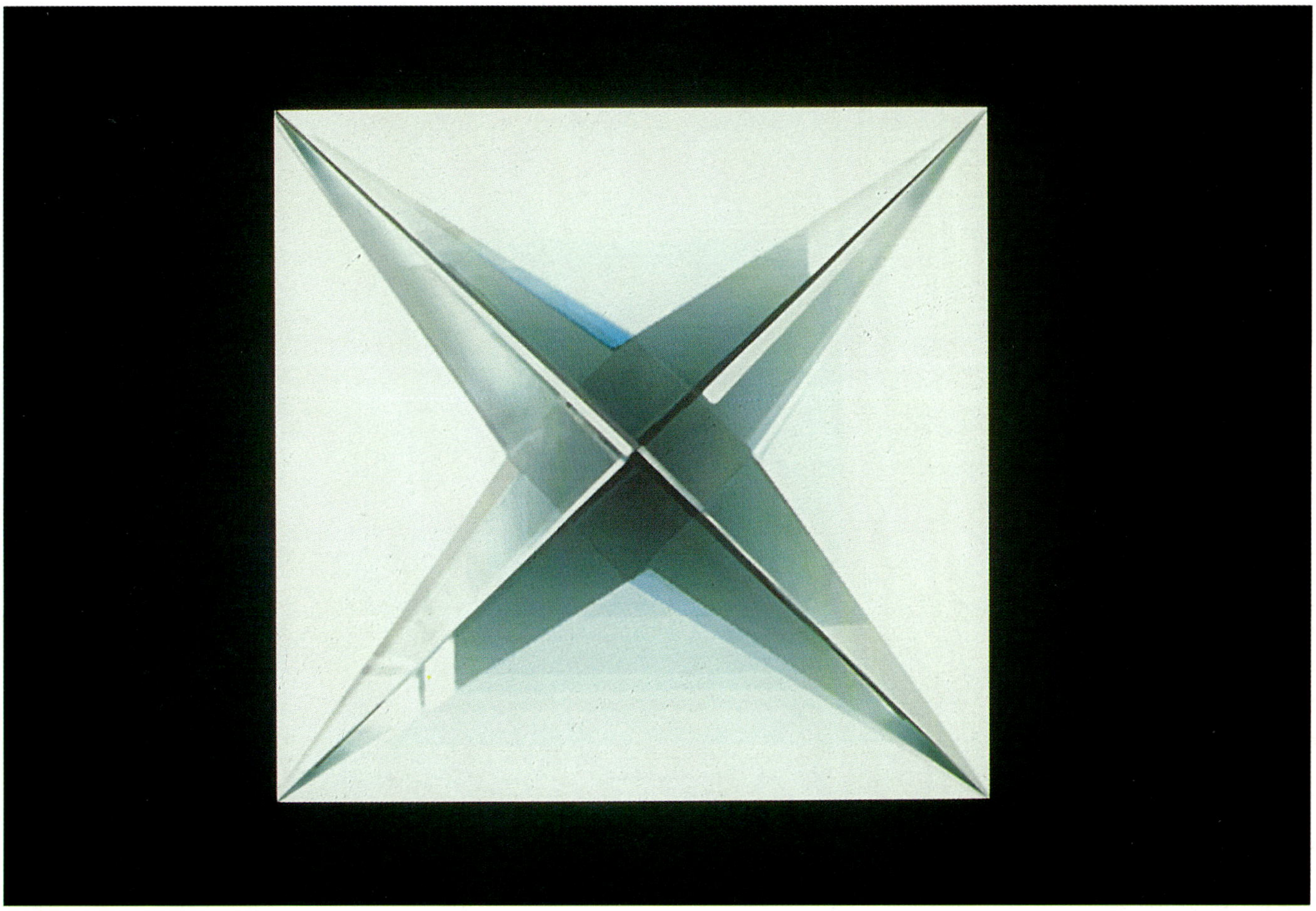

DR. ULRICH FREIESLEBEN: *"CONTEXT CUT"* Cut diamond.

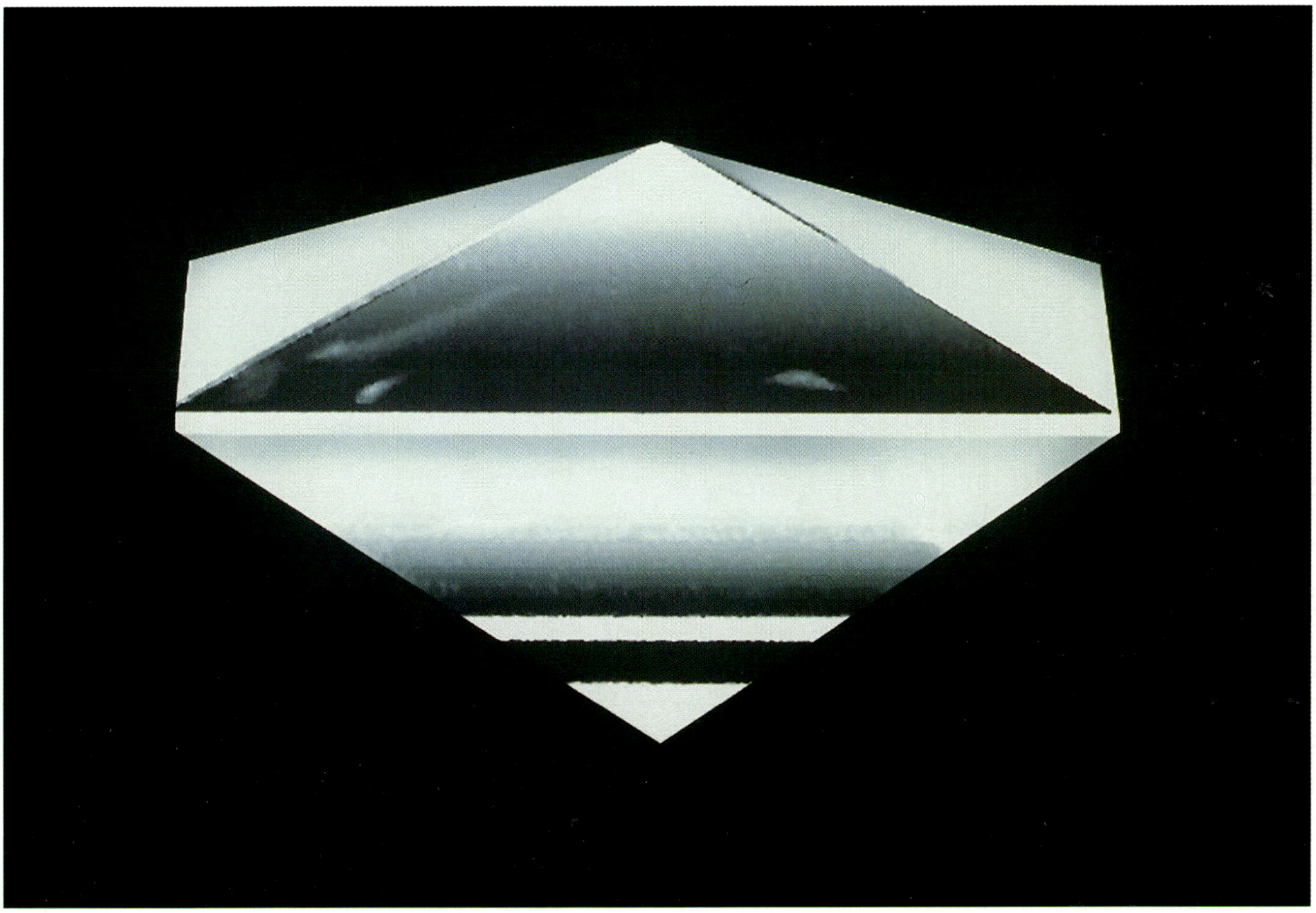

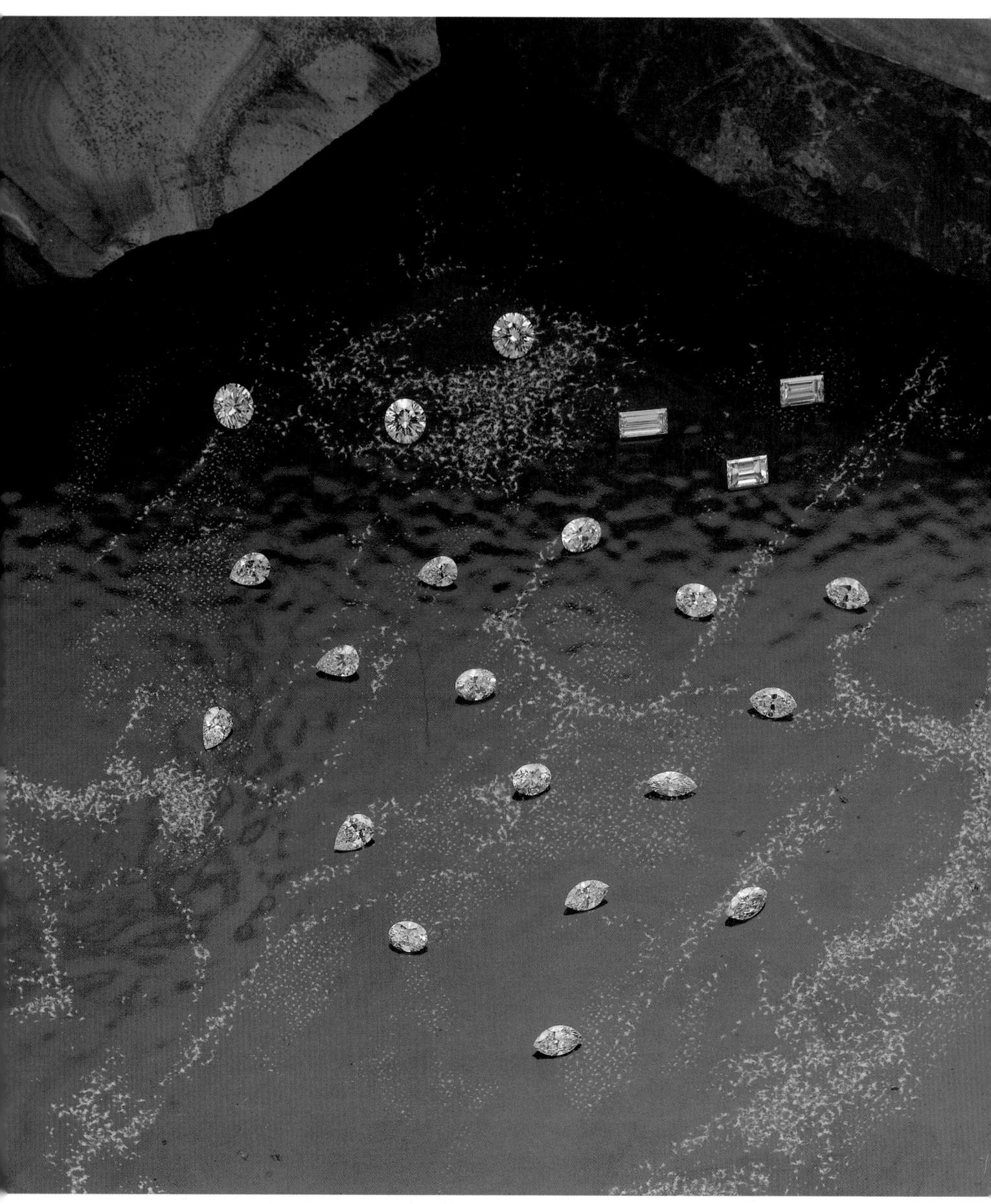

BRUNO PISANO.
Some of the classic cuts effected by the "master cutter" of Valenza Po (Italy).

Without exception, all certificates must be personally signed.

It is the practice of some laboratories to return the analyzed diamond in a transparent package sealed with data corresponding to the certificate.

See the facsimile on page 99.

Synthetic diamonds Nobel Prize winner for physics in 1946, P. W. Brigdman, a researcher in the field of high pressures and related instrumentation, was actually also one of the most important figures in the development of the synthetic diamond.

As early as 1930, with his diagram of the graphite-diamond state, Brigdman had foreseen the type of working conditions that would be required to achieve this structural modification; of course graphite is a carbon, just like diamond.

It was not until 1954, though, that the equipment (Belt) was developed, capable of working under extreme pressure and temperature. In effect, in February 1955 the General Electric Company announced the creation of a synthetic diamond, produced under the extraordinary conditions of around 100,000 atmospheres and about 3000 °C.

At present, besides the General Electric Company, other producers of synthetic diamonds are: a De Beers subsidiary, whose output represents about one-third of the world total; the Sumitomo Electric Industries of Itami (Japan); and the Academy of Sciences in Russia, which employs a technique defined as BARS.

And though initial production was destined for industrial use, today's output reaches a quality level that can be put to service as gemmological material.

Obviously the world diamond trade now faces the problem of deciding whether synthetic diamond, like synthetic ruby, sapphire, and emerald can be officially recognized and gemmologically classified… without disorientating the world diamond markets.

To set the record straight: the dramatic 1993 announcement by Chatam Created Gems of San Francisco, that they were about to present the world market with large quantitites of low-cost, gem-quality synthetic diamonds, proved unfounded or at least quite premature.

Up-to-date information excludes any possibility of finding colorless synthetic material on the market, though there are many examples of synthetic yellow diamonds in all the various tonalities and shadings.

Nonetheless, for the final guarantee of natural versus synthetic we must rely on laboratory analysis. Be assured: just as gemmological analysis is able to recognize synthetic versions of ruby, emerald and sapphire, it is equally reliable in setting apart the synthetic diamond from the real one.

When a gemmological analysis laboratory studies any variant of yellow diamond it regularly uses a spectroscope and ultraviolet rays either at 366 nm or at 253.7 nm and, of course, an attentive microscopic examination.

Having gathered a mass of data, the analysts then study them with scrupulously severe scientific methods.

In addition, a recent initiative of the De Beers management is also to be noted, who have contacted the most important of these laboratories offering assistance in the study of the evolution of the synthesis of diamond.

The goal of all concerned is to eliminate any element of doubt in the diamond sector.

As confirmation, De Beers has sent documentation on the topic to all laboratories concerned.

C.V.D. (Chemical Vapor Deposition) This is a process for obtaining a synthetic diamond from a large number of organic compounds. Without entering into the merits of this rather recent methodology, let us point out that it will not produce diamond in crystal structure, but can only create a very fine film, that may be deposited on various supports.

Hypothetically, at least, we have the following possibilities:

– adding a layer of colored synthetic diamond on a poor quality diamond;

– covering an imitation diamond with a layer of this synthetic diamond.

Detection of the deposited layer is easy enough, though a lens a bit larger than the usual 10x is suggested, through which the surface reveals an orange peel effect.

Imitations In theory, any colorless mineral or synthetic product can be used to imitate diamond.

By comparing the table of basic diamond data (page 98), with the data relating to its possible imitations, we must immediately recognize that the range of substances in this sector is large indeed, though the imitations most frequently employed constitute a much shorter list.

In any case, alarm bells should start ringing if you can observe: unpolished angles, surface scratches, angle doubling and an anomalous brilliance. It is time to get a careful data check, a density measurement in particular, if you are dealing with an unset stone.

For round unset stones, we can also calculate the characteristic number, by applying the formula:

TABLE COMPARING PROPERTIES OF THE DIAMOND WITH THOSE OF ITS POSSIBLE IMITATIONS			
GEM	HARDNESS	SPECIFIC GRAVITY	REFRACTION
Diamond	10	3.52	M
Yttrium Aluminum Garnet or YAG	8	4.55-4.60	M
Synthetic blend or synthetic sphalerite	3½-4	4.06	M
Synthetic cassiterite	6-7	6.80-7.10	U
Synthetic colorless corundum	9	3.98-3.99	U
Rock crystal (quartz)	7	2.65	U
Synthetic gahnite or synthetic zinc spinel	7½-8	4.40	M
Gadolinium Gallium Garnet or GGG	6½	7.05	M
Bismuth germinate	4	7.12	M
Goshenite (colorless beryll)	7½-8	2.69-2.72	U
Potassium Tantalate Niobate or KTN	6	6.43	M
Lithium niobate	5½	4.64	U
Yttrium oxide or yttria	7½-8	4.84	M
Synthetic rutile	6-6½	4.25	U
Synthetic scheelite	4½-5	5.90-6.10	U
Colorless synthetic spinel	8	3.61	M
Lithium tantalate	5½-6	7.30	U
Barium titanate	6½	5.90	M
Calcium titanate	6-6½	4.05	B
Strontium titanate	6-6½	5.13	M
Colorless topaz	8	3.56	B
Colorless glass	5½-6½	2.30-5	M
Colorless zircon	6½-7½	3.90-4.72	U
Cubic zirconia	8½	5.60-6	M

M = monorefringent
U = uniaxial birefringent
B = biaxial birefringent

$$n = \frac{w}{d \times d \times h}$$

where n is the characteristic number of a given material, w the weight in carats, d is the diameter and h the height, the two latter quantities measured in millimeters. Weight, of course, is obtained on a precision scale, and height is measured with a caliber.

So here are the key numbers for the most frequently encountered imitations, compared with diamond data:

STONE	CHARACTERISTIC NUMBER
Diamond	approx. 0.0060
YAG	from 0.0076 to 0.0086
Strontium titanate	from 0.0087 to 0.00936
Cubic Zirconium	from 0.0095 to 0.0118
GGG	larger than 0.0120

These characteristic numbers are closely connected to the density of the stone examined. Now, to give the reader an additional reference, we have set up a comparison of brilliant-cut stones having 6.5 diameter and a cut that enters in the norm:

STONE	WEIGHT
Diamond	about 1.00 ct
YAG	about 1.30 ct
Strontium titanate	about 1.45 ct
Cubic Zirconium	about 1.70 ct
GGG	about 2.00 ct

In today's market cubic zirconium is the most popular substance for imitations.

Instruments Above and beyond the check methods already indicated, the reflectometer helps detect imitations by measuring surface reflecting power (detailed instructions are supplied with the instrument), or even the thermoinertiameter, that measures diamond's thermal conductivity (and it is decidedly higher than that of other materials). None of these instruments will be of any use in analyzing imitations on which a thin synthetic layer has been deposited by the C.V.D. process (see the section "Synthetic diamonds").

As the reader will recall, we encounter the very same problem when examining the table of a doppiette in which the upper section is, in fact, diamond.

ANALISI CONSULENZE GEMMOLOGICHE
ESAME PIETRE PREZIOSE
Dr. CARLO CUMO
VALENZA (Al) Italy - Via Tortrino, 5 - Tel. (0131) 953161

CERT. N. 4*0005

VALENZA 28/03/1996

QUALITÀ: Diamante naturale

PESO: ct 0,520

DIMENSIONI: 5.10-5.16x3.26 mm

PROPORZIONI: BUONE

- Altezza totale in % 60
- Diametro tavola in % 60
- Altezza corona in % 13
- Altezza padiglione in % 44

GRADO DI PUREZZA A 10 X: puro IF
(Normative UNI)

PURO IF	VVS 1	VVS 2	VS 1	VS 2	SI 1	SI 2	P 1	P 2	P 3
X									

GRADO DI COLORE (Scala GIA): D

D	E	F	G	H	I	J	K	L	M	N	O	P	Q	R	S-Z
X															

CINTURA: SF.ST/M.

OSSERVAZIONI: 1 FS.

TAGLIO E FORMA
- Brillante rotondo **X**
- Brillante ovale
- Marquise
- Goccia
- Smeraldo
- Cuore

GRADO DI FINITURA
- Ottimo
- Buono **X**
- Medio
- Scarso

FLUORESCENZA UV
- Nulla **X**
- Debole
- Media
- Forte

RILEVAMENTI EFFETTUATI CON:
- microscopio American Optical e Zeiss - Schneider
- lente aplanatica e acromatica a 10x
- lampada UV 253,7 e 366 mm Eickhorst
- bilancia automatica Mettler
- diamond color checker Okuda e master color diamonds
- calibro Presidium
- proporzionoscopio GEM
- diamond checker Cultj

La manomissione dell'involucro trasparente sigillato, contenente la pietra analizzata, non invalida la presente analisi, in quanto questo laboratorio può, su richiesta, verificare la corrispondenza dei dati della pietra con quelli indicati nel certificato relativo e quindi risigillare la pietra.

Dr. CARLO CUMO
già Analista del Laboratorio Gemmologico di Stato di Valenza. Perito del Tribunale e della CCIAA di Alessandria

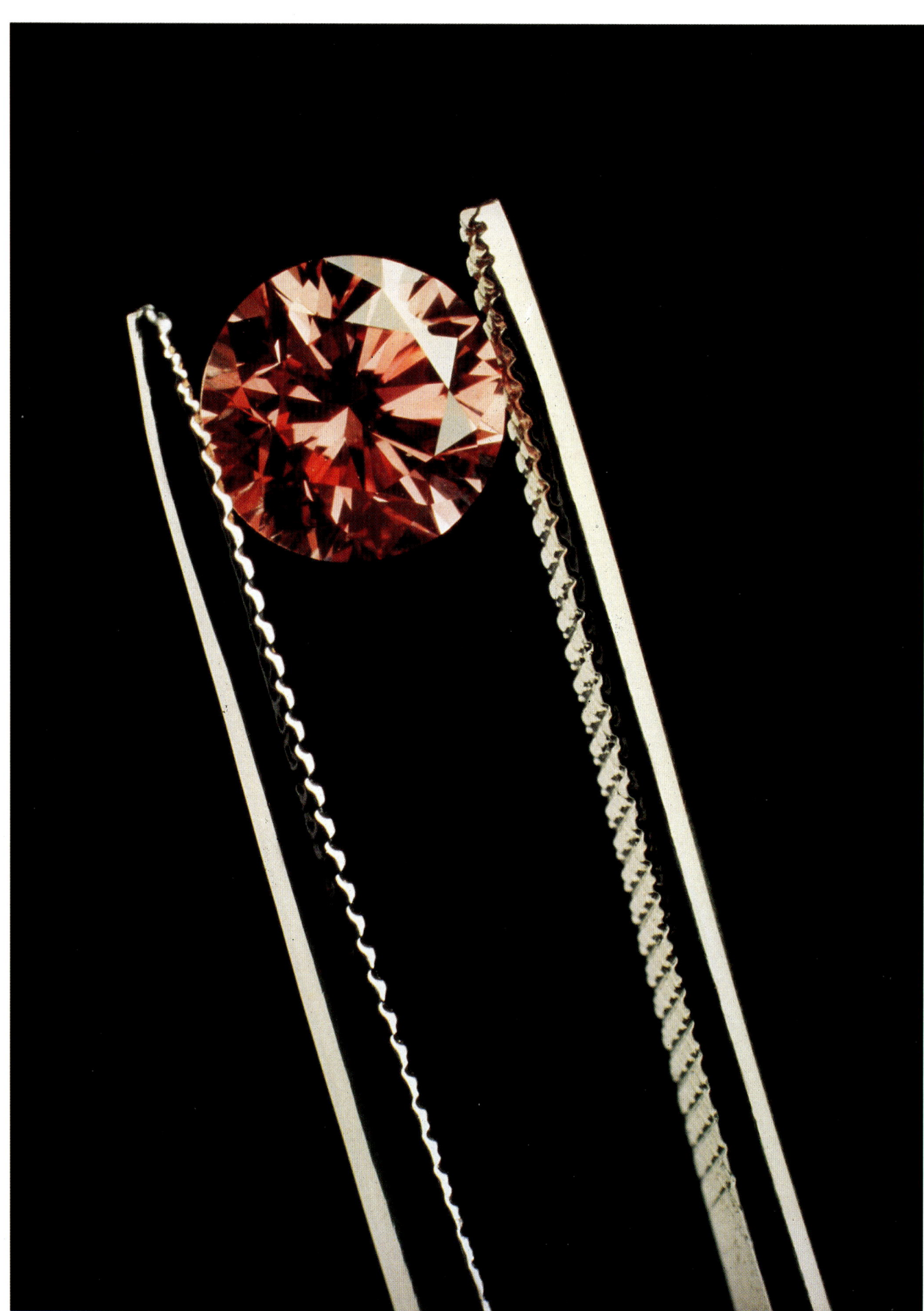

100 *Rose diamond from the mines of Argyle (Australia).*

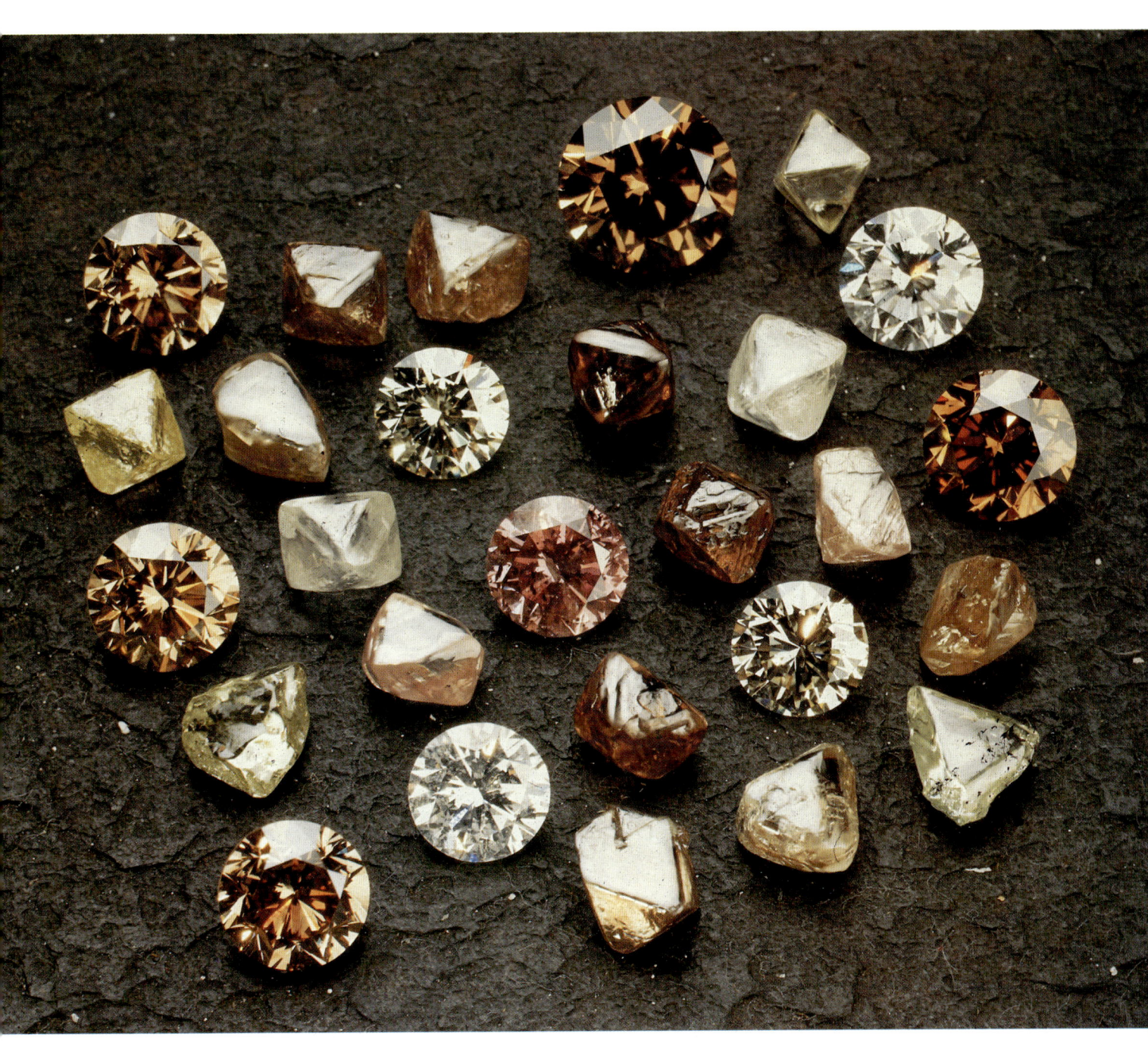

Cut and rough diamonds from the mines of Argyle (Australia).

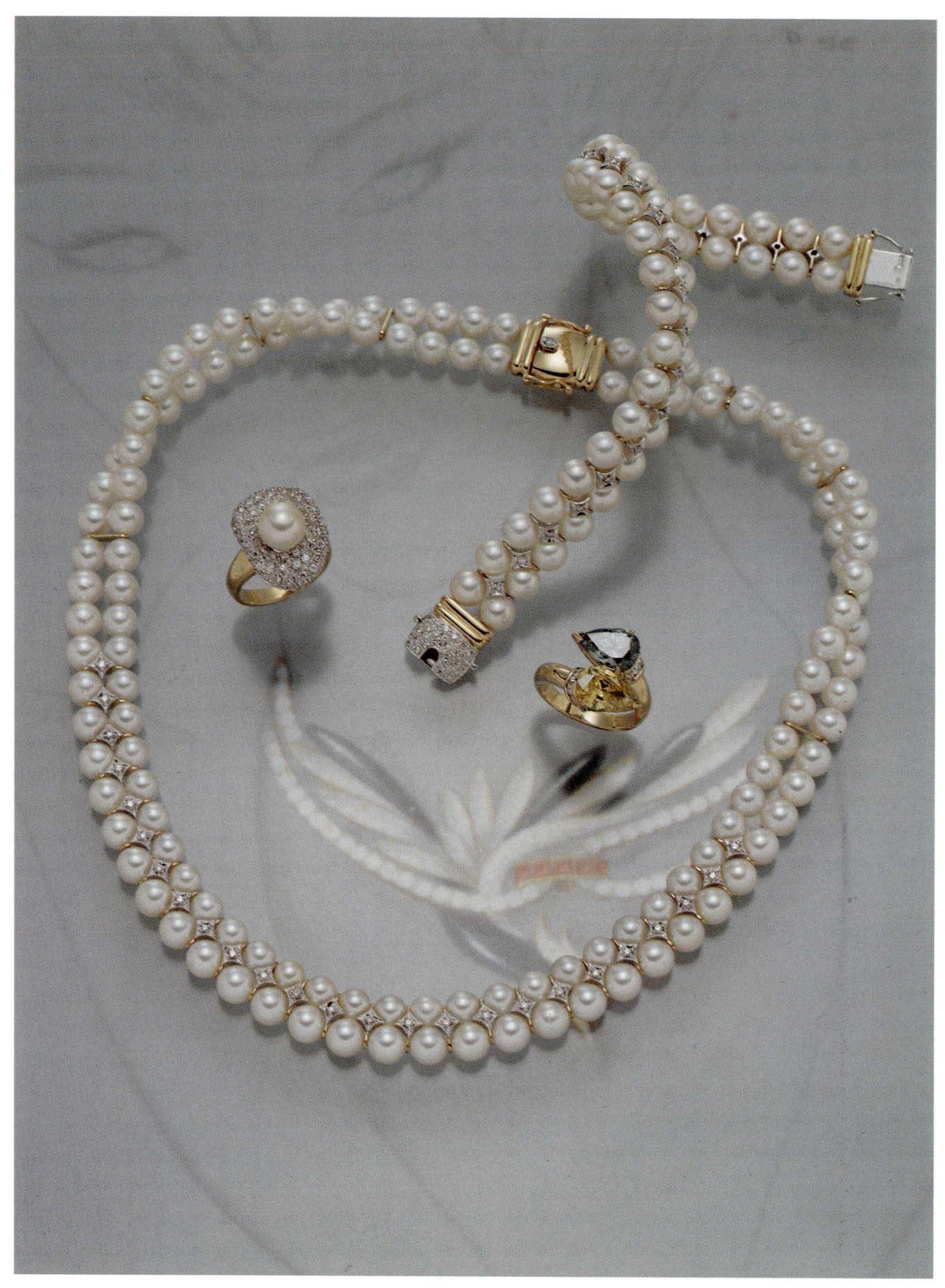

AURELIA GIOIELLI.
Ring consisting of two pear-shaped diamonds, one natural yellow and the other blue. Set of pearls and diamonds.

GIUSEPPE VERDI.
Bracelets in yellow, white, and pink gold enhanced with the purest of diamonds.

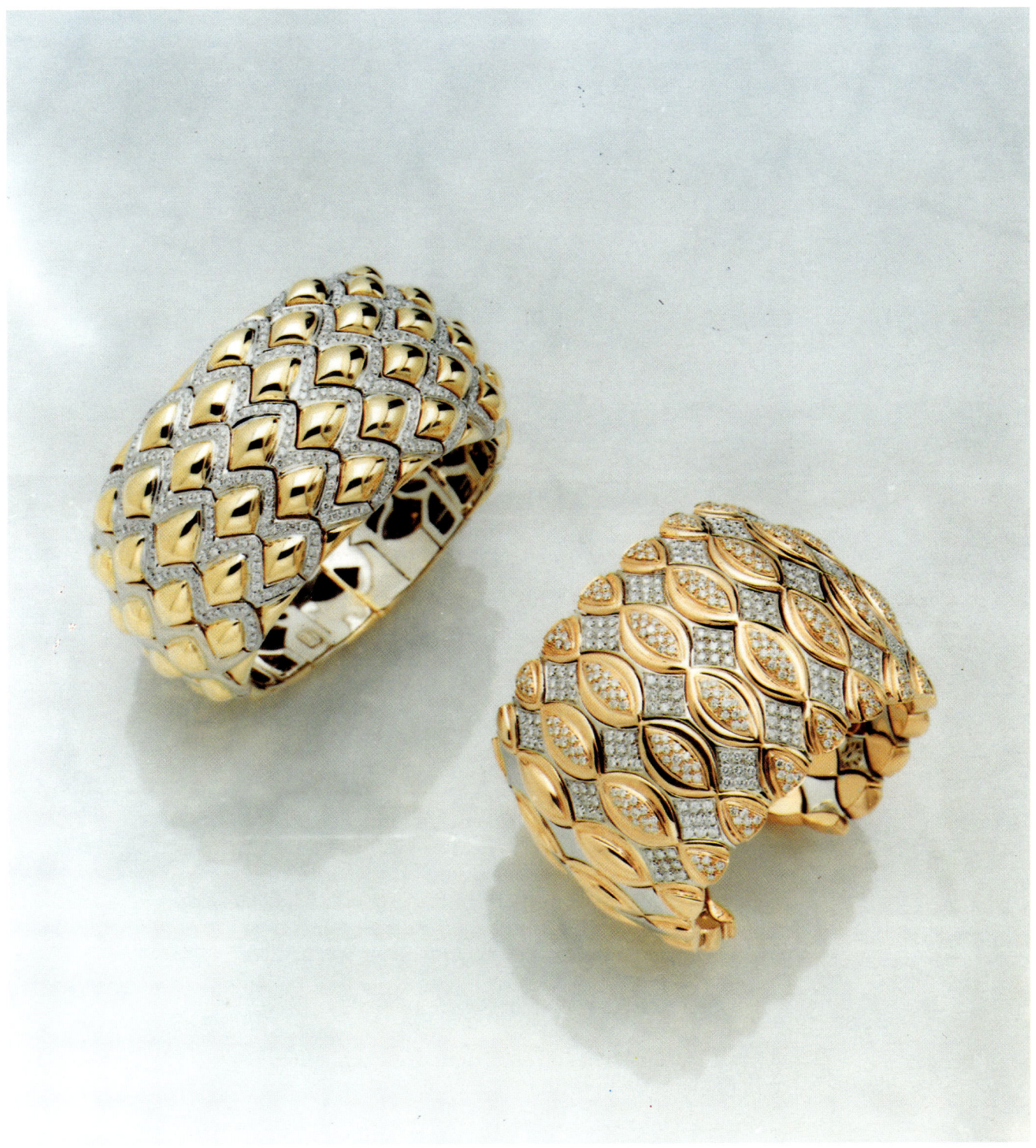

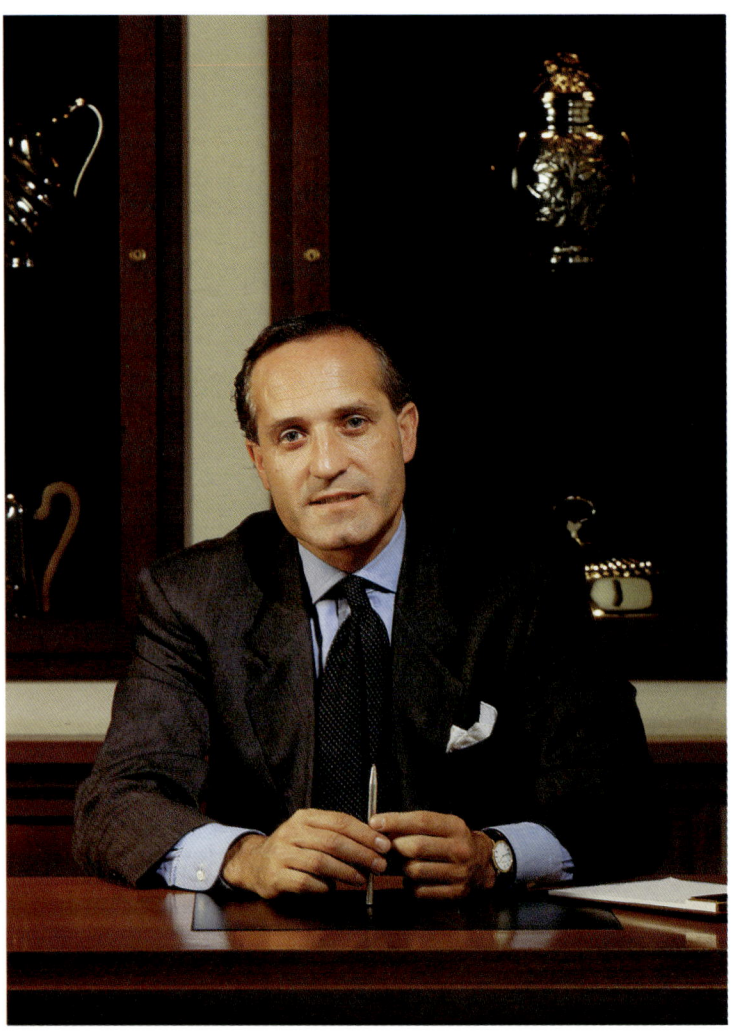

Roberto Boglietti, owner and designer of the firm.

Boglietti Gioielliere in Biella. Its origins can be found by tracing the history of a family that has lived in close contact with art. Eden and Walter Boglietti, sons of Melchiorre – at the beginning of the twentieth century a sculptor, by the forties he was working gold and silver, engraving, crafting, and inlaying in masterly fashion – in 1953 form the company by opening a goldsmith's intaglio workshop. In 1972 son Roberto enters the business, and two years later, Gigliola takes the place of her uncle Edon, assisting father and brother with the running of the workshop. In 1991 Roberto and Gigliola open "Boglietti Gioielliere in Biella," offering their own pieces of jewelry that are all created with an art that has steadily improved with time and are subject to scrupulous care throughout the entire process; from initial concept right through to manufacture. Accurate technical design and painstaking craftmanship offer modern creations that, like all unique works, stand up to the test of time.

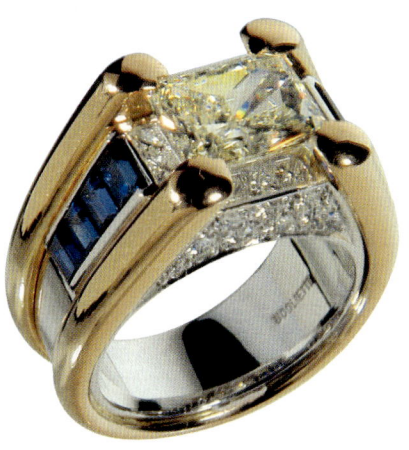

ROBERTO BOGLIETTI.
Rings with diamonds and sapphires.

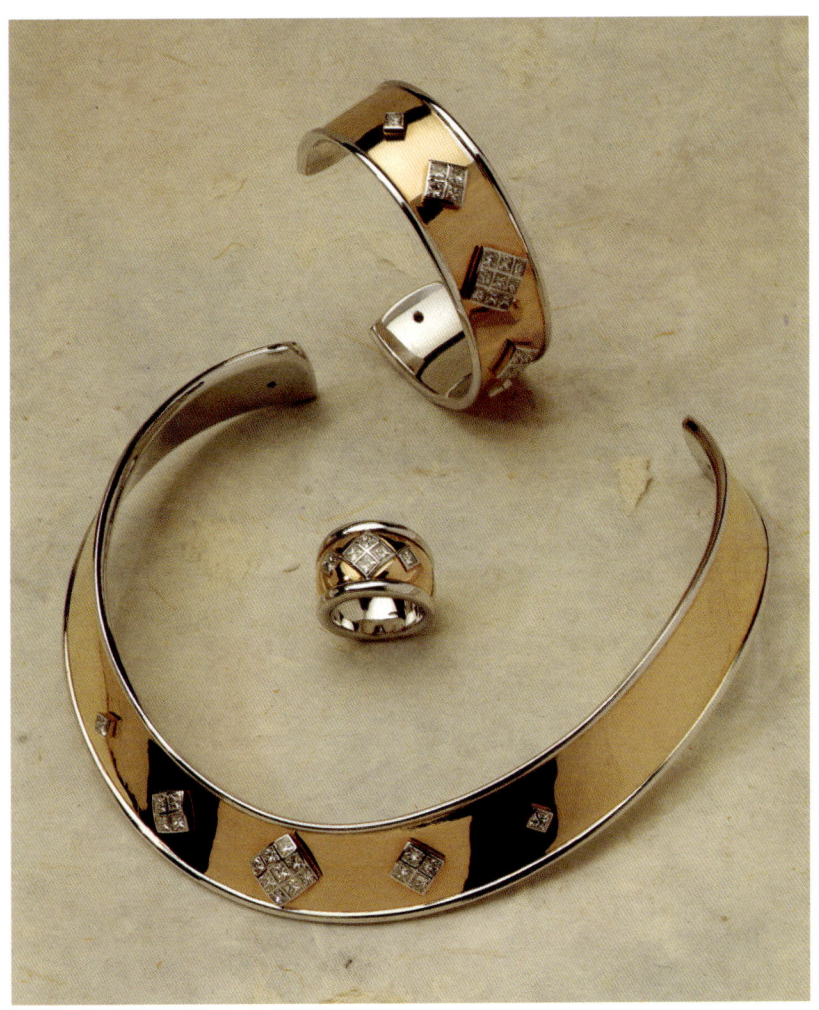

ROBERTO BOGLIETTI.
Set in gold and diamonds.

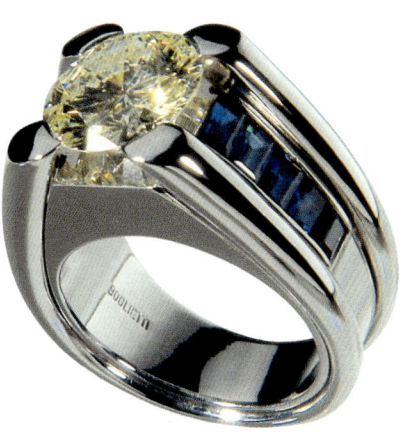

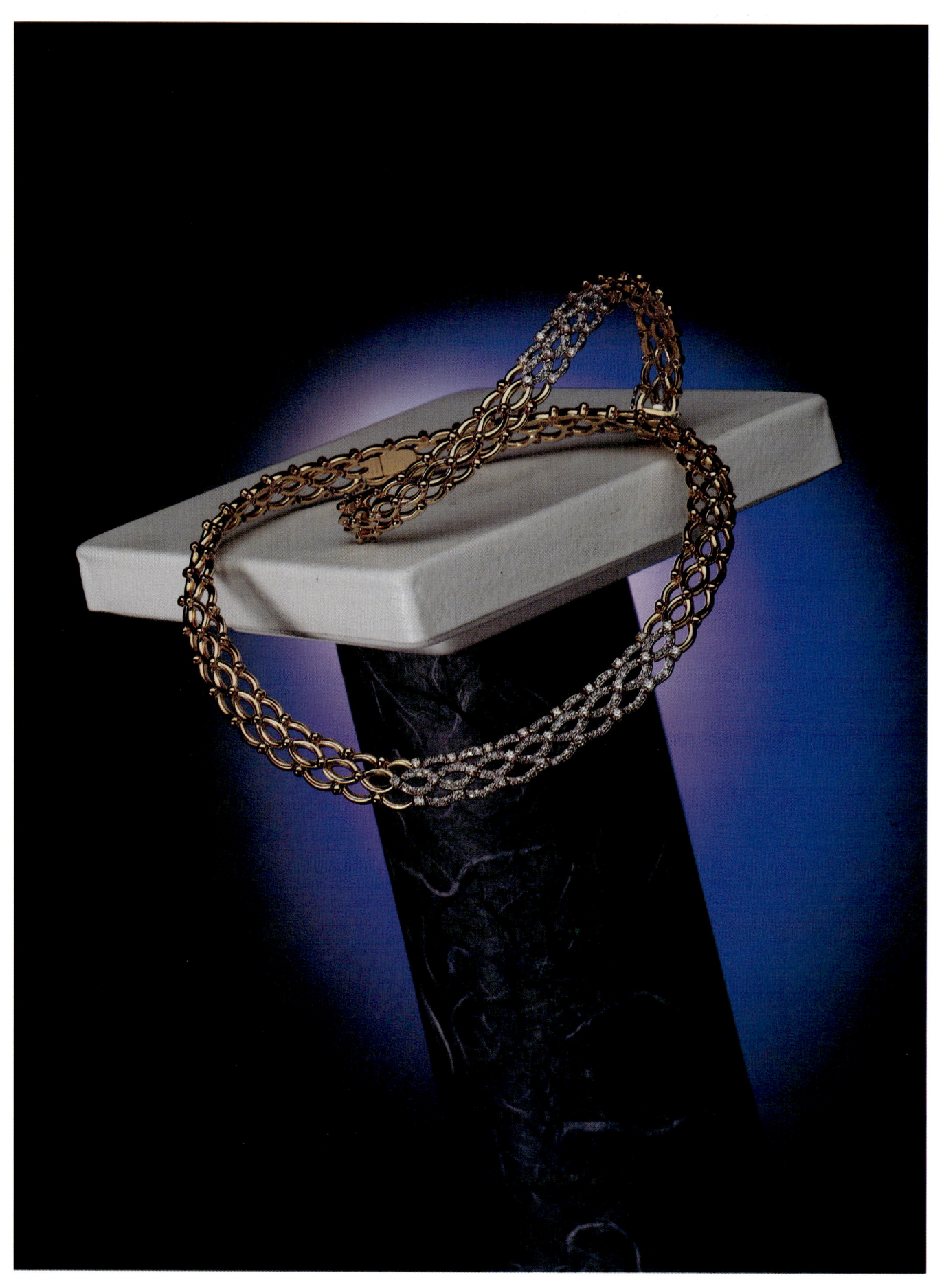

ALDO GARAVELLI.
Gold and diamond choker and bracelet.

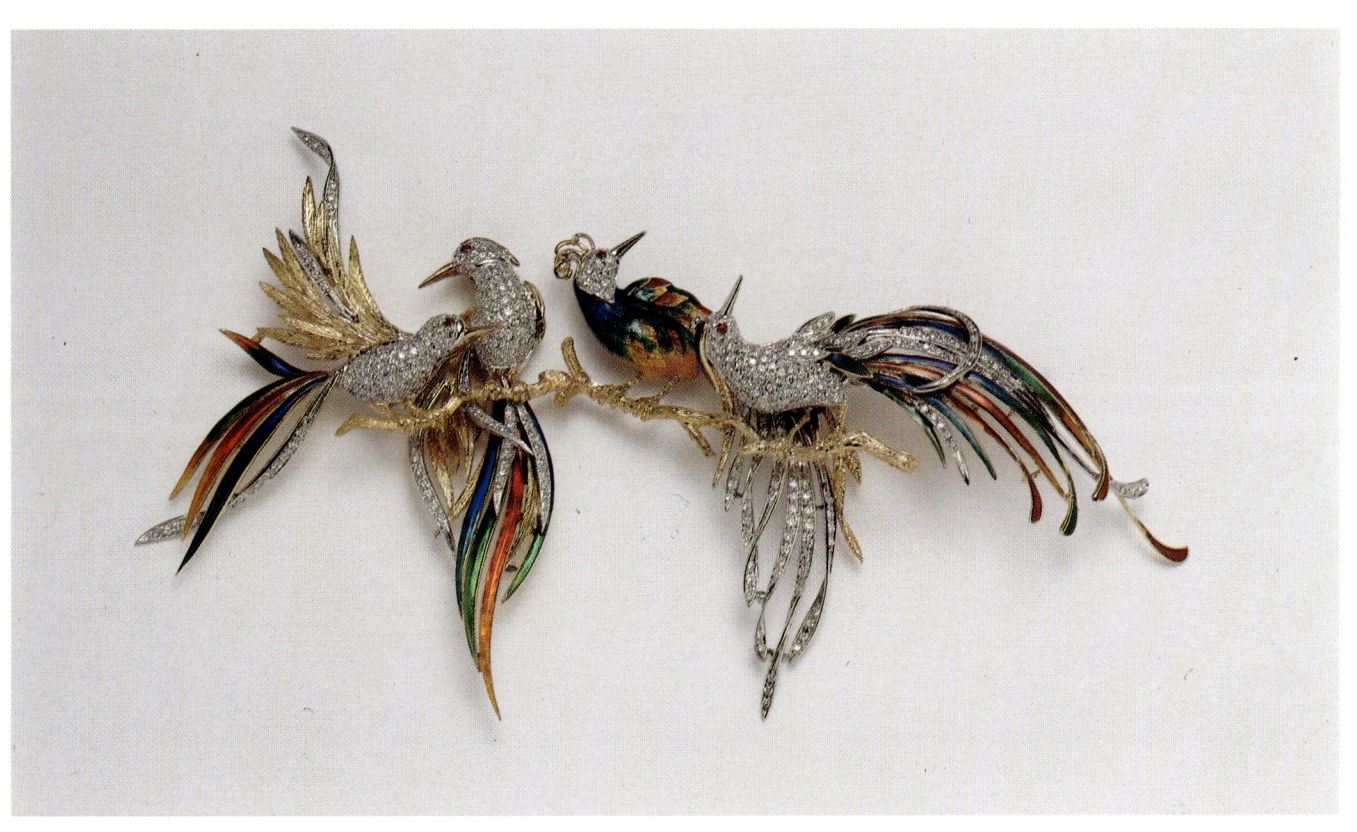

Aldo Garavelli: "Birds of Paradise"
Brooches in gold, diamonds, and enamel.

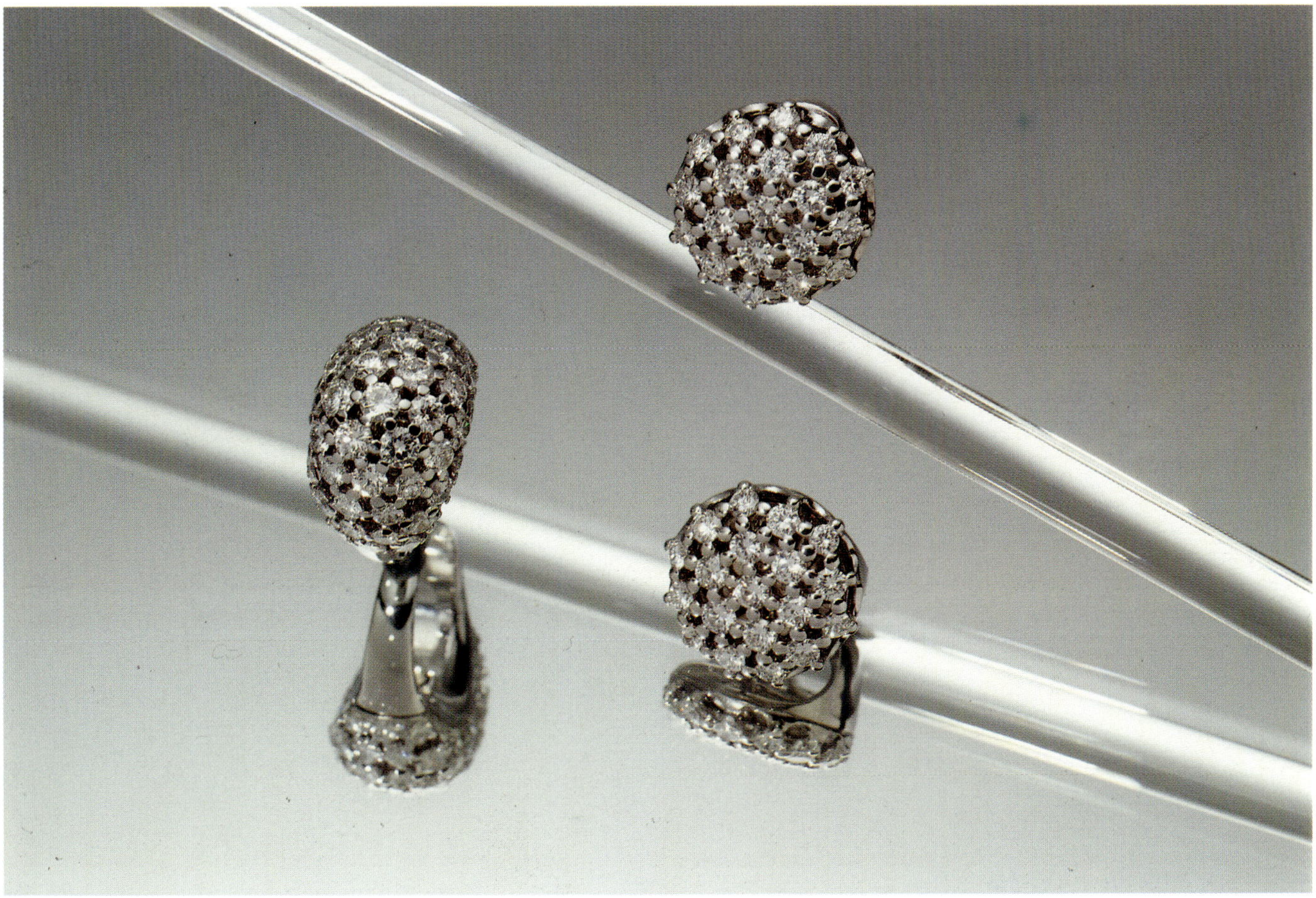

Aldo Garavelli.
White gold ring and earrings with diamonds set as if suspended.

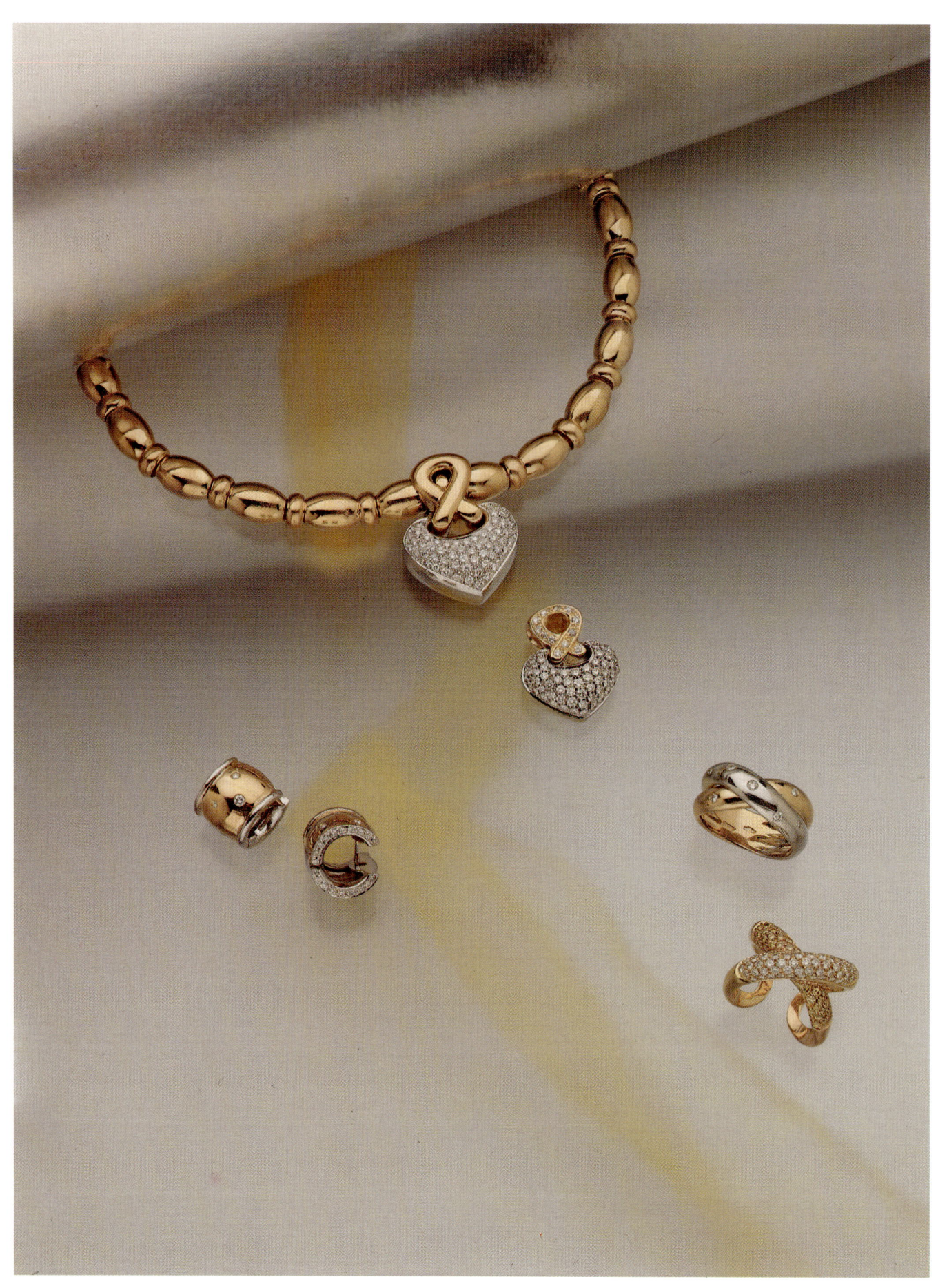

GALDIOLO.
Jewels in yellow, white, and pink gold set with white and yellow diamonds.

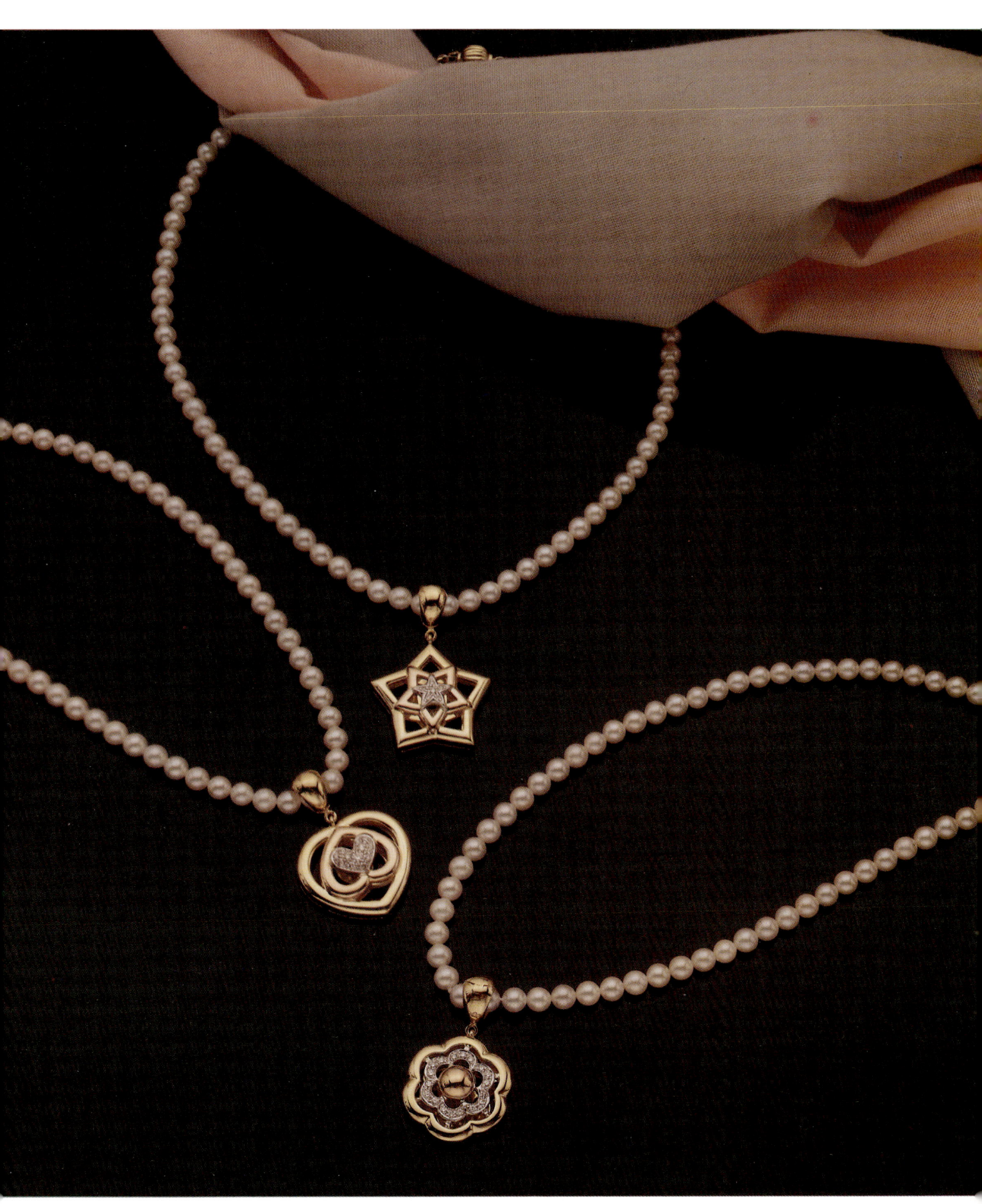

Ermes Marega.
Three pendants in gold and diamonds set on pearls.

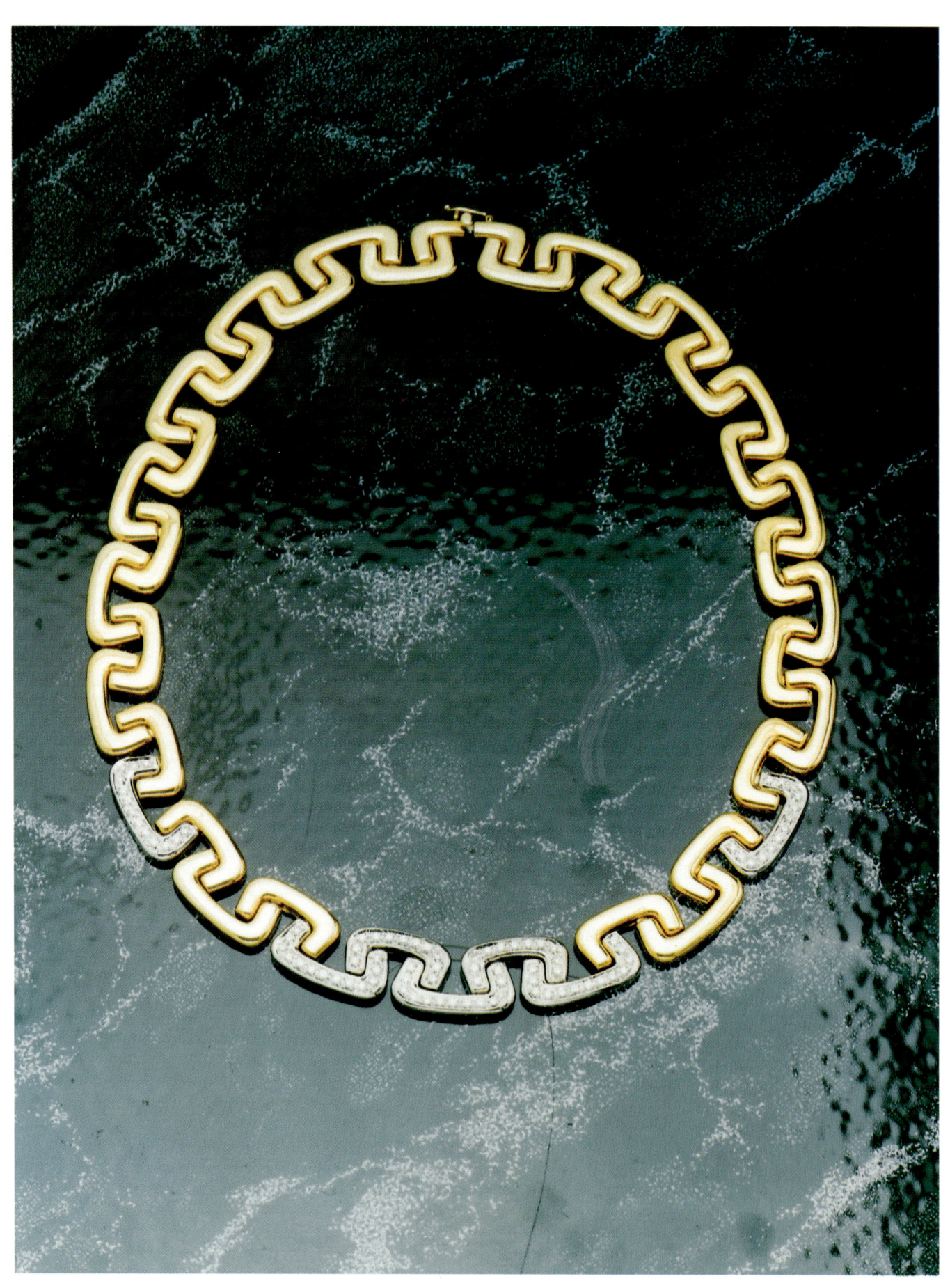

Ivo Robotti: "Greek"
Choker in yellow and white gold with diamonds.

New Italian Art: "Dunes"
Gold ring set with white, yellow, and pink diamonds. This jewel, created by Antonio Gié from Valenza Po, Italy, was winner of the Diamonds International Award in 1996.

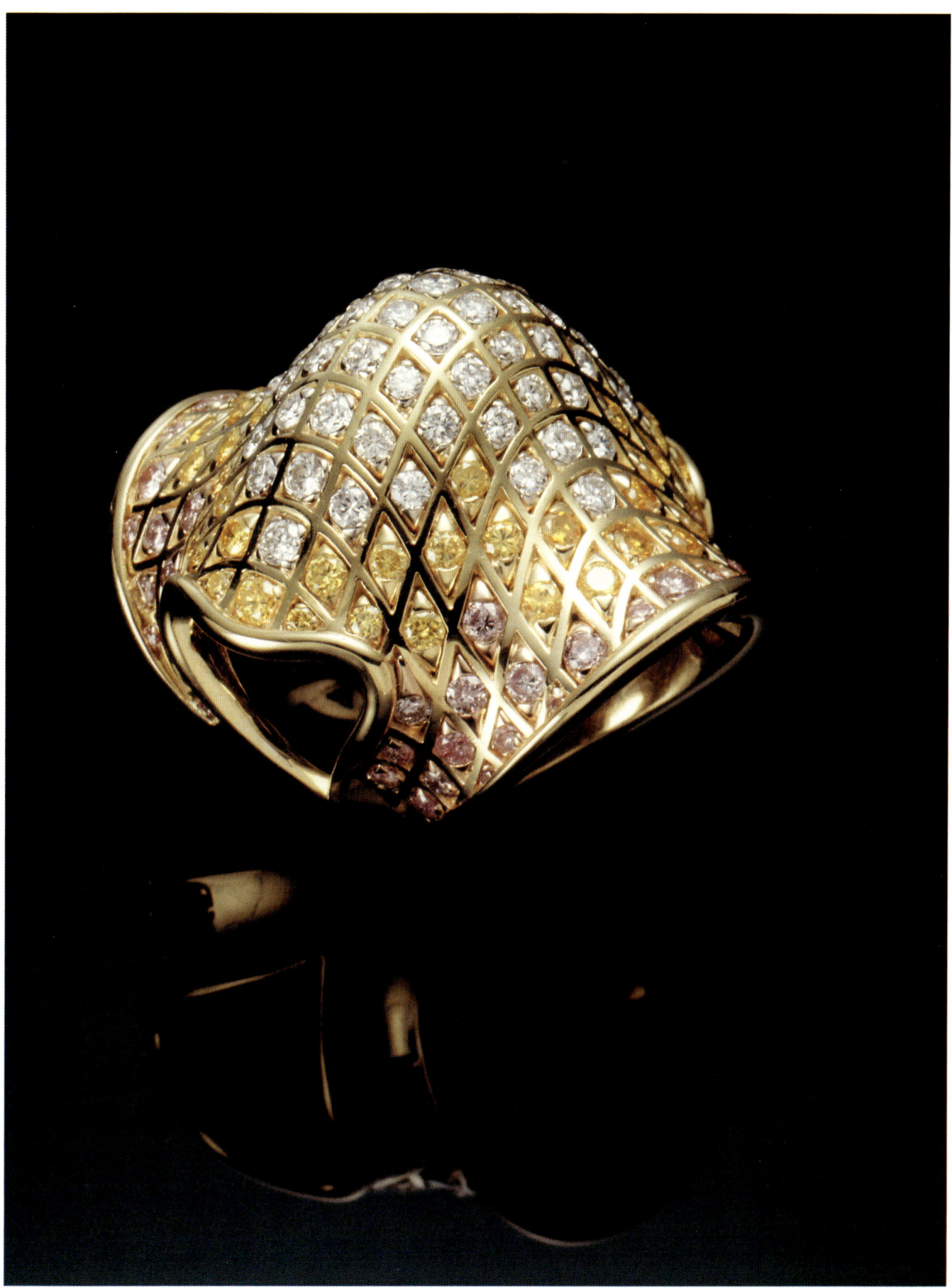

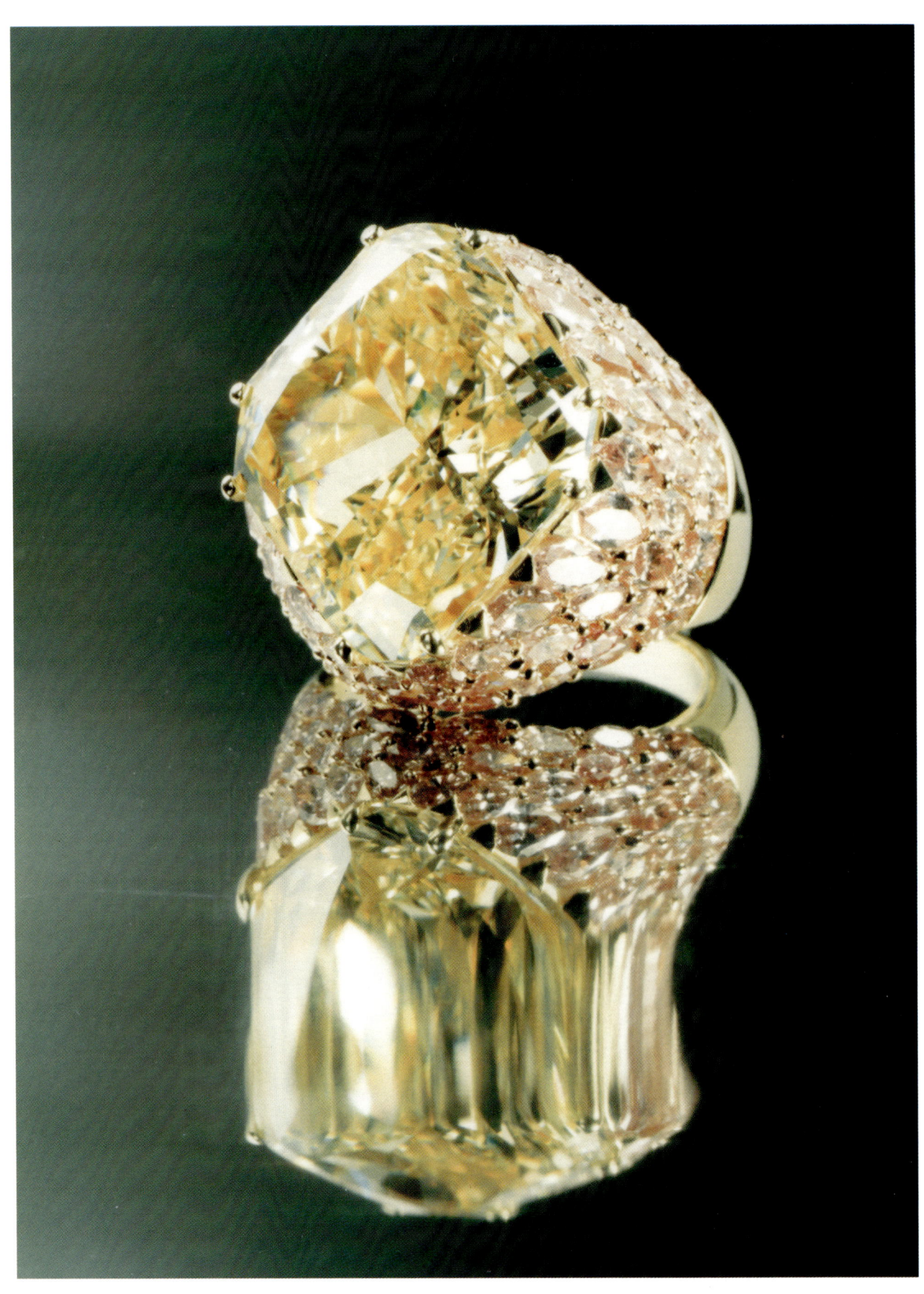

RCM.
Gold ring with yellow diamond, lozenge cut, weighing 21.06 carats.
The border is formed by pink diamonds, navette cut.

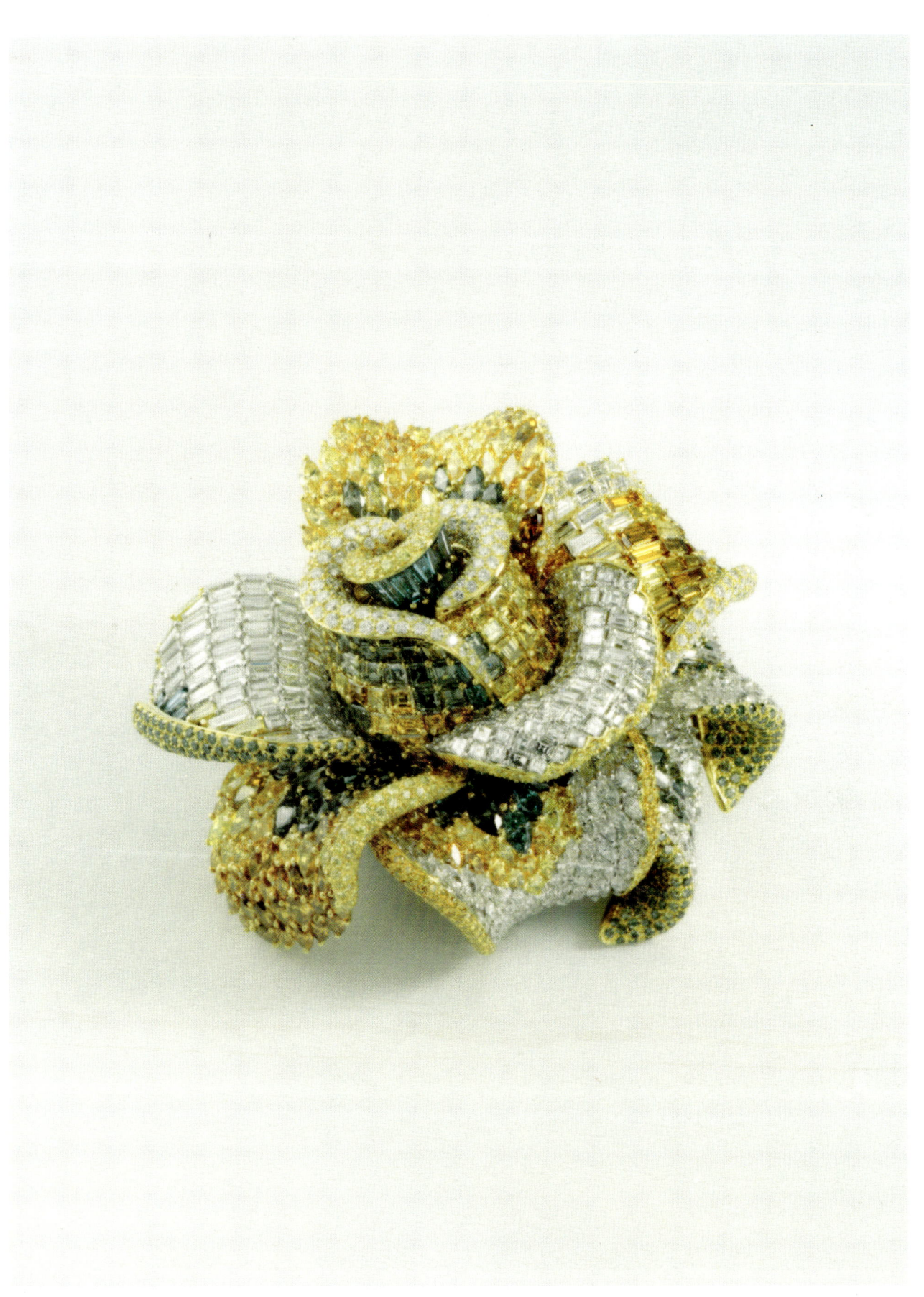

RCM: "Flower"
Gold brooch studded with 118 carats of variously sized diamonds.

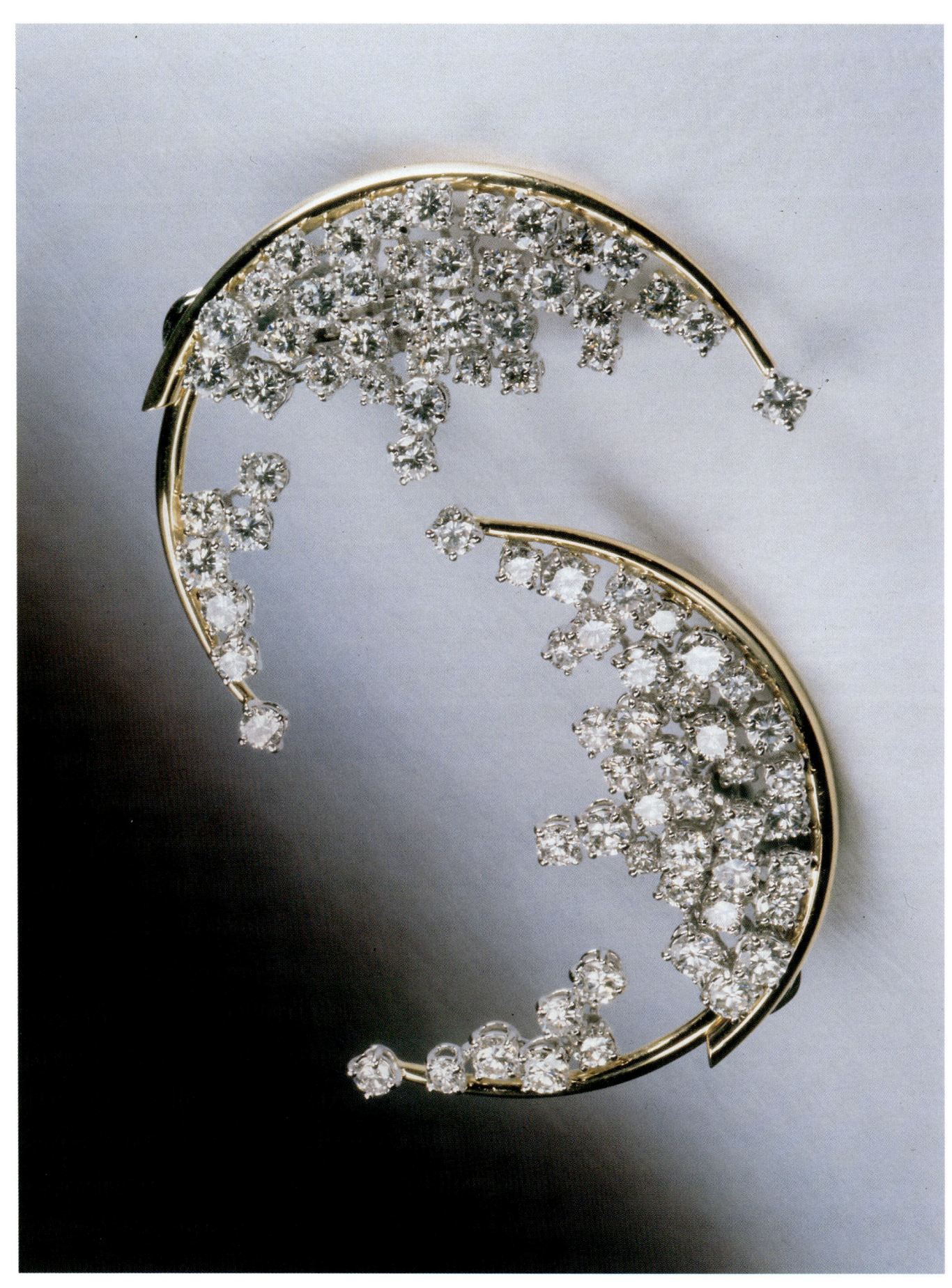

Damiani: "Blue Moon"
Gold earrings with 13.19 carats of diamonds that highlight the femininity and charm of a woman.
Designed by Silvia Maria Grassi, this jewel was the winner of the Diamonds International Award.

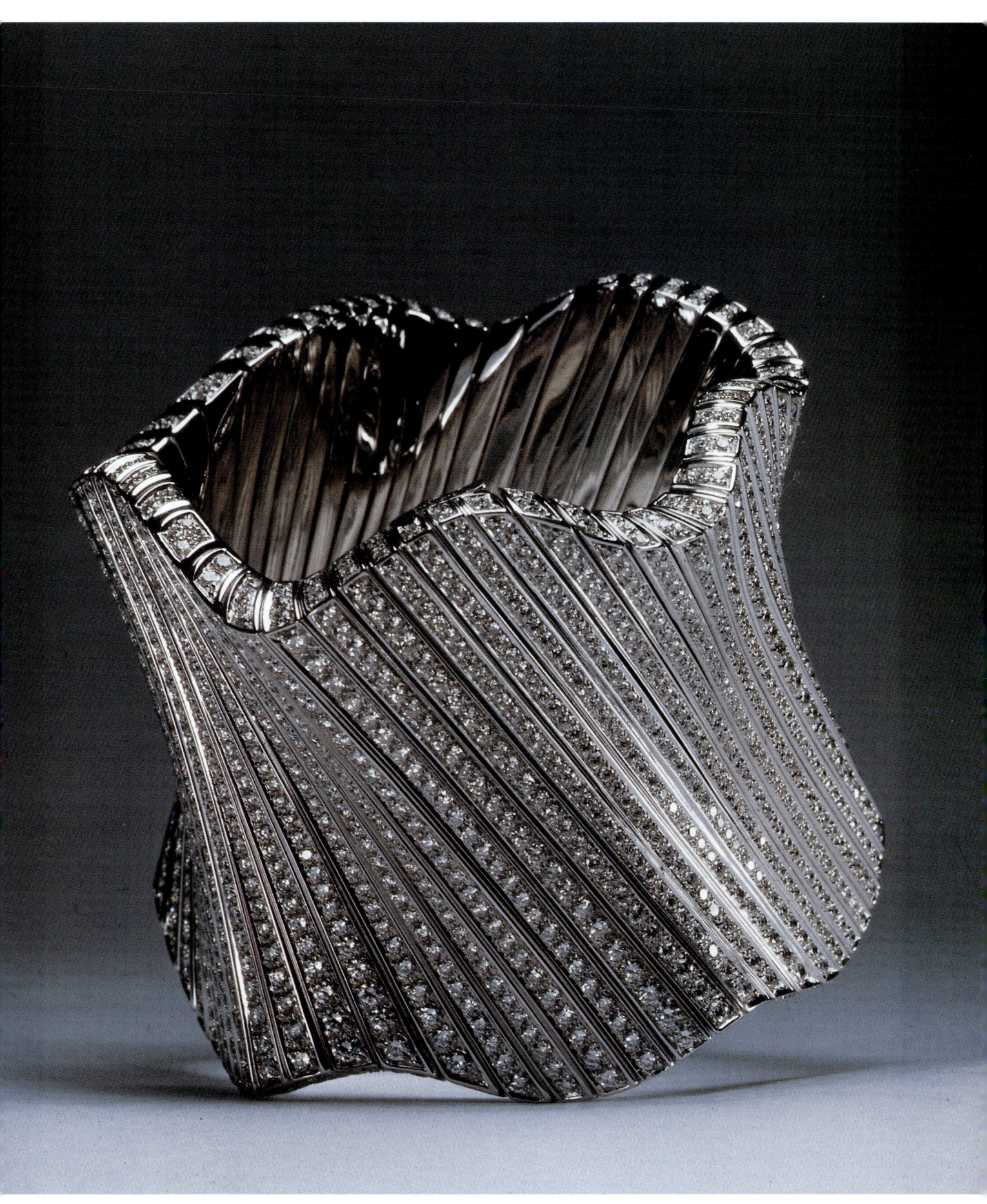

DAMIANI: "SAHARA"
White gold bracelet with 47.41 carats of diamonds, winner of the Diamonds International Award.

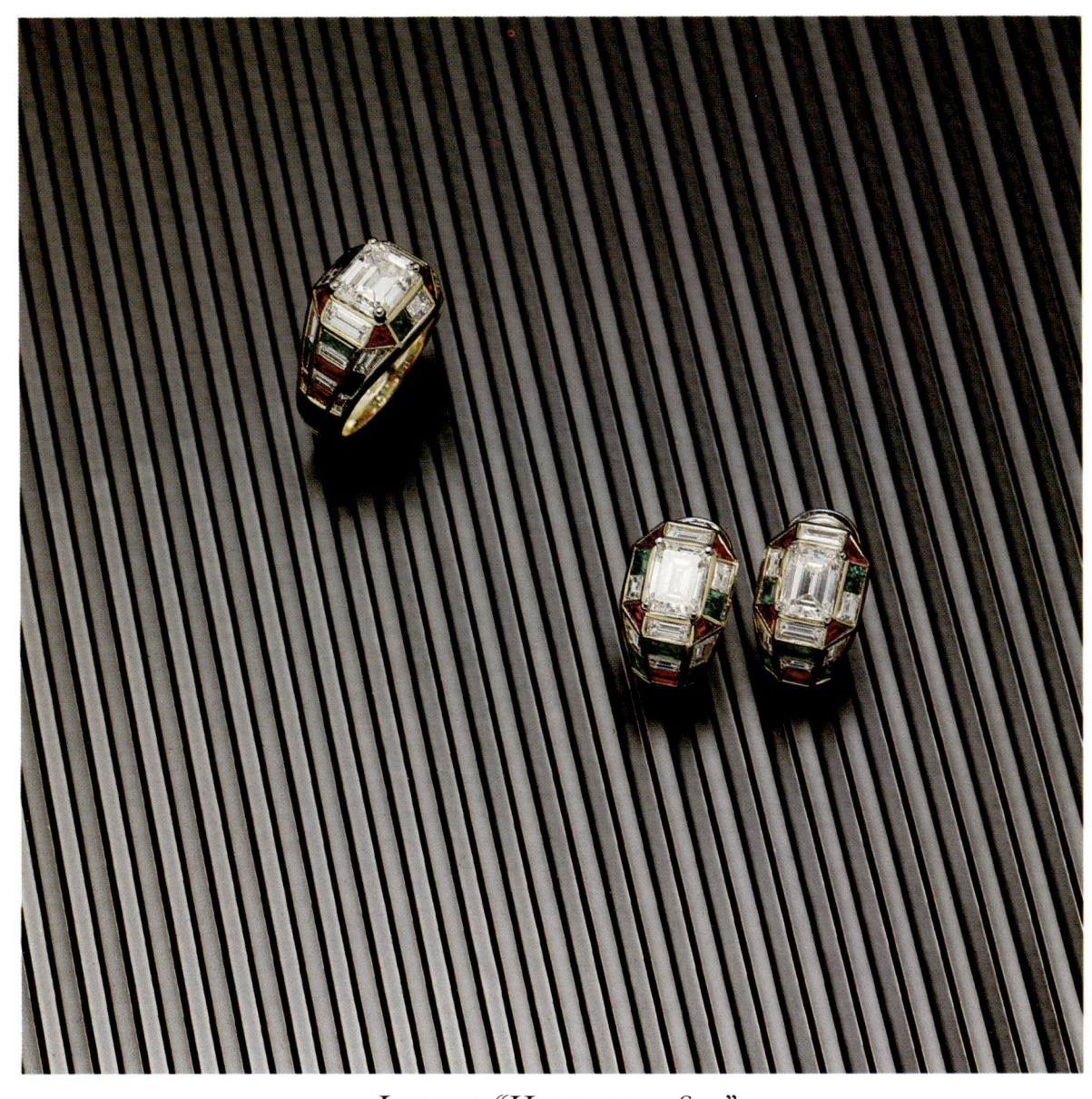

Lunati: "Harlequin Set"
Gold ring and earrings set with diamonds, rubies, and emeralds.

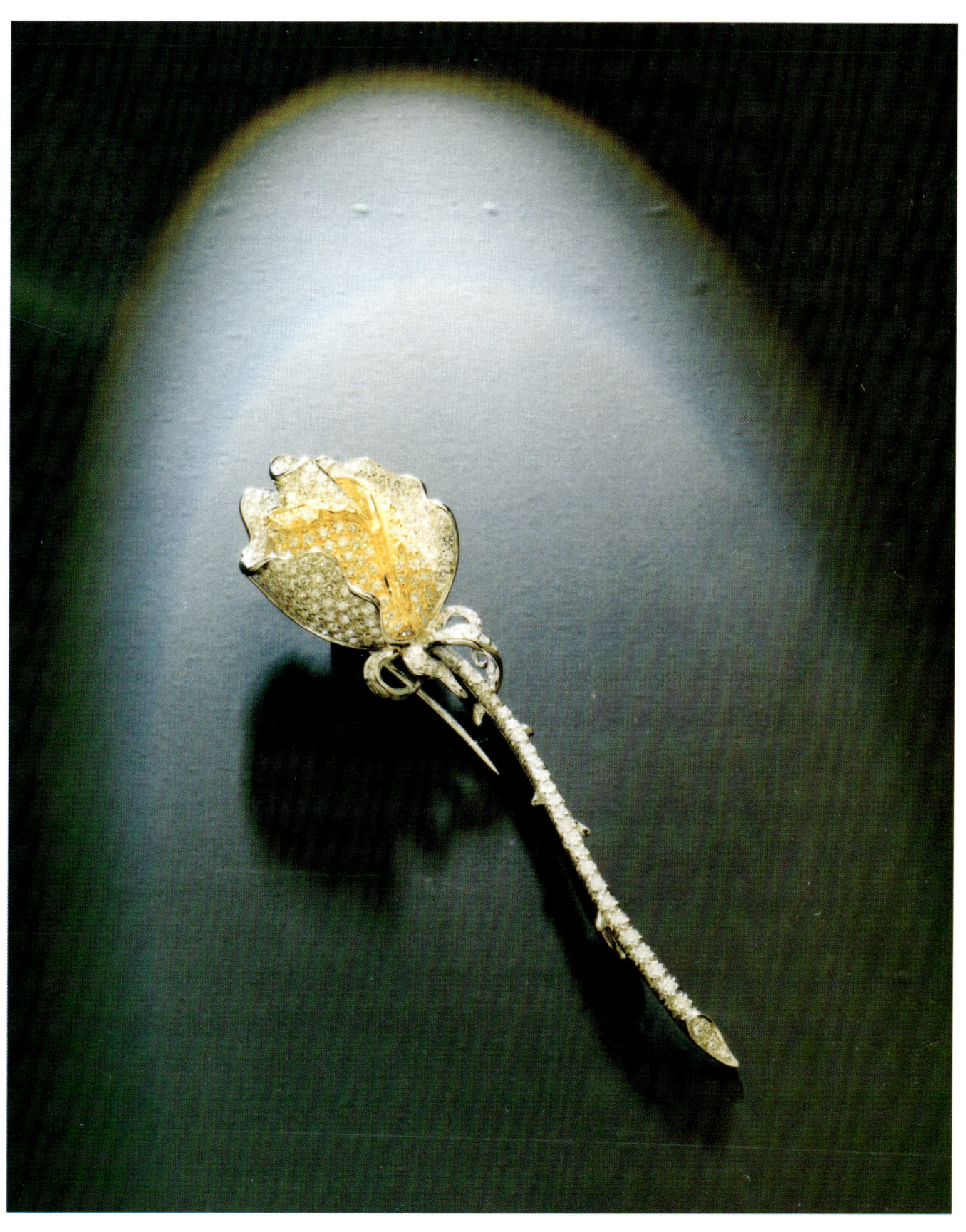

COSTANTINO ROTA: "ROSEBUD"
White gold brooch with 223 diamonds.

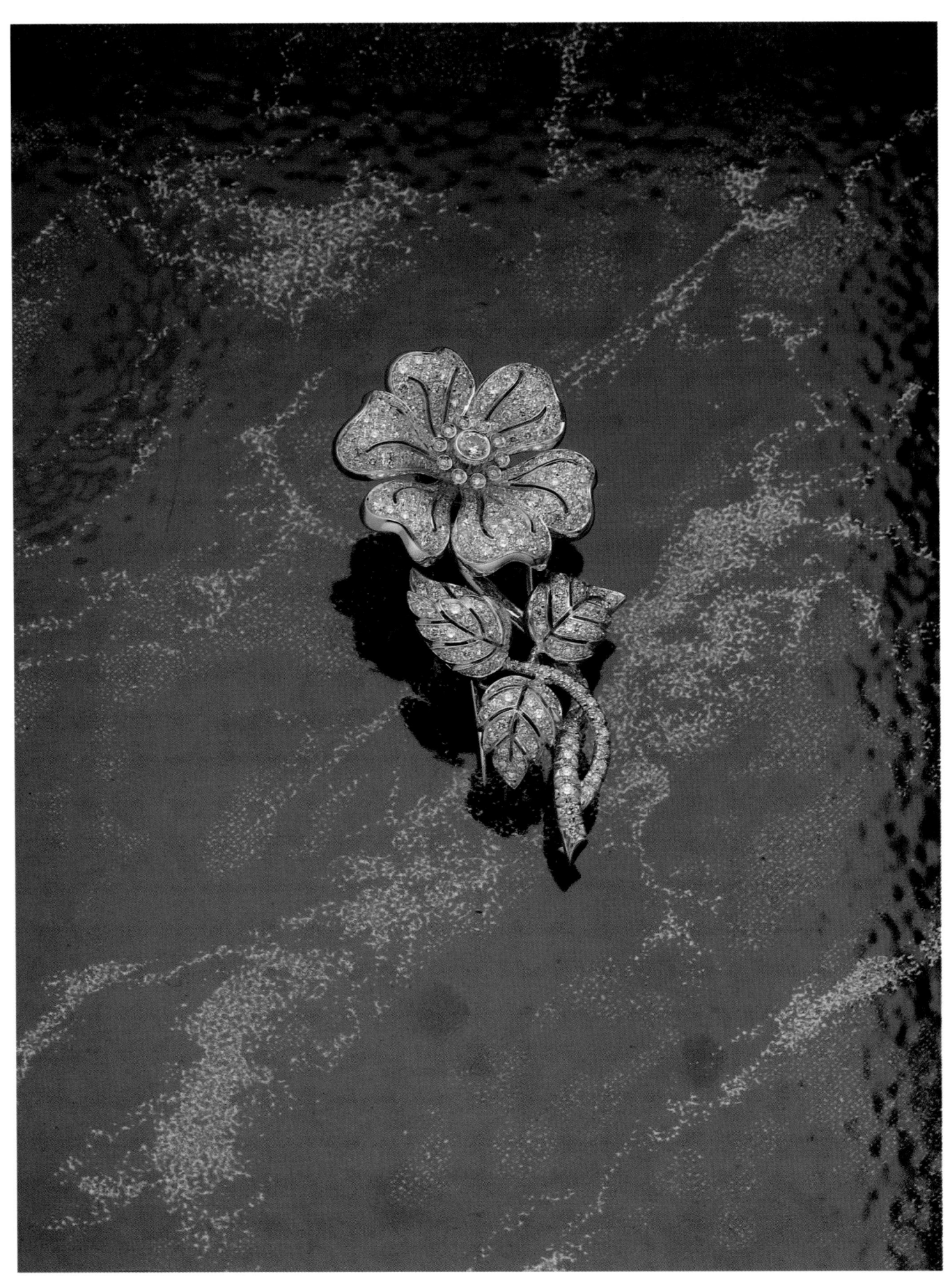

Dirce Repossi: "Art Deco"
White gold brooch with diamonds.

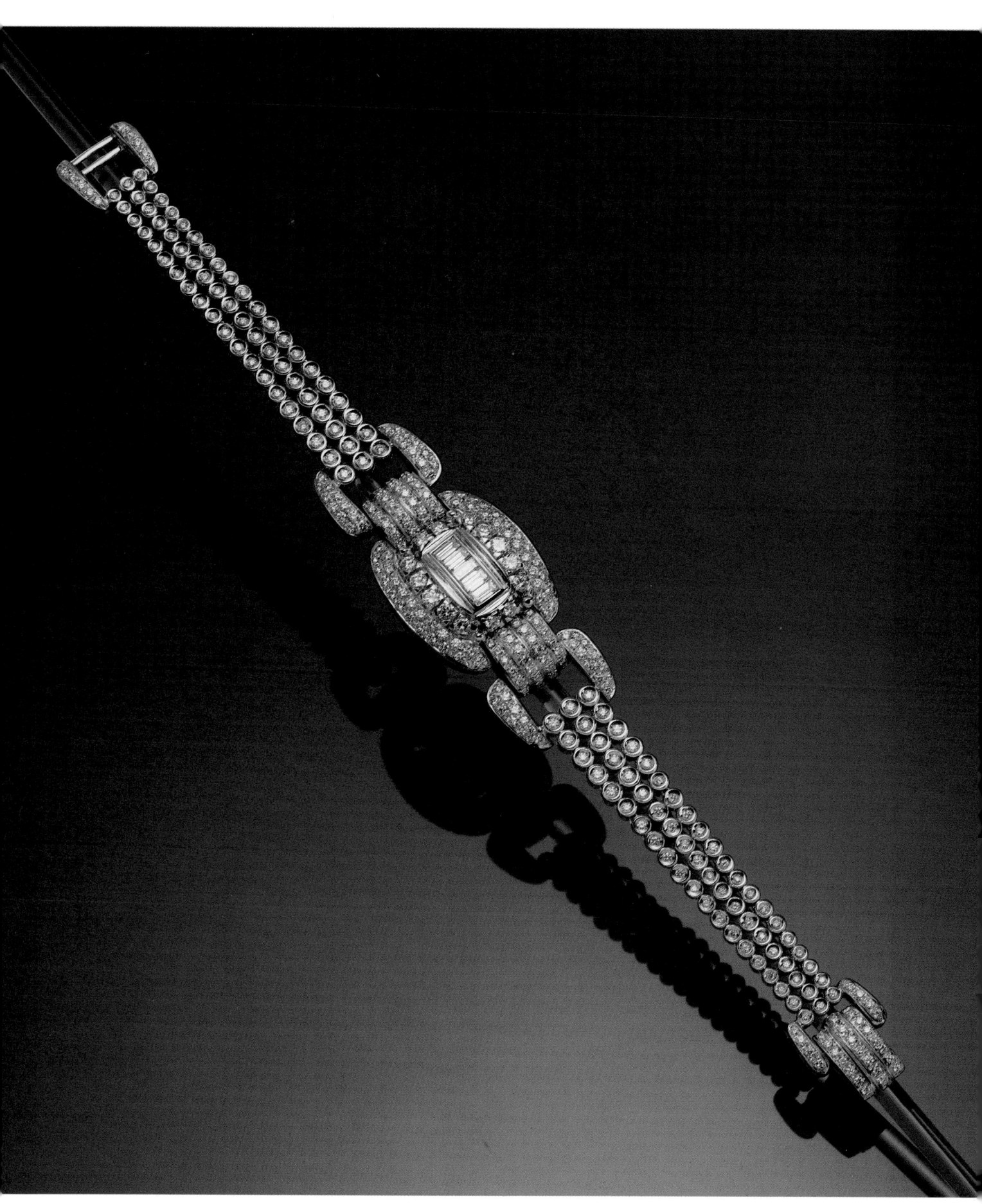

RECARLO.
This white gold bracelet, also inspired by art deco, is studded with over 200 diamonds.

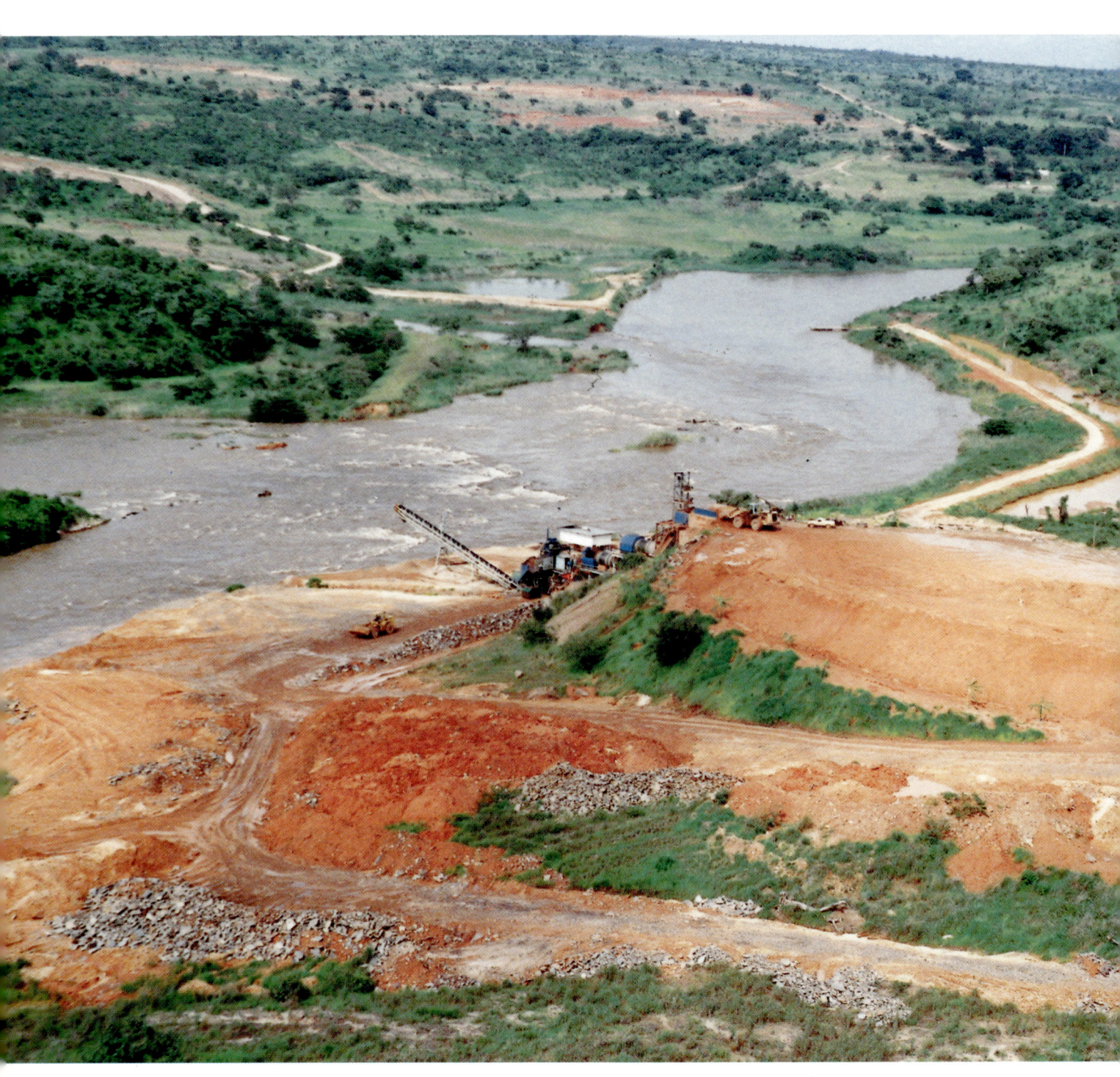

Aerial view of the diamond mine of Luzamba (near Kafunfo).

Angola:
Diamond Hunt

by Claude Mazloum

From the window of our Tristar I glimpse the first majestic dunes of the Sahara, like the golden waves of a vast burning sea, yet perfectly motionless. The plane is almost empty, we are only a few dozen passengers, all men, on our way to Luanda. I can even take four seats to myself and try to make up for last night's lost sleep caused by our ten-hour delay at the airport.

My objective: film the diamond mines in Angola. "Easier said than done..." had warned my friend Deborah Peterson, public relations officer of an American multinational oil company recently established in Angola. It was Deborah who had initially suggested I come and take a look at this country, slowly but surely opening up to the West.

Bartholomew Colombo, Deborah's secretary, is waiting for me at the airport with a VIP visa upon my arrival. And a good thing too, for I see there are no taxis to take me into town. I am reserved in a five-star hotel of a well-known international chain.

Unfortunately, when I finally arrive, the room still isn't ready yet and my stay begins with a big argument in the peeling lobby of the best hotel in the capital. This earns me the honor of being blacklisted at all the chain's hotels worldwide.

Here I find no electricity, very little water, and an abundance of cockroaches. Moreover, the room across from mine is occupied by the commander of the opposition forces who has just arrived from the distant jungle to settle accounts with the present leaders. The way to and from my room is therefore an obstacle course around kalachnikovs and tense soldiers.

I have fourteen days at my disposal, but my accommodation is certainly far from ideal, not to say downright depressing. For moral reasons it would be difficult in this country for Deborah to invite me to stay with her, so I try calling a childhood friend who has recently been transferred here as manager of a geological research company.

I'm in luck, my friend invites me to stay in his magnificent villa complete with electric generator and well. He even has a telephone and a car with a driver. "Make yourself at home," Damien Rispel tells me, unaware of the risks this will entail for him, or for me either for that matter. I have arrived on Saturday, I spend my second day, Sunday, with Deborah at the sea and discover the national dish: grilled royal lobster, absolutely delicious!

Invisible Diamonds

My first real contact with Luanda is a wild goose chase through its streets accompanied by Bartholomew as we try to locate supposed dealers in rough diamonds. He drives me from one end of the city to the other. We are told that the people aren't in, we are given other contacts, other addresses, and after four hours of impossible traffic in our VW Beetle which, has neither windshield nor brakes, we find a gentleman of mixed race whom we have been told deals in rough stones. He has nothing to show us, he says, and in fact has never seen a diamond in his life.

On our way back, Bartholomew tells me that the seller was simply afraid I was working for the police. Diamond dealing is, in fact, severely punished.

It is useless now to keep tracking diamonds in the city since I've been branded as one of the police, better to go directly to the mines, those in Kafunfo, famous for the quality and abundance of its diamonds. For years now funds from the sale of these diamonds have been used to buy arms for the civil war raging in the country between the UNITA and the MPLA.

The mines are located about 500 miles from the capital, about 45 miles of this road being a highway. After that, there are 300 miles of paved and unpaved roads up to Malanje and then 125 miles of just dirt track. Four days going, four days coming back, this is still feasible in the time I have left.

Deborah helps locate a jeep in good enough condition to make the trip, a man capable of driving it, a Portuguese ex-army commander familiar with the terrain, and a journalist well introduced in political circles. Damien sees to supplies of tinned foods, bread, water, etc., since in this country there are no stores where you can buy these provisions. No one thinks about gas since the jeep's tank carries enough for 250 miles plus a 10-mile reserve.

The Invisible Mines

We leave for Luanda at noon on Tuesday. Our party, consisting of two white men and two men of mixed race in a car that more or less runs normally, does not go unnoticed. We are stopped and undergo a few police and army checks. The excursion is pleasant though, on the whole, the mahogany and baobab trees beautiful, the rhythms of the music and the promise of adventure intoxicating.

In the evening, the journalist advises me to stop for the night to avoid any problems. We are a few miles from N'Dalatando, a small town located between the capital and Malanje. We look for a hotel, the best one in town is still shabby. We're in luck! There are two rooms still vacant, I take one and give the other to my men. There hasn't been a drop of running water in the taps for fifteen years; to wash, a plastic container filled with a dubious looking liquid is handed to us with the room keys.

It goes without saying that I sleep fully dressed because of the conditions of the place and the number of insects and reptiles that also abound. That night, truckloads of natives arrive and camp outside the hotel, singing and dancing until dawn to frenetic rhythms. Our windows have no panes and sleep is impossible.

We get off to an early start on the remnants of a paved road that had been used and abandoned by the Portuguese, then worked over by Russian and Cuban tanks. Only occasional strips of asphalt give any indication that we are on the right road to Malanje. Finally, in the afternoon we arrive there. The by now impending dread of the hotel, however, still threatens. Compared to this one, last night's hotel was paradise.

Our next stop is the state-owned company La Codian, which has a monopoly on all the mines. The La Codian authorities refuse to give us authorization to visit the deposits unless we first obtain a pass from the mine police. An officer from the latter, with an arrogant and condescending look, tells us," Our mines don't need any publicity, quite the contrary." Then, menacingly he continues, "In fact you don't belong here at all, return to Luanda immediately."

Overcome with fatigue and depression, we give up for the day.

The journalist in our party is a friend of the Governor of the province of Malanje. The next day, at 9:00 a.m. we're at the Governor's palace, at 3:00 p.m. we leave with an official authorization to visit the Kafunfo mines. However, it is too late to leave now, and moreover the little gas we have left is definitely not enough for a round trip.

Then begins the mad race to find gas. Impossible. In addition, I notice that after my visit to the mine police's headquarters, we are being watched. When we eventually do find some gas, two plainclothes men intervene and stop the attendant from filling up the tank. The gas is strictly reserved for military use.

No gas to continue the expedition, nor for the return trip back. No telephone to contact Deborah or Damien. Impossible to ask the Governor a second time for help. The Portugue ex-army commander goes to see if his old army buddies can help. That evening he comes up with nineteen precious gallons of premium. We celebrate the event by opening up several tins of corned beef. On Friday the thirteenth, for some reason hoping this will bring us good luck, we set off towards the province of Luanda Norte.

Local police stop us at the first road block, but the authorization we show them is irrefutable. At the second check point, this time the provincial police stop us and try to persuade us to turn back warning of various dangers such as the bad condition of the roads and the risk of bandits. But our destination is so close now that I won't be put off by anything or anyone. At 50 miles from the mines, we enter a valley before passing a mountain range that will lead to the volcanic plateaux of the diamond area. Suddenly, we see an excited group of people struggling around three trucks that cannot be driven forward nor backwards. Apparently just an hour before we arrived, there had been several violent explosions and the passage through the valley is now completely blocked. Talking with the people, I find a missionary from Guinea-Conakry who speaks perfect French. He tells me he is on his way to the village of Kafunfo. "The police themselves set off these explosions – if they had intended to block our way, they couldn't have done a better job. This is the only way to reach Kafunfo. I'm going back home, I can't stay in this crazy country any longer, it took me five days to get here!"

Just a coincidence? Destiny? Or perhaps the bosses of the mines, with their mafialike links with the mine police, who simply want to keep us from discovering the richness of these deposits? For, if I reveal their true yield, the dealers will no longer be able to hand over only part of the daily take and keep the rest for themselves. Having understood the situation all too clearly, I decide to call a halt to the expedition and return to Luanda. Again, impossible hotels, Malanje, N'Dalatando, then the capital, which we reach Monday evening.

Politician vs Dealer

Deborah and Damien, now having become friends as a result of the problems I have created for both of them, are extremely relieved to see me, but at the same time disappointed that after nine days in Angola, I have not been able to see one diamond. Deborah, feeling somewhat responsible for this unsuccessful trip, does everything in her power to find a solution. She has some contacts among government officials.

I spend Tuesday and Wednesday following her from one Ministry to another until we finally end up at the Ministry of Mining and Natural Resources. His Excellency Mr Arthur Ben, after a long discussion, personally arranges for me to visit Kafunfo as soon as possible and orders La Codian to issue without delay the authorization necessary to visit the mines.

In exchange, I promise him a complete and detailed report of the current situation of the deposits there. A call to the Minister of Interior and a helicopter as well as military protection is organized. On Thursday, we see to a few other administrative and technical details, and finally everything is set for early morning Friday.

My return to Europe being planned for the same day at midnight, I'm worried since if I miss the flight, there won't be another one for another week, which will fall right during the Christmas holidays.

Shadows of the Mafia

I see prowling shadows in the street, suspicious faces keeping a watch on the Rispel residence. I don't say anything to Damien about it, to spare him any more worries than he already has, knowing perfectly well that his problems will be over with my imminent departure.

However, since Deborah has special security protection, I ask her if she can spend the evening and night with us at the villa, since she will be taking me at 5:00 a.m. to the military heliport in any case. When she agrees, I feel safer and decide to have my observers' identities checked out and try to discover what their motives are. At about 6:00 p.m., I take my luggage and go to the hotel. Part of the group of spies follows me and the others remain around the villa. My departure creates some confusion and attracts the attention of Deborah's guards. They intervene and discover that my observers are in fact only common thieves convinced that I have money or diamonds in the villa.

After this "happy end" to the incident, Debora

asks to go back home, it's already 10:00 p.m.

Kafunfo at Last

The helicopter takes off at dawn with the first rays of the sun. At 8:00 a.m. we make our first refueling guarded by two MIG 21s. At 10:00 a.m. we're in Kafunfo!

A miracle, we should have done this before...the commander tells us we must leave no later than 2:00 p.m. to be in Luanda before nightfall. This is perfectly fine with me, since I have to be at the airport at 10:00 p.m. for my flight home.

So, I have a full four hours.

Some armed men search me apologetically and after a short ride around the village, they take me to the head of La Codian, who checks my papers and then asks, "Why do you want to film the mines?"

"Because I'm a gemmologist. I'm interested in learning more about them."

"Isn't it enough to just visit, do you absolutely have to film them?"

"Of course I have to film, otherwise I'll never be able to illustrate my lecture to my colleagues."

"In that case, I can authorize you to film solely from the helicopter, not from the ground."

"You are very kind, thank you very much."

I have thus lost all hope of seeing the diamonds, especially when the two soldiers accompanying me are replaced by three guards, an Englishman, a Brazilian and a South African. Soldiers are not allowed to fly over the monopoly's territories, except in time of war. We set off for Luzamba, a fifteen-minute flight. Someone points out from the aircraft the locations of the mines or former mines, the sorting facilities and the entrances to the diamond galleries. A ten-minute tour then, return to the base. Such a lot of time and money wasted for only ten short minutes! But I'm not the kind of person who gives up easily, and I decide to make one last try.

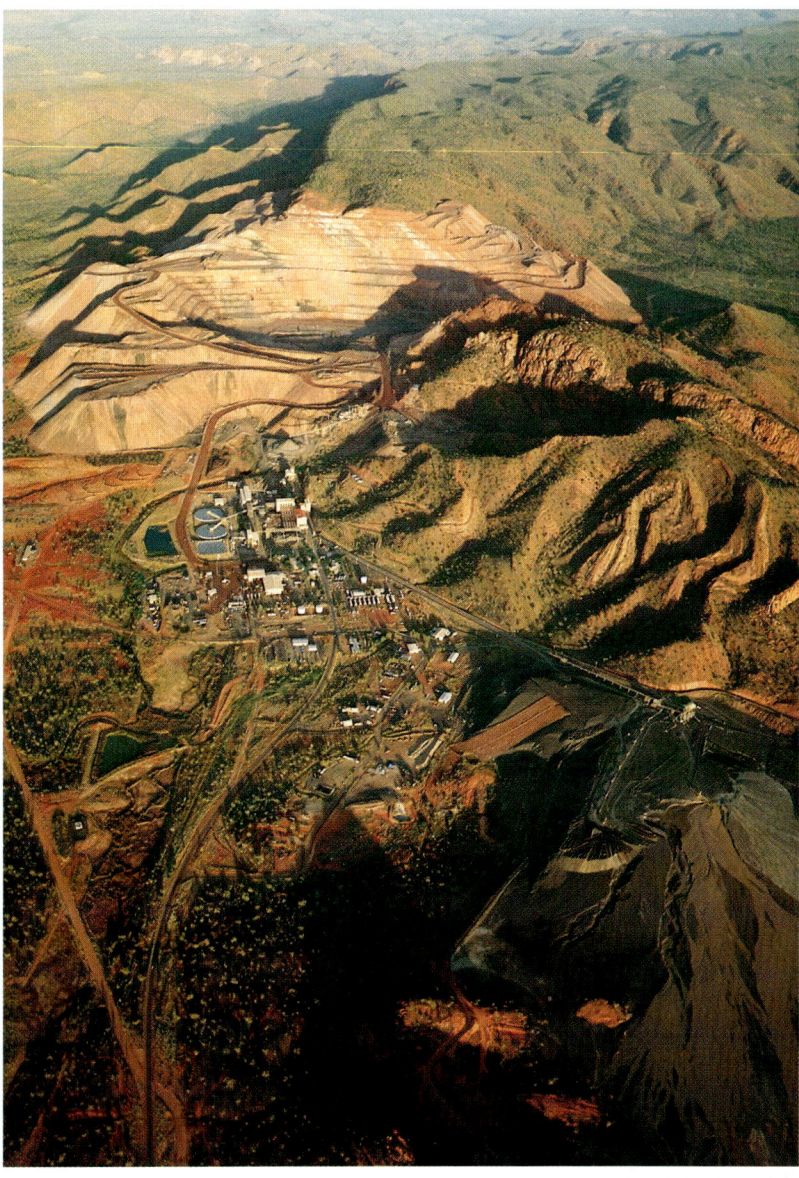

Aerial view of the diamond mine of Argyle (Australia).

Japanese Diamonds

It is noon, we are heading back to Luanda again, the two soldiers having returned to their places in the plane, while the roar of the propeller more or less helps cover up the sinking feeling of general disappointment. A few minutes after take off we are outside the territory of the mining concession, but still above the diamond zones where children search tirelessly for precious crystals.

The idea of returning to Europe without having seen one diamond bothers me and I'm dissatisfied with myself. I ask the pilot to land. He categorically refuses. It is almost Christmas Eve, I still have a thousand five hundred dollars in my pocket; I offer the soldiers a gift of five hundred each if they land. The money is barely out of my pocket that the commander is already requesting authorization to land, reporting a "technical problem."

I am allowed to stay on the ground for half an hour, using the supposed repair as an alibi. I'm just out of the plane when a dozen native children run up and invite me to follow them. A few feet away they point to several holes dug into the ground. "Diamonds! Diamonds!" *Mui* diamonds, *mui* diamonds!" the youngsters shout. At the same time, they scream down the holes in the earth. A few instants later children, all about ten or fifteen years old, begin climbing out of the holes, one after the other like little mice out of a big Swiss cheese. One of them, a little older than the others, half-covered in mud and bleeding, runs up to me with a little pouch in his hand, containing a nice lot of transparent and white crystals. "A thousand dollars for all!" He cries. What a deal! This lot should be worth at least a hundred thousand dollars!

I take out my magnifying glass to examine the large

piece, eight carats at least. But then I am immediately filled with disgust. Usually, I can converse with gems by the use of a special fluid that never lets me down. It is a false rough diamond. Is it possible? In a mine! I can't believe it. With my inseparable diamond pen, I test for hardness. A magnificent scratch, deep and powdery, on the side of the stone. Excellent "Made in Japan" imitation, how dreadful! Too bad I don't have any money left or I would buy them, if only just to show our laboratories as a curiosity.

High Altitude Diamonds

Now I don't even have the luxury of regrets left. I can think of nothing other than getting out of here as quickly as possible and going home. However, this is not going to be so easy. Suddenly the weather turns, forcing us to land at the civil airport in Malanje again.

Fortunately, though it is a violent storm, it passes quickly. We are just ready to leave again when a man of mixed race approaches the aircraft and politely asks if he can pay me for a ride, there's an empty seat in the back, and he offers me three hundred dollars.

I ask him to give a hundred to each of the men. We take off. The fatigue, the purring of the motor, and the monotony of the terrain lull me into a deep sleep. The men talk to the passenger about me, and as I wake up, he hands me a headphone and explains in English that he is a dealer in rough stones and that at that very moment he is carrying more than five thousand carats on him. I ask to see them. A real first – I have certainly never had the opportunity of expertising gems in a helicopter before, quite original.

There is absolutely no doubt that these are real diamonds, and of very good quality too. This lot has already been sold to some people in Lisbon for two million dollars, but if I can offer a little more, he could sell them to me instead...that would spare him from having to go through Customs, he explains nonchalantly.

Persecuted to the End

Yes, I have seen diamonds in Angola, but not in their gangue. The ones in their original rock mass were false. Out of genuine sympathy and so that I will not return home completely empty-handed, Deborah contacts some of her acquaintances to arrange for me to see some lots before leaving.

When I arrive at the villa, there is Deborah, Damien, a white man, a black man and a man of mixed race. A nice range of colors.

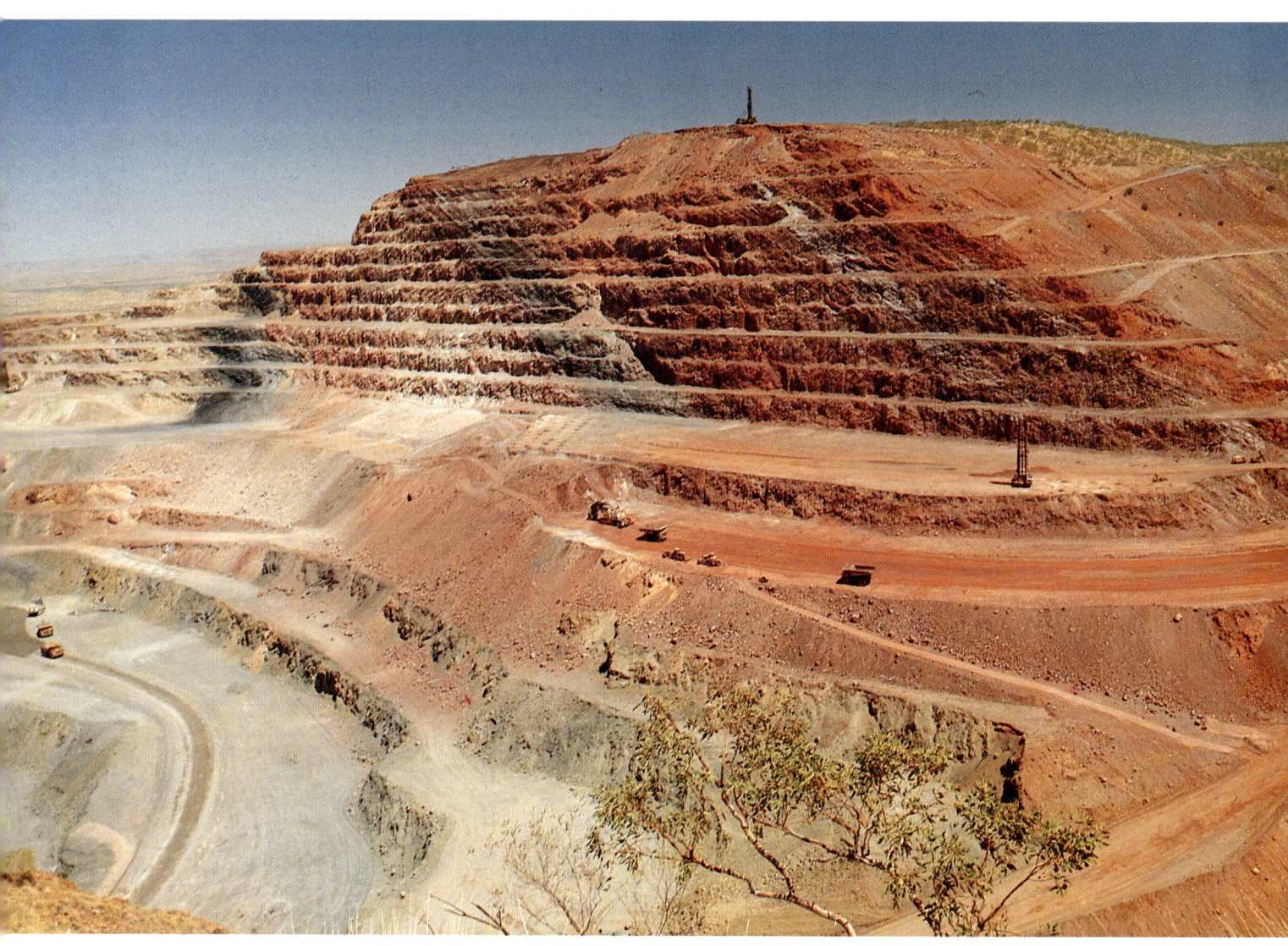

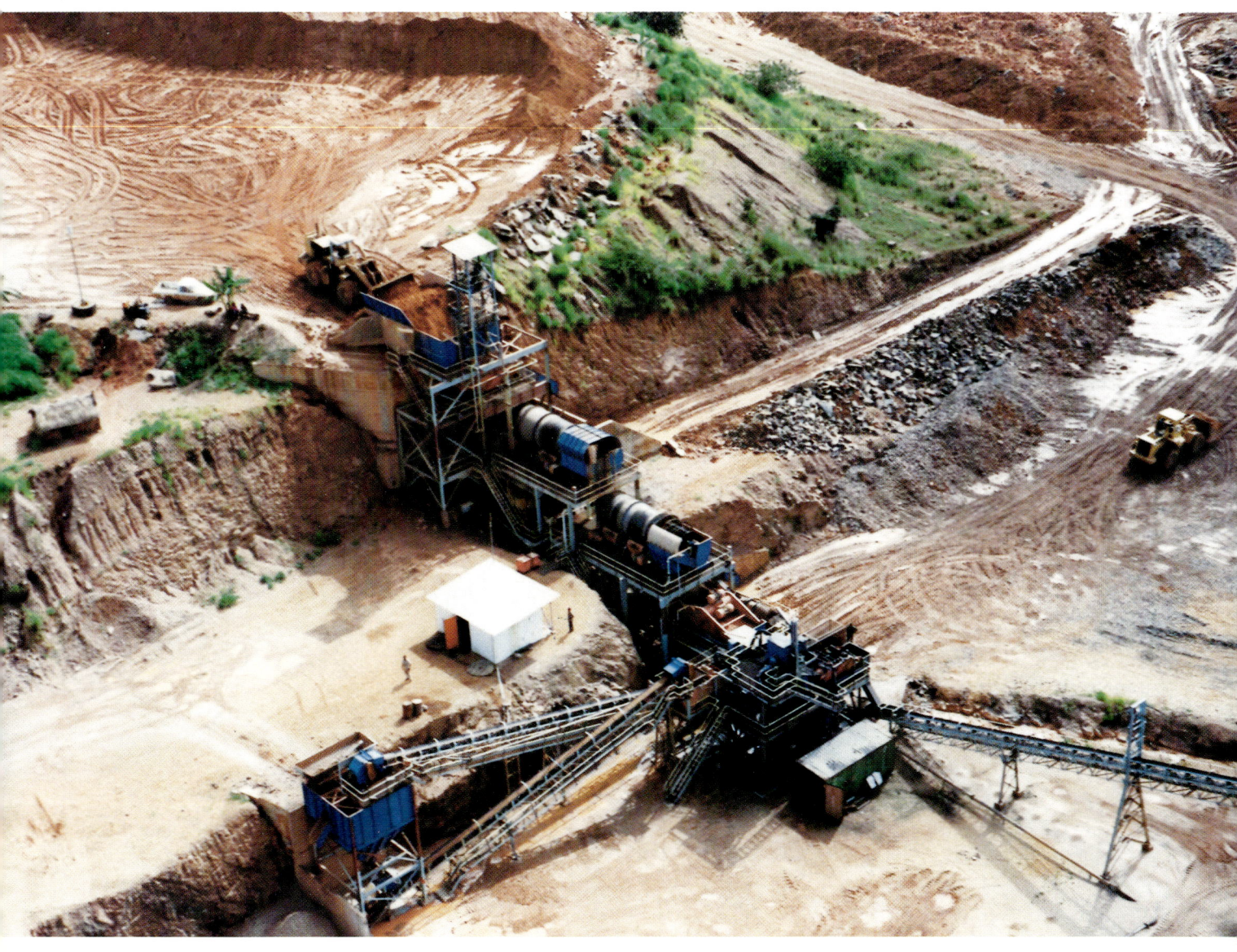

The three guests have small pouches of stones. The white man begins to show me some… it is no longer repulsion that I feel but downright nausea. Well, finally I understand why none of the cars in the city have windshields! So this is where the pieces of shattered glass go. The other two men have the same type of merchandise. Deborah is very upset, she is only consoled when I tell her the story of the Japanese diamonds.

As soon as I get home, I call my former professor and close friend in Antwerp to describe what I've seen.

"Rest assured, there is worse. A colleague received false rough rubies from Vietnam that had been manufactured in Austria, and they even had the typical inclusions of real corundums. They had been bought in the new mines of the golden triangle."

"Guess that'll be my next stop!" I tell him.

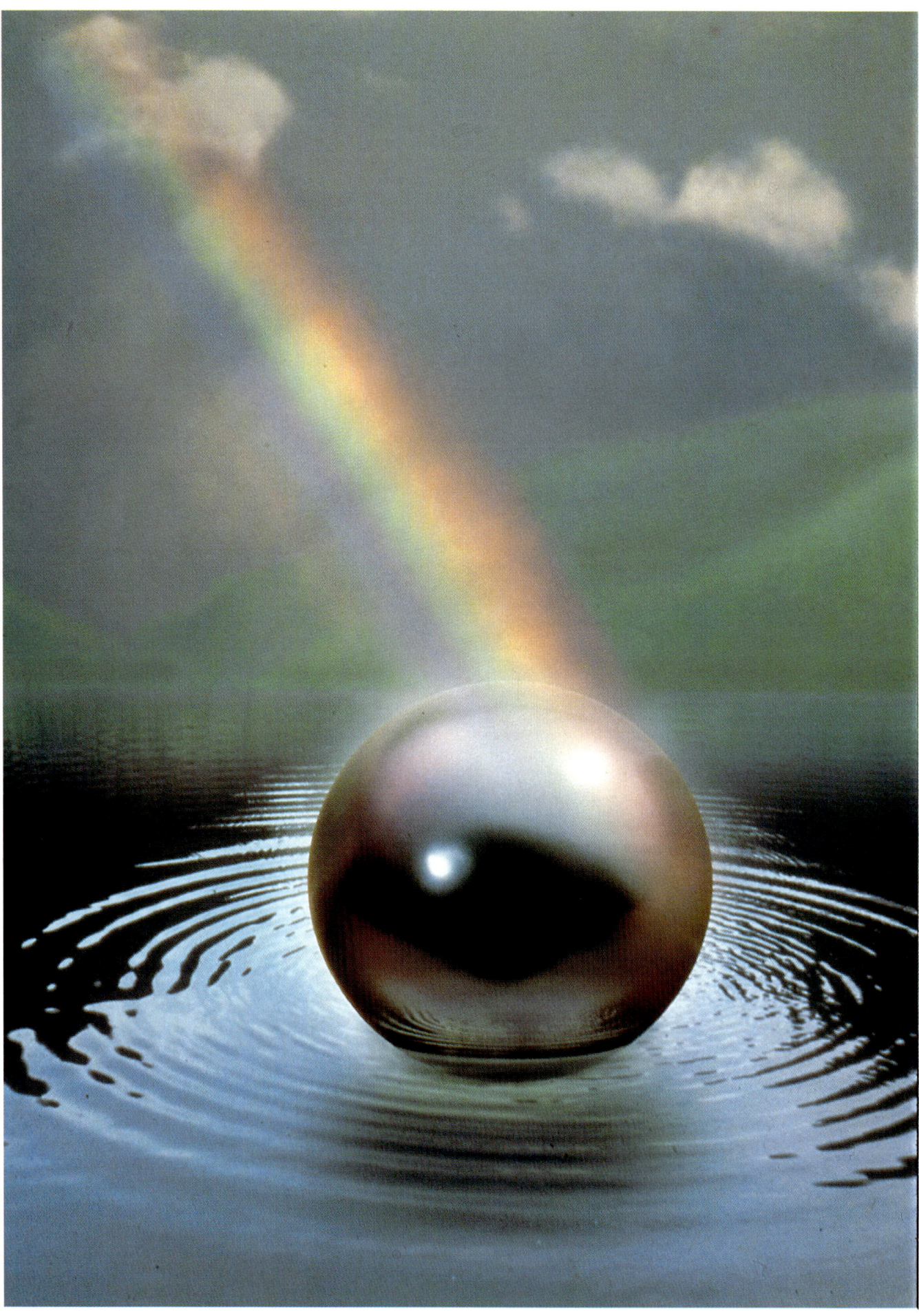

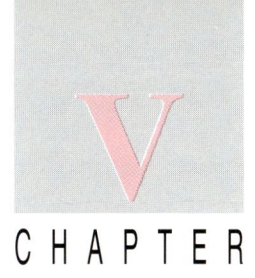

CHAPTER V

Pearl

GENERAL INFORMATION

How it got its name Apparent options are: the Latin *spherula* (little sphere) or *perula* (little pear); or possibly it comes from *perna*, the name of a mollusk. A gem whose fame dates back into man's ancient past, it has never known moments of decline, but instead has always characterized our most significant cultural and historic times.

Varieties Although the subdivisions here described could be introduced later, we list them now to emphasize a very clear-cut classification: natural pearls, cultured pearls, and imitation pearls. Strictly speaking, the term "pearl" should only be applied to the natural product; when we are speaking of the cultured variety, it is obligatory to label it as such. "Pearl imitations" refer to totally man-made products aimed solely at imitating the appearance of the gem. This concept bears repeating: the natural pearl, the cultured pearl, and the imitation are not three varieties of the same gem, but three completely different products that must be distinguished as such.

Natural and cultured pearls may be selected on the basis of color, shape, and the fact that they are produced by mollusks in a salt or fresh water environment.

Both natural and cultured are available in silvery white, white, pinkish white, a light pink, pink, creamy pink, pinkish cream, cream, greenish cream, golden, pinkish gold, yellow, greenish yellow, pinkish green, green, bluish green, a pinkish-lustered blue, blue, dark blue, silvery gray, gray, dark gray, and black; pearls that display truly vibrant colors are also defined as "fantasia."

We have a choice of many shapes: round, chiefly used for necklaces; pear or drop, a good choice for earrings and pendants; button, which has a flattened side; baroque or seed-pearl, in highly irregular contours; blister; mabe; and finally a pearl tagged "mostro" ("monster"), due to its unusual form.

According to expert Lovell Auguste Reeve there are 71 species of mollusks with a mother-of-pearl shell lining that can "mother" pearls.

Some interesting sidelights It is believed that pink pearls endow the wearer with fame and success, while the blue shades help make romantic dreams come true. Black pearls grant the gift of understanding yourself and others. And all pearls aid the wearer in overcoming psychosomatic disturbances, and prevent allergies and even poisoning.

The western world had its introduction to pearls when Alexander the Great defeated Darius III, last King of Persia, and gathered a fabulous booty that included some extraordinarily valuable pearls.

Some texts tell us that when Cleopatra wanted to pay homage to Marc Antony, she offered him a magnificently large pearl as it was dissolving in a glass containing wine and vinegar. Even if this chemical reaction is possible, it takes place

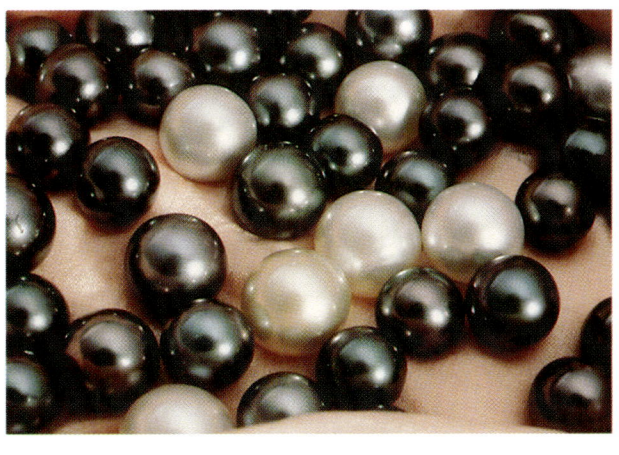

Chemical Formula: $CaCO_3$, $C_{32}H_{48}N_2O_{11}$ – calcium carbonate (82-86%), conchioline (10-14%), water (2-4%).
Hardness: 3 – 4 (Mohs scale)
Specific Gravity: 2.60 – 2.80
Color: white, pink, cream, gold, green, blue, grey, black

only over a long period of time, and therefore our charming anecdote would appear to be more fiction than fact.

Celebrated pearls

The private collection of Henry Thomas Hope contains a 450-carat pearl, nearly cylindrical in shape, 51 mm high, and with a maximum circumference of 114 mm and a minimum of 83 mm; as for color – it is three-fourths white and one-fourth bronze. The famous Peregrine Pearl, weighing 27.88 carats, and supposedly owned by Mary Tudor, daughter of Henry VIII, was bought at auction in 1969 by Richard Burton for 37,000 dollars; today, it is housed in the Moscow Museum. Philip II of Spain owned a 34-carat pearl of Panamanian provenance. Noted among the Crown Jewels of France we find La Reine des Perles, weighing 27.5 carats, and La Regente at about 84.25 carats. According to rumors, the world's largest pearl, at 1,595 carats, was found in 1934 in the Philippines, on the island of Palawan: some say it was sold in 1969 under the name "Pearl of Allah," for well over a million dollars. But all of this is just hearsay, for the very existence of this pearl is hotly debated.

Natural pearls

Though 4,500 years ago oriental peoples believed that pearls were born of drops of dew fallen into a mollusk, the birth of a pearl is actually an anomalous phase in a mollusk's biological development.

It's worth repeating this basic concept – that the formation of a natural pearl is a purely accidental and, obviously, natural occurrence since it is the product of a mollusk's extraordinary reaction when a foreign body penetrates within its shell. The foreign element may be a parasite (trematode or cestode), a tiny grain of sand, or even just a minuscule piece of seashell. From the moment the mollusk harbors an intrusive body it reacts by forming a calcareous concretion around it. And so a pearl is born, and will continue to grow until its mollusk producer dies.

As early as 1852 Filippo De Filippi (Assistant Director of the Museum of Natural History in Milan and later Director of the Museum in Turin) discovered that pearls produced by freshwater mollusks originated in intrusive parasites encysted in the mollusk mantle; later, Tokichi Nishikawa, from Japan, realized that a pearl forms around a foreign element only when it is also involved with the mantle's epithelial tissue. In fact, the foreign body may attach to the mother-of-pearl lining in the host mollusk to produce a blister pearl with a flat side where it has adhered to the shell lining; or it may encyst in the fold of the mantle, producing normal, more or less round pearls. Around the miniscule intruder concentric layers form, composed of foliations of calcium carbonate – aragonite – and fine films of conchioline, which confer that unique luster called "orient," or – to use a less fascinating but more scientific term – iridescence.

Pearl-producing mollusks are chiefly gastropods and lamellibranchs. Marine lamellibranchia include: the *Pinctada meleagrina, margaritifera, fucata, radiata, margaritifera/mazatlantica* variety, *maxima, Pinna nobilis*. For the gasterpod we could cite: *Strombus gigas* and *Haliotis*. Two important freshwater mollusks in pearl culture are the *Unio* and the *Hyriopsis schegeli*.

At this point, it becomes easier to understand the fact that pearl color can depend on:

– the pearl-producing mollusk;

– the mollusk's specific water environment;

– the coloring of the conchioline membrane nearest the pearl's surface.

Let's look at some examples. The presence of phytoplankton may produce a slightly greenish coloring. Among the minerals, azurite creates blue tones, smithsonite introduces a grey color and magnesite, the highly rated golden tone of Burmese pearls.

Pearl's prized quality is luster, a term denoting the brilliant effect created by its surface homogeneity, obtained by a polishing process.

Growth is slow: 2,000 layers are needed to increase thickness by just 1 mm; and since three or four layers are produced in a day, it takes six years before a pearl attains an 8 mm diameter. Difficulties in gathering pearls not only depend on the fact that only one oyster in forty will produce a pearl; a further obstacle is that out of ten pearls found only one will be suitable for jewelry making. So four hundred pearl-producing oysters would have to be fished in order to obtain one acceptable pearl. In reality, this is now a theoretical discussion, because the gathering of natural pearls has come to an almost total halt. We can get an idea of the current situation by recalling that as late as the start of this century there were 3,600 boats employed in pearl fishing in the Gulf of Persia; in 1925 that number had dropped to 600. Now there isn't even one pearl-fishing boat in this area; for in the Gulf War, massive quantities of petroleum were released and allowed to disperse and sink to the Gulf bottom, producing a probably irreversible ecological disaster. In fact, natural pearls are victims of environmental pollution.

Areas for pearl gathering

Though no longer active, the following areas are part of the history

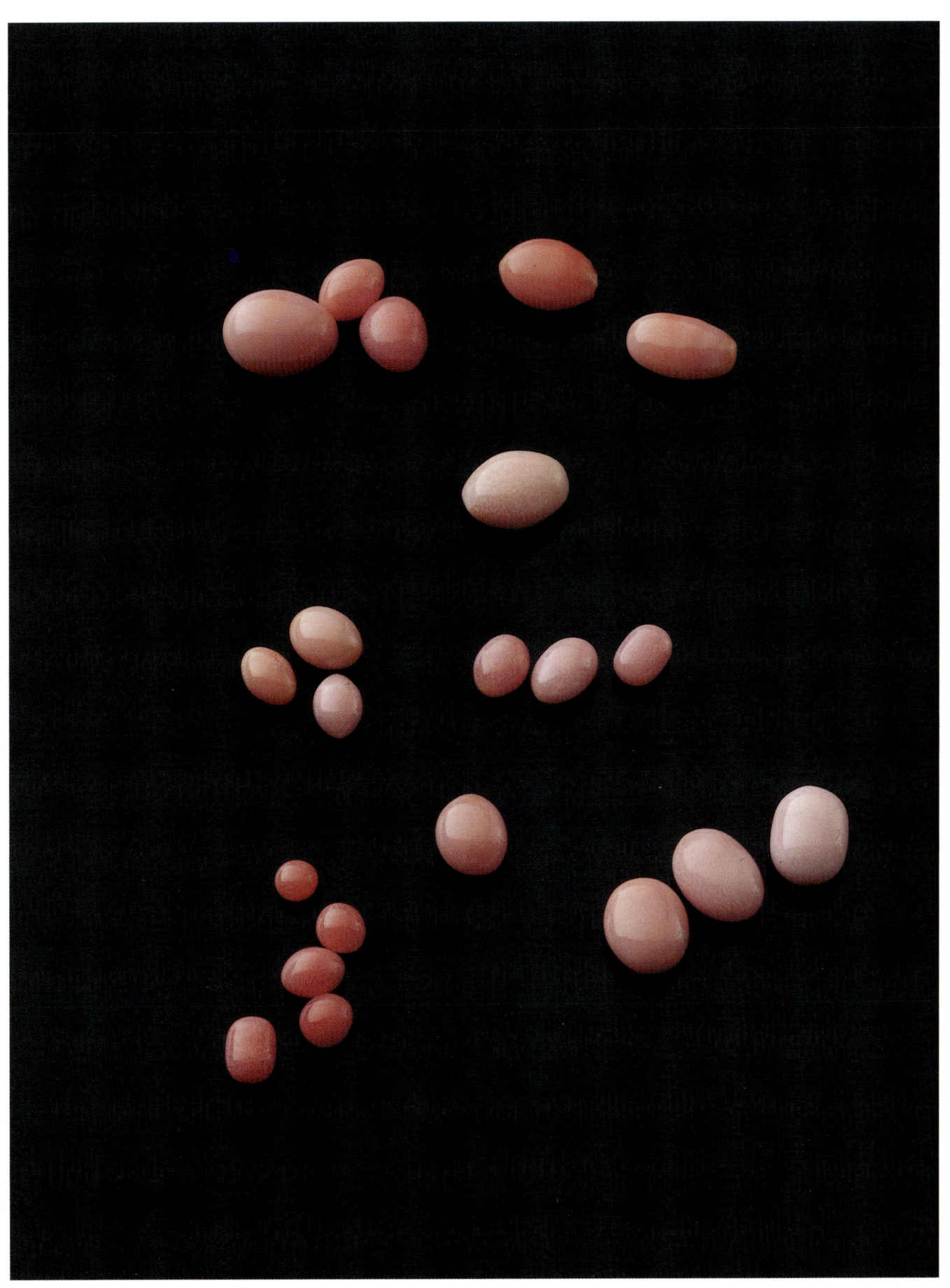

Aurelio Abrami.
Private collection of Conch pearls.
The "flame" effect can be noted which is typical of these fascinating pearls.

of pearls: the Persian Gulf; the Mannar Gulf, which separates Sri Lanka from India; and the Red Sea. The gems fished in these zones were called "oriental pearls." Less important locations are: the Arabian Sea; off the coast of Bombay; Shark Bay, along the northwestern coast of Australia; around the innumerable Polynesian and Micronesian islands; and in the waters off Tahiti, Venezuela, Mexico, and Panama.

Conch pearls A particular type of natural pearl produced by the gastropod *Strombus Gigas*. Conch may come from the Latin *concha* for pearl-producing seashell or it may derive directly from the fact that both the English and the Germans use the word *conch* to indicate gastropods. This mollusk can grow as large as 20 to 30 cm and weigh from 2 to 3 kilograms; its natural habitat is in the territorial waters of the Caribbean Sea and the Bermudas. Colorings here may range from varying shades of pink to white, yellow, or brown; salmon pink is very much prized, but the most sought-after varieties are the oval-shaped pearls in colors from deep pink to red. It is best to remember that the color of these pearls is not always stable and tends to lighten after long exposure to the ultraviolet rays in natural sunlight.

Normally these pearls are a bit irregular in shape, generally longer than the standard, and rounded off. Weight is about half a carat though Conch pearls weighing as much as ten carats have been found; the largest known weighs about 45 carats. For a while, smaller sizes had quite a success in Art Nouveau jewelry; but after the First World War when Art Deco took the stage, this minute size was seldom any longer used. Lovely to look at, but can we call them pearls in the full sense? For there is no conchioline in their chemical make-up. On the one hand the famous CIBJO says "yes," and suggests labelling them "Pink Pearls." Yet until recently the American GIA Laboratory defined them as simple calcareous concretions, though recent certificates carry the tag "Conch Pearl." Italian UNI adds its weight, affirming that pearls found in the *Strombus Gigas* have every right to the title.

Under the lens these pearls reveal an identifying spotty structure referred to as "flamelike."

So far, it has not been possible to obtain cultured Conch pearls; therefore those existing specimens that are outstanding for weight, color or shape must be categorized as rarities.

Cultured pearls As we have seen, the formation of a natural pearl is a totally spontaneous event; whereas human intervention is indispensable in producing cultured pearls. First attempts at obtaining this product were made by Linneo in 1748, and in 1761 he did at last manage to get some very small, almost round cultured pearls; but this research direction was later abandoned. The world waited until July 1893 for a similar success when, after five years of study, Japan's Kokichi Mikimoto finally produced seven half-pearls.

Analagous results were achieved by Tatsuhei Mise in 1904 and Tokichi Nishikawa in 1907. But it was only in 1914 that Kokichi Mikimoto hit upon the technique of first wrapping the intrusive nucleus with the mantle's epithelium and only then introducing the nucleus into the host mollusk. To fully grasp this explanation, the reader will need more details on the total process.

Japan's cultured pearls In the country of its birth, pearl culture found the best possible conditions in which it could develop and become a national patrimony, both commercially and culturally.

Here are a few basic points regarding the key culture phases:

1 – The *Pinctada Fucata*, discovered 130 years ago, is the most commonly used pearl-producing mollusk, familiarly referred to by the Japanese as "Akoya." *Pinctada Martenesi* is a new variation, quite recently selected. Just for the record: Japan's territorial waters contain about 5,000 types of mollusks.

The first phase in the culture, then, concerns Akoya breeding, which takes place in specialized farms that care for the mollusks until they are mature and follow their development with rigorous selection and testing. After approximately three years the Akoya is fished out of its bed since it is now ready to receive the intruder nucleus.

Until 1950 this task was performed by the famous *Ama*, who fished out the pearl-bearing oysters one by one. Today these Ama are employed in organizing oyster baskets and equipment or, more often than not, simply fishing for the benefit of the tourists.

2. A cultured pearl is produced by introducing a miniscule sphere, the nucleus, into a space already prepared within the shell of specific mollusks. In fact, once cultivators preferred the shell of a freshwater bivalve of Chinese provenance ("la Moule d'Eau Douce Tenshin"); then, after the Second World War the shells of certain Mississippi bivalves were highly prized ("la Orteil de Cochon" and "la Tête de Nègre," both Unio varieties). Currently, producers are studying the possibility of using plastic nuclei. Finding the right nucleus to insert in the mollusk

to cause it to produce a cultured pearl is made difficult by the necessity to reduce to a minimum the risk that the mollusk will reject the intruder.

3. With both mollusk and nucleus, the cultivator moves to the next, and highly delicate operation: inserting the nucleus. Specialized personnel open the oyster valve, cut the pearl-producing sac and insert this nucleus. But before insertion, a third of the nucleus's surface area is covered with a small rectangle of epithelium tissue taken either from the same mollusk or, more probably, from another. An expert in this field can insert about 500 nuclei a day.

And these may have varying dimensions: normally two are inserted at a time, though this depends very much on the development phase of the pearl-producing oyster.

4. Now the Akoya is kept in control conditions for six weeks, during which time there is a 60% possibility of rejection. Once this danger is over, those mollusks that still contain a nucleus are placed in heavy net baskets attached to special rafts and brought out to sea. It is important that this phase coincides with that period of the year when sea water temperatures range from 18°C to 25°C; or, in Japan, during the season running from early April to early July. The mollusks remain in sea water for varying lengths of time, according to the diameter of the inserted nucleus. For 8 mm nuclei the mollusks may remain as long as three years in all; for nuclei under 4 mm diameter the time period is clearly much shorter.

Throughout the entire period of cultivation the rafts are shifted around in a constant hunt for those areas richest in plankton. Water temperatures are checked daily, and every two or three months the oysters are cleaned one by one.

And all of this human work takes place while the mollusk builds a nacreous cyst around the intruder. The Akoya covers its guest nucleus with pearly layer upon layer until a cultured pearl is formed. So when we speak of such pearls we are talking about an artificially inserted nucleus upon which the mollusk performs its natural task. Because of the natural layer growth we are able to call the product a pearl, though always with a "cultured" tag. Referring to these layers, we have the following generic classification for such pearls, organized according to thickness.

excellent = a thickness of 0.6 mm or more
very good = a thickness of 0.5 to 0.59 mm
good = a thickness of 0.4 to 0.49 mm
fair = a thickness of 0.3 to 0.39 mm
poor = a thickness of less than 0.3 mm

Here it should be noted that the Japan Pearl Exporters' Association works assiduously to guarantee that cultivated pearls at less than 0.3 mm are not exported.

5. Once the time for attaining a suitable thickness has passed, mollusk gathering begins; and it is best if this phase takes place from the end of December to the beginning of February while water temperature is about 15° C. For, in cold water conditions, the Akoya produces a pearly layer with a more highly rated brilliance and sheen.

Following the gathering, extraction, and preliminary cleaning of the pearls, they are subdivided into three classes: high, medium, and low quality.

6. Finally, as long as six years after starting the first cultivation phase, the Akoya are ready to be sold at auction. In only two months of sales each year, the buyers must round up the purchases on which they base their annual work.

To give an idea of the quantity produced for each size, the table below is an instant guide:

Cultured Pearl Production in Japan (expressed in tons)					
Year	1986	1987	1988	1989	1990
Size					
8 mm and+	4,93 (7,4%)	6,42 (9,7%)	9,19 (13,1%)	10,26 (14,8%)	13,27 (18,9%)
6-8 mm	42,09 (63,2%)	43,72 (66,2%)	47,21 (67,1%)	45,93 (66,4%)	45,59 (64,8%)
5-6 mm	11,87 (17,8%)	9,39 (14,2%)	8,9 (12,7%)	7,92 (11,5%)	5,8 (8,2%)
– di 5 mm	5,2 (7,8%)	4,56 (6,9%)	3,36 (4,8%)	3,32 (4,8%)	3,95 (5,6%)
half pearls	2,45 (3,7%)	1,92 (2,9%)	1,66 (2,4%)	1,69 (2,4%)	1,73 (2,5%)
TOTAL	66,54 (100%)	66,01 (100%)	70,32 (100%)	69,12 (100%)	70,34 (100%)

Final classification of these cultured pearls is effected on the basis of: size, shape, thickness of cyst covering, color, sheen (also called "luster"), and how "clean" it is (i.e. degree of surface imperfections, if any).

In the end, high quality pearls comprise only 5% of total production; 45% have no commercial value; and the roughly 50% that remain, classified as good or fair quality, go into normal trade channels.

After classification, cultured pearls are pierced and strung and are sold in bundles consisting of several strands called chokers, each one formed of "uniform" diameter cultured pearls (i.e. varying no more than half a millimeter).

Strands, of course, may vary in length, and will thus be designated with special names such as: Graduation (14-16 inches, or 35-40 cm); Princess (16-20 inches, or 40-50 cm); Matinée (20-26 inches, or 50-66 cm); Opera (26-36 inches, or 66-90 cm); Rope (more than 40 inches, or lengths over one meter). A pearl necklace featuring a large central pearl with both sides formed of regularly diminishing sizes is termed "Chute."

In Japan, the official unit of weight for cultured pearls is the *momme*, which corresponds to 3.75 grams and, therefore, 18.75 carats.

Mabe pearls

A combination of culture and manufacture, they are also labelled "Japanese half pearls." *Mabe* is the Japanese term for the *Pteria Penguin* mollusk, which is put into service along with a specialized technique, to obtain these hemispheric pearls. In fact half an orb of agalmatolite – or currently even plastic – is attached to the shell's inner lining so that the mollusk will enclose it in a nacreous cyst. When the pearl is gathered, the half nucleus that had been tucked in is removed and in the fragile cavity a mother-of-pearl hemisphere is inserted in its place and attached with special adhesive. A surface mother-of-pearl disk is applied to the base to cover the insertion, and the Mabe is ready for sale. Diameters for these pearls range from 15-25 mm.

Cultured pearls without nucleus

A freshwater culture, it was first practiced in Japan in Lake Biwa (*Biwa-Ko* in Japanese, in which *"Ko"* means lake). All cultured pearls without nucleus are defined very simply as Biwa Pearls.

First experiments in this lake around 1920 adopted the bivalve mollusk *Hyriopsis Schlegeli*, which is still used today. The lining of this 20 cm-diameter greenish black oyster is grafted with strips of epithelium secretions, without addition of an artifical nucleus.

Usually about a dozen epithelium strips are grafted on, but in some cases, depending on the mollusk's development, as many as twenty may be employed. After two or three years, the mollusks produce about 7 mm pearls in the form of grains of rice. At times, to deliver more regular shapes, the pearls themselves, enclosed in epithelium secretions, are grafted into the mollusk lining, and the resulting second product may be as large as 12 mm.

This pearl-producing oyster has a very high yield, about 60% in terms of utility of final product; while grafting produces 100% results. Unfortunately, pollution in Lake Biwa waters has now severely reduced output, but there has been an important increase in freshwater culture production in recent years in China.

Keshi pearls

It should be added, to complete the above information, that if the empty mollusk is put back into the water after the pearl has been removed, then for some unknown reason, without nucleus insertion, the mollusk spontaneously produces slightly crushed 8 mm pearls, labelled *Keshi*. For certain fresh water bivalves this is a frequent phenomenon.

Regarding the Keshi (whose name stems from the Japanese term for poppy seed), it is hard to decide if they are natural or cultured products; for they are a spontaneous production, though in a mollusk previously manipulated by man in the initial stages.

Polynesian black pearls

Black pearls on today's market are cultured, produced with the techniques originating and developed in Japan. Their cultivation takes place almost exclusively in the Tuamotu-Gambier archipelago, in the waters off some of the French Polynesian islands, from whence their name.

Oysters used are the bivalve *Pinctada Margaritifera*, very common in the lagoon of

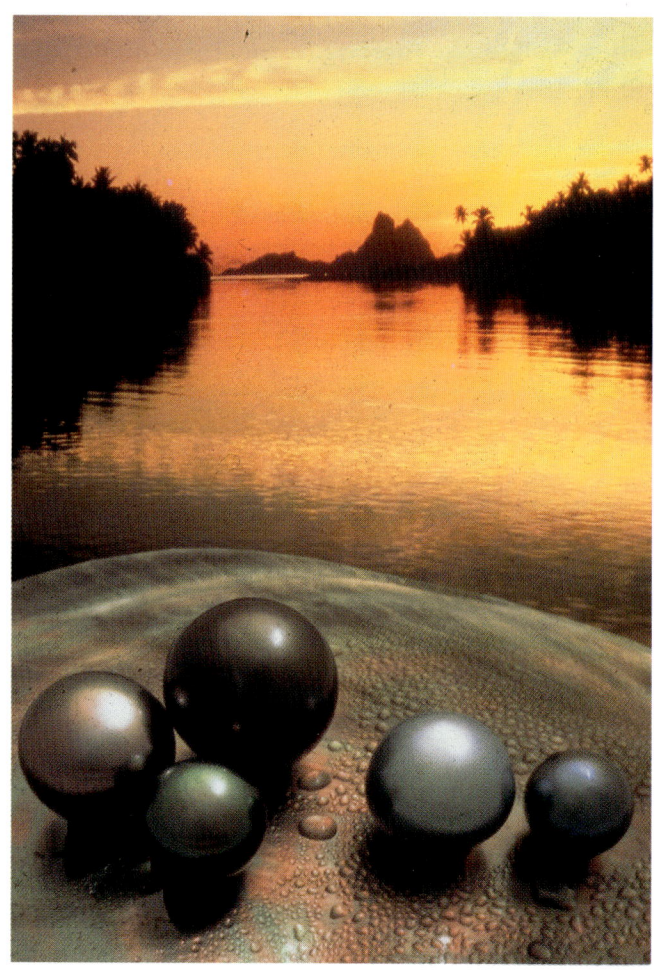

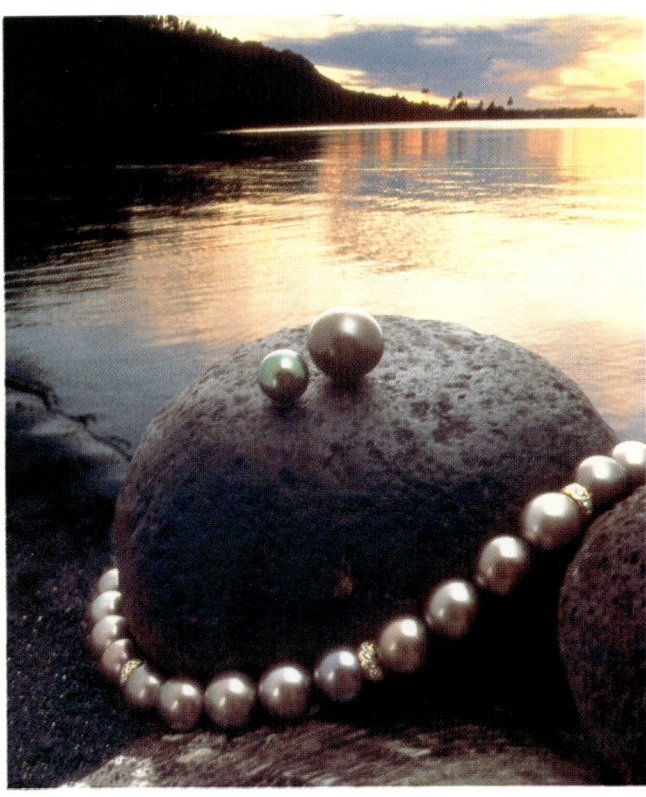

French Polynesia. They may weigh as much as 5 kilos and have a maximum diameter of 30 cm; the shell's lining is in a striking blackish green, which is often repeated in the color of the pearls.

To be precise, cultured black pearls have a blackish green tone, also called "peacock," as they shine with silvery, gray, and purple hues, an effect not to be confused with the Akoya blue variety. They have a fine size, often being as large as 18 mm in diameter, although the largest known cultured black pearl reaches 20.8 mm.

On average only 55% of the mollusks react positively to the graft; however, results are considered good if 30% of the cultured pearls gathered are idoneous for jewelry.

On the topic, some curious information: occasionally the *Pinctada Margaritifera* grafted for black-pearl growth loses the nucleus but exploits the remaining mantle fragment that enclosed it and proceeds to produce a pearl without nucleus.

Australian cultures Australia did not start cultivating pearls until 1956 when it began using Japanese techniques, adopting the *Pinctada Maxima* as pearl-producing mollusk.

At first only blister pearls were obtained, but now somewhat baroque-shaped cultured pearls are made, in a silvery white hue, weighing as much as 20 carats and having a 10 to 20 mm diameter. This mollusk graft to produce a blister pearl resembles the technique used for the Mabe: a mother-of-pearl nucleus fastened to the shell lining. Later dressing will result in a ¾ pearl since the attached part remains flat when filed away from the shell. And though the pearls are cultivated in Australia they are finished in Japan. There are also varieties of naturally produced blister pearls created when tiny animals or vegetable forms attach to the inner lining forming a protuberance around which the host mollusk deposits pearly layers. As these small bodies are covered, they degenerate creating gaseous substances. The final product is a perfectly hollow ampulla.

Distinguishing between natural and cultured pearls

First of all, it is best to keep in mind that the natural pearl is formed of concentric circles whereas the cultured pearl has quite a different structure, its most common form built on a nucleus of flat, parallel layers around which the mollusk secretes a nacreous veneer. One means of verifying natural pearls that are pierced is to use a simple lens to look down the hole and check the successive pearly layers, whose color intensifies going toward the center.

Examining cultured pearls in this way we note a distinct separation between the pearly surface layers and the nucleus, which is uniform and usually a diaphanous white. If performed by experienced operators, this examination usually provides adequate identification.

With unpierced pearls, however, we must turn to the well-equipped laboratory that makes X-ray photographs (which also show layer thickness in cultured pearls) or, for even better results, X-ray diffraction.

Imitations Imitation pearls were around more than three hundred years ago, when they were called "French pearls"; these were formed of hollow spheres filled in and covered over with a mixture of glue and fish scales, termed "oriental essence." Majorca pearls are actually imitation pearls, but have had great commercial success.

If you are looking to buy imitation pearls you might also run into Nikko pearls, formed of a spherical mother-of-pearl bead covered with a layer of resin – the surface does not react to artifical acids and has a nice iridescent effect.

At times we come across imitations labelled "pool pearls," to give the impression of a new sort of culture.

Aside from Nikko pearls, imitations usually have an orange peel surface that shows up under a 10x magnifier. If they are pierced, you will note that the membrane around the hole can be easily lifted with a common pin.

To conclude: if a pearl is to be evaluated, your first step must be to determine if it is an imitation, cultured, or natural creation.

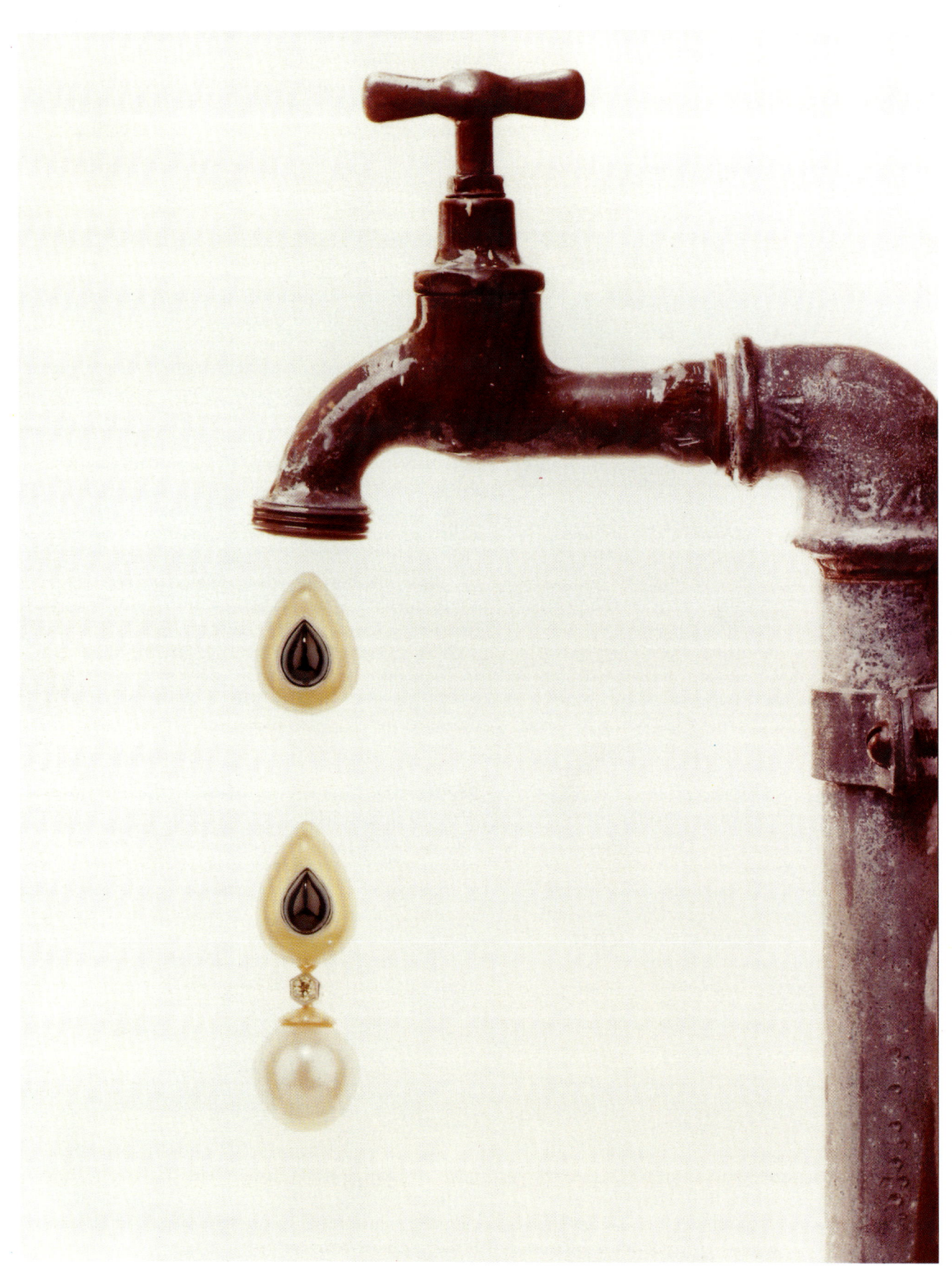

KRISTEN EHHALT-VUSEC.
134 *Pair of gold earrings with platinum, sapphires, diamonds, and pearls (interchangeable) of the South Seas.*

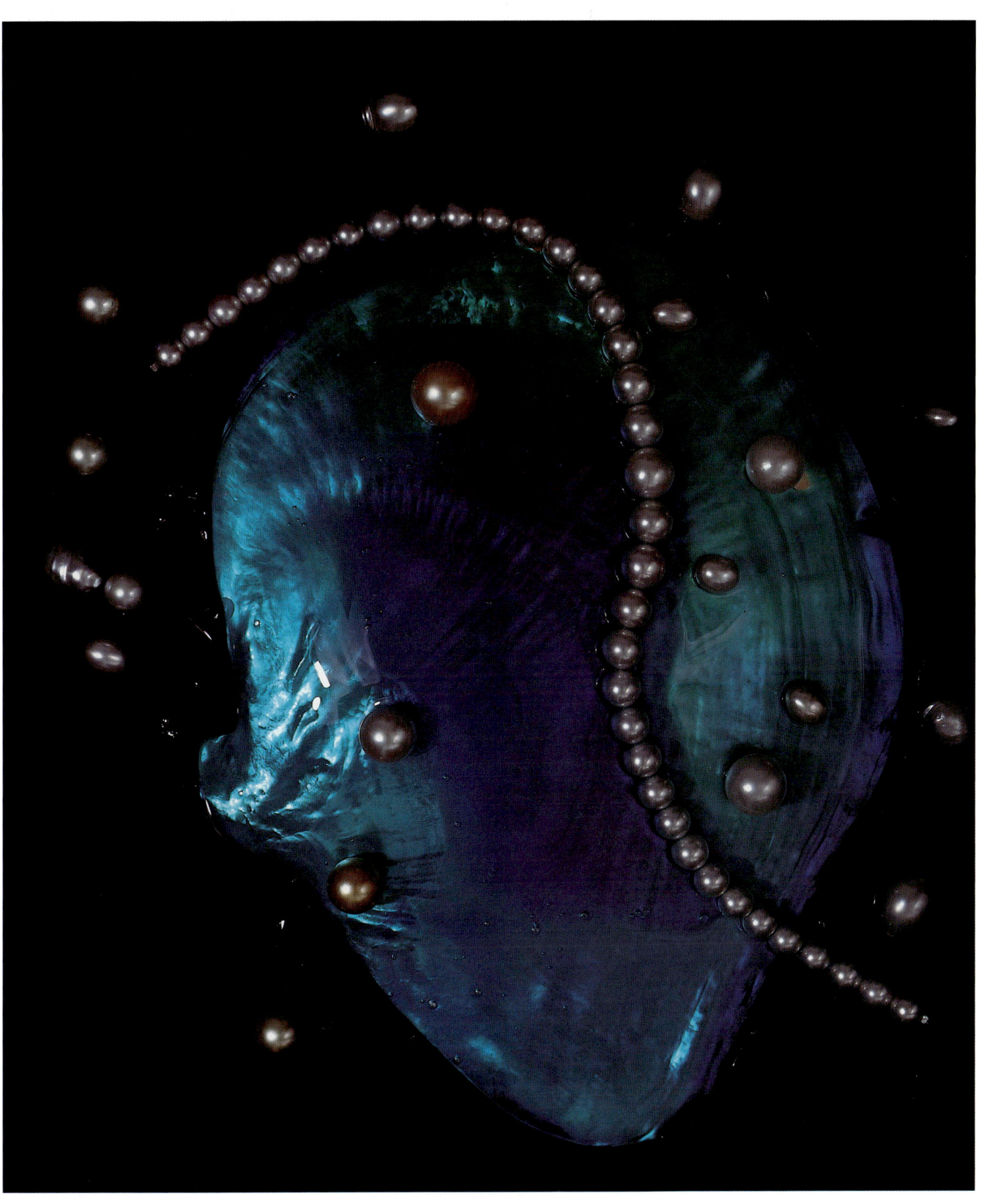

Rosario Autore.
Exceptional collection of Australian pearls.

Treatments Whether they be cultured or not, pearls can be artificially colored with quite simple substances; for a more sophisticated coloring treatment, experts turn to gamma rays or neutrons. In the former case, results are not homogeneous and simple lens observation can detect the simulation; if more sophisticated techniques have been adopted, we need a specialized laboratory to classify. Some commonly adopted procedures: light-colored cultured pearls turn black when treated with silver nitrate in an ammoniac solution; the resulting color is quite stable, though at times there are slight cracks on the surface due to the effect of silver salt.

Excellent results are obtained by the simple procedure of using artifically colored nuclei for grafting. The effect is quite pleasing for all shades, but pink is the most popular. A piece of

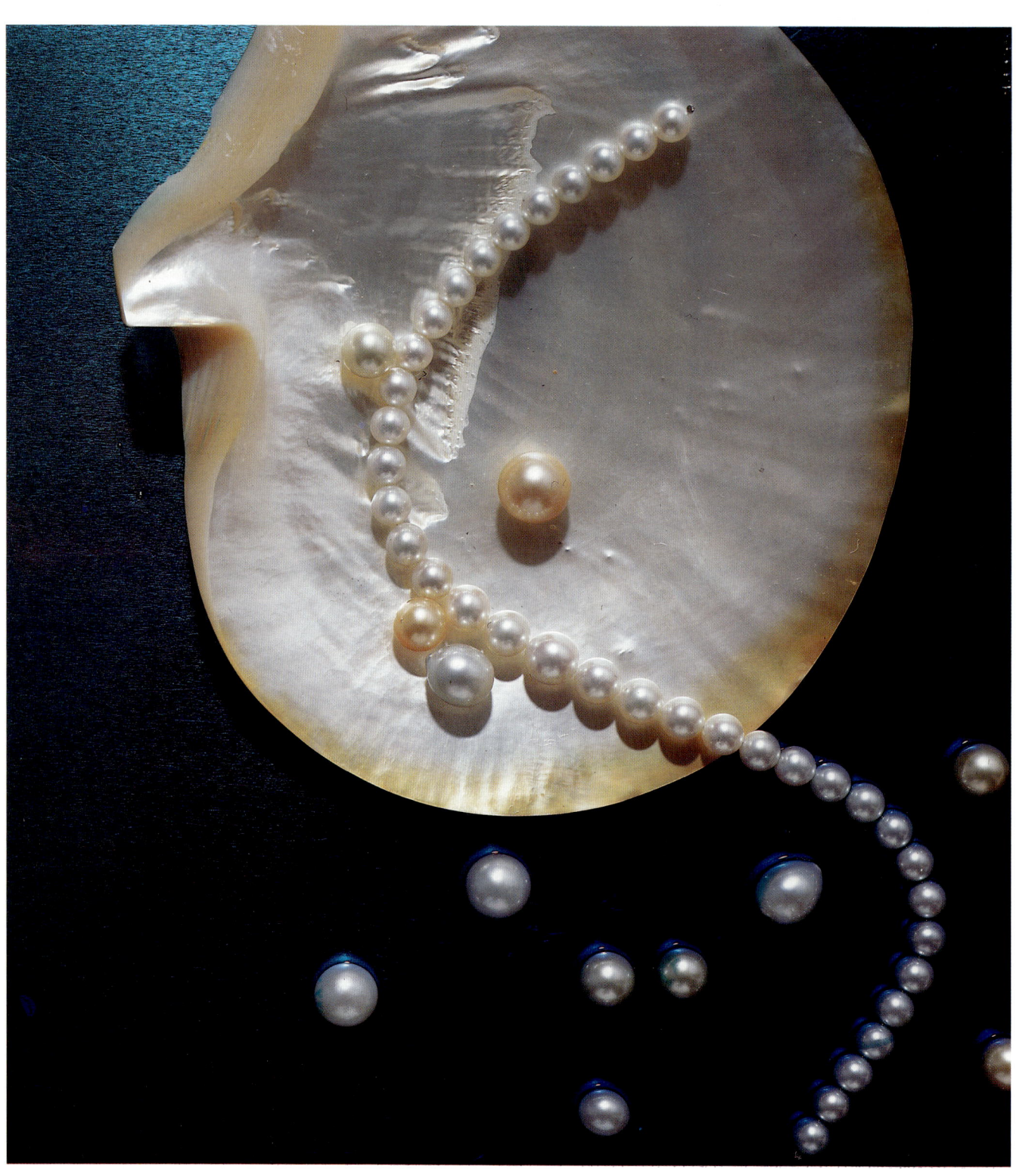

Rosario Autore.
Australian pearls.

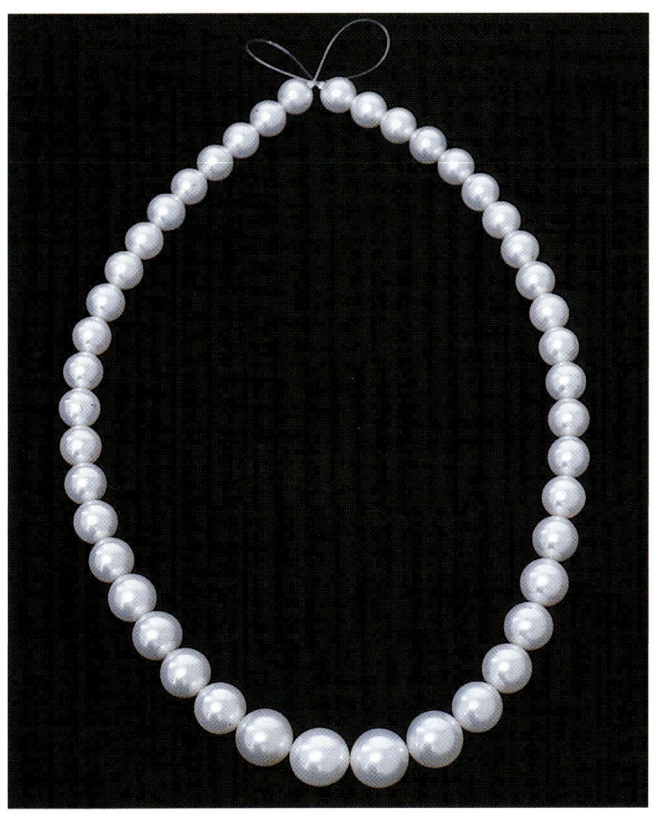

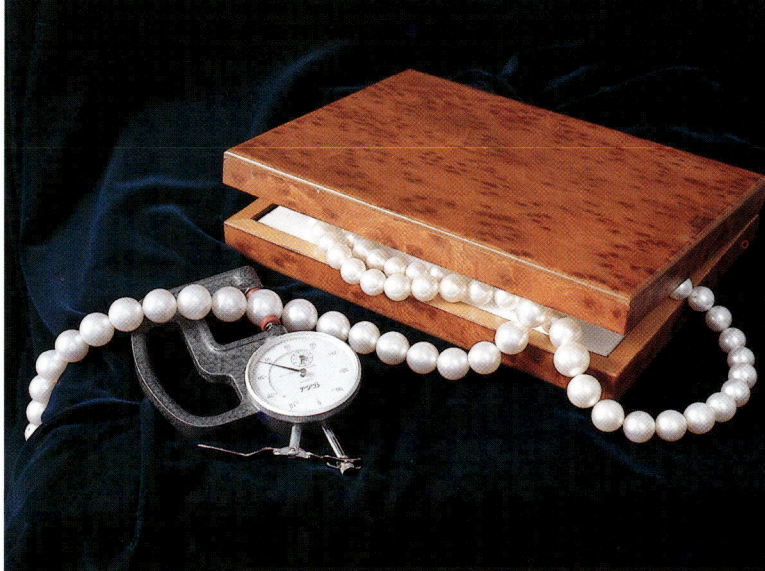

ROSARIO AUTORE.
Two superb necklaces of Australian pearls.

advice: ask for a check on all pearls that have an especially deep color. This is especially important for black cultured pearls, which may be the genuine Polynesian original but are so easily imitated.

How to care for your pearls Since they are not a very hard substance, you must always treat them with due care.

Do not keep them in overly arid climates as they will dehydrate and lose their typical luster.

They must not have direct contact with the skin during hot seasons if the wearer is prone to heavy perspiration (which is acid and can ruin the surface of a pearl; occasionally, a cultured pearl of scarce diameter may soon begin to show its nucleus). Do not use spray products when wearing your string of pearls.

If necklace pearls are worn regularly they should be restrung every year.

After wearing your pearls, clean them one by one with a soft cloth. And if they have come in contact with cosmetics, use a neutral cleansing agent; and when they are perfectly dry rub them with a soft cloth lightly moistened with oil, which helps to cover up any surface scratches.

If you follow these simple rules, your pearls will maintain a lasting beauty through the years.

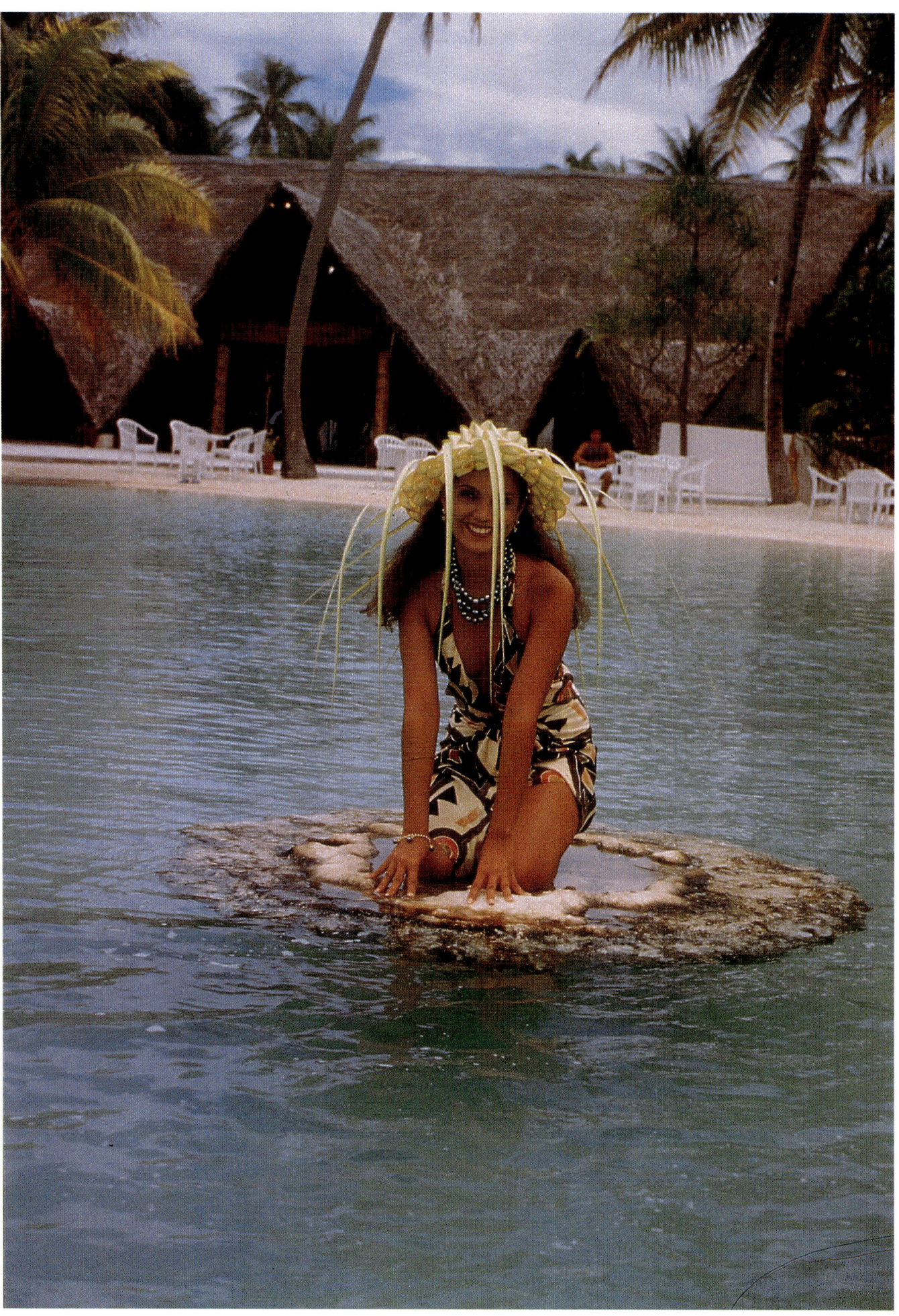

The Pearls of Tahiti

by Martin Coeroli

The Legendary Black Pearl

Better known as "black" or "gray" pearls, Tahitian pearls are found almost exclusively in the coral lagoons of French Polynesia

According to Polynesian legend, Oro, the god of peace and fertility, came down to earth riding a rainbow to offer this very special pearl to the beautiful Princess of Bora Bora as a token of his love.

Tahiti's pearl-oyster industry can be traced back to the last century as simple fishermen went free-diving for oysters in the shark-infested waters of the Tuamotu and Gambier island lagoons and atolls.

It was probably by sheer accident that natural pearls of such great worth were discovered in this way, for the odds were that more than fifteen thousand oysters would have had to be opened just to discover one natural pearl!

Because of their rarity, black pearls soon became famous and their value phenomenal. Often selected to adorn imperial jewels, they became known as the "pearls of queens" and the "queens of pearls."

The most famous of these natural black pearls was the famous "Azra."

A Pearl Industry in Tahiti

Since 1963 a thriving pearl-oyster industry has been developing in the lagoons of Tahiti and its neighboring islands. Three years are required for an oyster to reach sufficient maturity so that it may undergo pearl grafting, two more years for the pearl's gestation inside the oyster.

The growth of these pearls is identical to that of a natural pearl and Man's only role is to put this process into motion. The resulting cultured pearl is several layers thick, each layer characterized by a different shade of natural coloring ranging from pale gray to coal black.

Choosing a Tahitian Cultured Pearl

"Tahiti Cultured Pearl" is the official, internationally recognized commercial name for these gems which are classified according to five criteria: size, shape, color, luster, and purity. The size of Tahiti's pearls range from $5/16$ to $10/16$-inch (8 to 16 mm) diameters and the most frequent shapes are: round, button, pear, circle, and baroque. The luster, or brilliance, of a pearl depends

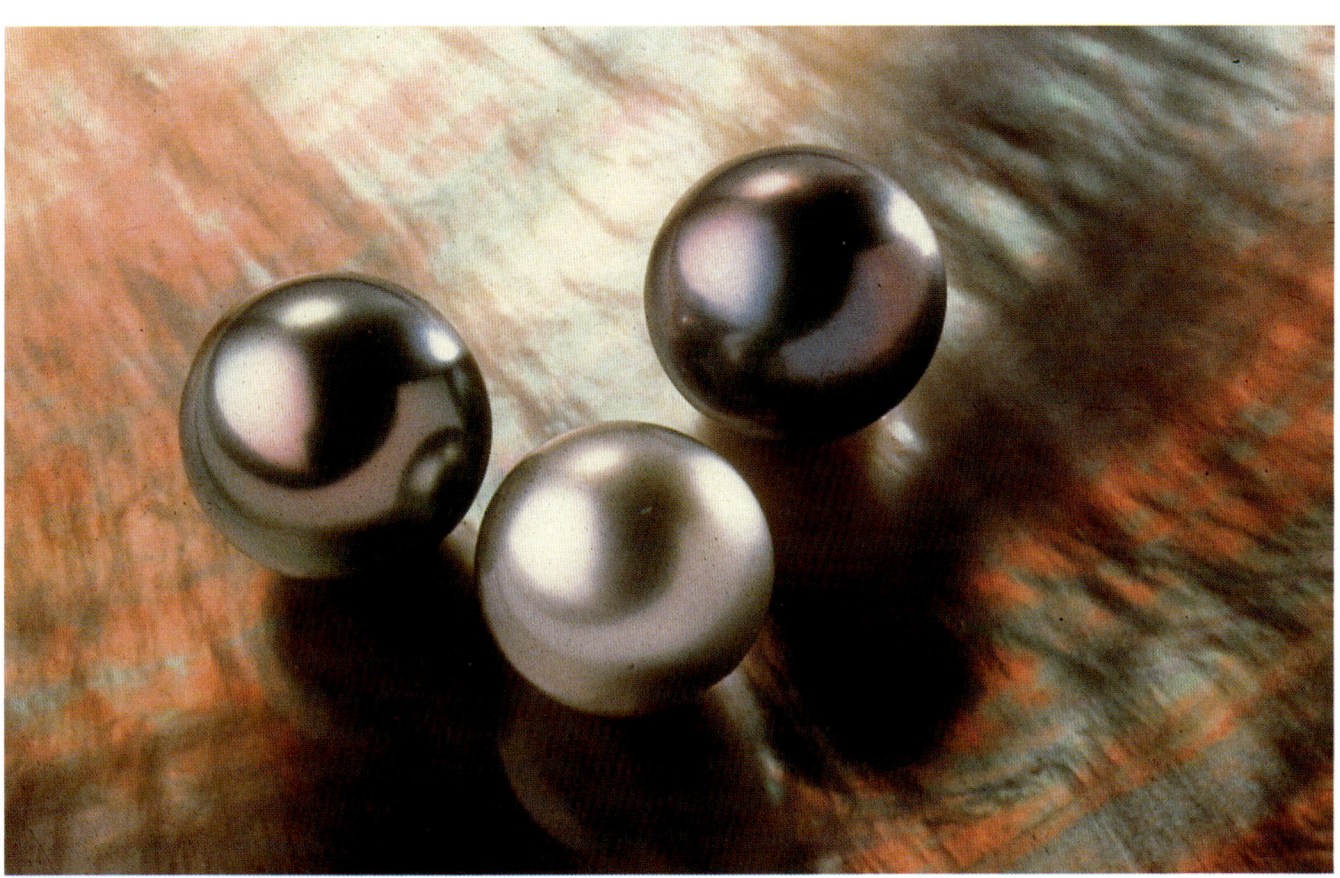

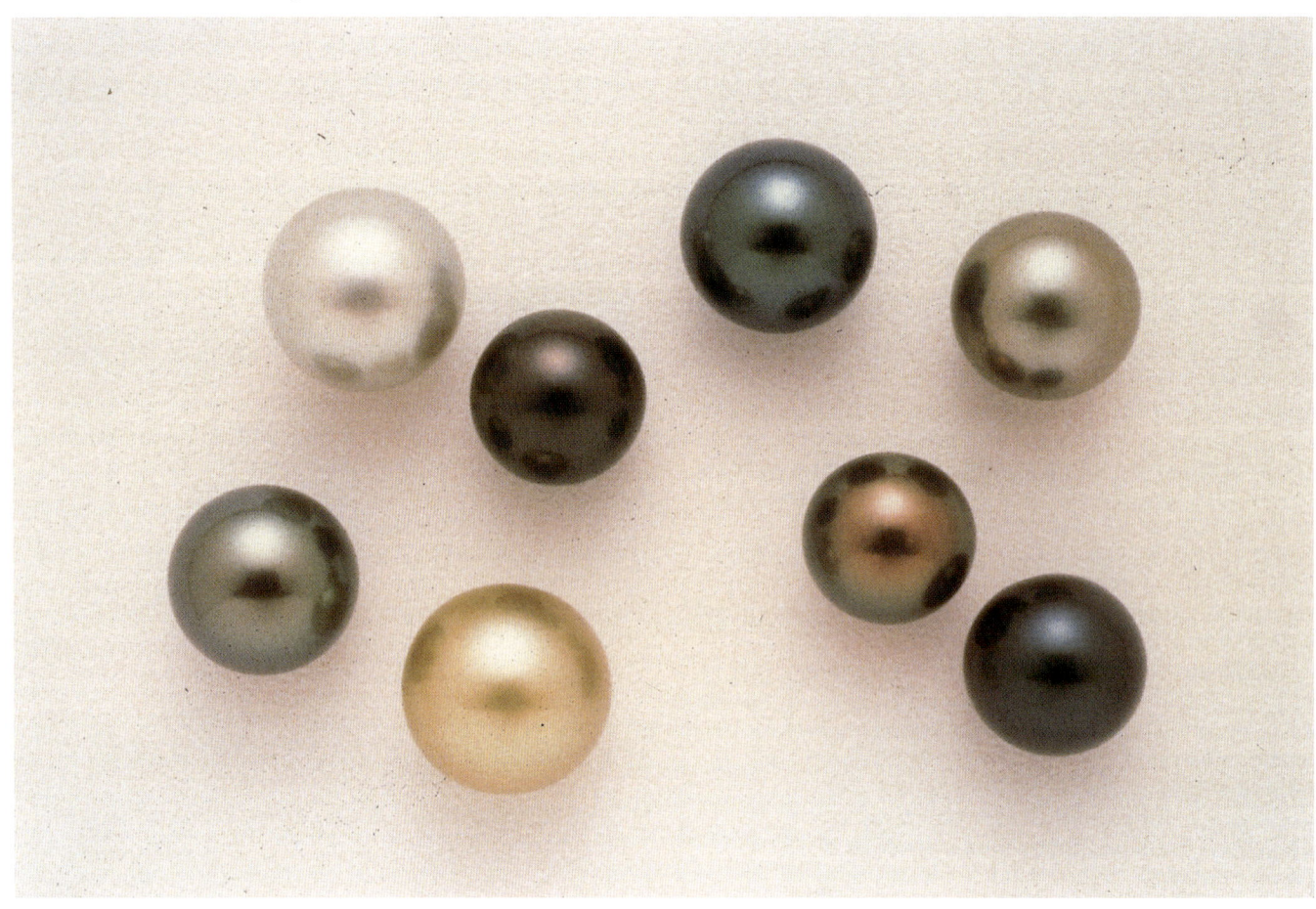

upon the intensity of the light reflected from the pearl's surface. Purity refers to the quality of this surface and is judged according to the blemishes, if any, visible to the naked eye and where they occur.

Consumer demand and preference, of course, influence the valuation of pearls as well as their rarity, and their use in jewelry making.

Of course, consumers' tastes vary from country to country and according to fashion trends. In Japan, for example, large round peacock-green pearls are popular, whereas in Europe smaller gray pearls are preferred.

In jewelry making, because of the uniqueness of each Tahiti pearl, obtaining a necklace of round pearls of the same color and size is a long and painstaking process and this explains why these types of necklaces are usually quite expensive.

Ranges of Pearls

Because of their special features and particular adaptability, Tahiti Cultured Pearls are used in all types of jewelry products, from popular commercial jewelry to high fashion creations.

The relatively large diameter of these gems gives them the visual impact normally only obtained by the use of precious stones or perhaps other types of special pearls. The different shapes of these pearls lend themselves to a variety of styles, from classic designs to the most avant garde.

They are appreciated for their wide range of shades and hues, including gray and black, that can complement a variety of wardrobe color combinations.

It is interesting to note how sensations and feelings are suggested by the different colors of pearls. For example, peacock-green pearls tend to give an impression of affluence and freshness, purple pearls inspire sentiments of nobility. Lavender pearls make us romantic, whereas bronze-shaded pearls are more active. Pale grey pearls exude warmth, while coal black or pigeon-gray pearls create a classic and professional appearance.

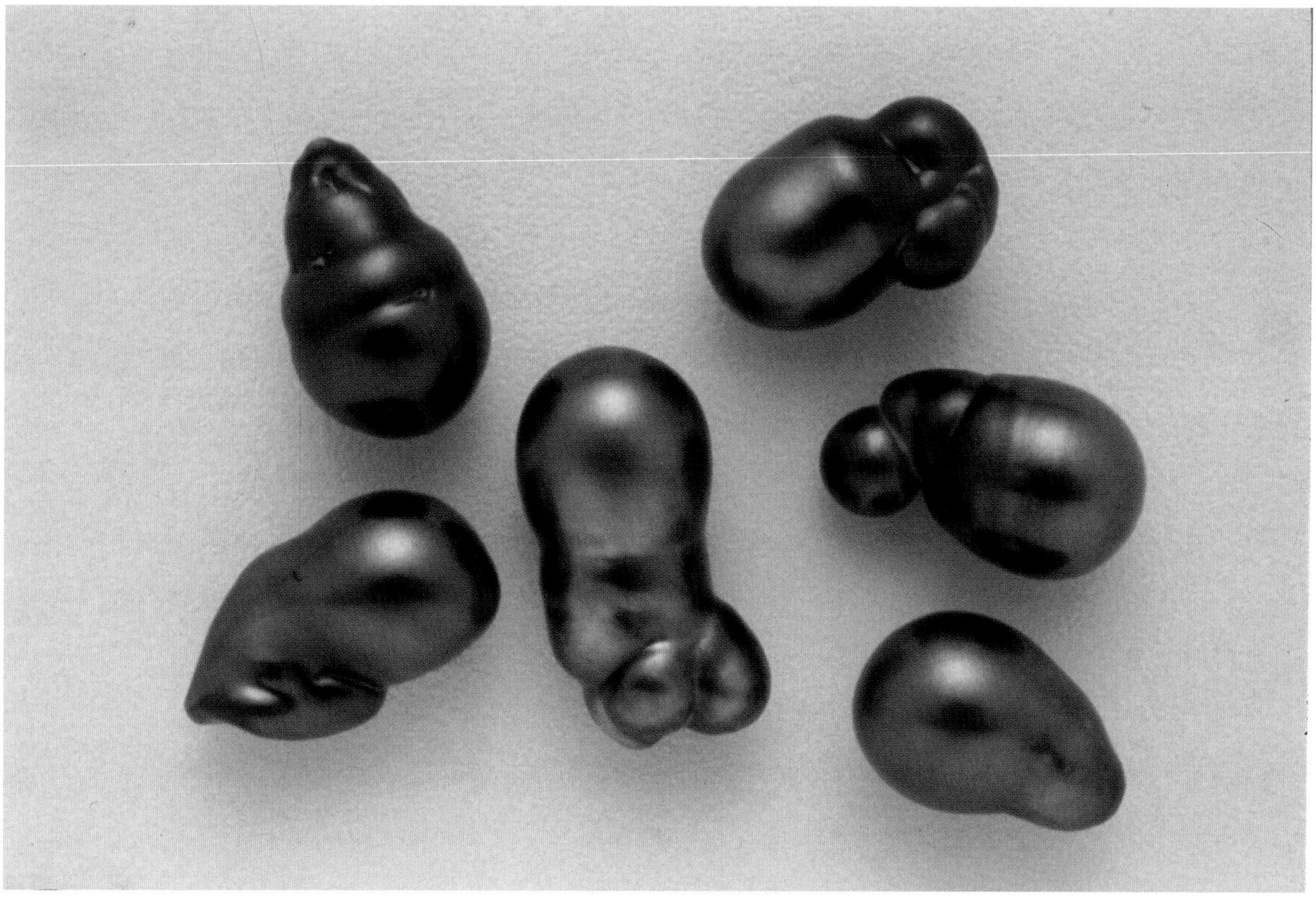

TAHITIAN PEARLS.
The "pearl of queens" or the "queen of pearls".

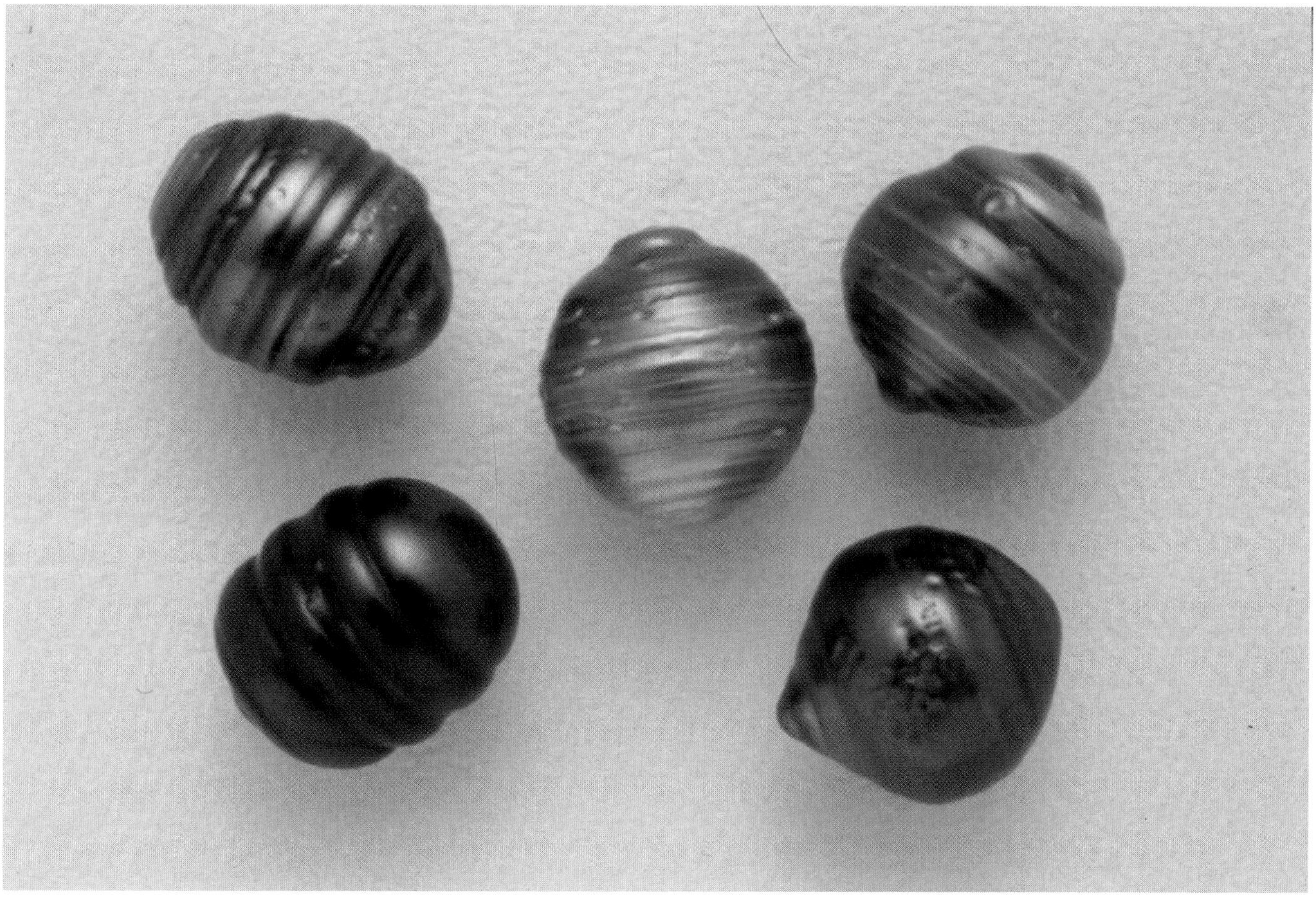

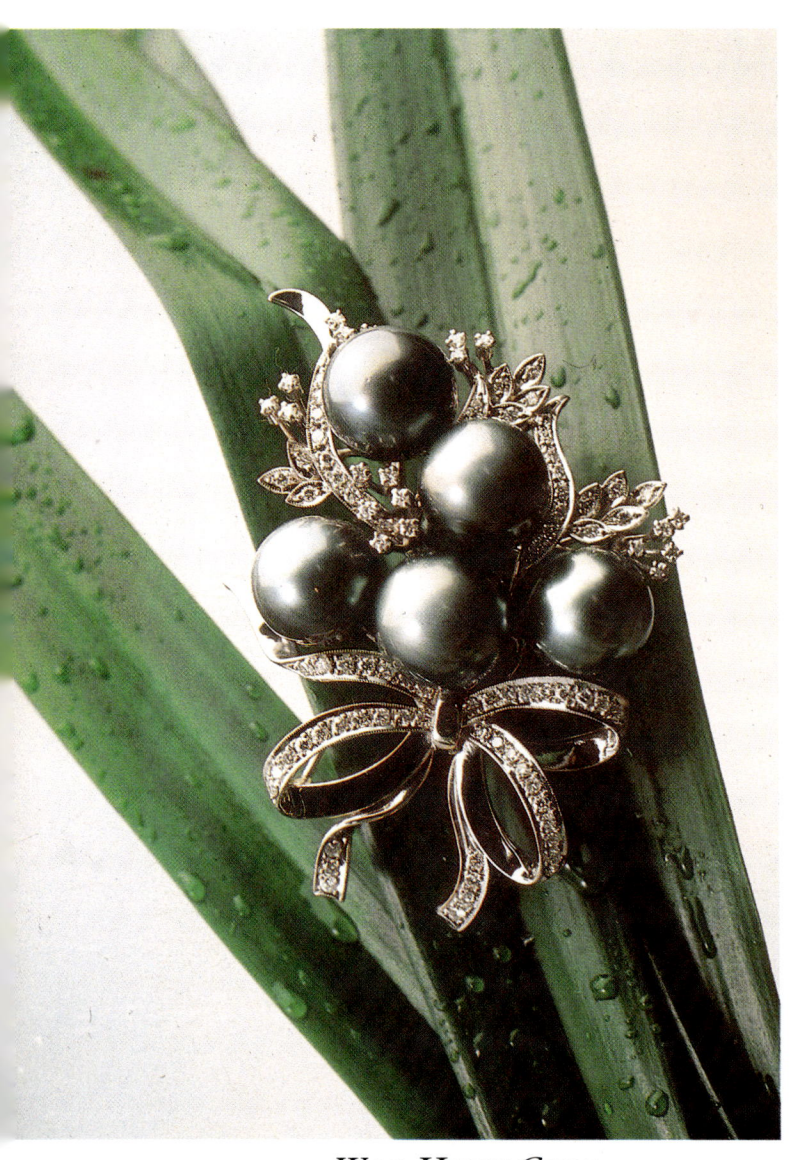

WOO HYUN CHOI.
Brooch in gold, diamonds, and pearls.

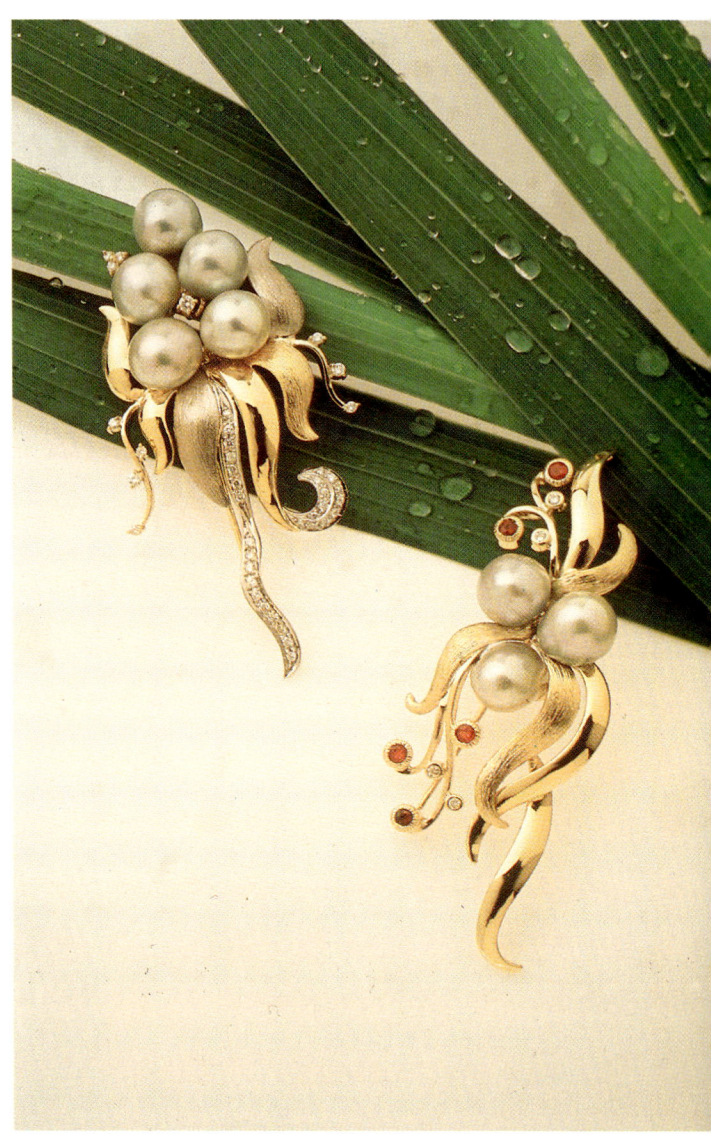

WOO HYUN CHOI.
Brooches in gold, diamonds, rubies, and pearls.

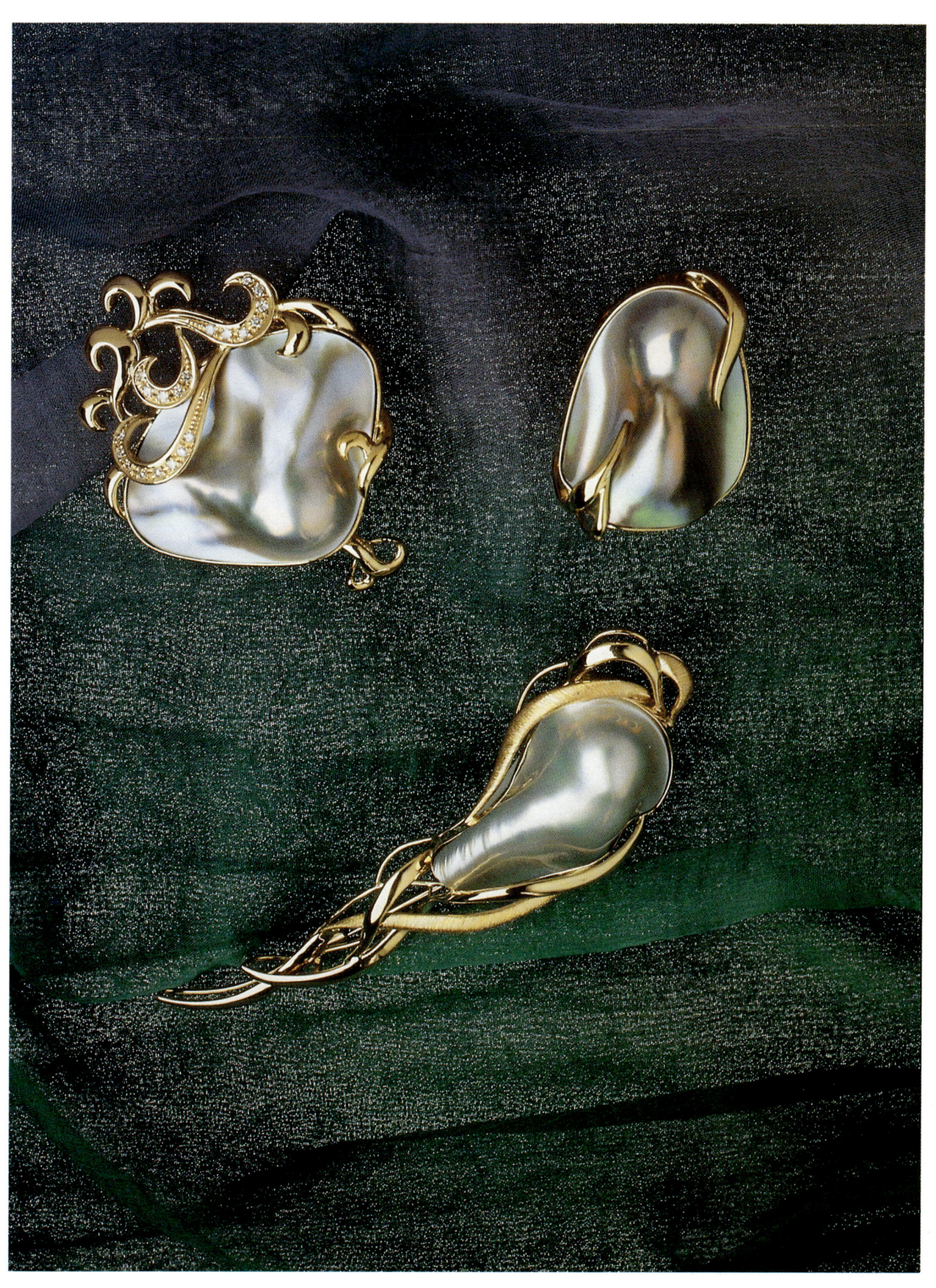

WOO HYUN CHOI.
Brooches in gold, diamonds, and pearls.

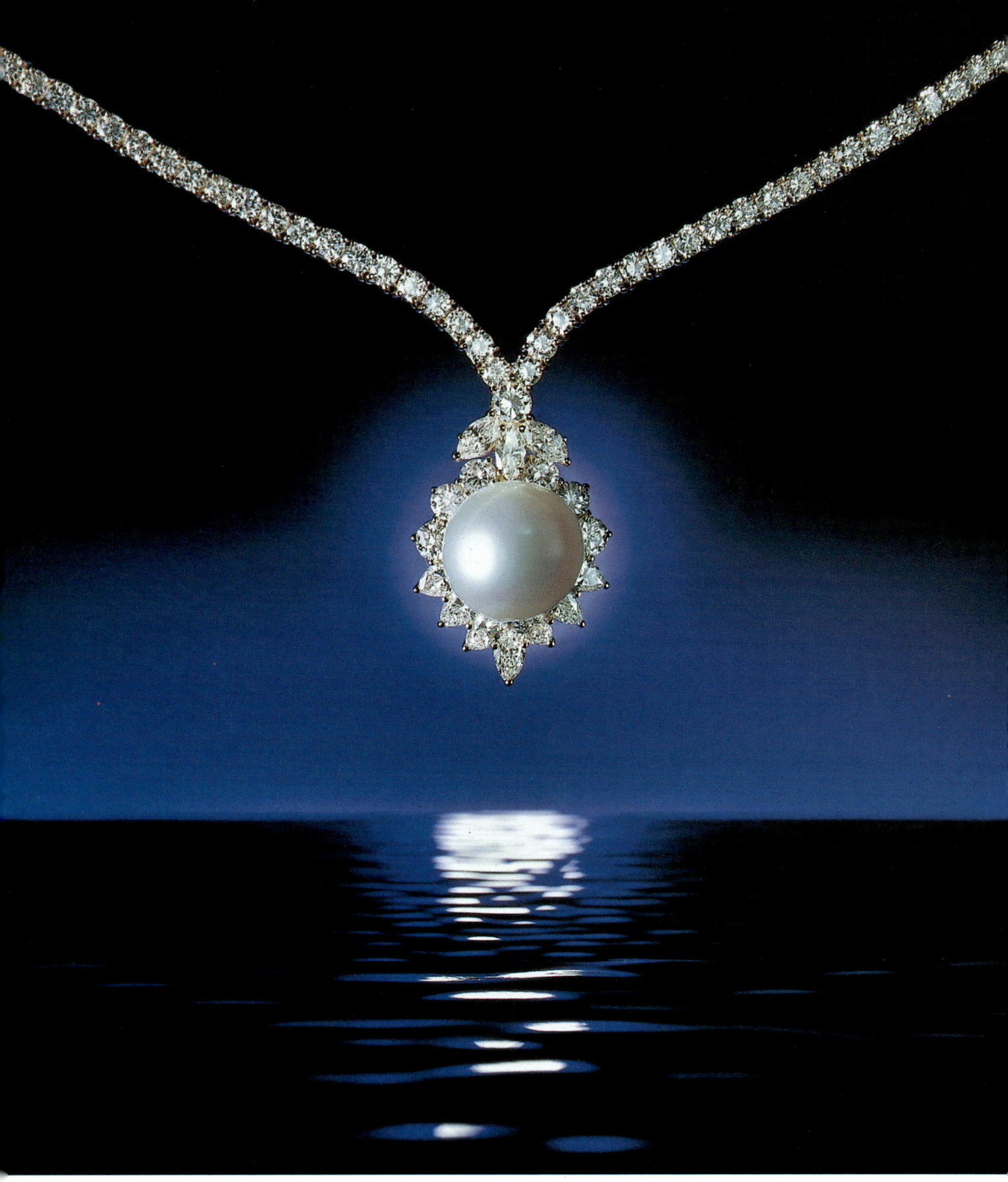

ASAYO: "FULL MOON"
From the sea surrounding oriental lands, from the light of diamonds and precious metals, this jewel is born, as rare as it is precious, since created with a South Sea pearl.

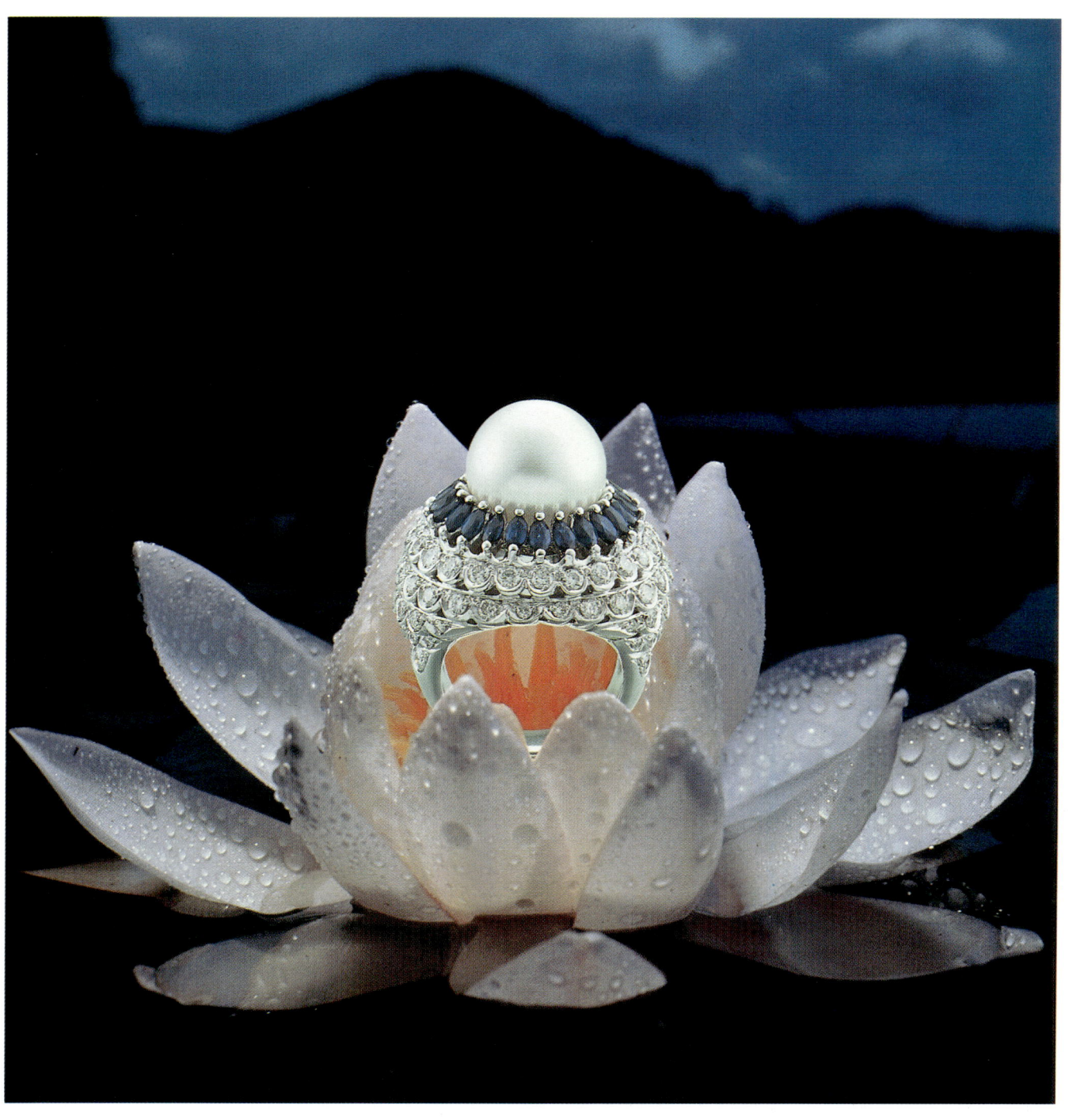

MIKAWA: "LOTUS FLOWER"
Platinum ring with an extraordinary Australian pearl, diamonds, and sapphires.

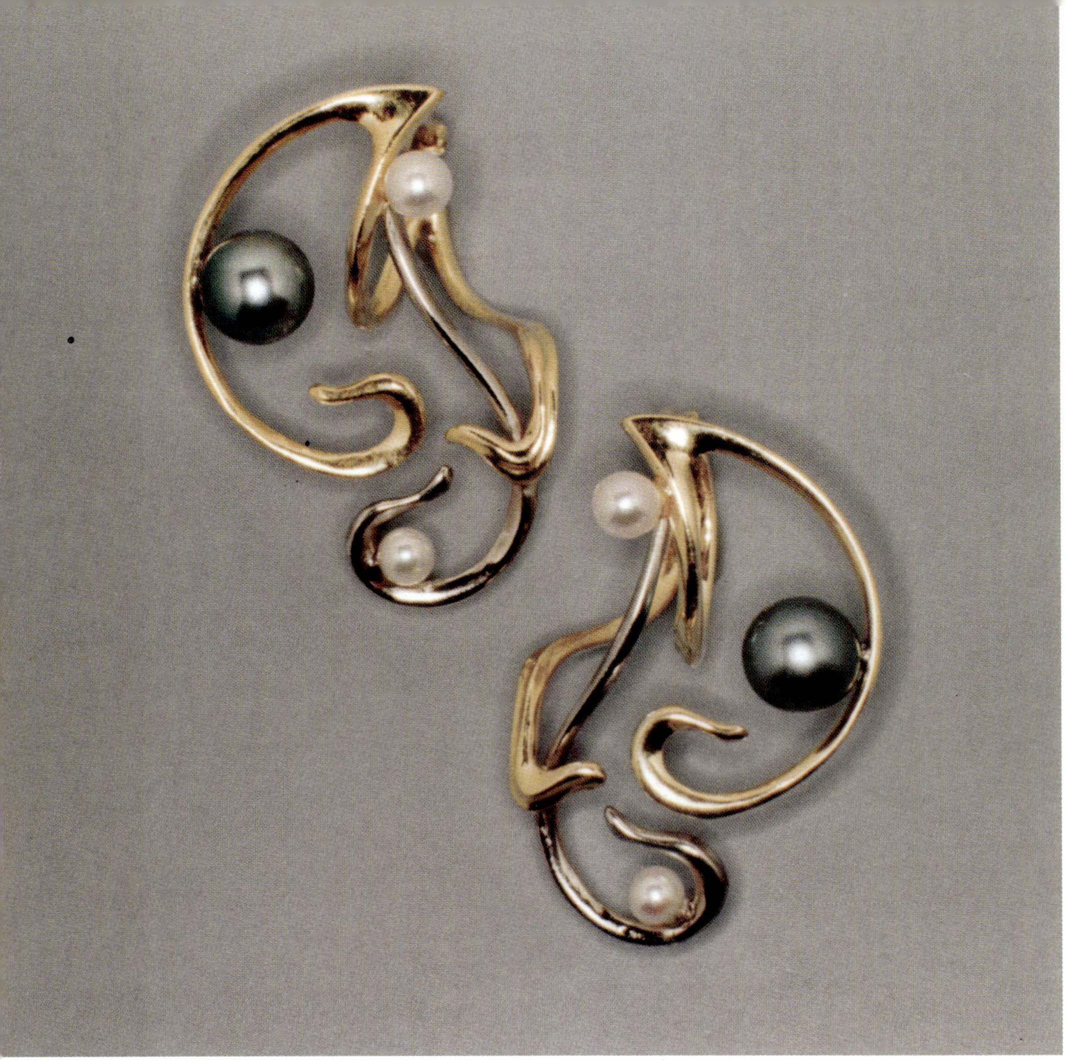

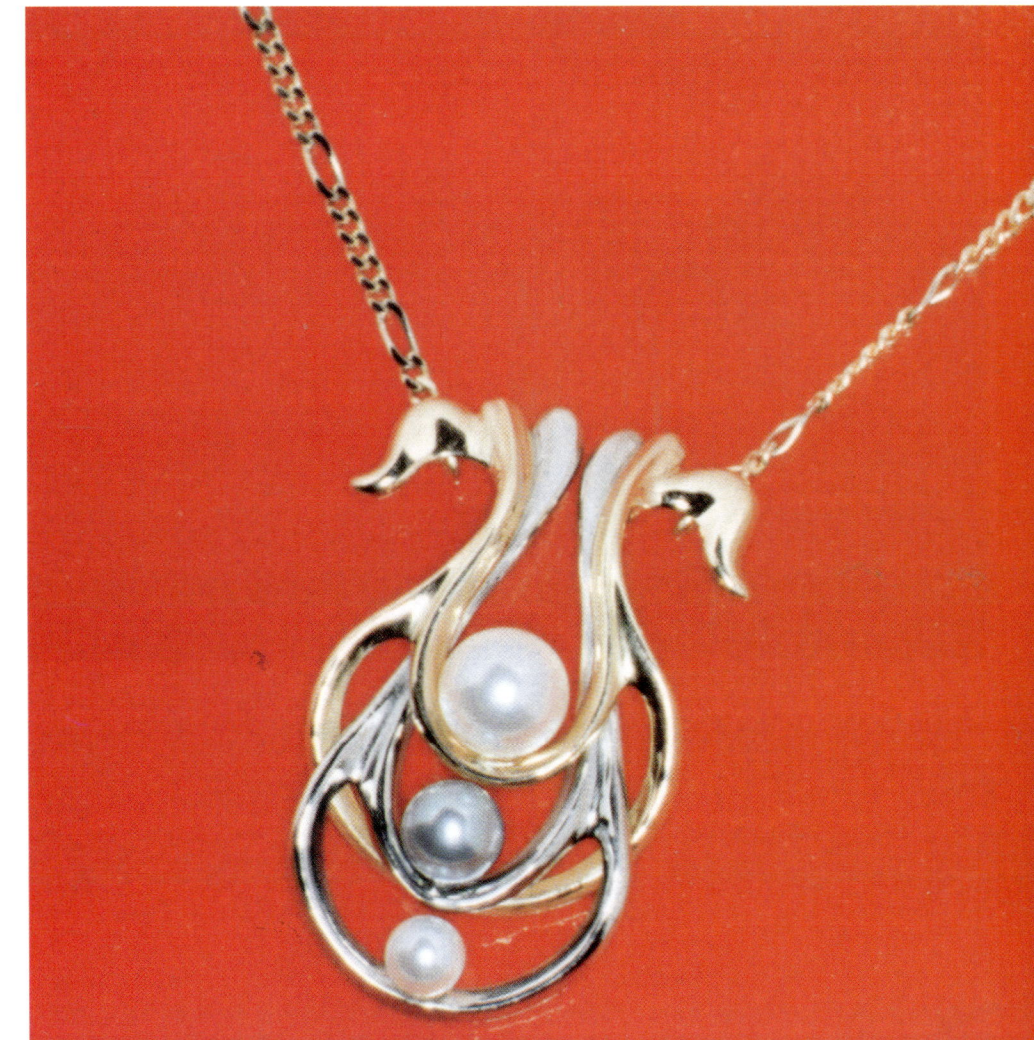

ALAIN DETRIXHE.
Set in gold with pearls.
"His jewels were in symbiosis with the ritual of wine, the joy of living, the ladies…"

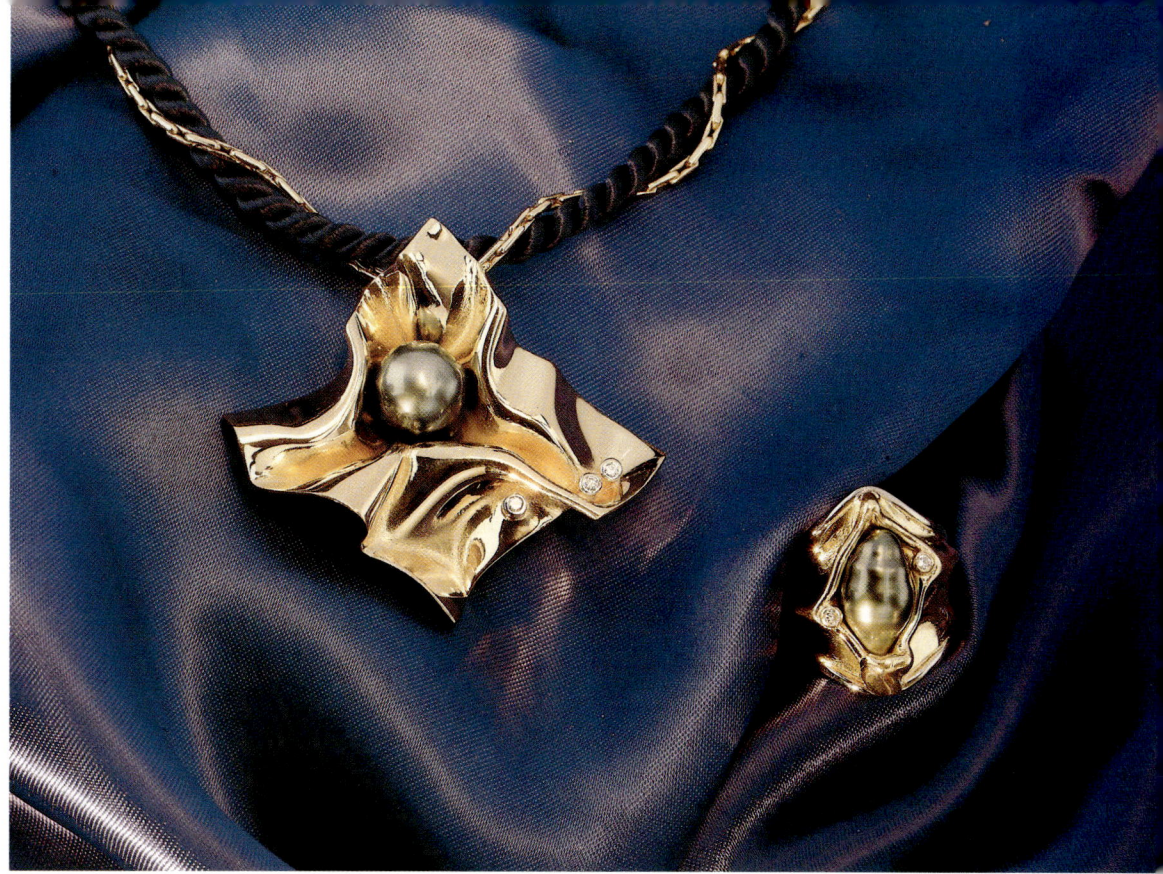

Pierre and Denis Deprez. Pendant and ring in yellow and white gold with black Tahitian pearls and diamonds.

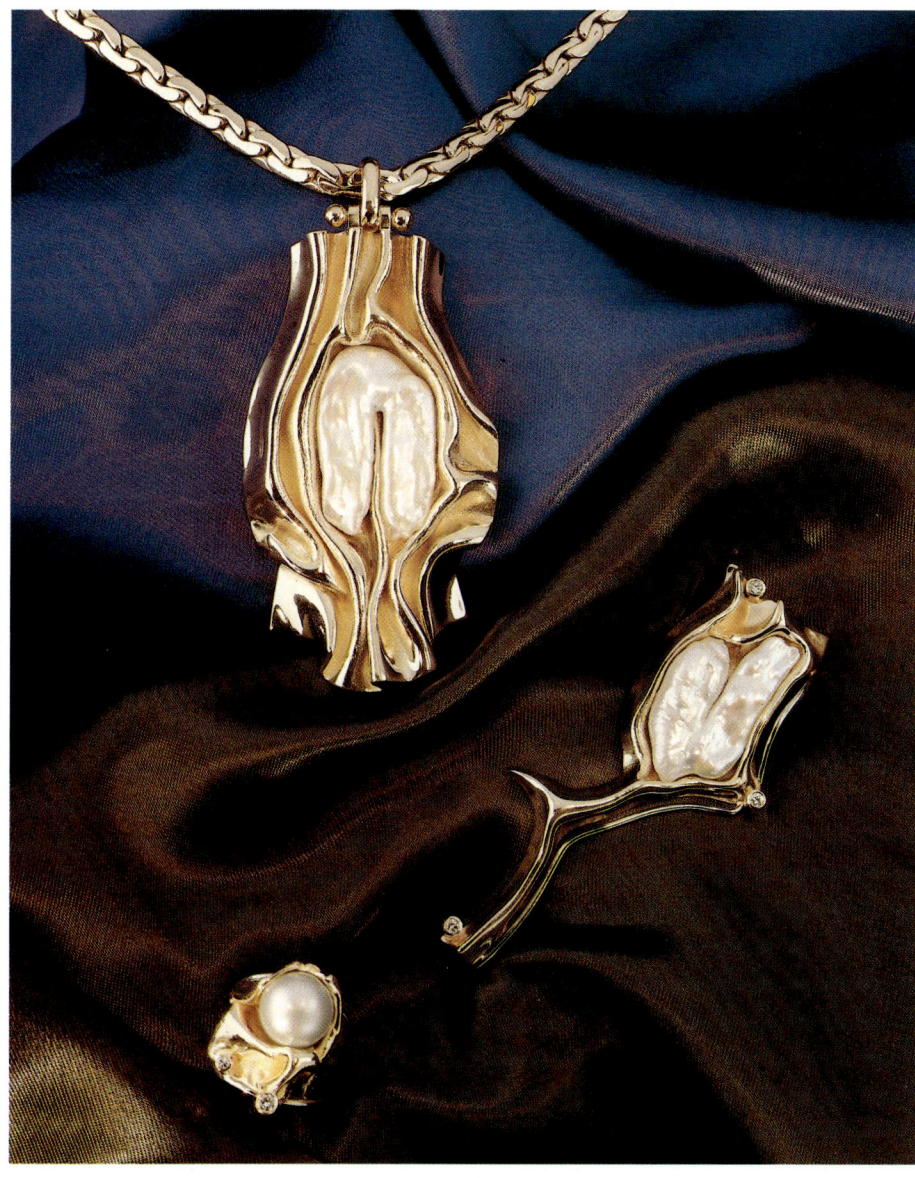

Pierre and Denis Deprez. Yellow gold pendant with Biwa pearl. Brooch in yellow and white gold, Biwa pearl, and diamonds. Ring in yellow and white gold, gray Tahitian pearl, and diamonds.

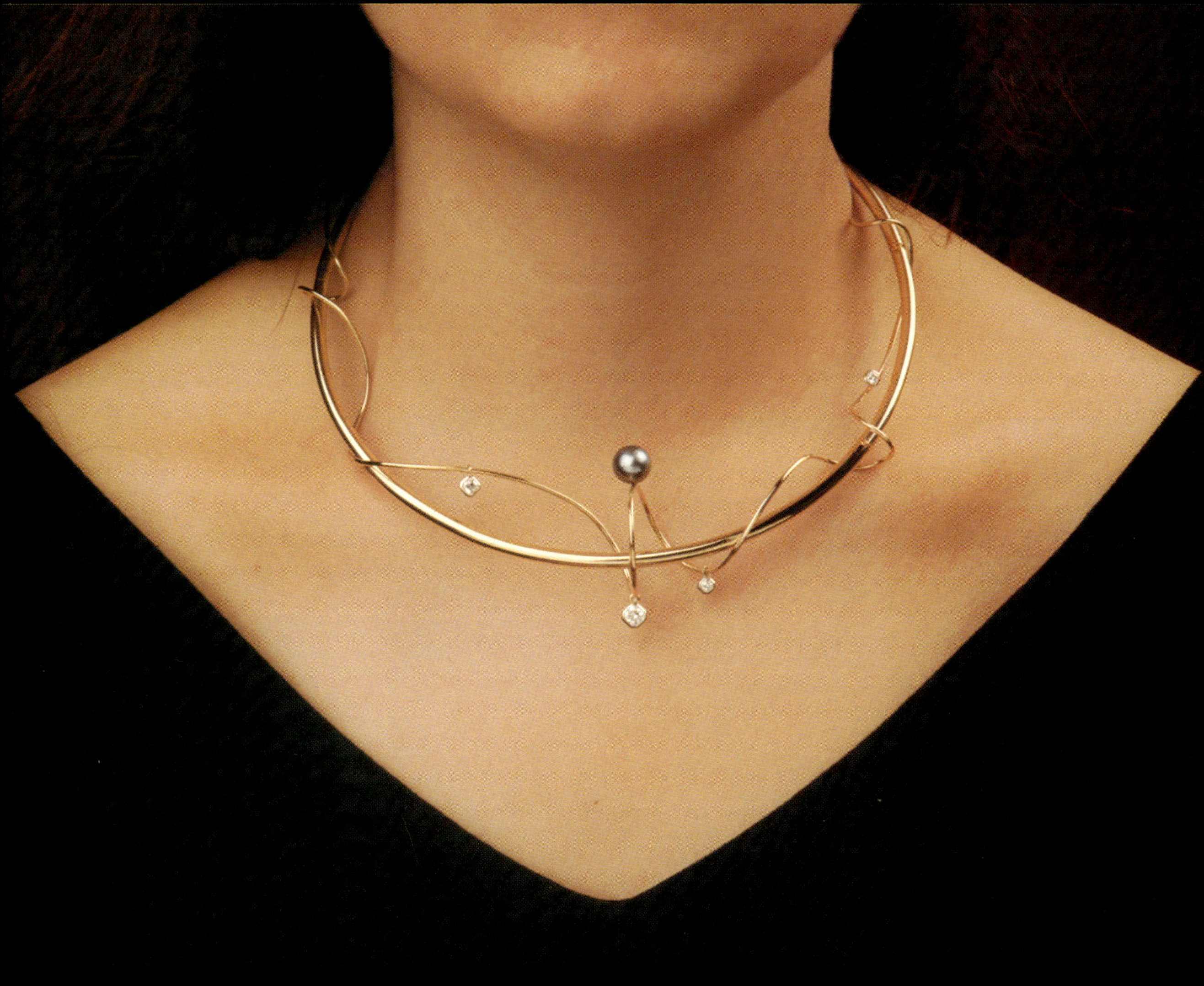

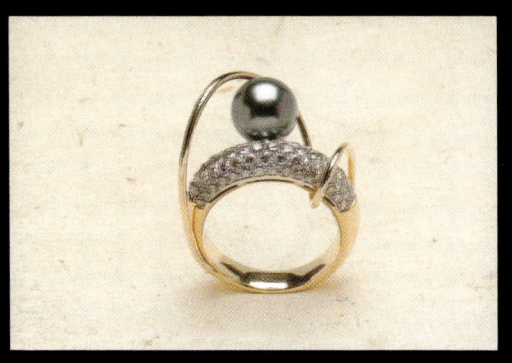

KRISTA AND GRETY VANDEVELDE: "EARTH DANCE"

The day God created Earth, it set about circling the sun. The evening Krista and Grety discovered the pearl, it set about dancing nine times around a circle of gold... and it was then that Woman was radiant. Gold necklace and ring with diamonds and pearls from Tahiti.

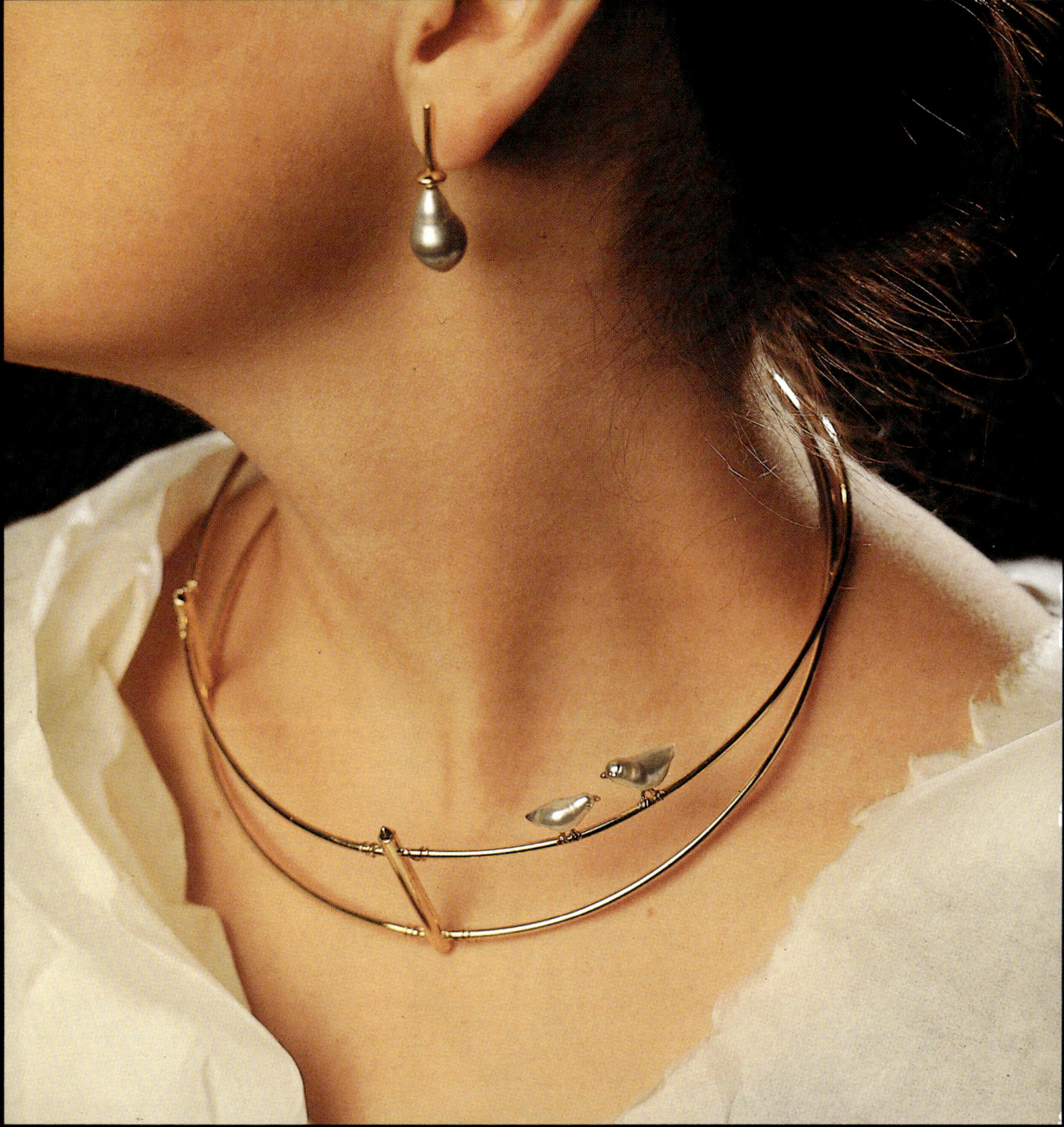

Krista and Grety Vandevelde: "Dialogue"

It is the natural shape of these pearls that inspired the Vandeveldes. The symbol of duality is expressed in the three-fold dialogue between the silence of the birds, the impossible fusion between gold and pearl, and the conspiratorial meeting between flesh and substance.
Gold necklace with diamonds and Keshi pearls from Tahiti which won first prize in the Design competition 1995/1996.

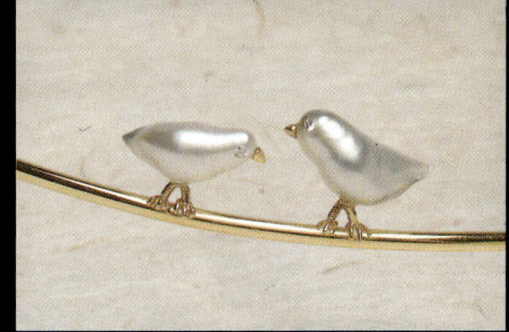

JAN VANSCHOENWINKEL.
Is it possible to talk about jewelry without imagining stones? Perhaps it is, but the stones are largely responsible for the strength and personality of the jewel. In the same way, they inspire the creator with the desire to produce a unique piece. It is then up to him to match the piece's various elements. Pendant and bracelet in yellow and white gold with black pearls and diamonds.

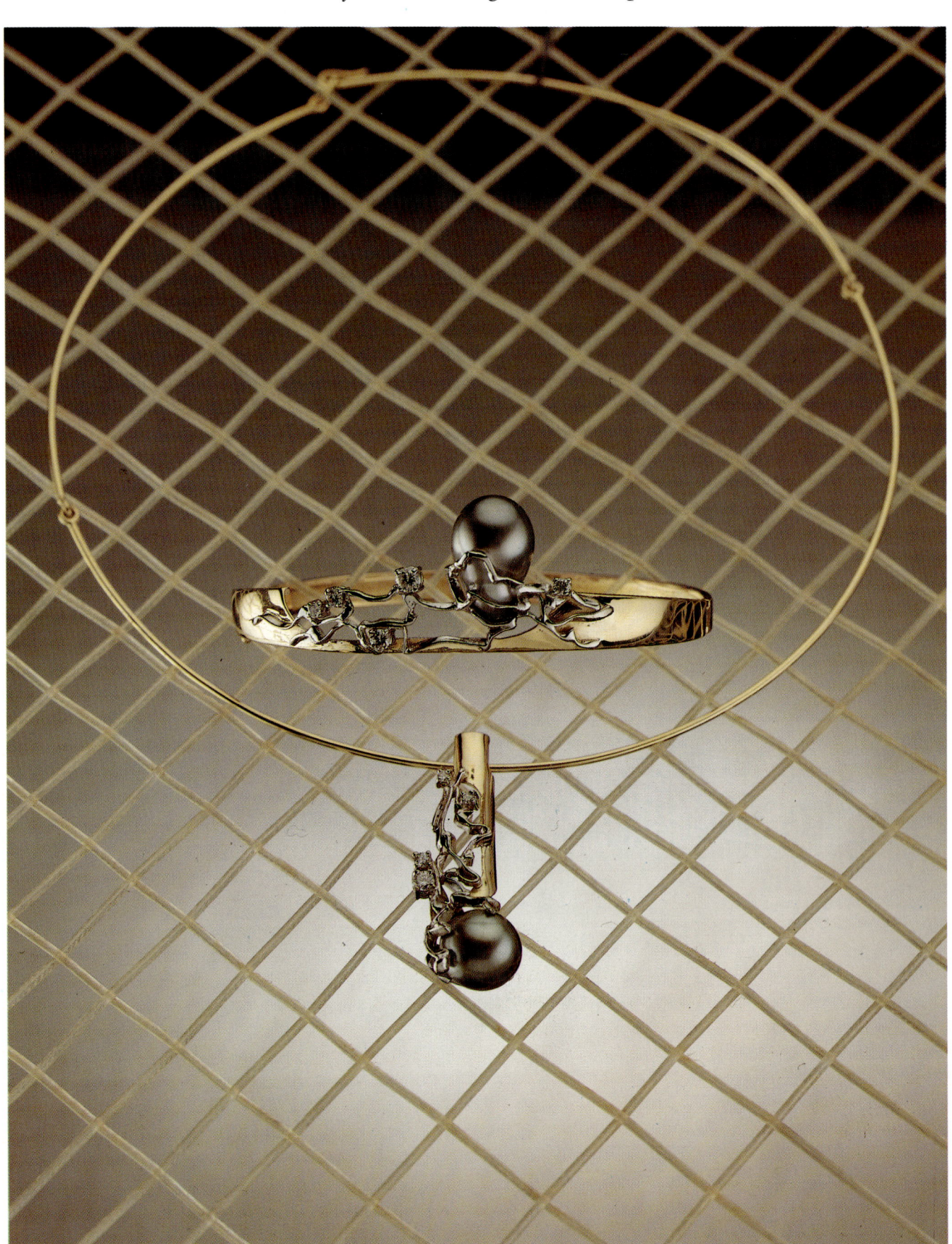

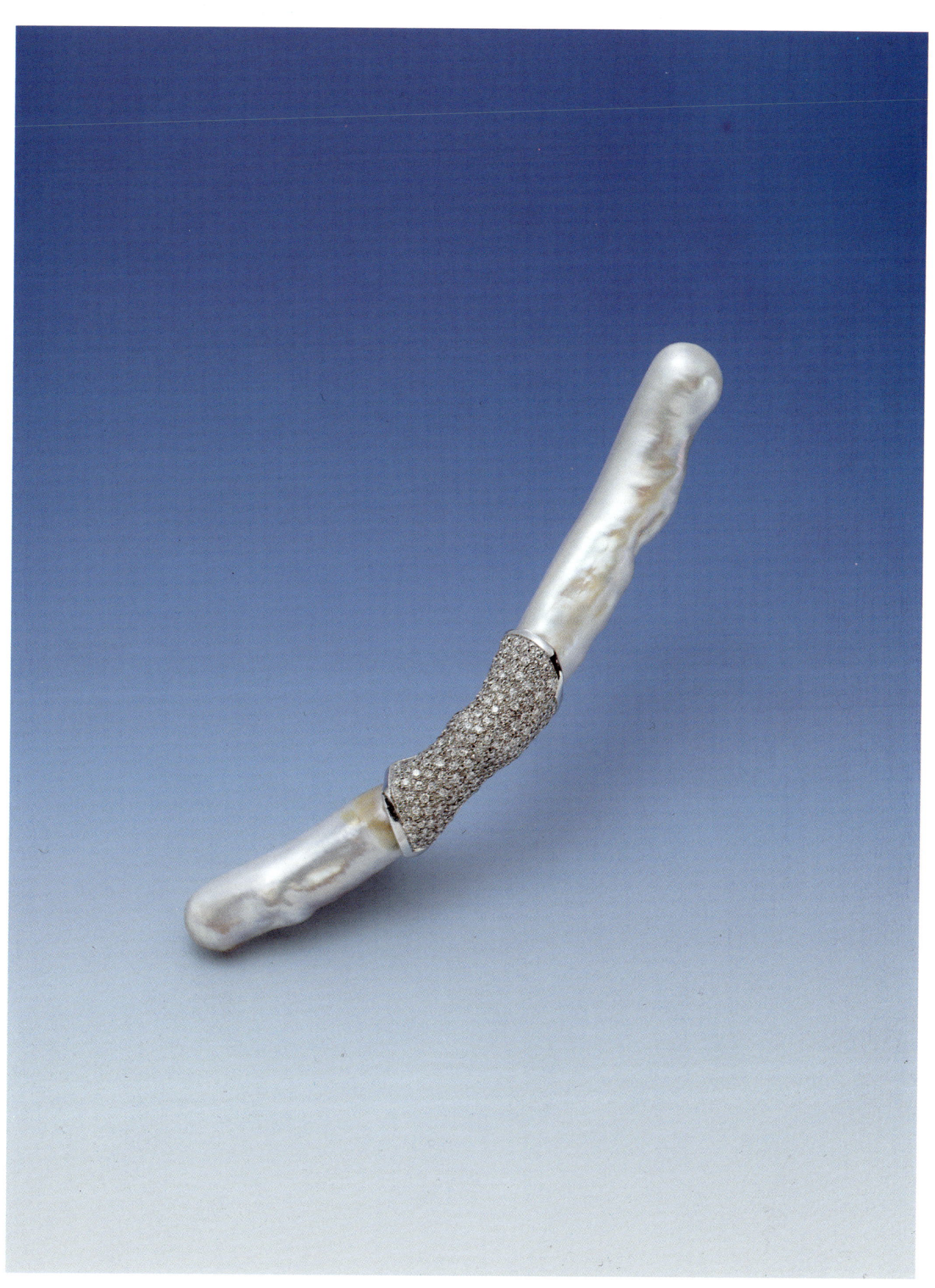

PAOLO SPALLA: "NATURAL LINE"
Brooch in white gold with diamonds and natural pearl.

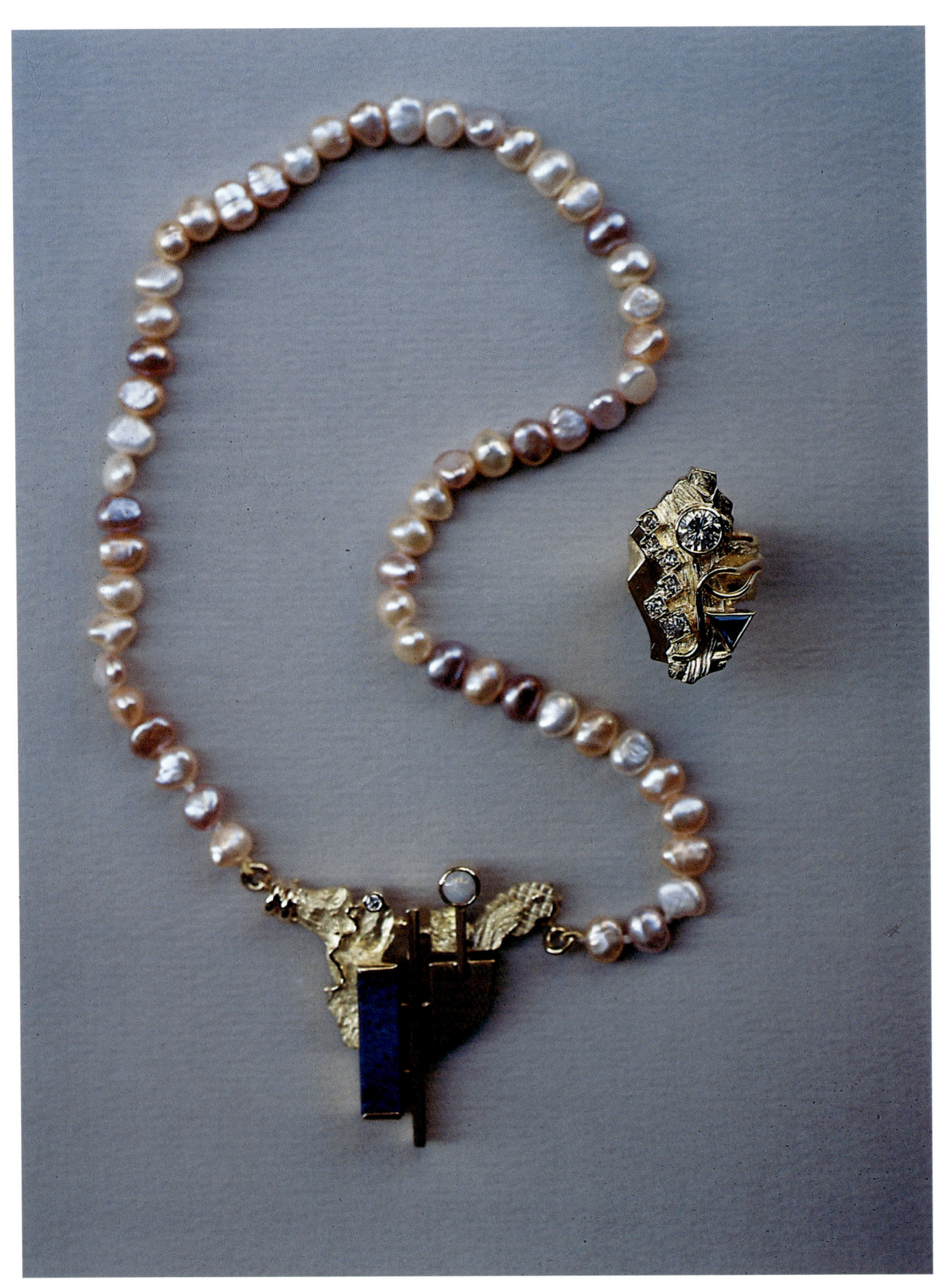

ROLAND TSCHIEGG: "UNIQUE CREATION"
Gold, diamonds, pearls, lapis lazuli, opal, and sapphire: necklace and ring crafted entirely by hand.

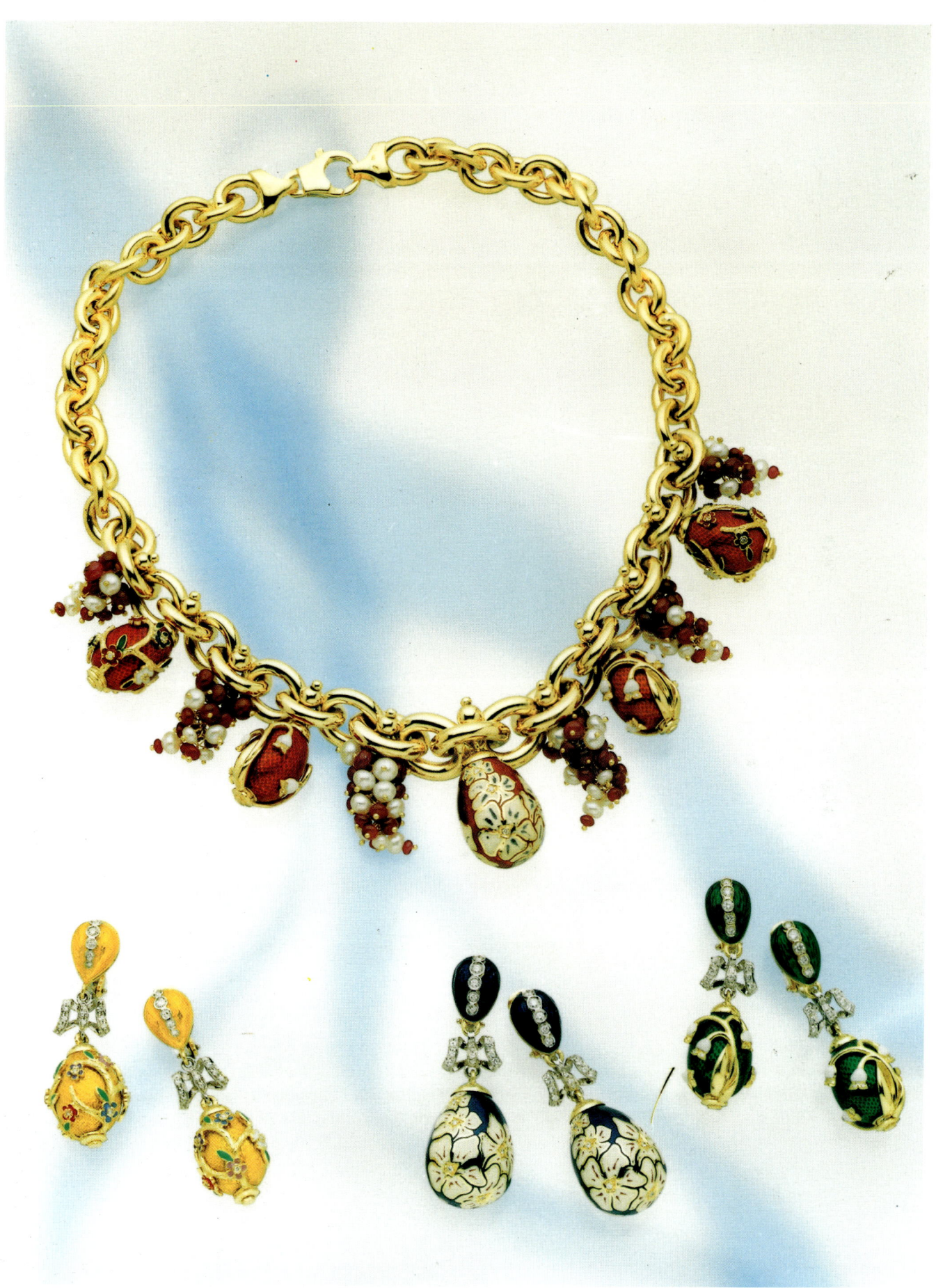

Roberto Gioielli.
Choker and earrings with enamelled eggs, gold, diamonds, rubies, sapphires, emeralds, and cultured pearls.

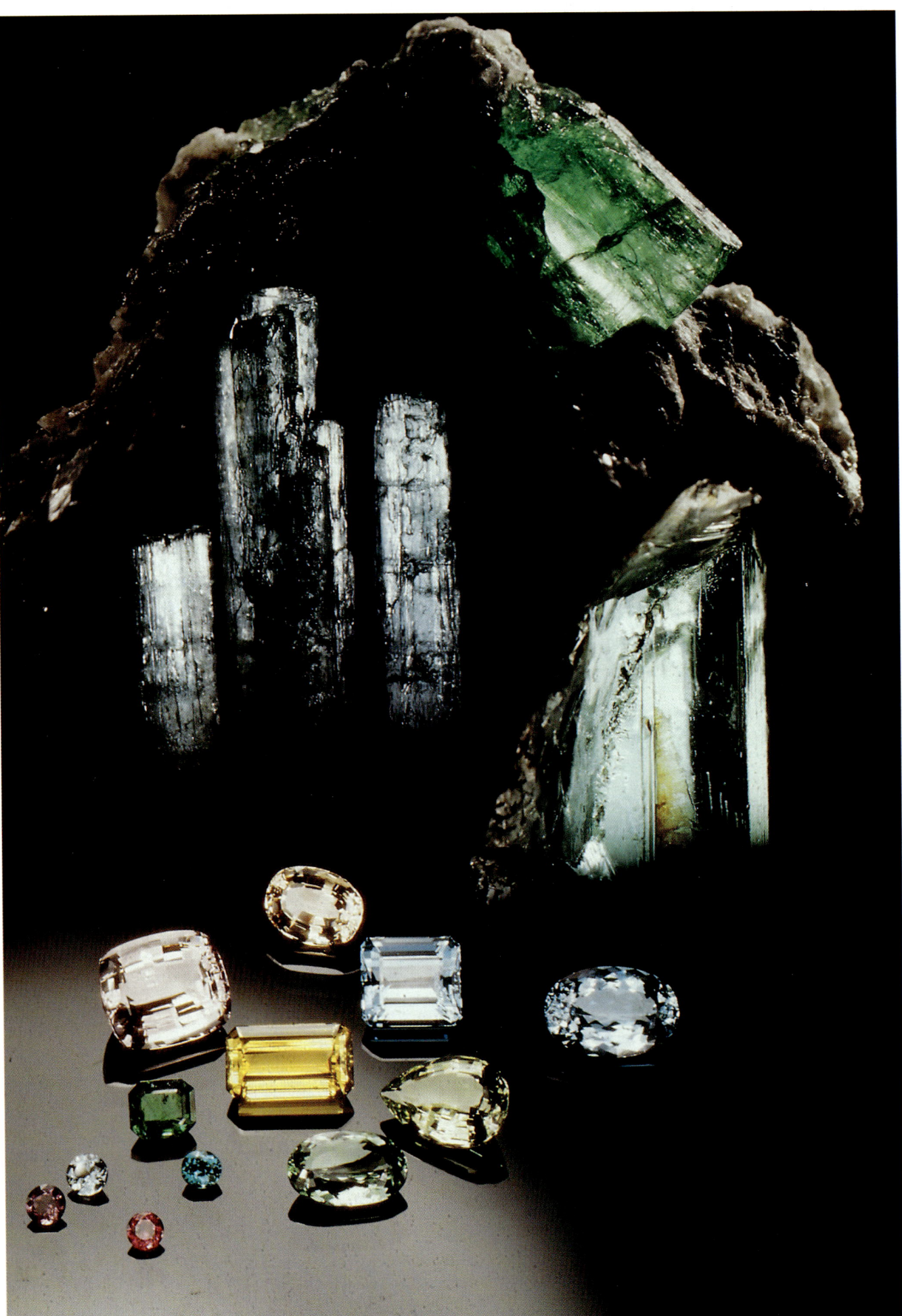

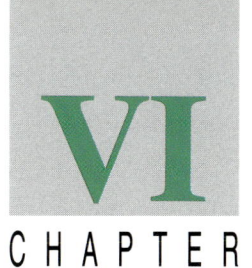

CHAPTER VI

26 Fine Stones

This chapter, of fundamental importance to our work, describes the most important fine stones and particularly the mineral families that group together gems almost identical chemically, though completely different in color. For example, in the tourmaline family, rubellite is a red tourmaline, whereas if it is blue it is called "indicolite."

All of these stones, commonly known as "semi-precious," are in fact very rare and in some cases, they may even be worth more than the four stones considered as truly "precious." Today, and even more so in the years to come, these semi-precious stones will be more widely known to the general public and are destined to become even rarer than the diamond, for example. A gem's preciousness or rarity is certainly not determined only by advertising campaigns or promotions but above all by its beauty and also by the actual quantities of the gem lying in waiting beneath the earth's crust.

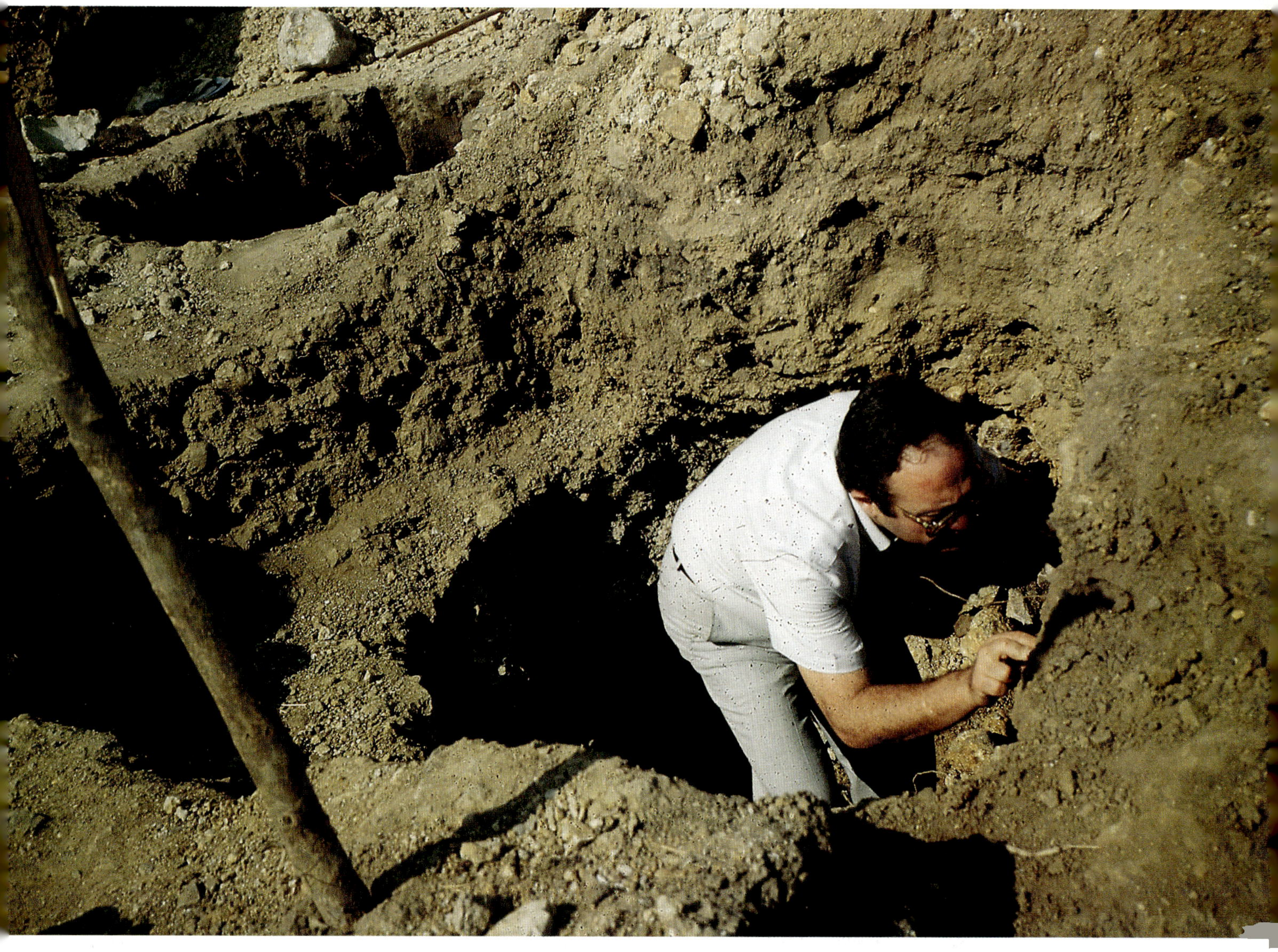

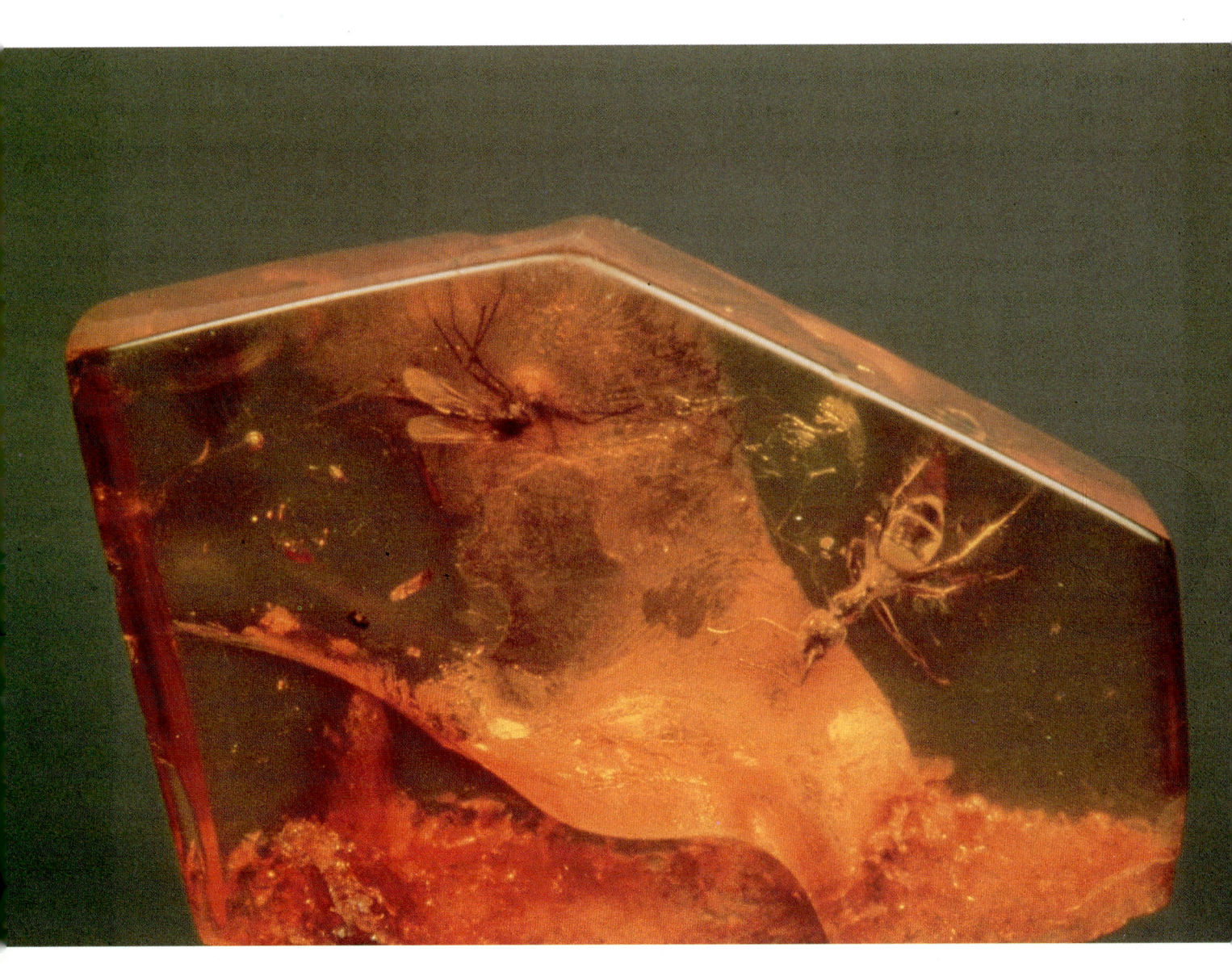

Amber

GENERAL INFORMATION

How it got its name Amber actually, traces to the Arabic denomination *al-anbar*. But the Germans dubbed it *bernstein* (the stone that burns); for when amber is ground to a powder and heated, it produces a pleasing aromatic fragrance, and this Northern people, like many others, used it as incense. Amber is considered an amorphous substance.

The Greek word for amber was *élektron*: if you rub amber with a soft cloth it is charged with static electricity and can attract small, lightweight particles; our word "electric" goes back to the same root. The ancient Romans, on the other hand, considered the substance *succinum*, a tree's vital juices.

Actually, amber is a resin generally produced by certain pine trees such as the *Pinus succinfera*, clearly linking to Roman terminology. These conifers exuded this natural resin during the Oligocene geologic period… more than thirty million years ago, to keep our dates straight. In the course of the passing geological eras the product hardened until it became what we call "amber," which may range in appearance from transparent to translucent, or even opaque, and exhibits a distinctly rich sheen.

Varieties Also called "gold of the North," it was the first gemstone primitive man adopted for self-adornment. When we speak of amber today, we normally mean the tawny stone of Baltic provenance, also called *succinite*, an amber-colored variety of grossulative (garnet) since it contains succinic acid.

This variety is classified as compact (the only sort directly useful in jewelry making thanks to its extreme transparency), opaque (at times markedly so), and porous. Other stones to be discussed in this framework include *retinite*, whose color ranges from clear yellow to a nearly red shade produced by oxidation on its surface; it comes from San Domingo (does not contain succinic acid, is a product of leguminous rather than coniferous resin, and has evolved rather more recently than succinic amber). In addition we have *birmite*, or *burmite*, coming from Burma; *rumenite*, from Romania; *gedanite*, from Poland (a name derived from *Gedanum*, Danzig's name in ancient times; *simetite*, of Italian provenance (from Simeto, the name of a river in Sicily).

Best keep in mind that though we have many varieties, only 15% of all amber that is extracted is used in jewelry making. The rest is employed in the production of succinic acid, amber oil, and colophonies utilized in preparing paints.

Some interesting sidelights Ovid reminds us that in Greek mythology amber bowls betokened the tears shed by Phaeton's sisters when their brother tragically plummeted to Earth in his father's chariot, the supposed cause of a series of important geological phenomena.

According to ancient traditions, amber is a potent amulet against a number of diseases, thanks to the positive field of energy created by its electrical properties.

Persuaded it could protect from contagion, Arab peoples constructed their *narghilé* mouthpiece almost exclusively in amber, for the waterpipe had to to be passed around, and, presumably, amber would not carry infection. Meanwhile in India amber was said to cure all sorts of lung problems.

At Benares, the sacred city of the Hindus, a temple is dedicated to the amber necklace it hosts, a relic called "The Necklace of the Goddess of Favors." For two thousand years believers have held that if you touch this talisman any favor you ask will be granted.

Deposits Generally, amber deposits lie in nodules, though it is sometimes possible to come upon entire blocks which may weigh up to tens of kilos.

Succinite is found in

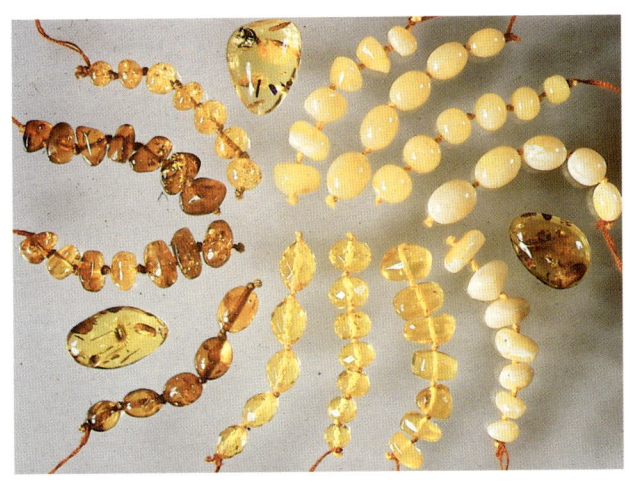

Chemical Formula: $C_{10}H_{16}O$ – fossil resin
Hardness: 2-2½ (Mohs scale)
Specific Gravity: 1.03 – 1.10
Refraction: monorefringent
Color: honey yellow, brown, milky white, almost colorless white, blue, black, red, greenish

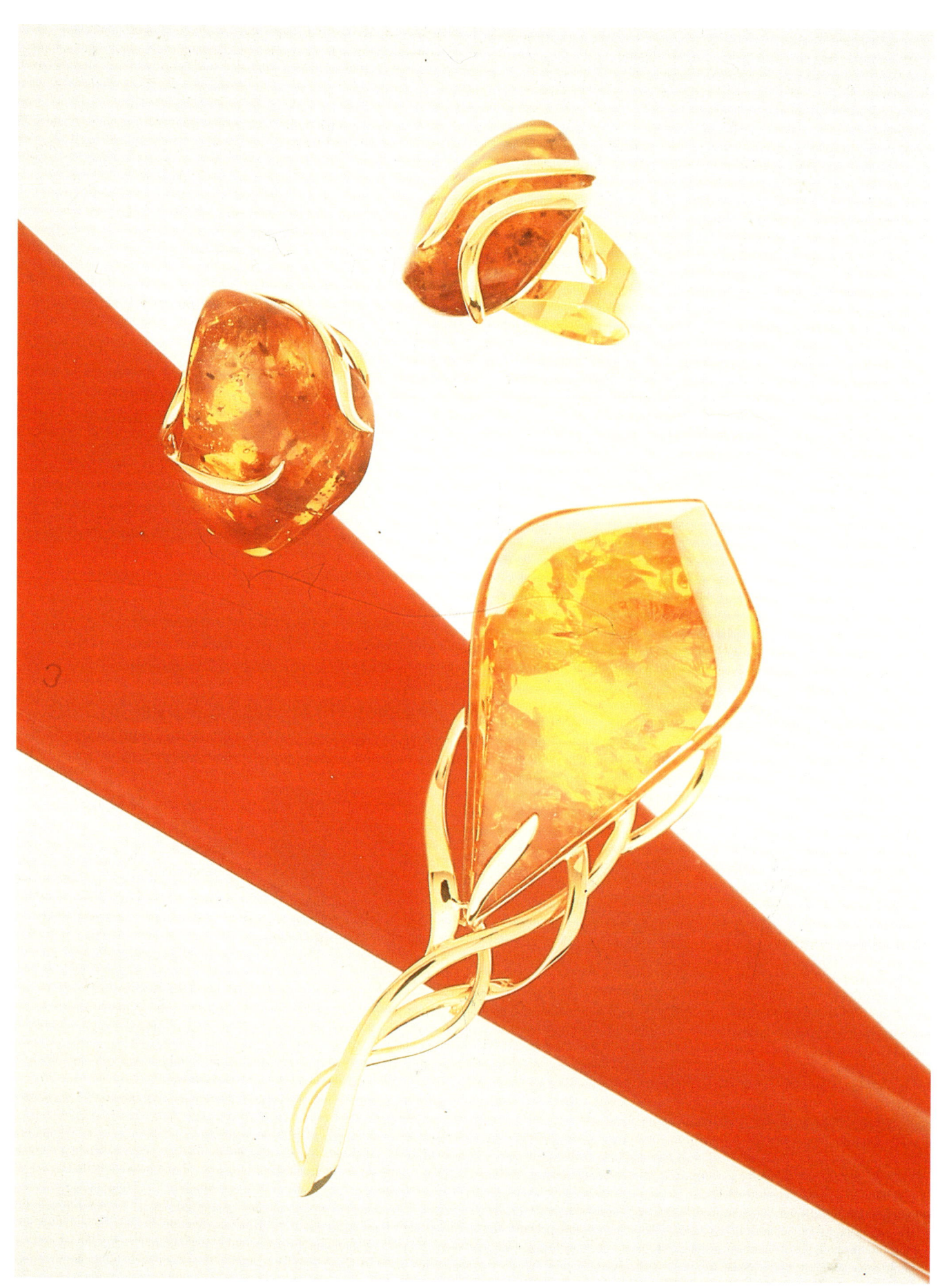

Woo Hyun Choi.
Set in gold and amber.

Russia along the coast of the Samland peninsula near Kaliningrad. Here both marine and quarry amber are available. The former is literally torn from the bottom of the sea by the erosive action of waves, which then carry it for considerable distances, as far, for example, the shores of Norway, Denmark, the Baltic Sea, and the eastern coast of England. Quarry amber is mainly extracted at Palmnicken, on the Baltic Sea, in specific locations defined as "blue earth" for their typical greenish-blue color. Steam shovels are employed to eliminate the layer of surface earth; after a forceful hosing down, the underlying amber treasure is revealed.

As briefly mentioned in the section on known varieties, amber also comes from the valley of the Hukong River (Myanmar, formerly Burma); Santo Domingo – famed for its deposits since Christopher Colombus made his second voyage to America – where there is a highly transparent quality which is currently processed on site; Sicily, along the banks of the Simeto river near Catania; Romania, at varying sites, the most productive lying in the province of Muntenia (or Greater Walachia); and Poland.

Of course amber is obtained from other spots as well, but they are of lesser importance.

Cut A vast gamut of possiblities: drop, pear, spherical, barrel-shaped with either smooth or faceted surface; en cabochon either round or oval; in addition, this gemstone is suitable for the sort of dressing aimed at producing creations of high artistic worth.

Under the lens When observing pieces of amber with a lens it is possible to make out air bubbles and even two-phase inclusions. What makes this inspection particularly interesting, however, is the chance that you may discover fossilized objects that were entrapped in the sticky resin eons ago, pieces of insects – even a whole one – or perhaps small fragments of vegetable origin. By examining the elements preserved in amber, zoologists, chemists, and paleontologists have been able to "spy" on life on Earth at the precise instant when these remnants were enclosed, millions of years past. By such observation, scientists have even been able to define percentages for various gases found in the air and discover the secrets of numerous forms of life among the flora and fauna of our prehistoric past.

Synthetics and similar substances Though no synthetic amber exists, nevertheless there is a technique for employing quite small but fairly transparent pieces of the stone which are fused when put under pressure and simultaneously brought to a temperature of about 180° C. First employed in Vienna in 1880, this procedure creates a compact product of rather good size that is normally called *ambroide*, *pressed amber* or *reconstituted amber*. As long as the pieces put into service have been carefully cleaned and chosen, it is not easy to discover the counterfeit unless it is possible to make out flow structure caused by intersoldered fragments, or oblong bubbles. In some instances, there is quite an unusual and particularly brilliant blue fluorescence.

Before it can be utilized, the nontransparent quality undergoes a clarifying process in which it is immersed in a carefully checked and moderately heated bath of linseed or rape oil, or even soluble fats. But that is not very new; as many as two thousand years ago, Pliny described a method for enhancing the beauty of this material. Today we have a dry version of the preceding treatment: the material is placed on a sand bed, which is moderately heated. In consequence, the material may reveal fractures which, due to their discoid form, are called "nasturtium leaves."

Actually, there are a number of substances that resemble amber. For convenience, we shall cite only the best known examples, that can be subdivided into two groups: natural resins and synthetic resins. *African copal resin* and the *kauri rubber* or gum *copal* belong to the first group. Neither type is fully fossilized, and they do not polish well. In technical terms they are quite similar to amber; however, if you apply a drop of ether or ethyl alcohol onto their surface it becomes quite sticky, whereas true amber suffers no such change.

Synthetic resins that are used to imitate amber are:
– *bakelite:* with a specific gravity of 1.26, it remains inert in UV, gives off acrid smoke during the hot pin test;
– *casein:* with a specific gravity of 1.33, which turns whitish under UV, and during the hot pin test gives off a smoke similar to that produced by burning corneous substances;
– *celluloid:* with specific gravity at 1.38, that becomes yellowish white under UV;
– *perspex* (or *plexiglass*): with specific gravity at 1.18;
– *polybern:* formed of tiny pieces of amber held together with a resin of colored polyester which, during the hot pin test, gives off a bitter smoke that smells like burning plastic;
– *bernat:* a plastic substance, with a specific gravity of approximately 1.23, at times containing inclusions of insects or small vegetable fragments which have obviously been added during processing.

In describing these synthetic resins, specific gravity measurements have been included as they offer clear data in making comparisons. For home testing: take a sample of authentic amber and place it in a normal glass of water to which you will add ten teaspoons of kitchen salt, one after the other; the density obtained will range from 1.12 to 1.14. Being less dense, the amber sample will always float to the surface. Since all amber imitations have a greater density than real amber, they sink to the bottom. Should they by chance float up, the solution may simply be less dense than what the procedure calls for, and you can rectify the test by slowly adding water and checking to see which substance sinks to the bottom of the glass first.

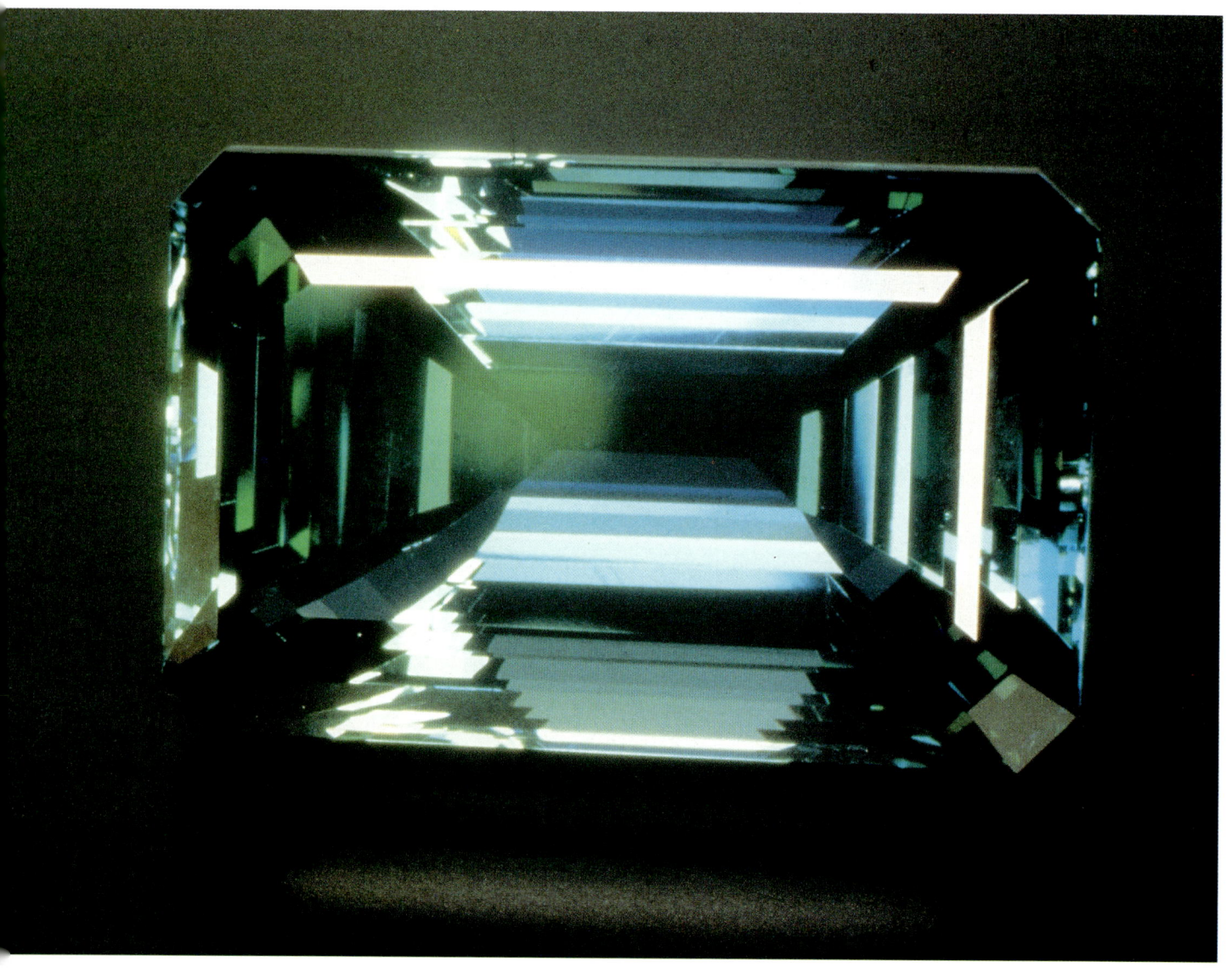

Aquamarine

GENERAL INFORMATION

How it got its name For once a common sense guess is the right one: the mineral recalls the color of sea water.

Varieties A variety of beryl (see entry), aquamarine is considered separately due to its choice position in the world of gems.

Heating yellow beryl (see entry) or greenish aquamarine there is a fair probability of getting an appealing azure shade.

Some specimens reveal an evanescent chatoyant effect; material with asterism, however, is an unusual find.

Coming from a Brazilian mine of the same name, the beryl called *maxixe* may be regarded as a special type of aquamarine and has a strong deep azure hue. Unfortunately, the brilliant shade of this stone decreases on exposure both to sunlight or particularly bright artifical light; as a result, this beryl has never had much success on the market.

Maxixe has a specific gravity equal to 2.80.

Some interesting sidelights Color here depends on the presence of iron atoms - trivalent - in the crystal lattice.

Pliny the Elder had an idea for judging the quality of this gem: place a number of aquamarines in sea water; the finest quality will so blend as to be almost invisible. It is easy to understand why this gem was held to be a sailor's good luck charm. In addition, however, it is reputed to create happy marriages and ought to make a nice wedding gift.

Recommended for thyroid problems, it also improves memory and relieves depression.

According to Ayurveda, aquamarine works upon respiratory problems and so can dispel all those typical symptoms of timidity such as repeated swallowing, increased salivation and blushing.

Celebrated aquamarines In 1910 in Marambya (Minas Gerais mines, Brazil) a superb greenish azure crystal was discovered, 48.5 cm long and weighing 110.5 kilograms. Another Brazilian find: an aquamarine crystal weighing an amazing 61 kilograms was extracted at Belo Horizonte in 1956.

A select gem on view at the Bibliothèque Nationale in Paris bears a carved likeness of Giulia, daughter of Emperor Titus; originally it was placed above the reliquary called "Charlemagne," which has since been lost.

A sea green flat oval-cut stone weighing 875 carats displays its splendor in the British Museum in London.

In the well-known Morgan collection in New York City (see the entry "Morganite"), there are three prize examples weighing respectively 160, 215, and 272 carats.

Deposits Brazilian sources maintain prime importance, notably those in the states of Minas Gerais, Alagoas, Ceará, Espirito Santo, Paraíba, and Rio Grande do Norte. However the city of Teófilo Otoni is the indisputable Brazilian capital for the gem as it boasts a surrounding bevy of deposits spread over a 100-kilometer radius.

Other significant deposits are found on the island of Madagascar in its central mountainous area.

Meanwhile, Russian locations in the Urals and Tranbaikalia, which once disclosed superb examples, now seem to be mined out.

Of minor value, but worth listing are the deposits in: Argentina, Australia, Myanmar, Mozambique, Namibia, Norway, Sri Lanka, the United States (California, Connecticut, Maine), Tanzania, and Zimbabwe.

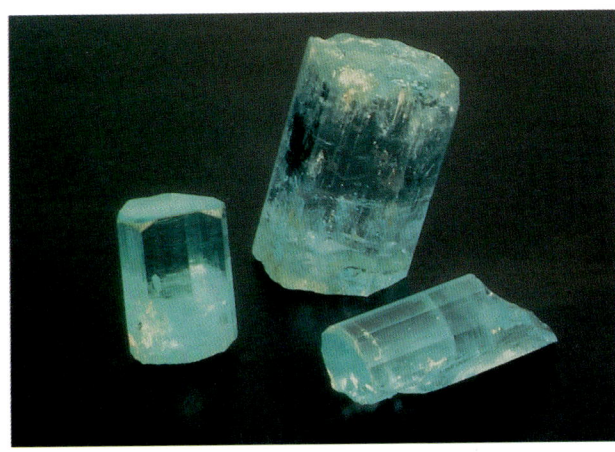

Chemical Formula:	$Be_3 Al_2 O Si_6 O_{18}$ – beryllium aluminium silicate
Hardness:	7½ – 8 (Mohs scale)
Specific Gravity:	2.68 – 2.74
Refraction:	biaxial birefringent
Color:	variable tones of azure or greenish azure

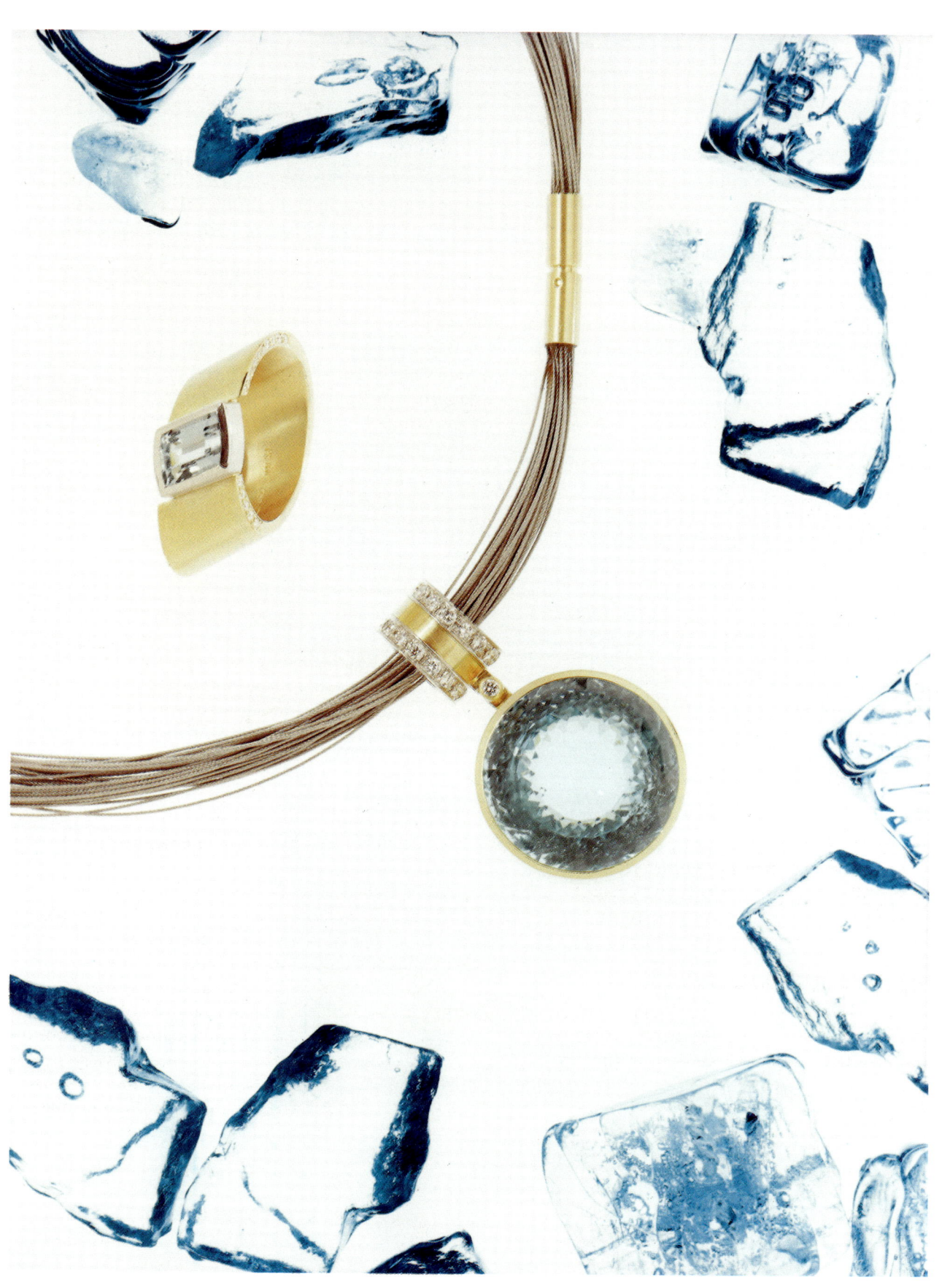

KRISTEN EHHALT-VUSEC.
Gold necklace in platinum, diamonds, and 62-carat aquamarine.
Gold ring, platinum, diamonds, and green-blue beryl.

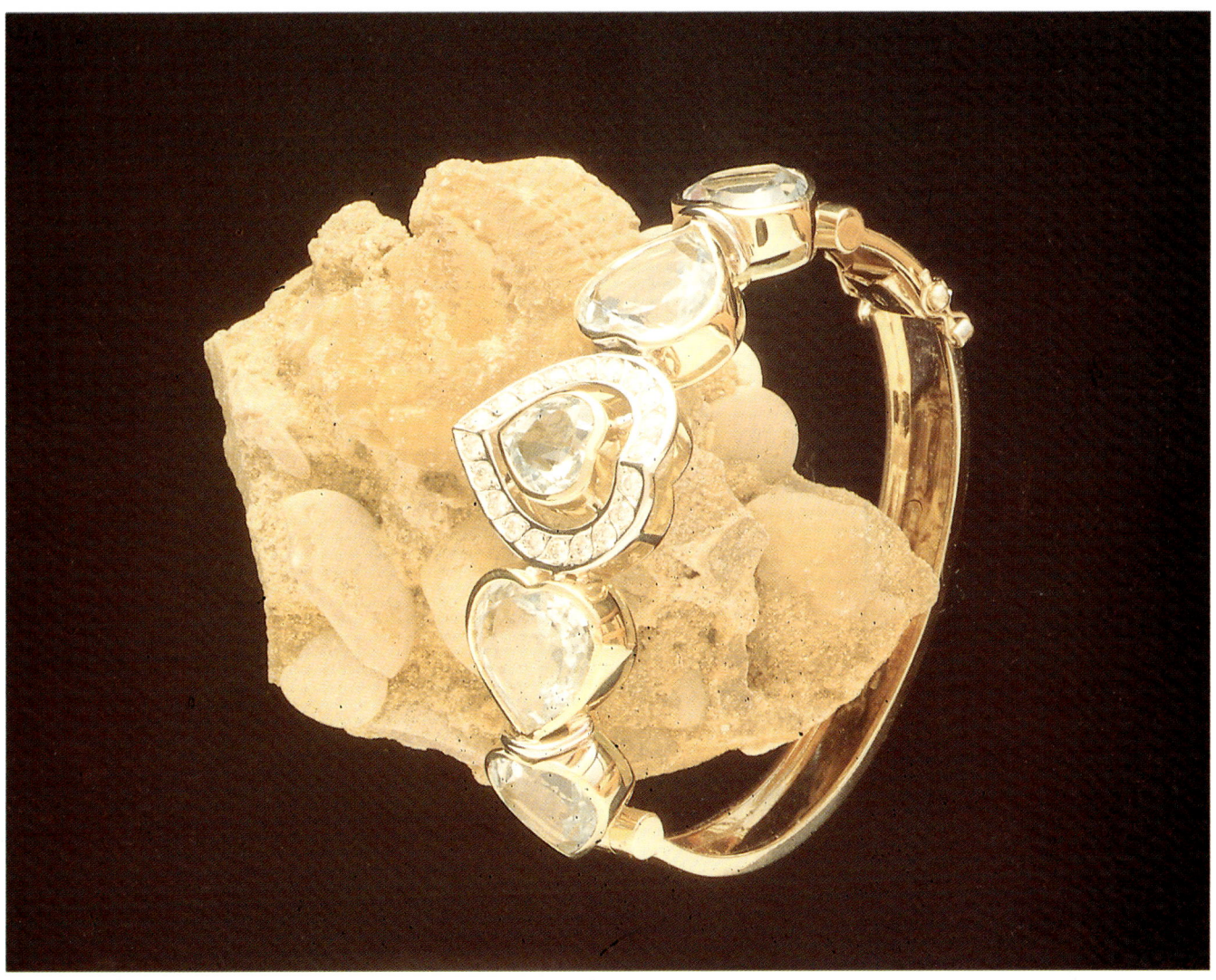

MARCELLO PIZZARI.
Gold bracelet with aquamarines and diamonds.

Under the lens Often aquamarine contains no inclusions, though we may sometimes note very fine needles, two-phase inclusions and certain typical inclusions termed "chrysanthemum," formed of round layers with jagged edges.

Synthetics and similar substances A synthetic aquamarine has been produced in Russia with the hydrothermic method; however, since it is rather costly the product is not well known on the market.

Under the lens the surface of this synthetic reveals a color fluidification similar to that observed in the synthetic Biron emerald (see entry).

Azure topaz, a much less valuable stone, is sometimes mistaken for aquamarine. Key technical data for differentiating: the specific gravity of topaz exceeds that of aquamarine by 35%.

Other problems of identification may occur between aquamarine and light azure corundum, euclase, azure topaz, azure tourmaline and zircon.

Here again we find that like-colored glassy substances are common counterfeits; and we must beware of synthetic azure spinel (see entry), which, however, is monorefringent.

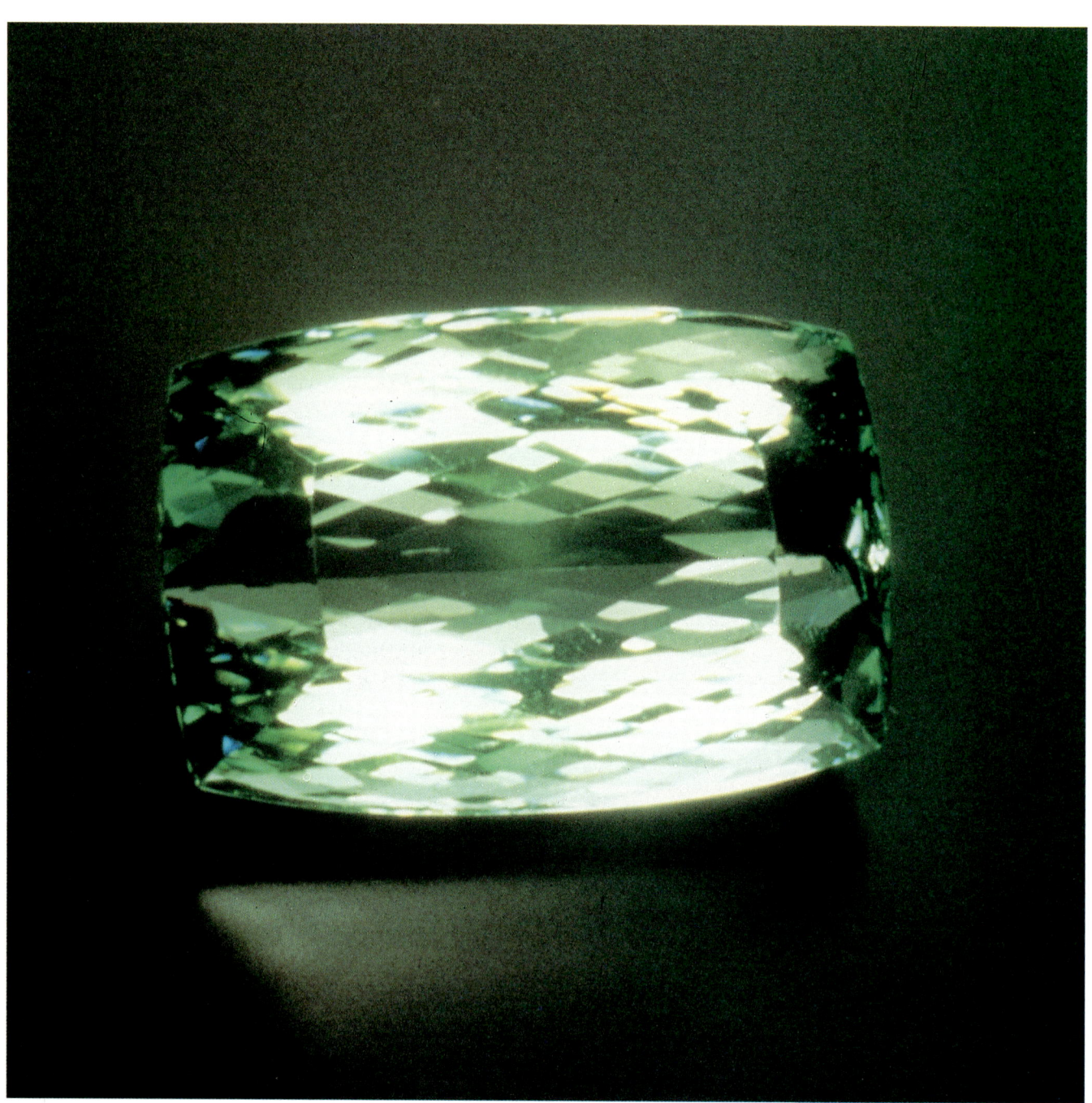

Beryl

GENERAL INFORMATION

How it got its name We can trace this to the Greek term *berylos* but have no key to its etymology; some experts suggest ancient India as a linguistic source.

Varieties To this mineralogical group belong two renowned varieties: emerald and aquamarine; both of these illustrious stones have been reviewed under separate headings.

Other varieties include *golden beryl*, (or *heliodore*), *pink beryl* (or *morganite*), *red beryl* (or *bixbiit*) and *colorless beryl* (or *goshenite*).

Note that when yellow beryl undergoes heat treatment from 300° to 600° C it may take on an aquamarine blue coloring, though the genuine aquamarine is certainly a more prized material.

The Greek words *élios* and *dóron* have given us this "gift of the sun."

Though it is unusual, there are instances when pink beryl evinces a chatoyant effect; at times the material is heated to deepen color.

"Morganite" was so dubbed by mineralogist G.F. Kunz in tribute to the eminent collector J.P. Morgan.

Among all the beryls, the red variety is quite rare, especially if you are looking for a specimen ideal for faceting.

The odd sounding "bixbiit" was named by Eppler, probably because this variety is usually found together with black bixbyite crystals. Absolutely unfounded is the story that allies this terminology with the Arizona city of Besbee.

Goshenite, however, does depend on a place name: the city of Goshen where the largest quantities are extracted.

Turning to the colorless variety, we must warn that there are few and rare specimens available.

Some interesting sidelights One line of exegetical interpretation insists that beryl is the Church's symbol for perfect prophecy. A unique example is the black star beryl discovered in Mozambique.

Celebrated yellow beryl A splendid specimen: a 2,054-carat processed stone is on display in the Smithsonian Institution in Washington, D.C.

Deposits
- *Yellow beryl:* Brazil, Madagascar, Mozambique, Namibia, the United States (Connecticut).
- *Pink beryl:* Brazil (Minas Gerais), Madagascar, the United States (California).
- *Red beryl:* Russia (Urals) and – mainly – in the United States (Utah, California).
- *Colorless beryl:* Russia (Urals) and – mainly – in the United States (Massachusetts).

Cut Transparent material over a certain weight can be cut with any technique; beryls extracted in Brazil are usually given a rectangular or square cut with rounded sides and lozenge-shaped facets.

Under the lens
- *Yellow beryl:* inclusions look very like those observed in aquamarine (see entry), and they often share the same deposit site.
- *Pink beryl:* at times we may observe very fine needles; chatoyant specimens have a thick network of tubular inclusions.
- *Red beryl:* in the infrequent faceted specimen we may observe liquid inclusions, or – rarely – two-phase and crystal inclusions; color is often in zones.
- *Colorless beryl:* two-phase and crystal inclusions.

Synthetics and similar substances Quite recently Biron International of Perth, Australia, has achieved a pink synthetic beryl by hydrothermal treatment. As is the case with Biron synthetic emeralds (see entry), of early production, examination

Chemical Formula:	$Be_3 Al_2 Si_6 O_{18}$ – aluminium beryllium silicate
Hardness:	7½ – 8 (Mohs scale)
Specific Gravity:	2.60 – 2.90
Refraction:	uniaxial birefringent
Color:	azure, yellow, pink, red, various shades of green, and colorless

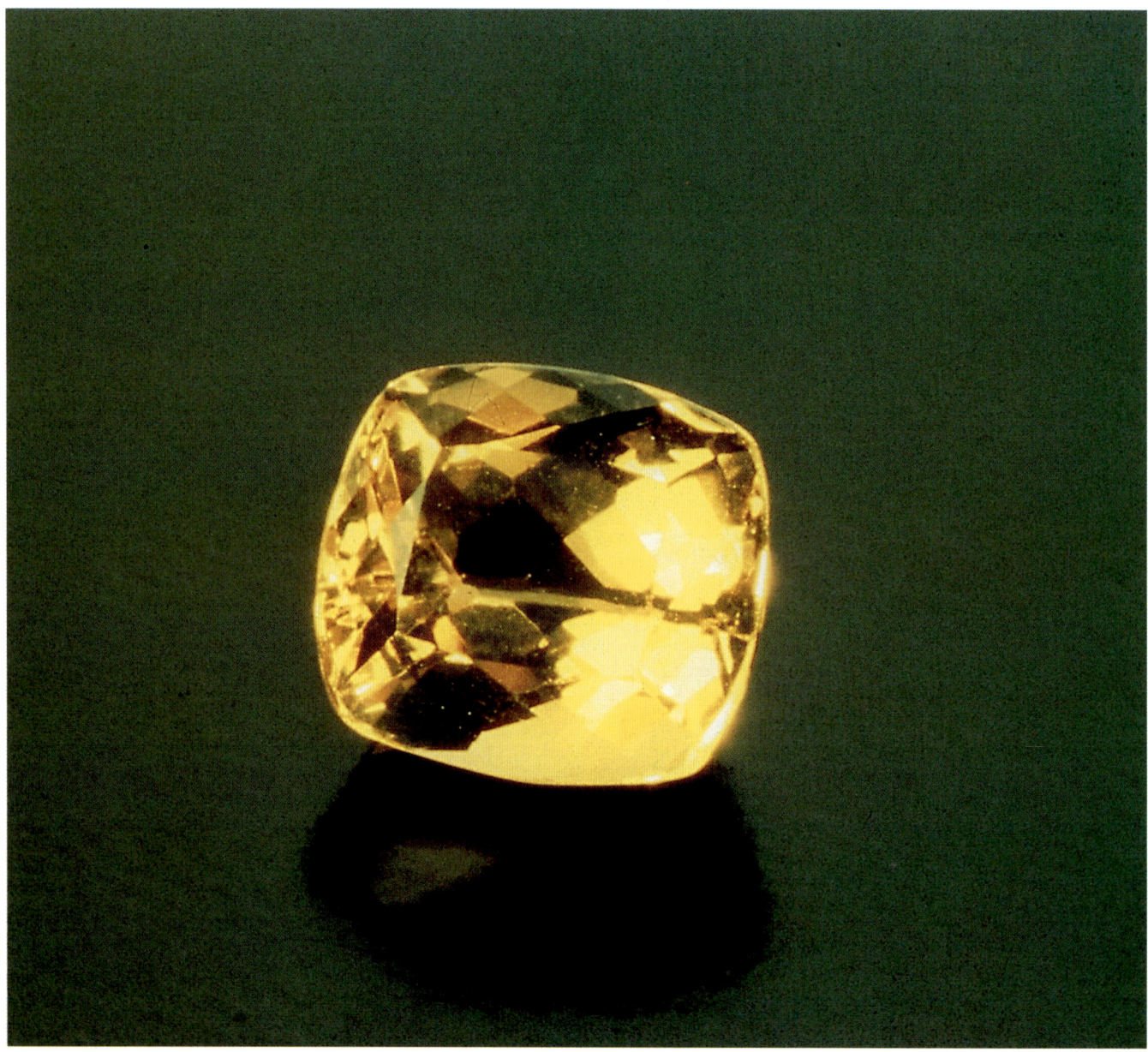

Golden beryl or heliodor.

with a 10x lens will reveal color fluidification and inclusions resembling the fingerprint category.

For a full account of this synthetic product, see an article by this book's co-author in the magazine "Antwerp Gems", edited by the HRD Institute; ample photographs are included.

To avoid confusion, a list of similar stones and their characteristics is essential:
- *Yellow beryl:* may be confused with brazilianite, datolite, olivine, citrine quartz, topaz, and tourmaline.
- *Pink beryl:* may be mistaken for natural and synthetic pink corundum, kunzite and pink topaz; and remember that there is a very deceptive doppiette on the market composed of a garnet layer on top and pink glass in the bottom section.
- *Red beryl:* when color shadings are the same, rubelite often passes for beryl.
- *Colorless beryl:* is easily confused with all other colorless stones and has even been used to imitate diamond; in this case the section of the stone inserted in a setting is given a partial metallic sheathing.

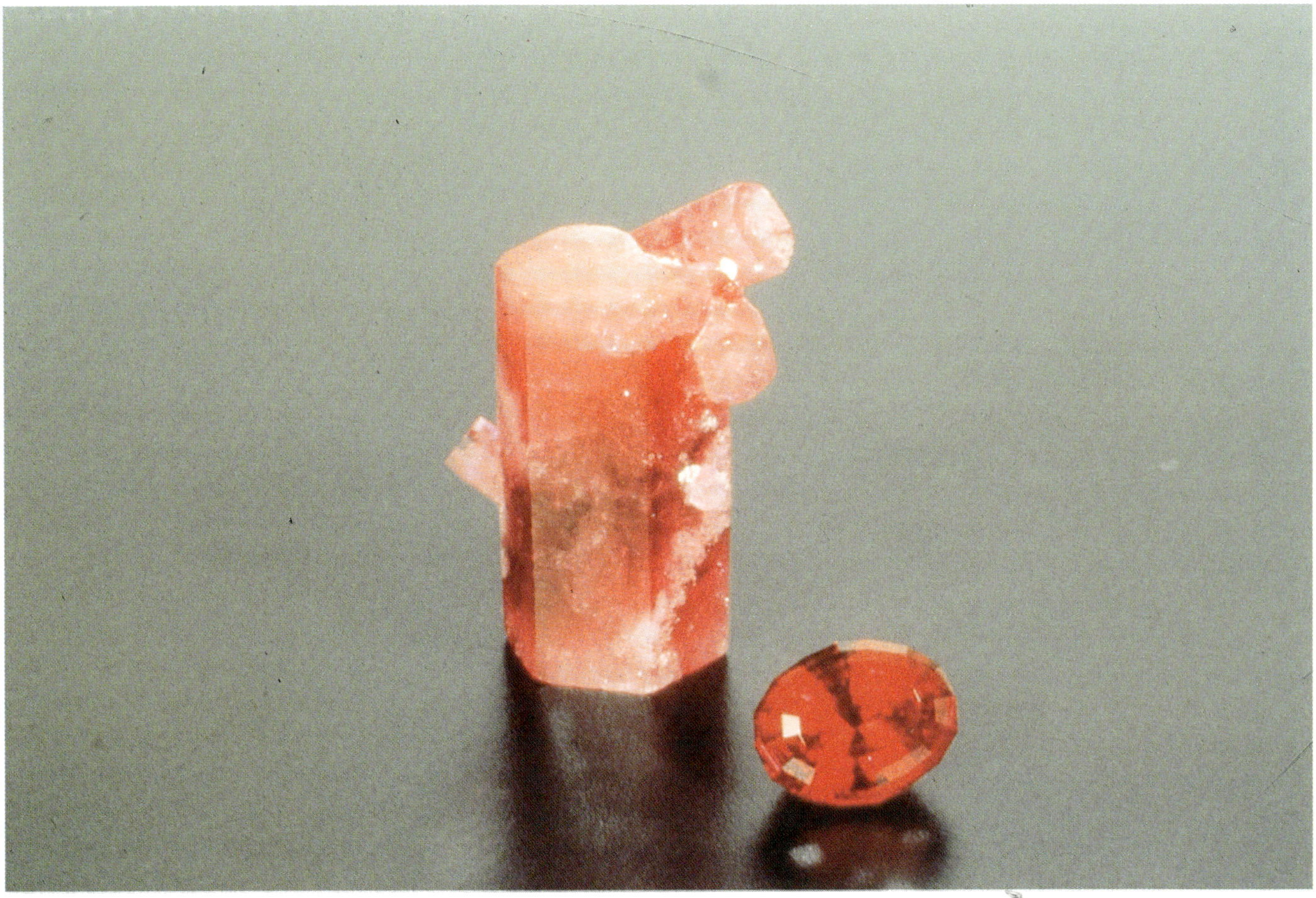

Red beryl from Utah, USA.

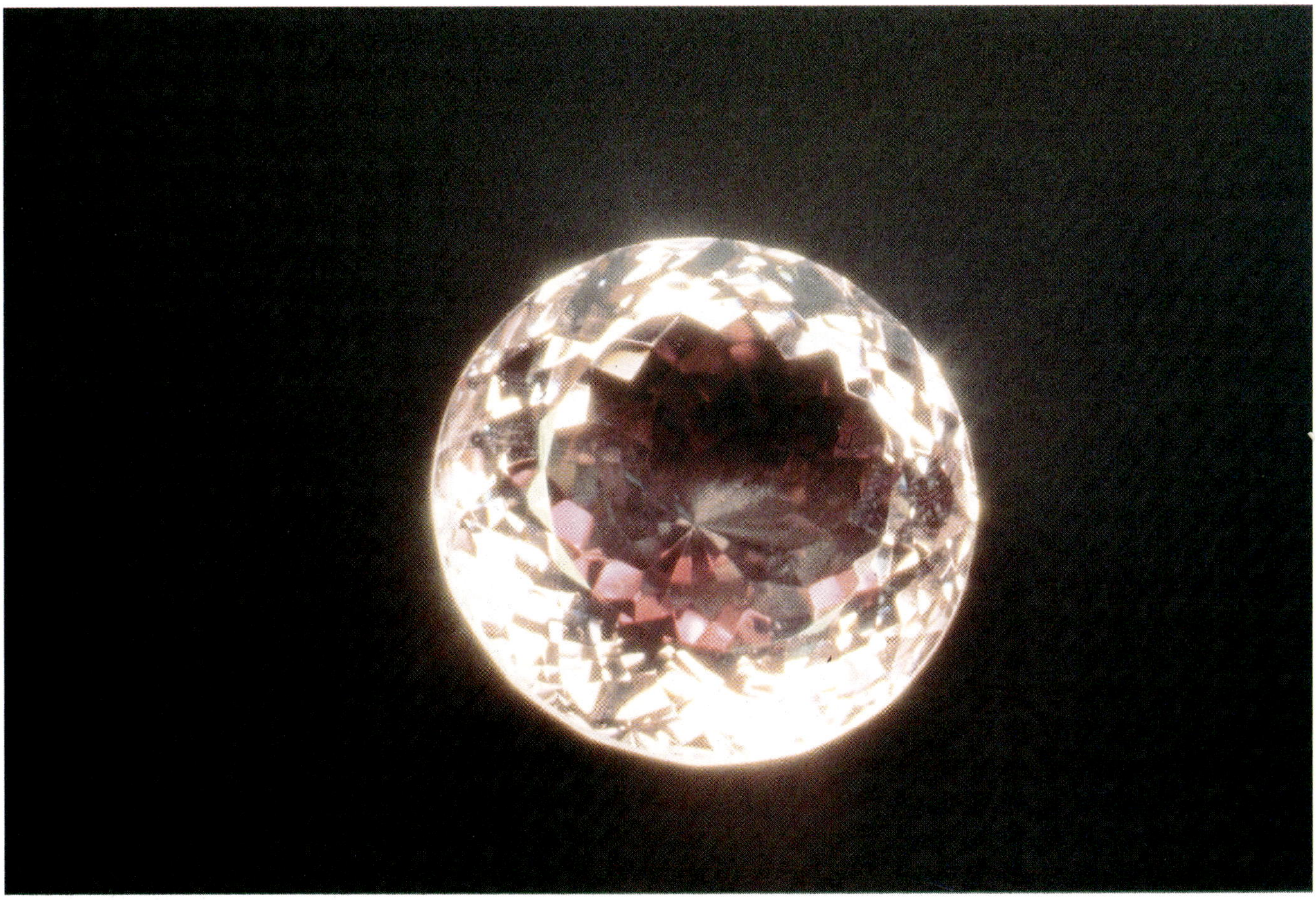

Rose beryl or morganite.

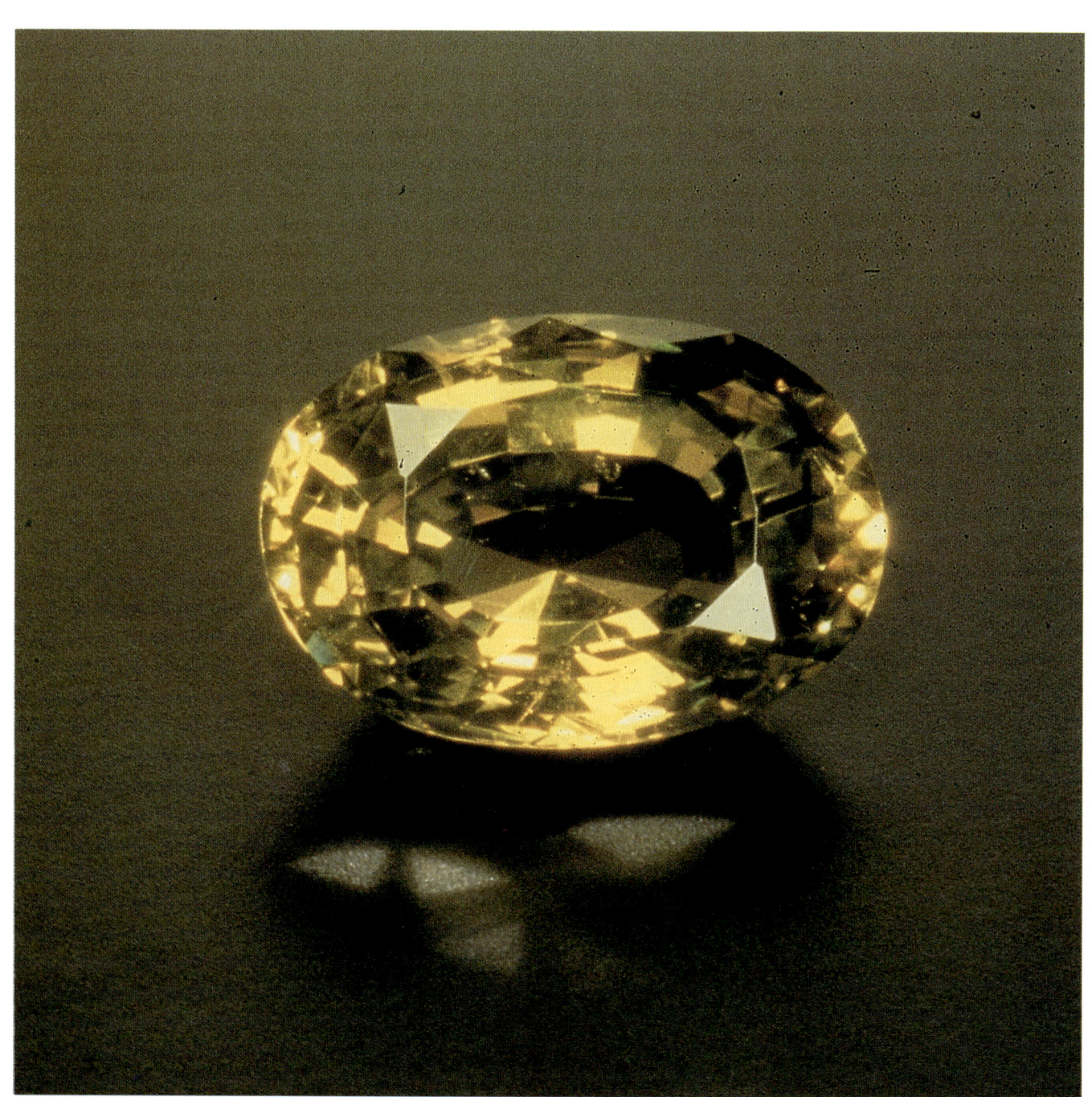

Chrysoberyl

GENERAL INFORMATION

How it got its name From the Greek terms *khrysos* (gold) and *berylos* (beryl). As discussed below in "Varieties," there are two quite distinct classifications: *alexandrite* and *cat's eye*. The former name was coined to record the stone's discovery in Russia in 1830 on the very day on which Tsar Alexander II came of age; cat's eye, on the other hand, refers to the ray which, when the stone is held to the light, resembles the glowing, contracted pupil of a feline's eye.

Varieties Current terminology mates *chrysoberyl* with the particular color of the stone defined. Exceptions to this rule are: the grass-green colored variety that is called *alexandrite*; and gems of other colors which, cut en cabochon because they are not transparent, suddenly display a cat's eye, undulating luster, and must be classified under that name.

It is important to remember that all other chatoyant stones are also identified according to their mineral category: for example, cat's eye quartz.

Once upon a time, cat's eye was called *cymophane*, Greek for "wavelike." As for alexandrite: it looks grass green in sunlight but becomes red or violet red under artificial incandescent light, a phenomenon called *cangianza* (changing colors). These two chrysoberyls are much sought-after and can be sold for quite high prices. The value of a cat's eye stone is judged by the sharpness of the "cat's eye" ray; while the most attractive color is a rich honey yellow.

Some interesting sidelights
Alexandrite is the favorite good luck charm for people seeking adventure or forced to make major life decisions. Its typical color changes are supposed to correspond to its capacity to aid and abet people who keep an open mind to all life's realities.

It is also said to facilitate mental development, eliminate memory problems, and impede the progress of arteriosclerosis.

Celebrated chrysoberyls The British Museum is the owner of a lovely yellow specimen known as "Hope," and an equally choice alexandrite, both of which weigh about 45 carats.

Sri Lanka was provenance of a 1,876-carat alexandrite, the largest example of this stone ever found. For the largest faceted specimen, 66 carats, visit the Smithsonian Institution in Washington, D.C., where you can also admire two gorgeous cat's eyes, weighing 58 and 172 carats respectively.

Should you be interested in further examples, there is always the Tsar's treasure collection in Russia where highly valuable chrysoberyls are on display.

And a private collector in Milan has an exquisite, 28.32-carat olive-green stone that was mined in Sri Lanka.

Deposits First discoveries were in Ekaterinburg, Russia, and later in the southern Urals, but these sources are now practically mined out. We do still obtain good chrysoberyls from the gemmiferous gravel pits of Sri Lanka; nevertheless, alexandrites mined in Russia maintain top value due to their color. Other important deposits lie in Brazil (Minas Gerais, Minas Novas, Bahía); and we must also mention the mines in India (Orissa), Madagascar, Rhodesia, Tanzania (at Lake Manyara), Zambia, and Zimbabwe. For the most important deposits of cat's eye, we are led back to Sri Lanka's gem gravels.

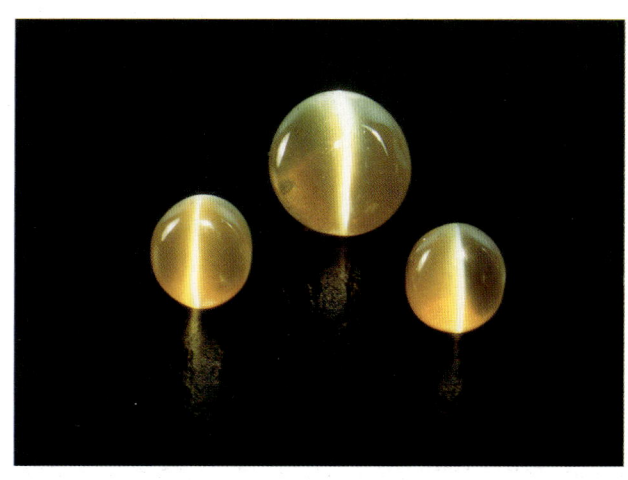

Chemical Formula: *BeAl$_2$O$_4$ – beryllium aluminium oxide*
Hardness: *8½ (Mohs scale)*
Specific gravity: *3.71 – 3.72*
Refraction: *biaxial birefringent*
Color: *colorless, brown, golden yellow, greenish yellow, green, green-yellow*

Cut A mixed cut is best for chrysoberyls, usually the brilliant cut with faceted crown and the pavilion step cut. A pure emerald cut is not normally used, even though it is generally employed for other important colored stones. Obviously if we want to

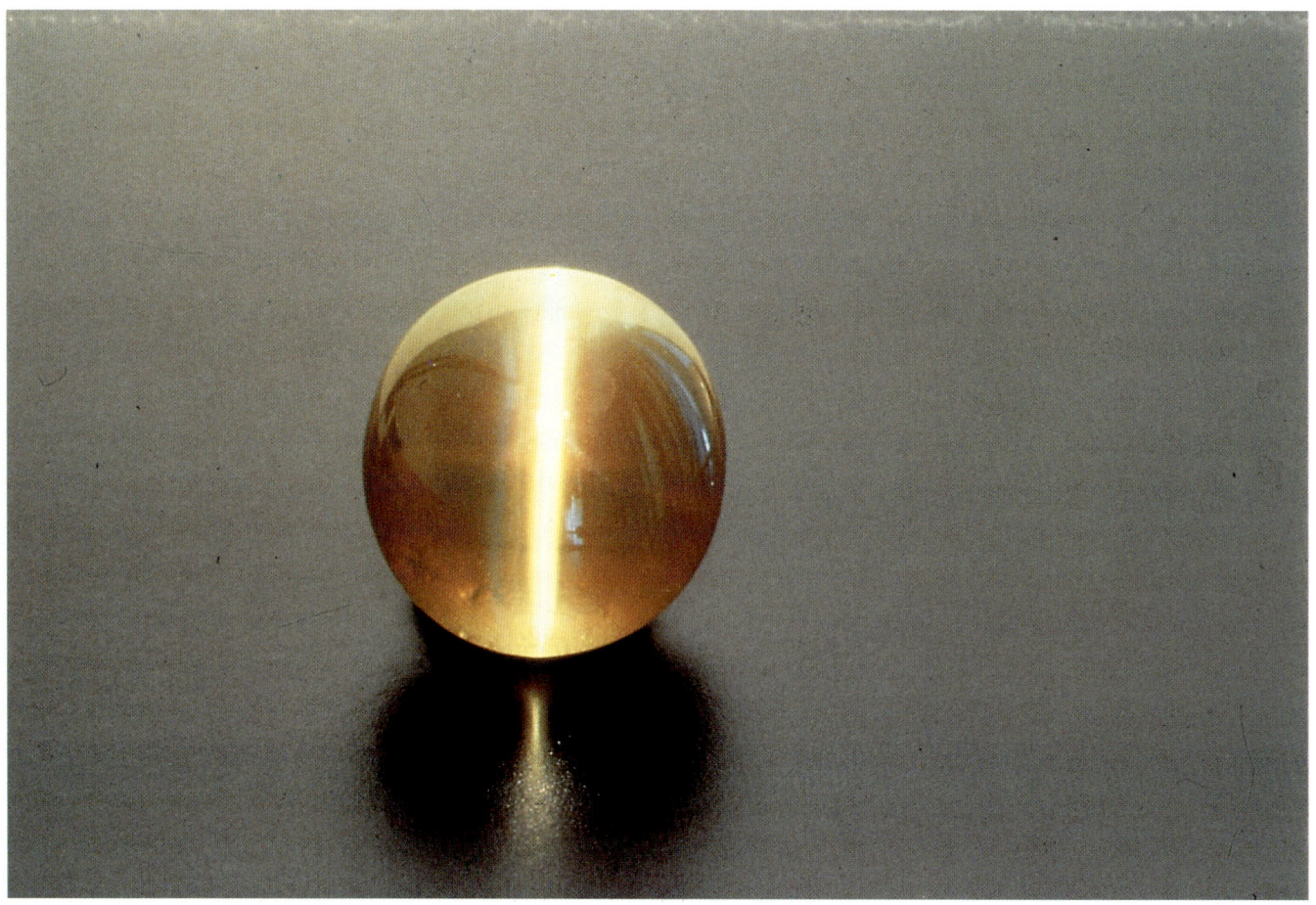

Sri Lankan cat's eye.

show off the brilliance of the cat's eye ray, the material must be cut en cabochon, with the part that will be visible in a set piece placed a bit higher than is usual for that cut.

Under the lens Close inspection can reveal short needles, very fine foliations, crystals, and two-phase inclusions (liquid with an air bubble), and even tubular cavities. It is precisely these cavities and needles that produce the optical effects in an en cabochon cut.

Synthetics and similar substances Alexandrite has been synthetically produced since 1973, with two basic procedures. In one type, lens examination will disclose curved striae on the surface, whereas the second type has two-phase inclusions which are similar in every way to those contained in the natural gems.

So, in order to confirm whether you have the synthetic or the real article, you had best ask for the help of an expert with a specially equipped laboratory.

Often travelers to Egypt purchase so-called alexandrites, which, in reality, are synthetic violet corundums (at times with a slight chameleon effect). Remember that in natural light alexandrite has a grass green and not violet color; therefore you must be on the alert for green-colored artificial glass which remains green under incandescent light and will not turn red, red-violet as, however, genuine alexandrite does. Or you may come across certain doppiettes (two-layer fakes) with a very attractive chameleon effect, such as those products that are garnet red on top with green glass on the bottom.

There is a quartz cat's eye that is occasionally taken for the genuine article, but it is certainly much less valuable.

Generally chrysoberyls may be confused with andalusite, brazilianite, spodumene, heliodor, hiddenite, olivine, yellow corundums, scapolite, sinhalite, spinel, topaz, tourmaline, zircon.

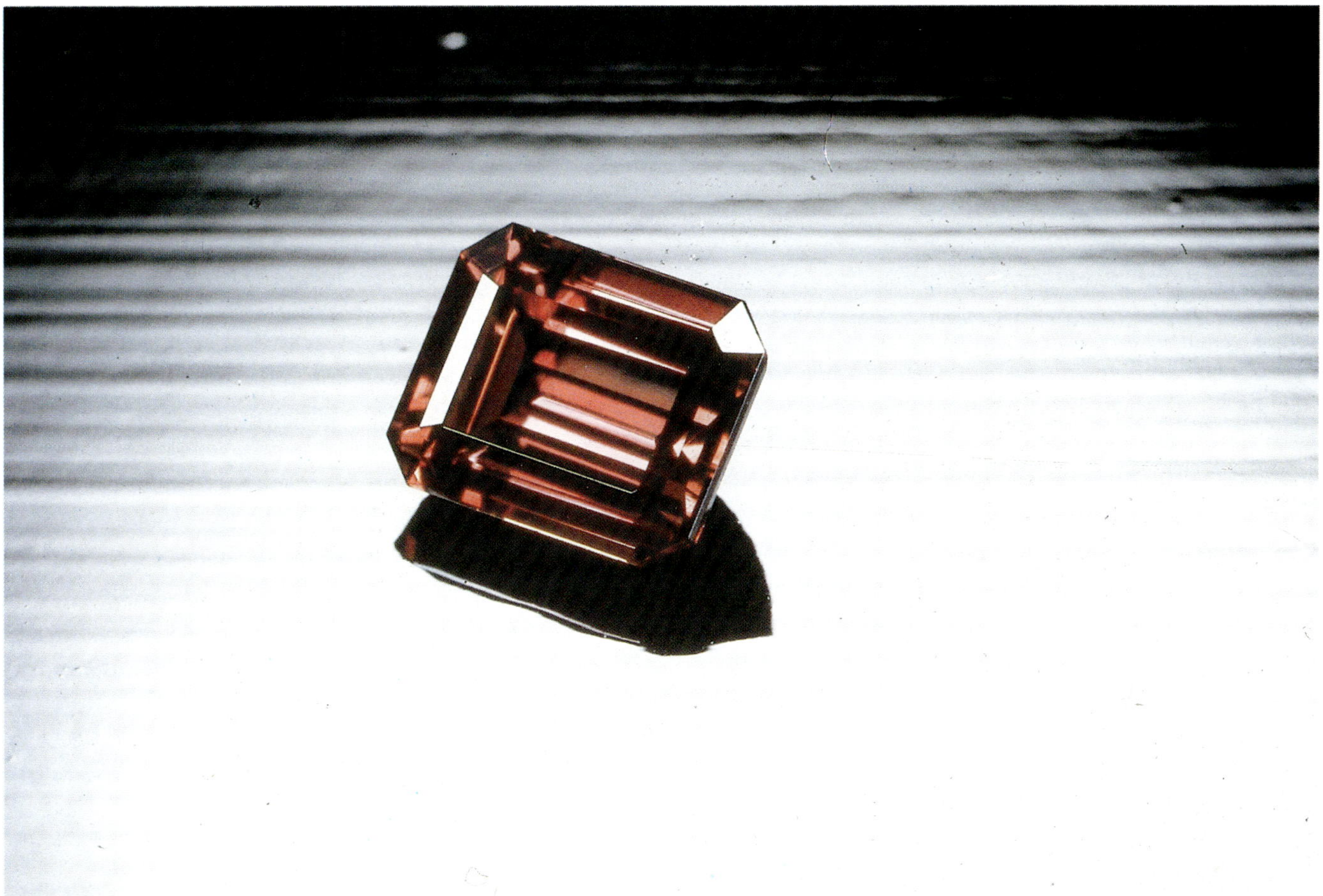

Alexandrite in natural light.

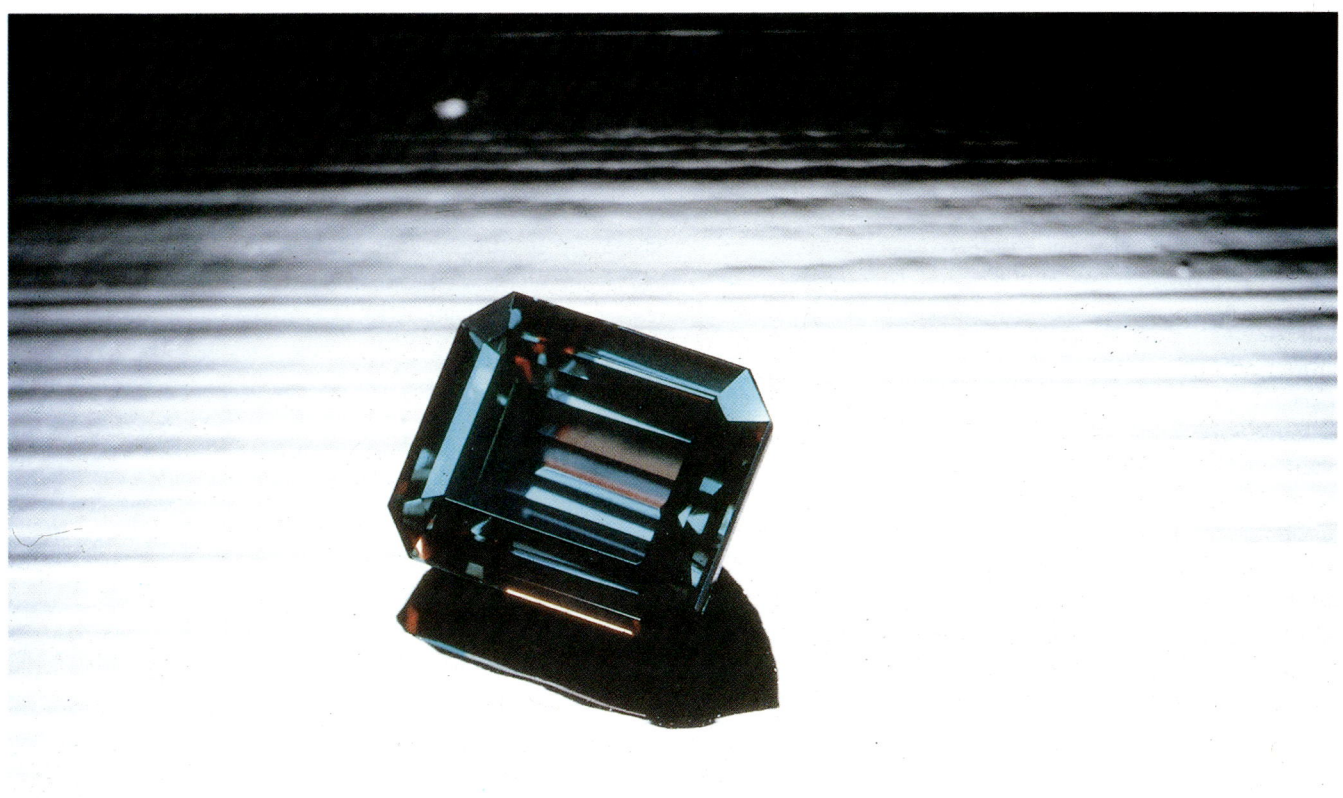

Alexandrite in incandescent light.

Coral

GENERAL INFORMATION

How it got its name The Greeks called it *korallion*. Their mythology has passed on a lovely tale according to which coral was formed from the blood of the Gorgon Medusa. After Perseus killed her, he supposedly tried to wash off her blood in the sea; according to the story, drops of the blood trickled from her severed head and fell on thin branches which turned into coral.

Varieties Men have fished for coral since prehistoric times. At the dawn of civilization this precious material was used as money by Sumerians, Assyrians and Phoenicians. The Chinese, Japanese, and Indians used it both as currency and adornment.

It is generally believed that coral is the skeleton of specific polyps, namely of the Coelentrates Type, Anthoza Class, Gorgonocea Order, and Coral Family. This is, in fact, the scaffolding on which these animals live in colonies, thereby attaching the calcium carbonate contained in sea water. Branched or arborescent formations are the most frequent. There are as many as 27 types of polyps that are capable of creating coral formations, but those whose material can be dressed and used for jewelry are: Elatius, Japonicum, Konojoi (Japanese and Chinese Sea); Secundum (Hawaii); Rubrum (Mediterranean).

When it is just gathered, coral's value depends on uniformity of color, the thickness of its branches, and its probable quantity as a finished product. Up to a year or so ago, Mediterranean corals were classified as: *choice pieces*, the largest and most uniformly colored; *barbaresco* named after its fishing site, and of about a 2½ to 3½ inch – (6 to 8 mm) thickness; and finally *terragno* about 1¼ to 2 inches (3 to 5 mm) in thickness. Each group, of course, had its own price range. Times have changed, and now all coral that is fished in the Mediterranean is sold in mass, and subdivision into groups is now only used for coral gathered from seas near Asia. Black coral was first encountered around 1960; it is produced by *Antipathes spiralis* and is mainly composed of a corneous substance. But there is even a blue coral, produced by the *Allopara subirolcea*; and this, too, is corneous.

Some interesting sidelights Ever since ancient times coral has been considered a marvelous amulet; Egyptians and Greeks spread crushed coral on their fields in the belief that it would produce abundant crops. In Africa it was looked upon as a symbol of wealth, fertility, and sexuality, its fame so widespread that even today the Masai use coral for their most important personal adornment.

Folk medicine in India has always advised the use of coral to cure anaemia; for coral, it seems, should stimulate the production of red blood cells. As adopted in Tantra yoga, this material is supposed to reroute erotic energy toward the brain, transforming sexual impulse into creativity, intuition, and imagination.

Areas where it is gathered Probably the best known coral is the small white variety found in the Mediterranean (offshore Tunisia and Algeria; off the coasts of Sicily, Campania (especially in the waters around Naples), Sardinia, Corsica, and France (in the waters off Cannes). Around 1970, Japanese coral appeared on the market; its provenance is the Ryukyu Islands and it is prized for its red color.

Since the Mediterranean area, and Italy in particular, is so important in this field, the coral fished in these waters is internationally called "Sardegna." There is, in fact, also a commonly accepted subgrouping

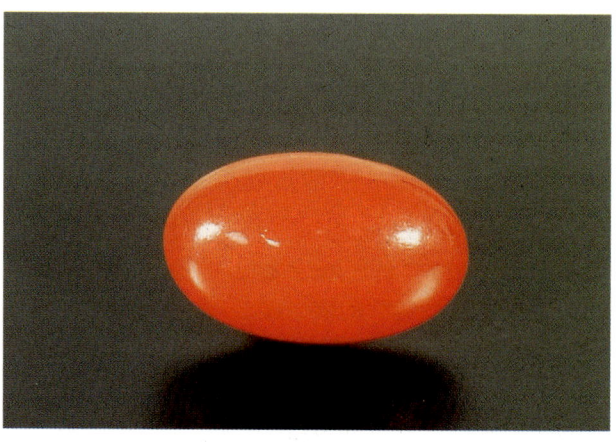

Chemical Formula: *mainly formed of calcium carbonate ($CaCO_3$), small percentages of magnesium carbonate ($MgCO_3$), and an organic substance of proteinous origin*
Hardness: *3½ (Mohs scale)*
Specific Gravity: *2.60–2.70; 1.34 (black color)*
Refraction: *monorefringent*
Color: *white, pink, red, black and blue*

based on color, with terminology in Italian, as indicated in the following table.

Commonly accepted name	Corresponding color
bianco	pure white
pelle d'angelo	light pink, uniform
rosa pallido	pink
rosa vivo	bright pink
secondo colore	salmon
rosso	bright red
rosso scuro	dark red
arciscuro o carbonetto	very dark red (oxblood)

One coral type is missing from the above table, and that is the Sicilian variety called "Sciacca," which was once gathered about thirty miles offshore from this village. After thirteen years of intense activity, in 1887 this variety was not for sale for five years. Unfortunately, at the end of this period it was found that the three coral reefs were completely depleted. This lovely material had a special pink salmon color, ranging from bright to the palest possible pink, with occasional delicate shadings.

The table for Japanese coral is also organized according to color, after which it is named, as shown in the table at the bottom of this page.

In today's coral market you may also encounter other designations referring to coral fished in the Pacific Ocean during the last thirty years. These names are internationally accepted and in common usage:

Midway (1965) – white color; or pink with red specks or striae;

Garnet (1970) – a deeply violet pink with some yellowish shadings;

Miss (1976) – pink color with a slight shading to violet;

Deep Sea (1979) – a red color which tends to lighten as the branch thickens;

Cut Be it of Mediterranean or Pacific provenance, most coral is dressed in Italy, and generally in the Naples area at Torre del Greco, site of a long and famous tradition in coral working, where the craft is mainly practiced by women. Production is varied, including various beads, small intaglio objects, cameos, and even pieces of indisputable artistic value.

Under the lens Observing an uncut branch with a lens you can note a number of grooves along its axis. Beads, on the other hand, may reveal foliations that radiate like the spokes of a wheel, or even a series of concentric circles. Coral from the Japan Sea presents color layers that occasionally alternate with white, marbled areas.

In black coral, which has a lower specific gravity, equal to 1.34, spiral-shaped fractures may be observed.

To check undressed pieces, the application of acids on red, pink, and white coral creates carbon anhydrite and produces an effervescence (a fact that reminds us to be careful that dressed pieces do not come into contact with acids, which will surely damage them).

When black and blue coral are touched by a hot pin they give off a distinct smell of keratin, like the odor of a burning fingernail.

Synthetics and similar substances A fairly wide range of materials are employed in creating coral imitations: gum and chalk mixtures; powdered marble; coral dust compressed with special binders. But there are even fairly simple imitation procedures involving glass, or plastic or porcelain substances. In some cases coloring is added, but this is easily detected since it dissolves in solvents such as acetone.

Another material placed on sale is produced by Gilson in France and is composed of calcite and artificial coloring; like those imitations cited above, it lacks coral structure. When real coral is of distinctly low quality, it is often stuccoed and its color improved by staining which generally penetrates more deeply into the fractures where UV inspection reveals a more marked purple-red. At times, the shell of the *Strombus Gigas* is used for coral imitations that display an appealing pink tone, usually quite uniform, though once in a while it may contain a barely discernable though characteristic flame-shaped structure. Take note that this particular imitation is not always easy to identify.

Name		Color
English	*Japanese*	
White	shiro	all white; occasionally has small spots
Rose or angel's skin	bokè	pink with white center (must have a uniform color when processed)
Bright red	momo	cherry red going from dark red to pale pink
Dark red	aka	dark red with white center (center disappears after dressing)

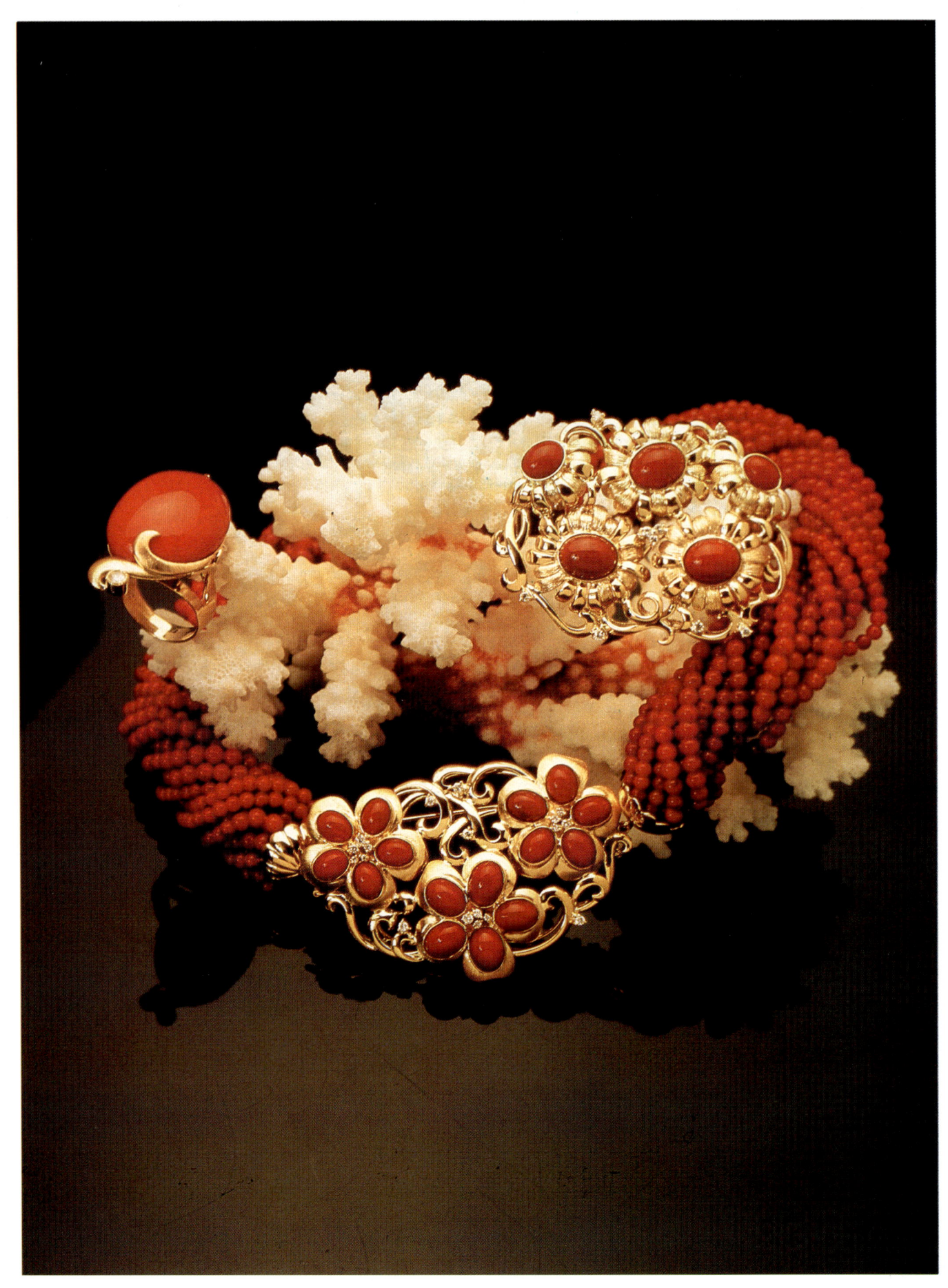

Woo Hyun Choi.
Brooch, choker, and ring in gold with coral of exceptional quality.

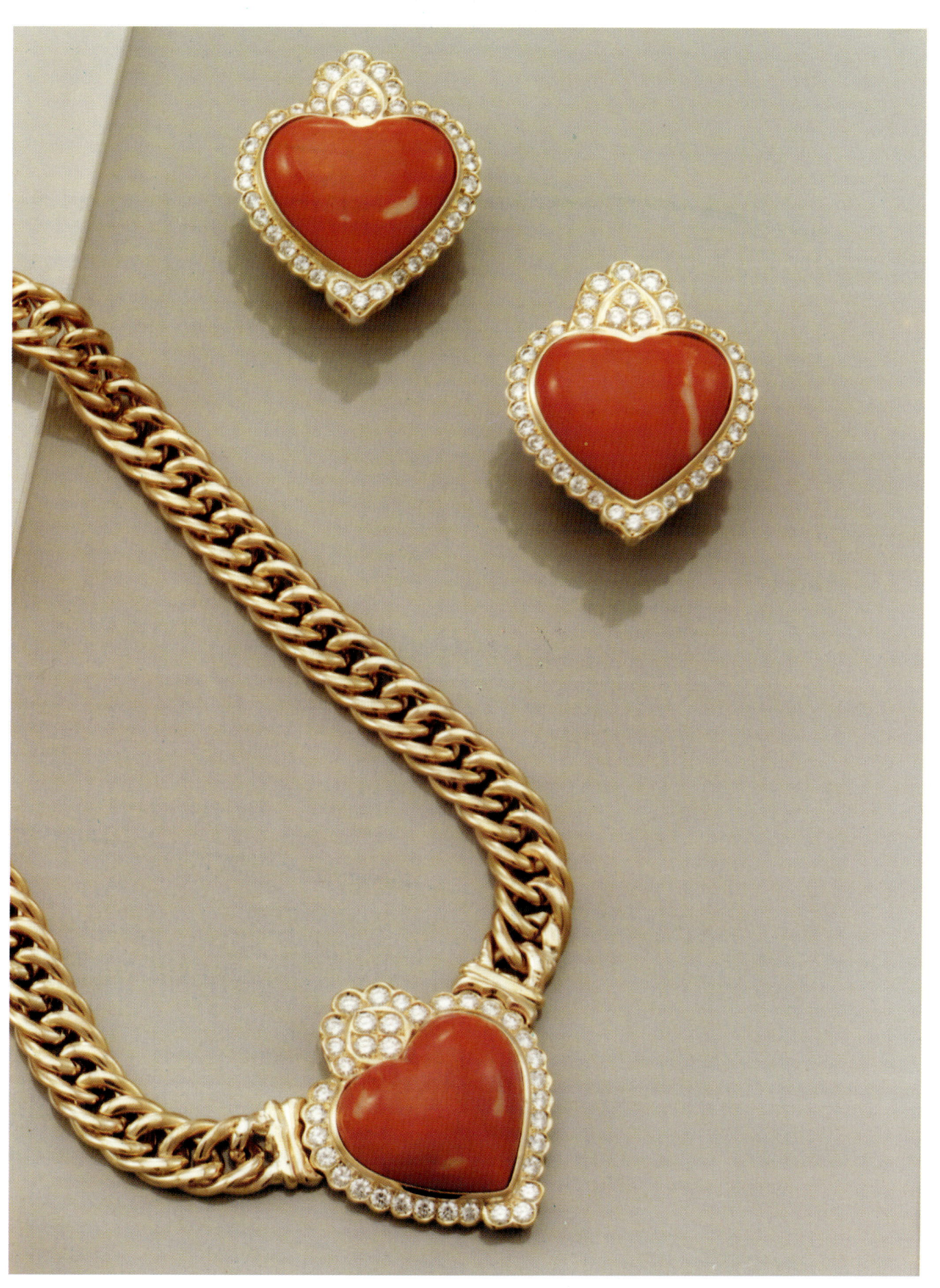

Julieta de Castro.
Gold necklace and earrings with diamonds and coral.

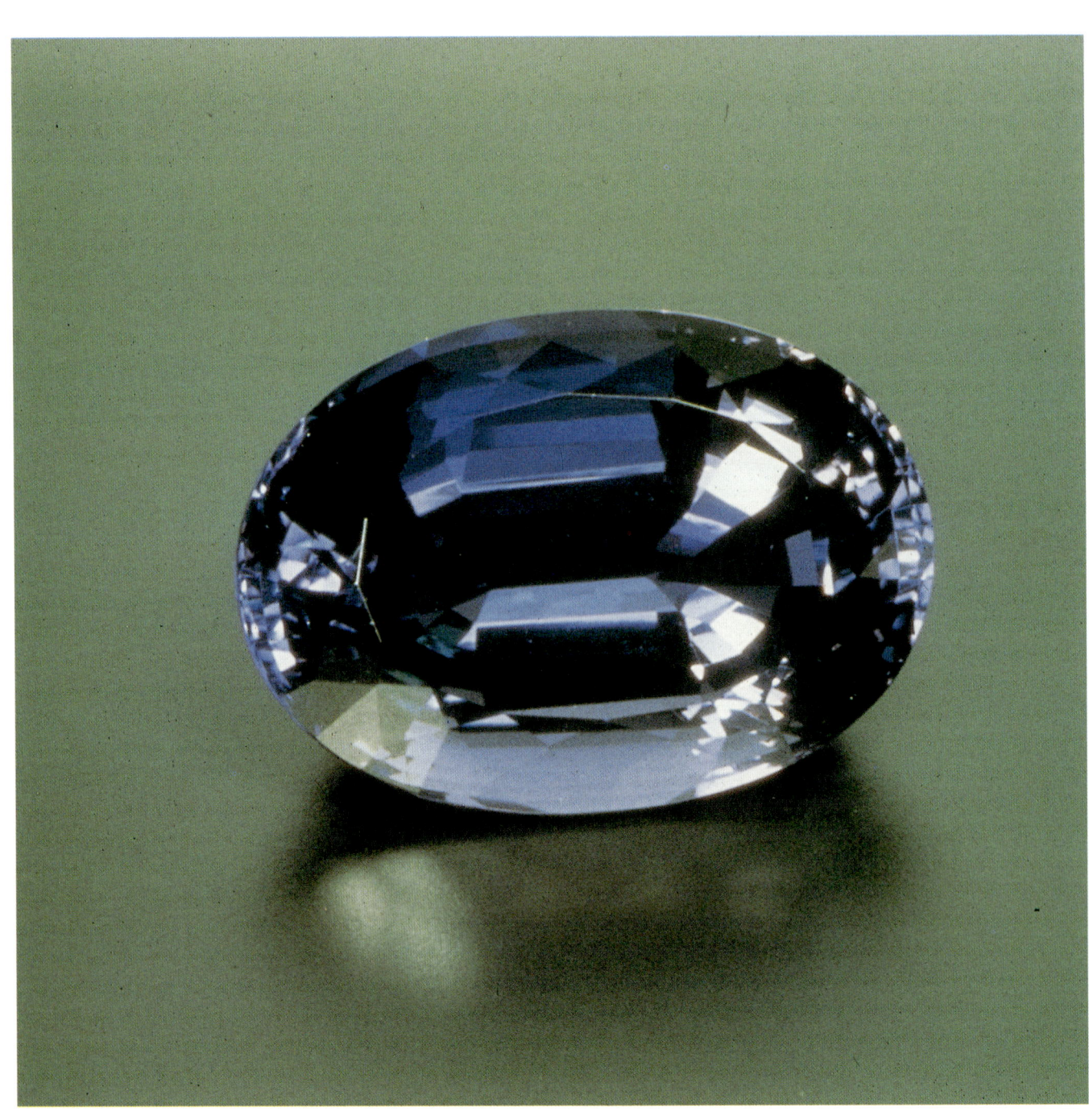

Cordierite or Dichroite or Iolite

GENERAL INFORMATION

How it got its name   Or names. Christened cordierite as tribute to the French geologist A. Cordier, dichroite goes back to the Greek *dyo cróos,* meaning "two colors," a reference to the material's clear pleochroism; the term "iolite" also comes from a Greek source, *ion* (violet).

Some interesting sidelights   The Vikings exploited its pleochroic value for travel on polar routes. During daytime hours the sun was a navigator's only reference, but was often obscured by heavy fogs. When the Vikings realized that this stone was lighter when turned toward the sun and remained darker when facing other directions, these courageous sailors used it to steer their routes; from whence yet another name, "the Viking stone."

Celebrated cordierites   The Mineral Gallery in the British Museum displays a dressed piece with an exceptional weight of 177 grams.

Deposits   For dressed stones most widely used as jewelry gems we must look to Sri Lanka, though very good quality material is also mined in Madagascar and Brazil. Less valuable mineral deposits are found in Canada, India, Burma, Namibia, and Tanzania.

Cut   The transparent quality used for jewelry usually has a mixed and bern cut; and whenever the number of inclusions reduces a piece's transparency, an en cabochon cut is adopted, either simple or double.

Under the lens   Multiform solid inclusions can be observed in this mineral, but it is especially noted for the presence of reddish-tinged thin hexagonal laminae, sometimes quite numerous. Formed by hematite or goethite, they constitute a typical feature for identifying the gem.

Here we may add that the characteristic and intense muddy yellow, azure, and deep violet-blue pleochroism is another reliable indication of the cordierite type. However, all identification hypotheses here are best confirmed by instrumental testing data.

Synthetic and similar substances   This mineral has no synthetic imitation. When first observed with the naked eye, cordierite is easily confused with sapphire, and was also called "water sapphire."

The following substances are sometimes mistaken for this mineral: *spinel*, however as this stone is monorefringent, it has no pleochroism; some *amethyst* samples with pale violet, purplish violet or lilac-violet pleochroism; *tanzanite*, though this gem's typical purplish reflections are quite different from cordierite's violet coloring; *benitoite*; *sapphirine*; *scapolite*; *tourmaline*.

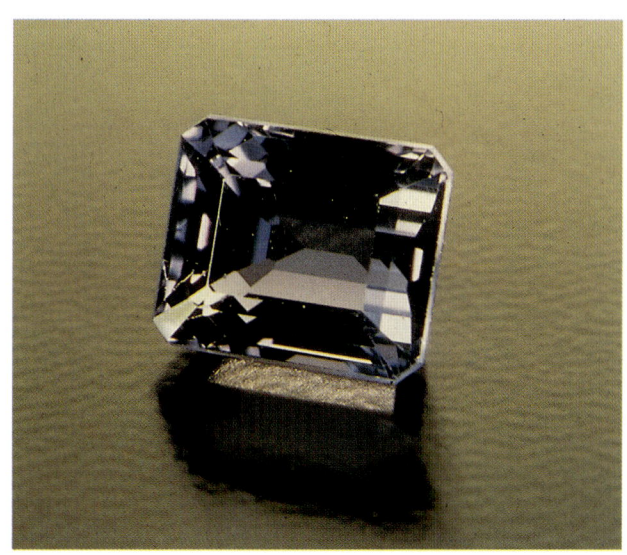

Chemical Formula:	*$Mg_2Al_2Si(Si_4Al_2O_{18})$*
	– magnesium cluminosilicate
Hardness:	*7-7 ½ (Mohs scale)*
Specific Gravity:	*2.57 – 2.66*
Refraction:	*biaxial birefringent*
Color:	*varying shades of violet blue*

Corundum

GENERAL INFORMATION

How it got its name Probably descended from the Hindu *kurand* or *korund*, or the Sanskrit word *kuruvinda*, all of which denote an extremely hard stone.

Varieties This mineralogical group contains two very well known varieties, *ruby* and *sapphire*, whose importance merits separate discussion (see respective listings).

There is only one other corundum that has its own denomination, the orangish-yellow and tangerine-colored *padparadscham*, a name taken from the Singhalese *padmaragay*, indicating the color of a lotus flower.

In gemmology, all other members of the mineralogical group are referred to with the dual name combining "corundum" with color. However, we must add that British and American usage tends to the old nomenclature: pink sapphire (instead of pink corundum), yellow sapphire (instead of yellow corundum) and so forth.

Many translucent and opaque corundums, when cut in round or oval cabochon, present a sparkling asterism formed by a six-pointed star glowing on the domed surface.

Due to this strikingly shaped gleam, these gems are defined as *star rubies* and *star sapphires*, though there are "star" stones in other color varieties as well.

Some interesting sidelights It is so resistant, that Mohs chose the corundum to represent 9 on his hardness index.

In Sri Lanka, natives hold "star" corundums to be among the most highly-prized talismans.

Celebrated corundums This category is almost exclusively devoted to star rubies and star sapphires:

– Long Star Ruby, weighing 100 carats, is on display at the American Museum of Natural History in New York.

– Rosser Reeves Ruby, a star ruby at 138.7 carats, part of the collection in the Smithsonian Institution in Washington, D.C.

– Star of India is a star sapphire weighing 536 carats, also on display at the American Museum of Natural History in New York.

– Star Midnight, an almost black star sapphire, weighs 116 carats, and is, likewise, at the American Museum of Natural history of New York.

These last two gems were stolen at the same time, in 1968, but luckily were recovered after just a few days.

– Star of Asia, a 330-carat star sapphire that is part of the collection of the famous jewelers Macan Markan of Sri Lanka.

Deposits Provenance is the same as for rubies and sapphires; padparadscham is, however, almost exclusively found in Sri Lanka.

Cut A mixed faceted cut is normally employed for all transparent gems, whereas substances displaying asterism are cut en cabochon.

Under the lens You won't need a jeweler's lens to identify a star ruby or star sapphire as asterism is visible to the naked eye, when the gem is displayed under proper lighting. In other natural corundums we find the classic inclusions: crystal, minute needles, curvilinear striae, and liquid inclusions referred to as "fingerprints" or tiny "fly wings."

Usually when at least one of these inclusions is observed, the sample

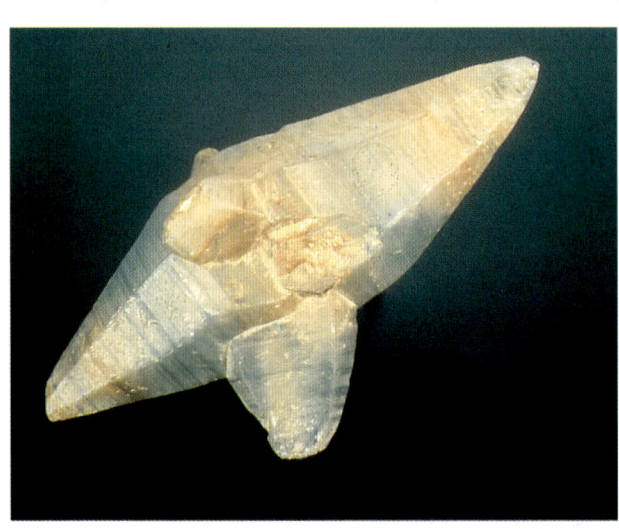

Chemical Formula: Al_2O_3 – aluminium oxide
Hardness: 9 (Mohs scale)
Specific Gravity: 3.90 – 4.10
Refraction: biaxial birefringent
Color: varying shades of red or blue, azure, orangish yellow, tangerine, light yellow, lemon yellow, pink, purplish pink, yellowish green, bright green, colorless, and black

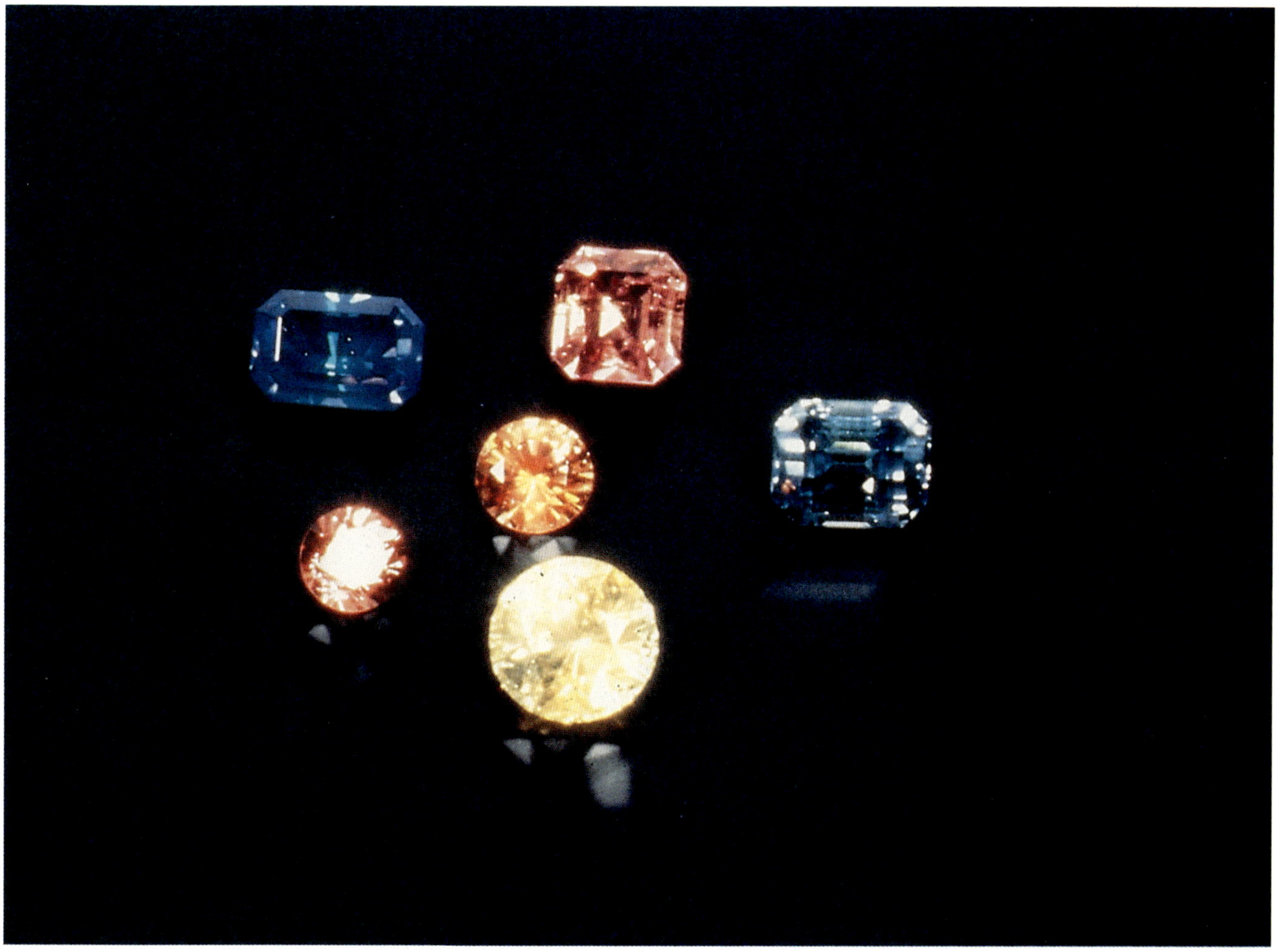

Sapphires of various size and colors from mines in Montana, USA.

examined may be securely claimed as a natural product.

Synthetics and similar substances All corundums, in the vast range of known colors, may be obtained by Verneuil synthesis.

In order to identify these synthetics, an expert has the none-too-easy task of searching for rounded striae and gas bubbles.

With the Verneuil method we can even obtain synthetic star rubies and star sapphires. However, the asterisms produced in these artificial stones are overly dramatic; and an examination of the base of the cabochon cut does reveal those curvilinear striae and air bubbles mentioned above.

Often violet-hued artificial corundums are offered as alexandrites, though the reader should recall that in clear sunlight this valuable material turns green (see "Chrysoberyl" under the section, "Varieties").

A multitude of stones may be mistaken for natural corundums because their great range of colors.

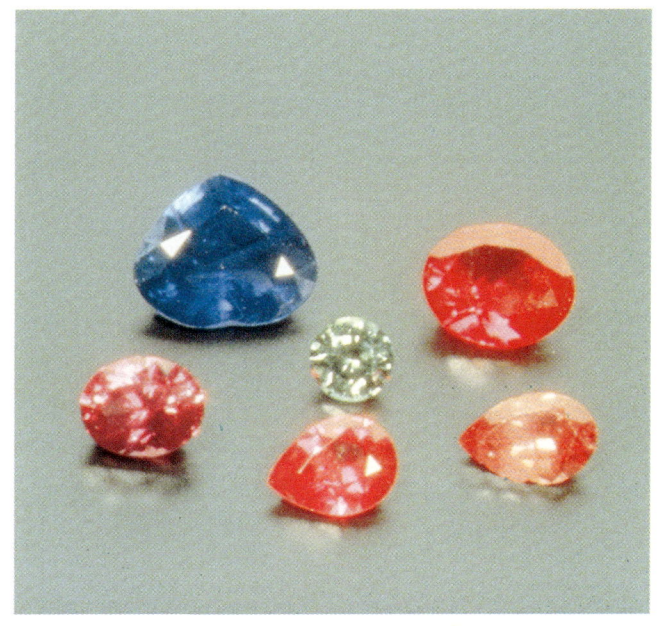

Sapphires and rubies found in Vietnam.

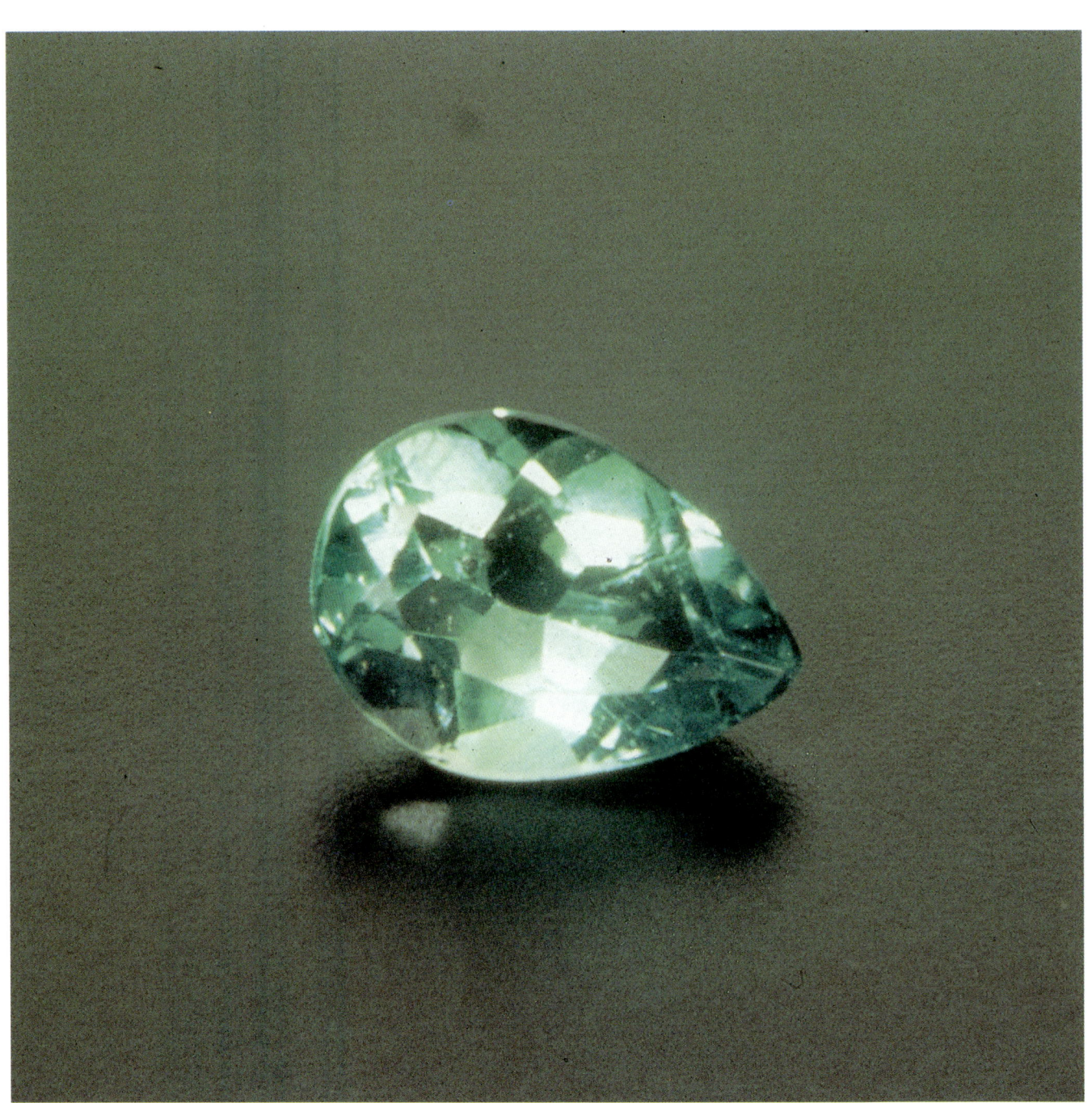

Fluorite

GENERAL INFORMATION

How it got its name Look to the Latin *fluor* (to flow) for this mineral, that melts down easily.

Varieties It is common usage to define each variety with the word *fluorite* plus its determining color, for example: *blue fluorite, violet fluorite, yellow fluorite,* etc. Multicolored versions of this material are simply called *polychrome fluorite.*

A rock variety named Blue John or Derbyshire spar used to be extracted in the Castelton area in England, but these deposits are apparently exhausted. Material of this provenance has curved zonings in blue, purple, and violet and is particularly suitable for making valuable and beautiful vases. Another rock variety exists, but it is almost colorless aside from a yellowish brown veining.

Fluorite is also available in a brilliant emerald green, offered as "South African emerald," an enticing but quite misleading label. Since it lacks hardness – Mohs deliberately chose it to indicate 4 on his scale – this quality is not used in jewelry making, in spite of its beautiful crystals.

Some interesting sidelights The famous murrine vases refer to *murra*, the oriental word for this mineral. Perhaps the best known of all fluorite objects, they were used by the ancient Romans to set out propitiatory offerings to the gods. In the 1700s, the columns and ornamental friezes on an architecturally prized fireplace were made from a special type of fluorite of English provenance.

"Fluorescence" refers to the fact that this mineral reacts strongly to ultraviolet rays, and takes on a different coloring when exposed to them.

Supposedly fluorite stimulates creativity and is a boon to artists and anyone who pursues an intellectual activity. Regarding therapeutic effects, it seems that fluorite stimulates calcification; if enclosed in earrings the wearer's teeth will stay beautiful.

If you remember to put it under your pillow at night, it will help you recall your dreams; and is thus considered a great aid in clearing up unconscious motivations.

Deposits Aside from the English minerals, which are the loveliest of all, some very attractive pink crystals are mined in Chamonix, France. Other important sources for this material are the United States, Switzerland, and Namibia (provenance of the emerald green quality cited earlier); whereas less important mines are located in Australia, Germany, Mexico, Norway, and the Czech Republic.

Cut Any sort of cut may be used though they are all a bit difficult to effect since the material is naturally flaky.

Under the lens If pincers are used in dressing the stone, their points must be protectively covered as the stone is not very hard and easily damaged.

Transparent, the material is usually free of inclusions, though you can sometimes find liquid inclusions, three-phase levels – like those noted in Colombian emeralds – and metallic-looking crystals.

Synthetics and similar substances Synthetic fluorite has been obtained and even cut for collectors.

At first glance, fluorite may be confused with other gems, especially the translucent opal, calcedonian, beryl, and quartz. These last two gems, however, reveal a pleochroism not present in fluorite since it is monorefringent.

Chemical Formula: *CaF_2*
– calcium fluoride
Hardness: *4 (Mohs scale)*
Specific Gravity: *3.18*
Refraction: *monorefringent*
Color: *colorless, orange, blue, yellow, pink, green, violet*

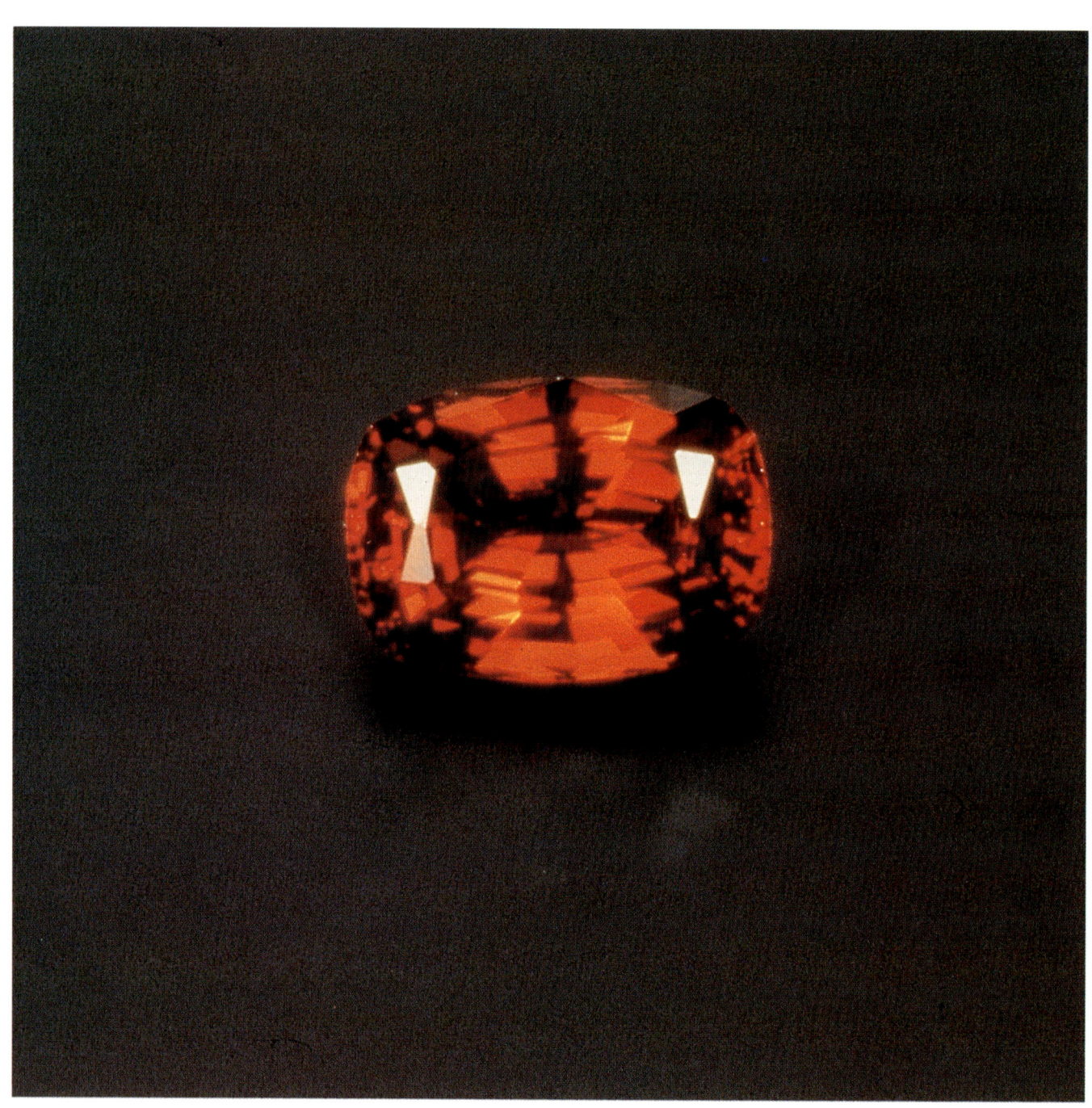

Garnet

In point of fact this term indicates a group of minerals – neosilicates – which though they may have varying chemical composition, exhibit structural analogies since they all belong to the same crystal system.

GENERAL INFORMATION

How it got its name A suggestive word that comes down to us from the Latin *granatum*, meaning "pomegranate," its name is a clear allusion to the striking red shade found in a number of garnet varieties, though some say it also indicates the rounded form of its crystals.

Varieties Highly variable in color: except for blue, it runs the whole spectrum from colorless to black. Garnet varieties belong essentially to two subgroups:
I. *Pyralspite*, includes: pyrope, almandine, and spessartite;
II. *Ugrandite*, includes: uvarovite, grossularite, and andradite.

Within the same subgroup solid mixtures may be encountered, a less probable phenomenon between the two subgroups.

Some interesting sidelights Many thousands of years ago garnets were already considered a prized gem; jewels set with this stone were found on ancient Egyptian mummies.

It seems Mediterranean civilizations were quite familiar with garnet, and the almandine variety in particular, in the period immediately following Alexander the Great's voyages in search of the Indies.

Victorians associated very dark or opaque garnets with funeral rites. But by the end of this period, garnets were considered a more auspicious stone and varieties such as demantoide were worked to produce small talismanic animal shapes.

It is widely held that the red variety is a potent magic stone.

A fine lady in the Middle Ages would give her knight a garnet as a token of love, and also to ensure that the beloved would not forget her.

It is often claimed that illicit possession of a garnet is punished by bad luck and failing health.

As so often with red stones, the garnet is held to stimulate the circulation of the blood, stop hemorrhaging and heal wounds.

For kidney problems, they say an orangish yellow garnet is curative.

Synthetic garnets Though synthetic specimens have been obtained – by J. Coes – they have not been commercially distributed. This information is offered simply for the record.

Synthetics with garnet structure In a laboratory, and by substituting silicon with specific chemical elements, it is possible to obtain compounds with a garnet structure.

Among these, the best known is undoubtedly yttrium aluminate (YAG) employed as imitation of diamond. If, however, iron is inserted in the molecule instead of aluminum, a deep green compound results (YIG) which is sometimes used as imitation of emerald.

Another possible diamond imitation is galliate of gadolinium (GGG).

Even if these products are recognized as garnets, the fact is that, aside from their similar structure, they are definitely not garnets.

Pyrope

Chemical Formula: *$Mg_3Al_2(SiO_4)_3$ – magnesium and aluminium silicate*
Hardness: *7 – 7½ (Mohs scale)*
Specific Gravity: *3.65 – 3.80*
Refraction: *monorefringent*
Color: *dark red, with occasional brownish tints.*

How it got its name From the Greek word *pýr*, for "fire."

Highly esteemed in the eighteenth and nineteenth centuries, it has also been known as "Bohemian garnet" or "Cape ruby," though these are totally unofficial labels and best disregarded.

Celebrated pyropes At the Grüne Gewölbe in Dresden a huge 468.5-carat garnet is on display; and the pigeon-egg sized gem possessed by the Hapsburg, Rudolph II, is legendary.

Deposits Pyrope has widespread sources: Australia, Brazil, Madagascar, the Czech Republic, Slovakia, Sri Lanka, the United States, South Africa, and Tanzania.

Generally, miners agree that when pyrope is present there is a good chance of finding diamond as well.

Cut All faceted cuts are suitable.

Under the lens Clearly visible crystal inclusions; blackish, jagged inclusions; possible intersecting needles; two-phase inclusions.

Similar stones There may be some confusion with almandine or spinel (see entries), and ruby (remember that this mineral is birefringent and therefore pleochroic).

Almandine

Chemical Formula: $Fe_3Al_2(SiO_4)_3$
– aluminium and iron silicate
Hardness: *7½ (Mohs scale)*
Specific Gravity: *3.95 – 4.20*
Refraction: *monorefringent*
Color: *red with violet shadings.*

How it got its name Traced to Alabanda, an ancient city in Asia Minor.

Deposits Almandine may be found in Afghanistan, Brazil, India (Rajasthan), Madagascar, Sri Lanka, and the United States. Mines of lesser importance are in: Austria, the Czech Republic, and Slovakia. India even produces four-point star garnets.

Cut A mixed cut is most often used, but samples with particularly lovely coloring are ideal for an emerald cut.

Less transparent material and pieces evincing asterism are worked en cabochon; in very dark almandines the lower section of the cabochon cut is hollowed out to lighten the color a little.

Specimens that lack transparency or have many inclusions may be simply polished by tumbling and the resulting pieces pierced to be used as necklace beads.

Under the lens With a 10x lens it is easy to make out crystals with a halo effect (most marked specimens from Sri Lanka), encrusted-looking crystals, needle inclusions intersecting at 70° and 110° (not at 60° as in Myanmar rubies), and liquid inclusions arranged in fanlike patterns.

Rutilated needles are rather clearly visible and have a fair extension; when they are thickly spread out, a slight asterism is produced.

Similar stones Almandine may be taken for pyrope or spinel (see entries) and ruby (keeping in mind, again, that this birefringent mineral is pleochroic).

Watch out for doppiettes composed of a thin sheet of natural almandine glued on a pavilion made of synthetic ruby.

Spessartite

Chemical Formula: $Mn_3Al_2(SiO_4)_3$
– manganese aluminium silicate
Hardness: *7 – 7½ (Mohs scale)*
Specific Gravity: *4.12 – 4.20*
Refraction: *monorefringent*
Color: *orangish yellow*

How it got its name Refers to Spessart, an area in Bavaria where this material is extracted.

For mineralogists, "spessartine" is the preferred term.

Celebrated spessartites Larger specimens are difficult to come across, and 7 to 8-carat stones are considered a superior size for this material.

The British Museum in London displays a fine 6.25-carat crystal. And we have information that two truly large specimens at 18.92 and 27.37 carats respectively were discovered in Kenya.

Deposits This garnet is extracted in Australia, Brazil, Germany, Kenya, Madagascar, Mexico, Myanmar, Namibia, Norway, Pakistan, Sri Lanka, the United States, Sweden and Tanzania.

Cut Transparent material is suitable for all cuts.

Under the lens Jagged liquid inclusions similar to those encountered in rubelite (red tourmaline).

Similar stones May be confused up with essonite, though only because of the color; technical data make an immediate distinction.

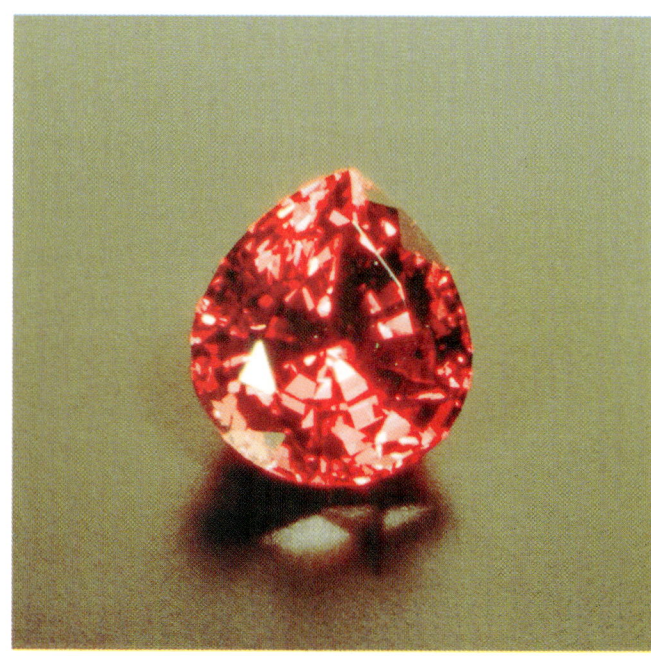

Rhodolite garnet, pear cut.

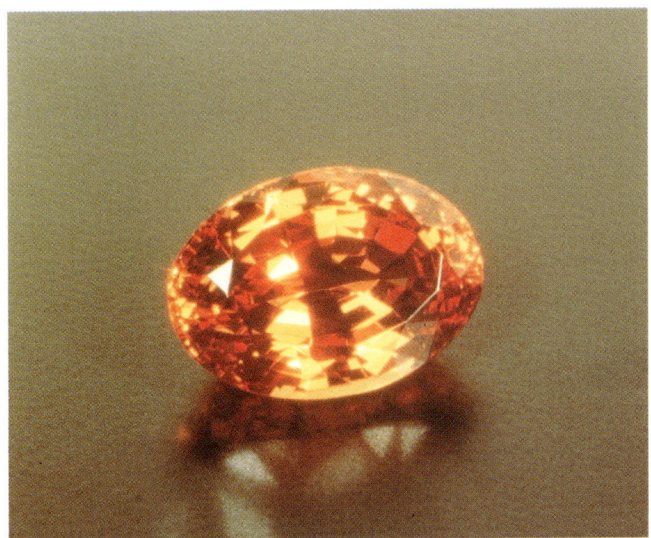

Tanzanian Malaya garnet with an oval cut.

Rhodolite

Mixture of pyrope (57%) and almandine (35%) with traces of andradite and grossularite.

Variable coloring from slightly pinkish red to purplish red.

A garnet variety found in the same mines from which pyrope and almandine are extracted. Thailand offers good-size crystals, and we know of rhodolite samples of that provenance weighing 9.41, 22.10, 27.39, and even 74.30 carats.

Malaya Garnet

Mixture of pyrope and spessartite with additives of almandine and grossularite. The denomination is not uniformly accepted. Color ranges from orangish red to orangish yellow.

Of Kenyan provenance, we know of two samples weighing 27.87 and 38.00 carats; while Tanzania is the source of a 42.33-carat exemplar.

Uvarovite

Chemical Formula: $Ca_3Cr_2(SiO_4)_3$ – calcium and chromium silicate
Hardness: 7½ (Mohs scale)
Specific Gravity: 3.41 – 3.55
Refraction: *monorefringent*
Color: *emerald green*

How it got its name In dedication to the Russian academic Sergej S. Uvarov (1786 - 1855). Quite rare, it is found in somewhat small crystals and varies from slightly transparent to translucent.

Deposits Extracted in Canada, Finland, India, Poland, and the United States.

Cut Given the size of its crystals this mineral is cut only on collector request.

Under the lens No characteristic inclusion has been identified.

Similar stones It may be confused with demantoide (see entry), but technical data make it easy to distinguish between the two. It may also be mistaken for emerald; remember that this mineral is birefringent and therefore exhibits a (not easily detected) pleochroism.

Grossularite

Chemical Formula: $Ca_3Al_2(SiO_4)_3$ – calcium and aluminium silicate
Hardness: 7 – 7½ (Mohs scale)
Specific Gravity: 3.28 - 3.65
Refraction: *monorefringent*
Color: *colorless, brownish orange, yellow, reddish, green, pale green*

How it got its name In Latin *ribes grossularia* is our "gooseberry."

Varieties This garnet variety has, in turn, many subvarieties, which are:
- *Essonite*. Color runs from cinnamon yellow to a bright orange.
  Specific weight more or less constant at 3.65.
  Deposits are located almost exclusively in Sri Lanka.
  A stone that may be mistaken for spessartite (see entry) and zircon (keeping in mind that this mineral is birefringent and therefore pleochroic).
- *Tsavorite*. Deep green or yellowish green coloring. In addition to good transparent material, there is some production of torbid quality. A subvariety discovered in the eighties.
  Deposits in Kenya and Tanzania.
  It may be mistaken for any other green stone with either good or slight transparency and brilliance.
- *Hydrogrossularite*. A further subvariety: a massive microcrystal, provenance South Africa (Buffelsfontein). Due to its appearance, it has been erroneously labelled "Transvaal jade." Additional massive material comes from Pakistan.
  Hydrogrossularite may also occur in yellow, pink, and red.

Under the lens Essonite reveals a peculiar molasses effect that can perhaps be compared to the moment that sugar dissolves in water; rounded crystal inclusions may also be observed.

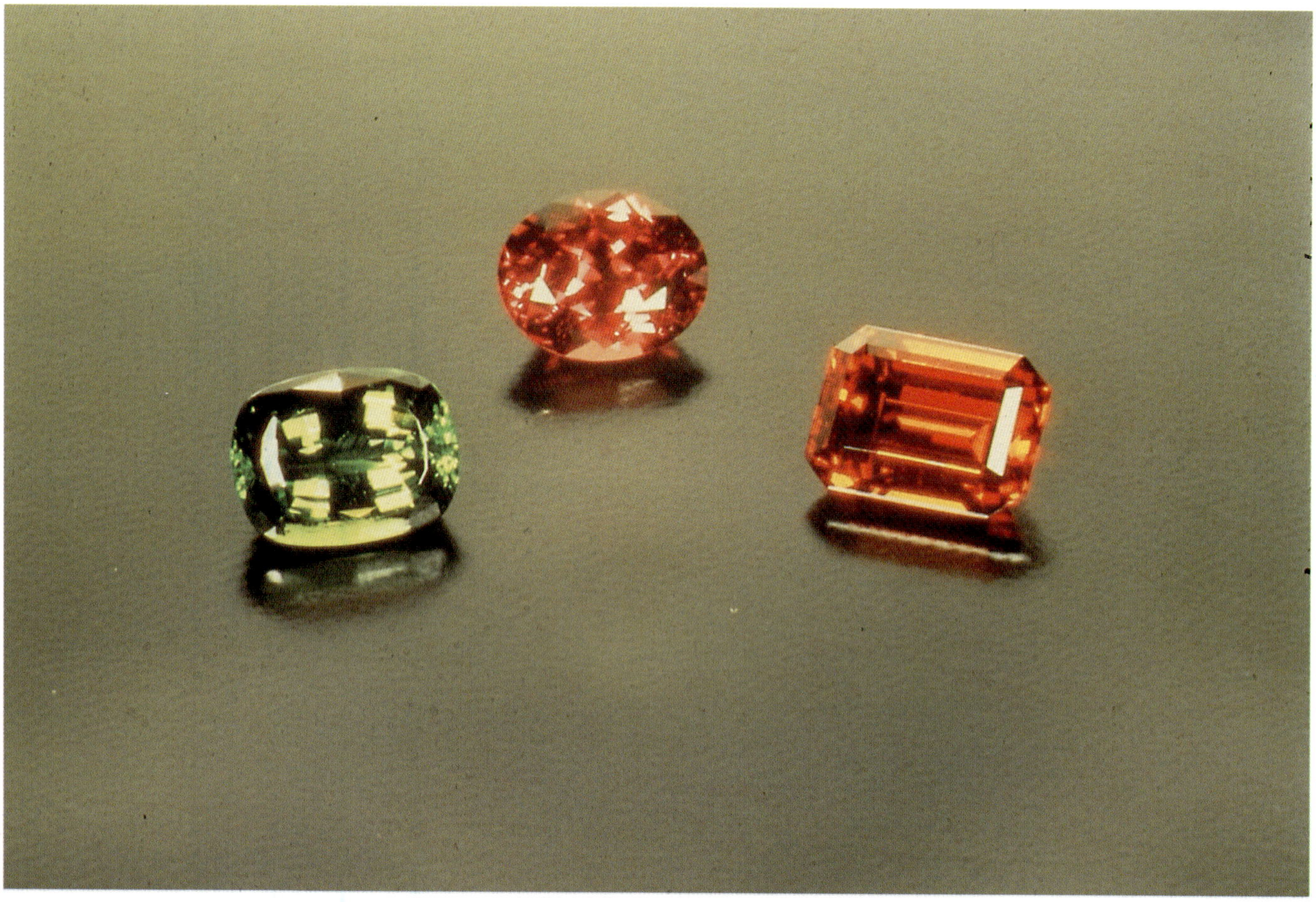

Three different garnets: tsavorite, rhodolite, spessartite.

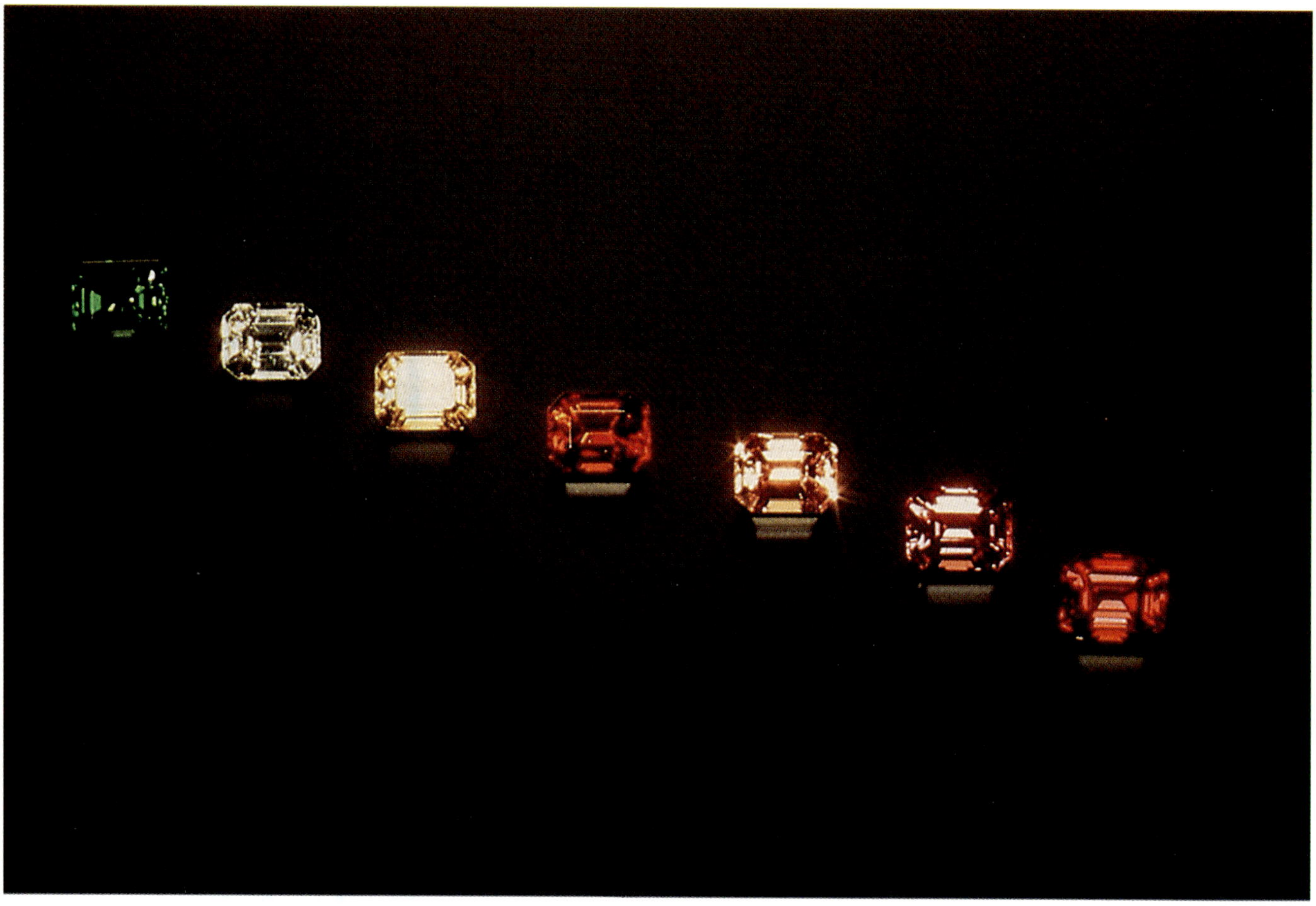

A rainbow of emerald-cut garnets.

Tsavorite contains small wandlike inclusions as well as opaque bands, haloed crystals, liquid inclusions and – in some samples – the slightly torbid effect already mentioned.

In less transparent specimens it is not possible to examine the interior of the mineral, but in the first few layers under the surface we can note dark spots and rounded strips.

Andradite

Chemical Formula: *$Ca_3Fe_2(SiO_4)_3$ – calcium and iron silicate*
Hardness: *6½ – 7 (Mohs scale)*
Specific Gravity: *3.75 - 3.85*
Refraction: *monorefringent*
Color: *almost colorless, brown, yellow, black, grass green, emerald green.*

How it got its name Attributed to mineralogist J.B. de Andrada e Silva (1763-1838) who first studied this variety and classified its subvarieties.

Varieties Subvarieties are:
- *Colofonite*. A name referring to the fact that it has the same brownish yellow and reddish brown coloring as colophony (resin).
- *Demantoid*. By far the most popular garnet for jewelry.

A name reflecting the fact that its dispersion is superior to diamond's; in fact, these stones display an extraordinary fire. Discovered in Russia in 1868. It runs the gamut of green tones since it contains iron and – on the atomic level – chromium, which determines the material's striking brilliance.

Under the magnifying lens, there is evidence of asbestos fibers arranged like the spokes of a wheel or in a special formation descriptively labelled "horse's tail."

It is extracted in Russia (the Urals) and Italy (Val Malenco).

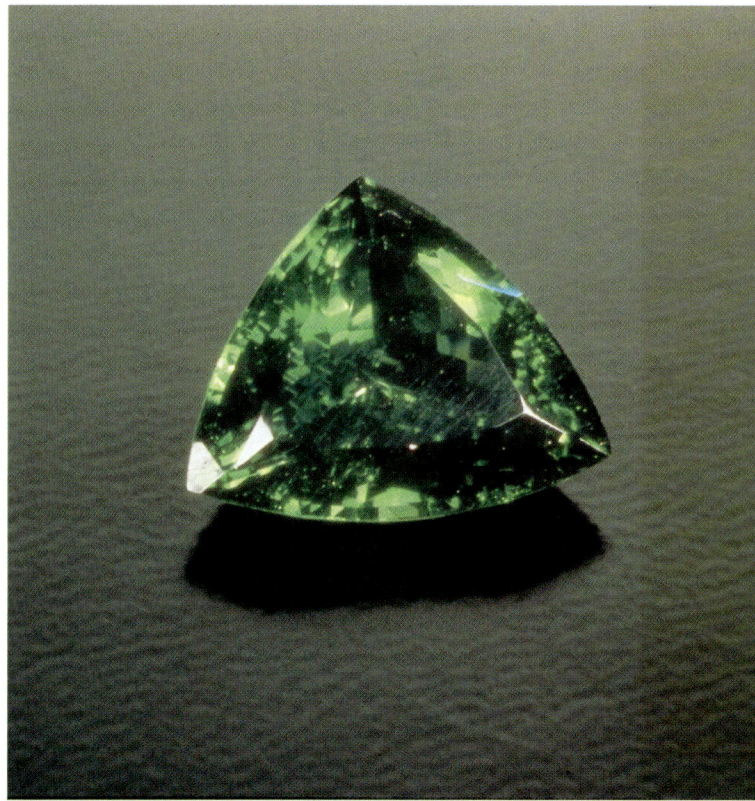

Tsavorite garnet with a shield cut.

Demantoid can be confused with olivine (and, in fact, was classified as such for a certain period), emerald, spinel, tourmaline, and vesuvian.
- *Melanite*. A name reflecting its mainly black, opaque and occasionally dark brown coloring.

While very popular in the Victorian era, it is not often employed in contemporary jewelry making; usually cut en cabochon. For splendid crystal specimens look to Chile.
- *Topazolite*. An orangish yellow, honey yellow or lemon yellow, similar to topaz, which suggested its name.

This garnet subvariety is mined in Switzerland and the the western sector of the Italian Alps.

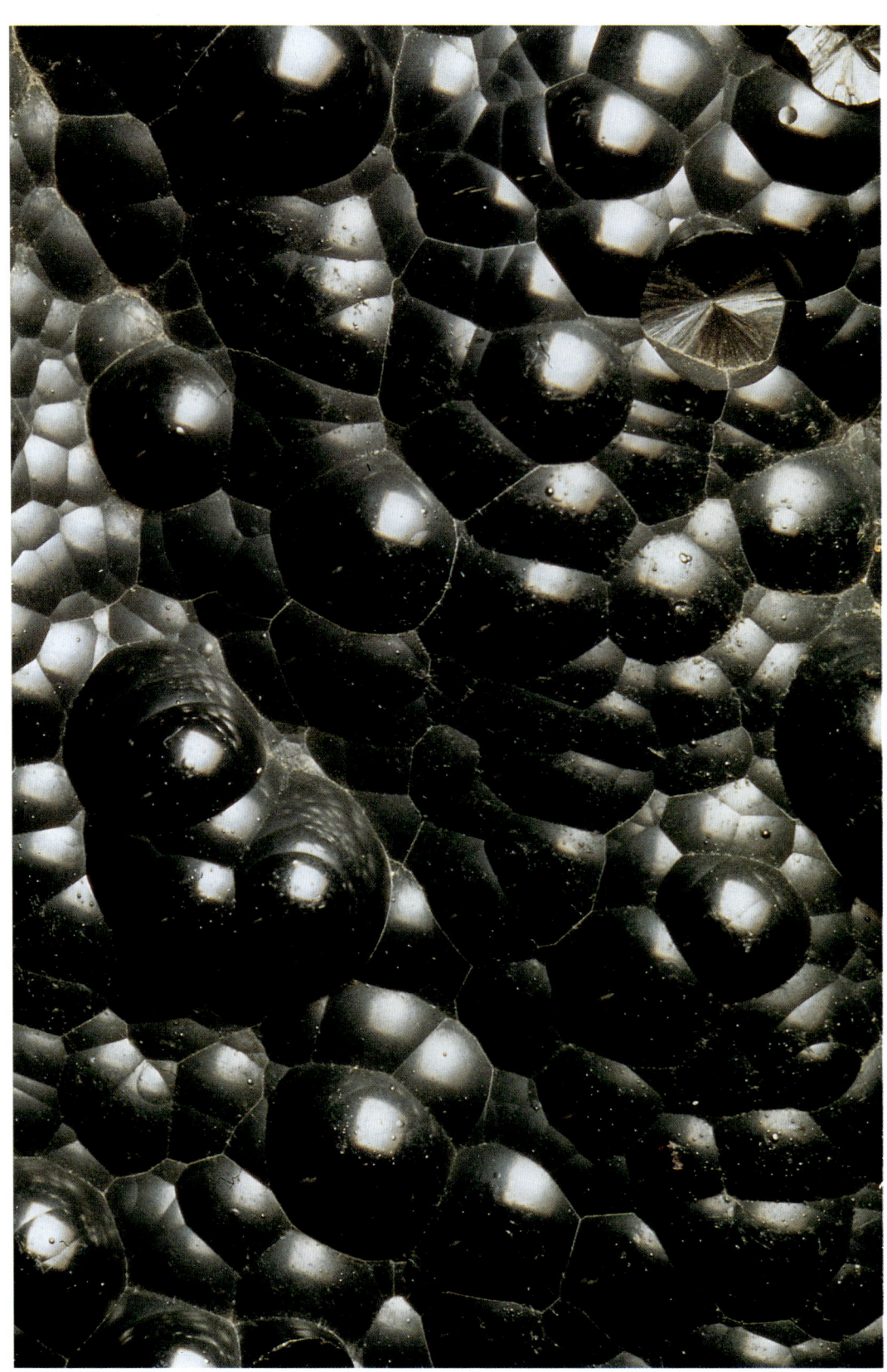

Hematite

GENERAL INFORMATION

How it got its name As the mineral produces a red dust, the Greeks dubbed it *aimatos*, meaning "blood."

Varieties It has several varieties including *oligist* (with an iridescent gleam), *micaceous hematite* (with foliated crystallizations), and *fibrous hematite* (found in oblong crystals).

Some interesting sidelights Before going into battle, the native American Indians used the soft variety for their war paint. In the distant past, hematite slabs were put to use as mirrors. When ground into dust it becomes the "rouge" that goldsmiths adopt for polishing golden objects. Hematite is a symbol of frankness and loyalty. Because of its high iron content, people say that it fights off blood infection; in fact, the ancient Egyptians adopted it for curing hemorrhages.

Deposits Hematite mines are situated in Brazil, Germany (Saafeld), England (Cumberland), Italy (the Isle of Elba), Norway, Russia, the United States, Sweden, and Switzerland (in the Ticino canton and the Grisons).

Cut It is likely to be faceted in an emerald cut and a round brilliant cut; or it may be worked as beads for necklaces. It is currently used in Brazil to produce animal figures.

Under the lens This densely opaque material will not reveal identifying characteristics under the lens. However, one sure way of testing for hematite is by rubbing it on highly polished porcelain; if the mineral leaves a brick red streak you can be certain it is hematite.

Be careful not to be fooled by hematite in a round brilliant cut, since at first glance it may look just like a black diamond. Another error to avoid: do not be deceived into mistaking a necklace of hematite beads for one of black pearls!

Synthetics and similar substances For some time now the market has been flooded with imitations with names such as *hematin* or other derivatives. Recently, however, they have been produced with alloys containing iron and titanium which are almost as hard and dense as hematite. Often these imitations are used for machine-cut objects that imitate hand-cut ones; so you must check carefully to see if these objects have blurred cuts rather than the fine incisions found in hand-cut pieces.

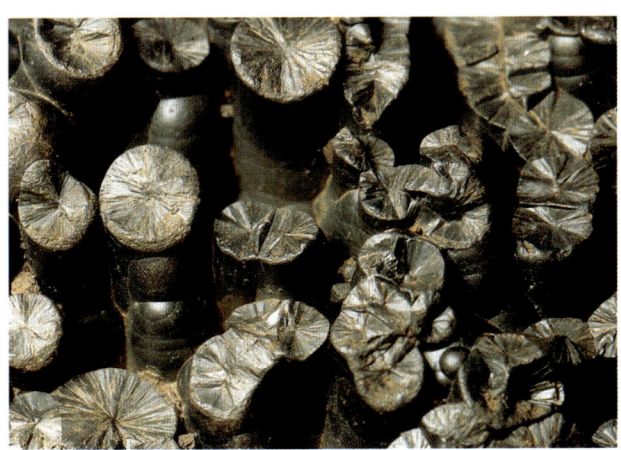

Chemical Formula: Fe_2O_3 – ferric oxide
Hardness: 5½ – 6½ (Mohs scale)
Specific Gravity: 4.95 – 5.30
Refraction: *uniaxal birefringent*
Color: *black, greyish black, deep red*

Jade

"Jade" applies to a group of minerals that includes *chloromelanite*, *jadeite*, and *nephrite*. Beyond a doubt the last two are the best known; of similar appearance, they are actually quite different in refractive index and specific gravity (jadeite 3.30-3.50; nephrite 2.90-3.10); rightfully, they each merit a separate discussion further on. It wasn't until 1863 – after jade had been around for about 7,000 years – that A. Damour demonstrated that the single term was being used to refer to two chemically distinct mineral species: jadeite and nephrite. This gives an idea of the difficulty of distinguishing between them with the naked eye.

GENERAL INFORMATION

How it got its name The term comes from the Spanish *piedra de hijada* or "stone of the flank" referring to its therapeutic application along the hip. Spanish adventurers in Cortez' day brought it back to the Old World. The South American natives believed that when placed on the hip, this stone was an amulet to ward off kidney disease. Another theory attributes the name to the fact that the material is found in certain kidney-shaped pebbles. Gradually the word "jade" gained worldwide usage, whereas the ancient Chinese word *yu* totally disappeared; yet about 1000 B.C. the Chinese had used the latter to signify a highly esteemed green material that was probably what we now know as jade.

Some interesting sidelights In Pre-Colombian Central America, jade was used for precious carvings considered more valuable than gold. Unfortunately this art disappeared at the time when the Spanish conquerors arrived.

In China, jade has played an important role in religious cults for thousands of years, because the material is used to create mystic symbols of enormous artistic value. Even today, China has maintained a thriving tradition in working nephrite. Since about 1750, Chinese craftsmen have sustained equally high standards in working the jadeite which comes from Burma. The Chinese have always loved jade and used to carry small jade objects in their pockets in the belief that the material assimilated energy emitted from the body and took on a life of its own, defending its carrier from misfortune or illness. They placed small pieces of jade in the foundations of a new house, avoiding adversity for both home and family.

Having mentioned its presumedly beneficial effects on the kidneys, we should add that carrying or wearing jade is also thought to be good for the liver, spleen, and nervous system.

What's more, it is believed that the wearer will be led toward an understanding of life's deepest meaning.

Celebrated jades Keeping in mind jade's importance all throughout Chinese history, we must specially highlight its role in the Shang epoch (1523-1028 B.C.) when it was regarded as the purest and most noble of all materials. This period gave us Pi disks, depicting Heaven and the emperor's immense power, and the Zong tubule representing Mother Earth. The Nelson Gallery in Kansas City contains a splendid example of a Pi disk in yellow jade.

The later Zhou period (1027-1256 B.C.) produced a pierced and engraved disk which is much esteemed. We should also note the musical instrument made of wood and jade called the Pien-ch'ing consisting of sixteen L-shaped pieces of jade of varying thickness which, when struck, emitted a range of different sounds. A jade piece dating back to 220 B.C. is worth noting. Engraved in its center is the Tao symbol and, on the sides, a series of three characters read with the same phonetic sound and representing, as expressed in the Chinese book of wisdom, the *I Ching*, the sky, water, mountains, thunder, wind, fire, earth, and the atmosphere.

Central America has given us the famous Olmec sculptures, small statues dating back to the first centuries of the modern era.

In India, during the Mogul dynasty (seventeenth century) the working of jade, inlaid with rubies, emeralds, and gold, was brought to a high level of perfection which we can admire visiting some of the museums where these pieces have been preserved.

Technologically advanced tools, which today are used in the working of jade, have nevertheless failed to bestow the same fascination on their creations as the works of these past artisans.

Synthetics and similar substances Other than devitrified green glass, there are many minerals (sometimes artificially colored) that can be confused with jade: green aventurine (a variety of quartz, erroneously called "Indian jade"); green amazonite; bowenite (erroneously called "Korean jade"); chalcedony dyed green; chrysoprase (a

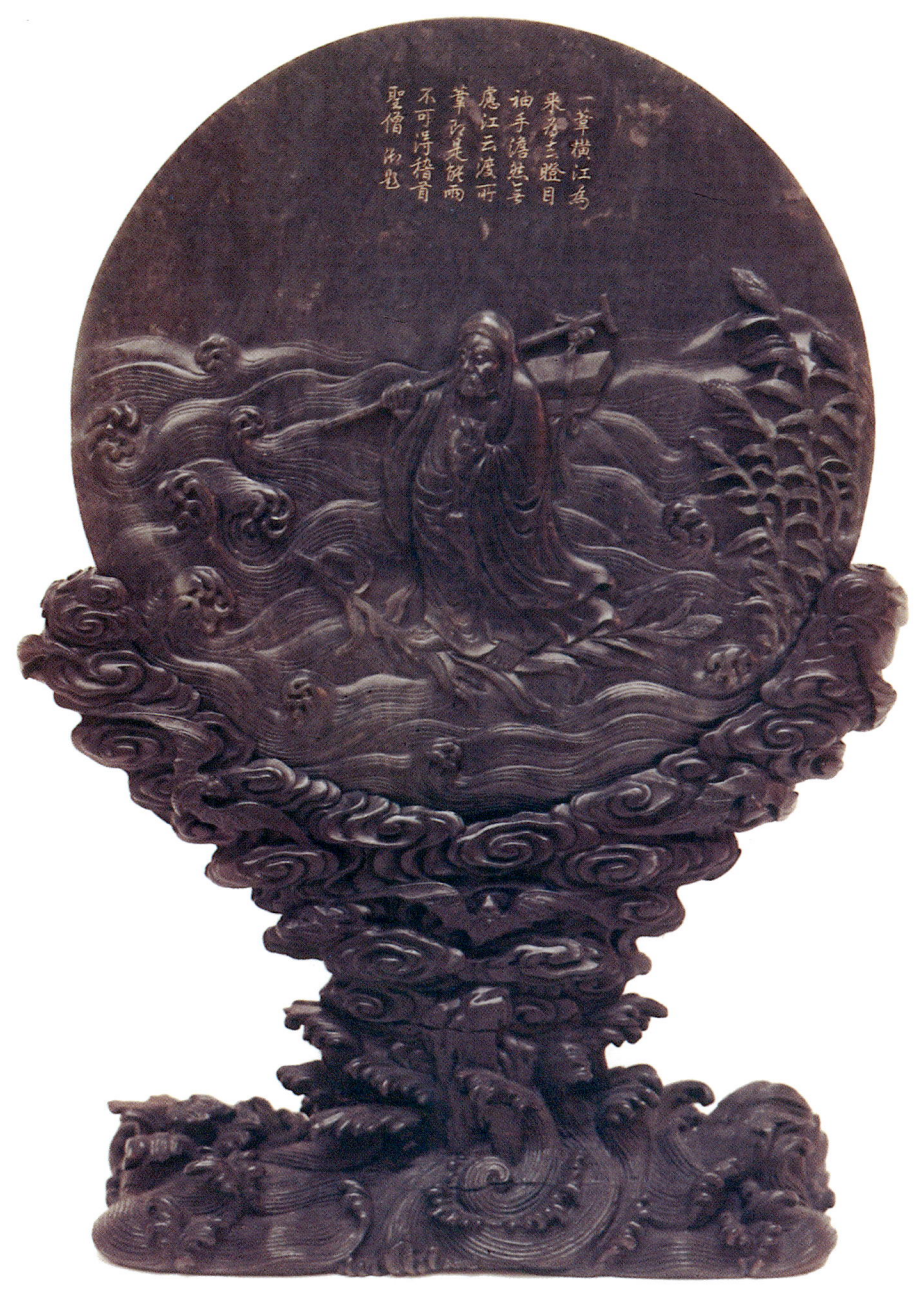

Chinese screen in jade.

variety of quartz incorrectly called "Queensland jade"); massive grossular garnet (incorrectly called "Transvaal jade"); green-dyed jasper (erroneously known as "Swiss jade"); pectolite; green vesuvianite rock (wrongly called "Californian jade"); and sausurrite.

Nor can we omit mentioning all the plastic materials used as imitations.

And the buyer had best beware of composite material: there is a triplette on the market today, its three layers composed of precious jade (erroneously defined "imperial"), a major component of less valuable jade, with a layer of green glue between the two pieces.

Treatments   Even a simple heat treatment can attractively lighten a jade or nephrite coloring; doubtless some unlucky goldsmiths can confirm this fact as it may occur during repairs made on a gold object set with jade.

To create artificially aged jade, the pieces are simply subjected to intense heating followed by a rapid cooling off in a concentrated acid solution.

Light violet jade, commerically called "lavender," may lose its tint if submitted to moderate heating at temperatures of 200-400° C; but the material in medium lavender maintains its color under temperatures up to 750° C.

Dyeing achieves a richer color for both jade and nephrite. In 1958 in Hong Kong there was already a procedure involving alcohol solutions containing, for example, yellow methanol and blue alizarin.

Small fractures present in the mineral are often hidden by the paraffin used in tumbling, which is the final phase, in working this material.

Jadeite

GENERAL INFORMATION

How it got its name A derivative of jade (refer to the preceding category in our list).

Varieties *Jadeite* is a pyroxene that is remarkably resistant thanks to its rather unique structure. Its best known variety is *chloromelanite* which is, in reality, a mix of jadeite and two other minerals. Though chloromelanite is usually a dark green almost black color, it occasionally is found in apple green with blackish specklings.

At times in the market you may pick up talk about a fantastic "imperial jade." However this is never an official designation, but only a simple reference to the emerald green quality preferred by the last Empress of China for its uniform coloring and rich sheen.

Market preferences often go to the quality that has a translucent appearance and a fine green color with bluish shadings, and to a few select chloromelanite specimens; oriental markets in particular follow this trend.

Deposits Extremely important deposits are located in Myanmar, in the north of Burma, near Tawmaw, but almost all of this material is brought to the province of Yunnan in China and goes on the market as "Yunnan jade". Other rich deposits are located in Guatemala, Mexico, and the United States; there are additional deposits in China and Japan, but they have little value.

Cut From jadeite we can obtain fine panels for carving; or it may be cut in rounded surfaces (en cabochon, or as necklace beads). It is especially suitable for inlay work that may result in exceptional artistic specimens.

Under the lens Since it is either translucent or, more frequently, opaque it discloses very little under the lens. But surface examination can reveal a certain discontinuity – not present in nephrite – since their constituent grains have different hardness values.

Synthetics and similar substances A dark green synthetic jadeite has been produced by the General Electric Corporation in the United States, though it hasn't yet gained much popularity on the market.

Again, as discussed in our section "Jade".

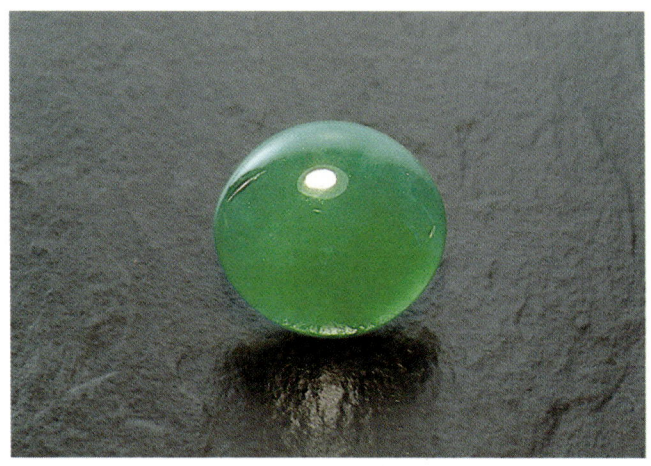
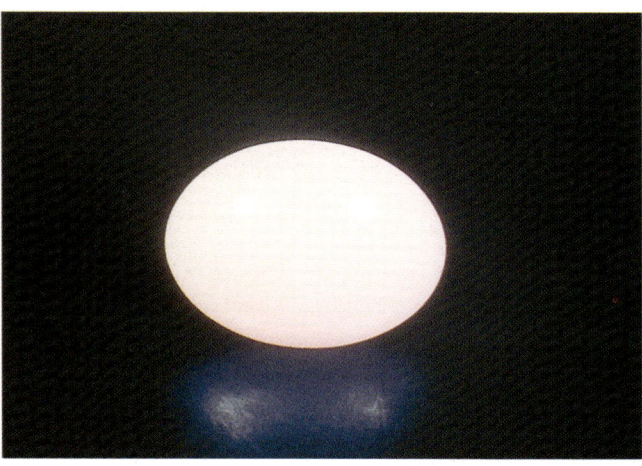

Chemical Formula:	*$NaAlSi_2O_6$ – silicate of aluminium and sodium*
Hardness:	*6½ – 7 (Mohs scale)*
Specific Gravity:	*3.30 – 3.50*
Refraction:	*biaxial birefringent*
Color:	*whitish, yellow, chestnut, reddish brown, pale violet, blackish, but usually green*

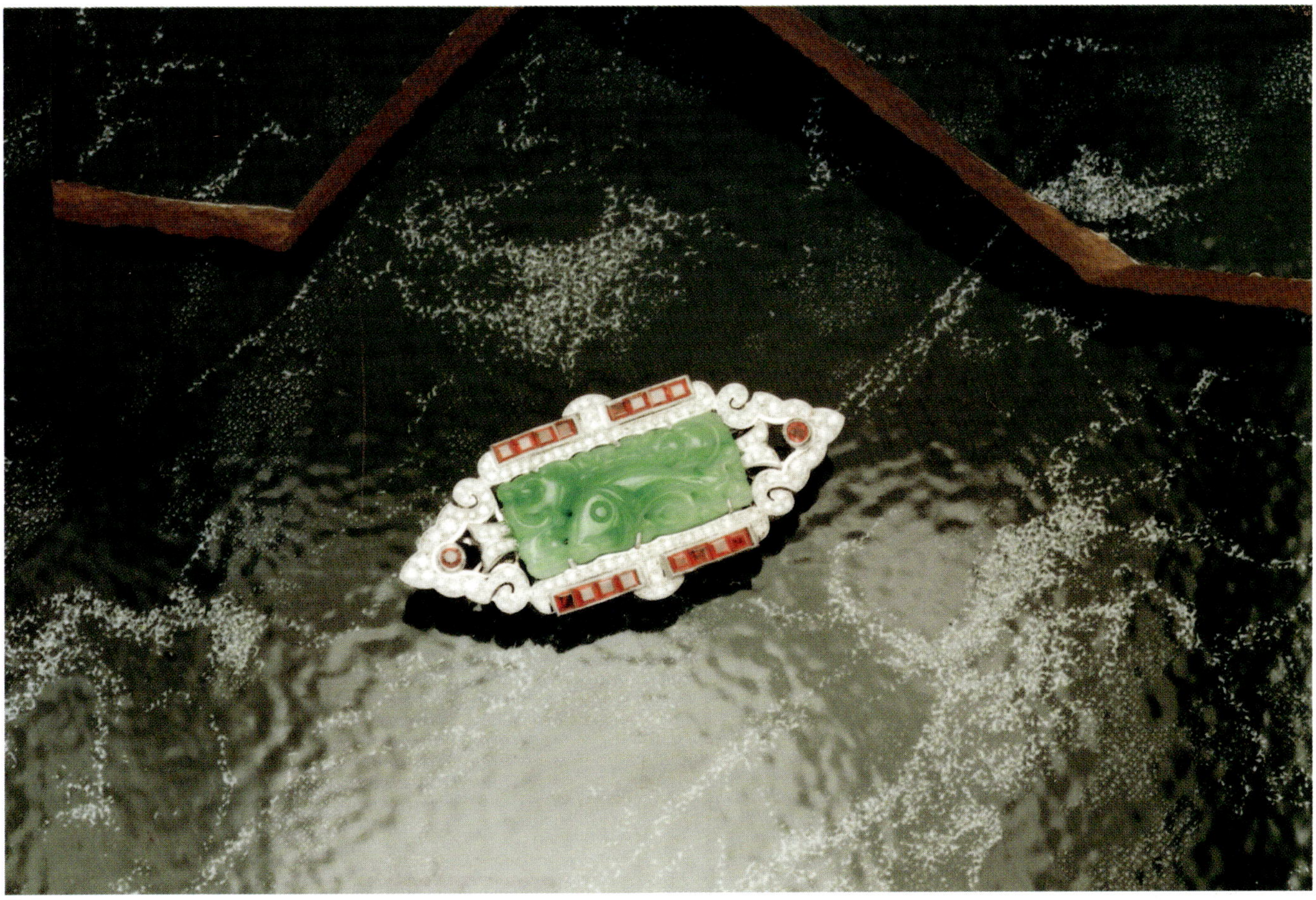

GILBERTO CASSOLA.
Brooches in gold and imperial jade (jadeite) with diamonds and corundums.

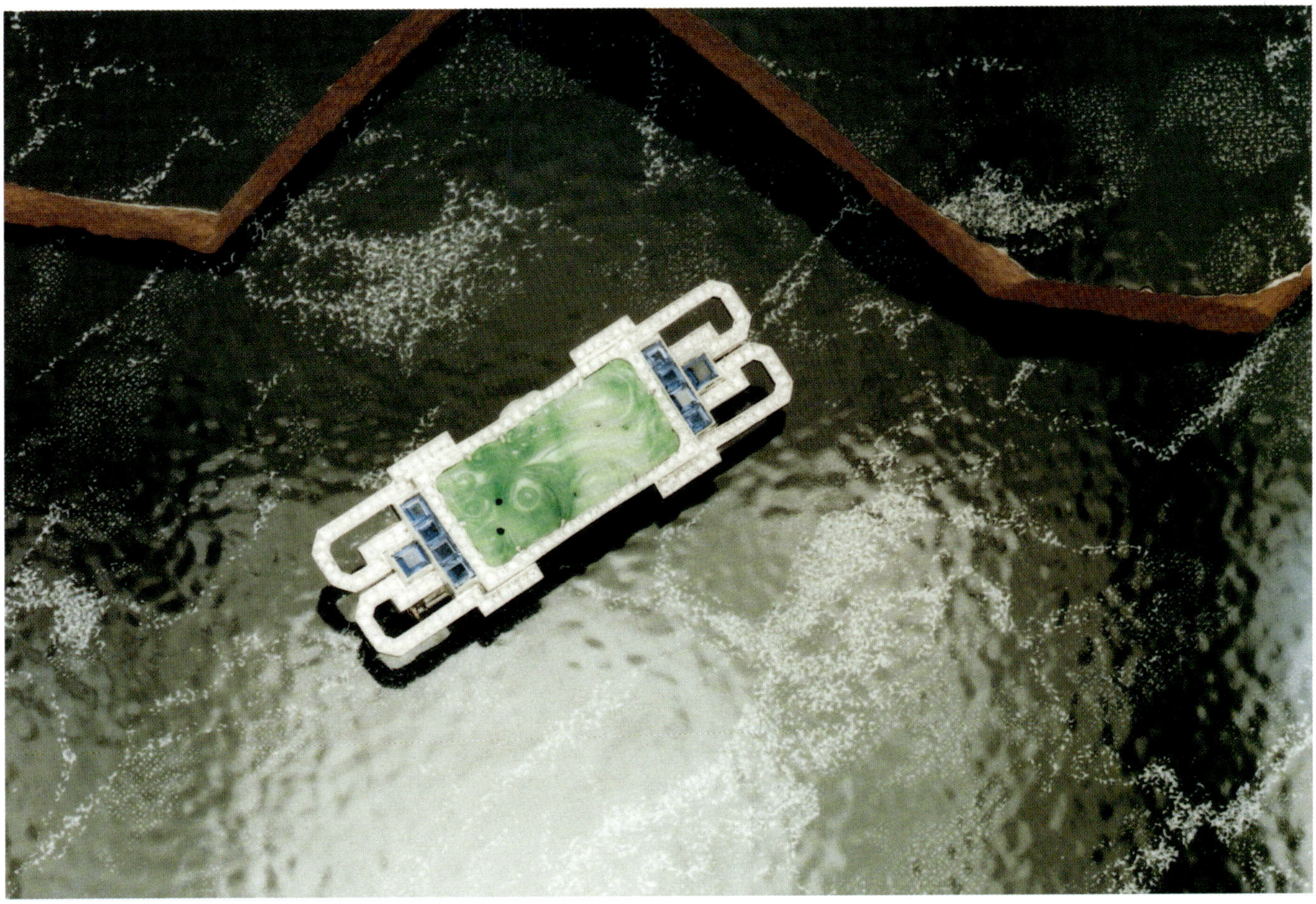

Lapis Lazuli

GENERAL INFORMATION

How it got its name Our root is the Persian word *lazhward* (blue stone), for a material that has been employed since antiquity.

Varieties There are no varieties; and it is best to underline the fact that lapis lazuli is not considered a mineral since it is a stone composed of many minerals: calcite, haüynite, noselite, pyrite, pyroxene, sodalite, and lazurite (the chief component).

Some interesting sidelights Excavations in Egypt revealed specimens from as early as the third century B.C. In fact, interpretations of hieroglyphic writings indicate that by this period the stone was already commonly imitated. From the Middle Ages till the start of the nineteenth century it was employed to obtain ultramarine blue, much sought-after by painters. Legend has it that the wearer lives in harmony with his or her surroundings and attains serenity. In ancient China, India, Egypt, and Persia it was a valuable talisman. Indian folk medicine still sets great store by the power of lapis lazuli to cure throat problems or even cleanse the entire organism. Also held to be a powerful food purifier; so the lapis lazuli displayed in American kitchens has more than just an ornamental function.

Celebrated lapis lazulis

Surely no such list is complete without the splendid lapis lazuli representing the planet Earth, on display in the St. Ignatius of Loyola chapel in the Gesù Church in Rome. Other well-known examples of its use: in a number of medieval castles whole columns and even entire walls are covered with this precious material.

Deposits The most important deposits of lapis lazuli are located in the Badakhshan district in Afghanistan where they have been mined for thousands of years. Marco Polo visited these mines in 1271 and left us a description in his book of travels. Of all lapis lazuli on the market, the finest is extracted from these founts.

Additional sources are located in the southwestern zone of Lake Baikal in Russia. Not very valuable, the Chilean variety is heavily spotted with white calcite. Deposits are located in the province of Coquimbo, north of Santiago.

Cut Since the material is highly opaque, it is almost exclusively dressed in round cuts (necklace beads), or table cuts (varying surface shapes); it is quite unusual to find faceted stones on the market. Remember that lapis lazuli has long been worked in intaglios that frequently have real artistic value.

Under the lens Even though you can usually judge quality and value with the naked eye, for confirmation use a 10x magnifier. Under this lens you may observe pyrite inclusions with a golden gleam; and it will be much easier to make out any whitish veining or calcite spotting. Keep in mind that these white marks diminish the beauty of the stone; therefore, they are often colored with appropriate solutions that penetrate more deeply into the indentations, but can be identified under the lens. If there is any doubt that the material has been so treated, you can do a general check by rubbing the pieces with a white cloth, which will pick up blue stains, indisputable evidence that the stone has been tinted.

Or else put some acetone on a cotton ball and apply it to the surface of the stone; blue marks on the cotton betray the presence of dye.

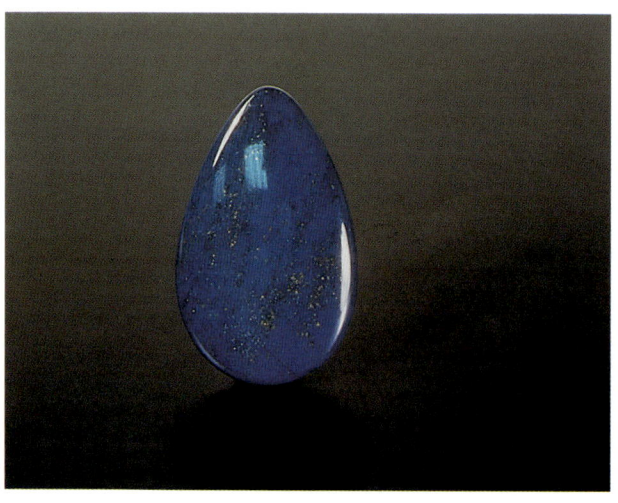

Chemical Formula:	$(Na, Ca)_8 (SO_4, S, Cl)_2 (Al\,SiO_4)_6$ – lazurite aggregate of various minerals with lazurite prevailing
Hardness:	5-6 (Mohs scale)
Specific Gravity:	2.70 – 2.90
Refraction:	monorefringent
Color:	indigo blue, deep blue

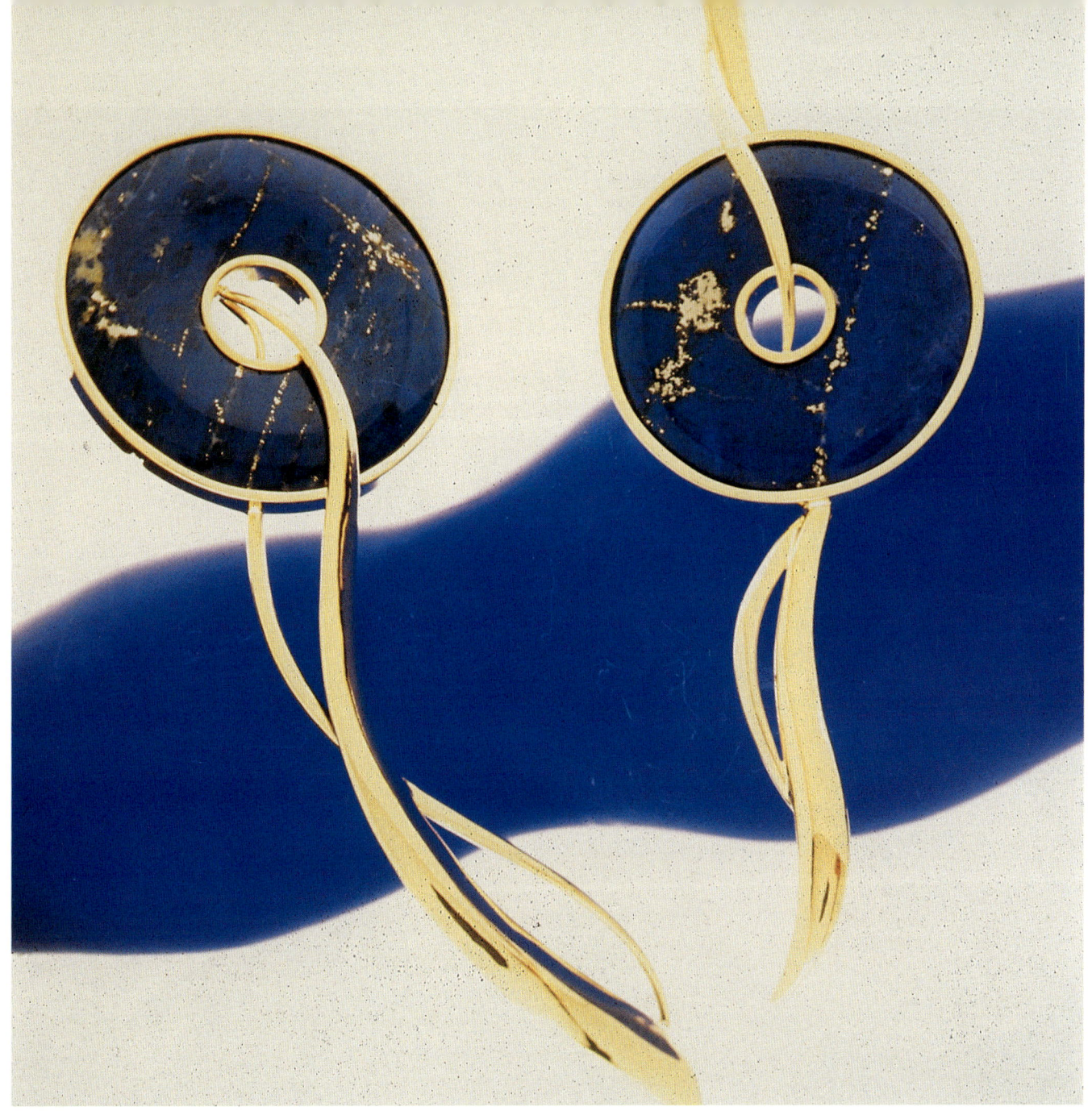

Woo Hyun Choi.
Gold earrings with lapis lazuli.

Synthetics and similar substances There is no corresponding synthetic, though the Gilson company has marketed an imitation produced by mixing various components. The most common facsimile is blue-dyed jasper, generally sold as "German lapis" or "Swiss lapis." Under careful lens inspection, this material even reveals small zonings with brilliant glints. But do not be fooled by them, as they are not the pyrite grains contained in real lapis.

In 1954 a grainy-looking blue-colored spinel appeared on the market, a troublesome imitation to identify as it contains fine gold strings. A somewhat easier counterfeit to identify is produced by opaque blue glass, sold as "blue quartz from India." Stones sometimes mistaken for lapis lazuli are: azurite, dumortierite, lazulite, and sodalite.

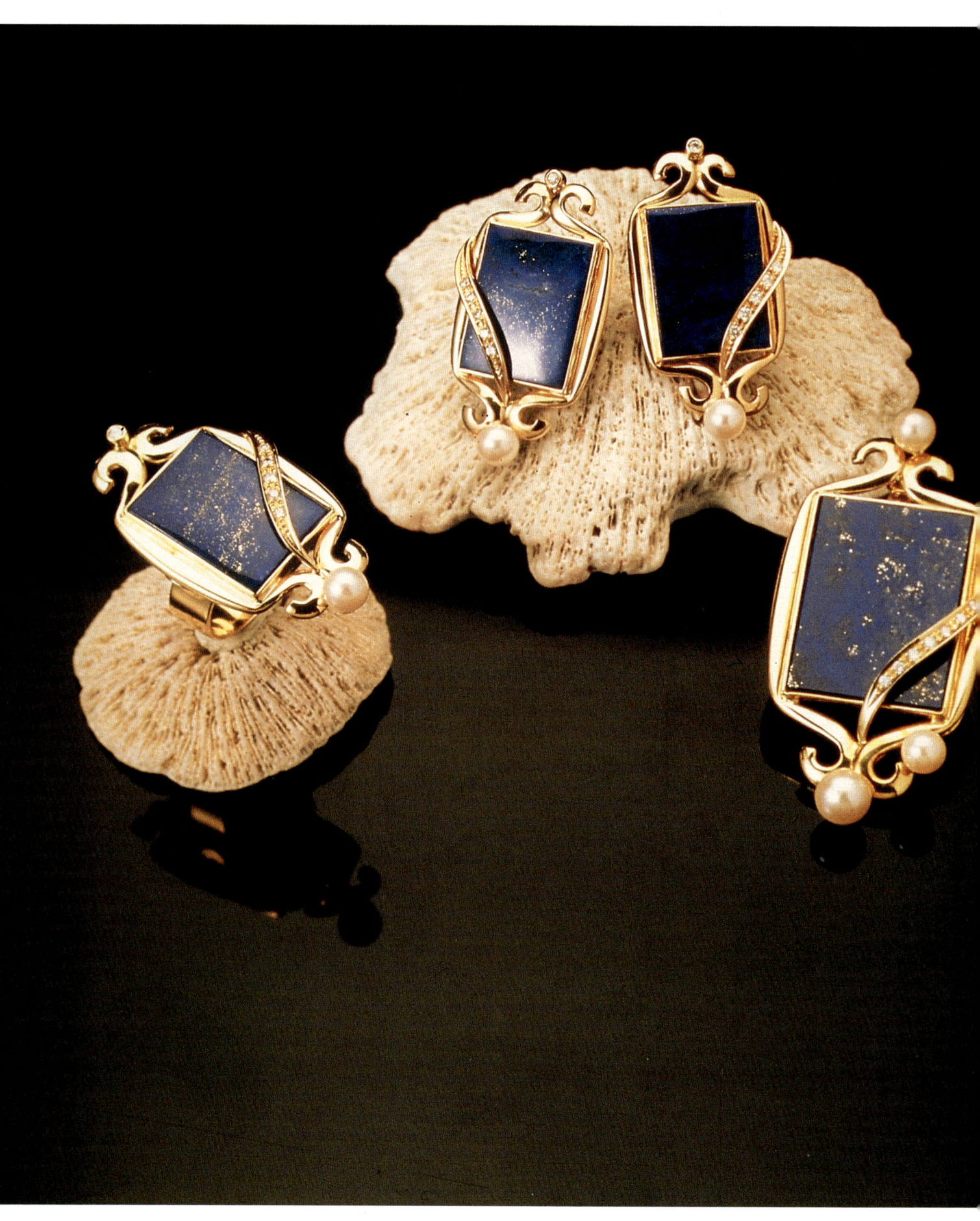

Woo Hyun Choi.
Set in gold and lapis lazuli.

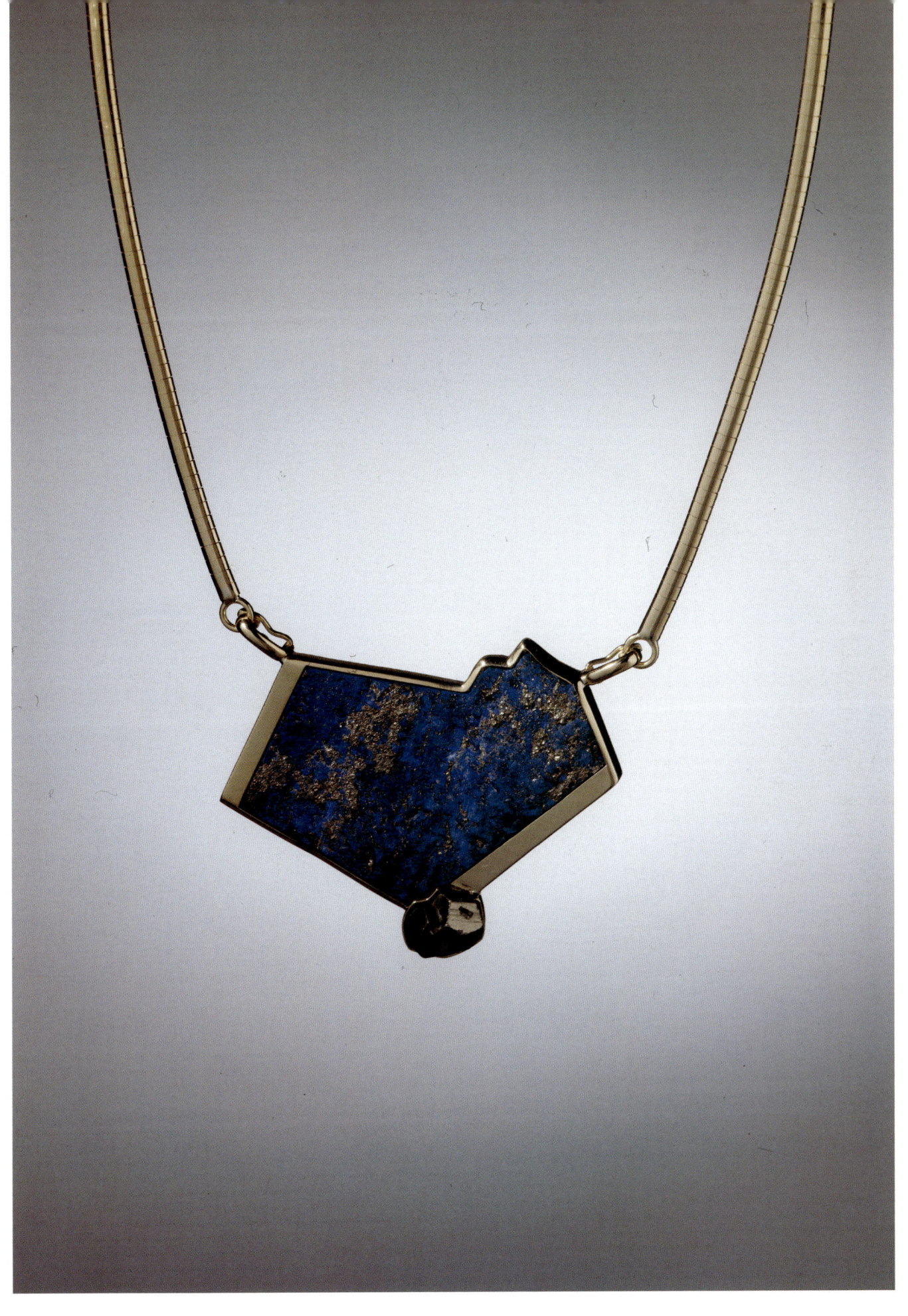

MIRIAM MAMBER.
Gold necklace with pyrite and lapis lazuli.

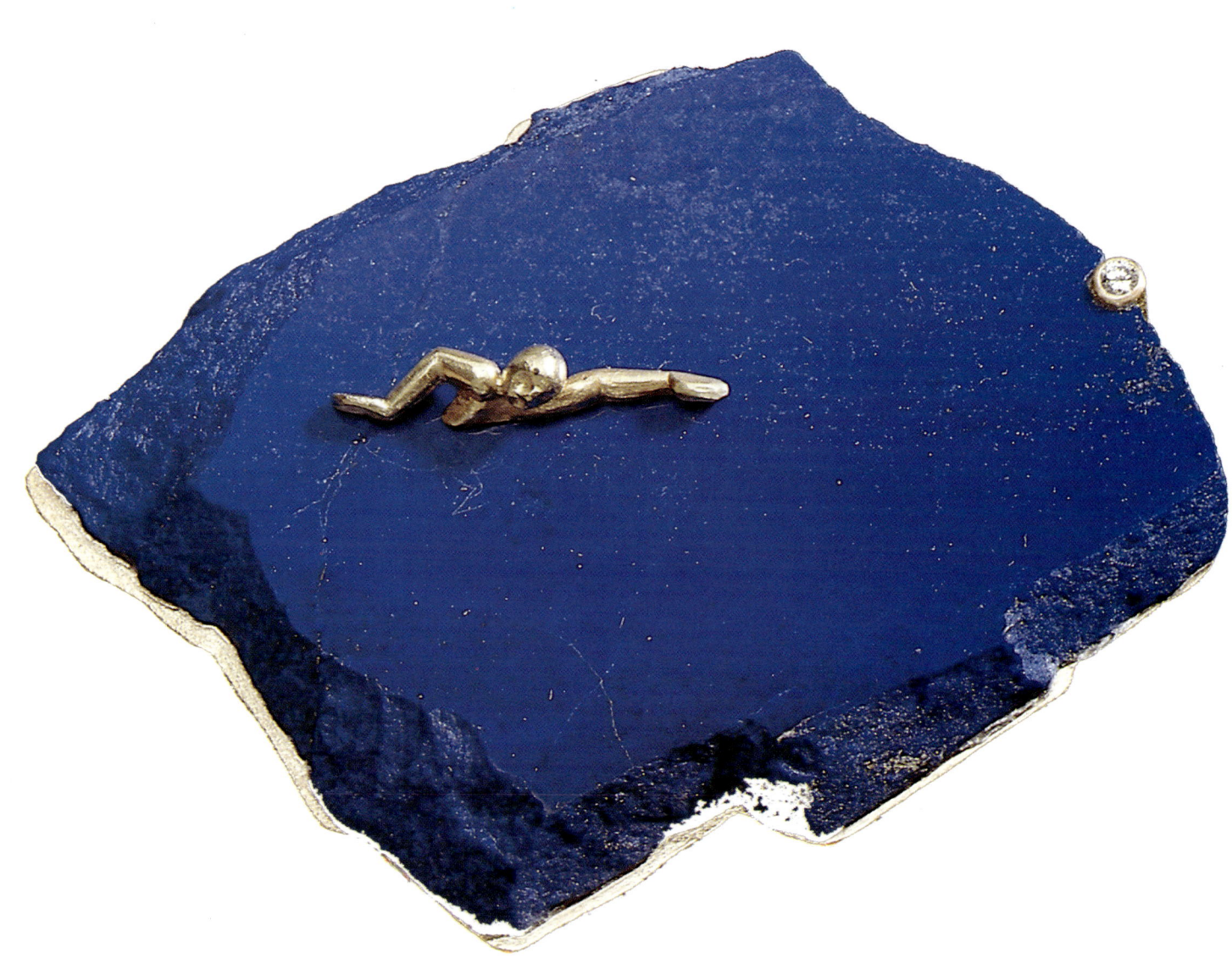

STEFAN PAULI.
Gold pendant brooch with diamonds and lapis lazuli.

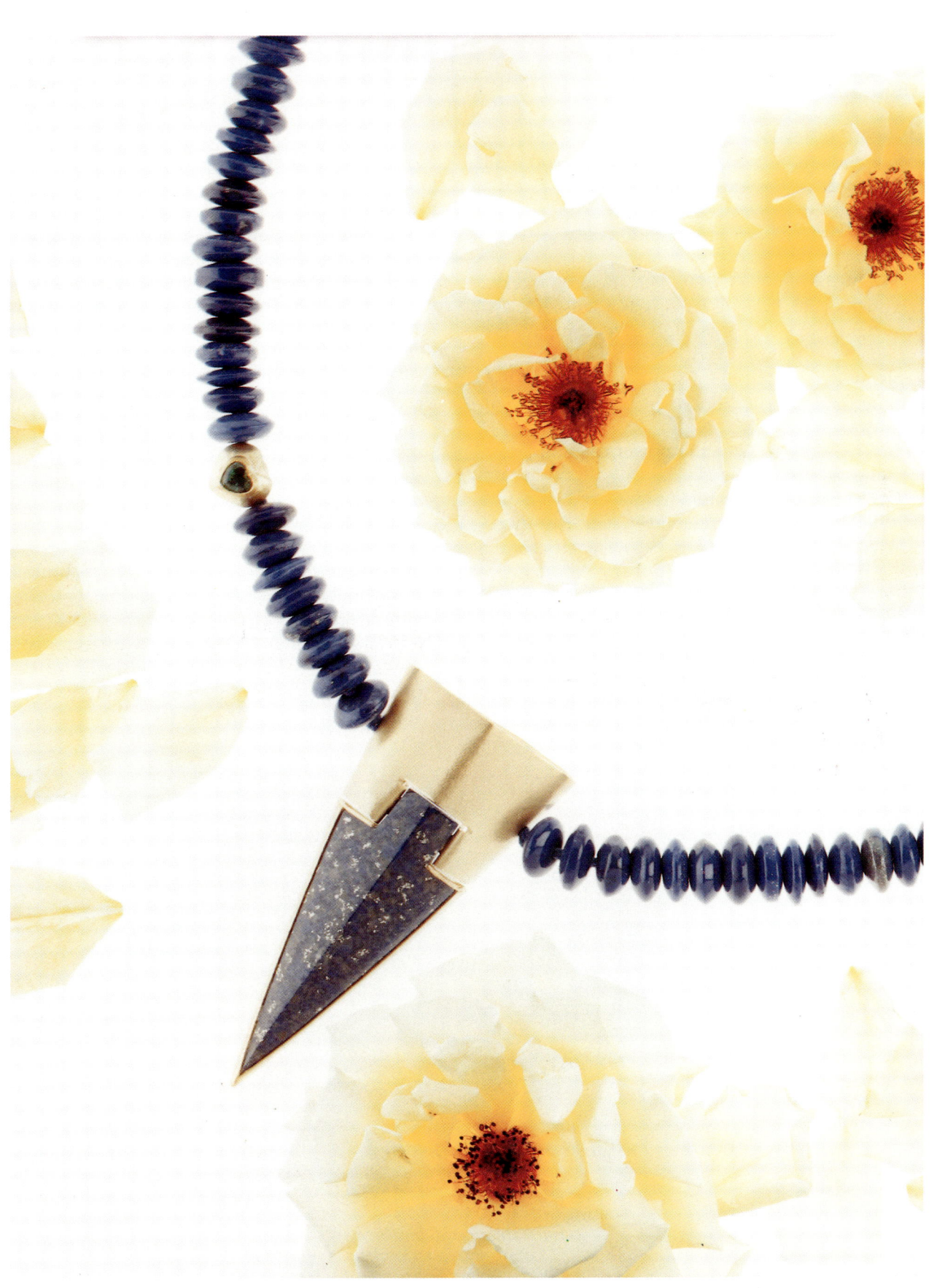

Heike Preuß.
Necklace in gold, with lapis lazuli and emeralds.

Malachite

GENERAL INFORMATION

How it got its name There are two theories: one that it comes from the Greek *malachòs* (soft) as it has a low hardness index; another theory refers to a different Greek word, *malachè* (mallow tree), and the particular green shade of its leaves.

Some interesting sidelights The ancient Greeks, Egyptians, and Romans used it as a talisman, an ornamental material, or simply as a cosmetic, for eye shadow. In those days it was held that applying malachite on a wound would speed its healing; later, in the Middle Ages it was adopted to stop vomiting.

It is believed to have the power to eliminate fear and indecision.

On the negative side, its fragility and lack of hardness means that it scratches easily. Another cautionary note: since it reacts to acids it can never be washed in acid solutions.

Deposits Our richest malachite mines are in the Urals. In fact, the two magnificent malachite vases in the Vatican Museum actually belonged to Tsar Alexander Nicholas. And the finest and most valuable malachite collections in the world are in Russia.

Today Zaire is the largest producer, though other bodies of the mineral are found in Australia, Chile, Namibia, the United States, South Africa, Zambia, and Zimbabwe.

Cut Malachite is particularly suited for jewelry, either en cabochon or table cut, but it also yields stupendous necklace beads.

In striking tonalities, the material is so elegant and glamorous that it is a favorite for ornamental and artistic objects.

Under the lens No need to use a lens to recognize this stone's typical concentric veining, running through a variety of shadings; any optical instrument can only confirm what is obvious to the naked eye.

Synthetics and similar substances Russia now produces a synthetic malachite that is impossible to distinguish from the real one by the usual analyses performed in gemmological laboratories.

Malachite may be confused with chlorastrolite – which is a rock – or, less often, with certain opaque green stones which contain multiple color shadings.

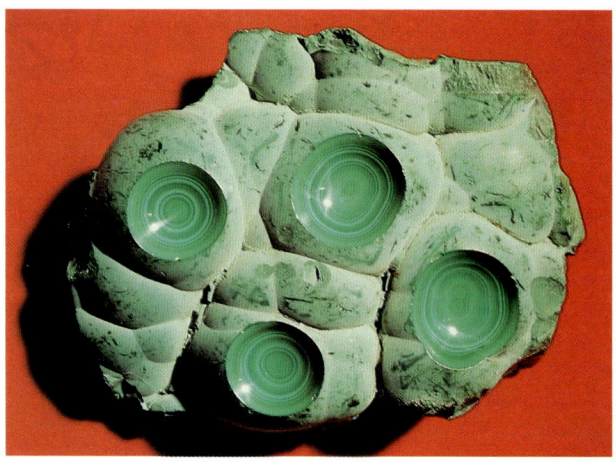

Chemical Formula:	$Cu_2CO_3(OH)_2$ – hydrous carbonate of copper
Hardness:	3½ – 4 (Mohs scale)
Specific Gravity:	3.75 – 3.95
Refraction:	biaxial birefringent
Color:	green stripings ranging from very light to quite dark

Nephrite

GENERAL INFORMATION

How it got its name Comes from the Greek *nephròs* (kidney) because it was deemed a cure for kidney ailments; further details are in our "Jade" listing.

Varieties Nephrite belongs to the group of amphiboles; according to the IMA (International Mineralogical Association), it must actually be considered a mixture of actinolite and tremolite. An opaque rock material, it has a greasy luster and a highly durable structure.

Since it is a fairly common substance its value mainly depends on the quality of dressing, the piece's age, and to which civilization it belongs.

Some interesting sidelights Nephrite was frequently adopted for producing combat or ceremonial weapons such as hatchets and knives.

Celebrated nephrites The Metropolitan Museum in New York has a decidedly rare specimen weighing 2,140 kilos, found in Poland by the mineralogist G.F. Kunz.

Deposits High quality bodies of this mineral are located in China, near Kashgar and Khotan; in Russia, in the western part of Lake Baikal, which has a characteristic spinachgreen variety; in the southern part of New Zealand, a quality placed on the market as "Maori jade" or "Maori stone," though in the past few years this raw material has no longer been exported.

Other deposits are situated in Australia (low value material); Canada, where it seems that Chinese workers in gold mines there, at the end of the nineteenth century found boulders containing nephrite in the Lower Fraze River, and sent them to China; Mexico; Myanmar; Poland (Lower Silesia); the United States (Wyoming, the Rocky Mountains), where chatoyant material is also found; Taiwan; Zimbabwe.

Cut Due to its opaque or translucent nature, the preferred cuts are rounded surface (en cabochon or as necklace beads); it is also suitable for sculpturing. Statues and vases carved in this material include many fine works of art. Nephrite has also been prized for carvings and dressed for jewelry making. Being very tough, it can be highly polished, a process once achieved with quartz sand but now effected with carborundum and even diamond dust.

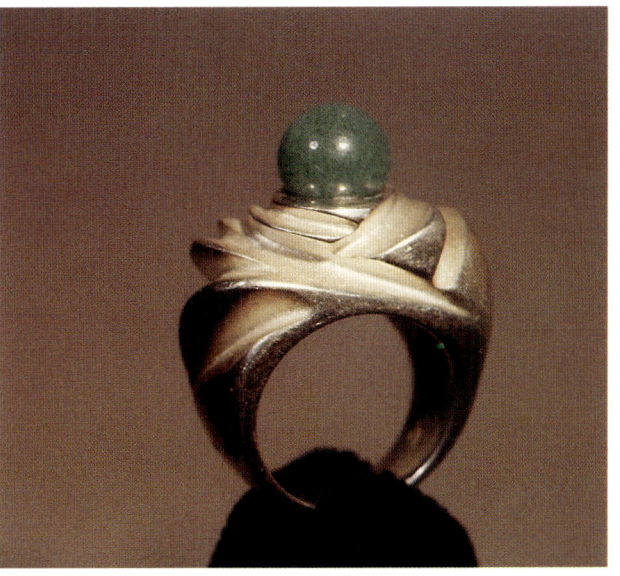

Under the lens Unlike jadeite, this material displays no surface irregularities; with a magnifier, however, observation reveals dark zonings of graphite, chromite or loadstone.

Synthetics and similar substances No synthetic form of nephrite has yet been obtained; there are similar stones, though, and they are discussed under "Jade."

Chemical Formula: $Ca_2(Mg, Fe)_5 Si_8O_{22}(OH)_2$ – hydrous calcium silicate with iron and magnesium
Hardness: 6 – 6½ (Mohs scale)
Specific Gravity: 2.90 – 3.10
Refraction: biaxial birefringent

Olivine or Peridot or Chrysolite

GENERAL INFORMATION

How it got its name Or, in this case, its many names. Most commonly found in olive shades, the logical name was "olivine"; the term "peridot" has no clear origin, though it may derive from Greek, referring to the crystals' multifaceted quality. Chrysolite has a definite Greek beginning in *khrysolithos,* or "golden stone," for a frequently extracted shade. The Germans use the term "chrysolite," though it was often used erroneously in the past, adopted in reference to other mineral species such as yellow chrysoberyl. However, even "olivine" has been wrongly used to indicate green demantoid granite.

Once upon a time, olivine (or peridot) was called "topaz," a general category then including all material of a certain color (such as real topaz) that came from the Greek-named island of "Topazos" in the Red Sea.

Varieties Olivine is actually a blend of forsterite (Mg_2SiO_4) and fayalite (Fe_2SiO_4); depending on the varying proportions of magnesium and iron, the mineral is classified as forsterite, chrysolite, hyalosiderite, hortonolite, ferrohortonolite and fayalite. Bear in mind, though, that these mineralogical subdivisions are not used in gemmology where the terms employed are, interchangeably, olivine or peridot.

Less popular is the variety with a brownish tinge; until 1952 many brownish green stones that had been classified as brown olivine turned out to belong to a totally different mineralogical species, later designated as "sinhalite."

In official nomenclature peridot and olivine are always listed by color type.

Some interesting sidelights

Ancient Egyptian sacerdotes incorporated this stone in religious rites, to take advantage of its supposed power to guarantee the gods' benevolent attention. During the Crusades, large quantities were brought to Europe, and it eventually became a stone symbol of the knights. Tracing its history, we find it is even cited in the Bible as one of the twelve apocalyptic stones.

Exaggerated as it may seem, some people have called olivines "heavenly stones" since they are found in meteoritic rocks that have fallen from space. As early as 1909 gemmologist Max Bauer cited in his text a number of olivine specimens of about a carat that had been discovered in meteorites; but it is also known that a number of olivines were extracted from deposits found in meteorites that fell in Eastern Siberia in 1749.

For those who believe the gem has mystic powers, it acts as a symbol of wisdom and purity.

Cornelius Agrippa claimed it could brush away unpleasant thoughts. And there are those who assert that the set gem inspires courage and brings wealth. What's more, it is supposed to offer a remedy for depression and feelings of solitude.

Its therapeutic qualities include disintoxicating the organism and specific cures for liver, spleen and pancreas; and if that's not enough, the gem is also considered a sort of tranquillizer to alleviate psychosomatic disturbances.

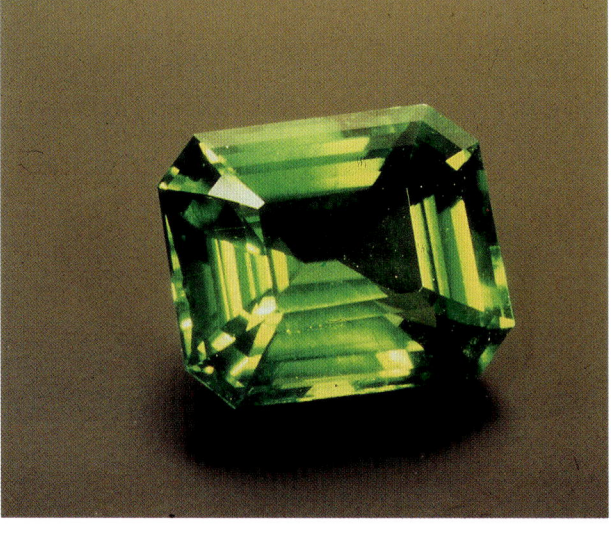

Chemical Formula: *(Mg, Fe)₂SiO₄ – magnesium iron silicate*
Hardness: *6 ½ – 7 (Mohs scale)*
Specific Gravity: *3.27 – 3.37*
Refraction: *biaxial birefringent*
Color: *greenish yellow (olive tone), green, brownish green*

Celebrated olivines The world's largest known faceted olivine, weighing 319 carats, is housed in the Smithsonian Institution in Washington, D.C. At the Museum of Diamond Treasury in Moscow there is a 192-carat olivine, and a 136-carat example on display at the London Geological Museum. In the Cathedral of Cologne in Germany the jewel box carried by the Three Kings is set with two peridots of about 200 and 300 carats respectively, which were long thought to be emeralds.

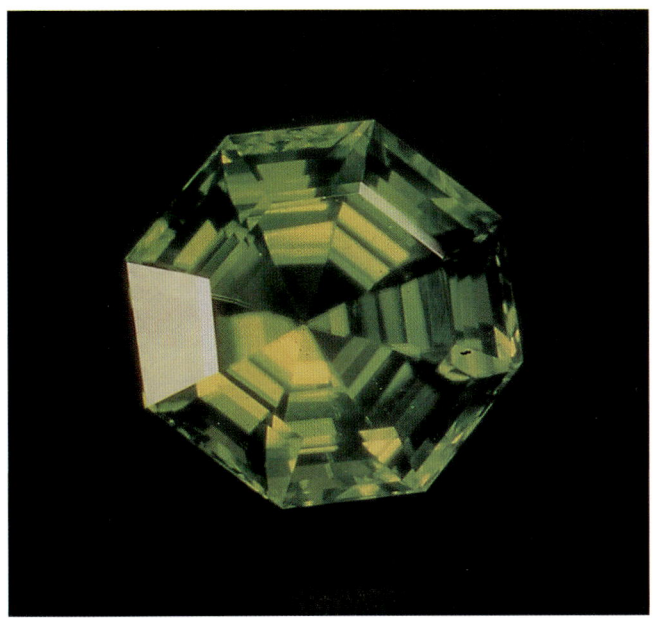
Peridot from Burma with octagonal cut.

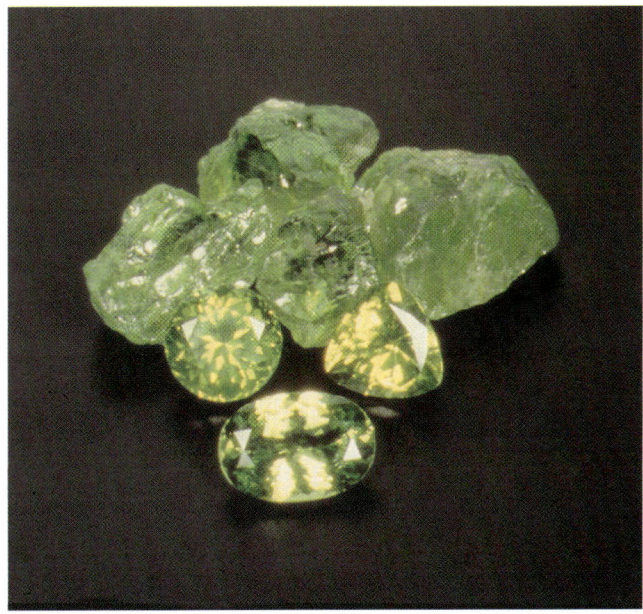
Cut and rough peridots from the mines of Ethiopia.

But for the most famous olivine collection of all, we must look to the Topkapi Museum in Turkey where we can admire the throne of Bayram, set with a bedazzling 954 large-sized peridots.

Deposits For going on 3,500 years now, our most important source has been the Egyptian volcanic island of St. John; there is also a quantity of good material extracted from the Kyaukpon mountain in the Mogok district of Myanmar.

Less important are the mineral zones in Australia, Brazil (Minas Gerais), China, Kenya, Mexico, Sri Lanka, the United States (Arizona, Hawaii, New Mexico), and South Africa, best known for its diamonds.

Should anyone have an incurable urge to walk on miniscule olivine crystals, there's plenty of such surface material on the island of Oahu, near Honolulu, and on the volcanic island of Lanzarote in the Canary Islands.

Cut During the Baroque period, olivine was greatly admired and frequently pressed into service, at times with special cuts. Since it is not a very hard stone, it does have limited use and is currently no longer popular. Normally, it is dressed with a rectangular step cut, but it is also suitable for a mixed oval, round, and drop cut; the brilliant cut is infrequent. In handling the stone, it is important to treat acids with care as they can diminish a peridot's polish.

Under the lens Usually olivines do not contain inclusions; at times, though, careful inspection may reveal minute dark, crystalline inclusions, light brown mica laminae, glass drops that look like air bubbles (of Hawaiian provenance), and discoidal markings.

Angle splitting caused by a high degree of birefringence is one of this gem's most important identifying characteristics.

Synthetics and similar substances Word got around of a synthetic olivine produced in 1851 and, again, in 1881; but there is no evidence that it was ever put on the market. The following substances may be mistakenly identified as olivine: beryl, chrysoberyl, demantoid, diopside, dioptase, moldavite, prasiolite, prehnite, sinhalite, emerald, spodumene, hiddenite, tourmaline, vesuvianite, synthetic corundum, doppiette (two layer counterfeit), synthetic spinel.

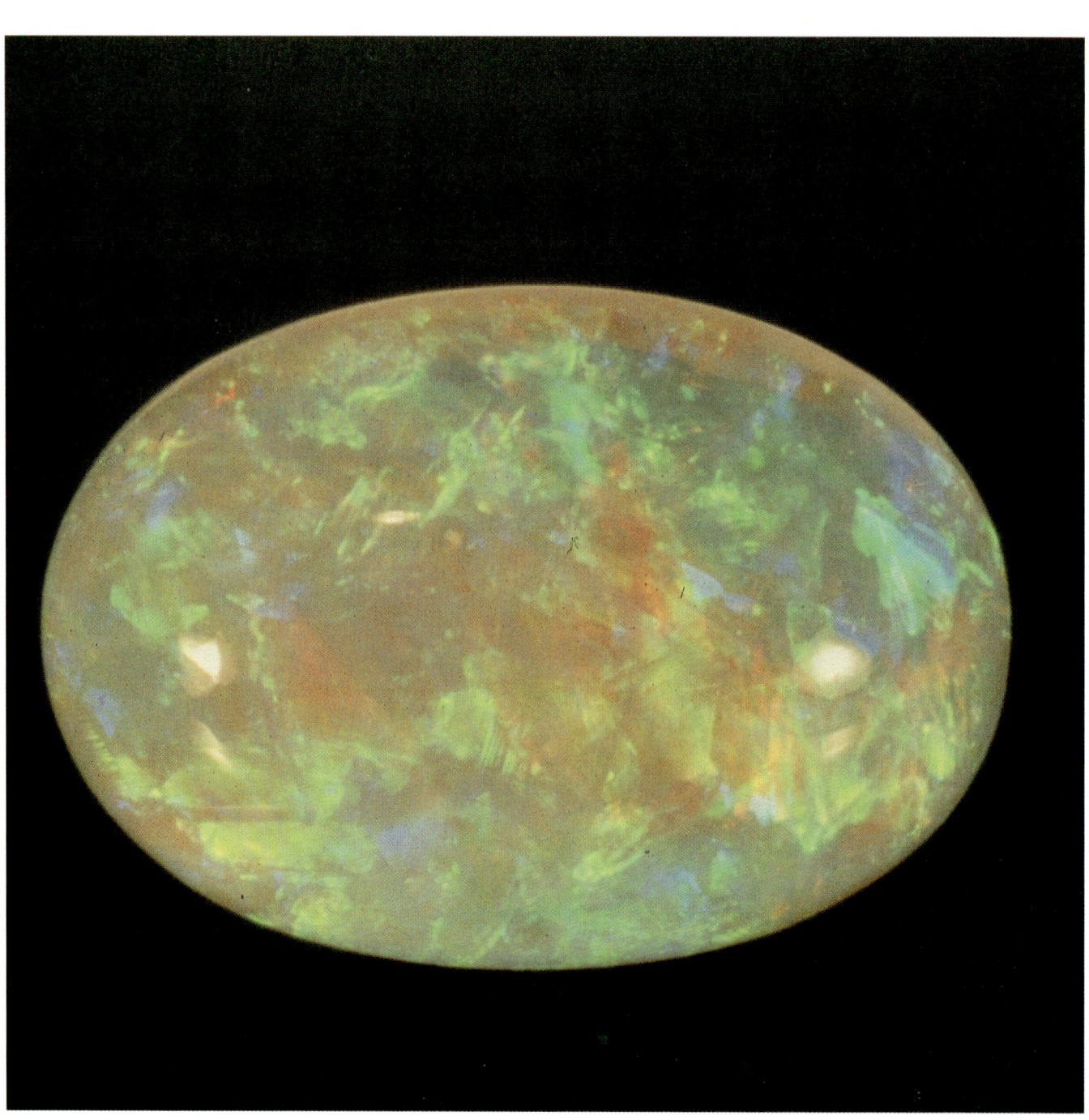

Opal

GENERAL INFORMATION

How it got its name Apparently traces to the Sanskrit *upalas* (precious stone). However it was *opalus* for the Romans and had an appreciable value for them as early as the second century B.C., given the plentiful deposits in their mines in Cervenica – once part of Hungary and now known as Slovakia.

Varieties Opals may be divided into three groups:
– *noble opals* that have a fantastic flash of varying colors, for which they are often called "harlequin"; without a doubt, these stones are considered the most beautiful;
– *fire opals*, having a decidedly typical flame orange color;
– *common opals*, which lack a color play, and are often almost opaque with a typical milky glow evoking a theoptical phenomenon called opalescence.

By now it must be clear that the harlequin and opalescent opals are distinctly different phenomena. The harlequin effect is created by minute spherules contained in the opal's silica mass. On the basis of the size of these spherules, which have a geometric disposition in the stone, we may observe a dazzling blaze of varied colors simply by looking at the same stone from different vantage points.

Common opals have several denominations, for example: *casciolongo* (a whitish stone with a mother of pearl sheen); *hyalite* (almost as transparent as glass); *hydrophane* (an opaque whitish material; when immersed, it absorbs water – and so got its name); *prase opal* (an apple green opaque stone).

Opals extracted in Australia are classified as:

White Opal. It may be transparent, translucent or opaque, with delicate shadings; obtained from mines in the southern part of Australia.

Boulder Opal (found in rock formations). A material that has formed on ferrous rocks; gleaming color play, partly owing to the fact that it lies on a brown matrix included in the extraction. Queensland is the almost exclusive source for this variety.

Black Opal. Surely the most sought-after type, this stone is really not black at all; actually, the color glints off a dark gray silicon base that may at times look blackish and displays a pronounced harlequin effect. Prices can reach dizzying heights for stones with predominantly red or fire orange colorings.

Some interesting sidelights The ancients believed that the stone's wide-ranging color effects meant it could unite all stones in its single form. Later on, in the early seventeenth century, it was quite popular, particularly as it was thought to bring good luck to the wearer. By the following century, however, its reputation had fallen and it was then considered bearer of ill fortune, some claim because of a Teutonic superstition, others because of its evil role in the Sir Walter Scott story *Anne of Geierstein*. The fact remains that today the opal has dual fame: though coming to the aid of all generous personalities, it is bad luck if you are only interested in acquiring material wealth. Its medicinal powers include invigorating the vital functions and stimulating the heart.
Moreover it is thought to eliminate envy and greed, and help create sincere friendships.

Celebrated opals The Australian government presented Queen

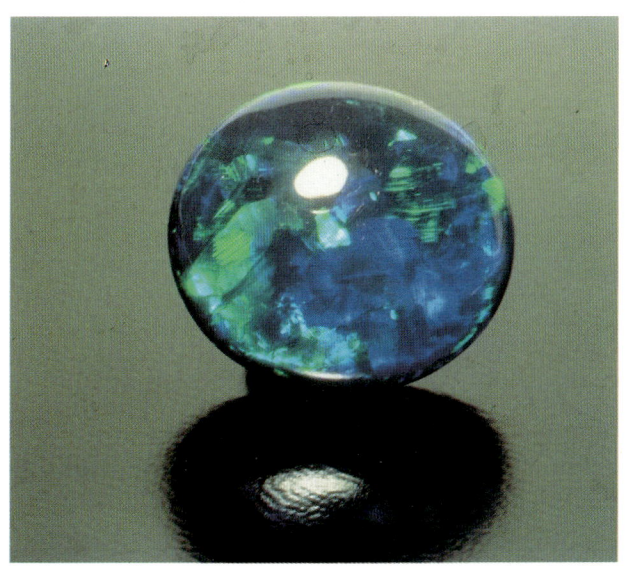

Chemical Formula: $SiO_2 \cdot nH_2O$ – hydrous silicon dioxide
Hardness: 5½ – 6½ (Mohs scale)
Specific Gravity: 1.98 – 2.20
Refraction: monorefringent
Color: a rich play of colors from basically white, blue, grey, black, green or orange stones

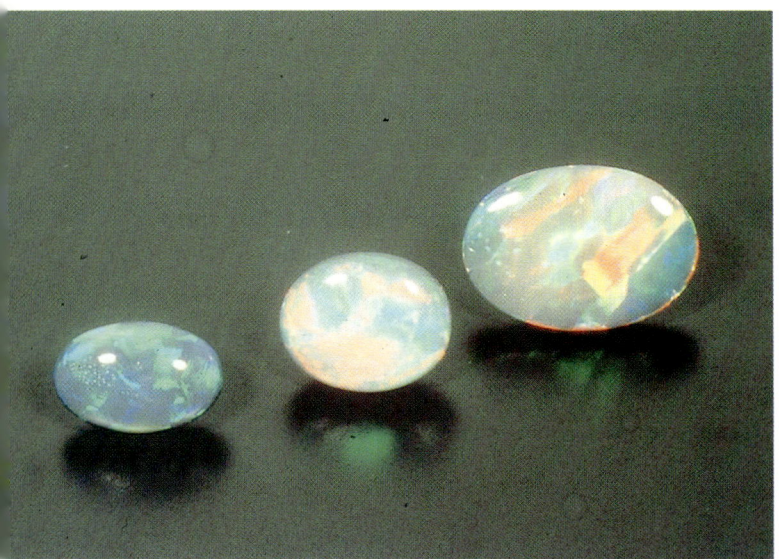

Black opals.

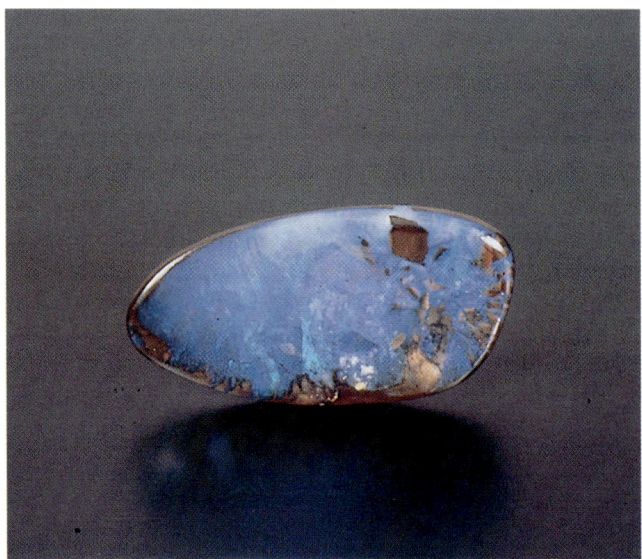

Boulder opal.

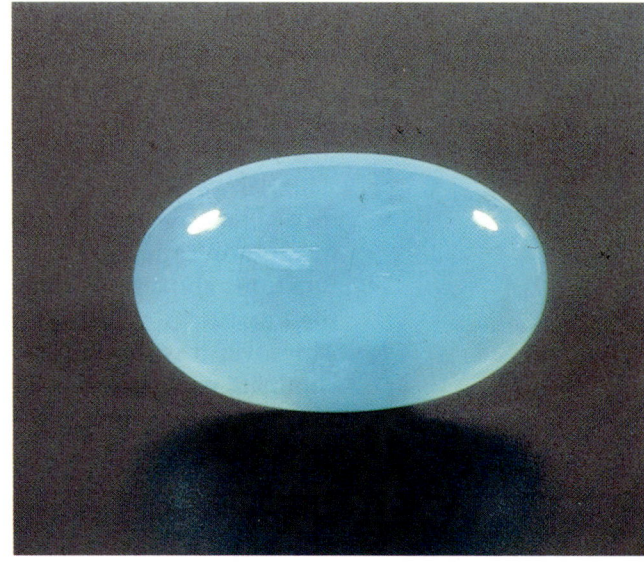

Blue opal from Peru.

Elizabeth II of England with a 203-carat opal called "Andamooka Opal," after the mine where it was discovered. Another gift of the Australian government: a 55-carat opal to the king of Cambodia; a particularly fine green gemstone presenting a stupendous play of red, orange and blue. Like as not, the most famous of all opals was the one called "the burning of Troy"; it is known to have belonged to Napoleon's Empress Josephine, but has since mysteriously disappeared.

Deposits Indubitably, Australia has the most important deposits, seemingly discovered in 1849, though the only documentary evidence we have dates to 1872. The great importance attributed to this body of minerals is demonstrated by the fact that its name stands for the classification of all such materials coming from the Australian continent.

In search of fire opals, the best sources are the Mexican mines.

Other deposits of this mineral are located in Brazil (in the States of Piaui and Bahia, and in the Pedro II district); less important varieties are situated in Abyssinia, Ethiopia, Honduras, Indonesia, Poland, Slovakia, the United States, and Tanzania (provenance of prase opal).

Cut As the gem is fragile, great care must be taken in the cutting phase. Usually it is cut en cabochon, which heightens harlequin and opalescent qualities; often, though, jewelers strive to keep the look of the stone in its natural state, rounding it slightly to emphasize its play of light and obtaining the most oddly shaped gems.

Only the fire opal is ever faceted.

Under the lens Evidently, the typical play of color and light is clearly visible to the naked eye; but when we use the lens, the slightest movement, and the colors seem to overlap and become illegible. Simple visual observation is always best, therefore, followed up by an analysis producing physical optical data. When studying a fire opal under the lens, it is sometimes possible to see red flamelike reflections.

Synthetics and similar substances Synthetic opals have been produced that create almost the same play of colors seen in the natural stones. In 1974 the first synthetic opals appeared on the market, made by Pierre Gilson, who has continually perfected his product right up to the present day. In fact, the early production reveals a mosaic structure surface (called lizard scales) whereas more recent products are extremely difficult to unmask. The Japanese, too, have obtained some excellent synthetic opals.

To imitate the real stones, double and triple

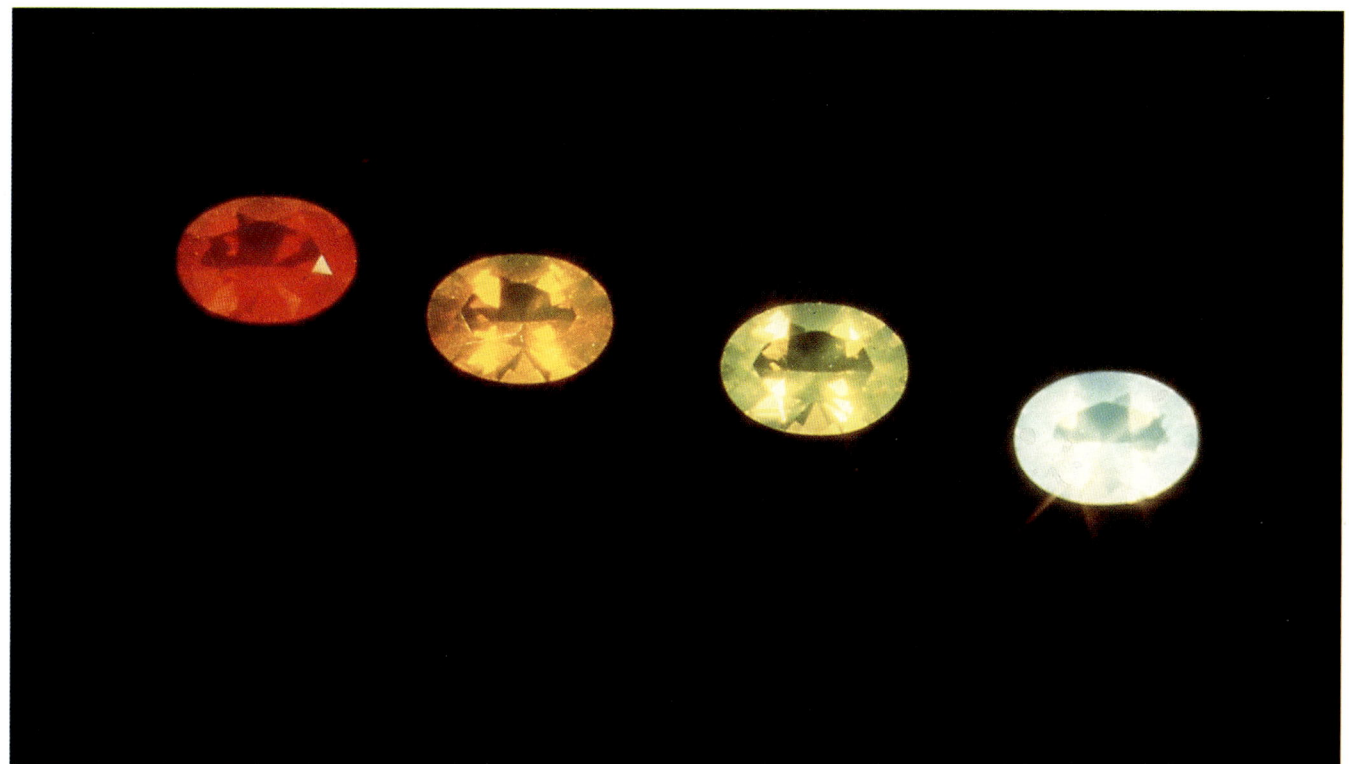

fused layers are employed. The former have as a base a thin band of natural opal topped by an en cabochon cut rock crystal glued to it. By attaching bands of black glass or even onyx under the natural opal of the double, we obtain the triple-layer synthetic; occasionally a piece of iridescent seashell is glued on as a substitute. Examining the side of this layered product with a lens, the different strata are easily discerned.

A very distinct type of glass is produced in the United States to obtain certain stones, called "Slocum stones" for the name of their inventor; and this imitation looks very, very similar to the real thing.

Faceted and cut en cabochon, quartz is sometimes covered with an extremely thin layer of gold, generating a quite attractive iridescent effect. Finally, our list of imitations even includes a specially developed type of plastic.

The opal mineral may be confused with: chalcedony, chrysocolla, and obsidian.

Fire opals.

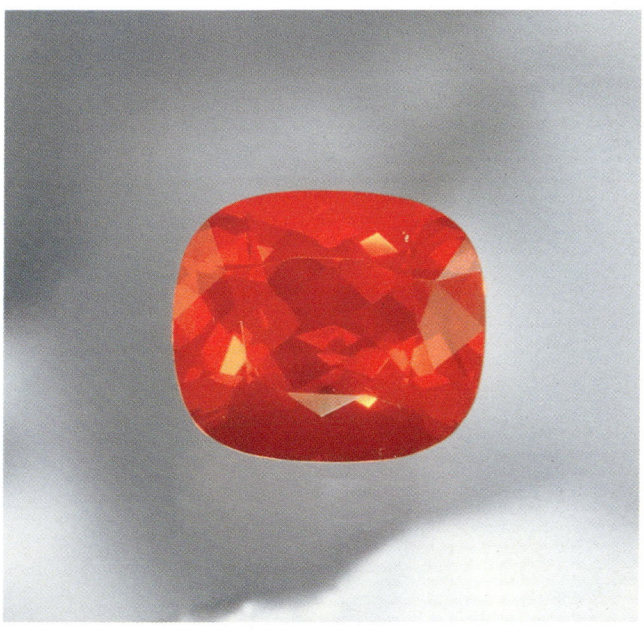

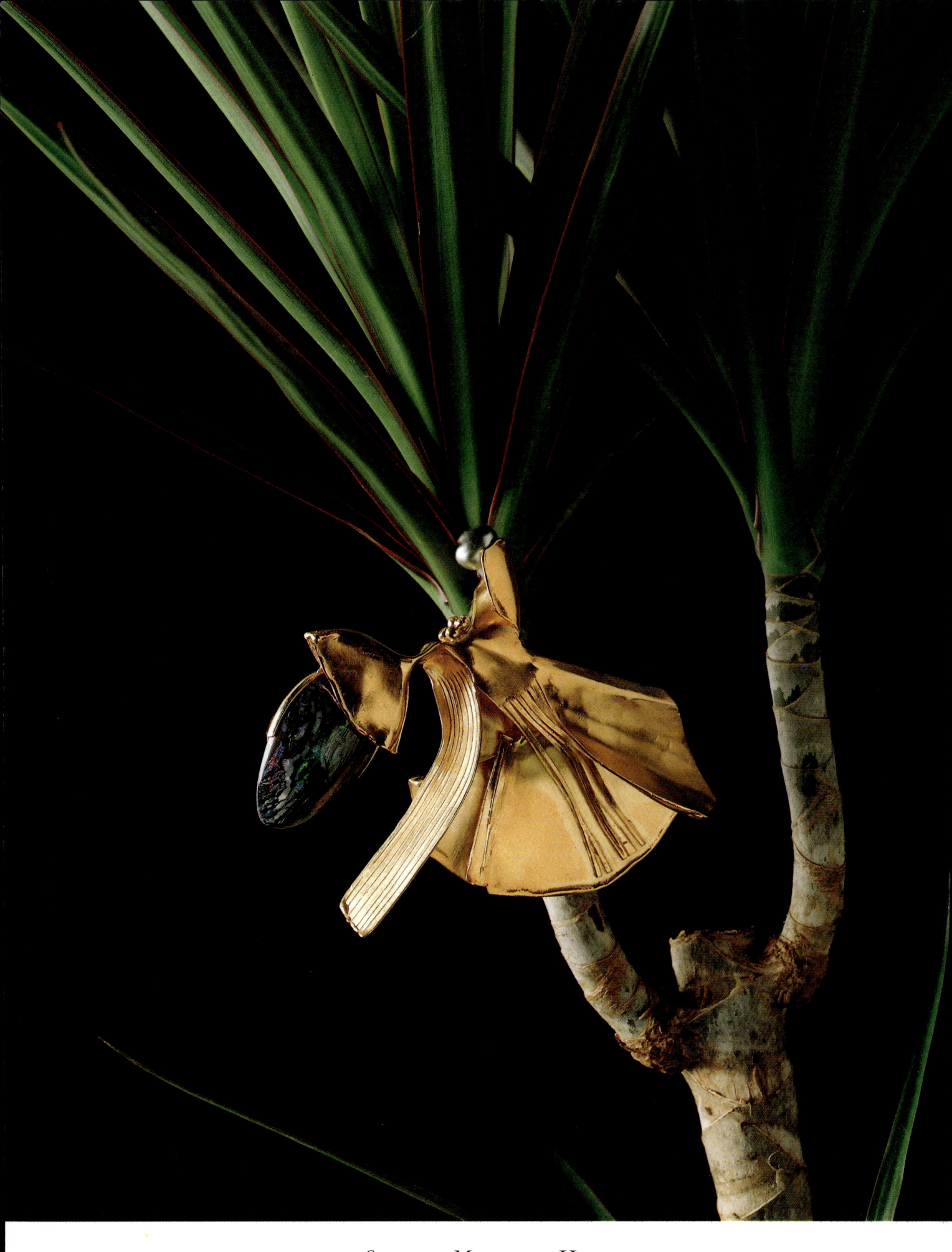

SIMONNE MUYLAERT-HOFMAN.
Gold pendant brooch with opal and Tahitian pearl.

JEAN-MARC SIEGL.
Creator of BIJ'ART, the contracted form of "Bijou d'art," and heir of a family of jewelers established in Cannes since 1880. These two works are identifiable thanks to the visible signature, open circles, and clasp (registered model and trademark).

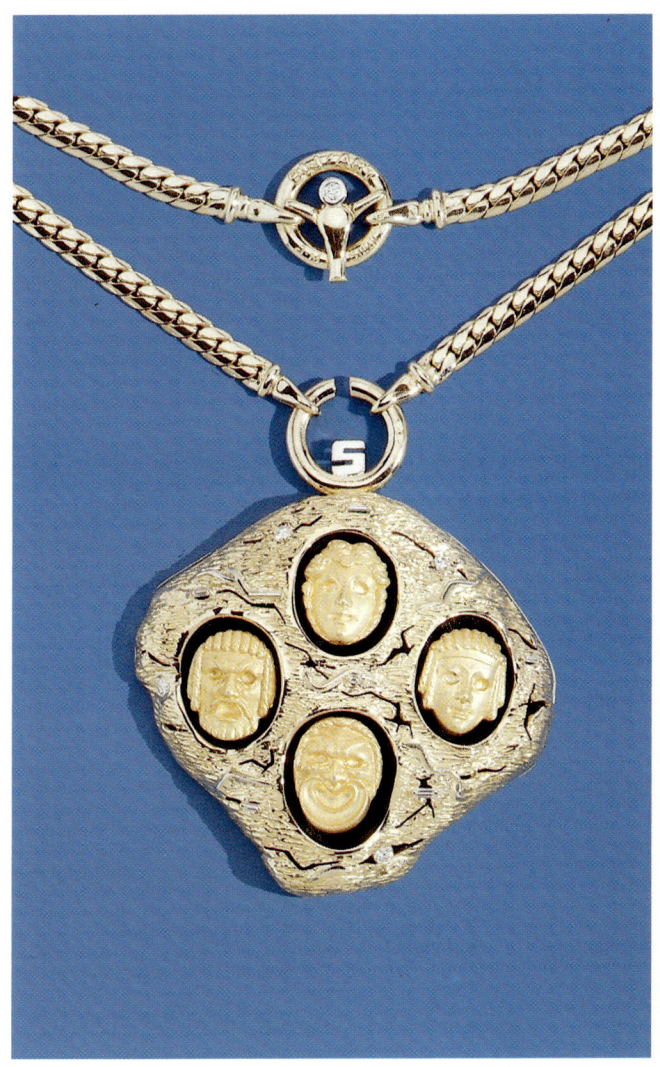

BIJ'ART "ANCIENT THEATER"
Gold and platinum pendant with 4 movable masks.

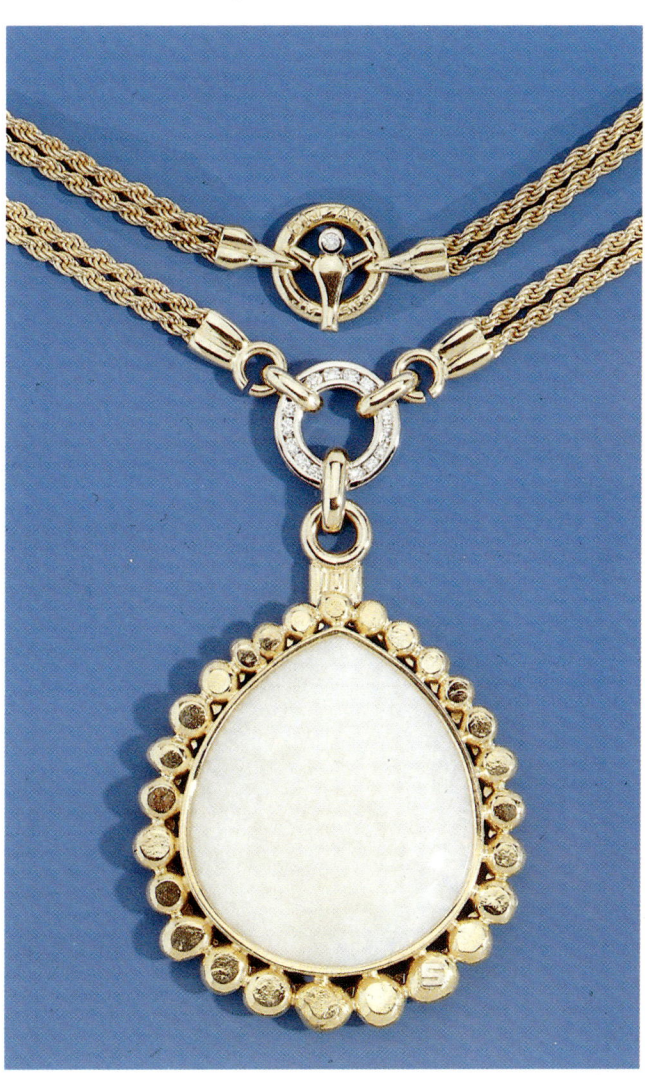

BIJ'ART "LAGON"
Gold pendant with diamonds and 105 carat opal.

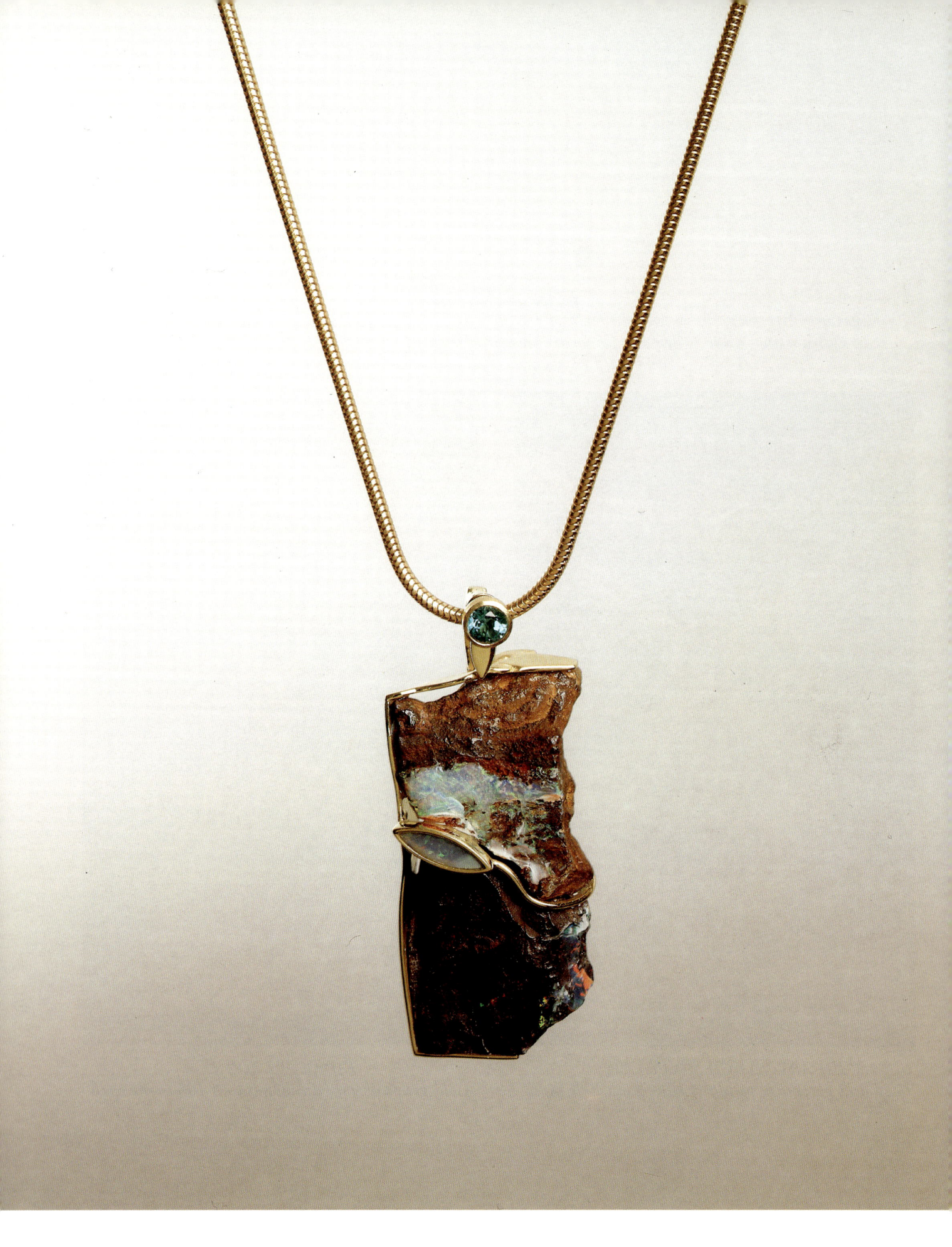

WIGBERT STAPFF.
Gold pendant with tourmaline, and rough and cut Brazilian opals.

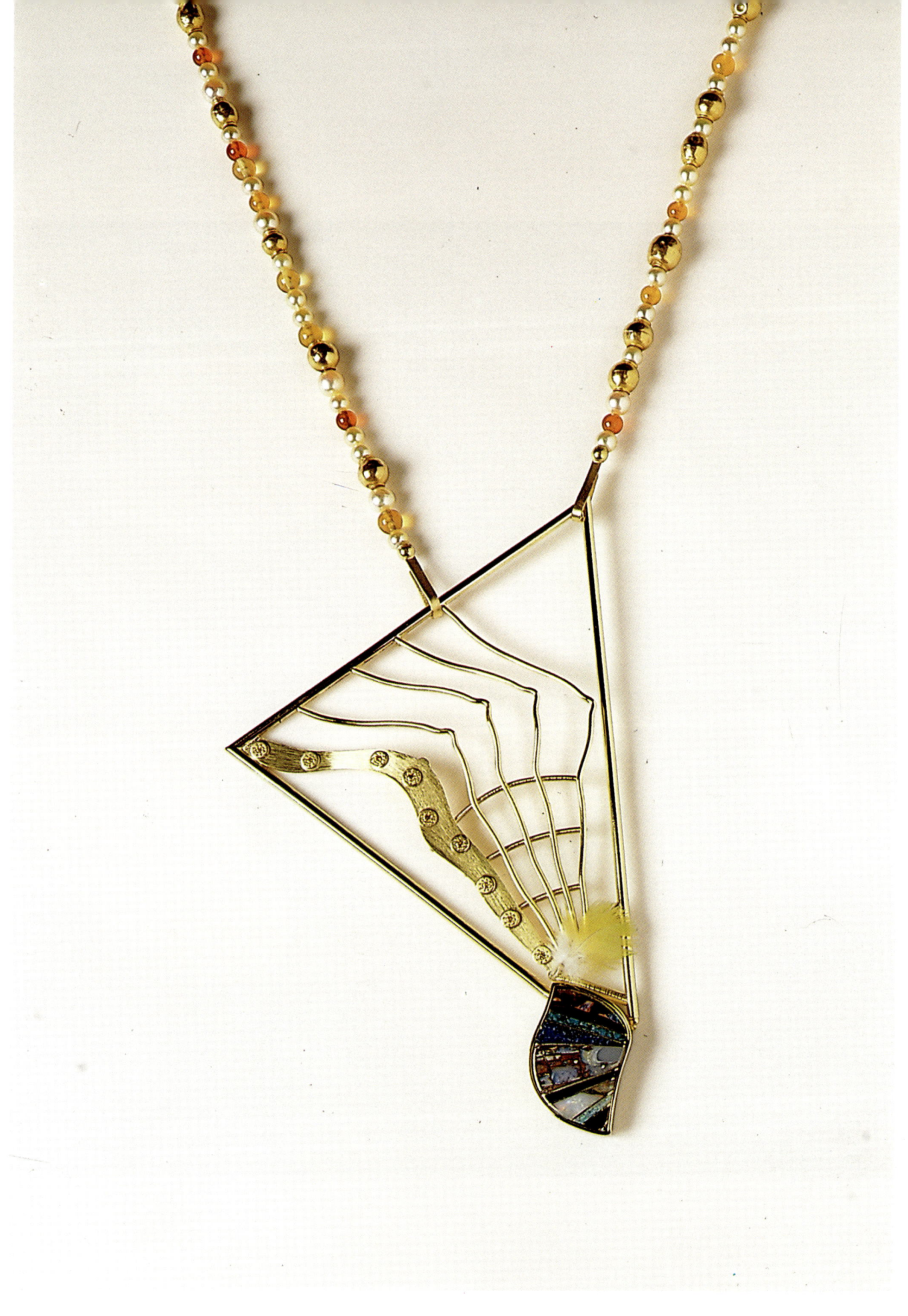

GABRIELE WEINMANN.
Gold pendant and brooch with diamonds, feather and mosaic in turquoise, opals and lapis lazuli.

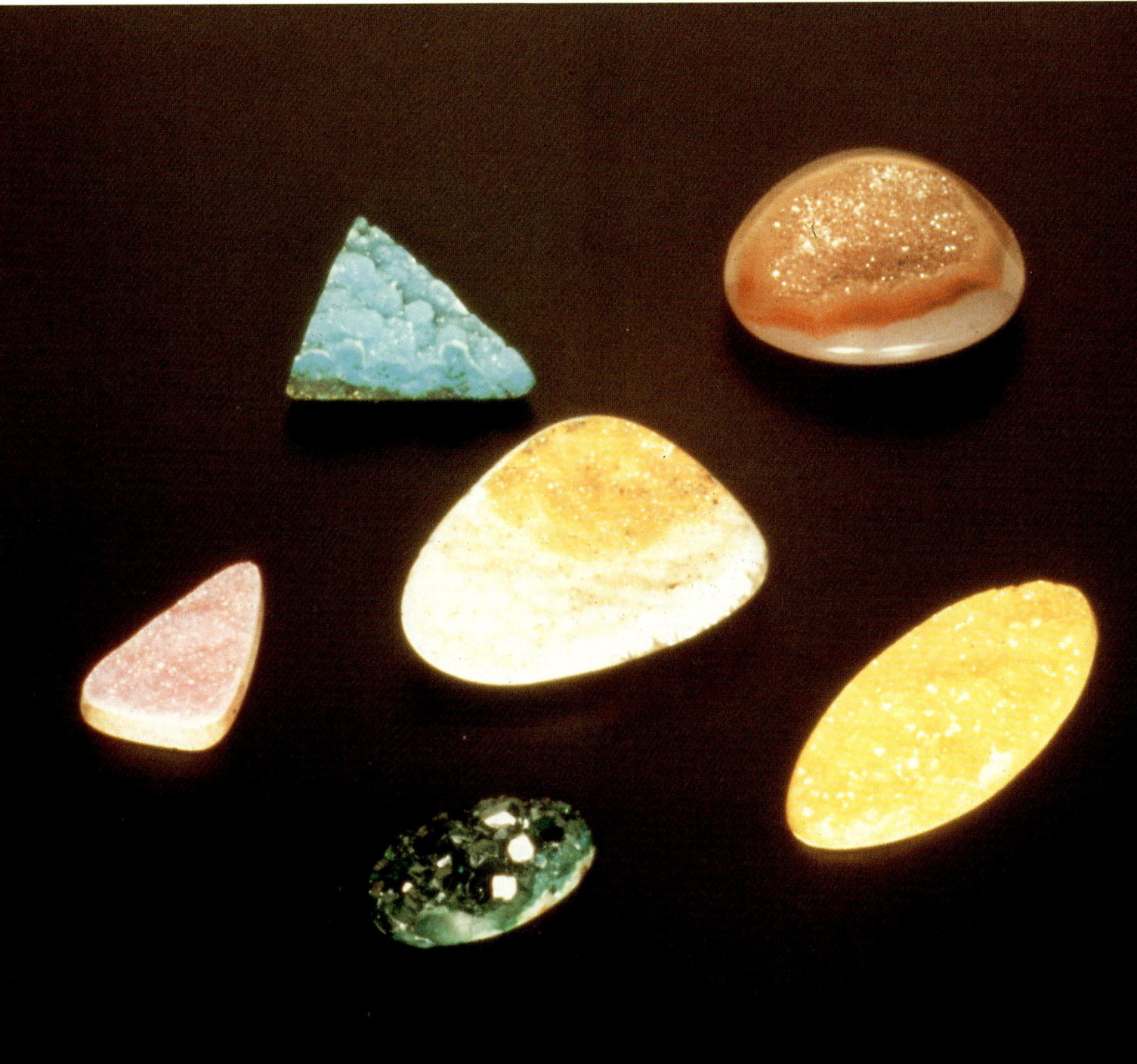

Quartz

GENERAL INFORMATION

How it got its name Apparently traces to the German *querkluftertz* for "mineral that runs in veins."

Varieties "Quartz" refers to a group of minerals covering quite a number of varieties.

Before going on, let's look at a summary of the basic classification of subgroups to which we shall be referring:

– Macrocrystalline quartz, which is almost always transparent, with rough crystallization.

– Microcrystalline quartz, containing reduced-dimension crystals grouped in compact masses, it may be found in translucent or opaque specimens.

– Cryptocrystalline quartz, formed of microscopic crystals enclosed in silicagel, a translucent or opaque material.

– Siliceous rock, with a high percent of silica, which is usually opaque.

Further on, a separate discussion will be dedicated to each subgroup and the quartz variety examined in detail.

Some interesting sidelights

- *Agate.* In ancient history it was treated as a sacred stone. Today some claim that it makes a male wearer so personable and attractive, that any woman he loves will have eyes for him alone.

Also assumed to cure stuttering and tobacco addiction.

Folklore assures that you may rely on this quartz variety to strengthen your immune system and aid your children's growth.

- *Amethyst.* A very old legend narrates the tale of the nymph Amethyst who was pursued by Bacchus, god of grapes and wine; to evade his overtures she called upon the goddess of chastity who turned her into a colorless crystal, which Bacchus promptly transformed to a purple hue of wine. In time, not by chance, the stone was presumed to cure immoderate drinking.

Definitely suggested for those seeking mystical revelation and spiritual uplift. Or as a charm to focus your powers of concentration.

Oriental peoples place it between the eyebrows, over the "third eye," where it can act directly upon the hypophisis.

- *Aventurine.* Perhaps because so easily confused with jade, talisman of well-being, it was inserted as the "eyes" in ancient Tibetan statues.

Many believe the crystal is a powerful charm for your economic affairs.

It is also a mineral that may bring to light its owner's artistic talent.

Aventurine is thought to act directly on the nervous system, producing happiness and dispelling anxiety. And it may be advised for psychosomatic suffering brought on by stress.

In the Orient it was also adopted to improve eyesight.

- *Chalcedony.* A chalcedony carved in your zodiacal sign and set in a ring worn on the ring finger of the left hand is supposed to create a positive influence by your dominant planet.

- *Cornelian.* According to an ancient Transylvanian belief, wearing a cornelian necklace will protect you from vampires.

Ancient Egyptians placed the stone in burial tombs as a good luck amulet accompanying the dead on their voyage towards eternity.

Indians receive it as a sign of peace.

But in the Middle Ages an engraved cornelian was placed on swords to ward off bad luck and evil spells.

This quartz variety is said to help those who suffer from anemia or heart problems, and it may even cure intestinal disturbances.

- *Chrysoprase.* Old tales refer to it as a symbol of loyalty.

It was once prescribed to cure envy and egoism and promote sincerity.

In particular, the stone was thought to cure impotence and frigidity and, in effect, resolve any sexual problem.

- *Rock crystal.* Nero is supposed to have owned sheets of rock crystal engraved with highlights from the *Illiad*.

Ancient Egyptians employed this colorless mineral to represent eyes in their statues while the Chinese processed the stone to produce religious ceremonial objects. The Romans, on the other hand, created elaborately engraved plates and cups that had a rare artistic value.

If you use a computer, wear this stone as it will absorb its electromagnetic emissions.

Wear the mineral for your skin's sake if you want to rejuvenate or slow down signs of aging.

- *Jasper.* Called "the witches' stone" by Italians, who gave it to children to protect them from evil curses.

In the second century A.D. a jasper necklace

was deemed a great help for stomach problems, and is apparently still so considered in England today.
- *Heliotrope.* Used by the ancients to bring rain in periods of drought.

An aid to eloquence, it will help keep your audience's attention. Thanks to heliotrope, yoga practitioners claim they can harmonize nature with higher forms.
- *Onyx.* African tribes once put it to use in celebrating fertility rites.

Since it simultaneously presents two opposing colors, Orientals imagined that it represented an equilibrium between two opposing but mutually dependent fields of energy.

Said to produce a loud, clear voice, this gem is a suitable adornment for singers. Take care though: this stone is not suggested for high-strung personalities.
- *Citrine and rose quartzes.* Catherine De' Medici possessed a belt bejewelled with twelve precious stones, each representing a specific month of the year. Since the citrine quartz in this belt stood for November, we can only surmise that its bright happy yellow was chosen to offset the natural melancholy of the season.

Rose quartz presumably wields a positive influence over introverted, timid personalities, and holds aid and comfort for the lonely.

Citrine quartz is assumed a lucky charm for kidney problems as it is said to help eliminate kidney stones.

Back to rose quartz, however, if you suffer from heart or lung problems.
- *Cat's eye and tiger's eye.* As far as we know, the term "tiger's eye" was born in a very old South African legend.

Both stones are considered powerful talismans, enabling the wearer to foresee imminent dangers.

Some say they sharpen your sense of direction, in a figurative sense as well.

Cat's eye quartz encourages introspection, and is believed to correct bad habits.

Macrocrystalline Quartz

Chemical Formula: *SiO_2 – silicon dioxide*
Hardness: *7 (Mohs scale)*
Specific Gravity: *2.63-2.65*
Refraction: *uniaxial birefringent*
Color: *see subgroup varieties*

GENERAL INFORMATION

Varieties This subgroup is also referred to as "monocrystalline quartz".

Each designation in the list below is, if not already, regularly followed by the term "quartz":
- *Smoky quartz* (a smoky gray). Designation according to its unique color. When heated to temperatures from 300°- 400° C the mineral tends to lighten; but colorless or yellow specimens may also be obtained.
- *Amethyst* (pale violet, purplish violet, lilac). This is undoubtedly the best known and cherished quartz type. Taken from the Greek word *améthystos*, for "drunken," in homage to its deep winey tone. A biblical citation indicates it was one of the twelve stones on which the names of the Tribes of Israel were carved.

In the past, the stone was the almost exclusive property of noble or clerical estates.

Amethyst changes color dramatically when

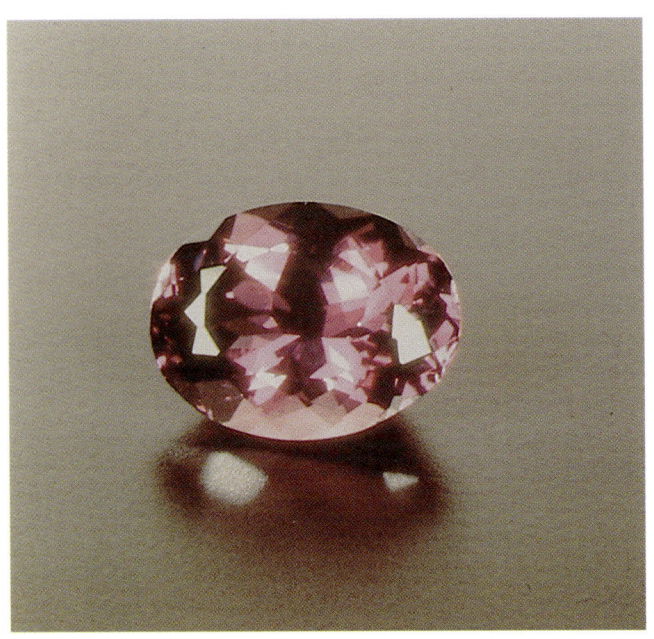

Amethyst with an oval cut.

Crystallized amethsyt.

heated: under 300° C the violet hue deepens, whereas higher temperatures may effect a complete color change, producing even yellow or colorless specimens.
- *Amethyst quartz* (purple with milky white striping). Though usually in rock form, it is occasionally found as crystals.
- *Amethyst-citrine quartz*. Specimens which contain colors typical of both amethyst and citrine, it is also known as Ametrina. The formation of such double colorings is the result of factors rather too complicated to go into here.
- *Citrine* (lemon yellow, orangish yellow, golden brown). Its lively yellow color suggested its name; today most specimens are obtained by heating smoky quartz or amethyst material in the less valuable shades. However, it is not at all easy to distinguish a naturally colored citrine from a heat-formed product; we may occasionally find a very slight reddish streak in the latter, which is never present in the naturally colored material.
- *Rock or hyaline crystal* (colorless). Mainly employed in making artistic and ornamental objects. Its name? Look to the Greek *krystallos*, for cristal. Some truly large examples have been found, actually weighing hundreds of kilograms.
- *Morion* (a dark, smoky brown verging on black). Darker than smoky quartz, it is also usually less transparent.
- *Praselite* (green). Its color is the key to its origin, the greek *prasios* meaning leek green. Most such specimens are obtained by heating amethysts and light-toned, yellowish quartz. Recently, natural, supposed volcanic examples in this color have been found in California.
- *Rose quartz* (a wide range of pinkish shadings). Its wide range of pinkish shadings give lovely but unstable color which changes notably when exposed to ultraviolet light and less dramatically when exposed to sunlight. Specimens have been unearthed with six-point star formations.
- *Reddish quartz* (true red, purplish red). Generally found in rock form; occasionally in crystals.

Celebrated macrocrystalline quartzes Two splendid crystals of smoky quartz at 133.5 and 127.5 kilograms, denominated respectively the "Grandfather" and the "King," are both on display in Switzerland at the Berne Museum.

The British Museum hosts three precious amethysts: one of Brazilian provenance weighing 343 carats. The other two are of Russian origin, weighing in at around 75 and 90 carats.

Rock crystal has been employed through the ages in priceless examples of glyptic art such as the Crucifix in the British Museum and *La storia della Vita di Cristo* by Valerio Belli, on display in Florence's Silver Museum. And we cannot forget to mention the "Pyramid" composed of five pieces of rock crystal, housed in the Museum of History and Art in Vienna.

Deposits Far and away the largest producer of this material is Brazil (Rio Grande do Sul, Mato Gross do Sul, Minas Gerais, Espírito Santo, Goiás, Bahia Ceará).

Important mining areas also lie in: Madagascar, Mexico (sites known from the Aztec period), the United States, and Uruguay.

And even if they are much less significant, we cannot overlook the deposits in: Australia, Austria, France, Germany, Japan, India, Iran, Italy, Namibia, the Czech Republic, Scotland,

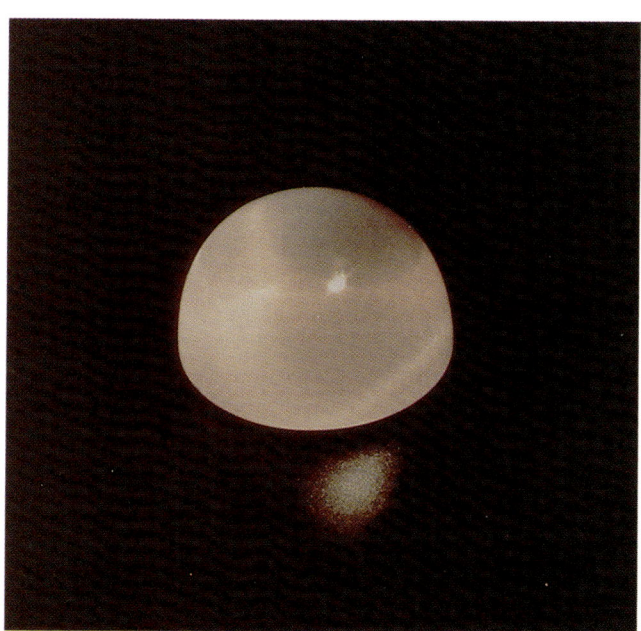

Rose quartz with a cabochon cut.

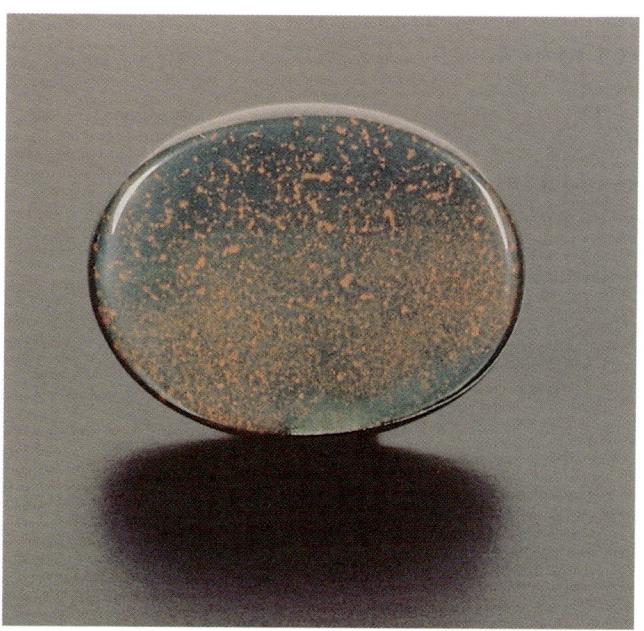

Blood jasper with a flat cabochon cut.

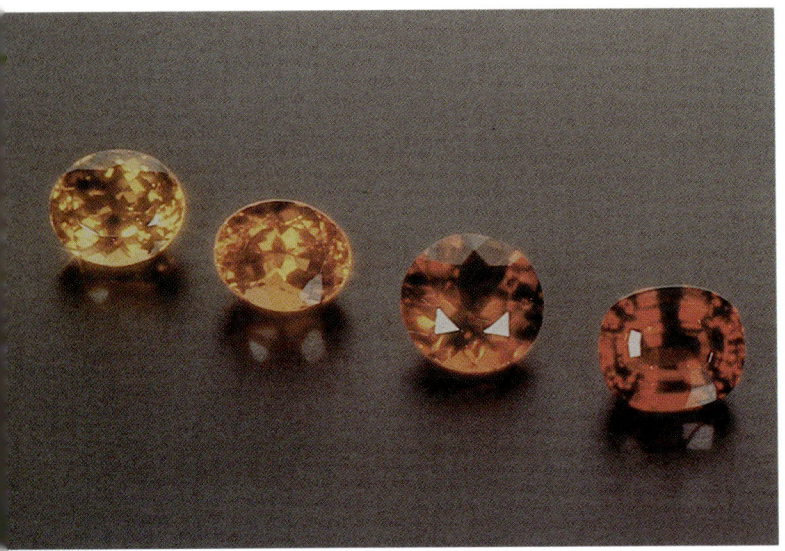

Varieties of citrine quartz.

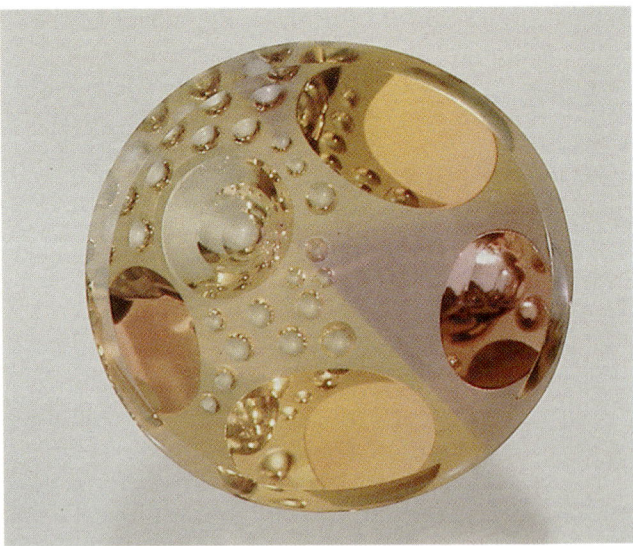

Ametrina from Bolivia weighing 55.65 carats. This stone was cut by Michael M. Dyber.

Spain, Sri Lanka, South Africa, and Switzerland (where smoky quartz is extracted in very large specimens).

Cut Only the finest examples of this subgroup are faceted, using bern, mixed, and Brazilian cut. Less valuable materials are polished by tumbling, then drilled, and strung as necklace beads.

Under the lens

- *Amethyst.* Short-needle inclusions; barely visible fractures so situated that they create a highly typical surface, somewhat like a tiger skin.
  Some Brazilian amethysts may also reveal liquid inclusions.
- *Smoky quartz and morion.* Crystal inclusions frequent; in addition, the darker variety will reveal bituminous remains.
- *Citrine quartz.* Paintbrush-color streaking; two-phase inclusions.
- *Hyaline or rock crystal.* Possible inclusions: crystals, two-phase needles of other minerals, and liquid inclusions.

Many of these inclusions will be obvious to the naked eye, and there is a useful classification of subvarieties:

- *Cacoxenite quartz,* named for the mineral inclusion, arranged in groupings of yellow tufts;
- *Tourmaline* hair quartz, evincing inclusions that resemble balls of dark green yarn;
- *Venus hairstone* sagenitic quartz, charaterized by the presenze of needlelike inclusion of rutile. Also known as rutilated quartz in a fine yellow shade suitable for valuable ornament (e.g. the precious vases sculpted in this material by Harold Van Pelt);
- *Water agate,* easily visible liquid inclusion (usually water);
- *iris quartz,* so named in reference to a luminous iridescence;
- *moss agate,* containing green dendritic inclusions.
- *Rose quartz.* Very often contains rutilite needles.

Synthetics and similar substances All transparent varieties of macrocrystalline quartz – excluding the rock crystal subvariety – may be obtained through hydrothermic processes; finally, even amethyst-citrine quartz has been produced in synthetic version.

These laboratory results can be produced as crystals weighing up to several kilograms. At times we find inclusions that look like breadcrumbs or are nail-shaped; nevertheless, not all synthetic quartz is easy to identify as such.

Rock crystal may be employed as raw material producing some striking imitations.

In fact, if we take a stone of this quartz variety, heat it in a liquid and then cool it off quickly, the entire surface is covered with fine cracks. And if we adopt a colored liquid, the stone absorbs this color through the cracks. By clever use of dyes, a laboratory can supply quite pleasing imitation rubies and emeralds. From citations by Pliny the Elder in his *Naturalis Historia* we know that ancient peoples were familiar with this process, though only recently has it come into use once more.

The possibilities of confusion with other stones are as follows:
- *amethyst:* synthetic purple corundum, fluorite, kunzite, and glass;

- *citrine quartz:* yellow shades of beryl, corundum, topaz and tourmaline. Quite often citrine quartz is wrongly offered to the public as topaz. Do keep in mind that these are two completely different minerals, of which the clear variation on the hardness index is one example; obviously, their prices are equally different. And considering topaz's real investment value, identifying quartz as topaz is an unpardonable error;
- *rock crystal*: all colorless stones, and glass;
- *praselite*: tranparent jade and olivine;
- *rose quartz:* kunzite, morganite, synthetic pink spinel (also used to obtain imitations).

Microcrystalline Quartz

Chemical Formula: SiO_2 – *silicon dioxide*
Hardness: *7 (Mohs scale)*
Specific Gravity: *2.64 – 2.71*
Refraction: *birefringent*
Color: *see "Varieties" for this subgroup*

GENERAL INFORMATION

Varieties Minerals listed are all quartzes with their respective color ranges:
- *aventurine:* reddish brown and an iridescent green with metallic sheen;
- *blue:* blue, purplish azure;
- *milky:* white, grayish white;
- *ox eye:* dark read, mahogany red in layers;
- *falcon's eye:* dark base with dark blue and greenish azure highlights; chatoyant not very striking that may be confused with quartz chatoyant;
- *cat's eye:* alternating stripes of dark and mahogany red in one type; glints of dark blue and greenish azure on a deep ground, with a very slight chatoyant gleam in a second type; in the more prevalent version we have olive green, brownish grey and greenish gray arranged on parallel fibers and a clear cat's eye;
- *tiger's eye:* golden yellow and brownish hues; a chatoyant gleam that can be taken for cat's eye quartz;
- *prase:* a not very bright green with whitish zonings.

Records tell us that the the name "aventurine" was due to a mishap ("chance") that occurred in Murano around 300 years ago when a glass blower dropped extremely thin bronze sheeting by mistake into glass paste; the resulting glass had the same striking iridescence typical of this quartz variety.

Deposits South Africa is home of our main deposits of microcrystalline.

Other sources are located in: Australia, Austria, Brazil, India, Russia (our most precious aventurine comes from the Urals and Siberia), and Sri Lanka (cat's eye).

Cut As these are dense gems with a chatoyant gleam, the en cabochon cut is usually employed.

Under the lens Whenever a quartz variety presents a cat's eye phenomenon, we need no more than observation with the naked eye, accompanied by the confirmation offered by technical data, which is obligatory for nontransparent stones.

However, to identify aventurine we need a 10x

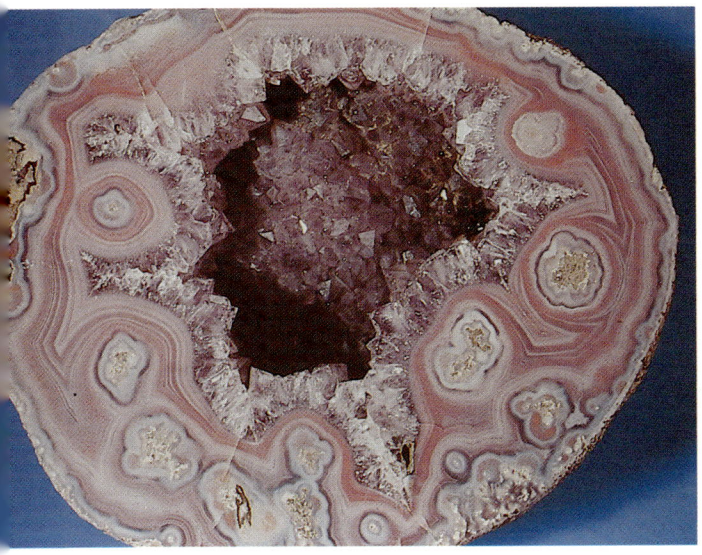

Agate geode with central amethyst.

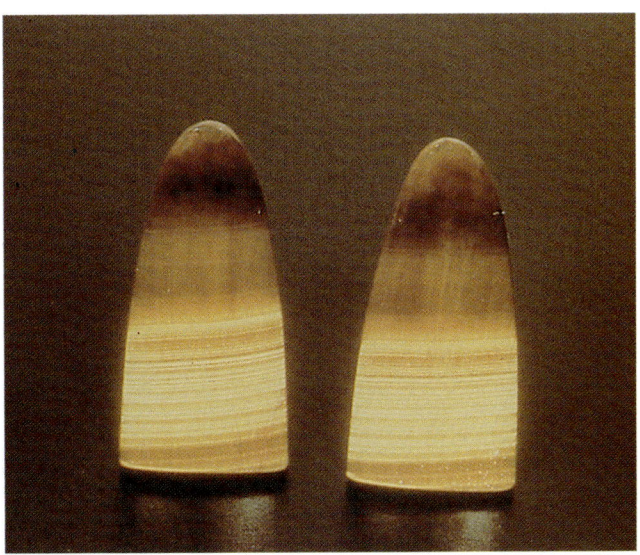

Tiger's eye quartz with cabochon cut.

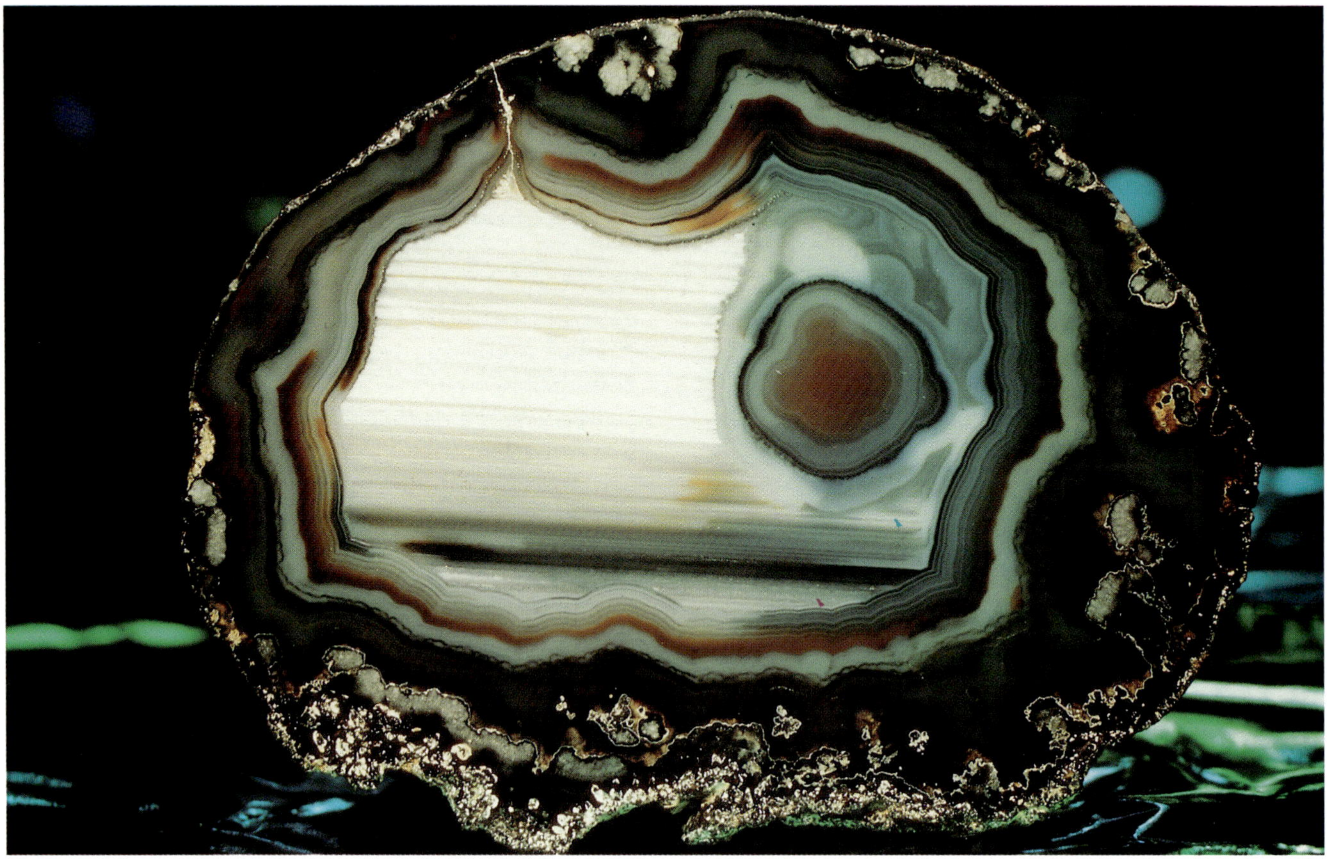

Agate.

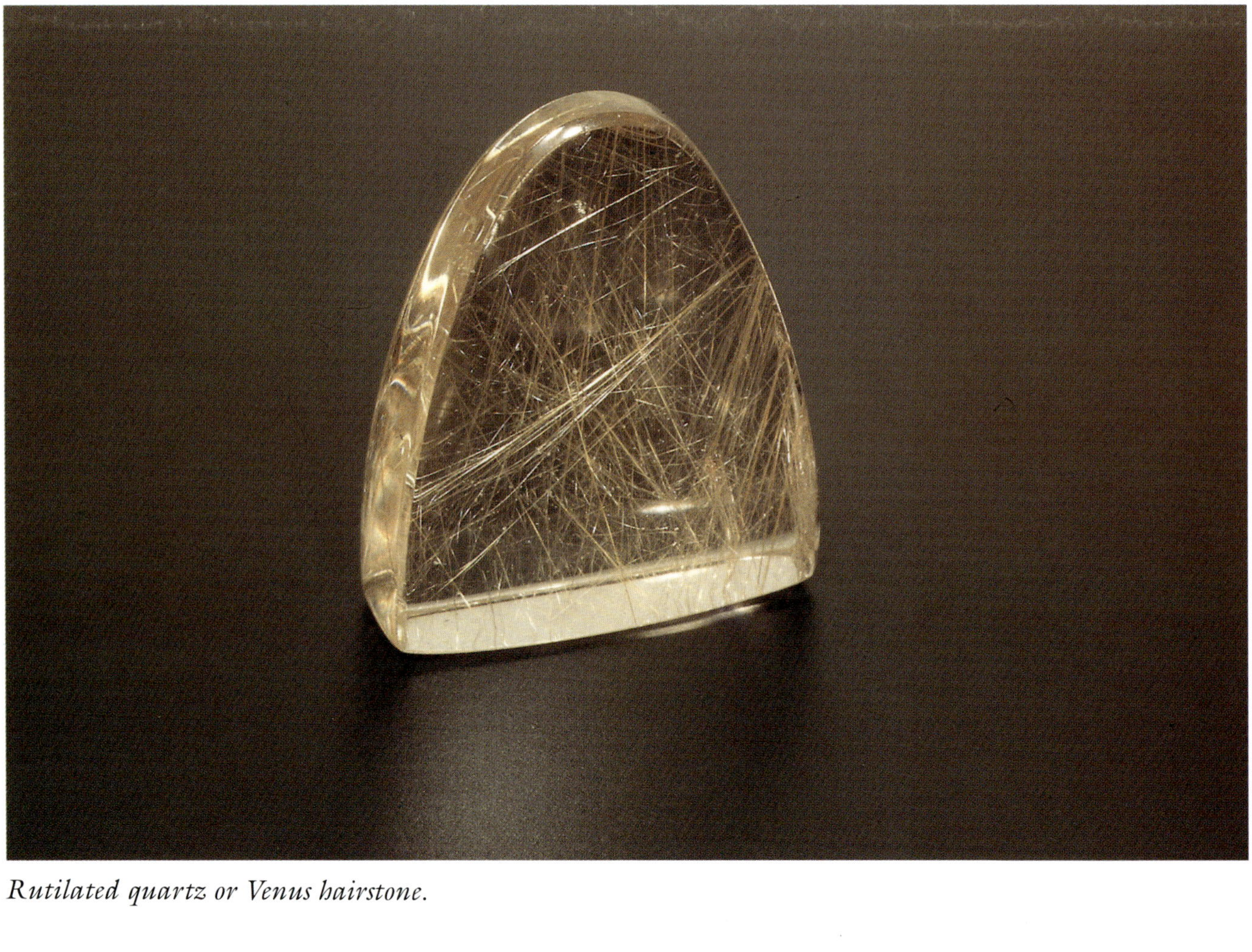

218 *Rutilated quartz or Venus hairstone.*

magnifier to hunt out green foliations (mica fuchsite) in the green variety and red foliations (hematite) in the brownish red type; it is also possible to see tiny crystals.

Synthetics and similar substances There are no synthetics for this quartz subgroup.

Green aventurine is at times confused with jade, and was once called "Indian jade"; imitations are offered in the form of like-colored glass aventurine.

Brownish red aventurine may be confused with oligoclase (see entry) and can be imitated by like-colored glass aventurine.

Cryptocrystalline Quartz

Chemical Formula: SiO_2 and $SiO_2 \cdot n\, H_2O$ – silicon dioxide and hydrous silicon (silica gel) dioxide
Hardness: 6½ – 7 (Mohs scale)
Specific Gravity: 2.58 – 2.65
Refraction: uniaxial birefringent
Color: see "Varieties" of this subgroup

GENERAL INFORMATION

Varieties This subgroup is also referred to as "polycrystalline" – or, more simply, chalcedonian.
- *Chalcedony.* Bluish, whitish, navy-bluish, milky gray, greenish. Khalkedon, an ancient city on the Bosphorus, gave this stone its name. Being slightly speckled, it is artificially dyed to produce a surprisingly rich range of tints, and is adopted to imitate other varieties in this subgroup.
- *Agate.* A wide range of colors with multiple shadings of azure, brown, yellow, gray, green. Supposedly, the term is traced to *akhátes*, the Greek name for a river in Sicily. Noted for its layering of colors, it does have some highly unusual patterns with intriguing names such as "water agate." Dendritic agate (also termed "tree stone") and moss agate (also called "Mokka stone" in honor of the Yemenite port from which the material was shipped) are two appealing names, though the mineral specimens are actually chalcedony.

Landscape agate is the result of a play of inclusions so arranged as to create the illusion of a natural landscape.
- *Cornelian.* Brownish red, light red, dark red. Named after its cornelian cherry coloring, which becomes even brighter if subjected to a heat treatment.

Sometimes chalcedony dyed a darkish red is offered as cornelian.
- *Chrysoprase.* Color shading from leek green to dark greenish yellow. Two Greek words at work here, meaning "gold" and "leek." A sought-after quartz type that had its peak popularity in the Victorian period, it has often been utilized as ornamental stone for interior decorating. After exposure to sun rays, its color lightens; and heat processing will lighten the shade even further. With the use of a chromium salt solution chalcedony can be dyed green as imitation chrysoprase.
- *Heliotrope.* Dark green, speckled with red. Another Greek derivation: this time from *helion-trópion* (turned toward the sun), whose significance leaves modern linguists puzzled. On the gem market it is also known as "blood jasper," though it has nothing to do with that mineral.
- *Onyx.* Parallel stripes of black and white. Only that material displaying black and white banding can truly be called an onyx; a pure black example is dyed chalcedony.
- *Plasma.* A shade of green, generally dark with light spots. Not often adopted in jewelry making; its Greek origin signifies "to mold."

The material that comes from Oregon, in the United States, is erroneously denominated "Oregon jade."
- *Sard.* Varying from orange-brown to dark brown. Named after *Sardeis*, the Greek city in Asia Minor where it first came to light.

Deposits

- *Chalcedony:* Brazil, India, Madagascar, Namibia, Sri Lanka, Uruguay.
- *Agate*: Brazil (Rio Grande do Sul) India, the United States, Uruguay.
- *Cornelian:* the best quality comes from India; other sources are all secondary.
- *Chrysoprase:* Australia (the top quality is extracted in Queensland), Brazil, India, Madagascar, Poland (deposits here are almost exhausted), Russia, the United States (Arizona, California, Oregon), and South Africa.
- *Heliotrope:* Australia, Brazil, China, the United States.
- *Onyx:* Egypt, Madagascar.
- *Plasma:* Egypt, India, Germany, Madagascar, and the United States (Oregon).
- *Sard:* Brazil, India, Germany, Japan, Russia.

Cut A dense, nontransparent material that is idoneous for rounded cuts, or even flat surface disks.

Ideal for all decorative objects and costume jewelry.

Under the lens Aside from the heliotrope variety with its typical red speckling, this quartz

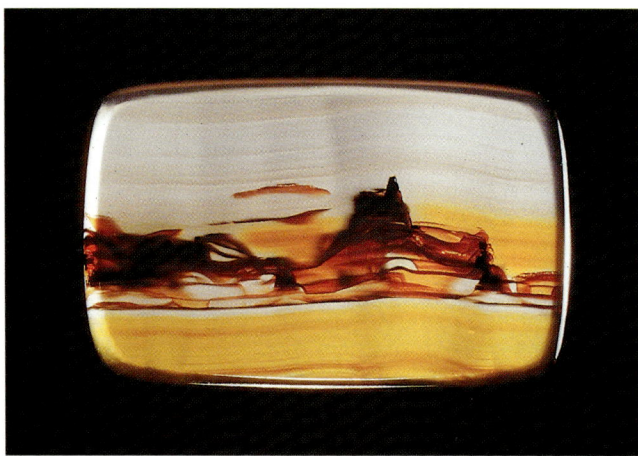
Agate "paesaggio".

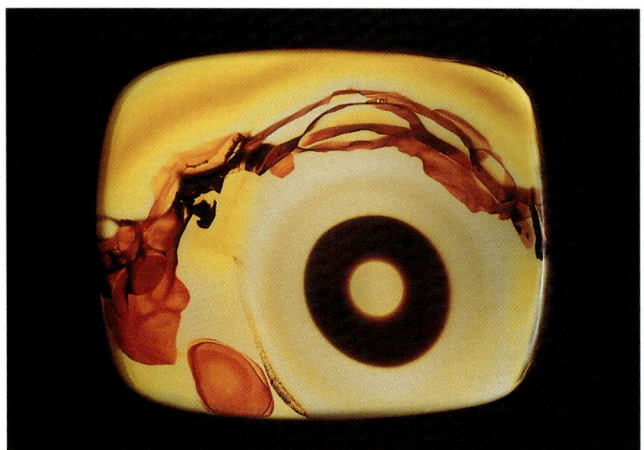

subgroup is not susceptible to identification by the usual 10x lens, and we must turn to our technical laboratory for data.

Synthetics and similar substances So far we have no synthetic version of this quartz subgroup.

Chrysoprase may be confused with jade, prehnite and artificially dyed chalcedony.

Be aware that there are frequent sales of a doppiette formed by laminating two layers of gray chalcedony in order to imitate moss agate. And remember that dyed chalcedony is apt to be employed to imitate some of the subgroup varieties.

Cameos A type of agate formed of successive color layers is utilized to create "cameos," a term deriving from the Arabic *gama'il* (flower bud) and referring to a specific intaglio work.

Cameo carving owes its technique to the fact that all layers except the white may be colored, thus effecting a dramatic contrast. Once the material is notched, the white layer is engraved into an attractive decorative motif. A buyer should be careful to ascertain that both the worked layer and the one immediately

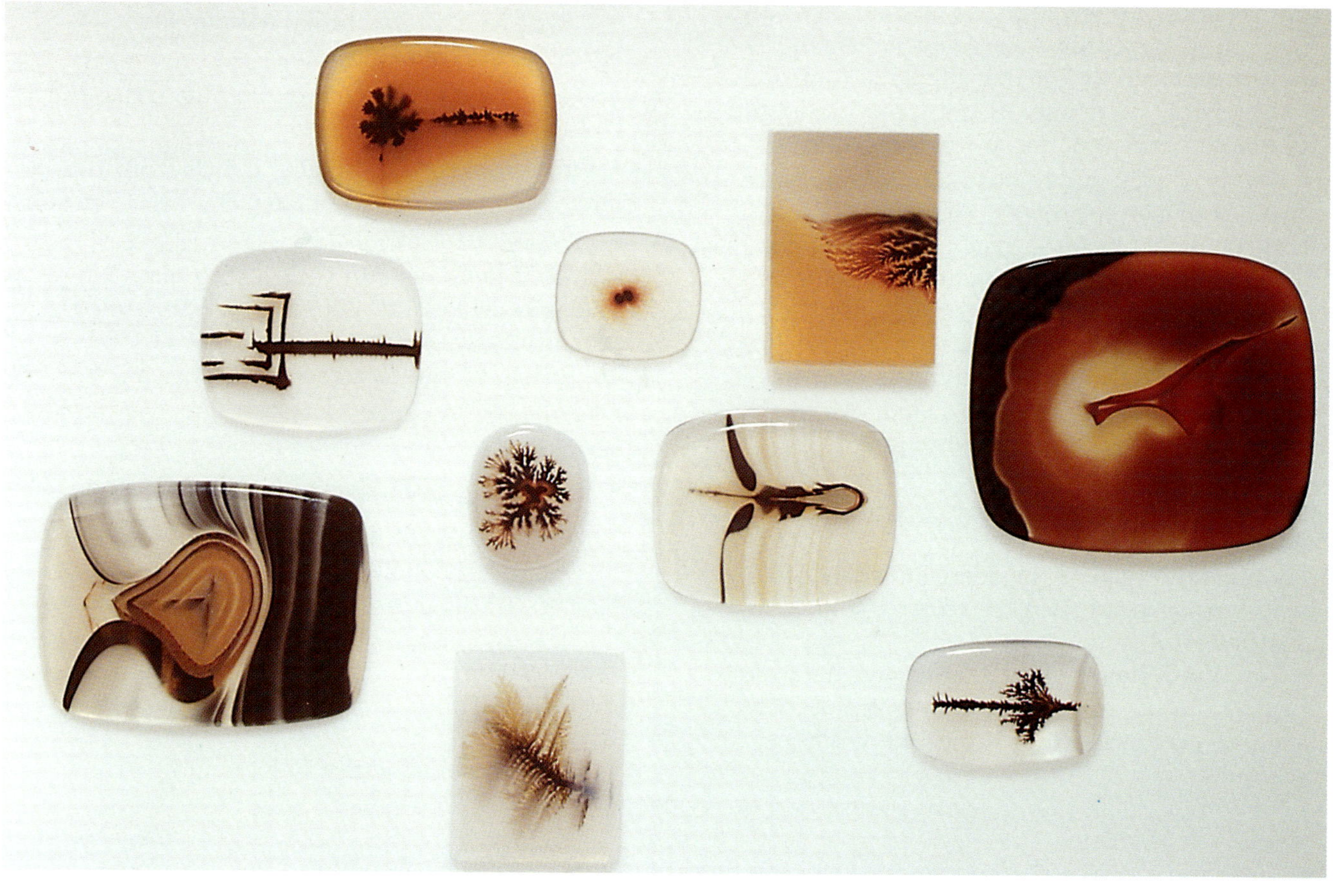

Brazilian agates with inclusions.

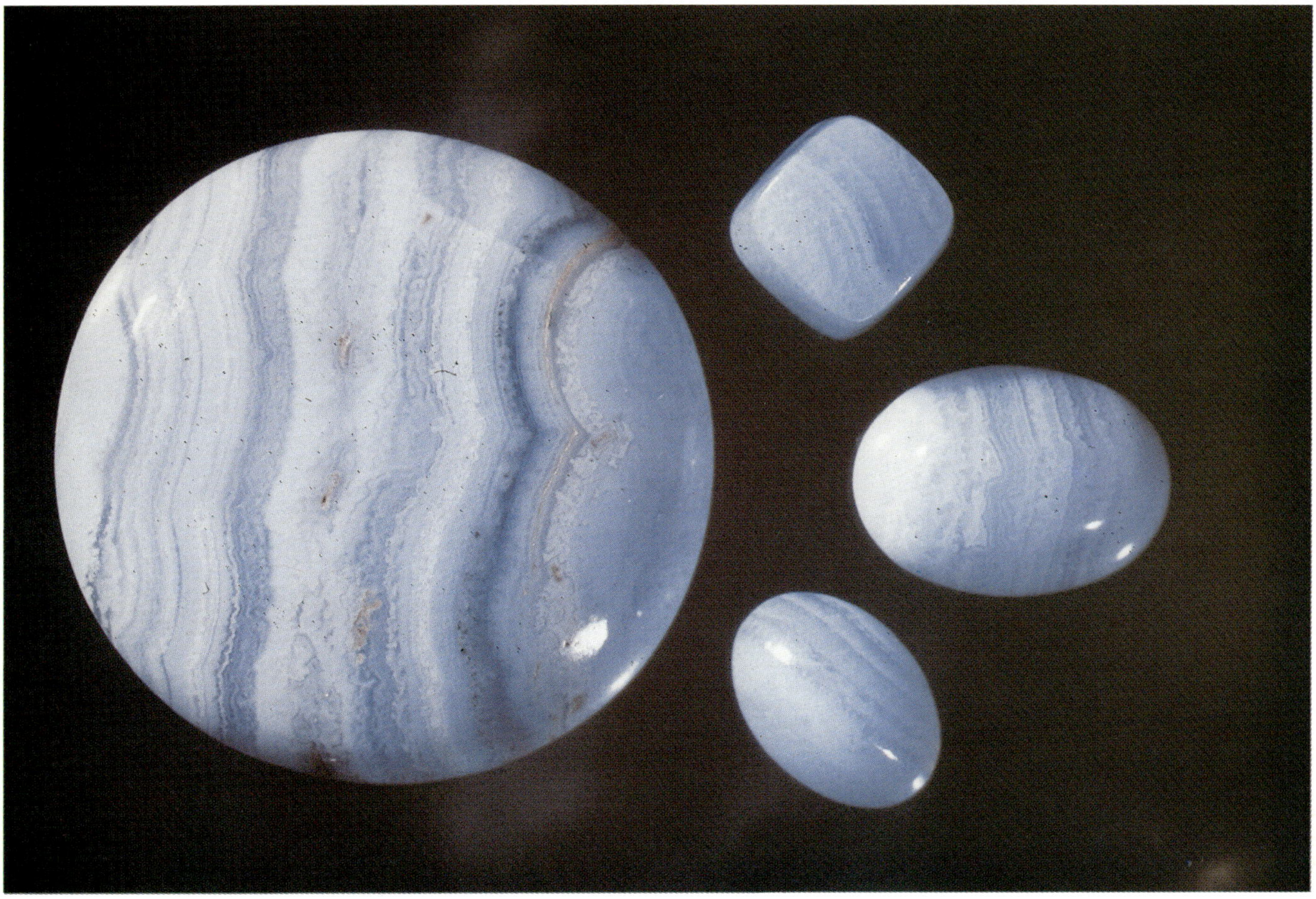

Blue chalcedony.

underneath are of a single piece rather than two separate sections held with adhesive, as the latter is clearly less valuable than the genuine article.

Silicious rocks These rocks are formed of micro and cryptocrystalline quartzes cemented with hydrous silicon dioxide (silica gel). Their structure is fibrous but granular. For our purposes, only the jasper variety will be discussed. In Late Latin, *diasprum* stood for "spotted stone." In fact, it is very hard to find specimens with only one coloring. A vast gamut of denominations is used to indicate differences in coloring or structure.

For deposits, look worldwide, including the bottom of the ocean.

Ornamental objects, mosaics, and at times even en cabochon cut stones are obtained from this attractive rock.

Once upon a time it was held to be a marvelous amulet.

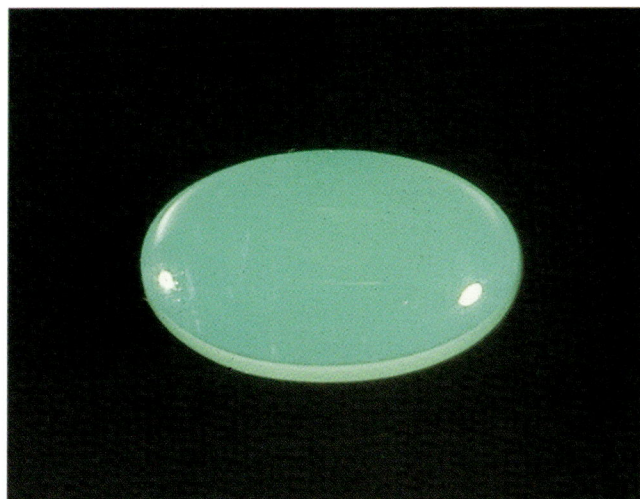

Chrysoprase with a cabochon cut.

Of course jasper can often be recognized on sight, but it is best to get precise technical data for a further, definitive confirmation.

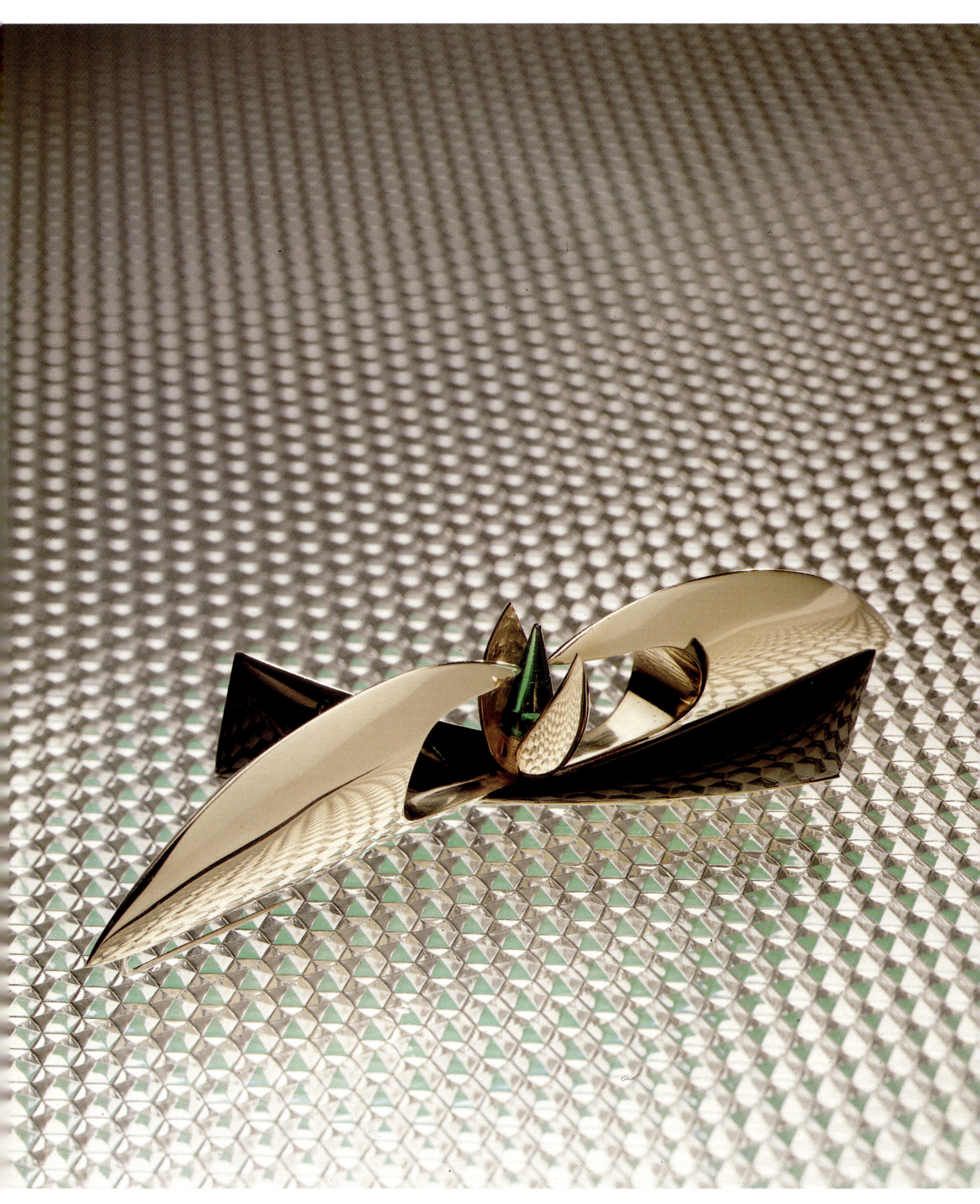

ALBERTO ZORZI: "AIR"
Gold brooch with black agate and green quartz.

Lena Antabi.
Gold earrings with diamonds,
amethyst, and tourmaline.

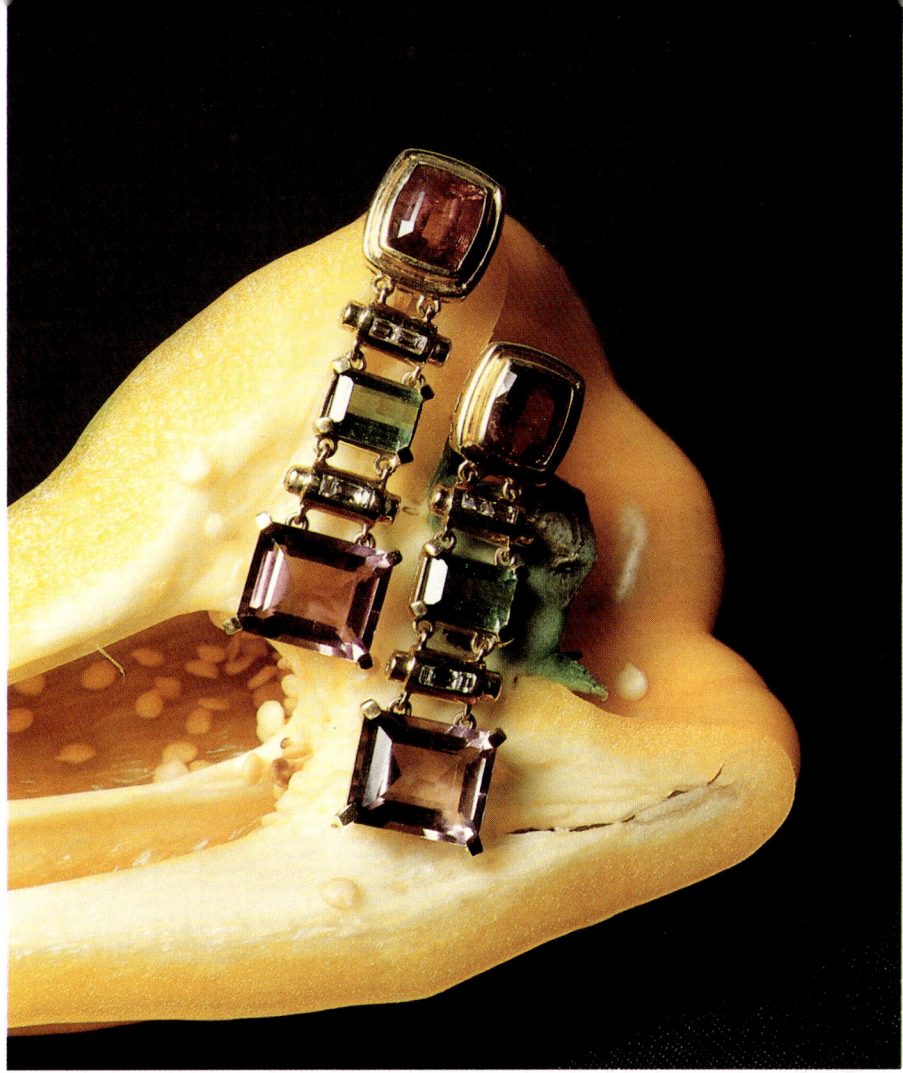

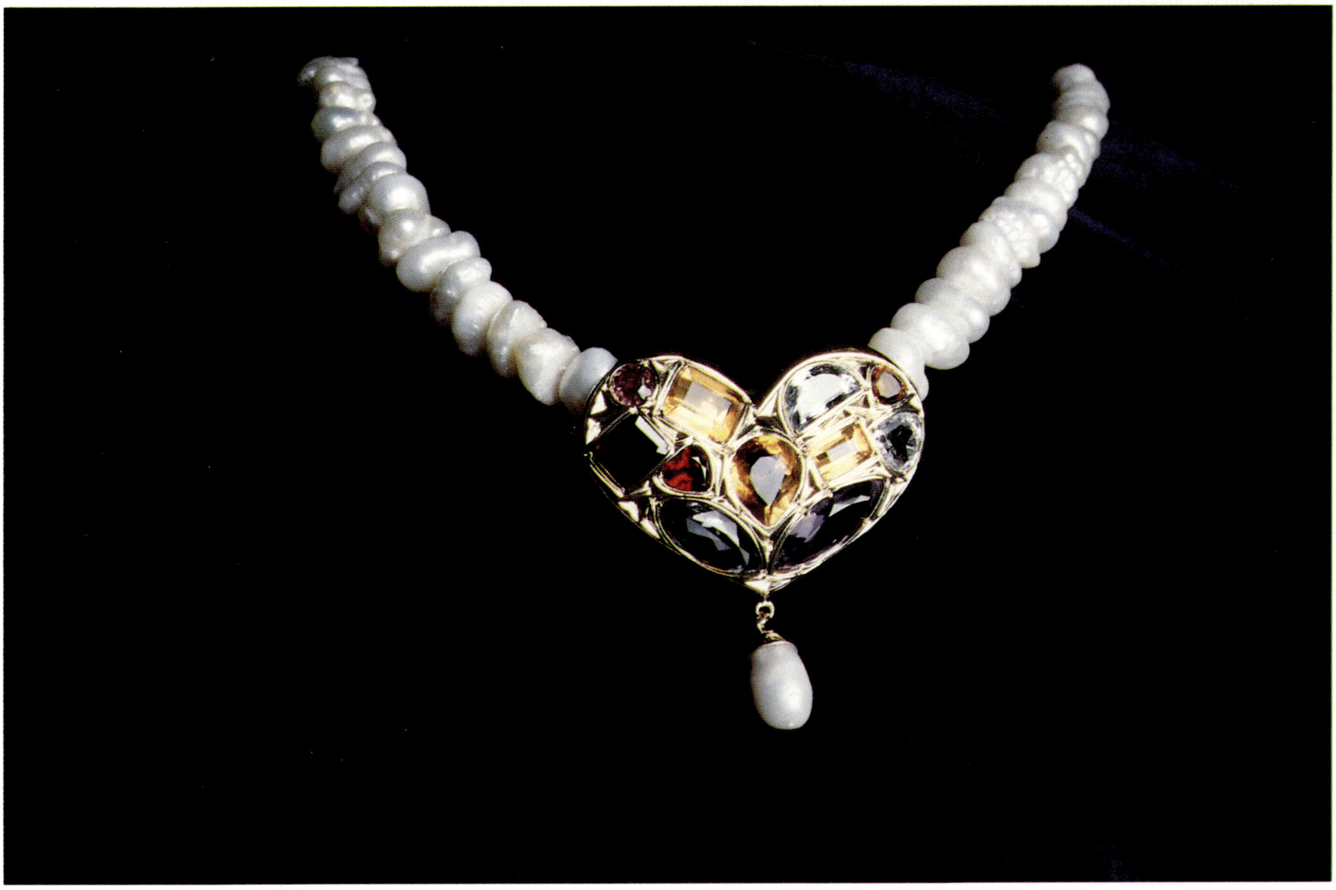

Lena Antabi.
Pearl choker and pendant in gold with pearl and a variety of fine stones in polychromatic harmony.

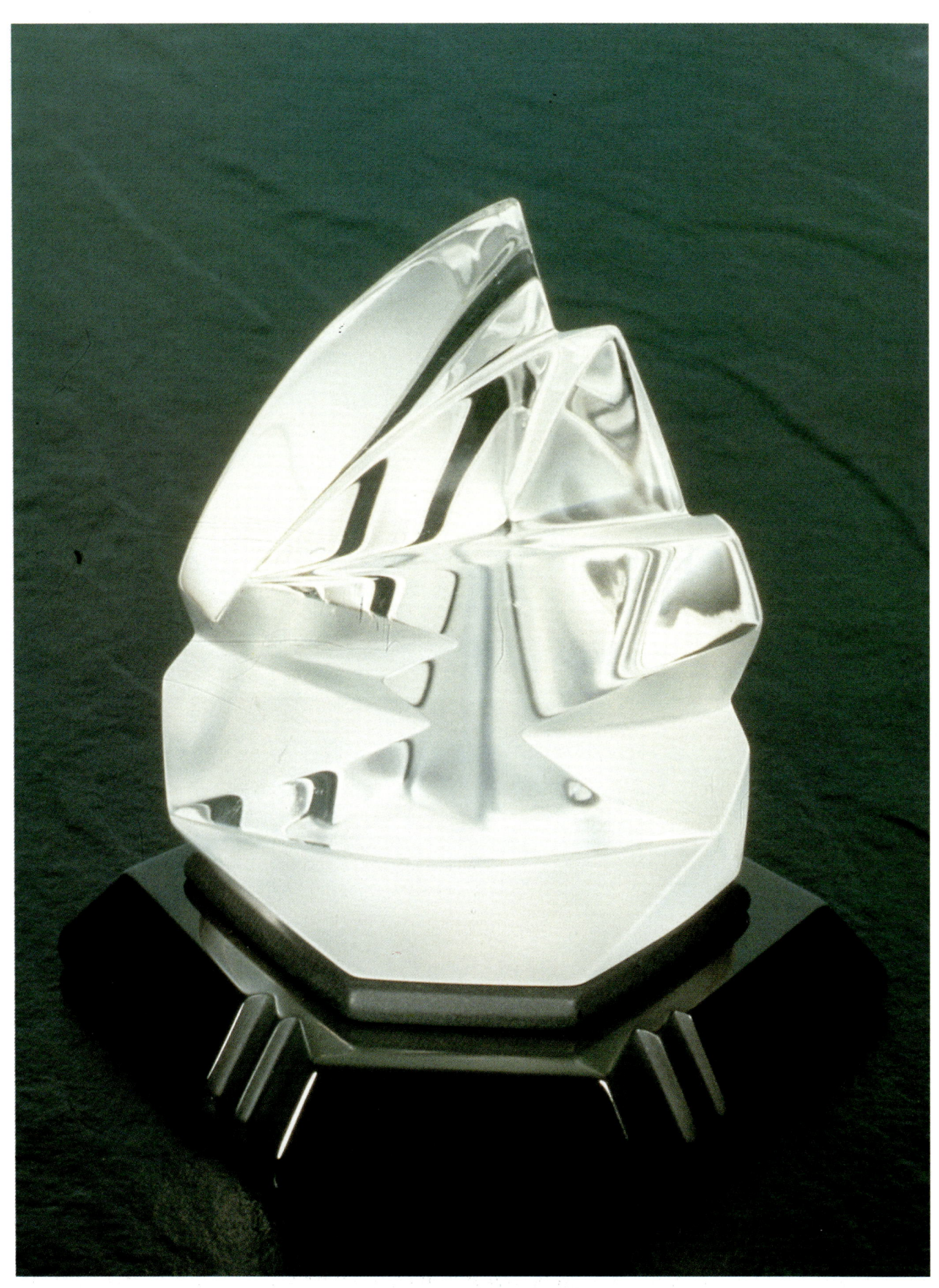

BART CURREN.
Rock-crystal sculpture.

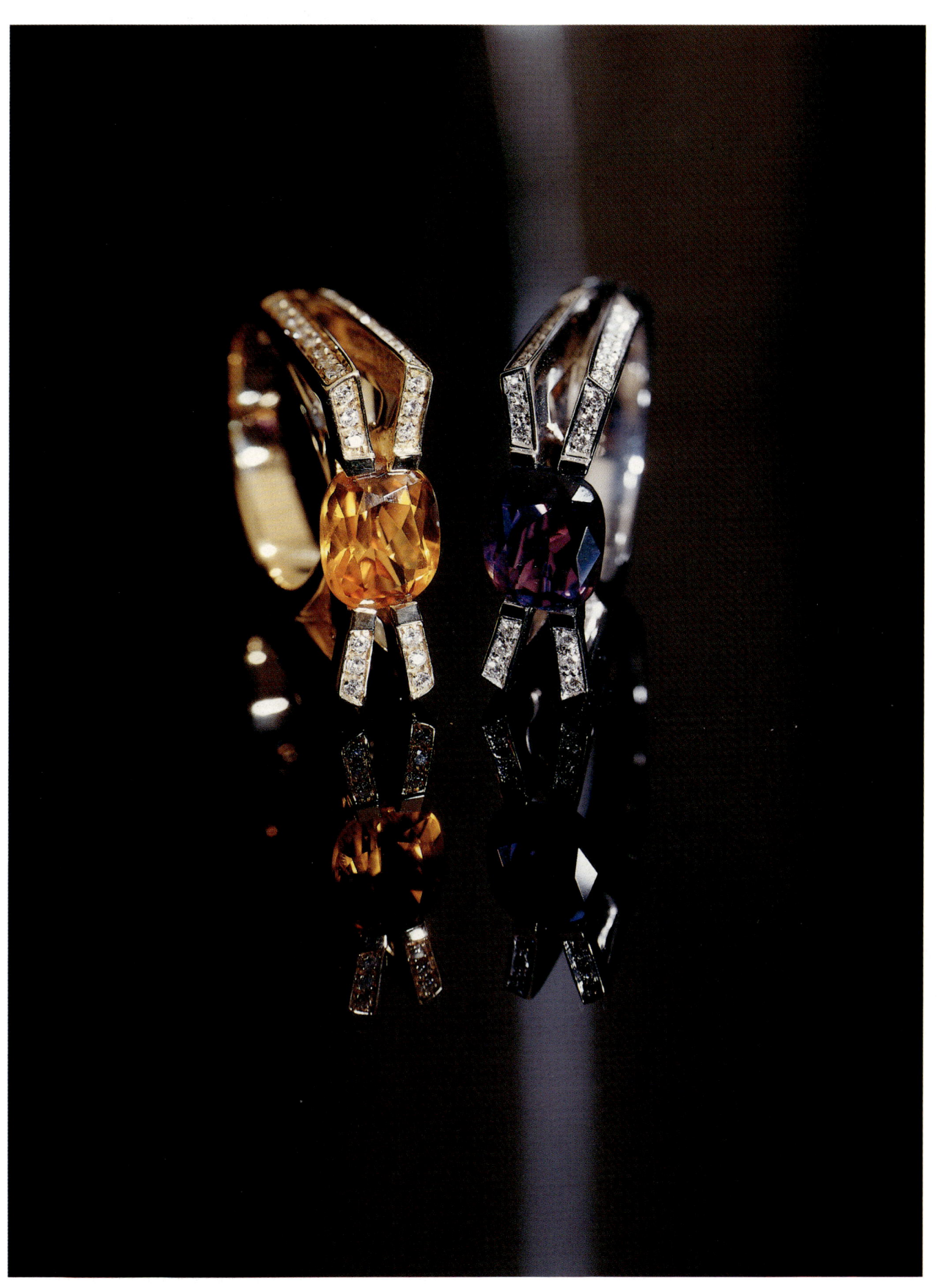

Andrea Galassini: "Mariposa"
Gold rings with diamonds, amethyst, and citrine quartz.

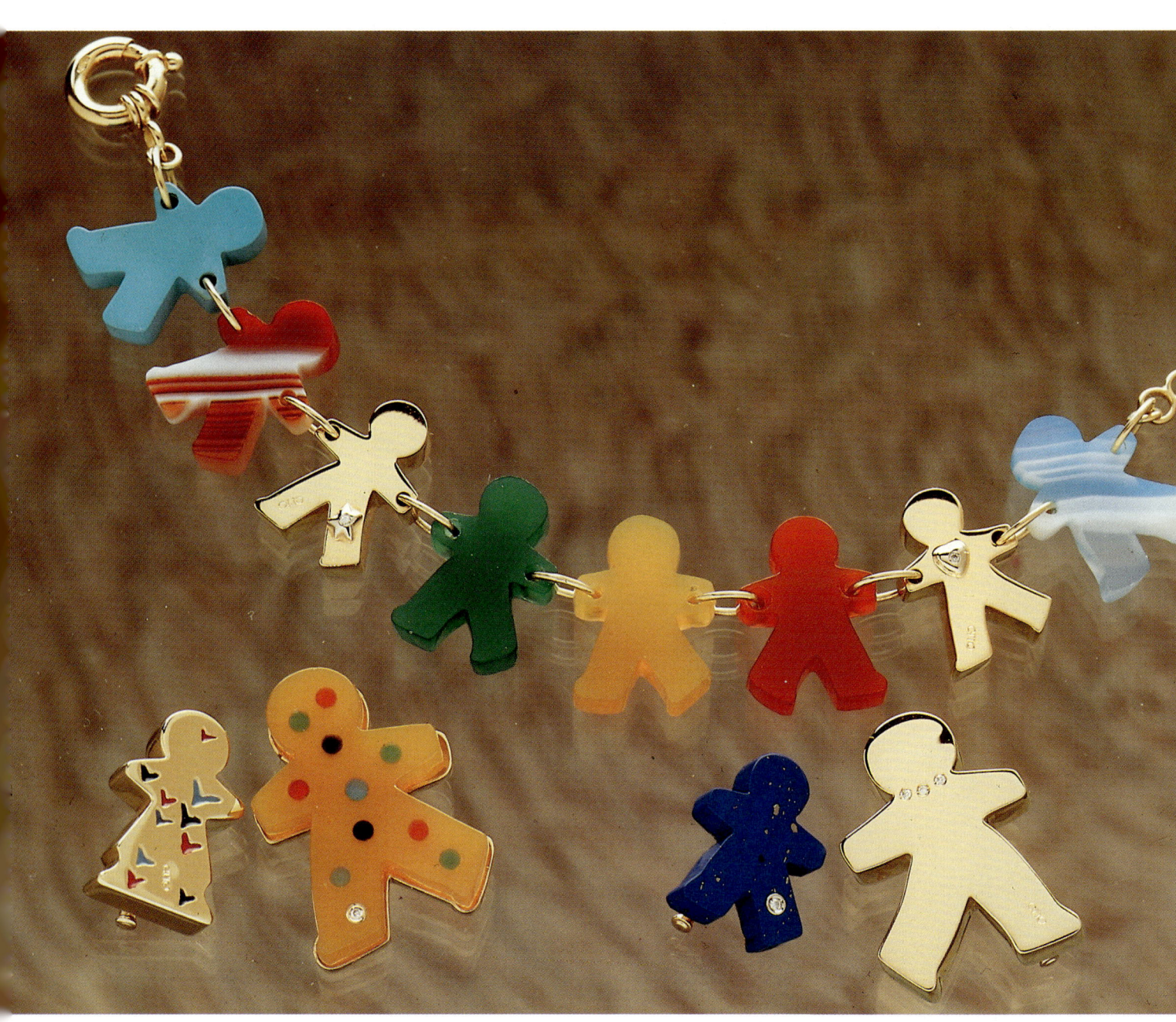

BIBIGÌ: "RING-AROUND-THE-ROSY"
*Series of amusing objects from childhood memories in a blend of color and light.
Gold, lapis lazuli, turquoise, enamel, and diamonds.*

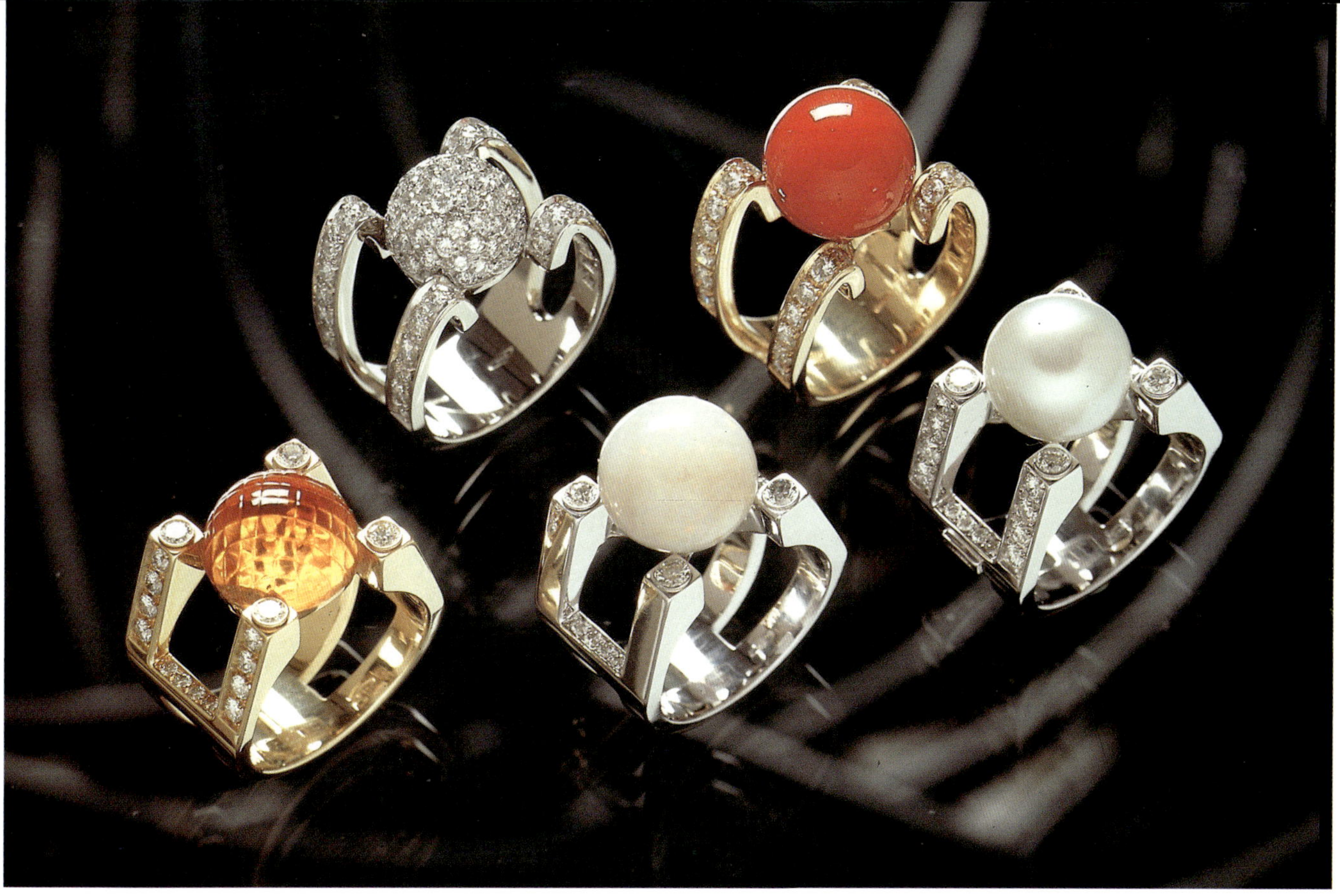

BIBIGÌ.
Series of gold and platinum rings with coral, pearl, quartz, tourmaline, and diamonds shining bright.

BIBIGÌ.
Rings in white gold and platinum with diamonds.

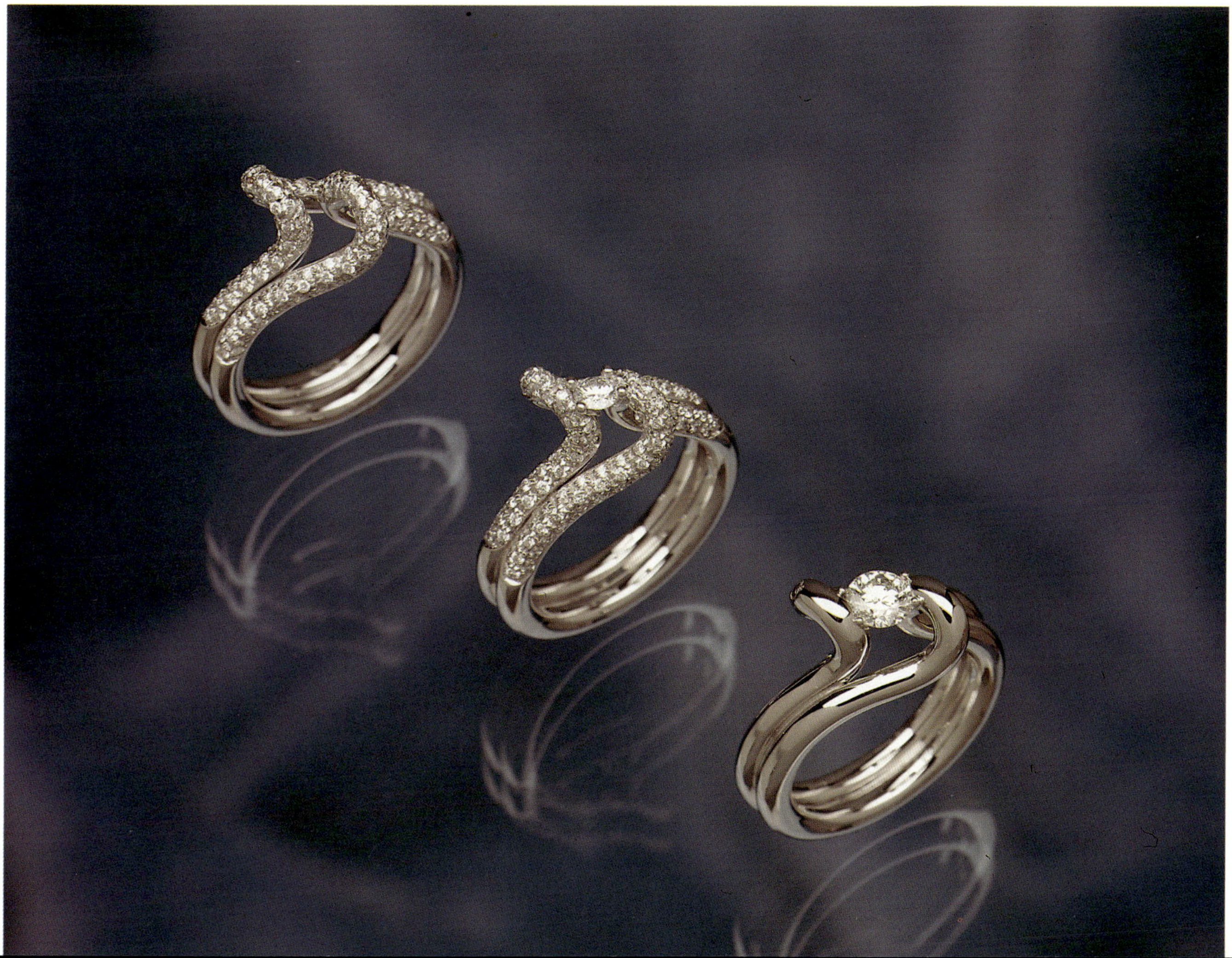

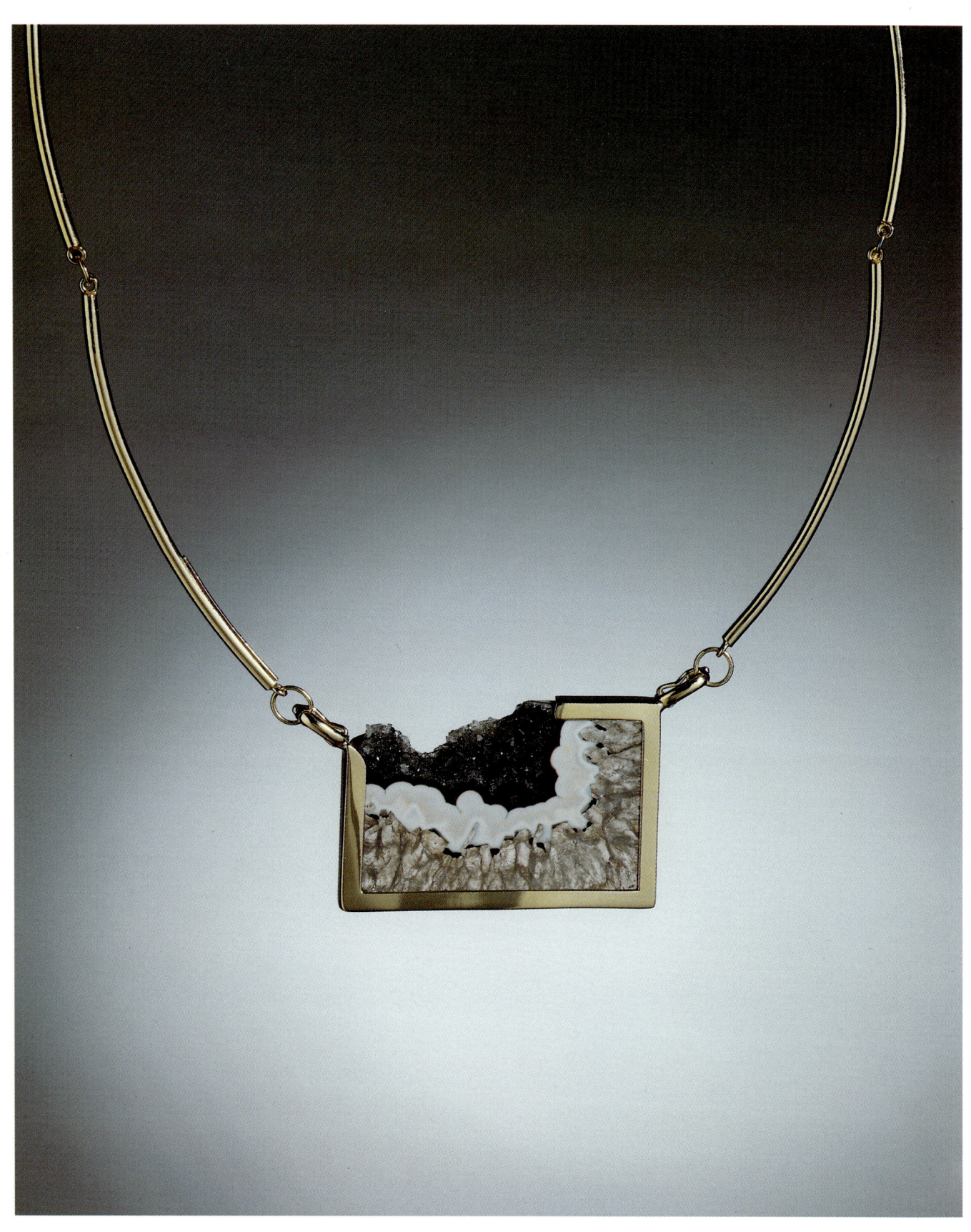

MIRIAM MAMBER.
Gold necklace with agate.

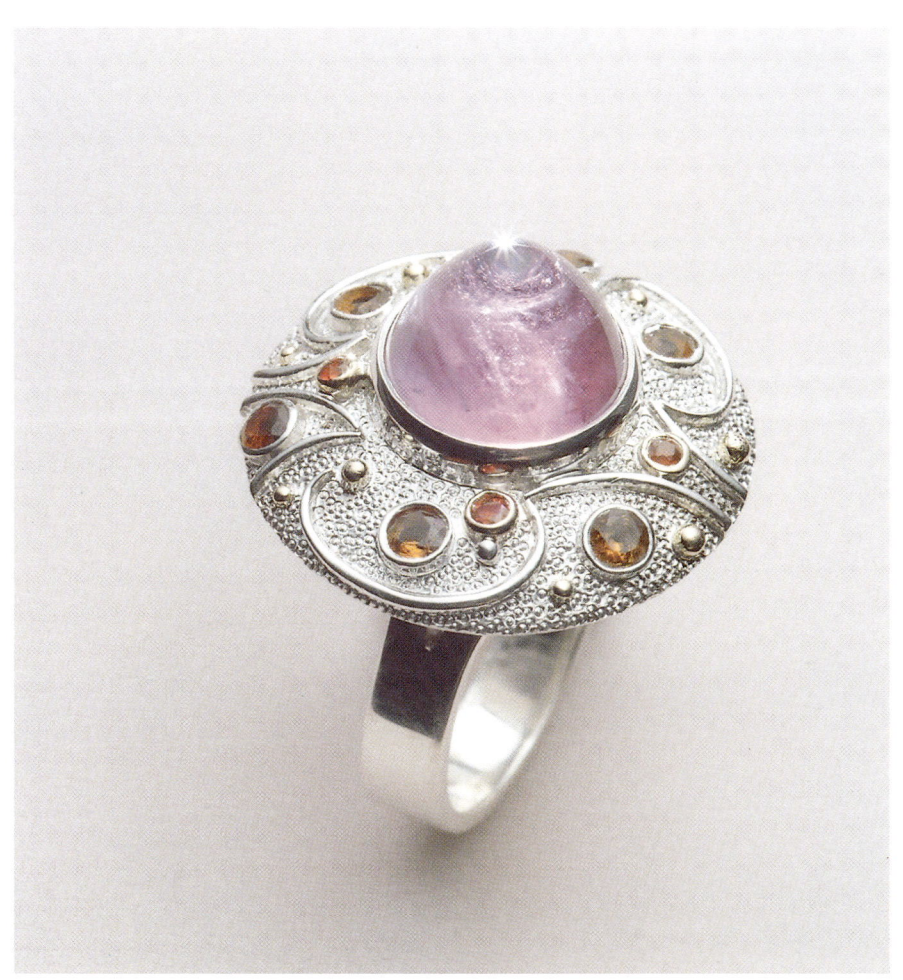

PHILLIP MAYNARD:
"NO RETURN"
Gold and silver ring with amethyst, citrine quartz, and ruby.

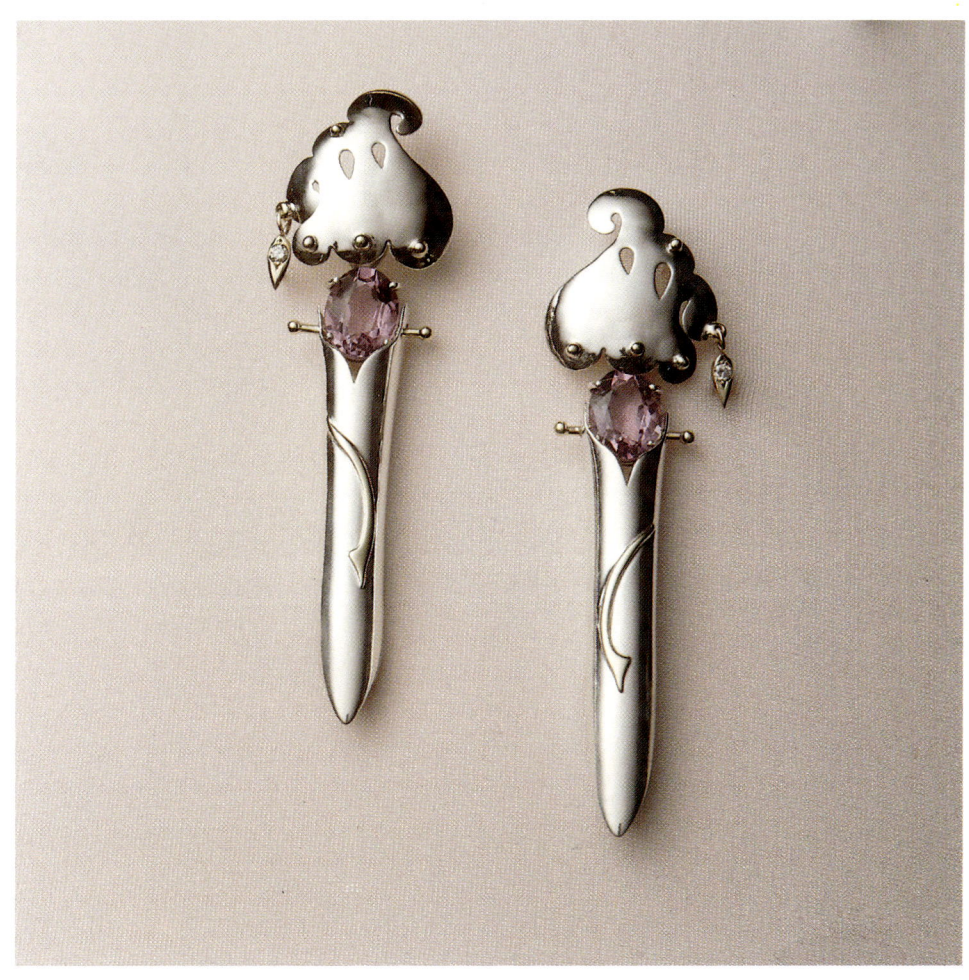

PHILLIP MAYNARD:
"BEAUTIFUL WOMEN"
Gold and silver earrings with amethysts and diamonds.

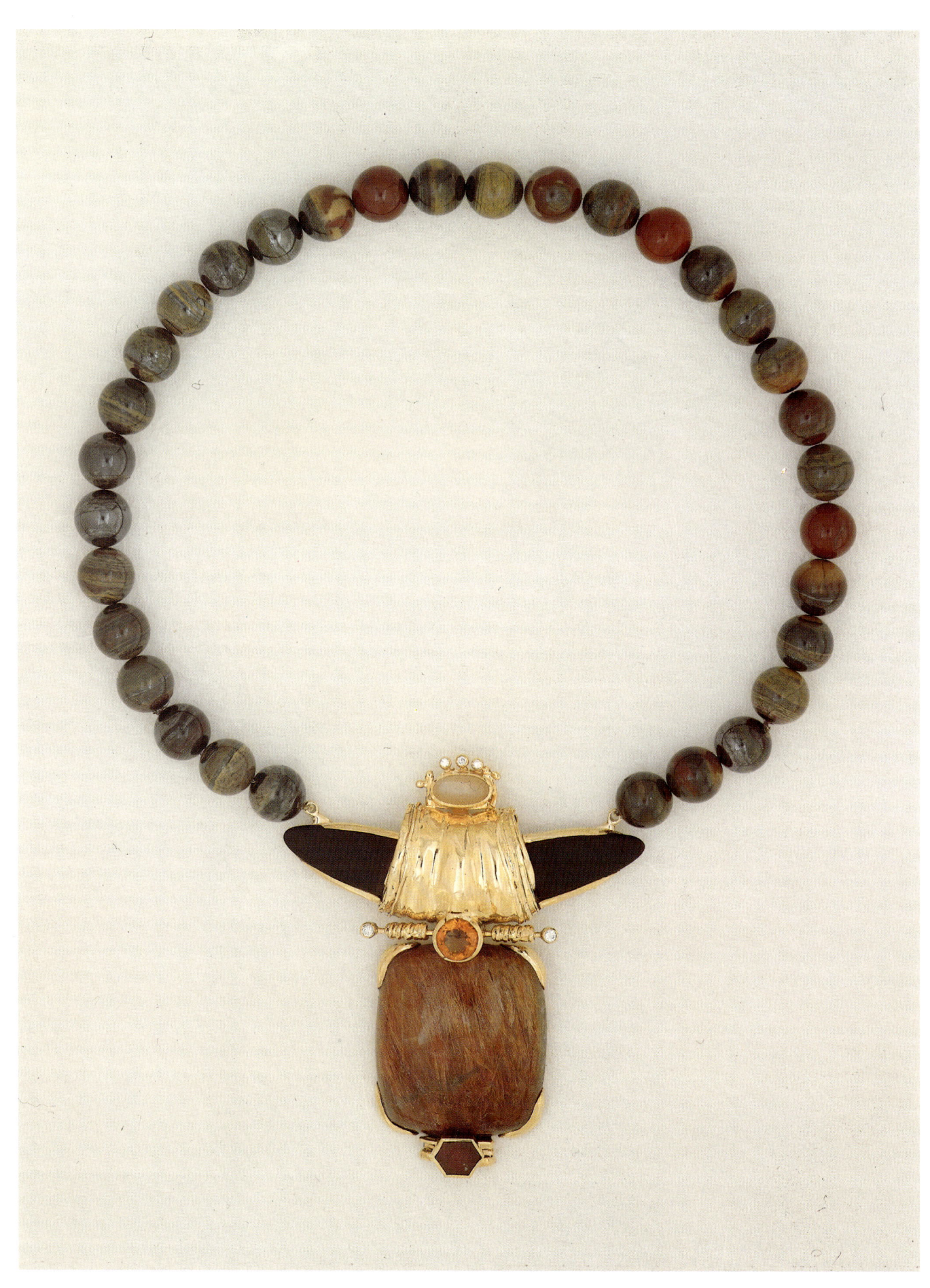

SIMONNE MUYLAERT-HOFMAN: "JASPER"
Gold choker with rutilated quartz, black agate, moonstone, citrine quartz, and diamonds.

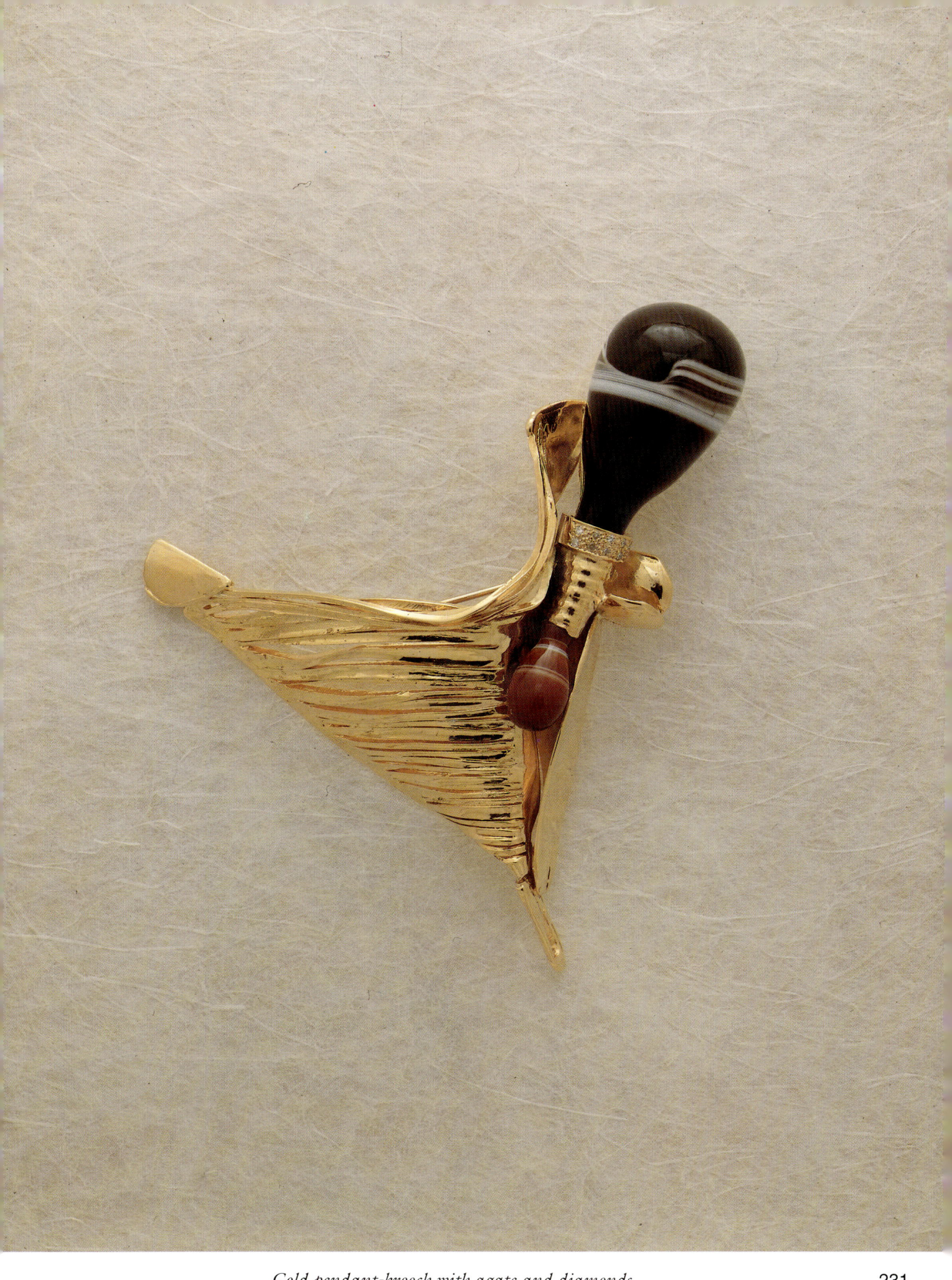

Gold pendant-brooch with agate and diamonds.

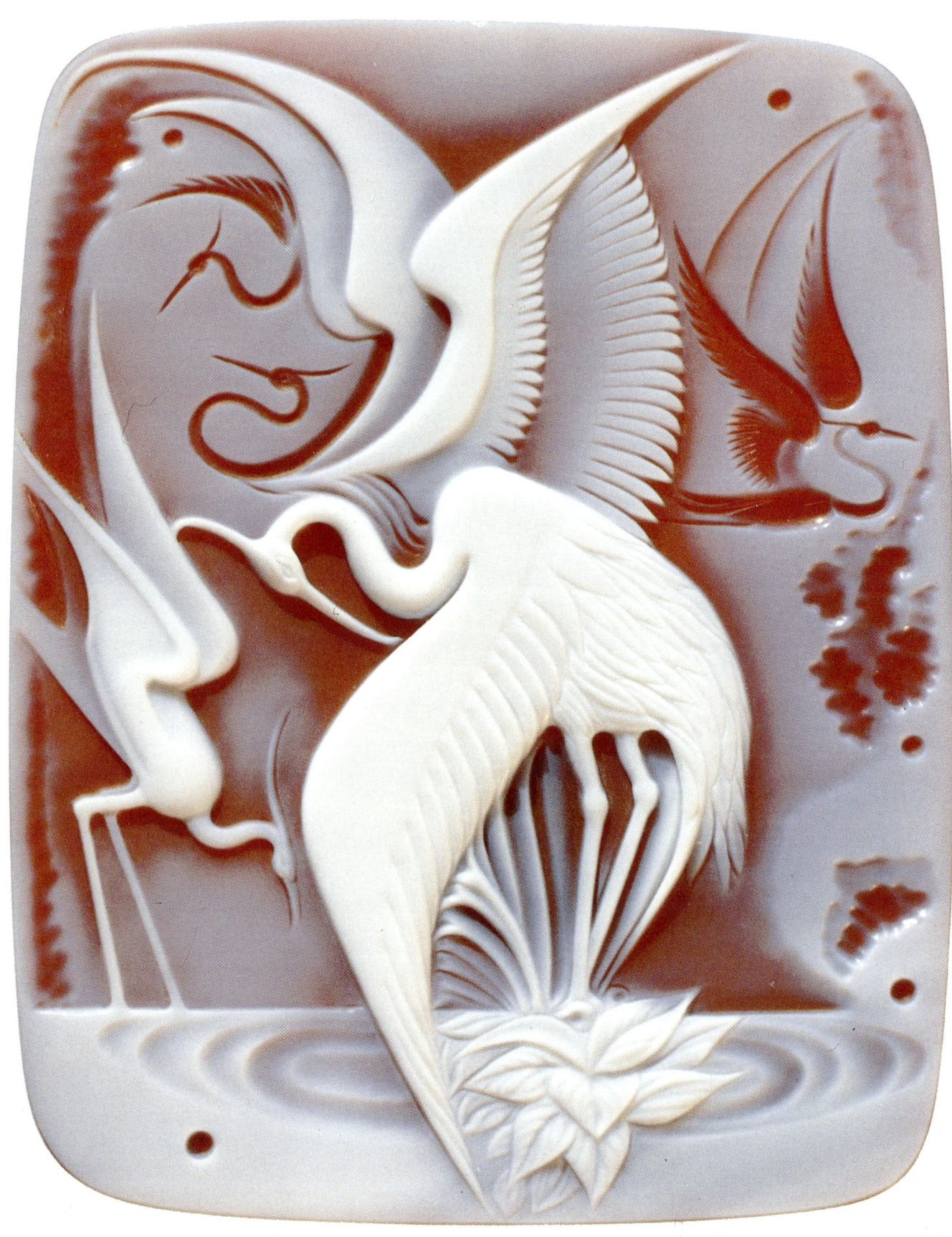

ERWIN PAULY: "THE CRANE"
Bas-relief in red and white agate from Brazil.

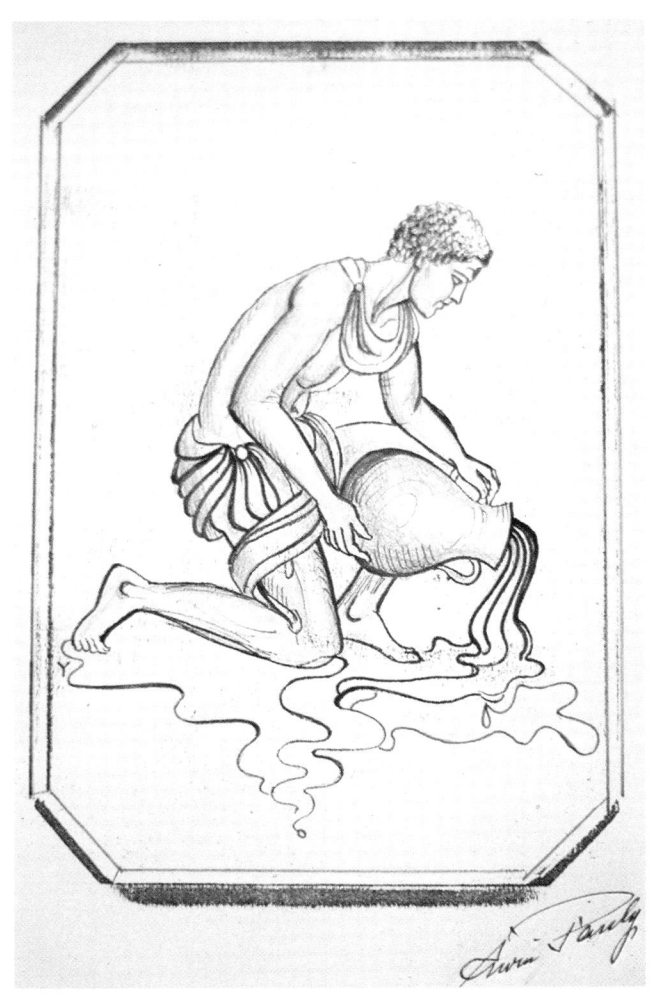
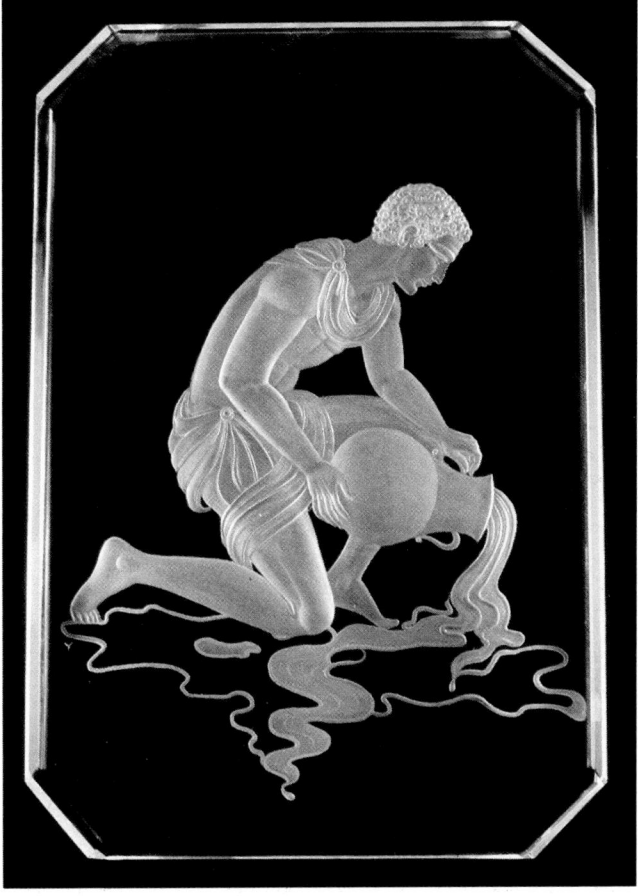

ERWIN PAULY:
"THE WATER GENIE"
*Object in carved rock crystal
(150 x 100 mm).*

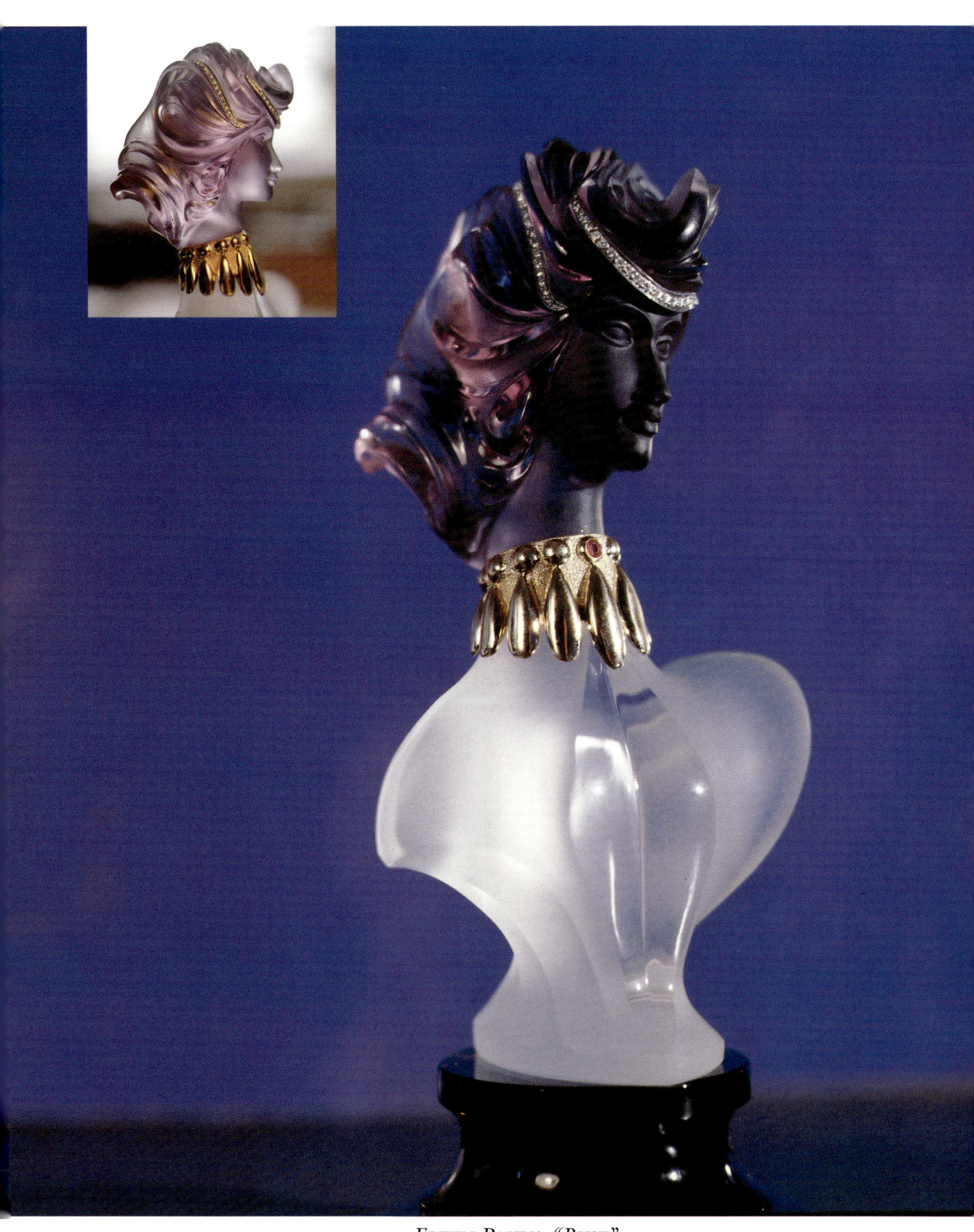

ERWIN PAULY: "BUST"
Rock-crystal sculpture with amethyst, gold, and diamonds.

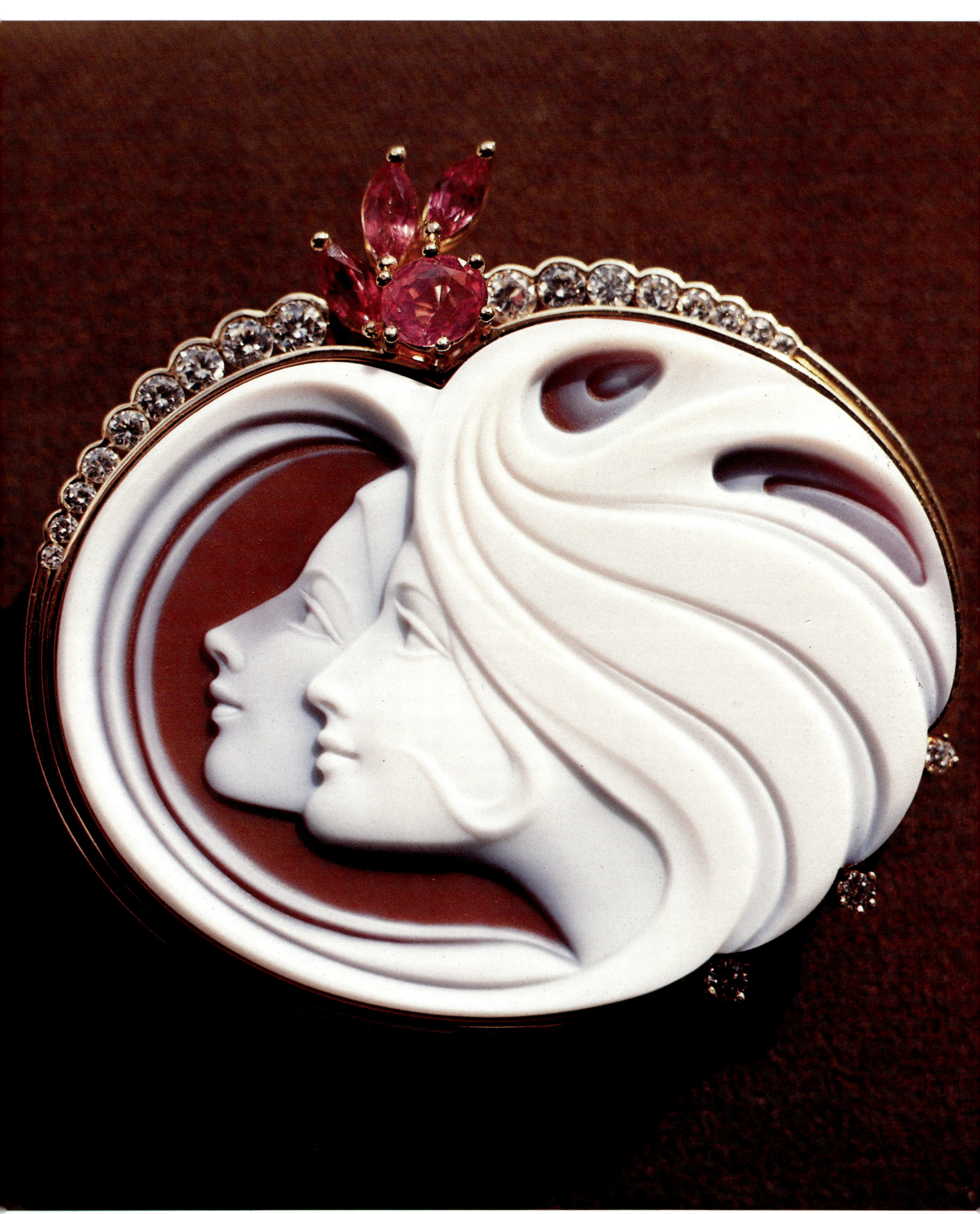

ERWIN PAULY: "HARMONY"
Cameo in red and white Brazilian agate with gold, diamonds, and rubies.

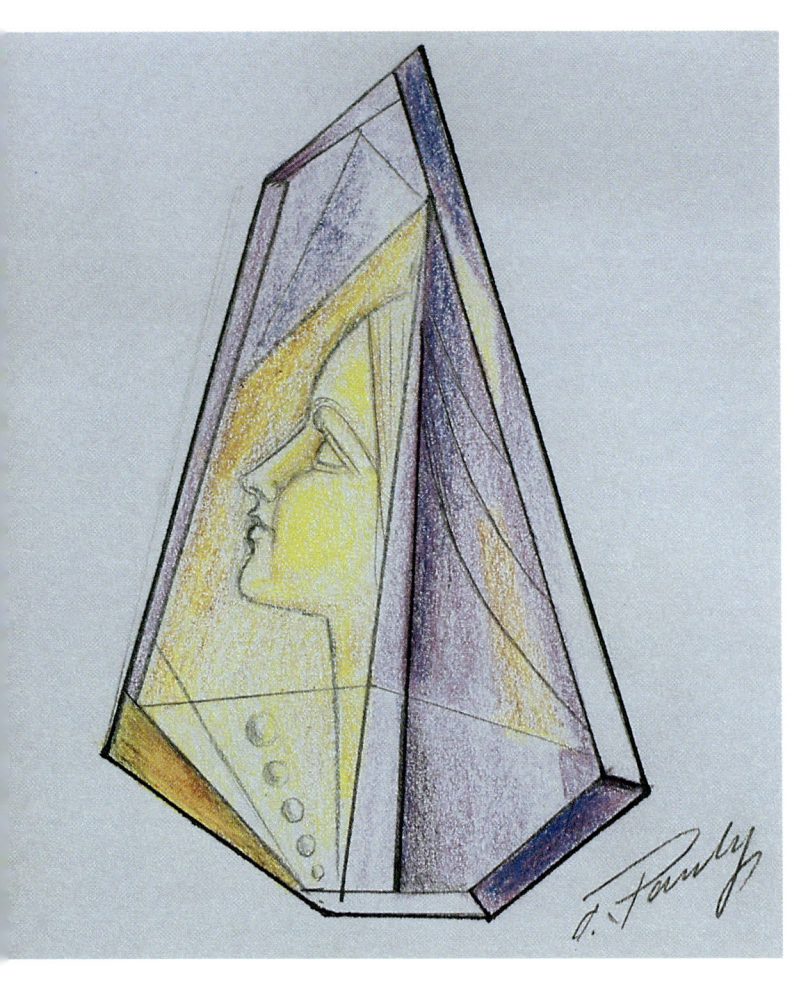
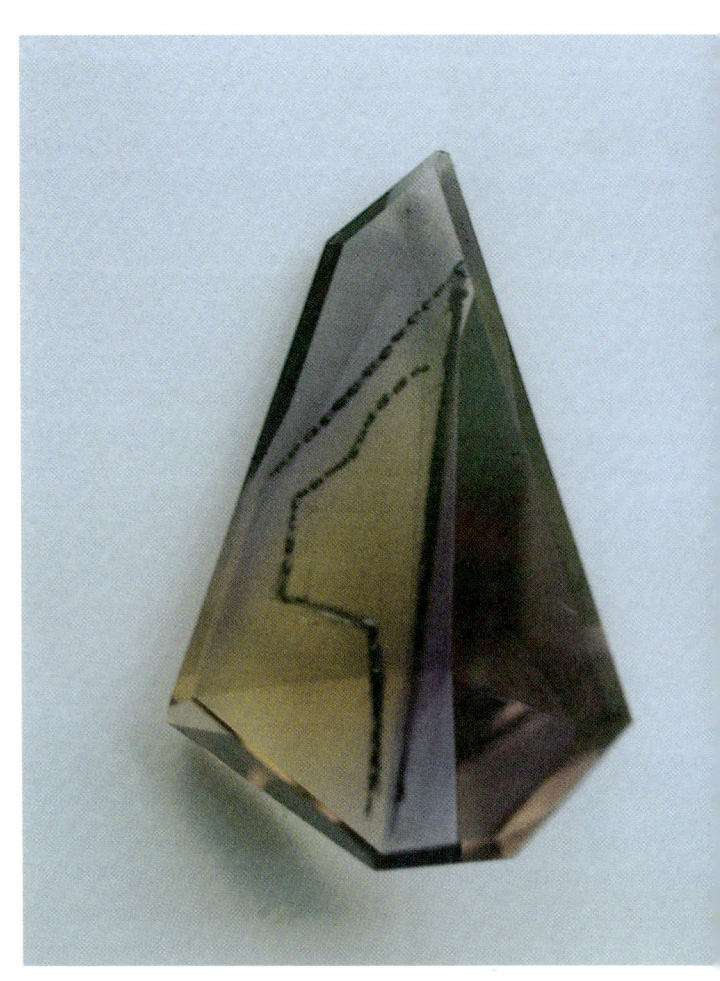
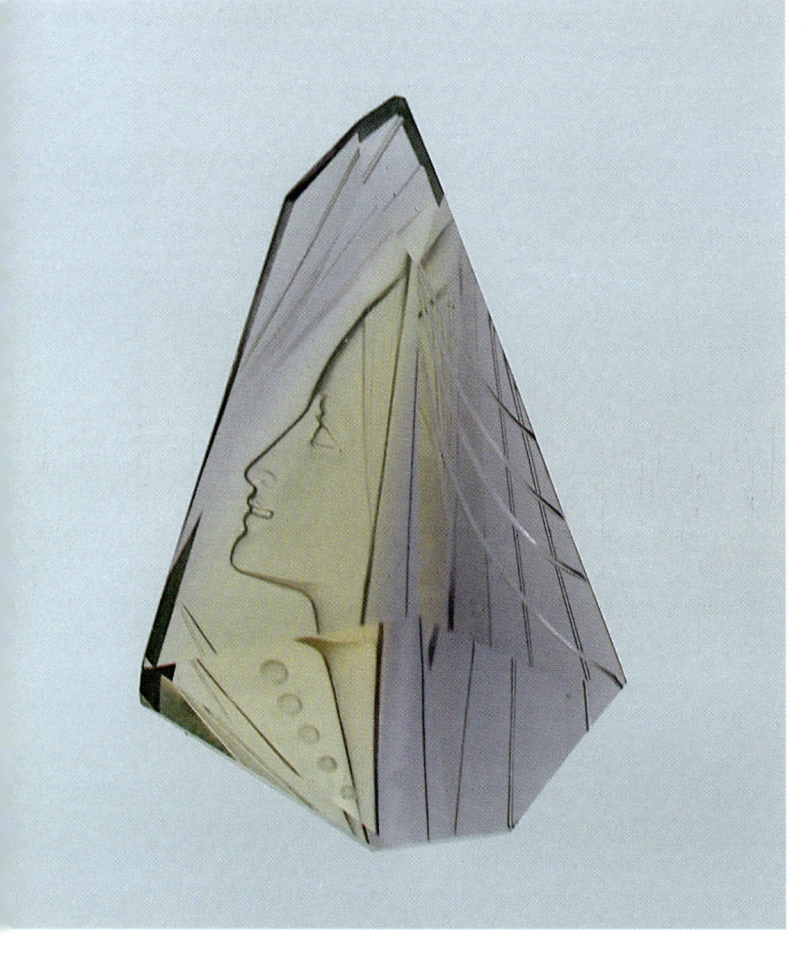
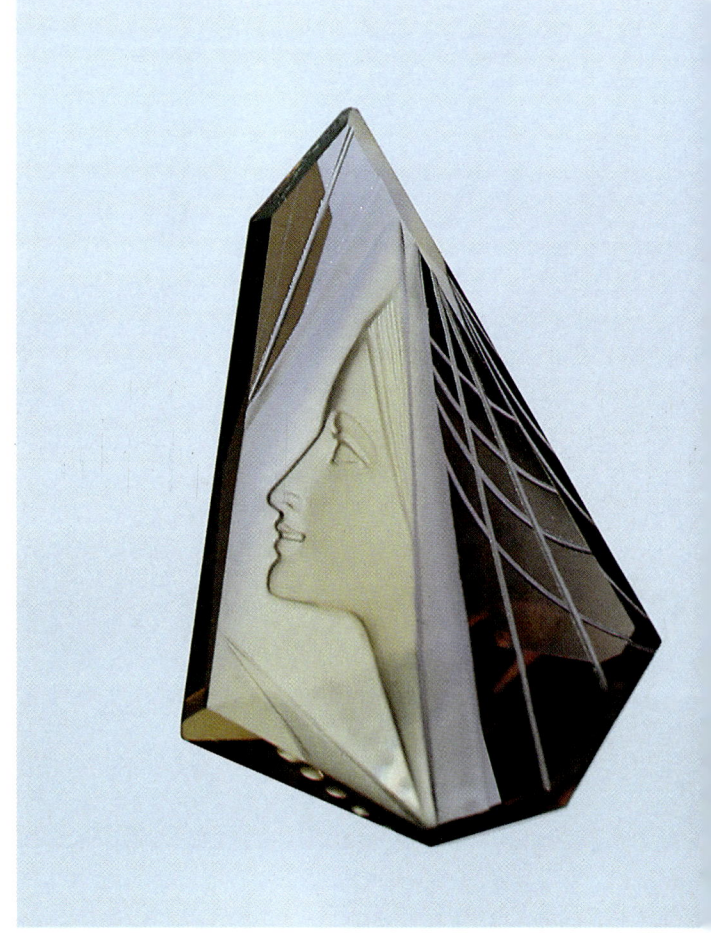

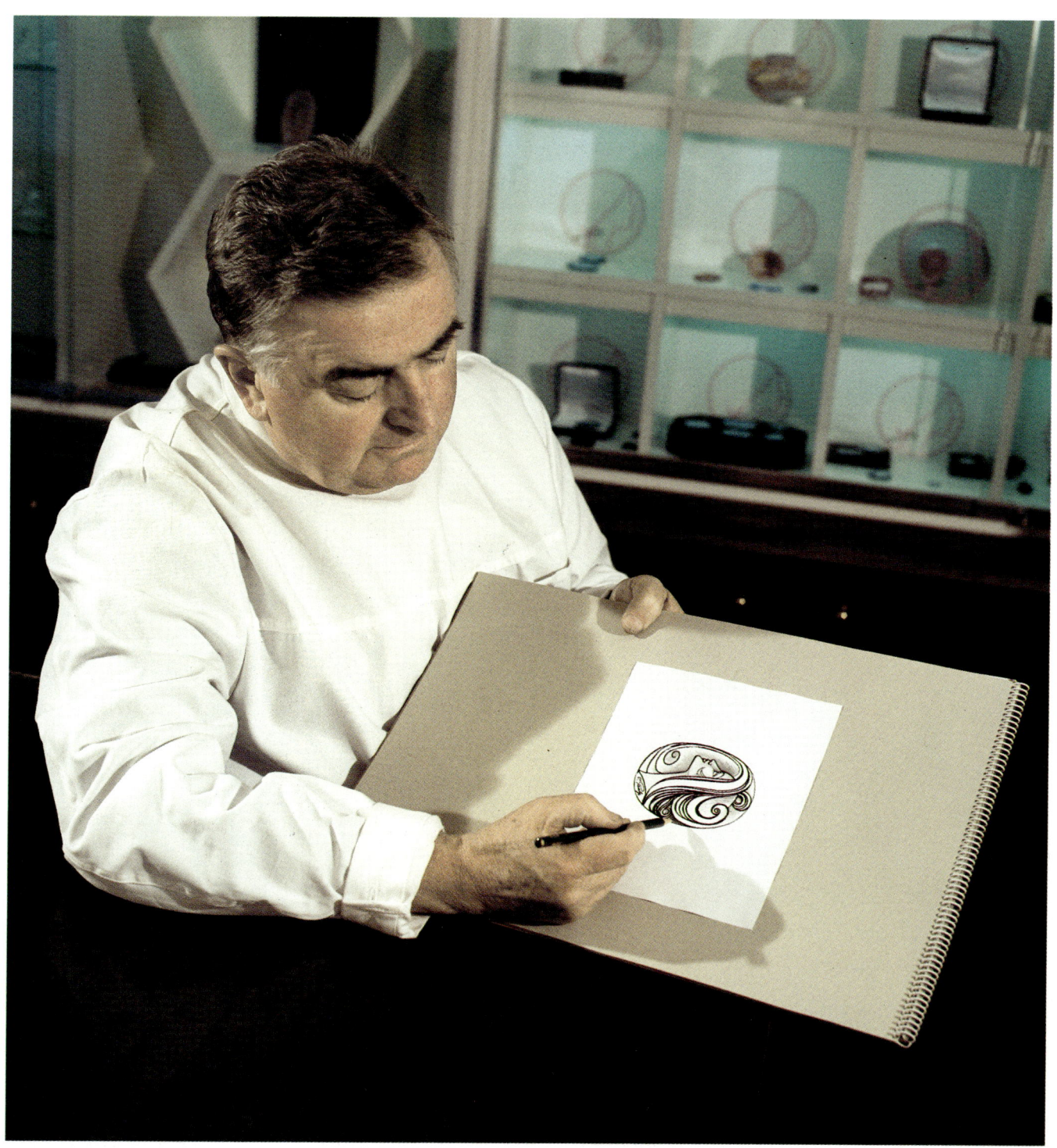

ERWIN PAULY:
"FEMALE PROFILE"
Carved ametrina, from design
to finished object, front and back.

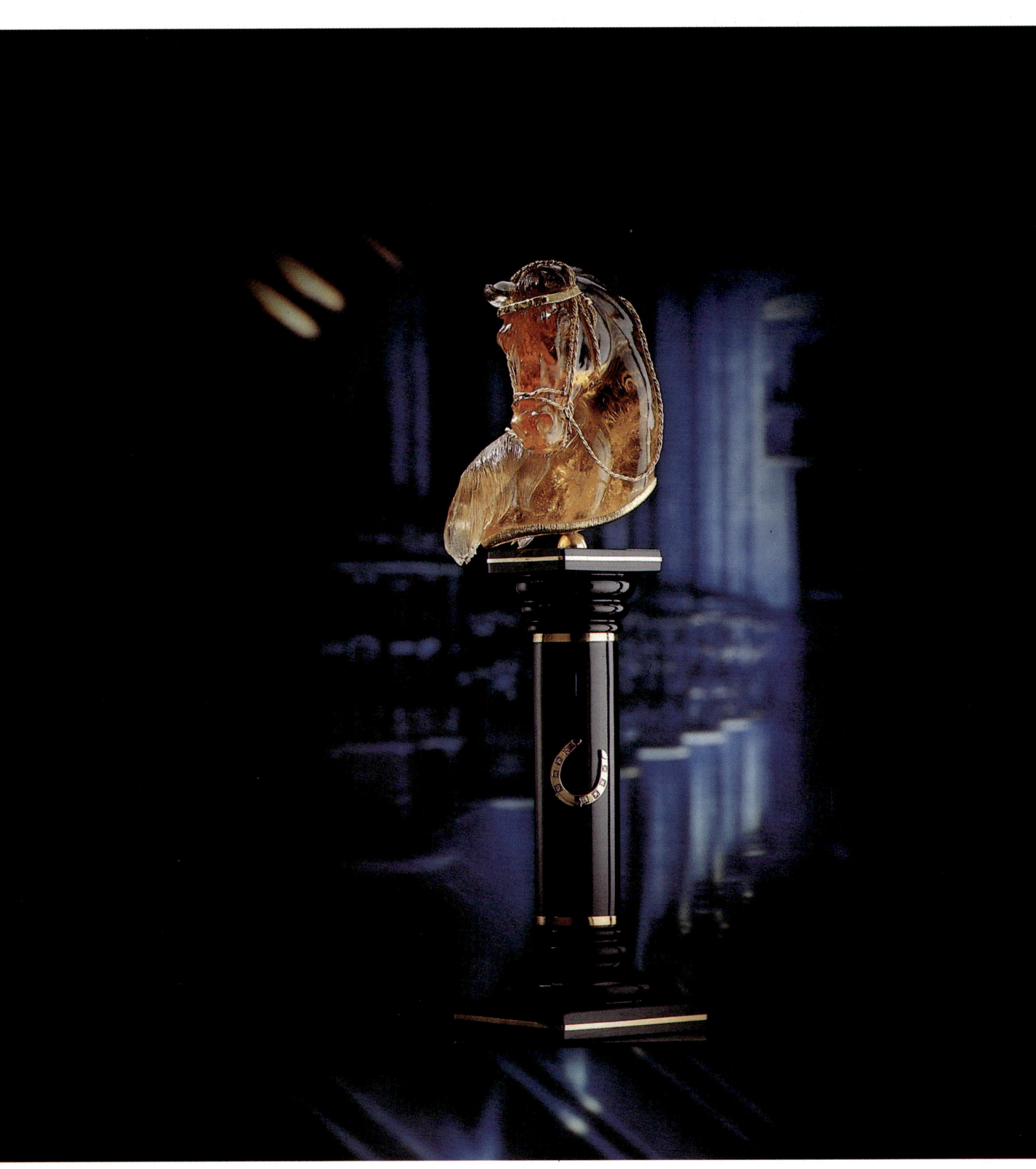

REINER STEIN.
Equestrian sculpture in citrine quartz, obsidian, gold, and diamonds. Height: 275 mm.

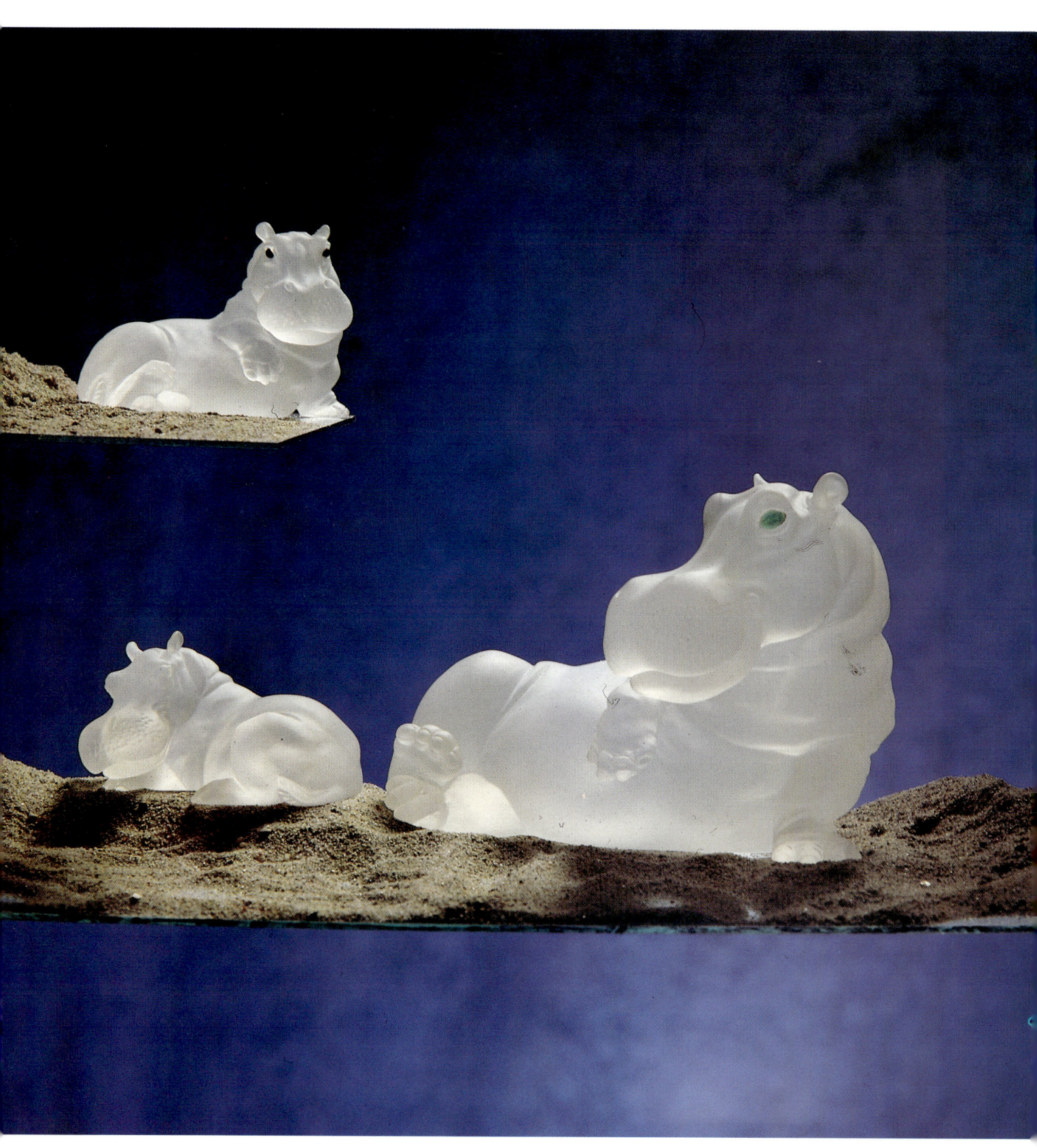

REINER STEIN: "FAMILY OF HIPPOPOTAMUS"
Sanded rock crystal.

Rhodochrosite

GENERAL INFORMATION

How it got its name From the Greek *ròdon* (pink) and *chròos* (color).

Some interesting sidelights Known on the market since 1950, rhodochrosite is suggested for people with an overwhelming urge to communicate their feelings – artists such as musicians, poets, and writers. In theory, it can help you overcome psychic trauma and emotional unbalance; and if you wear it on your wrist they say you'll no longer feel sleepy. A practical note: do not wash this gem with acid solutions as it will provoke a reaction.

Deposits At the moment the most important bodies of this mineral are located in Argentina. For other sources we look to Australia, India, Romania, the United States, South Africa, and Hungary.

Cut Normally the rounded surface cut is employed as it shows off the zigzag light-to-dark striae to good effect. It's possible to meet up with translucent or, quite rarely, transparent specimens; the latter comes in a uniform pink shade and is suitable for faceting.

Under the lens Because of its structure, rhodochrosite has a quite distinctive appearance (in this respect it is like malachite, although certainly not as regards coloring); so it can be quite easily identified with the naked eye. As regards the rare transparent specimen, any classification must be obtained by a gemmological laboratory that can analyze the mineral and produce relative technical data.

Synthetics and similar substances So far, no corresponding synthetic material is known, though the stone itself may be confused with rhodonite and hydrogrossularite.

A dyed pink imitation is on the market, obtained with calcite; nevertheless, observation by lens clearly reveals that the added color is more heavily concentrated in surface fractures.

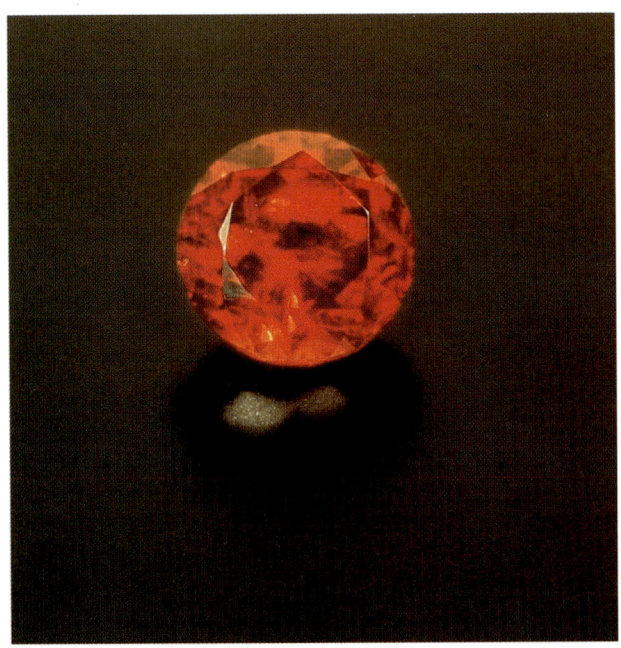

Chemical Formula:	*$MnCO_3$*
	– manganese carbonate
Hardness:	*3½ – 4½ (Mohs scale)*
Specific Gravity:	*3.45 – 3.70*
Refraction:	*uniaxial birefringent*
Color:	*pale pink and varied tonalities of dark pink*

Spinel

GENERAL INFORMATION

How it got its name Some argue that it comes from the Late Latin *spina* (thorn). Others think it goes back to the Greek *spinter* (spark; flash), describing a flame tone in the mineral's red variety. For just over a century and a half, "spinel" has finally been recognized as a separate and distinct mineralogical group.

Varieties Best known is the red variety, with its tonal gradations. Precise nomenclature is formed by a composite of the group name and its color type. Therefore, we hear of: *red spinel, reddish orange spinel, brick-red spinel, reddish pink spinel, violet spinel.* As with other mineral categories, many different names may have been used in the past, quite erroneously, such as: balas spinel, almandine spinel, ruby spinel, and nobel spinel, this last referring to the top quality. A last note: asterism is rarely observed in any of the red variety.

Blue is another prized subgroup; once called "kandite" (from Kandy, a city on the island of Sri Lanka) or even "sapphirine" (for its sapphirelike color), its correct name is *blue spinel*.

Dramatic color differences are due to the presence of trivalent chromium in the red mineral, and bivalent iron in the blue.

Other varieties, having their own specific names are: *pleonaste* (black), *gahnite* spinel (azure), *picotite* (deep green), *galmite* (grayish blue, blackish brown, dark green); once again a technical denomination prevails, for these names change according to any even partial substitution of a chemical element in the mineral's composition.

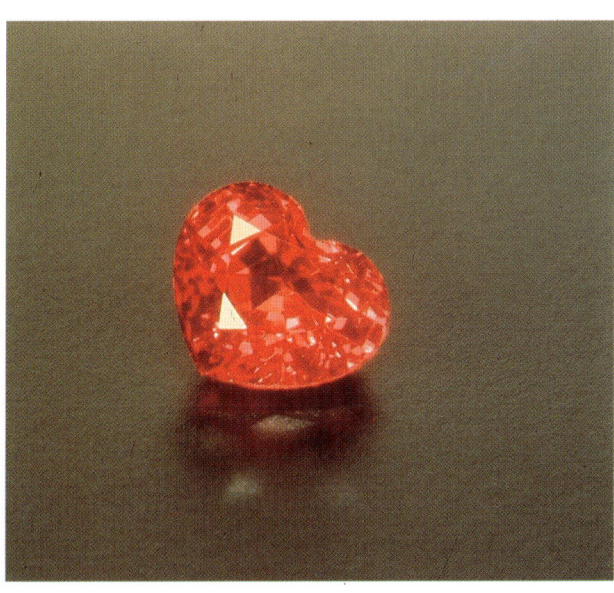

Chemical Formula: $MgAl_{12}O_4$ – magnesium aluminate
Hardness: 8 (Mohs scale)
Specific Gravity: 3.50 – 4.40
Refraction: monorefringent
Color: varying shades of red, blue, azure, yellow, orange, black, green

Some interesting sidelights There is a gem called the Black Prince's ruby set in the royal British crown, but it is actually an irregularly shaped red spinel about five centimeters long. The Timur ruby is another stone belonging to the British Crown Jewels which is really a spinel, all 361 carats of it; once the prized treasure of royal Shahs, the names of its six earlier owners are engraved on it, from Shah Jahangir (1612) to Shah Durr i-Dauran (1754).

The very idea that two such famous stones could have been falsely identified as rubies all goes to prove our earlier point: in the past, the correct spinel classification was not used. A spinel shaded from red to violet pink, once termed "balas spinel" in homage to its provenance, Badakhshan, ancient name of an Afghanistan province: it seems that by touching the border of gardens, vegetable plots, and fruit groves with this gem, you can keep the plants free of parasites.

Bright red spinel – once "noble spinel" – chases away sad thoughts, and can bring about reconciliations between parents or friends. In apparent contradiction – red shades of spinel were generally symbols of war and victory. According to Scodrero, "Worn or as drink, a spinel immunizes against poisons and the plague and protects against melancholy, lasciviousness, and evil thoughts."

Blue spinels bring serenity, whereas the black variety helps its wearer intuit the true meaning of existence, though it is not a stone for people with weak characters.

Therapeutic properties abound. Green spinel staves off wrinkles and keeps your skin young and fresh; it

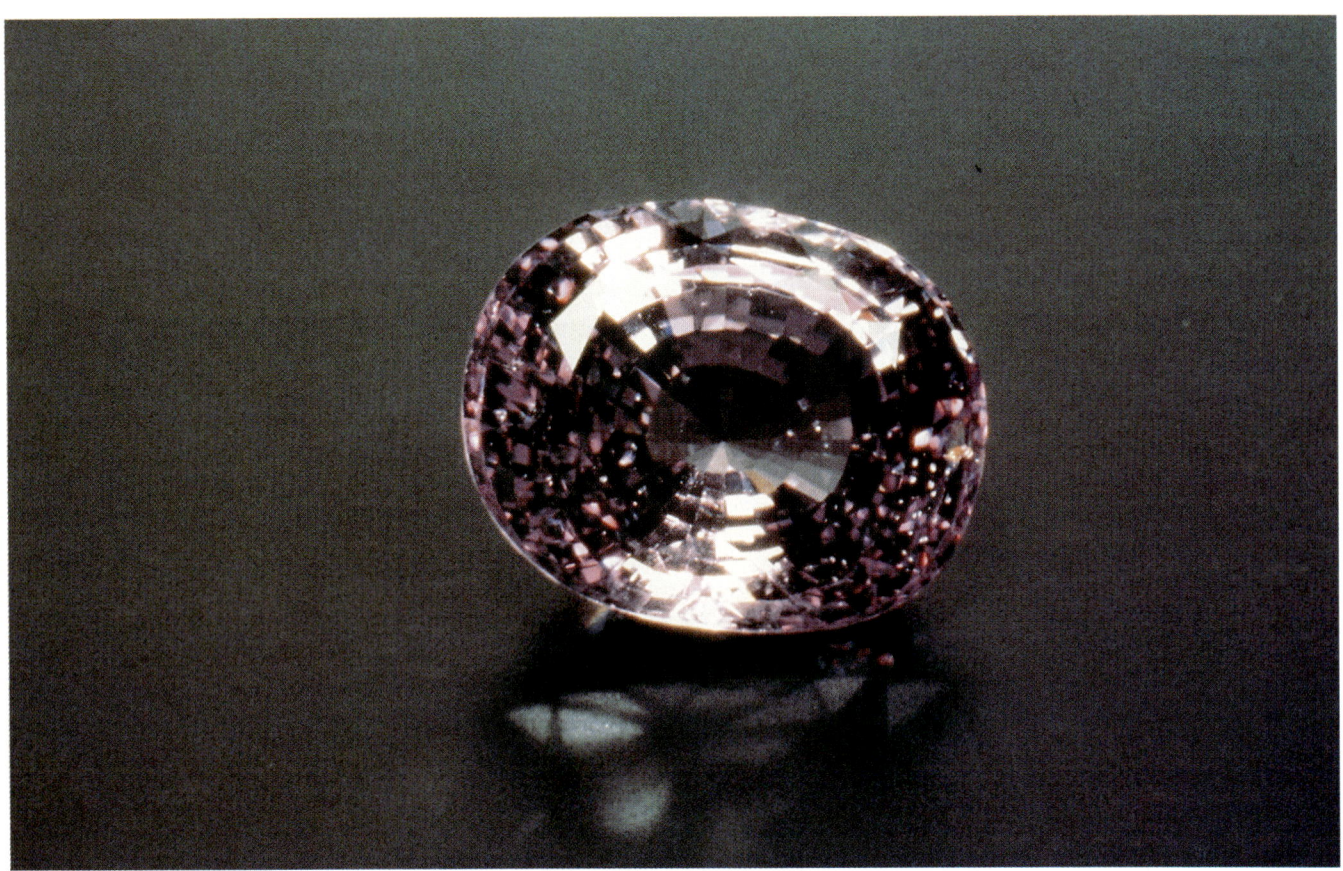

Spinel from Sri Lanka.

also animates the functions governing the genitals and the endocrine system. Red spinel purifies your blood. And, like all spinels, it has a positive influence on the nervous system and encourages social relationships.

Celebrated spinels Besides the Timur Ruby and the Black Prince's Ruby, the British Crown Jewels collection contains another two brilliant red spinels, weighing about 102.25 and 72.50 carats respectively. Further famous specimens: drop-shaped spinels set in the Wittelsback Crown (1830) were initially described as rubies; and there is an extraordinarily beautiful spinel weighing 400 carats in a Russian collection.

A gorgeous blue spinel is housed in the British Museum, which also has the two largest red spinels ever extracted, weighing about 520 carats each.

And the Iranian Crown Jewels include two very lightly polished stones at 270 and 500 carats.

Deposits Spinel normally turns up in deposits containing corundum; in consequence it is extracted in Myanmar (in the Mogok area) and in Sri Lanka (at Ratnapura). Less significant bodies are located in Afghanistan, Australia, Brazil (Minas Novas), Madagascar, Thailand, Turkey (Anatolia), the United States (New Jersey), and Sweden.

Cut In ancient times, spinels were set without any sort of dressing; the stone setter simply took care to place it in such a way that one of the crystal's octahedral points was to the top.

Today a mixed cut is adopted for less important stones whereas prized specimens are given an emerald cut.

Under the lens Red spinels may reveal dark hercynite crystals (a variety particular to spinels), negative crystals, and – very rarely – tabular crystals probably made of calcite. At times octahedron-shaped crystal inclusions are arranged in striking patterns in the host crystal. Blue spinels contain small dark crystals organized like the wing-shaped inclusions present in corundums.

However, you will look for a long time before encountering spinels with the "silk" effect displayed by corundums. In spinel crystals extracted from Sri Lankan gem gravels there are tiny zircon crystal inclusions surrounded by a vaguely brownish halo, a result of the fact that these tiny zircon crystals are slightly radioactive.

Synthetics and similar substances Synthetic spinels can be obtained by the Verneuil method

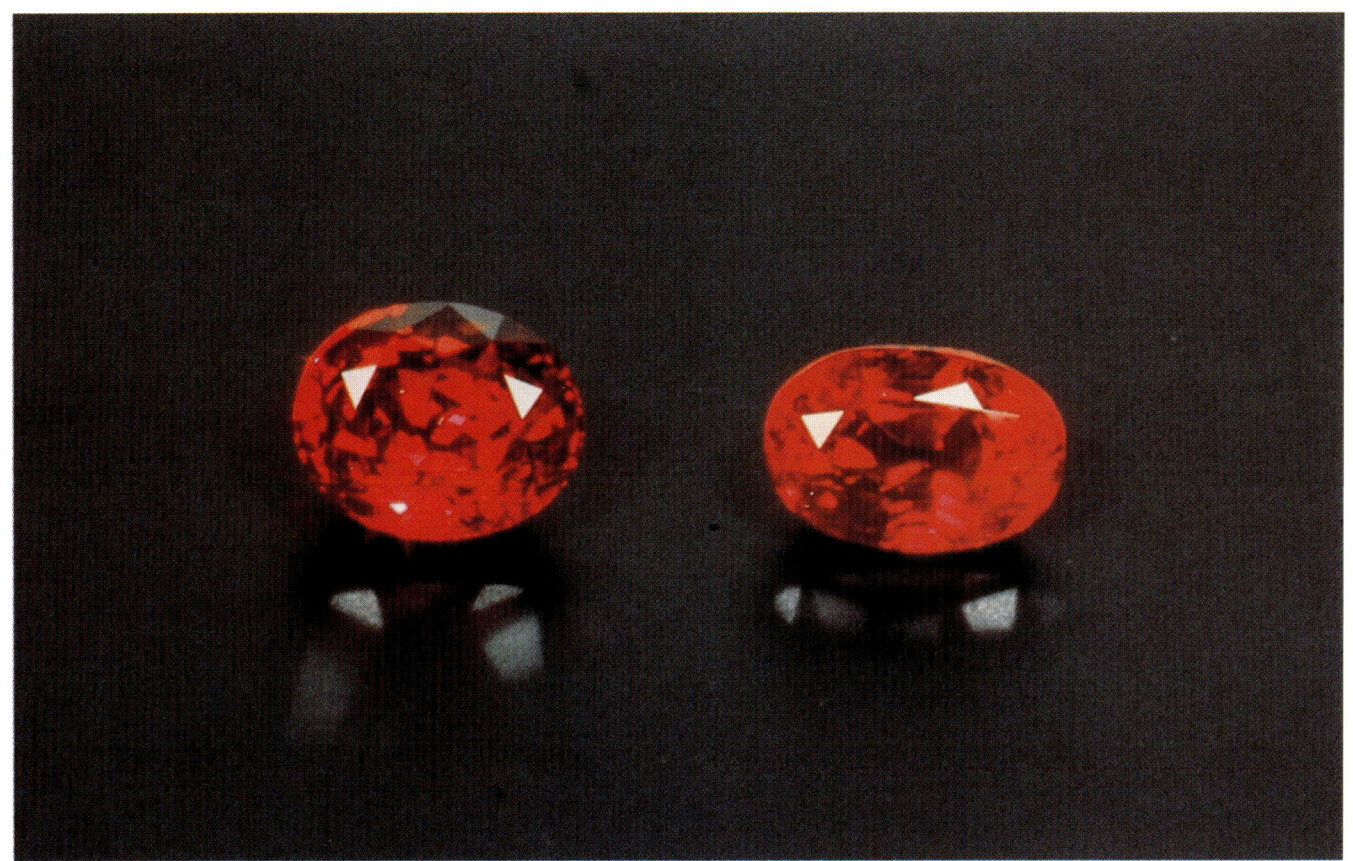

Spinel (left) and ruby (right).

and by a melting and fusing process. The classic "boule" produced by the Verneuil method is composed of 3.5 parts alumina to one part magnesium oxide, instead of the classic relationship of one part alumina to one part magnesium oxide. Some gemmologists, in fact, claim it is incorrect to call the product of this method a synthetic; for the material exhibits an internal tension that causes a characteristic anomalous birefringence. When analysed by cross-polarizers these anomalies cause a phenomenon defined as slurred termination. Some samples display curved striae with minute air bubbles, which are almost always isolated.

In addition to the red variety, synthetic spinels also come in azure and blue, as imitations of acquamarine and blue zircon respectively. In fact, if we add the right oxide to the base mix we can obtain materials at very low cost with a wide range of colors.

To identify a synthetic, simply look for the inclusions just mentioned; or check the refractive index, which normally ranges from 1.725 to 1.728, but is most often fixed at 1.727. A further test verifies the fluorescence either at 253.7 nm or 366 nm. In fact, at 366 nm (long wave), synthetic spinels turn a bright red, whether they be red, blue or azure, whereas green and greenish-yellow synthetic spinels turn a bright green. On the other hand, under short wave (253.7 nm) some of the colored synthetics listed above become a bright pale green. Many older objects and pieces were set with colorless spinel synthetics that can be identified under short wave, where they clearly display an azure-tinged white fluorescence.

Another synthetic on the market looks green under natural light and turns red under artificial light; in fact, it reacts like an alexandrite.

Several substances may be mistaken for red spinels: red and brick-red zircon; ruby; almandine garnet; pyrope and essonite; topaz; and rubellite tourmaline.

Blue spinels can be confounded with blue zircon, sapphire, sapphirine, tanzanite, dumortierite, or cordierite.

Spodumene

GENERAL INFORMATION

How it got its name With common spodumene having grayish crystals, the Greek word for it was *spodós* (cinders); in the recent past the accent was on the *u*, but today it is placed on the first *e* (spodum*e*ne).

Varieties Belonging to the pyroxene group, this mineral offers three distinct varieties: *common spodumene* in a grayish tint; greenish yellow and yellowish green *hiddenite*; and *kunzite*, coming in pink, violet, and pale violet. Common spodumene does not interest gemmologists, since it is mainly used for extracting lithium.

Hiddenite owes its name to its discoverer, W.E. Hidden, who came upon the first samples in North Carolina in 1879. The mineral has unstable coloring and though very popular in the United States it is not well known in Europe.

Kunzite honors the American expert G.F. Kunz who, in 1902, first gave us a thorough description of this gem. Once again, a stone that is very popular in North America, but is not much thought of on other continents.

Some interesting sidelights Thanks to its winning color it has been established as a symbol of sincerity and loyalty; in addition, it is thought to strengthen your powers of concentration, eliminate stress, and prevent psychosomatic illnesses.

Celebrated spodumenes Only the kunzite variety is on this quality level; a quite valuable faceted example, of Brazilian provenance, and weighing 542 carats, is on display in the Natural History Museum in New York City.

Deposits Hiddenite and kunzite are extracted from mines in Brazil, Madagascar, Myanmar, and the United States.

Reports have it that a blue specimen of spodumene weighing 35 carats was found in Mogok; and even a chatoyant white spodumene has been unearthed.

Cut Both hiddenite and kunzite are best suited for the step cut; in very rare cases, a brilliant cut has been employed. Cutting difficulties depend on a perfect cleavage, on the stone's fragility, and on the fact that in order to obtain the greatest color intensity, the table of the stone must be placed perpendicularly to the crystal's direction.

Under the lens Though this material is normally free of inclusions, both hiddenite and kunzite may display exceptions. In the former you might occasionally make out inclusions arranged in such a way that they resemble the rungs of a ladder; the latter could reveal liquid or even three-phase inclusions, occasionally formed of crystals.

Synthetics and similar substances So far this material has no synthetic counterfeit.

Hiddenite may be mistaken for light green beryl, chrysoberyl, diopside, euclase, peridot, tourmaline.

And kunzite is often confused with pale amethyst, pink beryl (morganite); synthetic spinel, artificial glassy substances, topaz.

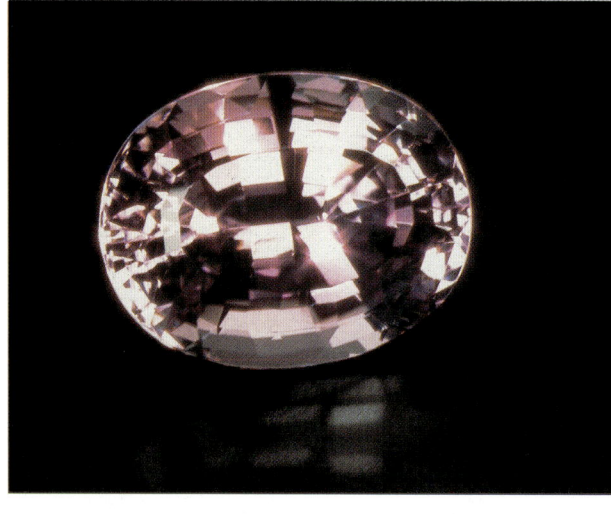

Chemical Formula: *LiAlSi$_2$O$_6$ – lithium aluminium silicate*
Hardness: *6 – 7 (Mohs scale)*
Specific Gravity: *3.16 – 3.20*
Refraction: *biaxial birefringent*
Color: *pale gray (almost colorless), greenish, yellow, yellowish, green, violet pink, pale, violet*

Topaz

GENERAL INFORMATION

How it got its name Let's look at the two contending theories. Pliny the Elder insisted the Latin *topazium* derived from the Greek *topazos*, name of a Red Sea island now identified with Zebirged or Zararjad, which had long furnished the Romans with precious stones, usually of olive green or yellowish green color. According to the second hypothesis the word traces back to the ancient Sanskrit *tapas* (fire). In the past, *topaz* was applied to all yellow gems. Even today citrine quartz is sometimes erroneously identified as topaz, though both minerals have very distinct physiochemical characteristics and, therefore, clearly defined properties and differing values.

Remember that the appellation "imperial topaz" is not official gemmological terminology and was probably born from the need to distinguish this gem and set it apart from other similarly-colored stones.

Varieties For proper identification, the color category is always added to the gem's general denomination. Chief varieties are: *azure topaz* (second only to colorless topaz for quantity available), *yellow topaz* (the best known), *pink and red topaz* (the most valuable). Sherry-colored stones from Ouro Preto range in tint from pinkish yellow, to honey yellow, and straw yellow, owing to the phenomenon of pleochroism.

If reddish brown crystals are heated to about 450 °C, when cooling off they turn to shades from salmon pink to purplish red.

Topaz takes a very fine polish, so the worked stones have a brilliant sheen and are slippery to the touch. Seems the well-known English gemmologist, A. Church, established the latter criterion as, without looking, he was able to put his hand in a bag of varied gems and take out the topaz, identifying it only by touch.

Some interesting sidelights During the Plague of 1348 Pope Clement the Sixth went around the lazarets bringing comfort to the sick; but he wore a huge topaz ring.

Documents from the time affirm that a few days after his visits a number of plague victims were actually cured. And some period reporters claimed it was the topaz that did the job, not Pope Clement.

Before leaving the story of the topaz and the Church, let's not forget that in the Early Middle Ages a condition for consecrating church altars was that they be set with the seven gems symbolizing the seven gifts that the Holy Ghost had given to the Church; among these, the topaz stood for knowledge.

Looking to the church fathers, we discover a further interpretation: topaz also represents one of the basic virtues of the Church itself – contemplation.

The ancient Indian folk medicine, Ayurveda, recognizes topaz's curative powers, helpful in building heart tone, revitalizing the circulation of the blood, preventing wrinkles and varicose veins, and keeping the skin young and fresh.

Reportedly, topaz also shores up the nervous system and eliminates fear and insomnia.

And whoever wears a topaz finger ring should become wise and judicious. Ages past, in China, topaz was hung on the doors of houses in the belief that the stone absorbed energy from the sun in order to transmit health and serenity to all the members of the family.

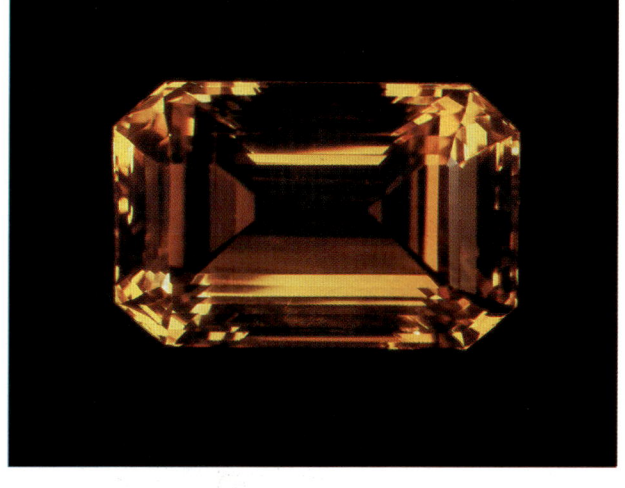

Chemical Formula: $Al_2(F,OH)_2SiO_4$ – aluminium fluosilicate
Hardness: 8 (Mohs scale)
Specific Gravity: 3.53 – 3.56
Refraction: biaxial birefringent
Color: yellow, honey yellow, azure, greenish azure, blue, colorless, pink, red, cherry red, brown

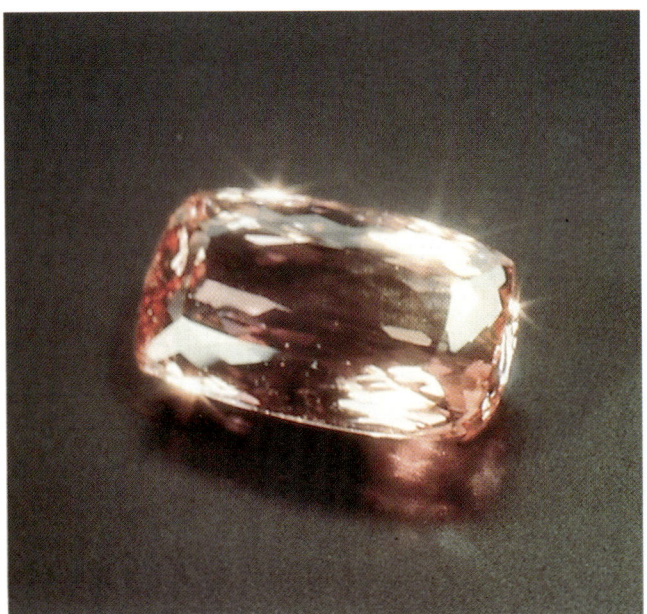

Rose topaz cushion cut.

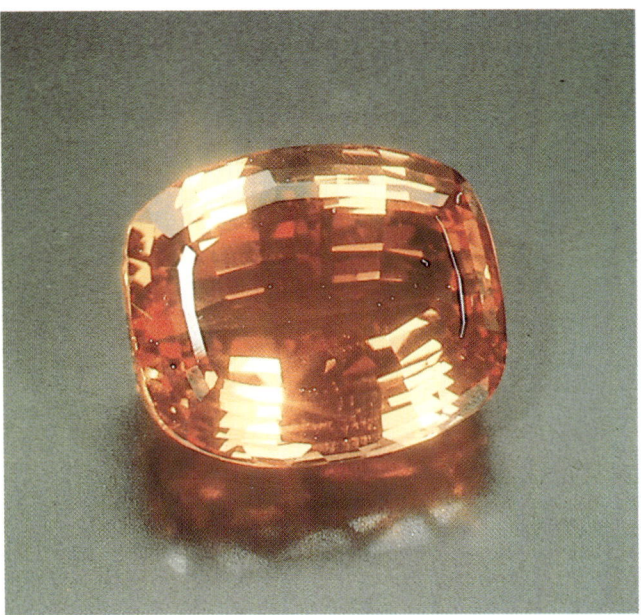

Golden topaz cushion cut.

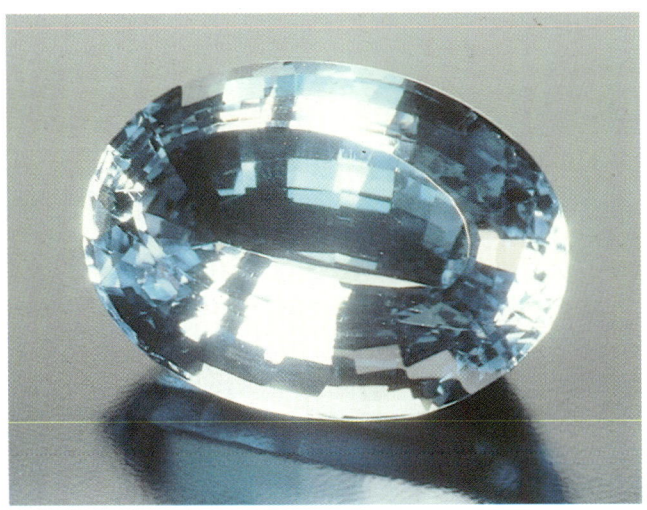

Blue topaz oval cut.

Celebrated topazes A 21.327-carat azure blue topaz, the Brazilian Princess, is on show at the New York City Museum of Natural History. Braganza, a colorless 1,640-carat stone, long held to be a diamond, embellishes the crown of Portugal. Two more famous stones, both in the collection at the Smithsonian Institution in Washington, D.C. are the Mineral Kingdom, a 3,273-carat azure topaz; the Porter Rankin Topaz, a 333.5-carat blue topaz.

Florence, Italy, hosts a colorless crystal weighing an amazing 151 kilos; it was discovered in Brazil in the noted Minas Gerais mines.

One of the authors personally had the chance to analyze a huge honey-yellow topaz of Brazilian provenance that weighed 1,374 carats.

Deposits Dye Bel Sabara deposits in Egypt are the oldest known, but are now exhausted. The Schnekenstein mines in western Germany and the mines near Gottersburg in eastern Germany also date far into the past. A sherry-brown variety highly prized in jewelry making hails from Ouro Preto, Brazil, in the state of Minas Gerais. As we've mentioned, these materials undergo a specific heat treatment.

Colorless and azure topaz are extracted in the Brazilian district of Diamantina, where diamonds are also located; whereas in Minas Gerais bodies of topaz mineral lie alongside beryl and chrysoberyl.

Yellow and colorless stones are mined in Durango, La Paz and San Luis Potosi in Mexico. Various colors are extracted in Russia, both in Siberia and the Urals. But Nigeria, too, has rich deposits of minerals offering a good color range.

Yet other mineral sources are in Algeria, Australia, Burma, England, Japan, Madagascar, Namibia, Nigeria, Scotland, Sri Lanka, the United States (California, Colorado, New Hampshire, Texas, Utah), and Zimbabwe.

Cut Square, rectangular, octagonal, oval, round, and droplet faceted cuts are the most commonly adopted. In older pieces of jewelry, topazes were set in closed mountings that blocked inspection of the pavilion; and frequently the metal setting was internally colored to enhance the color of the stones.

Under the lens No significant inclusions are observed though it is possible to note the presence of rhombic crystals, fibers, and irregular cavities in droplet or tubiform shapes. Occasionally, however, the examining lens may disclose areas literally covered with two-phase (gas and liquid) inclusions. On the other hand, it is common to find gemination and linear structure planes.

Synthetics and similar stones A not very successful synthetic has been produced for technical purposes, and no commercial use was ever intended.

Depending on its color, you might mistake topaz for granite, corundum, brazilianite, chrysoberyl, kunzite, morganite, fluorite, datolite, and ortoclase. Odds on to confuse azure topaz with aquamarine, euclase, and the azure synthetic spinel.

All topaz varieties can be imitated with artificial glass.

Modifying the color From the end of the seventies into the early eighties careful research came up with procedures that could alter the color of topaz.

To be exact, it's been known since the end of the seventeenth century that topaz shades can be altered in heating. Such treatments chiefly produce pink and colorless stones; in the past, the colorless variety was more popular than today, as it was employed as imitation diamond the two minerals having similar densities. Unfortunately, heat-treated stones become flaky.

Current, more sophisticated methods for modifying topaz colors are: gamma rays, high energy electrons and nuclear reactors.

Through the use of gamma rays, obtained from cobalt isotope 60, and alternating heat between 200°-300° C and radiation, it is possible to change colorless or almost-colorless topaz into azure or even bright blue specimens.

Azure remains stable up to temperatures of 450-500° C. Beyond that, the mineral becomes colorless again. So beware: if a ring with a treated azure topaz is worked to change diameter, the strictest precautions must be taken, for any heat, even a tiny flame, can make the once bright stone quite colorless. Frankly, the artificially produced bright blue has an unnatural look that workers in the field term "steely" or "inky."

Obviously techniques using high energy electrons or nuclear reactor-produced neutrons are not too often put into service as they are simply too expensive and could, besides, create slight radioactive waste due to impurities in the basic materials, even though only a tiny percentage of all samples have ever contained such traces. For the moment, only research laboratories with highly sophisticated and costly equipment are able to spot treated topaz. Paradoxically perhaps, where the usual gemmological laboratory instruments fail, a real expert comes into play, as he is trained to detect the steely tone of a treated topaz with just the naked eye.

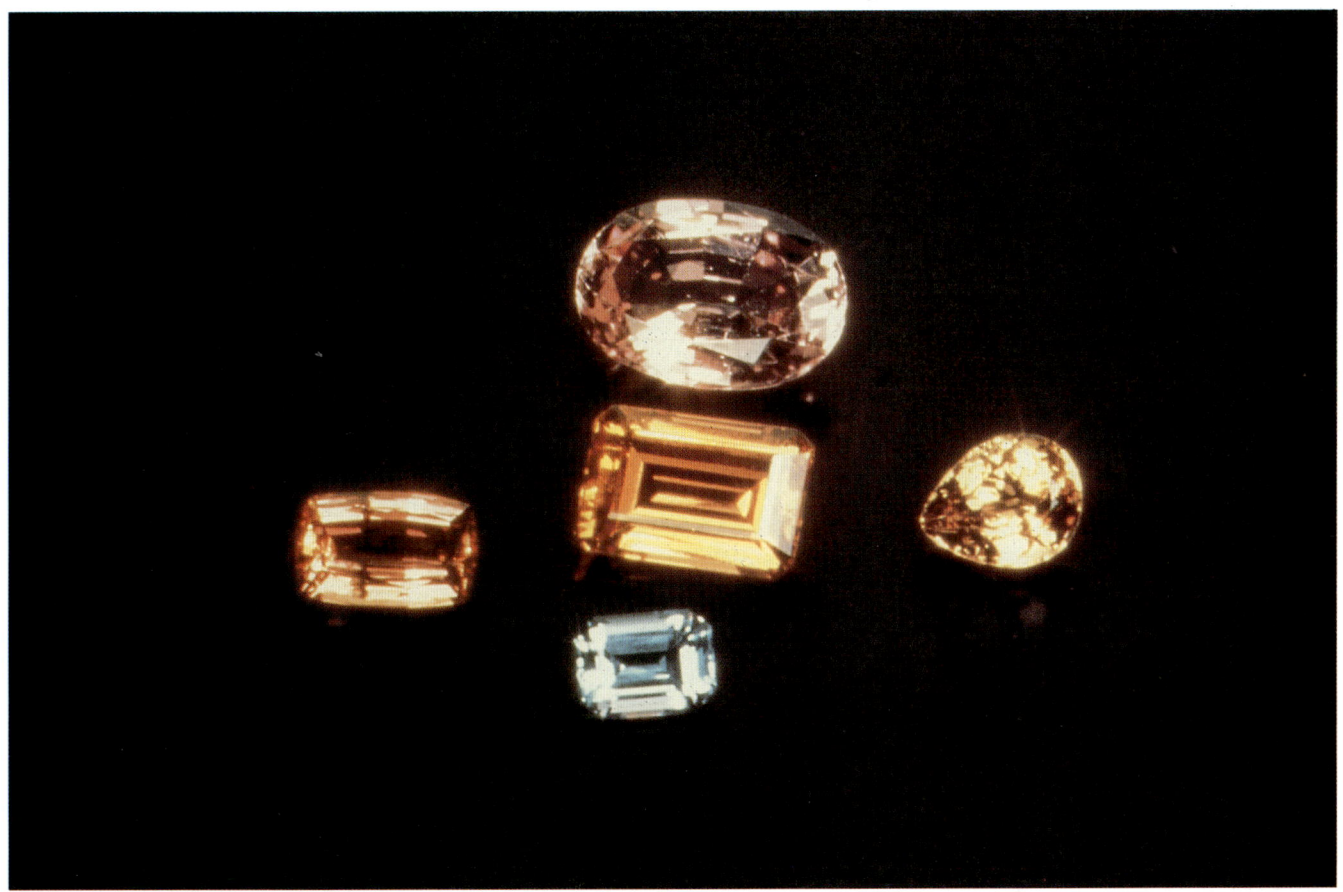

Various cuts and colors of topaz.

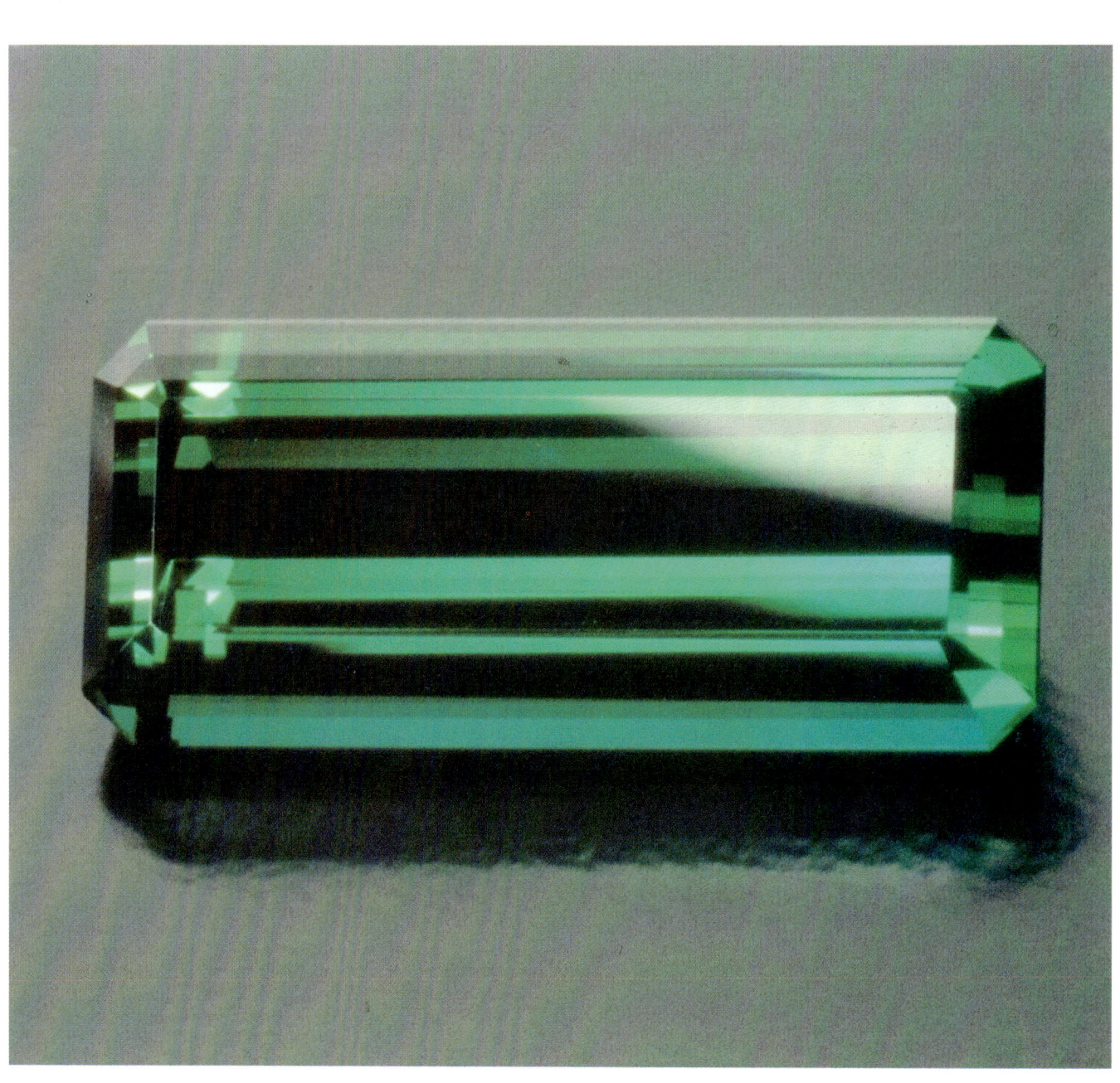

Tourmaline

GENERAL INFORMATION

How it got its name One possibility: it evolved from the Singhalese term *tormalli* or *turmali* for "mixed colors," referring to the stone's polychromatic possibilities. Or perhaps a purely local idiom prevailed when, in 1703, a large shipment of tourmaline, the first ever seen in Europe, arrived in Amsterdam, erroneously labelled with the Singhalese dialect term for yellow zircon.

The strong pleochroism characterizing this mineral gives it a dazzling allure.

Varieties Official nomenclature for both the green and yellow varieties includes stone category and color; thus, *green tourmaline* or *yellow tourmaline*. Pink and red varieties are called *rubellite*; varying shades of blue, *indicolite*; brown is *uvite*; reddish violet, *siberite*; black, *schorl*; blackish brown, *dravite* (note that these last two varieties are little used in jewelry making); and a colorless variety, *achroite*.

A glance at this gem's rather complex chemical composition, suggests the truly numerous variations of constituent elements that may be encountered, and explains why so many different terms have come into being. A final word: the true *polychrome* variety must contain two or more colors.

In the world of jewelry making, this striking gem was the preferred stone of René Lalique, master French jewelry designer and one of the finest and most important exponents of the Art Nouveau style in vogue around the turn of the century. More and more contemporary jewelry makers are adopting this exquisite mineral for their creations: Jean Vendôme is one leading name that comes readily to mind. Tourmaline with its myriad varieties, is frequently employed in that type of modern jewelry designed to bring natural stones back into style.

Some interesting sidelights When heated to a temperature of about 100° C, some tourmaline crystals develop electrical polarization at their terminations. This phenomenon is called "pyroelectricity," and was already well known to the Dutch when they imported tourmaline to Europe.

Piezoelectricity is another special phenomenon characterizing this gem; when a specimen receives a slight pressure, an electric charge is created. Thanks to this feature, tourmalines are adopted in making oscillators and sounding lines and rods.

Tourmaline so easily takes on an electric charge that even a light rubbing makes it capable of attracting other minute materials of reduced specific weight. The Dutch called it *aschentraken* ("ash taker") when they noted that it attracted ash from their pipes which were, of course, what one smoked at the time.

Brazilian lore has it that tourmaline had an extraterrestrial birth and was brought to Earth by beings with superior intelligence. Therapeutic properties have been suggested in texts divulging ancient practices and studies of the esoteric. Above all, these documents underline the importance of strict hygienic procedures: before and after each therapeutic application, the stone must be thoroughly washed. According to these sources, untreated green tourmaline favors cell regeneration when there is a wound or scar tissue; even burns can be cured, though the stone

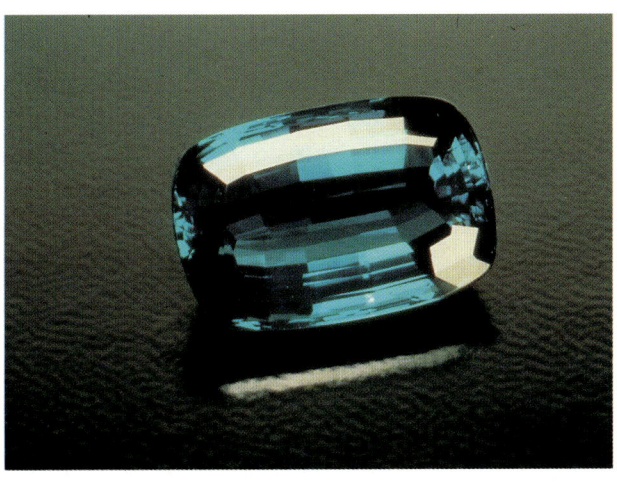

Chemical Formula:	$Na(Mg,Fe,Al+Li)_3Al_6(Si_6O_{18})(BO_3)_3(OH,F)_4$
Hardness:	7 – 7½ (Mohs scale)
Specific Gravity:	2.99 – 3.30
Refraction:	uniaxial birefringent
Color:	colorless, pink, red, dark brown, chestnut brown, green, blue, violet, reddish violet, black, polychrome

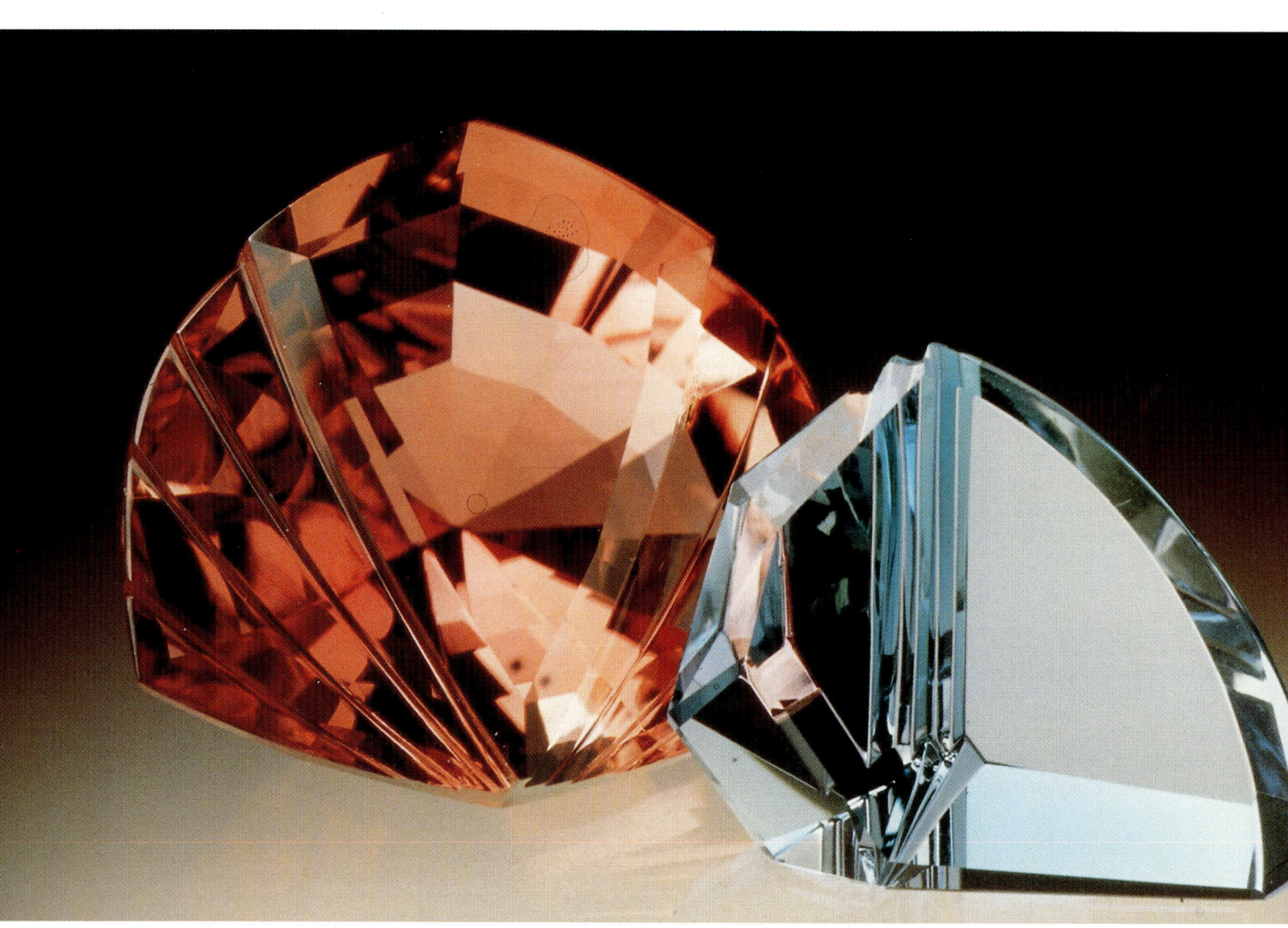

EKKEHARD F. SCHNEIDER: "CINEMA"
Aquamarine and pink tourmaline cut to seem in continual movement.

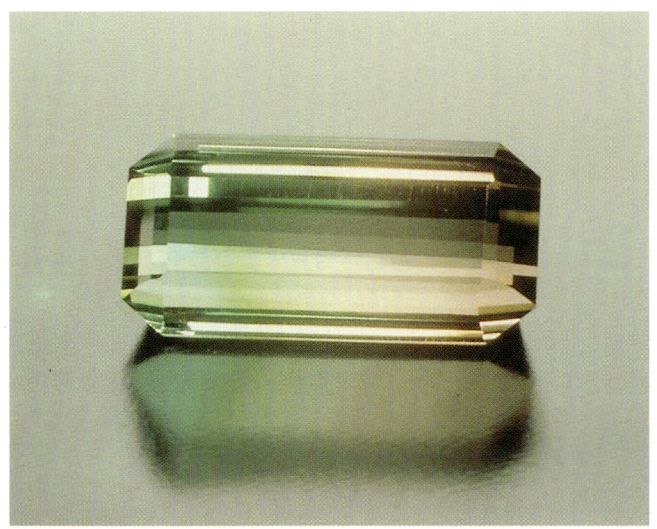

Exceptional tourmaline from a Nigerian mine weighing 58.08 carats.

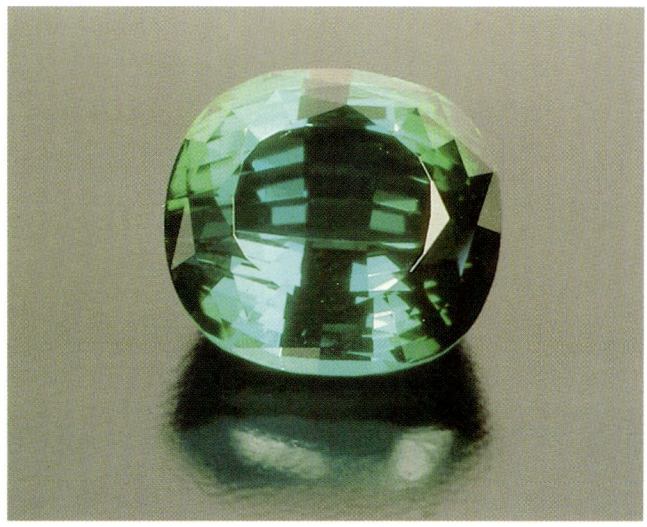

Green tourmaline with a cushion cut.

cannot be applied directly to the burnt tissue as its touch would provoke unbearable pain. Or, put one or two tourmalines to steep for at least twelve hours in your cup of camomile or tea, or in any other drink as long as it is not effervescent or alcoholic, and your beverage will heal scar tissue and even help cure ulcers. Whether your skin cream fights wrinkles, or is a simple detergent or moisturizer, augment its efficiency by leaving a tourmaline in the preparation.

Special therapeutic qualities are attributed to rubelites; supposedly, they help increase awareness of your body and free you from impulsive behavior. Indicolite purportedly keeps off lung diseases. Meanwhile the brown and black varieties protect us from dangerous radiation and should be particularly useful to people who work with computers. If you are sad or depressed, yellow tourmaline will come to your aid; but polychrome stones will actually make you more extroverted and sociable.

In India practicioners of yoga affirm that this gem helps rebuild *prana*, our vital energy, now so dangerously menaced by pollution levels.

Deposits Not only is Sri Lanka probably our oldest provenance for these stones, it is also one of the major producers in the world today, offering both brown and yellow varieties. In Russia, the Ural Mountains provide good quality red and violet-red material; and good quality tourmaline is mined in Transbaikalia as well. In the Ukraine, north of Ekaterinburg, splendid red crystals are extracted. While Madagascar offers a rich source of tourmalines in a wide range of colors: besides red, which is certainly the most precious variety – there are fine examples of blue, violet, yellow, brown, pink, and green deposits. Supplies from Brazil are esteemed both for quantity and quality, a production that includes blue, red, and green, as well as a polychrome mineral: main deposits are in the the northeastern sector of the State of Minas Gerais, in the Rio Doce, Rio Jequitinhona and Rio Acaçui river beds; an additional production of good quality and good color range stones comes from the State of Bahia. Namibia markets a slightly dark green tourmaline which turns a blazing emerald green when heated to temperatures between 450° and 650°C. Tanzania mines a brilliant bright green tourmaline that has a lovely transparency.

Other bodies of this mineral are found in the United States (San Diego, California; Haddam, Connecticut; Hebro, Paris, and Auburn, Maine); Australia, Burma, China, Mozambique, Thailand, Zambia, and Zimbabwe.

Cut Keeping in mind its evident pleochroism, the stone may be cut in many ways, though the mixed cut is most popular: this simply means that the pavilion is faceted in a step cut while the crown is subjected to a brilliant cut. For large-sized stones that are worth collecting, the emerald cut is practiced. But crystals with flaws are used for making necklace beads.

Under the lens Very fine cavities can be detected; under strong enlargement with a microscope it is clear that they are composed of two phases: liquid and gas. When these tiny rods are numerous and run parallel they create a ray effect that produces the cat's eye phenomenon.

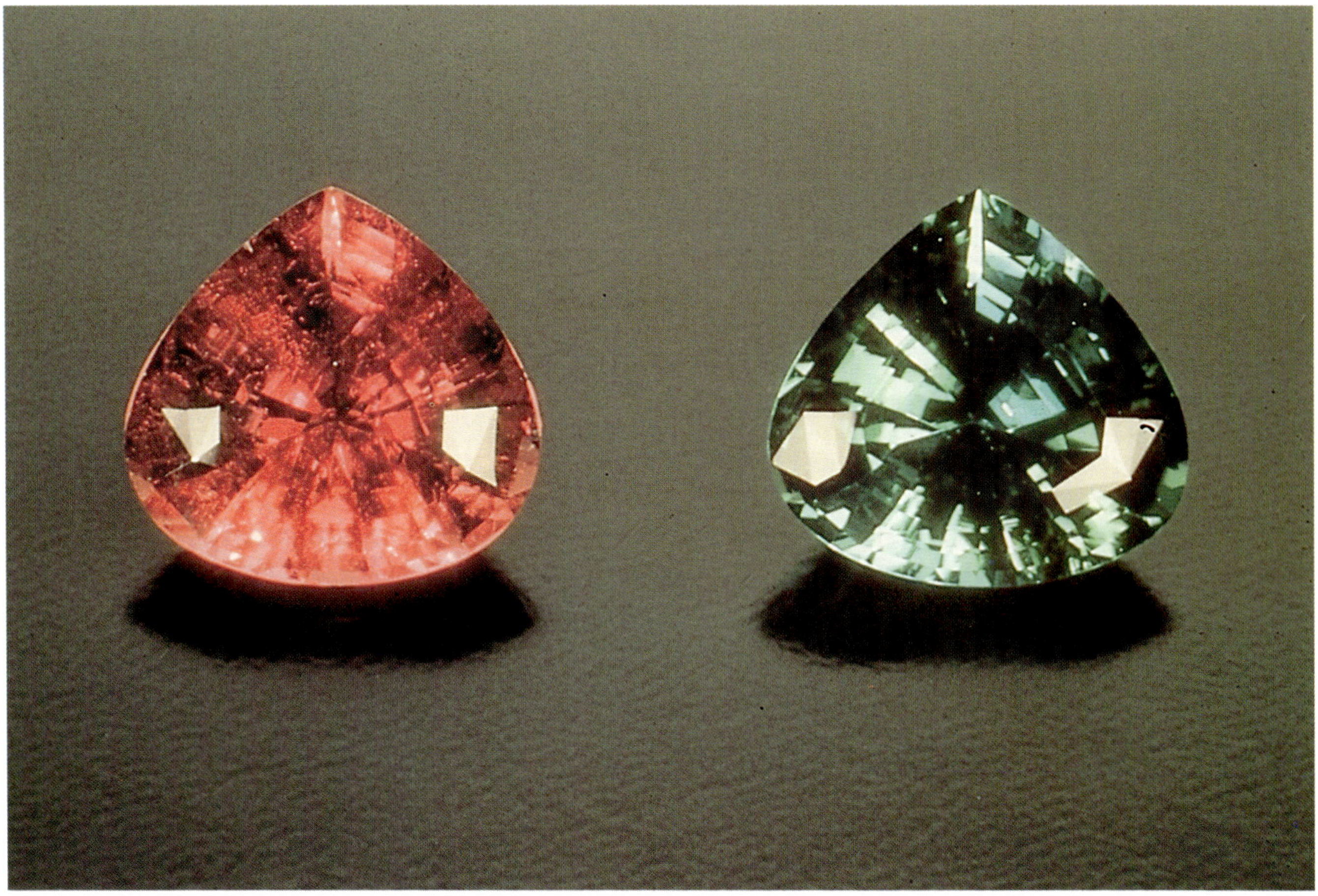

Two tourmalines with a pear cut, one pink and the other green.

Rubellite is a special case: if the jagged inclusions that may be observed totally reflect incident light, they resemble black speckles. For any decisive identification we must keep in mind the gem's two chief characteristics: a high level of birefringence and its accentuated pleochroism.

Synthetics and similar substances There is a production of synthetic tourmalines, but they have not been suitable for jewelry making.

Since tourmaline occurs in a wide range of color gradations, it is easy to confuse it with quite a number of other materials, such as: andalusite, brazilianite, yellow and pink corundum, chrysoberyl, azure fluorite, quartz – in all its vast color range – obsidian, ruby, emerald, natural and synthetic spinel, topaz, vesuvianite, zircon. Moreover, it may be imitated with any sort of vitreous paste.

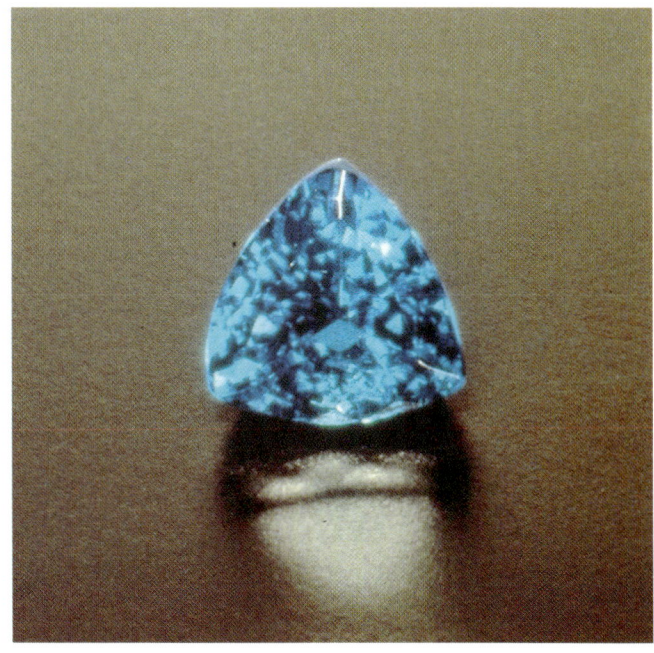

Blue tourmaline "Paraiba."

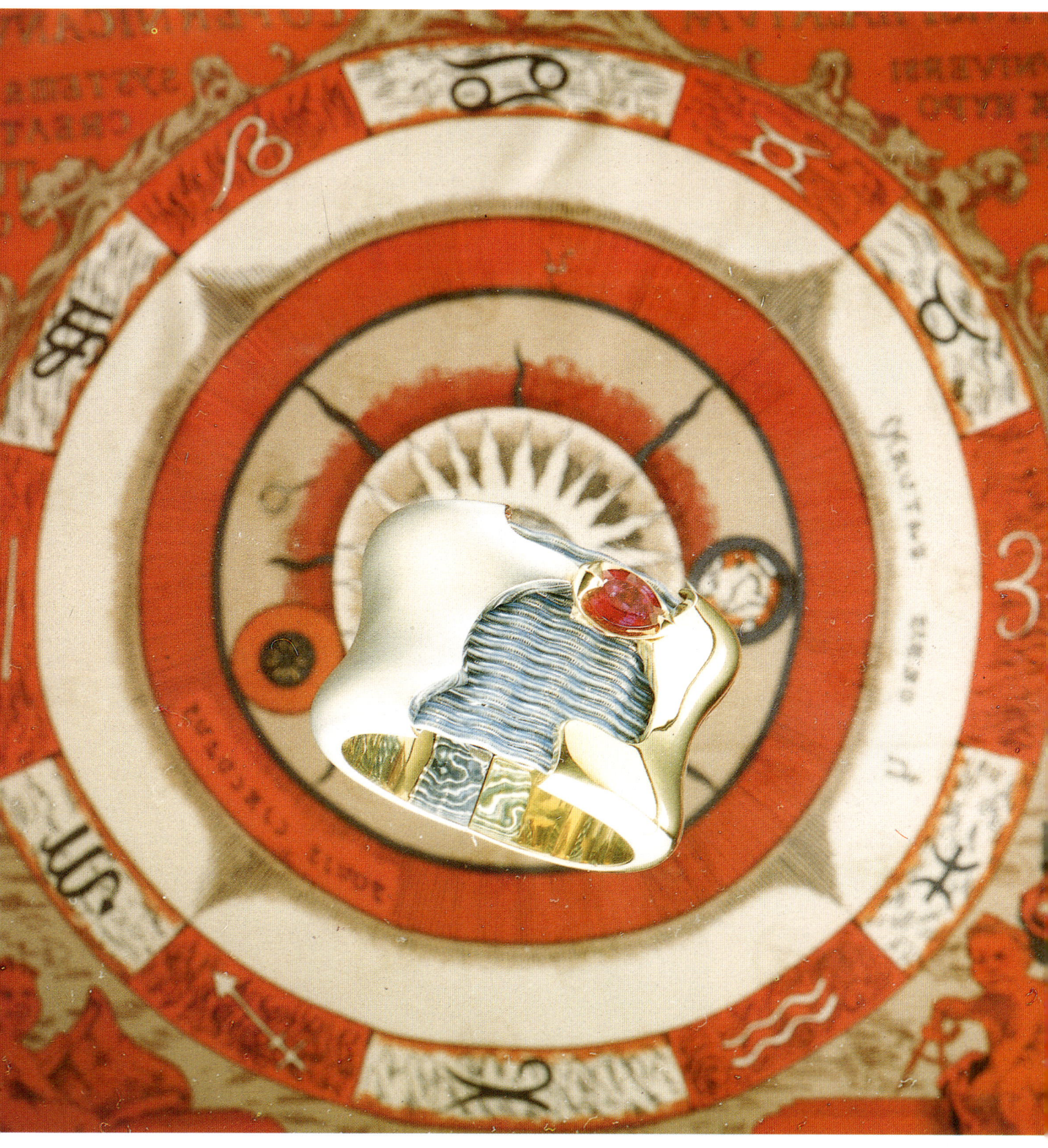

ARATA GIOIELLI: "IMAGE"
Bracelet created to mark the occasion of the five-hundredth anniversary of the discovery of America by Christopher Columbus. This jewel tells the story of a man of courage who challenged the unknown. Platinum, gold, rubellite, and nylon thread. Winner of the competition "Platinum Celebration 1992."

Turquoise

GENERAL INFORMATION

How it got its name From the French phrase "pierre turquoise" ("stone from Turkey"); because, long ago, turquoise arrived in Europe shipped from Turkey, though actually of Persian provenance. Our information comes from the renowned seventeenth century French traveller J.B. Tavernier who published his fact-filled memoirs *Voyage en Turquie, en Perse et aux Indes*, in 1676 describing how this material was extracted from the Firuzkuh Mountain in Persia. A further note: turquoise is called *firuzedi* in Persia and *firuze* in Turkey. It seems that the Romans called it *callaite* or *callaina* from the Greek word signifying a beautiful stone, at least this is what Pliny the Elder seems to have had in mind when he spoke of a beautiful azure-colored stone. In point of fact, however, the Greeks more frequently referred to the gem as *bòria*, or "the wind that comes down from the mountains," in reference to the color of the sky on the days when this cold wind blows.

Varieties For this particular gemstone we cannot talk of a classification in the narrow sense of the word; what we are referring to is a way of considering the material, based on provenance, visual appearance and certain specific technical data.

Persian turquoise has a decidedly uniform and compact appearance, with an attractive whitish cloudiness throughout; its hardness varies from 5 to 6 (Mohs scale), whereas specific gravity ranges between 2.75 and 2.85.

Talking about the American turquoise, we have quite a different set of coordinates: this stone has a waxy look and a bluish base color that can vary through to shades of green; there are frequent irregular whitish fractures, minute colorless crystals and brownish yellow zonings. Markedly porous, this material has a hardness index that varies from 4 to 4½ (Mohs scale) and a density from 2.60 to 2.70.

Keeping the above in mind, it will be possible to define the provenance of a turquoise sample with a fair degree of accuracy, a distinction of some importance since the Persian stone is certainly more appreciated on the market.

Remember that a mixture of turquoise, chryscolla and malachite is also available in an attractive streaked variety termed the "Eilat stone."

Some interesting sidelights Turquoise was well known even before 3000 years B.C. and was used in jewelry compositions in Mesopotamia in the Neolithic Age.

In ancient Egypt this mineral was extracted from the Sinai Peninsula, which was, historically speaking, our primary source. The ancient Egyptians rated it very highly and always adopted it for their most precious jewelry. An example of their outstanding work is seen in a splendid Egyptian royal breastplate on display in the Metropolitan Museum of Arts in New York. On a more prosaic level, the Egyptians commonly ground turquoise into powder for cosmetic use.

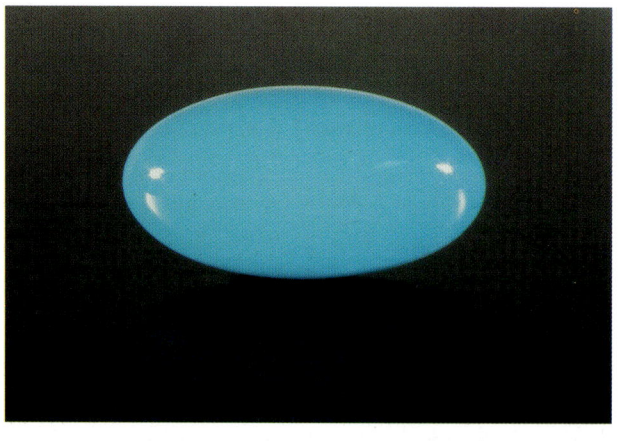

Chemical Formula: $CuAl_6(PO_4)_4(OH)_8 \cdot 5H_2O$ – hydrous phosphate of copper and aluminum
Hardness: 4 – 6 (Mohs scale)
Specific Gravity: 2.60 – 2.85
Refraction: biaxial birefringent
Color: from azure sky blue to pale green, with intermediate shadings and possible dark zonings

Deeming it a powerful talisman, Oriental peoples engraved most appealing and attractive good luck symbols on it. American turquoise was employed by the Aztecs to obtain jewels and valuable mosaics of which the British Museum has an admirable collection.

It was treasured by the Navajo Indians in America as an efficacious lucky charm; the great affection and respect they had for this gem is reflected in a production of splendid silver jewelry embellished with these stones as well as in its use in the simplest ornamental objects.

While taking a view of the distant past, it must be noted that the ancient

Greeks and Romans did not attach much importance to this gem. But in Tibet it was held to represent "divine azure"; in fact both *gau* (special reliquaries) and *perak* (rich headdresses for women) are the most precious objects that can be obtained with the use of this gorgeous gem.

Stories have it that turquoise instills courage and the strength of personality needed to face any and all risks; for more down-to-earth matters, it's supposed to favor business enterprise in general.

Used as therapy, it stimulates all respiratory functions. In ancient Islamic medicine it was ground into powder and applied to cure bites by scorpions or other poisonous insects.

Celebrated turquoises

We've already mentioned the pleasures of a visit to the British Museum or the Metropolitan Museum in New York; the Silver Museum in Florence's Pitti Palace displays a turquoise bust of Tiberius, a much esteemed work of art.

Deposits

Today our finest quality still comes from the ancient deposits in Nishapur in Iran (once Persia), though the quantity is much reduced.

Valuable samples are mined in Tibet in the Gangs-chan mountains near Nagari-Khorsum, in the eastern part of the country. For quantity, our most important founts are in the United States (Arizona, California, Colorado, Nevada, New Mexico, Virginia). Minerals from these mines are usually lighter in color.

Other deposits, commerically less important, are located in Australia, Chile, China (usually tending to green tones), and Mexico, whereas the once rich Egyptian mines are almost totally depleted.

Cut

Since it has a limited hardness, the stone is dressed quite easily and simply with a good polish. Turquoise is not faceted but dressed in a rounded surface (spheres for necklaces, cylinders, or en cabochon); or it may be cut in small plaques on which Orientals and Mexicans traditionally carve intricate designs representative of their cultures.

Occasionally, you may note that the base of a piece cut en cabochon is formed of the matrix on which the unprocessed stone was deposited; in the market these pieces are called "turquoise matrix."

Under the lens

Let's take a look at what we have said regarding the varieties; for turquoise is an opaque rock in which the lens cannot penetrate in depth, and we shall have to rely on characteristics as described.

Synthetics and similar substances

Gilson has produced a synthetic turquoise, and this synthetic and the natural stone present very similar technical data. To the naked eye the surface of this synthetic product looks like porcelain, or even Persian turquoise; but under the lens it is clear that the surface is a mosaic patterned like a beehive, even covered with a flecking of tiny white dots.

Other minerals often taken for turquoise are: amazonite, chalcedony, lazulite, pectolite (larimar), variscite, and wardite. Buyer beware: turquoise has many imitations made of simple blue-colored glass, ceramic, porcelain, neolite (a mix of bayerite and copper phosphate produced in Germany in 1957), Vienna turquoise (produced by compressing aluminum phosphate colored with copper salts), howlite (stained hydrous borosilicate), odontolite (fossilized teeth and bones colored in azure), magnesite (dyed magnesium carbonate, on the market as "turquerenite"), dyed jasper, dyed marble, or even plastic.

An additional offering hails from Arizona where turquoise dust is gummed together with resin; sometimes these synthetics even contain artificially produced fissures or flaws that make the counterfeit better than the original.

Glancing over this truly long list of materials we begin to understand how difficult it is to distinguish natural turquoise from its counterfeits.

Treating the stones

Some types of turquoise will get lighter or assume a greenish color as they age; to solve this problem a tint-enriching or restoration treatment adopting specific coloring substances is used. However, you can always check to see if a stone has been so treated by wiping it lightly with a cotton ball dampened with ammonia; wherever the cotton touches a treated area, a lighter patch of stone is evident.

If porous, even natural turquoise may be treated with silica, paraffin or plastic gels containing coloring substances. When the pores of the stone are filled with this mix, the gem seems to offer a highly uniform surface. A hot pin test will check for paraffin or plastic filling; wherever the hot pin touches there will be a partial fusion occasionally accompanied by a slight yellowing.

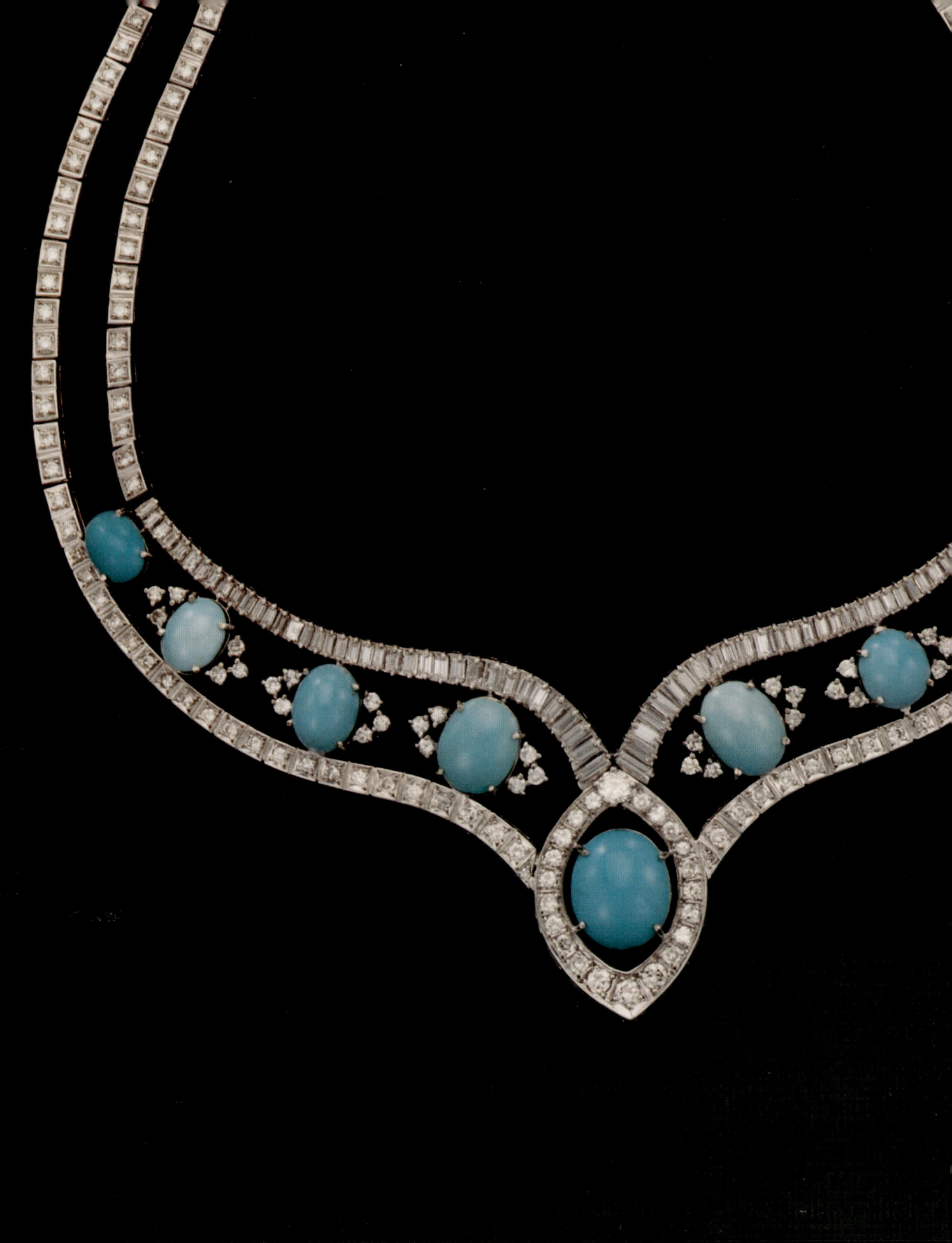

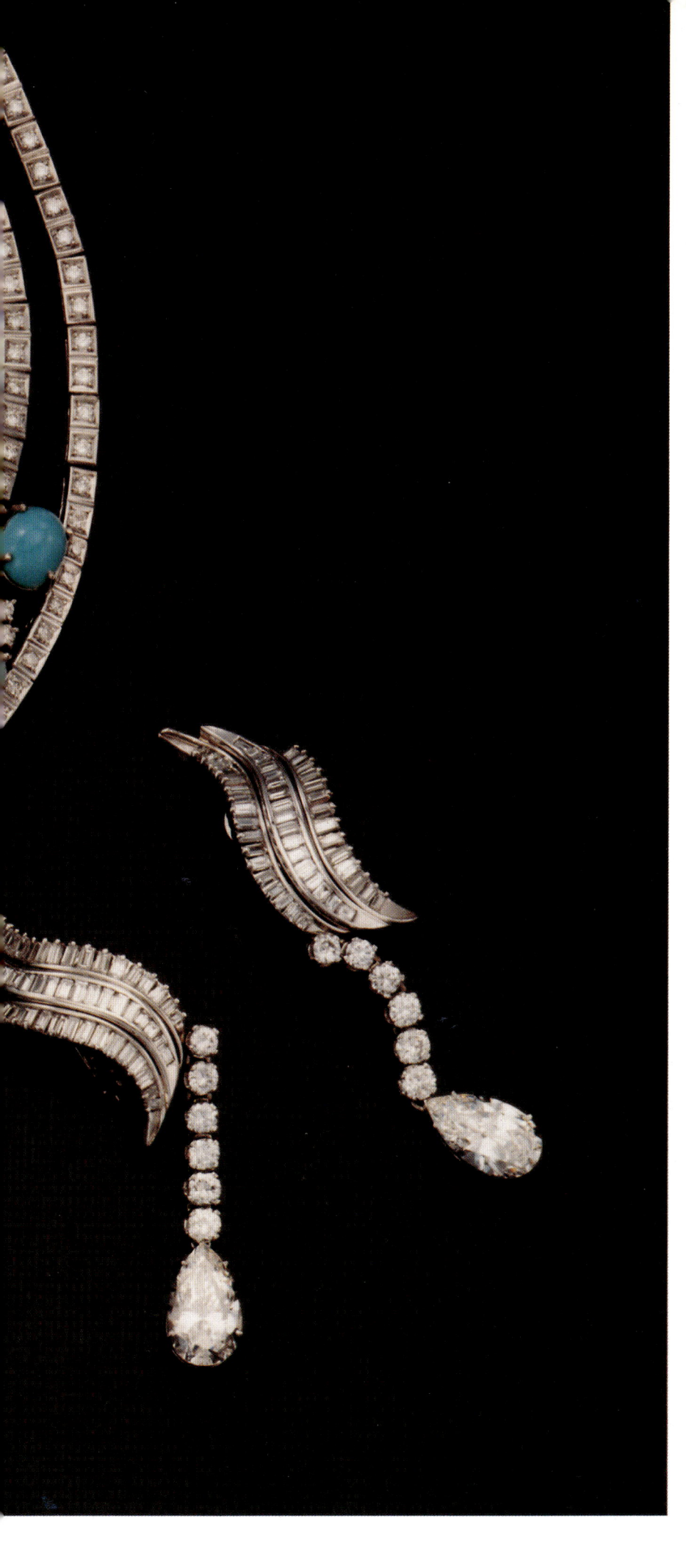

JULIETA DE CASTRO.
Set in turquoise and diamonds.

Zircon

GENERAL INFORMATION

How it got its name We have two possibilities here: the first is the Arab term *zarkum* for vermilion; the second refers to the gold tone described by the Persian word *zargun*.

Varieties In official nomenclature the term zircon is always associated with appropriate color designation, as: *blue zircon, yellow zircon, green zircon* and so on. Some very appealing names have come into use for different varieties: hyacinth, malacon, Matara diamond, Siam diamond, Siam acquamarine and starlite; but these attractive terms are commercial jargon and must give place to official nomenclature.

The once snubbed zircon began to come into its own about 80 years ago when the blue variety appeared on the international market. Extracted in the region of the Mekong River, this material is actually dark brown when mined and becomes blue only after heating. K.F. Chudoba and M. Von Stackelberg have supplied us with a significant variety of optical physical data: under X-ray examination, some zircons reveal the presence of radioactive atoms that, due to a decay effect, are able to provoke the collapse of the crystal lattice. This fact, for example, also induces a diminution of specific gravity; and so it is possible to clasify zircons as "high" (specific gravity between 4.67 and 4.72) and "low" (specific gravity between 3.90 and 4.10). Medium classification zircons also occur, specimens in which the crystal lattice has undergone a slight modification: such zircons present values of specific gravity that lie midway between the high and low figures cited above.

Zircons in the following colors usually have high specific gravity levels and are therefore classified as "high": azure, greenish azure, blue, yellow, orangish yellow, red, brownish red, and colorless. In contrast, green zircons have low specific gravity values and are classified as "low zircons." Unfortunately, schematic classifications are not infallible; for this material is often subjected to heat treatments that will change its color to a shade that sells better on the market. It is very unusual, but occasionally a chatoyant example turns up.

Some interesting sidelights It's been claimed that the orangish red zircon could protect against the plague; and Cornelius Agrippa recommended the same variety as an amulet for all those who wanted to make quick and easy profits.

With similar assurance, it has been asserted that yellow zircons cure intestinal disturbances, while the blue stones stimulate the function of our endocrine glands. Apparently, orangish red zircons help chronic insomniacs get a bit of sleep.

Deposits From the gem gravels of Sri Lanka we obtain material of real gemmological interest. Red zircons come from the Haute Loire in France, whereas in Arendal in Norway brown specimens are mined. Important bodies of these minerals are found in Cambodia, Madagascar, Myanmar, Thailand, and Vietnam, with other sources in Australia, Brazil, Canada, the United States, and Tanzania.

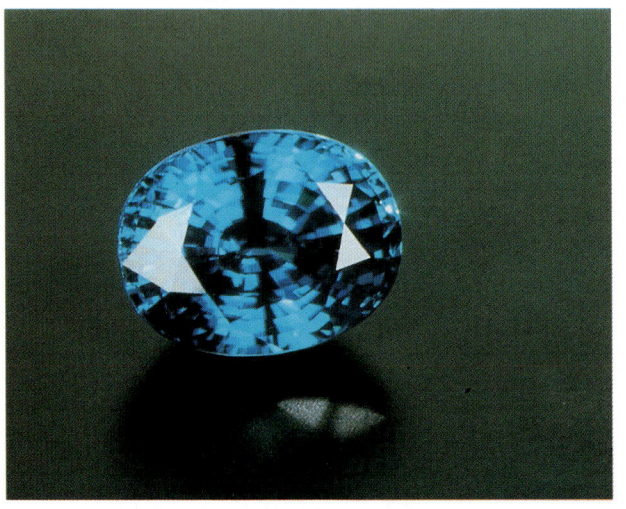

Chemical Formula:	$ZrSiO_4$ – zirconium silicate
Hardness:	6½ – 7½ (Mohs scale)
Specific Gravity:	3.90 – 4.72
Refraction:	biaxial birefringent
Color:	colorless, orange, azure, blue, dark brown, yellow, greenish yellow, red, green, and – rarely – even violet

Cut In general it has a fairly good transparency – particularly noted in the colorless variety after heating – so a brilliant cut may be put to good service, obtaining more facets in the pavilion than normally expected; the emerald step cut is also adopted. The mixed cut, however, is even more popular as it enables the stone cutter to underline the great beauty of this mineral which is greatly coveted by collectors. Given the fact that a high

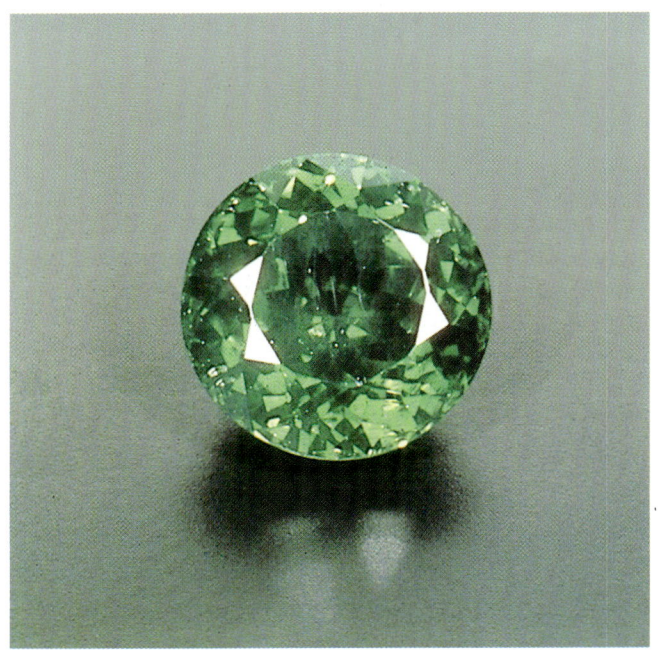

Green zircon.

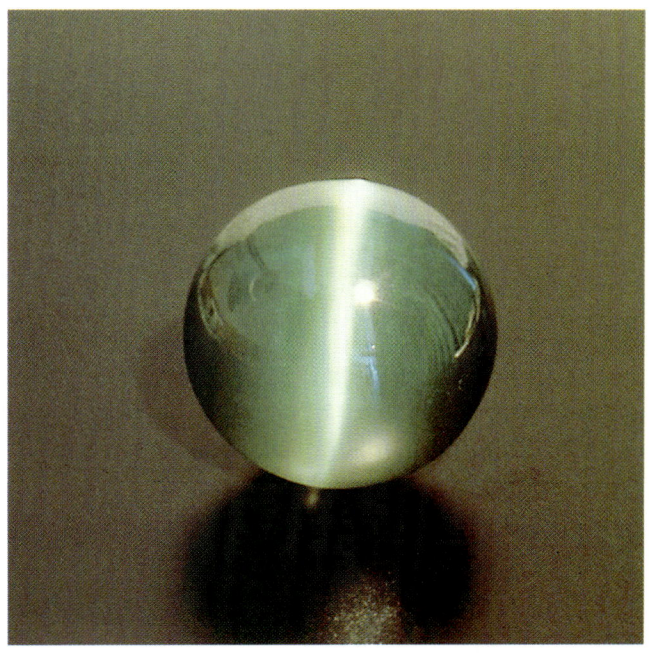

Cat's-eye zircon from a Sri Lankan mine.

percentage of all zircon is subjected to heating that makes it more brittle, particular care must be taken of faceted examples whose angles become more fragile and can easily chip off. Stone setters obviously are well aware of this problem and use great caution when attaching a zircon to an object.

Under the lens With the exception of green zircons the other varieties reveal a clear-cut angle-splitting in the pavilion when the table is examined under a lens, a decisive indication for identifying a faceted zircon.

Again, with a lens, we might make out liquid and crystal inclusions which can appear split when seen from the table. However, in the green variety in which the crystal lattice is almost totally disintegrated, it is not possible to note angle-splitting or possible crystal inclusions, though we can observe light colored bands.

Unheated colorless stones present a more or less cloudy appearance.

Synthetics and similar stones Synthetic zircons have been around since 1890, though they have had no commercial use and were only obtained for purposes of scientific research.

Depending on the color type, zircons may be taken for aquamarines, cassiterites, chrysoberyls, corundums, diamonds and all their various imitations, essonite, sinhalite, synthetic spinel, spessartite, topaz, tourmaline, vesuvian, and glass in general.

Changing a zircon's color As we have said, zircons are often subjected to heat treatments to change their color. The process is effected where they are extracted, and the temperature applied usually ranges from 800° to 1000° C.

We have to add, though, that the new colors are not always stable. In fact both ultraviolet rays and even natural sunlight may cause further color changes, not all of them desirable.

Zoisite

GENERAL INFORMATION

How it got its name Discovered in 1805, it was named in honor of the Austrian mineralogist S. Zois.

Varieties Until 1967 the known varieties were: *thulite*, a rose-colored massive form recalling "Thule," the ancient name for Norway, where this material first came to light; and another called *green zoisite* or *anyolite* from *anyoli*, or "color green" in the Masai tongue – another rock form that is little adapted to jewelry making, though it has many qualities including the presence of opaque ruby crystals, which makes it quite handy as ornamental stone.

Around 1967 rich deposits of transparent quality were discovered near Arusha in Tanzania. In standard terminology this material is *tanzanite*, after the country of origin – and was so-dubbed by Tiffany's in New York. But it is also known as *blue zoisite*, as this is the most sought-after color. Other transparent varieties include: green, yellow, pink, light brown, yellowish green, colorless, and a highly distinctive yellowish shade of persimmon. Oddly enough, when this mineral is put to temperatures between 380° and 450° C, no matter which of the above colors is concerned, it is possible to obtain blue tanzanite in varying shades.

The defining characteristic of this blue variety is the trichroism that can even be identified with the naked eye; but with careful examination, you can always observe a typical, slightly purple reflection.

By now it should be evident that only tanzanite has any real interest for jewelry.

Some interesting sidelights Noted for her deep violet eyes, the renowned actress Elizabeth Taylor happens to possess a stunning five-strand necklace of large, magnificent tanzanites. The astonishing similarity beween the glowing tint of her dramatic eyes and the purplish reflections in the tanzanite necklace create a portrait of glamorous allure.

Celebrated tanzanites The Smithsonian Institution in Washington, D.C. has a very large stone weighing in at 122.7 carats. Oddly enough a National Museum in one of the East African countries houses a stone of exactly the same weight. In the prized blue shade, we must highlight a 26.90-carat specimen on display in the Royal Ontario Museum in Canada.

While on the topic, remember that the loveliest and most precious blue tanzanites rarely exceed 20 carats.

Deposits Currently we get tanzanite almost exclusively from the Merlani Hills mines, 65 kilometers southeast of Arusha in Tanzania; recently, however, some bodies of this material have been discovered in small quantities south of Morogoro, again in Tanzania.

Thulite, mentioned previously, is extracted in Norway, the western part of Australia, the State of Carolina in the United States, and the Austrian Tyrol.

For anyolite, back to Tanzania once more, and to a number of alluvial deposits located in Kenya.

Cut As long as the jewel is made to orient the table in the direction in which the blue coloring is most evident, tanzanite will take any of the faceted cuts. Obviously this limits the degree to which the raw stone can be used to advantage, and is another reason why it is so difficult to find such gemstones weighing over 20 carats.

Thulite and anyolite offer a different opportunity: they are

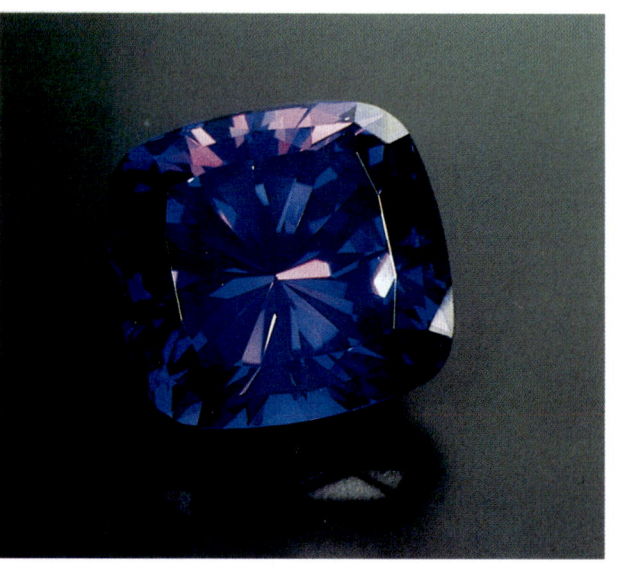

Chemical Formula: $Ca_2Al_3Si_3O_{12}(OH)$ – silicate of calcium and aluminum
Hardness: 6 – 7 (Mohs scale)
Specific Gravity: 3.09 – 3.38
Refraction: biaxial birefringent
Color: blue, light brown, yellow, yellowish green, green, colorless, pale pink

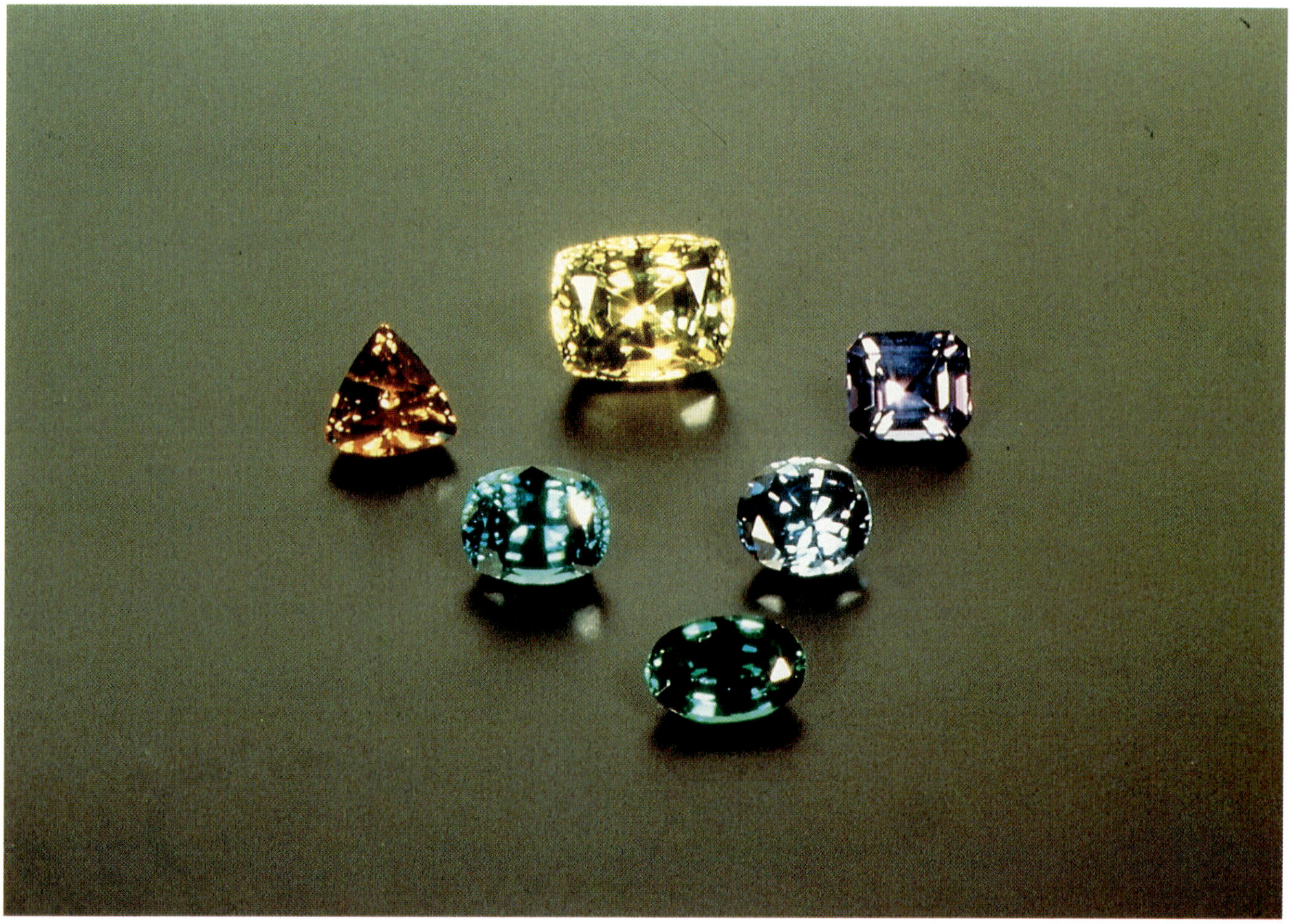

Various cuts and colors of tanzanite.

principally adopted for ornamental objects and may be worked in any form.

Under the lens   Usually, tanzanite is inclusion free, but some samples contain very fine needles arranged in parallels. Less often, we can make out crystals, probably zircon, with a sort of halo effect, or two or three-phase inclusions, or even a sort of fingerprint (or "little wings").

Since thulite and anyolite are massive – or rock – materials, a lens will not penetrate their depths, so we must rely on data from all other available instrument testing.

Synthetics and similar substances   There are no known synthetics for this mineralogical variety.

Similarities do exist, and tanzanite may be confused with: sapphire, synthetic violet-blue corundum, benitoite, and candite (though there is less confusion with the latter which is monorefringent and therefore has no pleochroism).

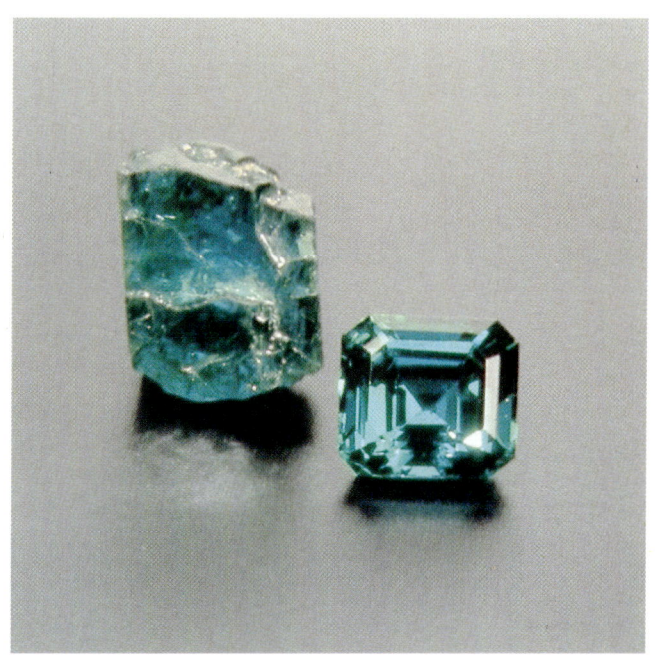

Rough and cut green tanzanite.

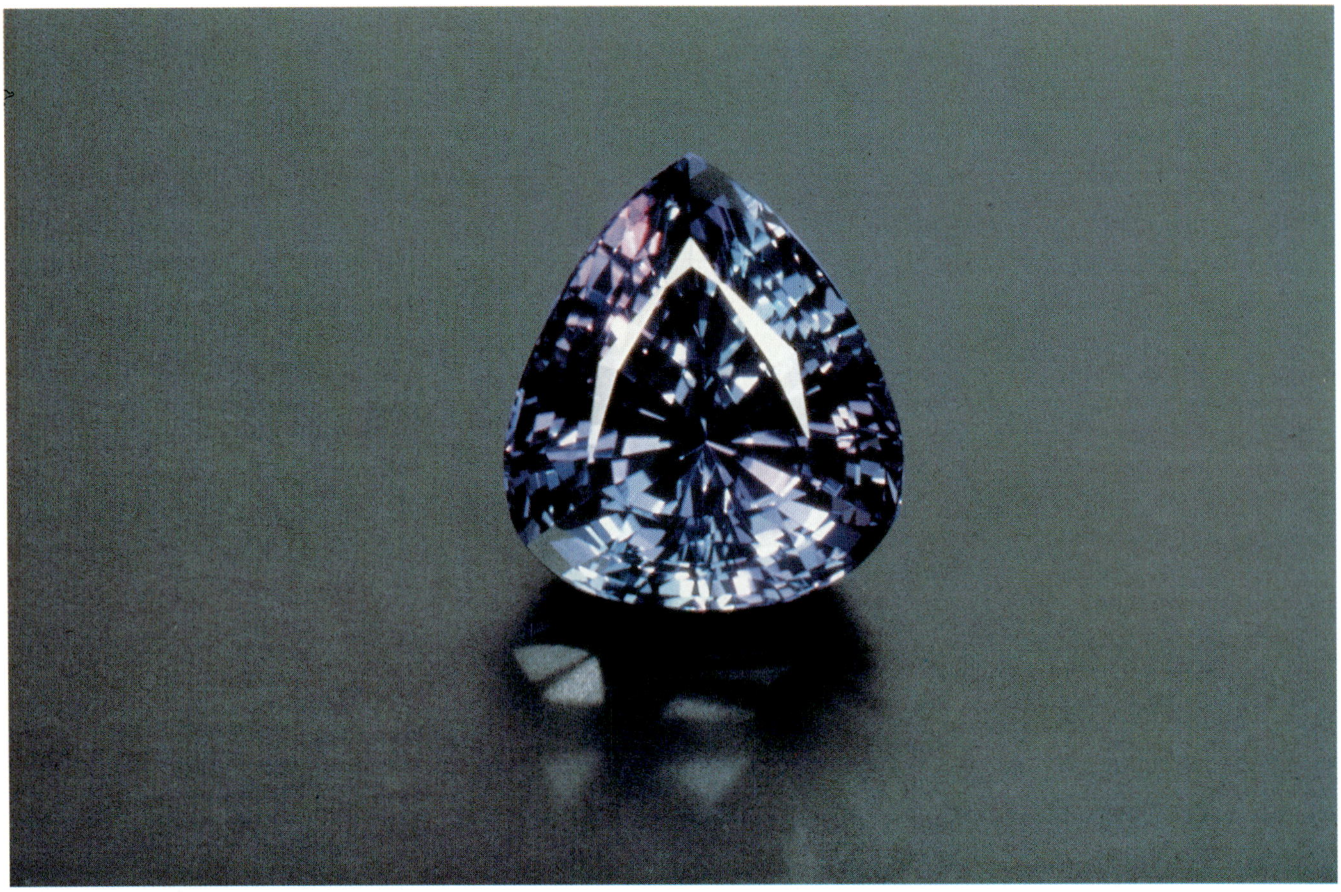

Pear-shaped tanzanite.

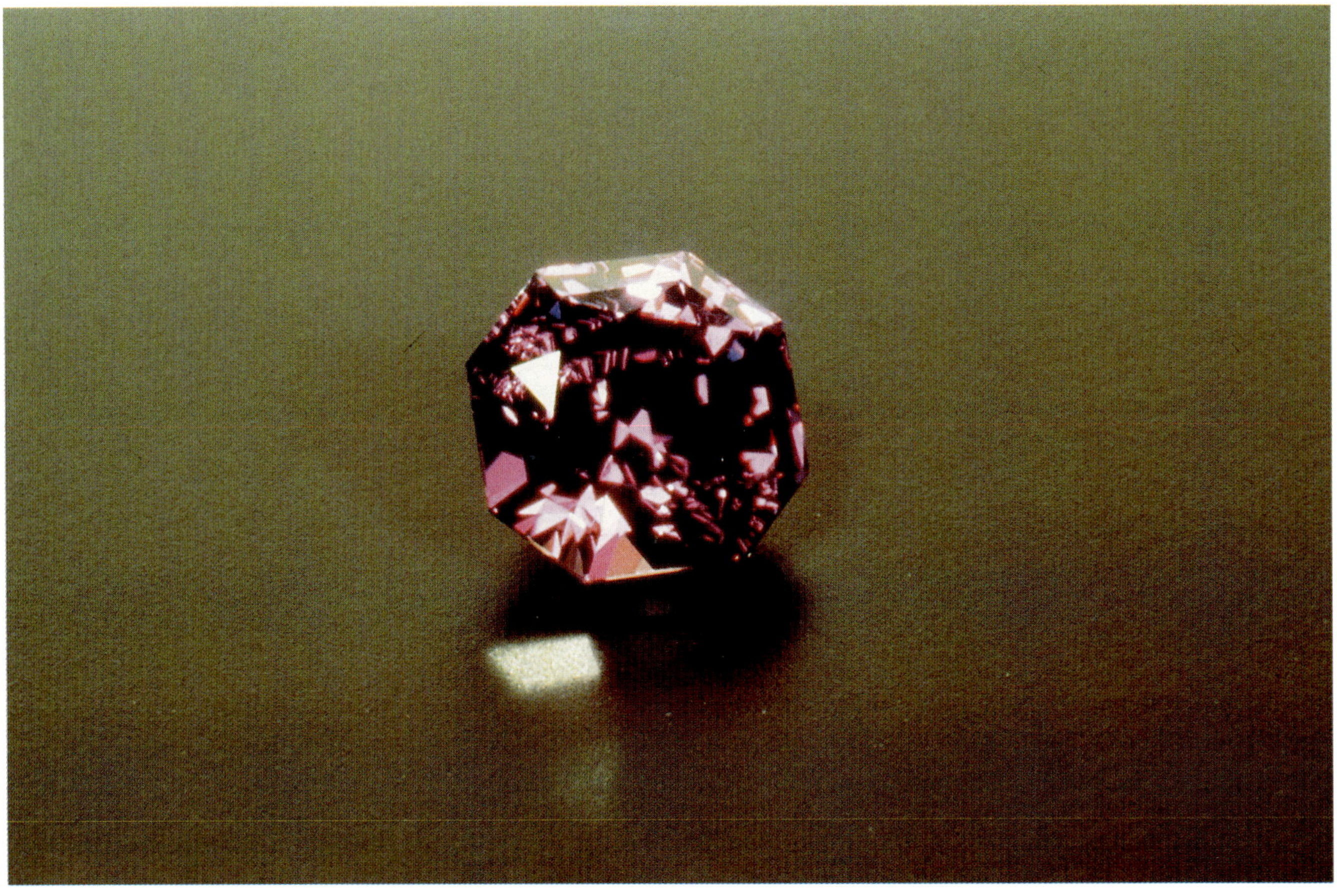

262 *Purple tanzanite with a square emerald cut.*

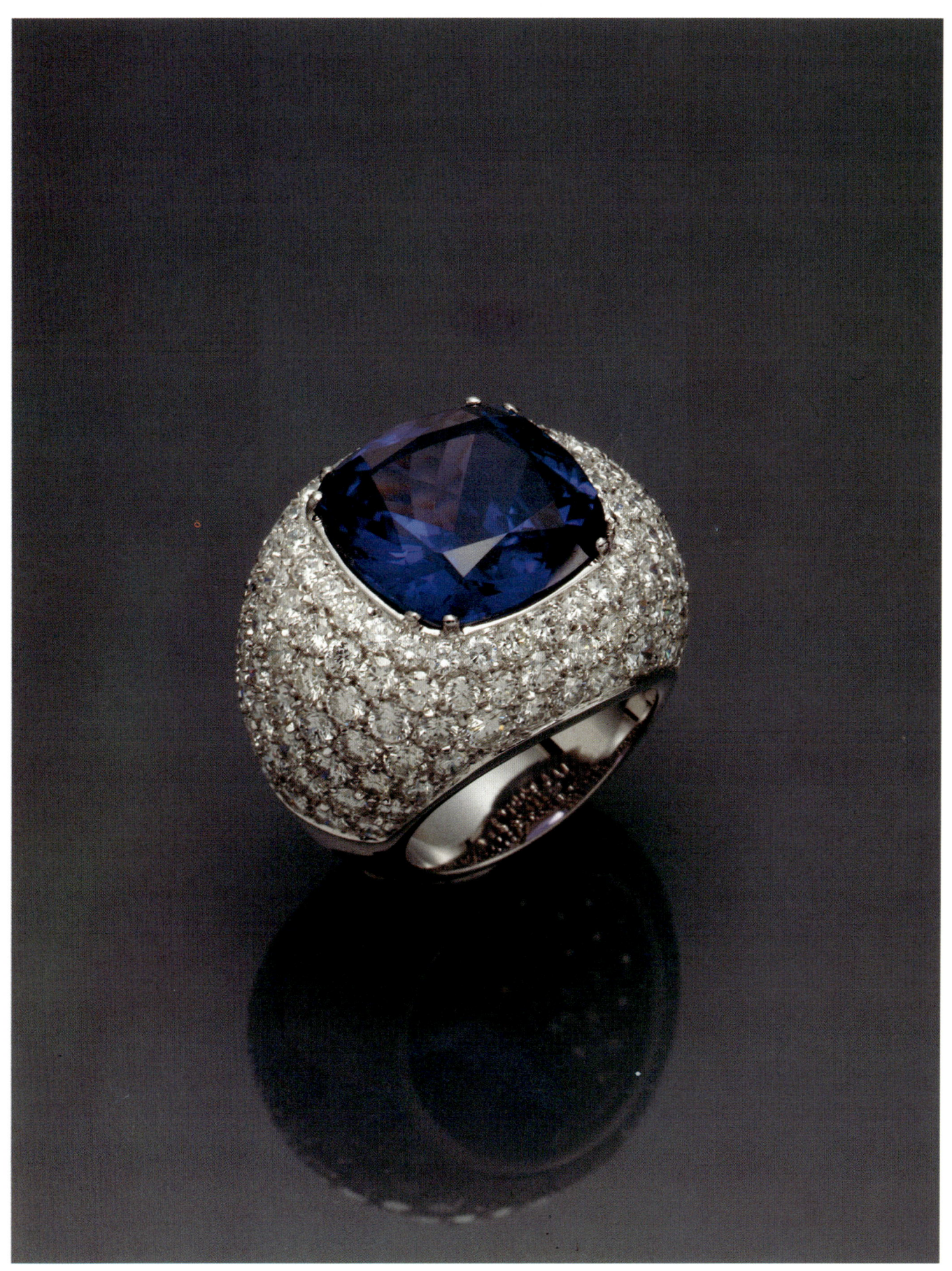

PREZIOSISMI.
White gold ring with a large tanzanite weighing 13.36 carats, in turn surrounded by 7.14 carats of diamonds.

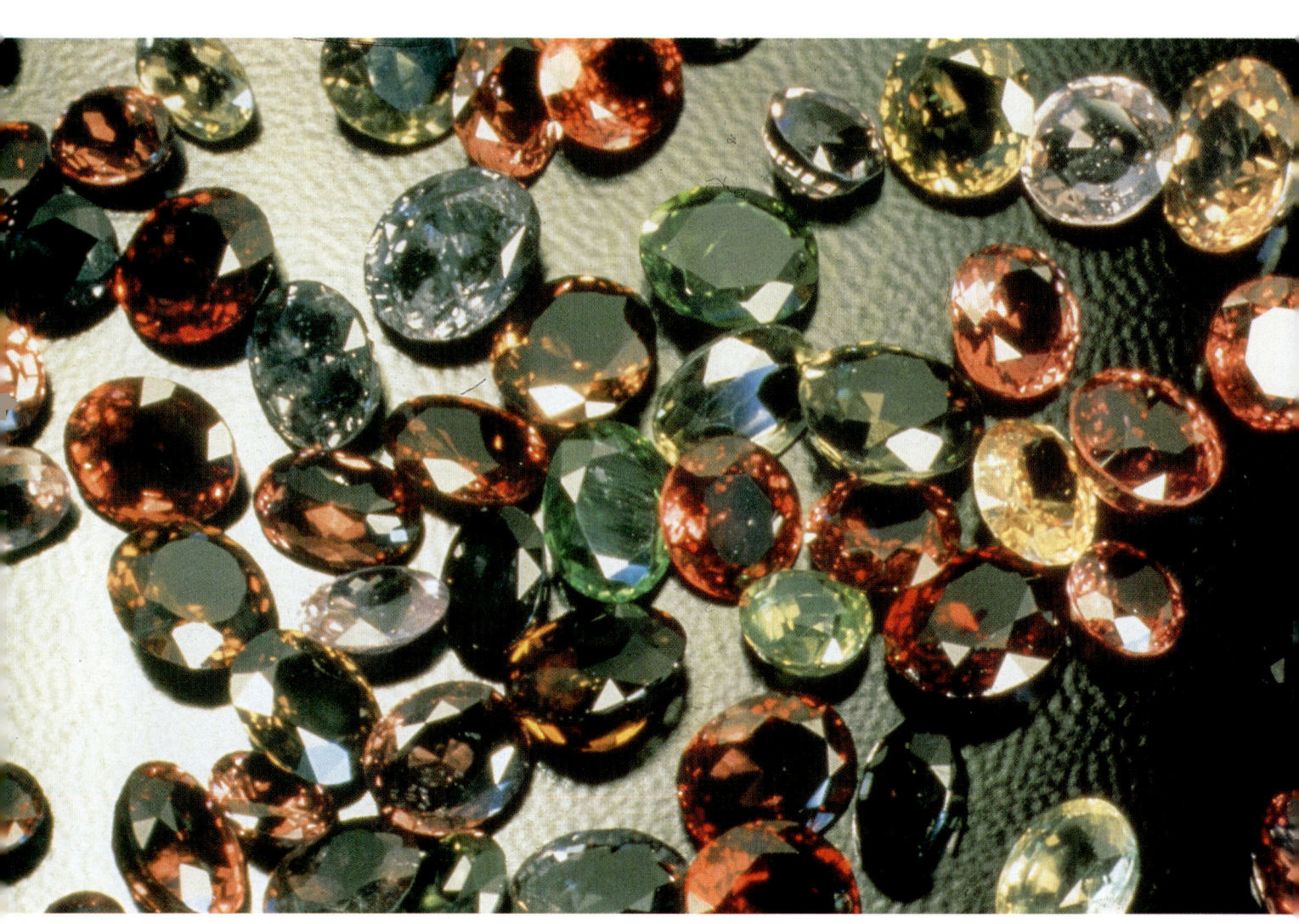

Chapter VII

Other Stones

Actinolite

Derived from the Greek *aktis*, for "ray"; its color may be black, yellow, or greenish yellow. At times the presence of its raylike optical phenomenon leads to mistaken identification as cat's eye jade.

Smaragdite is the label for the emerald green variety; and *nephrite* is actually a microcrystalline variety of actinolite. Those stones displaying a chatoyant effect may be taken for apatites or tourmalines that gleam with the same cat's eye ray.

Note: these are collectors' gems.

Deposits are located in Canada, the United States, Taiwan, and Tanzania.

Amazonite

Another member of the feldspar group; its name alludes to the Amazon Rio, though as far as is known the area has no deposits.

Categorized as ranging from translucent to opaque, amazonite is put to use in necklace beads, or may be cut en cabochon: various colors are available from grayish white to red, brownish red, or shades of green. In green or bluish green it may be confused with turquoise or jade; and, indeed, these are its best colors and the only ones used in jewelry making.

The stone is believed to have the power to make any woman beautiful and fascinating; but it is also helpful for people with memory problems and can even improve one's general psychophysical development.

In the past the most valuable stones were mined in the United States, but at the present moment our best sources are in a number of Indian locations and Kashmir; additional mines are in Australia, Brazil, Canada, Madagascar, South Africa, Tanzania.

A sea green variety with whitish veining has its provenance in the Ural Mountains.

Amblygonite

Due to its particular cleavage, the name became in Greek *amblys* and *gonia* ("obtuse angle"). Generally colorless, it may occasionally be found in golden yellow or light brown.

Amblygonite may be confused with brazilianite and scapolite.

Deposits are in many spots round the world: Australia, Brazil, France, Namibia, Norway, Spain, the United States, or South Africa (source of an unusual lilac shade).

Andalusite

It was first found in the province of Andalusia from which it took its name and a marked pleochroism is evident in all available colors: brownish yellow, greenish yellow, greenish brown, bright green, brownish red.

Green-hued stones may be confused with green

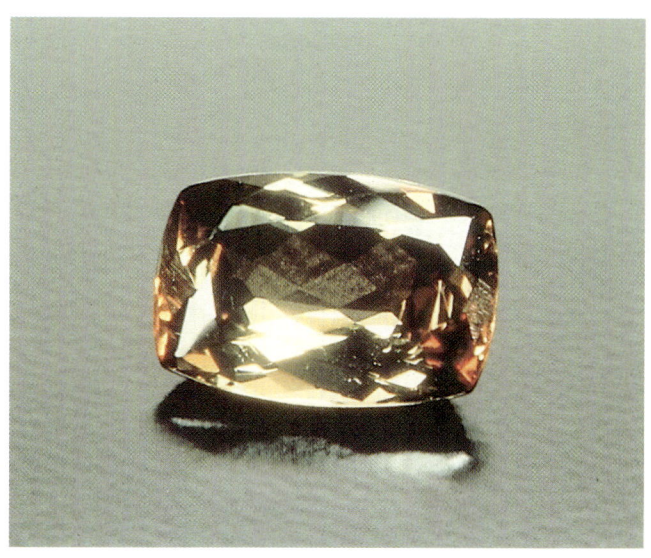

Andalusite.

tourmaline of Brazilian provenance; according to the color variety, the mineral may be taken for chrysoberyl, danburite, smoky quartz, or topaz.

In Spain there is an ancient legend recounting the tragic love between a young prince and a beautiful gypsy. Nature herself was so deeply moved by the prince's enormous grief that it created this gem as an eternal remembrance of their love. Logically enough then, it is recommended to the melancholy and the introverted. Noted deposits are in Brazil, Canada, Russia, Spain, Sri Lanka, the United States, and Zimbabwe.

Anorthite

Belonging to the feldspar group, its name goes back to the Greek and signifies "oblique," a probable reference to its particular crystallization.

It is rarely facet cut and generally only upon a collector's specific request. Pink and white are the only colors.

Mines are located in Canada, Finland, Kenya, Madagascar, the United States, and Switzerland.

Apatite

Mohs chose this stone to stand for 5 on his hardness index; and since it is a relatively soft material it has limited use in jewelry making.

It is on the market as a colorless stone, but is also available in pink, yellow, green, blue, or violet. Moreover, there is a chatoyant yellowish green variety, of Brazilian or Myanmarian provenance, called the "asparagus stone" for its characteristic coloring.

At times apatite may be confused with beryl, danburite, topaz or tourmaline.

Besides the above-mentioned deposits, mines are also located in Canada, Madagascar, Mexico, Norway, the Czech Republic, Spain, Sri Lanka, and the United States.

Artificial Glass

Our first artificial glass dates back to 4,000 B.C. Nowadays we distinguish two basic types: crown and flint. Crown glass is formed of a silica containing sodium oxide, potassium oxide and calcium oxide, and it is the glass commonly used for household articles.

Lead oxide is substituted for calcium oxide to form flint, a more valuable glass utilized for eye glasses, optical instruments, and with the addition of appropriate coloring oxides, gemstone imitations. One sector of this variety is known as "strass," or "paste."

Azurite

Inspiration for the term? Its intense azure tonality.

In a cabochon cut it is often used in jewelry making; alternately, its densely opaque quality makes it suited for ornamental objects.

Its natural partner in deposits is malachite, since it is a product of the latter's alteration. Owing to this common dual occurrence, the rock in which they are found is termed "azurite-malachite." It may be mixed up with dumortierite, lapis lazuli, or sodalite. In legend, this stone is deemed a great aid to eloquence and is suggested for those who have trouble expressing themselves or difficulties in

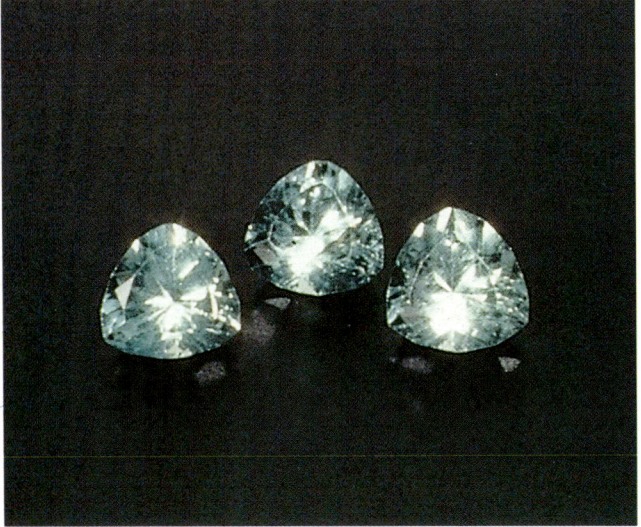

Apatite.

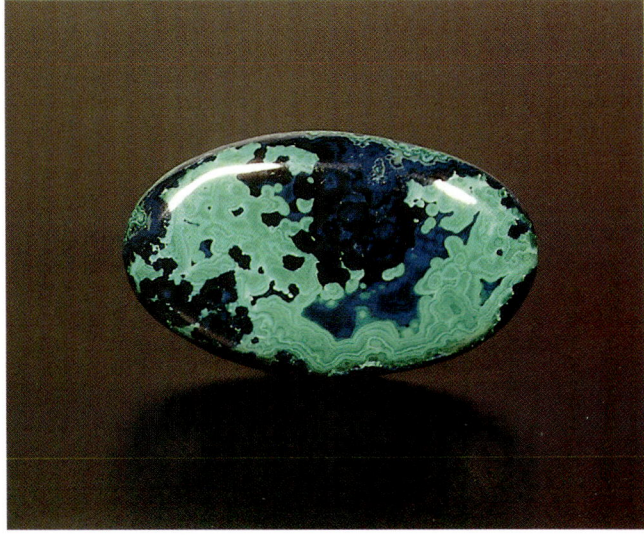

Azurite-Malachite.

communicating with others. Moreover, it is said to prevent respiratory diseases and reduce stress.

For our main sources we look to: Australia, Chile, France, Mexico, Namibia, Romania, Russia, the United States, and Zaire.

Benitoite

No totally transparent specimens exist. It was first discovered in 1906 in California, near the sources of the San Benito River, to which its denomination pays tribute. A blue variety bears very close resemblance to sapphire – so much so that the men who first spotted benitoite mistook it for its considerable resemblance. It may also be confused with azurite. San Benito is the unique deposit site and contains only very small crystals. Much sought-after by collectors.

Brazilianite

Once more, a name related to the original discovery site. Available colors are yellow and greenish yellow. At times, it may be mistaken for beryl, chrysoberyl or topaz. Besides Brazil, deposits are also found in the United States.

Bytownite

A feldspar dubbed for Bytown, the old name for Ottawa, capital of Canada. Labradorescence is the key identifying quality, and it may be had in yellow or varying shades of red. The stone's provenance is Canada and the United States.

Cassiterite

A term from the Greek *kassiteros* (tin), as it contains a proportion of this metal, which inspired its English name "tin stone." Usually the material has a blackish cast owing to iron impurities, but it may also be mined in brown, reddish brown, yellow, or even a colorless variety with an adamantine sheen.

Often confused with zircon, it may also be mistaken for the diamond; and, in effect, its artificial production was originally intended as diamond imitation. However, since it has a very high specific gravity at 6.95, it is easily identified when examined. Sources are: Australia, Bolivia, Germany, Indonesia, Malaysia, Mexico, Namibia, Spain, and the United States.

Celestite

As the first crystals found were in a celestial blue tone, the gem took its name accordingly, though it may also be quite colorless, yellowish, or – more rarely – a bright orange.

Being rather soft, it has little use in the jeweler's trade.

Considered a choice purchase by collectors.

Mines are in Canada, Egypt, England, Italy, Namibia, the United States, South Africa, and Switzerland.

Chrysocolla

Its gold streaking gained its Greek name *chrysos*, for gold.

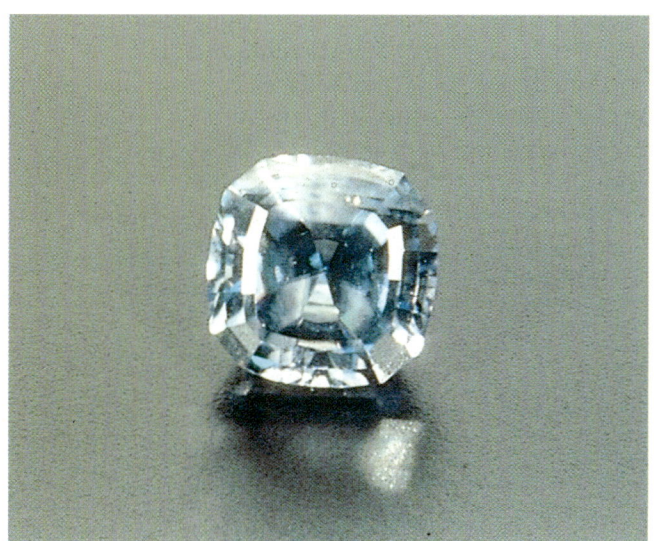

Benitoite.

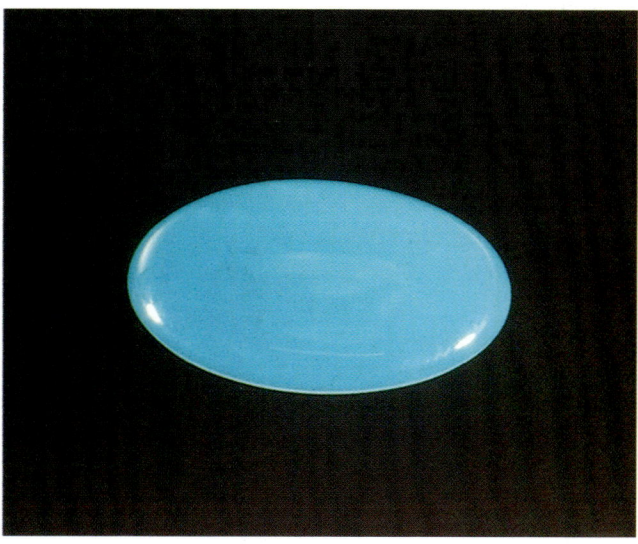

Mexican chrysocolla.

Base shades are blue, greenish blue, and green.

As the blue variety purportedly develops a clear, bell-like voice it is considered ideal for singers; some say it also conquers stress. Often confused with opal, blue chalcedony, and turquoise. For sources we can look to Chile, Russia, the United States and Zaire.

The best known variety is the Elat Stone, extracted near Elat, Israel. A mixture of chrysocolla, turquoise and malachite, it is usually cut en cabochon; alive with streaking, its base color ranges from blue to green.

Cornerupine

Named in tribute to the Danish geologist A.N. Kornerup, it is sometimes spelled with a *k*. Though colorless specimens have been found the mineral is usually mined in brown, yellow, green, or brownish green.

Standard examples are easily confused with enstatite and tourmaline; in addition, there are less frequent findings of a chatoyant variety and, more rarely, of a stone presenting asterism.

Deposits are located in Greenland (where it was first found), Kenya (where a strong green color suitable for faceting is mined), Madagascar, Myanmar, Sri Lanka, Tanzania.

Danburite

First found in Danbury, Connecticut, whence its name; it is often colorless, but also available in brown, a pale yellow, or – quite rarely – even pink.

At times it may be mistaken for quartz or topaz, though there may also be some confusion with andalusite and tourmaline.

Deposits in Japan, Madagascar, Mexico, Myanmar, and the United States.

Datolite

In Greek *datéomai* stands for "to divide," a reference to the grainy look of many samples. A list of tonalities includes: colorless, pale green, yellowish, orangish brown, pink.

Datolite with a granular appearance is cut en cabochon, whereas the transparent variety is faceted, for it is considered a quite valuable collector's piece.

Chief deposits are located in Australia, Austria, Canada, Germany, England, Italy, Mexico, Norway.

Diopside

Coming to us from the Greek term meaning "dual appearance," directly linked to a particular type of crystallization. Rarely colorless, it is more commonly found in a brownish hue, in violet, yellow, light green, black, and – most frequently – bottle green. One high chromium content variety comes in a strong emerald green and is labelled *chrome diopside*: "Violano," another variety, is named in recognition of its dark purplish blue tonality. A cat's eye effect is present in a number of varieties, and is quite marked in a green type mined in Myanmar (Stone Tract). In 1964 a new variety appeared on the market: diopside examples in a brownish, almost black hue, with asterism in the form of a glinting four-pointed star.

Remember that asterism in corundums displays six rays.

In addition to hiddenite, this stone may also be confused with olivine, emerald, and vesuvian.

Diopside with an asterism is advised for those who must undertake a dangerous voyage, though it is also believed a resource for people forced to make difficult choices. It has a range of therapeutic properties: containing both calcium and magnesium, it will strengthen the wearer's bones; it stimulates heart tone, tranquilizes the nervous system and intensifies the curative power of antibodies.

Beyond those deposits already cited, we may look for sources in Austria, Brazil, Canada, India, Italy, Madagascar, Russia, Sri Lanka, the United States, and South Africa.

Dioptase

Credited to the Greek *dia* and *optasia*, meaning "seeing through." Mined in a bright green, the stone is often highly transparent, and such specimens are subjected to facet cutting. However, it is a fairly soft stone, with an overly saturated color and is not very important in jewelry making; though it is highly rated by collectors.

May be taken for emerald, diopside, and peridot.

Mine locations are in Chile, Kazakistan, Namibia, the United States, and Zaire.

Dolomite

A mineral labelled in honor of geologist and mineralogist Dèodat-Guy de Dolomieu. Most prevalently mined as a colorless variety, it may occasionally contain light pink or yellow shadings.

In the Dolomite Mountains of Italy this mineral is the basic building block.

Dolomite rock, also referred to as "dolomite marble" is used to create objects ranging from the artistic to the useful, small handcrafted products.

Look for deposits in Austria, Brazil, Spain, the United States, and Switzerland.

Dumortierite

Coined in tribute to the French paleontologist Eugène Dumortier, most prevalent hues are blue and violet, but specimens in green and brown have also been encountered; a brownish red crystal has been found in Sri Lanka, and is now facet cut.

A gem that may be confused with azurite, lapis lazuli and sodalite.

Main sources are in: Canada, France, Madagascar, Norway, and the United States.

Enstatite

Highly flame resistant, it is intractable to the fusion process and so borrows its name from the Greek *enstates*, or "opposer." It may be found in green, brownish green or gray (the latter color evidencing a fine chatoyant effect when cut en cabochon); there is also a variety of enstatite which displays a six-point asterism.

The *blue ground* of African mines is fertile territory for a mating of diamonds and a stunning green enstatite. It may be confused with cornerupine.

Best-known sources are in India, Myanmar, Sri Lanka, and South Africa.

Epidote

In addition to epidote, the group of epidotes is composed of *allanite, clinozoisite, piedmontite, tawmawite*, and *zoisite*, whose importance merits the separate discussion we have dedicated to it.

Without a doubt, the origin of the term lies in the Greek *epidosis*, signifying "increase." But what sort of increase is intended? Some interpret it in terms of the crystal's unusually large number of facets; others insist that "increase" points out an imbalanced growth along one side of the crystal.

A brownish green gem with marked pleochroism and a fine sheen.

Allanite is brownish red, but clinozoisite is an opaque dark red, and tawmawite comes in deep green.

For this gem we have a truly long list of countries of provenance: Austria, Brazil, Finland, France, Italy, Kenya, Mexico, Myanmar, Norway, the Czech Republic, the United States, Switzerland, Zimbabwe (most interesting gemmological production).

Euclase

Adopted from the Greek *eu* and *clasis*, standing for "good break," its ease of cleavage unfortunately also makes cutting quite a difficult operation. Even if there are occasional colorless specimens, the stone is more commonly found in azure, blue, light yellow, greenish yellow, and sea green.

Euclase may be mistaken for green spodumene, hiddenite, sillimanite, blue topaz, or – in the case of a specific material mined in Zimbabwe – with sapphire.

Collectors rate this gem very highly.

Besides the deposits in Zimbabwe already mentioned, additional sources are located in Brazil, Colombia, Russia, and Tanzania.

Fibrolite

A variety of *sillimanite*, often used as alternate designation. Fibrolite comes in sapphire blue, bluish green and grayish green; in the latter two shades a chatoyant phenomenon is occasionally present. It is a gem that can be mistaken for jadeite.

Sources are located in Myanmar, Sri Lanka, and the United States.

Gypsum

Mohs selected this mineral to represent number 2 on his hardness index; it is found in both transparent and opaque varieties.

In rock form it is known as gypseous alabaster and is employed in the manufacture of artistic and ornamental objects. Alabaster has been known from the time of the ancient Phoenician, Assyrian and Eyptian civilizations; vases made of this material were unearthed in the tomb of King Tutankhamen.

The presence of iron oxide impurities frequently produces orange or lightish brown veinings. North African mines often contain a special reddish aggregate dubbed "the desert rose." In general, alabaster is found in many locations, but is especially abundant in the area of Volterra, Italy.

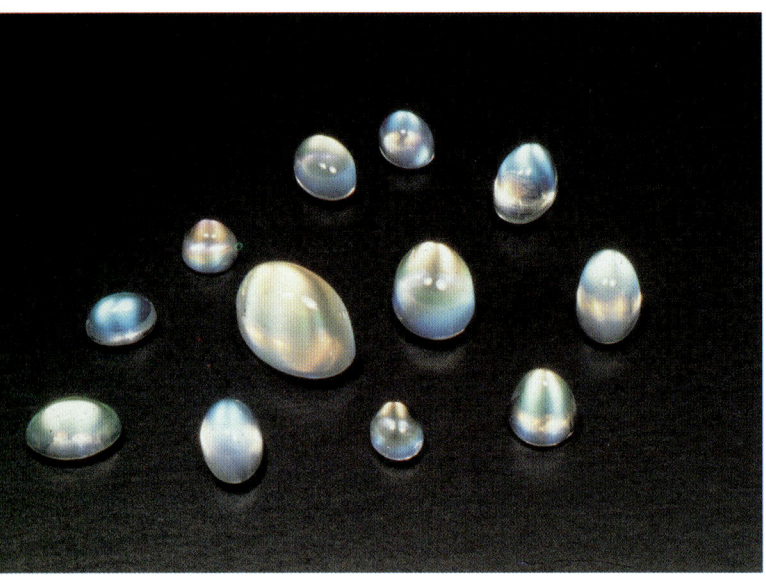

Labradorite

Labradorite

A feldspar named after the Labrador Peninsula in Canada, where it was first discovered in 1770. This mineral presents an appealing play of light on a dark gray ground; green and blue light reflections are the most popular; but the most prized specimens are those which give off the largest number of visible field colors. This optical phenomenon has been entitled "labradorescence." Among the different varieties there exists a very dark sort which can display a cat's eye phenomenon and is – quite improperly – defined as "black moonstone."

Labrador is believed to endow its wearer with seductive allure; moreover, it is claimed that the mineral has a tranquilizing effect on the nervous system. Sources for labrador are located in Canada, Finland (provenance of a material termed *spectrolite*), Australia (fount of a colorless or yellow material that can be faceted), Madagascar, Mexico, Russia, and the United States.

Lazulite

Credited to the Perisan word for blue, *lazuard*. Available in various blue tonalities with marked pleochroism; the rock variety often contains white spotting.

May be confused with azurite, lapis lazuli, sodalite, or turquoise.

There are deposits in Angola, Austria, Brazil, India, Madagascar, and Sweden.

Marcasite

Though it has the same chemical composition as pyrite, it crystallizes with different habit, and has a brassy yellow coloring.

Ancient Greeks and fabled Incas made fine use of this material, but its true burst of fame did not arrive till halfway through the eighteenth century.

In current fashion, you will find it in a round cut, with a flat base and a low crown in six facets, like the rose cut; in this form it is adopted for costume jewelry or as an ornament in silver objects.

Deposits may be found throughout the world.

Moldavite

Belonging to the group of tektites, moldavite is a distinct natural glass of meteoric origin. Despite various explanations offered, the most accredited theory is that this glass was formed as a consequence of the impact of meteorites falling to earth. Its name traces to the location where it was first found, an area near the Moldava River in the Czech Republic.

Most frequently encountered colors are: green, brown, and greenish brown; all specimens present a pitted surface.

This gem may be confused with artificial glass, diopside or olivine. On examination it reveals concoidal fractures typical of glass.

Moonstone or Adularia

Adula, in tribute to the homonymous Swiss Mountain, belongs to the feldspar group of minerals, and though often colorless it is also found in pink, yellow and light green.

Oriental fortune-tellers were wont to hold one of these stones in their mouths whenever they had to divine the future on a night with a full moon.

This evanescent gem was recommended to women in labor, seafarers, and anyone with a fickle humor; it was also assumed to improve family relationships.

Internal interference creates a light phenomenon suited to en cabochon cut, which will emphasize a surface gleam with bluish white or silvery white reflections. If this phenomenon is not strongly marked, the gem may look opaline; however this latter optical effect is actually an "adulescence," referring to the mineral.

Because of these suggestive milky white gleams

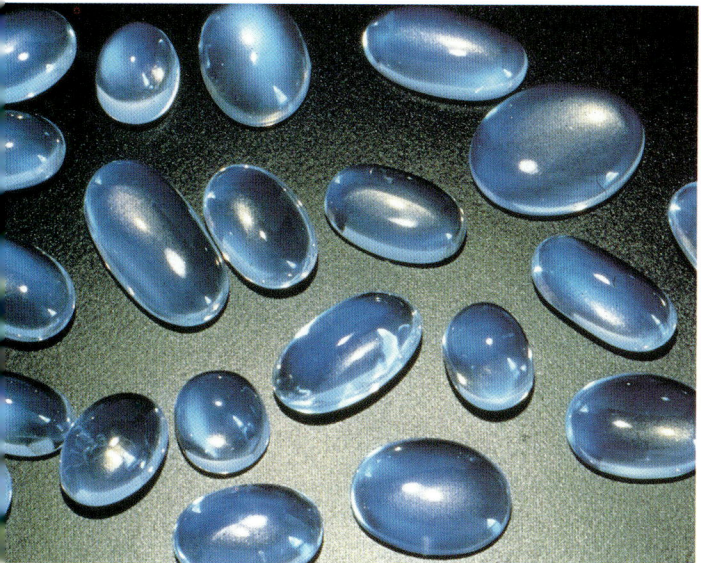

Moonstones.

the gem is often sold under the label "moonstone."

An interesting imitation is produced by heating a colorless synthetic spinel, a treatment resulting in an emulsive white surface; however even milk glass is used as counterfeit.

Sri Lanka contains the most important deposits; others are found in Australia, Brazil, India, Madagascar, Myanmar, Tanzania, and the United States.

Obsidian

A volcanic glass, this is a perfectly natural product as it is a rock with a high silicious content formed by rapid cooling. Usually found in gray or black, it has a fine golden or silvery iridescence owing to the many inclusions of air bubbles. An additional variety is called *flowering obsidian* or *snowflake obsidian* for its white spotting. Reputedly some transparent specimens have been found in a grass green shade. Obsidian may be taken for opals or artificial black glass, and it presents conchoidal fractures typical of glass.

Ancient Egyptians believed that obsidian carved as a scarab acted as a potent talisman; and so rings of these precious objects were placed on the fingers of the dead as guarantee of another life to come.

Many hold that this mineral eliminates intestinal inflammation and claim it is a great help for highly emotional and sensitive personalities as it induces calm and reflection.

Our best known deposits are in Ecuador, Mexico, and the United States, though the mineral may be encountered in any area containing active or even extinct volcanoes.

Operculum

This is a designation attributed to a type of marine gastropod.

Many thousands of years ago, this material was put to use in oriental countries where it was believed that the substance could prevent eye disease.

Operculum looks a bit like porcelain, has an almost spiralform structure and is found in orangish yellow with white streaking. Even today it is still commonly used in areas of Australia and Asia, and is labelled "Chinese cat's eye" or "seashell cat's eye."

Pectolite

Since its crystals appear quite compact, it was given the Greek name for that quality, *péktos*. It may be found in grayish white, green or blue; but in the last two instances, the material also presents multicolored shadings. The pectolite variety discovered in the Dominican Republic in 1974 in the Sierra de Baoruco area is called *larimar*. It may be mistaken for turquoise, chrysocolla, and jade.

In addition to the above cited Canadian sources, there are also deposits in the United States.

Phenacite

Phénax is the Greek word for trickster, since this mineral is easily mistaken for hyaline quartz. Various colors are on the market: it is colorless, but also light yellow, brownish, pink, and (rarely) greenish blue.

Besides its similarity to quartz, it may also be taken for euclase, spodumene, and topaz.

The largest known faceted specimen weighs 569 carats, having been cut out of a 1470-carat raw mass; it is in a pleasant oval shape, but, unfortunately, has so many needlelike inclusions that its transparency is greatly reduced. At times these needle inclusions can create a slight cat's eye effect.

Phenacite may be synthetically produced; in fact, finely shaped crystals can be observed in synthetic emeralds.

Look for deposits in Brazil, France, Mexico, Namibia, Rhodesia, Russia, the United States, Switzerland, and Tanzania.

Pollucite

First discovered on the Isle of Elba later, in 1846, it was found in association with another mineral; together they were named "Castor and Pollux," after Helen of Troy's twin sons. After a while, in mineralogy, the word "pollux" smoothed off into "pollucite"; meanwhile, it was learned that castor had previously been found and labelled as "petalite," its most common name. Colorless, white, gray, and blue are the known colors for this mineral.

For deposits, turn to the United States or Sweden.

Prehnite

From the name of its discoverer, the Dutch Hendrik van Prehn.

Chief colors are brown, brownish yellow and yellowish green.

Translucent specimens, cut en cabochon, occasionally display a chatoyant effect.

Prehnite may be confused with chrysoprase, jade, and olivine.

Sources for this gem are: Australia, Canada, China, France, the United States, and South Africa (where it was first found).

Rhodonite

Comes from the Greek *rhodon*, for "rose"; generally found in compact translucent or opaque masses, rarely in crystals. Due to its very deep pink color and black veining it is quite a striking gem.

Usually it is cut en cabochon, but it may also be employed to produce artistic carved objects, or just simple boxes or ashtrays.

The variety called *bistamite* may display a cat's eye ray.

Rhodonite is easily confused with the name and qualities of rhodochrosite, and it is at times also taken for pink hydrogrossularite.

Sources are identified in Australia, Canada, Mexico, Russia, South Africa and Sweden.

Sapphirine

Since the first specimens ever unearthed bore a strong resemblance to sapphire, the gem was

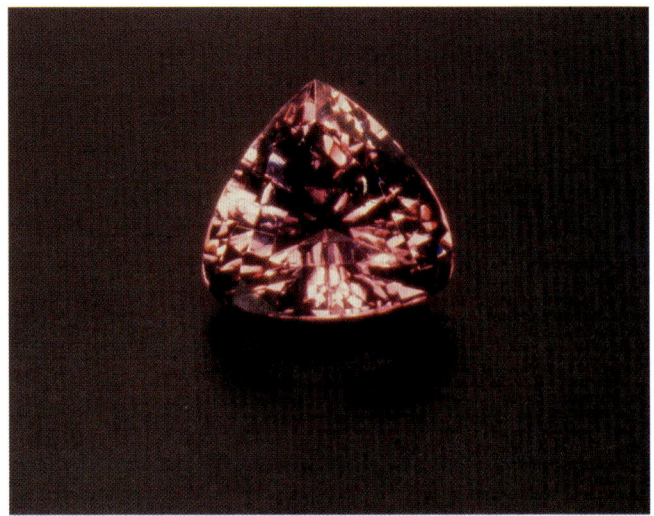

Scapolite.

ultimately given this nickname; along with this blue sapphire shade, it is also available in a greenish or even pinkish brown hue.

Only 25% of material mined is suitable for cutting.

For deposits, we may look to Australia, Canada, Madagascar, or Sri Lanka.

Scapolite

The Greek *scaps* (to dig) gave the stone its name; first discovered in 1913, it has various gemmological uses, and is also known as *wernerite*. Its color range runs from blue, to yellow, pink, or violet; however, colorless specimens have also been brought to light. And the transparent pink variety when cut en cabochon displays a chatoyant phenomenon.

The stone may be confused with amblygonite, yellow beryl, cordierite and chrysoberyl.

Brazil, Kenya, Madagascar, Myanmar, Namibia, and Tanzania have deposits.

Sepiolite or Meerschaum

Since it looks quite a bit like the bone of the cuttlefish ("osso di seppia" in Italian), and is so porous it floats, it is often referred to as "sepiolite."

Meerschaum (or sepiolite) pipes are famous, though the material is also put to good use for ornamental objects.

Deposits are in Greece, the Czech Republic, Somalia, Spain, the United States, and Turkey (Anatolia).

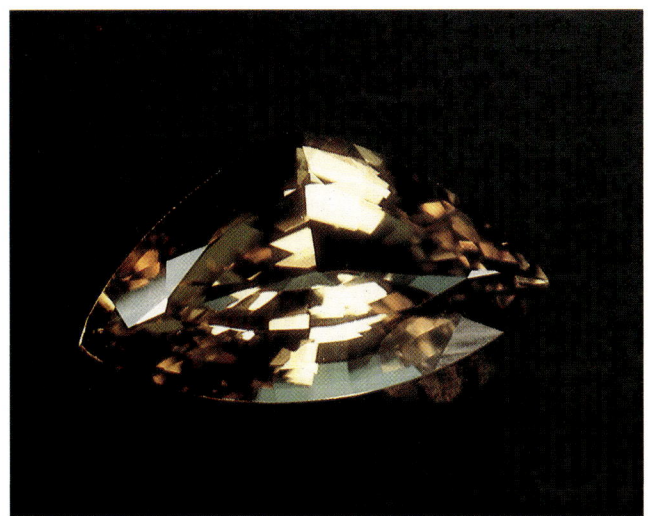

Sinhalite.

Sinhalite

In Sanskrit *sinhala* stands for the land of Sri Lanka, site of many deposits. The gem comes in golden brown, yellowish brown, greenish brown, or an almost totally black tonality. Easily confused with chrysoberyl, zircon, or olivine; and, in fact, until 1952 it was considered an olivine variety rather than a separate mineral.

Known deposits are in Sri Lanka, Myanmar and the United States.

Sodalite

It owes its name to sodium material in its chemical composition. Found in blue, grayish blue, or purplish blue, sodalite has the appearance of an opaque rock. Idoneous specimens are cut en cabochon; examples suitable for inlay are simply sold as "blue stone." It is said to induce restful sleep if you remember to place a specimen of the material on your night table; in cone or pyramid shape it stimulates creative thought. In crystallotherapy sodalite is used as kidney adjuvant. Meanwhile, oriental folk medicine affirms its power to maintain a balance between male and female energies, *yin* and *yang*.

Though lacking the velvety blue tone of lapis lazuli, it has been mistaken for the latter, as it is one of its components. Remember that pyrite sparkles are much more pronounced in lapis lazuli than in sodalite. For decisive identification, lapis lazuli has a much higher specific density.

The material can be also be confused with azurite, dumortierite, and lazulite.

Deposits are in Brazil, Canada, India, and Namibia.

Sunstone or Oligoclase

A feldspar identified by the Greek terms *oligos* and *klasis*, to indicate great difficulty in cleavage.

The variety employed as a gem is categorized as *sunstone*, referring to its brilliant metallic gleam. Red tints are the most common extraction, but there are also, more rarely, blue and green varieties. It may be mistaken for aventurine, (a special type of glass produced by chance in 1700), or with aventurine quartz. Canada, India, Norway and Russia have deposits of this mineral.

Taaffeite

An exceedingly rare mineral, its name is a credit to

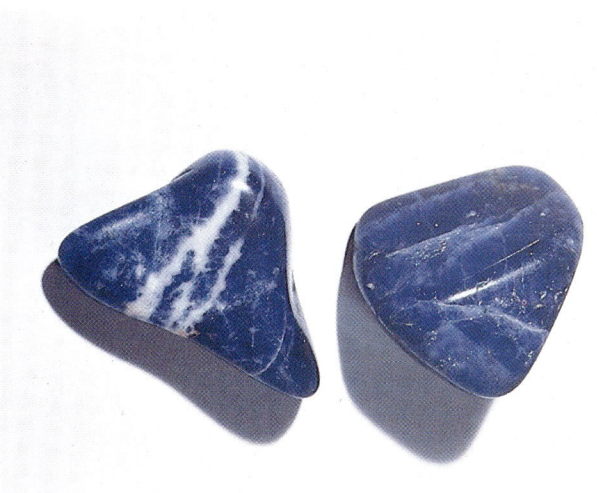

Sodalite.

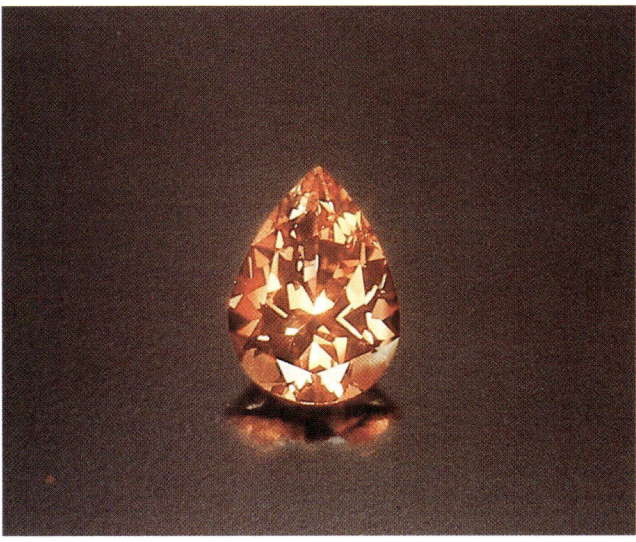

Sunstone from Ponderosa mines.

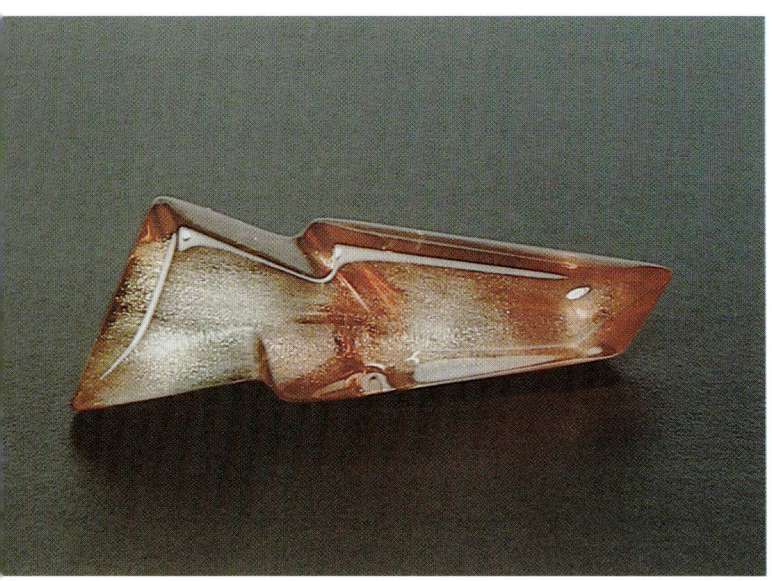

BART CURREN.
Carved sunstone. The rough stone comes from the Ponderosa mines in Oregon, USA.

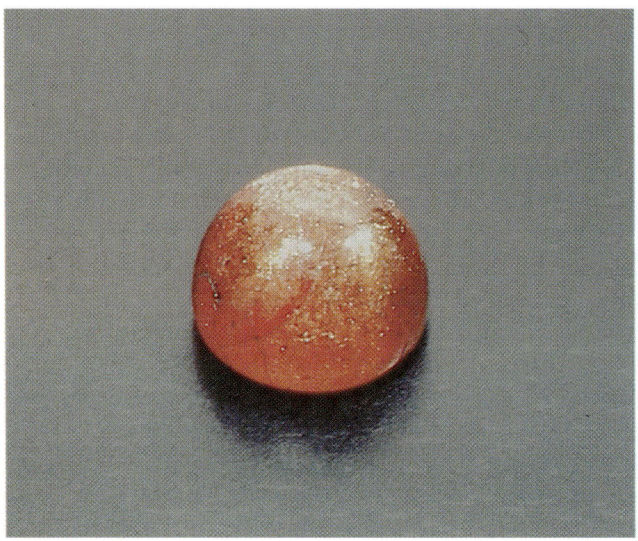

Sunstone with cabochon cut.

Count Taaffe of Dublin who came upon a cut example of this hitherto unknown gem in a jewelry shop in 1945.

Following a fairly complex process of analysis, its chemical composition was determined and it is officially classified as indicated.

Aside from the 1.42-carat mauve stone first noted by Count Taaffe, the only other examples discovered so far have been a 0.89-carat stone in Sri Lanka in 1949, another crystal in 1957, and in 1969 a fine brownish purple 5.30-carat example.

Later some isolated stones came to light in colors going from blue, to gray, pale pink, red, and reddish violet.

Finally in 1982 a number of crystals were discovered simultaneously, all in Sri Lanka; nevertheless, this gem remains a great rarity, especially for examples of more than 10 carats.

Quite recently a really large taafeite at 12.47 carats was put on sale in an important auction, and the established starting bid was 36,000 U.S. dollars.

Obviously, the gem is greatly prized by the most important collectors. Our only known sources have been Myanmar and Sri Lanka.

Vesuvian

Its name alludes to the volcano Vesuvius, near Naples in southern Italy; a second name is *vesuvianite*, and a third *hydrocrase*. It may be on offer in green, yellow, or a bluish brown hue.

Among its most noted varieties are: *californite*, a green rock material that can be mistaken for jade; a blue *cyprine*, so labelled for the island of Cyprus where it was mined in antiquity. It may be taken for demantoid, diopside, epidote, olivine, smoky quartz, tourmaline, zircon, or zoisite.

However rare, there have been specimens evidencing asterism, aventurine spangling or a cat's eye phenomenon.

A list of deposit sites includes: Austria, Canada, Italy, Norway (chief current source for cyprine), Pakistan, Russia, the United States and Switzerland.

Wardite

This term is tribute to H.A. Ward, the American collector and naturalist. A bluish green concretion, the stone has been sometimes used to imitate turquoise. Mines are located in Utah, in the United States.

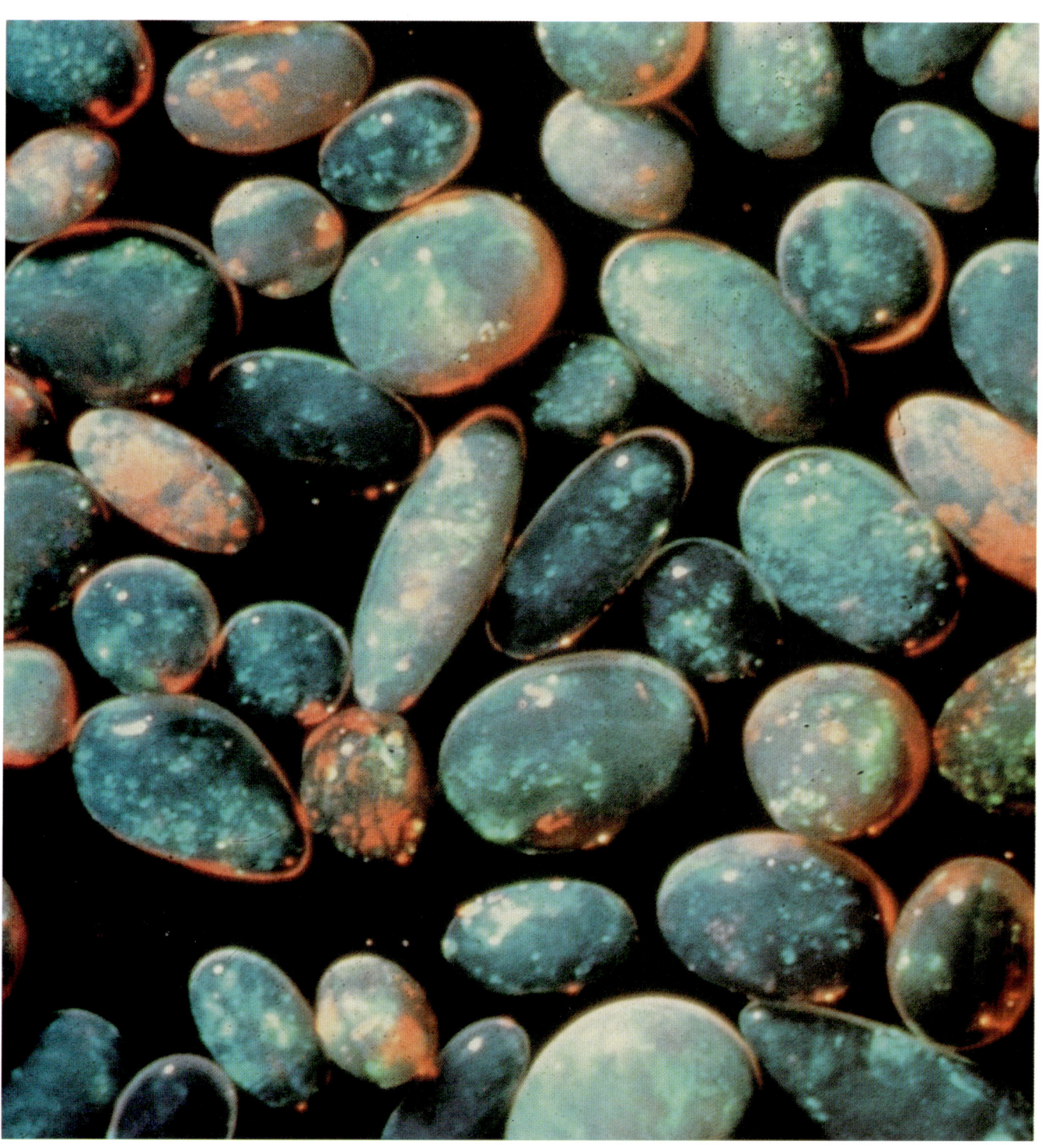

Glossary

Adularescence. The silvery white and bluish white reflections with a deep glowing luster that we see in adularia (also called "moonstone").

Allochromatic. Describes a mineral whose coloring depends on the presence of one or more elements defined as chromophores, impurity on the atomic level, which imparts color. For example, pure corundum is quite colorless: the presence of chromium atoms introduces a red shade (thus producing a ruby); while iron and titanium atoms create a blue sapphire. A list of other allochromatic minerals includes beryl, quartz, spinel, and tourmaline.

Amorphous. A greek term signifying lack of definite form. All substances whose particles are chaotic – not arranged, like crystals, with some degree of regularity – are called amorphous. Glass is a classic example.

Anisotropic. Materials whose physical properties depend on the direction of the crystal; crystals from Group II (also called dimetric) and from Group III (trimetric) are anisotropic.

Artificial product. Referring to gems: a man-made product intended as ornamental stone resembling those natural gems spontaneously formed in deposits.

Asterism. An optical phenomenon observed on the surface of a stone evoking the effect of a four to six-point star on a stone's surface. Caused by the presence of needle-shaped inclusions, it is strikingly apparent in en cabochon cuts (*see* Cabochon), when viewed in the crystal's direction.

Atom. Every chemical element is characterized by whole particles, defined as atoms, which are different for every element.

Atomic number. Qualifying number for every chemical element; it corresponds to the number of protons in an atomic nucleus.

Aventurine. This refers to the glittering spangles on a mineral surface created by miniscule foliated inclusions present in aventurine quartz, and oligoclase or sunstone.

Bern cut: May be square or rectangular; the angles of the girdle may be plane cut or not; however, all the crown and pavilion facets must be parallel to the girdle (*see* Girdle).

Biaxial. *See* Optical Axis *or* Biaxiality.

Biaxiality. Refers to crystals of Group III which are birefringent but offer two particular monorefringent directions, indicated as optical axes.

Birefringence. Phenomenon observed in Group II (uniaxial) and Group III crystals (biaxial) – excluding direction of the optical axes – when there is a refraction phenomenon that actually gives rise to two refracted rays. This birefringence produces an "ordinary" and an "extraordinary" ray which are polarized and exhibit differing velocities within the stone. Crystals containing such birefringence are optically anisotropic (*see* Anisotropic).

Birefringent. *See above.*

Brazilian cut: May come in different shapes: rectangular with curved sides; oval, or round. Crown and pavilion have a lozenge-shaped faceting which increases the stone's brilliance.

Brilliance. A major quality which is determined by the sum effects of reflection, refraction and dispersion in a faceted stone seen in clear white light.

Brilliant cut: Typical for diamonds, the brilliant cut in general may have a round or oval shape. In order to exploit brilliance to the maximum, specific proportions must be observed in the cutting. At times the term "brilliant" will be mistakenly used as synonym for a diamond: actually, such a usage is acceptable when we are dealing with 33 facets on the crown and 25 on the pavilion, including the base cut and the table cut, which is the largest of the facets.

Briolette cut. Term uniquely employed to denote a pear or drop-shaped diamond with innumerable tiny facets covering the surface which greatly increase the stone's brilliance.

Cabochon. A special cut producing a domed top and a convex, concave or flat base. The finished shape may be oval or round.

Chatoyant. An effect very similar to rays gleaming in the pupil of a cat's eye appears on the surface of certain gems observed under full light. This phenomenon is emphasized by an en cabochon cut and is the result of a dense, parallel arrangement of certain inclusions (needle, tubular cavity, filament). Though we can find the same phenomenon in other materials, quartz is surely the mineral identified with this effect, to the point that varying plays of light perceived in quartz have come to be identified as bull's eye, falcon's eye, and tiger's eye. In chrysoberyls this phenomenon is so famous that it is common to say "cat's eye" without naming the mineral.

Chemical element. Substance composed of a single chemical type with characteristic and distinctive properties. Each chemical element has a different atomic number.

Chemical formula. Every substance can be expressed by

the symbols for the atoms that form its molecule, determined according to precise and constant whole quantity relationships.

Chromophore. *See* Allochromatic.

Cleavage. This is a split that leaves the surface of a solid substance flat and regular, in contrast to fracture (*See entry*).

Composite stone. Doppiette (*see entry*) and triplette (*see entry*) gem fakes: the double and triple-layer technique in imitation.

Crown. Upper part of a stone: precisely, the area between girdle (*see entry*) and table (*see entry*), it may be either faceted or bern.

Cryptocrystalline. A particular structure formed of very fine crystals. Certain quartzes, such as chalcedony, are an example.

Crystal. When particles forming a substance are arranged in a precise, constant and definite order, the substance is a crystal. For a mineralogical crystal species, the aspect, or shape, is generally respected.

Crystalline group. All crystals are classified in one of three distinct groups: Group I (monometric), Group II (dimetric), and Group III (trimetric); these, in turn, are subdivided into seven systems in all.

Cut. An astonishing variety of cuts are available, all designed to make the most of a stone.

Dendritic. Branchlike in appearance.

Density. Result of the relationship between a body's weight and its volume; expressed in grams per cubic centimeter.

Dichroism. Such an effect is present in Crystal Group II (uniaxial) in both transparent and colored stones. Observed in different crystal directions, these gems display two different color shadings.

Dispersion. Phenomenon in which a single ray of white light crossing a particular medium is separated into the seven basic colors (red, orange, yellow, green, blue, indigo, violet).

Doppiette. A "constructed" stone made of two parts of the same or different material glued together.

Electron. Elementary particle, having a negative electric charge, contained in an atom.

Emerald cut. This is the same as a bern cut (*see entry*), but has come into use since the bern is an emerald's typical cut.

Fire. A sparkling effect of light and flashes of color glinting off a stone's facetings, caused by light dispersion within the stone itself. The term is most often applied to faceted diamonds.

Fluorescence. Emission of light occurring when a substance is subjected to ultraviolet rays (either short wavelength at 253.7 nm or long wavelength at 366 nm), or to X-rays; the phenomenon disappears when the substance is no longer exposed.

Fracture. We speak of fractures when the separation surface of a solid body is irregular in contrast, (*see* Cleavage). Fracture is typical of glass and is defined as conchoidal, for it looks almost as smooth and curved as the valve of a seashell. Jade, on the other hand, has a decidedly chipped fracture.

Fragility. The tendency in a substance to fracture or split when worked with mechanical techniques. Extremely hard materials are usually very brittle; diamonds, the hardest of all minerals, do have a significant fragility.

Gamma rays. Electromagnetic radiations similar to X-rays, but with a shorter wavelength. Such particles may be produced by particle accelerators.

Girdle. Periphery at the widest part of a stone, dividing the upper from the lower zone.

Grain. One-fourth of a carat. This unit of weight was widely used in the past. Today, however, the carat is the only referent.

Hardness. Degree of a mineral's resistance to chipping and scratching.

Harlequin. An image-rich term to describe the noble opal's fantastic play of light.

Idiochromatic. Refers to a mineral whose coloring depends on the presence of atoms that are an integral part of its composition (as expressed by chemical formula). Garnet, malachite, olivine and turquoise are examples of idiochromatic minerals.

Imitation. A substance which resembles a more valuable material in appearance only. A clear example would be a piece of green glass used to substitute an emerald.

Inclusions. Foreign substances within a mineral; they may be solid, liquid or gas. It is important to study inclusions since they may identify a mineral type or distinguish a natural product from a synthetic one.

Inorganic. Not belonging to organic chemistry.

Iridescence. A lustrous, rainbowlike play of colors.

Isotropic. Alludes to a material whose physical properties have the same values when measured along axes in all directions. For example, crystals from Crystalline Group I exhibit the same properties in all directions under optical examination (same refractive index). Glass behaves in the same way and is also isotropic.

Labradorescence. Indicates the play of metallic green and blue lights visible in a number of stones, labradorite for one, the source of this term.

Lens. A very simple optical instrument that is quite easy to use; a 10x lens (ten magnifications) is employed in the jeweler's craft. It is convergent and produces a virtual image, enlarged and direct when the stone under observation is placed exactly between the lens and the source of light.

Light. Electric and magnetic energy (or electromagnetic) capable of travelling through space, vibrating on all planes situated perpendicularly to the direction of light-ray source. Thanks to this energy we are able to see our surroundings. All optical phenomena are contingent on light.

Luminescence. By this term we refer to the phenomenon in which a mineral emits visible light when it is exposed to certain types of radiation. Resulting effects are fluorescence and phosphorescence (*see* Glossary *for both items*).

Luster. Corresponds to the quantity and the quality of reflected light and depends on a mineral's refractive index, hardness, and the technique used in polishing. We may observe a high luster (adamantine in diamonds, subadamantine in almandine, metallic in pyrite); medium (vitreous in transparent gems in general, subvitreous in the opal) or low (greasy in the nephrite, waxy for coral, and resinous in amber).

Medium. This generic term is employed in physics to designate a body through which a given phenomenon passes.

Metric Carat. International unit of weight adopted for gems, corresponding to 1/5 of a gram; its symbol is *ct.*

Mineral. Substance whose chemical composition is generally homogeneous in all of its parts.

Mixed cut. One cut for a stone's upper section and another for the lower: the crown may be faceted in a brilliant cut with the pavilion in a step cut, or vice versa.

Mohs Scale. In gemmology, as in mineralogy, hardness is indexed on an empirical scale (not belonging to the decimal metric system) composed of a series of ten minerals ranged in ascending order: 1- talc or graphite; 2- gypsum; 3- calcite; 4- fluorite; 5- apatite; 6- orthoclase; 7- quartz; 8- topaz; 9- corundum; 10- diamond. The scale was invented by the mineralogist F. Mohs to whom it owes its name.

Molecule. Within any substance, the smallest constituent part.

Momme. Unit of measure for weighing cultured pearls used in Japan, it corresponds to 3.75 g and 18.75 ct.

Monochromatic light. Term used to designate light composed of a single wavelength and, therefore, of a single basic color.

Monorefringence. A particularity of metals in Crystalline Group I (monometric) and to non-crystallized, and therefore amorphous substances. As these materials contain a single refracted ray and are optically isotropic, they are called monorefringent.

Monorefringent. (*See above*)

Neutron. Uncharged sub-atomic particle contained in an atomic nucleus.

Opalescence. Describes the iridescence of the common opal.

Opaque. (*See* Transparence)

Optical axis. The direction along which a birefringent crystal (i.e. either from Group II or III) behaves like a mono-refringent crystal (i.e. from Group I). Hexagonal, trigonal and, tetragonal crystals (Group II) have only one optical axis and are defined as uniaxial; rhombic, monoclinic, and triclinic crystals (GroupIII) have two axes and are defined as biaxial.

Organic. Describes any chemical compound belonging to carbon chemistry. Amber, coral and pearls are examples of organic substances.

Orient. Refers to that particular play of light found in pearls as result of internal reflection and iridescence.

Pavilion. The lower part of a stone, extending from the girdle to the base; it may be cut in facets or steps.

Phosphorescence. A light emitted from a substance when it is exposed to special radiation. Such emission may last for a period of time even after radiation is over.

Pincers. Tiny tweezers adopted to hold precious gems when they are held under a 10x magnifying lens for observation.

Plastic. Term denoting all artificial organic materials similar to resins.

Pleochroism. Terminology generically adopted to indicate dichroism (*see entry*) and trichroism (*see entry*). This phenomenon is typical of transparent gems and colored gems from Crystalline Group II (dimetric) and Group III (trimetric), birefringent crystals.

Polarized light. Light which diffuses in space vibrating on a single plane. When double refraction (or birefringence) occurs the two refracted rays are polarized on a plane lying perpendicular to them.

Proton. Positively charged subatomic particle, contained in the atomic nucleus.

Radioactive decay. Either spontaneous or provoked emission of subatomic or electromagnetic particles by an atomic nucleus.

Radioactive. Alluding to any unstable atom which, emittng particles or radiation, changes into another atom.

Reflection. Optical phenomenon occurring when a light ray (called an "incident ray") moving through the air (the prime medium) meets a flat-surfaced body having a greater optical specific gravity; an example of the latter might be a mineral, in this case referred to as second medium. A part of the incident ray's light energy is returned off the surface and passes through the air, according to specific optical laws, so producing what is called a "reflected ray" and consequently the reflection phenomenon per se (*see also* Refraction).

Refraction. An optical-physical phenomenon that takes place when a light ray passes through an air medium and hits another medium that has a different optical specific gravity - a mineral, for example. Generally a part of the ray's light energy is reflected (*see* Reflection) and the remaining part enters into the second medium (in this case, the mineral), undergoing a deviation in respect to the incident ray. The term refraction stands for this deviation of the ray.

Refractive index. Corresponds to a number signifying the refringent capacity of a specific substance. In reality it furnishes the relationship between speed of light through the air and speed of light in a material under observation. An easy-to-use optical instrument, the refractometer is a tool for

specific evaluation; for each refracted ray we obtain a refractive index, which can be of fundamental importance for gemmological analysis aimed at defining a material in question.

Resistance. Quality of hardness in a solid body: its capacity to withstand an opposing force without shattering or breaking.

Rock. An aggregate of various minerals, it is chemically heterogeneous.

Synthesis. Process by which we obtain a synthetic mineral.

Synthetic stone. Man-made material produced in the laboratory and subsequently cut. It has the same chemical composition and the same optical-physical data as the corresponding natural stone. Obviously, it is not always easy to distinguish between synthetic and natural stones.

Table. The upper flat surface of a cut stone.

Total reflection. Optical phenomenon in which an incident ray does not undergo refraction but – solely and uniquely – reflection. For diamonds, total internal reflection of a faceted stone is indispensable if we wish to display a stone's maximum brilliance.

Translucent. *See* Transparence.

Transparence. Refers to a substance's capacity to let light pass through it. A material is transparent when objects placed behind it are clearly visible; translucent when only the outlien of objects can be seen due to diffusion of the light; opaque when objects cannot be seen because the medium is impervious to rays the light.

Transparent. *See* Transparence.

Trichroism. An effect present in both transparent and colored stones belonging to Crystalline Group III (biaxial). In gems of this type, if pleochroism (*see entry*) is notable, we may observe as many as three tonalities of different colors.

Triplette. "Constructed" stone composed of three layers, usually different materials, glued together.

Tumbling. A special term for polishing; especially refers to the technique practiced on opaque materials, which are placed in a revolving barrel containing lightly abrasive substances employed for polishing.

Ultraviolet light. Light whose frequency is superior to that of the visible field. Gemmology employs long wave (366 nm) and short wave (253.7 nm) ultraviolet lamps to stimulate gem fluorescence.

Ultraviolet rays. Obtained by using special lamps (*see* Fluorescence *and* X-rays).

Uniaxiality. Denoting Group II crystals that are birefringent with a particular monorefringent direction, indicated as optical axis.

Uniaxial. *See* Optical Axis *and below,* Uniaxiality.

UV. Symbol for ultraviolet rays (*See above and* Fluorescence).

X-rays. Extremely short wavelength radiation.

The World's Finest Creators

Aurelio ABRAMI
Via Alfieri, 14
15048 Valenza-Po (AL), Italy

Lena ANTABI
Rua Batatais, 507/61
CEP 01423-010 São Paulo, Brazil

ARATA GIOIELLI
Viale Manzoni, 17
15048 Valenza-Po (AL), Italy

ASAYO
Corso Magenta, 82
20123 Milano, Italy

AURELIA GIOIELLI
CO.IN.OR.
Lotto 4A Circ. Ovest
15048 Valenza-Po (AL), Italy

Rosario AUTORE Pty Ltd.
117-121 Reservoir Street
2040 Surry Hills, NSW, Australia

BERCA & Co.
Via C. Battisti, 7
15048 Valenza-Po (AL), Italy

BIBIGÌ
Via del Pratone, 10
15046 San Salvatore Mto. (AL), Italy

BOGLIETTI GIOIELLI
Via Italia, 11
13051 Biella (VR), Italy

Fabrizio CANTAMESSA
Viale Dante, 43
15048 Valenza-Po (AL), Italy

Gilberto CASSOLA
CO.IN.OR.
Lotto 13A Circ. Ovest
Valenza-Po (AL), Italy

CEVA GIOIELLI
Via Camasio, 4
15048 Valenza-Po (AL), Italy

Woo Hyun CHOI
808–5 Yeukusam-Dong
Kangnam-Ku
Seoul, Republic of Korea

Bart CURREN
3910 West Clement Road
Boise, ID 83704, U.S.A.

Casa DAMIANI
Corso Magenta, 82
20123 Milano, Italy

Julieta DE CASTRO
Rua Rio de Janeiro, 67 ap. 92
CEP 01240-010 São Paulo, Brazil

Jean-Pierre DE SAEDELEER
Rue du Chêne, 33
5537 Sosoye, Belgium

Pierre and Denis DEPREZ
6, Rue du Gravier
4032 Chenee (Liège), Belgium

Alain DETRIXHE
Av. Brigade Piron 30/A
4020 Liège, Belgium

Kristen EHHALT-VUSEC
Brückenstraße, 30
69120 Heidelberg, Germany

Ulrich FREIESLEBEN
Postfach 460209
48073 Munster, Germany

Andrea GALASSINI
Vicolo M. del Pero, 8
15048 Valenza-Po (AL), Italy

F.lli GALDIOLO
Via XXIX Aprile, 11
15048 Valenza-Po (AL), Italy

Aldo GARAVELLI
Viale Dante, 24
15048 Valenza-Po (AL), Italy

P. Carlo LENTI
Corso Garibaldi, 143
15048 Valenza-Po (AL), Italy

LUNATI
Via Trento, 5
15048 Valenza-Po (AL), Italy

Miriam MAMBER
Al Gabriel Monteiro Da Silva,
1046, Jardim Paulistano
CEP 01442 São Paulo, Brazil

Ermes MAREGA
Via Pisacane, 10
15048 Valenza-Po (AL), Italy

Phillip MAYNARD
34, Hammer Street
Christchurch, 1, New Zealand

Claude MAZLOUM
Schupstraat, 9/11(B.P. 23/C),
2018 Antwerp, Belgium

MIKAWA
Corso Magenta, 82
20123 Milano, Italy

F.lli MORAGLIONE
Via Sassi, 45
15048 Valenza-Po (AL), Italy

Bernd MUNSTEINER
Wiesenstraße, 10
55758 Stipshausen, Germany

Simonne MUYLAERT-HOFMAN
36, Nieuwstraat
9300 Aalst, Belgium

NEW ITALIAN ART
Via Trieste, 6
15048 Valenza-Po (AL), Italy

Stefan PAULI
Gerechtigkeitsgasse, 13
Bern 8, Switzerland

Erwin PAULY
Blumenstraße, 39
55758 Veitsrodt, Germany

Bruno Pisano
Via Lega Lombarda, 22
15048 Valenza-Po (AL), Italy

Marcello Pizzari
Via della Cappelletta
della Giustiniana, 24
00123 Rome, Italy

Jacques Prades
228, Ratchadaphisek Road
J.P. Bldg.
Chongnonsee, Yannawa,
Bangkok 10120, Thailand

Heike Preuß
Brückenstraße, 30
69120 Heidelberg, Germany

Preziosismi
Via Benvenuto Cellini, 36
15048 Valenza-Po (AL), Italy

RCM
Via Camurati, 45
15048 Valenza-Po (AL), Italy

Recarlo
Via Tortona, 22
15048 Valenza-Po (AL), Italy

Dirce Repossi
Viale Dante, 49
15048 Valenza-Po (AL), Italy

Roberto Gioielli
Via Amisano, 26
15046 San Salvatore Mto. (AL),
Italy

Ivo Robotti
Via Camurati, 27
15048 Valenza-Po (AL), Italy

Costantino Rota
Via San Salvatore, 64
15048 Valenza-Po (AL), Italy

Hans Schindler
Salzgasse, 3
59494 Soest, Germany

Ekkehard F. Schneider
Mühlwiesenstraße, 31
55743 Kirschweiler, Germany

Jean-Marc Siegl
54, Rue d'Antibes
06400 Cannes, France

Paolo Spalla
Viale Dante, 10
15048 Valenza-Po (AL), Italy

Wigbert Stapff
Kapellenweg, 3
69121 Heidelberg, Germany

Reiner Stein
Haupstraße, 4b
55758 Veitsrodt, Germany

Roland Tschiegg
11, Rue Mercière
68100 Mulhouse, France

Krista and Grety Vandevelde
Hoge Steenweg, 33
1850 Grimbergen, Belgium

Jan Vanschoenwinkel
Varkensmarkt, 5
3590 Diepenbeek, Belgium

Giuseppe Verdi
Via XXIX Aprile, 8
15048 Valenza-Po (AL), Italy

Gabriele Weinmann
Kapellenweg, 3
69121 Heidelberg, Germany

Alberto Zorzi
Via Malfattini, 17
35010 Loreggia (PD), Italy

Photographic Credits

Aazet 76, 77, 79

Alessandra Aliperti 223

Vicente Alves 15

Argyle 100, 101, 123, 124

Atelier Photo 209

André Barsamian 150

Ditmar Bollaert & Karel Moortgat 208, 230, 231

Jacques Breuer Photographe 147(a and b)

Anna Cella 201

Chris Colemont 55

Courtesy of GIA 81, 82, 88 (above)

Courtesy of the University of São Paulo, Brazil 188, 189 (Fabio Colombini)

Courtesy of the Metropolitan Museum of New York 191

Monica Cumo 13

Bart Curren 224

Damiani 14, 114, 115, 144, 145

Das Atelier 238, 239

Vincent De Jaegher 127

Alain Detrixhe 146

Ricardo De Vicq De Cumptich 197, 228

Alexander Ehhalt/Lossen Foto 134, 162, 199

Gigi Fantoni 253

Fotolineadieci 226, 227

GIA and Hrd/De Beers 32

Jean-Jacques Goldfar 37

Karl Hartmann/Messeverein 154, 157, 214(rt), 217(rt), 218(a), 220 (all), 245

Hrd/Aazet 73

Hrd/De Beers 4, 79, 88, 89 (b/rt and b/lft)

Hrd/De Beers/Goffin Visual 86-87

Ica 11, 29, 49, 67, 275

Ica/Bart Curren 12 (all), 17, 26, 27, 28 (all), 32, 38, 39, 41 (a/rt, a/lft, b/lft), 42, 46 (b and a), 50, 53, 56, 57, 58, 62, 67, 72, 141(b/rt), 156, 160, 161, 164, 165, 166, 167(a and b), 168, 169, 172, 176, 177, 178, 179, 179 (b), 180, 182, 184, 185, 186 (a and b), 187, 192 (rt and lft), 194, 202, 203 (lft and rt), 204, 205, 206 (all), 207 (a), 212, 214 (lft), 215(rt and lft), 216(lft), 217(lft), 221(a), 240, 241, 242, 243, 244, 246 (all), 247, 248, 249, 251(rt and lft), 252 (all), 258, 260, 261(a and b), 262 (a and b), 265, 266 (rt and lft), 267 (rt and lft), 270, 271, 272, 273 (a and b/rt), 274 (a and b), 299

Ica/Gembureau Europe 221(b)

Ica/Intergem 200, 207(b), 273 (b/lft)

Ica/Suwa & Son 171(a and b)

Pol Leemans 64, 148, 149

Lee Seoung Gon 33, 142, 143, 158, 174, 195, 196

Lorne Liesenfeld 210, 211

Archivio Lunati 116

Studio Marigrafica 104, 105

Damon Mc Phail 229

Peter Michel 175, 257

Gabriela Noris 163

A. Nyssen 139, 140, 141(a and b)

Orlando Pastorello 109

Stefan Pauli 198

Erwin Pauly 232, 233, 234, 235, 236, 237

Photo 2000 108, 117, 119, 123, 153, 165, 225

Studio Photocrom End paper, 17-63, 18, 19, 20(a, b), 21(a, b), 22, 23, 24, 45, 106, 107(a), 107(b), 111, 151, 263

Jacques Prades 44

Burghard Reihs 94, 95

Foto M. Roudnitska 126, 132, 133, 138

Gary Sarre / Rosario Autore Pty Ltd. Cover, 135, 136, 137

E. Schneider 250

Sandro Sciacca 112-113

Massimo Sormonta 222

Spectrum Fotodesign 66

Studio Tecla 43, 96, 102, 103, 110, 118, 193

Van Cauwelaert Back cover

Claude Vest 152

Robert Weldon 216/rt

All other photos are from author Claude Mazloum's private collection.

Index of Stones

Actinolite	265
Amazonite	265
Amber	157
Amblygonite	265
Andalusite	265
Anorthite	266
Apatite	266
Aquamarine	161
Artificial Glass	266
Azurite	266
Benitoite	267
Beryl	165
Brazilianite	267
Bytownite	267
Cassiterite	267
Celestite	267
Chrysoberyl	169
Chrysocolla	267
Coral	172
Cordierite or Dichroite or Iolite	177
Corundum	178
Cornerupine	268
Danburite	268
Datolite	268
Diamond	73
Diopside	268
Dioptase	268
Dolomite	268
Dumortierite	269
Emerald	57
Enstatite	269
Epidote	269
Euclase	269
Fibrolite	269
Fluorite	181
Garnet	183
Gypsum	269
Hematite	189
Jade	190
Jadeite	192
Labradorite	270
Lapis Lazuli	194
Lazulite	270
Malachite	200
Marcasite	270
Moldavite	270
Moonstone or Adularia	270
Nephrite	201
Olivine or Peridot or Chrysolite	202
Opal	205
Operculum	271
Obsidian	271
Pectolite	271
Phenacite	271
Pollucite	272
Prehnite	272
Quartz	213
Rhodochrosite	240
Rhodonite	272
Ruby	27
Sapphire	39
Sapphirine	272
Scapolite	272
Sepiolite or Meerschaum	272
Sinhalite	273
Sodalite	273
Spinel	241
Spodumene	244
Sunstone or Oligoclase	273
Taaffeite	274
Topaz	245
Tourmaline	249
Turquoise	254
Vesuvian	274
Wardite	274
Zircon	258
Zoisite	260

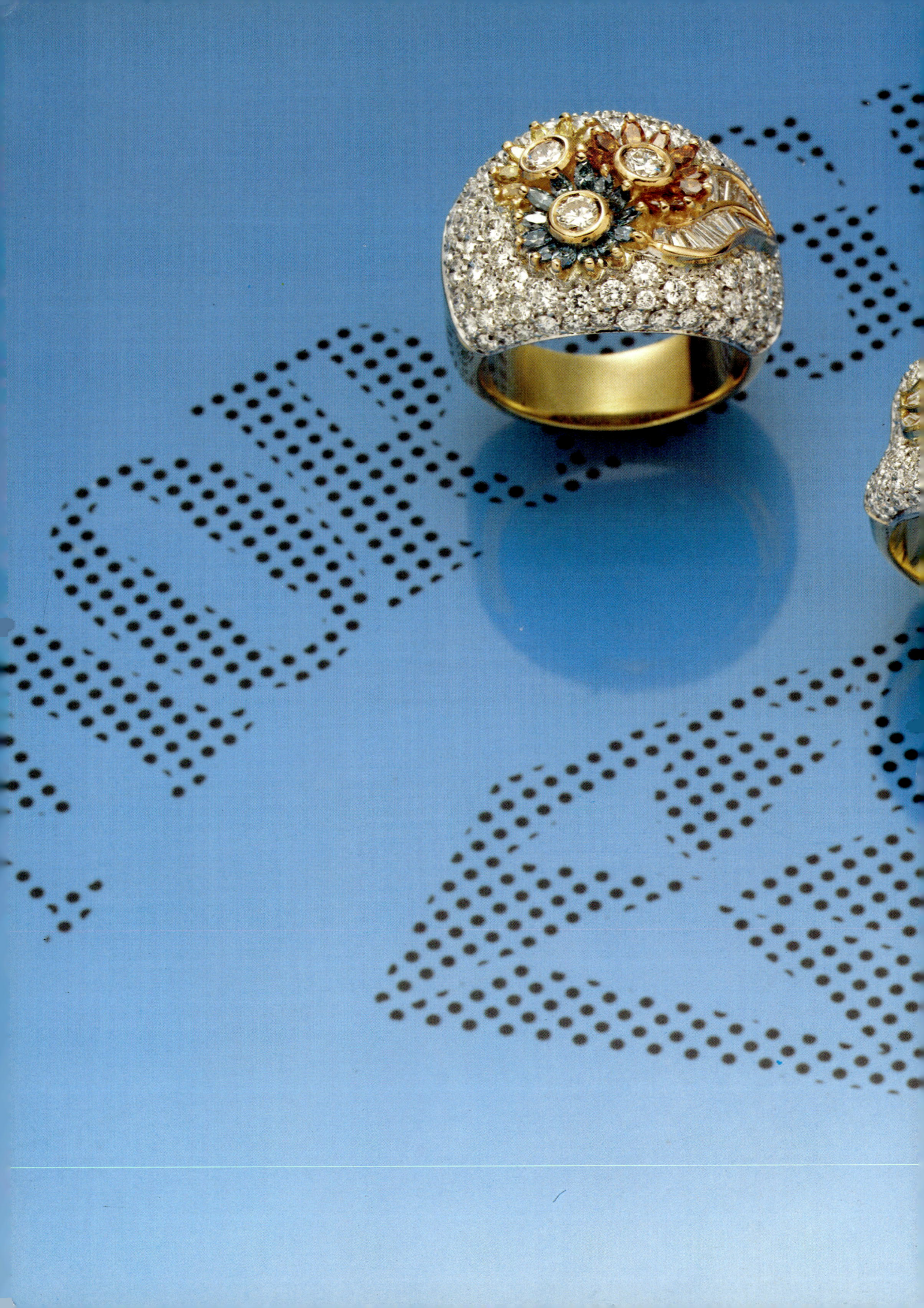